INTRODUCTION to OPERATIONS RESEARCH and MANAGEMENT SCIENCE:
A General Systems Approach

McGRAW-HILL SERIES IN INDUSTRIAL ENGINEERING AND MANAGEMENT SCIENCE

Consulting Editor
James L. Riggs
Department of Industrial Engineering
Oregon State University

Gillett   METHODS OF OPERATIONS RESEARCH

Riggs and Inoue   INTRODUCTION TO OPERATIONS RESEARCH AND MANAGEMENT SCIENCE: A General Systems Approach

INTRODUCTION to OPERATIONS RESEARCH and MANAGEMENT SCIENCE: A General Systems Approach

James L. Riggs, Ph.D.
Professor and Department Head of Industrial and General Engineering
Oregon State University

Michael S. Inoue, Ph.D.
Professor of Industrial and General Engineering
Oregon State University

McGraw-Hill Book Company
New York St. Louis San Francisco Auckland Düsseldorf Johannesburg
Kuala Lumpur London Mexico Montreal New Delhi Panama
Paris São Paulo Singapore Sydney
Tokyo Toronto

Library of Congress Cataloging in Publication Data

Riggs, James L
   Introduction to operations research and management science.

   Bibliography: p.
   Includes index.
   1. Operations research. 2. Management. 3. System analysis. I. Inoue, Michael Shigeru, joint author. II. Title.
HD20.5.R47   658.4′034   74-31423
ISBN 0−07−052870−5

**INTRODUCTION to OPERATIONS RESEARCH and MANAGEMENT SCIENCE:
A General Systems Approach**

Copyright © 1975 by McGraw-Hill, Inc. All rights reserved. Printed in the United States of America. No part of this publication may be reproduced, stored in a retrieval system, or transmitted, in any form or by any means, electronic, mechanical, photocopying, recording, or otherwise, without the prior written permission of the publisher.

1 2 3 4 5 6 7 8 9 0 KPKP 7 9 8 7 6 5

This book was set in Times Roman by Textbook Services, Inc.
The editors were B. J. Clark and M. E. Margolies;
the designer was Ben Kann;
the production supervisor was Sam Ratkewitch.
The drawings were done by B. Handelman Associates, Inc.
Kingsport Press, Inc., was printer and binder.

CONTENTS

PREFACE ix

CHAPTER 1 *Toward Better Decisions: Operations Research and Management Science* 1
  1-1 *A Way of Thinking* 1
  1-2 *What Is in a Name ... ?* 2
  1-3 *Multidisciplinary Approach* 3
  1-4 *Scientific Approach* 9
  1-5 *Foreword and Forward* 15

CHAPTER 2 *Problem Investigation: Cause-&-Effect Diagrams* 19
  2-1 *Getting Started* 19
  2-2 *Problem Portrait* 20
  2-3 *C & E Analysis Procedures* 21
  2-4 *Variations of C & E Diagrams* 26
  2-5 *History and Theory* 30
  2-6 *C & E Benefits and Applications* 32

CHAPTER 3 *Data Analysis: Pareto Pattern* 38
  3-1 *Data Deluge* 38
  3-2 *Vilfredo Pareto* 39
  3-3 *Pareto Diagram* 40
  3-4 *Pareto Patterns* 42

CHAPTER 4 *Problem Formulation: Resource Planning and Management System* 60
  4-1 *Value of Resources* 60
  4-2 *Model Construction* 61
  4-3 *General Systems Theory* 64

4-4	*RPMS Postulates*	*71*
4-5	*RPM Network Construction Procedure*	*75*

CHAPTER 5 *Model Experimentation: Graphic Introduction to Linear Programming*   *84*

5-1	*OR/MS Experimentation*	*84*
5-2	*Construction of E^2 FSS and Its Role in Optimization*	*86*
5-3	*Adaptivity Analysis*	*95*
5-4	*Minimization*	*99*
5-5	*RPM Network Interpretation*	*104*

CHAPTER 6 *Normative Model Formulation: Programming LP Problems*   *112*

6-1	*Origin of Programming*	*112*
6-2	*Standard Forms of LP Problems*	*114*
6-3	*Diet Problem*	*117*
6-4	*Using Dominance to Simplify an LP Model*	*125*
6-5	*Using Basic Nodes to Simplify LP Models*	*129*
6-6	*Values of Leftovers*	*136*
6-7	*When Nature is Hostile*	*140*

CHAPTER 7 *Applied Normative Models: Linear Programming Paradigms*   *151*

7-1	*Golden Rules of RPMS Linear Programming*	*151*
7-2	*Basic RPM Network Patterns*	*153*
7-3	*Technological Constraints*	*158*
7-4	*Blending Problems*	*161*
7-5	*Cyclic Scheduling*	*165*
7-6	*Potpourri: Traditional LP Paradigms*	*175*
7-7	*Double Trouble: Common Problems and Cures*	*181*

CHAPTER 8 *Network Programming: Transportation and Transshipment*   *199*

8-1	*Hitchcock-Koopmans Transportation Problem*	*199*
8-2	*Relating Supplies to Transfer Costs to Demands*	*200*
8-3	*Feasibility Analysis*	*208*
8-4	*Optimality Analysis*	*215*
8-5	*Extensions of Transportation Models*	*226*
8-6	*Branch-and-Bound Method*	*231*

CHAPTER 9 *Simplex Tableau: A Table for Resource Exchange*   *243*

9-1	*Climbing a Convex Hull*	*243*
9-2	*Economic Interpretation of the Dual Flows in RPM Networks*	*246*
9-3	*Simplex Tableau Format*	*248*
9-4	*Dimensional Scaling*	*253*

9-5	Standard Simplex Procedure	255
9-6	Nonfeasible Initial Solution	266
9-7	Complications in Simplex	269
9-8	Incorporating a Tableau within an RPM Network	280

CHAPTER 10 Sequential Decision Process: Dynamic Programming — 288

10-1	One Thing at a Time	288
10-2	Characteristics of DP Models	296
10-3	Longest- and Shortest-Path Problems	299
10-4	Resource Allocation	304
10-5	Planning Horizon	316
10-6	Combining Linear and Dynamic Programming	328

CHAPTER 11 Implementing the Implementation: Project Planning and Management — 336

11-1	Value of OR/MS	336
11-2	History of Project Management	337
11-3	Planning Phase	341
11-4	Scheduling Phase	349
11-5	Resource Management	364
11-6	LP Interpretation of Scheduling Problems	370
11-7	Time-Cost Tradeoff	371
11-8	PERT Probability Analysis	380

CHAPTER 12 Systems Evaluation: Queuing Models and Simulation — 394

12-1	Diagnostic Tools for Systems	394
12-2	Basic Queuing Theory	395
12-3	Finite-queue Single-server Models	398
12-4	Infinite-queue Single-server Models	405
12-5	RPMS Representation of Queuing Models	409
12-6	Multiserver Systems	416
12-7	Monte Carlo Simulation	419

CHAPTER 13 RPMS: A Tool for General Systems Analysis — 425

13-1	Think Ahead—Think Behind	425
13-2	Think Big—Think Small	430
13-3	Think Again	443

APPENDIX A Conversational Computer Programs for Linear Programming — 452

A-1	Time-Sharing Terminals	453
A-2	LINPRO***	453
A-3	Customized Conversational Linear Programs	462

APPENDIX B *Mathematical Programming System: The Product-Form Approach*   473

B-1 *Revised Simplex Production Form*   473
B-2 *MPS*   475
B-3 **REX*   482

ANNOTATED BIBLIOGRAPHY   485

INDEX   492

PREFACE

This book differs from other texts on operations research (OR) and management science (MS). It is an introduction to traditional OR/MS subjects, but it advocates a new, general systems approach to them. This approach is based on methods collectively called *resource planning and management system* (*RPMS*). RPMS encourages more precise formulation of problems and provides a format for analysis and display of the solutions. It is visually apparent in the form of RPM networks, which are used both in describing and in solving the problems. The simulation and optimization properties of RPMS constitute a potent service to promote the general systems approach to OR/MS education and practice.

THE ROLE OF OR/MS

Operations research and management science have had short, explosive histories. OR was created to guide wartime decisions through collective expertise drawn from diverse experience; MS evolved as a discipline encompassing techniques directed toward the quantification of managerial decisions. Both OR and MS rode the boom of computerization in gaining recognition, and today there are OR and MS departments in universities, corporations, and government.

The OR/MS umbrella covers an impressive collection of systems analysis and design techniques. Their wide applicability is attested to by the way OR/MS tools have been adopted by disparate professional disciplines. Just as the science of physics spawned multiple areas of application that became branches of engineering, OR/MS applications are currently being exploited in many systems-oriented disciplines. Whether OR/MS was the cause or effect of interest in systems analysis is less important than an awareness of its role and potential. There is a need for both OR/MS specialists and for engineers, managers, and social scientists whose familiarity with OR/MS complements their professional competence and broadens their outlook. Scientists still search for the secrets of nature, and OR/MS specialists seek even more sophisticated ways to guide decisions. Physicists work with engineers to convert theory into practice, but OR/MS specialists are often expected to do *both* research and development, which is a difficult duty. Theorists stretch the boundaries of OR/MS with energetic thrusts toward elaborate refinements, but few comparable advances are evident at the core where practitioners operate. The message and methods in this book are dedicated to bridging the gap between theory and practice.

THE DEVELOPMENT OF RPMS

About 10 years ago the authors were attracted by the similarities of the objectives and analysis techniques employed in business, industrial and systems engineering, economics, and other professional fields. Yet, there were difficulties in communication among disciplines. Some tools popular in one field were virtually unknown in another; other tools were well accepted by all fields. Critical-path scheduling (CPS) was an especially engrossing topic. It grew from being just a concept to having proliferate applications within half a dozen years. Almost overnight, it became an accepted management tool for businessmen, engineers, consultants, contractors, and administrators.

Why did CPS receive such recognition? Was it the intuitively logical structure? The fact that it is easy to learn? The availability of computer assistance? Its graphic appeal? Its economic usefulness? All these qualities likely contributed, but other OR/MS tools possessing many of the same qualities did not receive such rapid acceptance and widespread adoption. Through repeated short courses in CPS that were offered to a wide variety of participants, the answer slowly crystalized. *Communication* was the key word. The main advantage of CPS is its ability to transcend disciplinary boundaries by lucidly portraying not only the problem, but also the solution to the problem.

Focusing on the value of graphics as a key attribute to increased usefulness, the authors experimented with network representations of standard OR/MS techniques. It was found, for example, that the difficulty associated with the identification of activities and dummies in a CPS project could be alleviated by explicitly representing both the activities (processes) and states (resources) of the system before and after processing. Next, a similar network model was built to describe a linear programming (LP) problem visually. The value of pictorial displays was confirmed in university classes, industrial courses, consulting engagements, and conference presentations. It became apparent that most OR/MS problems can be represented by a universal network configuration that is independent of the solution procedure to be applied. Thus, an OR/MS analyst can start describing the problem by identifying cause-and-effect relationships among its elements before having any idea of what solution procedure to employ.

An RPM network describes how resources are converted through processes. Flows of resources are portrayed by many traditional network models: time flows through critical-path networks, signals through signal-flow graphs (SFG), products through flow-process charts, and data through computer flow charts; authority is delegated through organizational charts. A common property of all these models is that only one type of flow is *simulated* in each. The networks reveal whether or not a system is feasible by tracing the flow of a resource from its source to the sink. The exceptional advantage of a CPS network is that the constraining resource (time) is also the evaluation criterion for optimality. Thus, the same network can be used for both simulation and optimization.

Unfortunately, most OR/MS problems must be stated in terms of an objective that is different from the set of resources constraining the feasibility; thus a feasible solution is not necessarily optimal, and an optimal solution is not necessarily feasible. A breakthrough occurred when it was realized that one RPM network could represent both the feasibility and optimality conditions. There is the *primal* resource-conversion process and the corresponding *dual* value-assignment process; the former ensures the feasibility, while the latter checks the optimality.

Any resource-conversion system that can be described by a set of linear equations and inequalities is easily portrayed by an RPM network, and this book considers only such systems. A path in an RPM network alternates between the two types of nodes, resource and process nodes. Each pair of nodes describes a relationship between a resource and a process. Successive stages of development in a system are described by connecting many resource-process pairs. When the network is used for evaluating the system's feasibility, primal flows are tracked from one process node to another, ensuring that no resource is overdrawn at any resource node. When the network is used for evaluating the system's optimality, dual flows are tracked from one resource node to another, ensuring that no deficiency is created at any process node. The same transmittance effect is apparent in going from a feasibility analysis to an optimality analysis.

Perhaps the most valuable attribute of RPMS is the new perspective it fosters for systems analysis. The process-resource sequence helps users see the economic effect of allocations. And the economy is not limited to finance. In society we observe scarce resources attracted by prices and laws toward uses that best fulfill societal needs. If two processes are available to produce the same end product, resources will be allocated to the most efficient process until that process operates at capacity or its productivity drops below that of an alternative process. Ultimately, the economic value of any resource is affected by the productivity of associated processes. Economic considerations are integral to most OR/MS techniques, but they are usually masked by tableau manipulations, standard formulas, and computer programs. The same considerations are very evident during the construction of RPM networks and the computations conducted on them.

THE PRESENTATION OF OR/MS AND RPMS

In this text, the traditional aspects of OR/MS are treated parallel with the introduction of RPMS. Experienced OR/MS practitioners will encounter familiar subjects augmented by RPMS concepts. Newcomers to OR/MS will be exposed to complementing OR/MS and RPMS discussions that build from investigative procedures through deterministic models to a brief treatment of stochastic models. A thorough presentation is attempted by weaving standard approaches with new ones.

The vulnerability of using a new approach is described nicely by William H. Huggins:

> *There is a growing awareness that the traditional symbolism of our conventional mathematics leaves something to be desired. Experience has repeatedly shown that advances in knowledge depend heavily upon the creation of a concise terminology and an efficient notation . . . . Yet, experience has also shown that efforts to introduce new mathematical notations usually meet with resistance.*

The reception of the OR/MS RPMS approach by the limited audience that has been exposed to it so far has been most encouraging. Students not already familiar with OR/MS subjects grasp the concepts quickly and utilize them effectively. Those with exposure to traditional methods are sometimes slower in accepting the RPMS approach but soon recognize its value. The situation can be likened to the wariness of many adults toward the unfamiliar metric system until its value is proved.

The flow of this book gradually leads the reader from general principles to specific techniques and back to general systems analysis. While presenting the OR/MS tools that are expected in an introductory text, two themes are emphasized. The first is *problem formulation:* how to set up a problem so that the appropriate solution method(s) can be identified and applied. Too often students adopt a pet technique and attempt to force all problems into the same solution mold. RPMS procedures are the suggested deterrent. RPM networks can describe systems without guidance from a preconceived solution procedure. The second theme that is emphasized is *duality*. Beginners have little difficulty understanding the simulation concepts based on the primal flows. They often fail to realize the importance of dual values in examining the options available to a decision maker. Both themes are explored through novel developments of the subject matter.

In maintaining an introductory presentation, basic concepts are developed where needed and explained in detail; readers should not need calculus or special competence in statistics to comprehend the material. Mathematical rigor is sacrificed for intuitive reasoning when there is minimum danger of misuse. The text is thus suitable for undergraduate courses. However, a judicious selection of chapters combined with deeper conceptual and mathematical probes can yield a stimulating graduate course. It has been utilized effectively at both levels and in industrial short courses.

Several features are included to make the book engaging and versatile. It is hoped that this book will serve to enhance social consciousness in OR and MS courses that traditionally emphasize quantitative aspects, and, equivalently, to bring quantitative techniques into advanced social science courses where an appreciation of such tools has been lacking. Abundant examples are drawn from several disciplines to emphasize the adaptability of OR/MS tools. *Tune-ups* are provided for appropriate sections within the chapters to enlarge upon or provide depth to the subject being discussed. Worked out solutions to the tune-ups are then given at the end of each chapter. An instructor's manual is available to provide extra problems, solutions and suggestions for course development to ease the transition from traditional course structure or inclusion in a non- OR/MS curriculum.

Acknowledgments

The development of RPMS has spanned several years, and the authors are indebted to the many individuals who have influenced its development. Not enough space is available to acknowledge them individually. Special gratitude goes to our colleagues and students who were exposed to the initial versions of this text and offered improvements. Professors Robert M. Stark and Kostas N. Dervitsiotis have made direct contributions to the manuscript. Kuei-Lin Chen worked on the verification of Kuhn-Tucker conditions and other algorithms that are not included in this book but served as the foundation for it. General Electric Company, International Business Machines, and Professor H. Lynn Scheurman of Oregon State University are gratefully acknowledged for the release of materials related to computer programs.

James L. Riggs
Michael S. Inoue

TOWARD BETTER DECISIONS: Operations Research & Management Science

Chapter 1

1-1 A way of thinking

Long before anyone thought of making decisions "scientifically," prehistoric Homo sapiens were forced to solve problems with harsh consequences for wrong answers. With their limited brainpower and meager physical resources they competed for survival in a world seemingly weighted against them. That we are here today confirms the ability of some prehistoric "cave managers" to make the right decisions. Humanity's quest for improved decision-making continues because the consequences for wrong solutions are still harsh.

Modern managers probably face fewer life-and-death decisions than their prehistoric counterparts, but the pace and complexity of today's decision-making are surely greater. Information, requests, and orders are transmitted swiftly anywhere on our planet. Informed groups are ready to line up on both sides of any issue under consideration. Laws, traditions, and political pressures influence the options available. Advances in technology offer an ever expanding choice of resources and methods to accomplish objectives. These and many other factors challenge decision makers at every level from executive boardrooms to isolated offices.

2 Introduction to Operations Research and Management Science

In this chapter we shall explore the response of the management community to the challenge for better decision-making. The reader will recognize how the concepts and techniques presented can contribute to improved problem-solving at all managerial levels through

Disciplined thinking	Concentration on what is realistic and feasible
Objective thinking	An unbiased evaluation of data
Systematic thinking	A step-by-step analysis of the entire problem
Action-oriented thinking	A thorough search for the solution that can be implemented most economically

1-2 What is in a name?

A "legend" suggests that the term OR/MS was first created from the desperate chant of Romans when they were faced with unsolvable problems: "Oremus!" ("Let us pray!"). Although the legend is facetious, it must be admitted that the definition of OR/MS is still debatable. It is almost impossible to distinguish between OR (*operations research*) and MS (*management science*). Not only do both fields deal with unsolvable (or almost unsolvable) problems usually associated with complex man-machine systems, but they are also supported by professional societies [Operations Research Society of America (ORSA), founded in 1952, and The Institute of Management Sciences (TIMS), founded in 1953] composed largely of the same membership and belonging to the same international federation [the International Federation of Operational Research Societies (IFORS)].[1] In addition, many other professional societies are directly or indirectly concerned with OR/MS subjects. Among them are the American Institute of Industrial Engineers (AIIE), the American Institute for Decision Science (AIDS), the Society for General Systems Research (SGSR), and the Systems, Man, and Cybernetics Society [formerly, the Systems Science and Cybernetics Professional Group of the Institute of Electrical and Electronic Engineers (IEEE)]. Members of these and other groups have contributed to the development and dissemination of OR/MS concepts.

For the purpose of this book we shall define OR simply as the science devoted to the study of the behavior of man-machine systems. Similarly, we shall define

---

[1] In 1972 the IFORS (established in 1959) had 23 nations represented among its 26 participating societies. There have always been proposals to merge ORSA with TIMS, the first of which, by J. B. Lathrop, dates back to 1957. In 1973, the two societies decided to start sharing their journals and functions.

MS as the science that deals with the application of OR techniques to management problems. Thus, in OR we explore the mathematics of model manipulation, while in MS we attempt to solve business problems using mathematical models. These definitions conform to those generally accepted by the professional societies. However, we shall not restrict our discussion to subject matters that are strictly man-machine or business oriented. We shall consider also ecological, societal, and energy systems and even other general systems whenever they can be treated by OR/MS methodology. Let us regard OR/MS as providing tools for general systems and not artificially restrict applications to traditional areas.

The practice of OR/MS is usually characterized by two approaches resulting from its system orientation:

1. *Scientific approach:* The use of mathematics as the language of study

2. *Multidisciplinary approach:* The use of more than one discipline to overcome suboptimization resulting from the ignorance of the complete system

Unfortunately, these two approaches are not always compatible. The use of mathematics as the official language of study often frightens the people who *know* the problem and discourages them from joining the task force organized to *solve* the problem. This dilemma can be avoided either by educating managers who are most likely to have OR/MS problems or by using models that are more easily understood by nonmathematicians but that are rigorous enough to be mathematically interpreted. We shall address ourselves to both of these possibilities.

1-3 Multidisciplinary approach

The terms OR and MS were unknown before World War II, and yet the concept of a multidisciplinary approach was used in important decision-making processes as long ago as ancient Greece.

DELPHIC ORACLES The great Temple of Apollo (the god of prophecy as well as of the sun), located in Delphi at the foot of Mt. Parnassus, Greece, was renowned as a place where oracles were spoken by divinely inspired priestesses. These oracles helped shape the destiny of Greece as early as the sixth century B.C.

The priestess Pythia sat on a golden tripod and received gift-bearing supplicants. In a frenzied trance, she uttered sounds in response to their questions. Although Pythia supposedly pronounced oracles while analyzing omens discerned in such things as the flight of birds or the entrails of a sacrificed animal, no one understood the meaning of those oracles until they were interpreted by a council of priests much later, and usually in verse.

What actually happened could indeed qualify for what we would today call a "think-tank" operation. Hidden by the smoke of incense and stage props members of the "multidisciplinary" council of priests listened carefully to the pleas and queries of the supplicants. The council then convened, under the pretext of translating Pythia's oracle into meaningful verse, to analyze data and decide on the best solutions to the problems that were presented. Often, when the priests lacked certain data, they would send out spies to collect and bring back more information. The verse they finally spoke hinted at the optimal solution procedure.

Thus, the analysis procedure used by the "Delphi team" can be summarized as (1) identifying all possible solutions, (2) selecting the best one, and (3) communicating it to the user. The perceived and actual sequences are shown in Figure 1-1. Note the graphic portrayal of resources by circles and activities by rectangles. This format is used extensively throughout the book to describe problems and situations. It is a schematic approach, called RPMS (resource, planning, and management system), designed to assist decision makers.

BLACKETT'S CIRCUS Probably the earliest record of a modern OR team is the antiaircraft command research group, which solved a number of military operational problems for Great Britain during World War II. This research team was assembled by a Nobel Prize winner, Professor P. M. S. Blackett of the University of Manchester, and was known as *Blackett's circus* because of its makeup of eleven scientists representing seven disciplines. It included three physiologists,

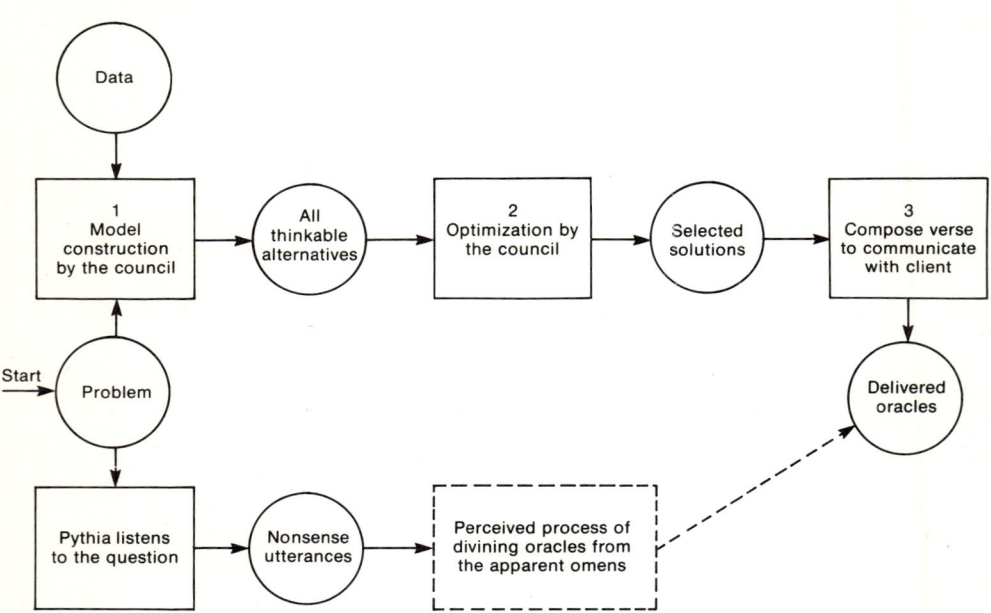

What actually happened at the Temple of Apollo . . .

. . . versus what supplicants believed and observed

Figure 1-1   RPM model of the actual and perceived workings of the Delphic oracles.

two mathematical physicists, one astrophysicist, one army officer, one surveyor, one general physicist, and two mathematicians. Though the team members were not military experts, the mixed-discipline-team approach was so successful in solving military problems that it was soon copied for other types of problems. The success stemmed from following a systematic investigation and using quantitative evaluation based on the team's varied experiences with scientific research.

NEW YORK ELEVATOR LEGEND In OR/MS circles one well-known story involves a consulting firm which was requested to solve the problem of office workers complaining about slow elevator service in a New York building. Many ideas were tossed around by mathematicians, engineers, and statisticians about how to eliminate the complaints concerning the long wait for elevator service. Increasing the elevator speed, adding extra elevators, having some elevators skip floors, and several other costly ideas were being discussed when the psychologist in the team asked exactly which workers were complaining about the elevator service. When it was revealed that the majority of the population using the elevator and complaining about service were secretaries, the psychologist proposed a simple and inexpensive solution which was subsequently adopted. A full-length mirror was installed opposite elevator doors at each floor. No more complaints about slow elevator service were heard either from the female or male employees.

This story illustrates that solutions developed by OR/MS teams do not always include mathematical models. Most problems necessarily require mathematical formulations, but OR/MS analysts consider behavioral factors whenever they are important.

SOLUTION SPACE The reasons why OR/MS studies rely on a multidisciplinary approach are now apparent. Since these studies are frequently directed at complex systems problems, it is not reasonable to expect a single individual to possess all the background training necessary to find the best solution. The multidisciplinary team approach utilizes the expertise of individuals from several areas.

Solution space is a concept that is useful in portraying the problem-solving mechanism. Picture the universe of Figure 1-2a, where tiny circles represent isolated solutions. It includes both very good and very bad solutions, economical as well as prohibitively expensive ones, some obvious and others nearly undetectable. Even simple problems may have an enormous number of theoretically possible solutions where no limits are set on expending resources. Usually, one of those circles represents a present solution which needs to be improved. It is not unlike trying to find a less polluted planet for our children's sake.

The problem solver tries to extract the best solution from the total solution space but may encounter constraints imposed by laws of nature as well as laws of society. Other handicaps may include lack of funds and ignorance of pertinent data and technology. Finally (and worst of all) the problem solver may be blinded by past experience and fictitious constraints. As depicted in Figure 1-2b and c, constraints reduce the number of alternative solutions that are available.

6   Introduction to Operations Research and Management Science

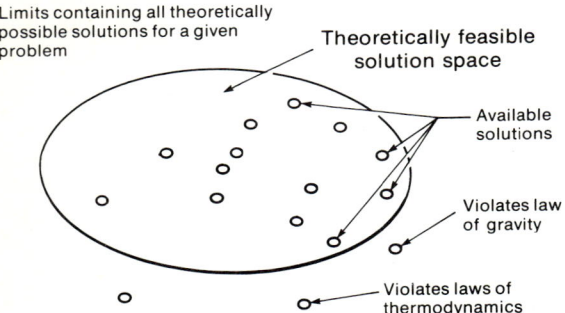

Laws of Nature

Limits containing all theoretically possible solutions for a given problem

Theoretically feasible solution space

Available solutions

Violates law of gravity

Violates laws of thermodynamics

(A) The total solution space includes all physically possible solutions allowed by unlimited resources.

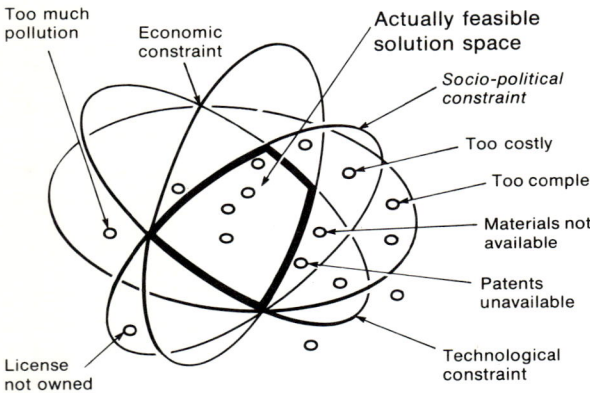

Too much pollution

Economic constraint

Actually feasible solution space

Socio-political constraint

Too costly

Too complex

Materials not available

Patents unavailable

Technological constraint

License not owned

(B) Real constraints characteristic of an individual solution seeker include technological limitations (lack of awareness that something is possible), economic constraints, and socio-political considerations.

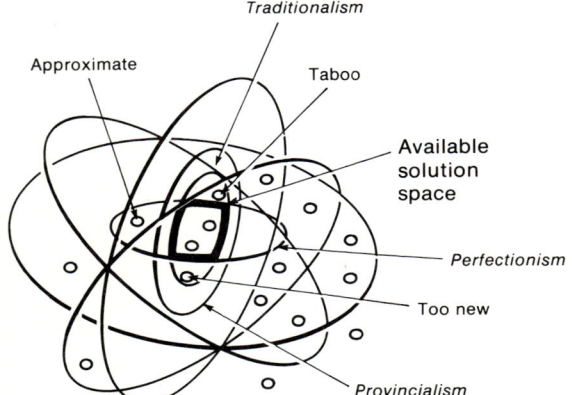

Traditionalism

Approximate

Taboo

Available solution space

Perfectionism

Too new

Provincialism

(C) Fictitious constraints make it impossible for the solution seeker to take advantage of the entire available solution space. These constraints may be products of cultural and social upbringing, as well as the psychological handicap experienced by the solution seeker. Fictitious taboos create forbidden regions within solution space.

Figure 1-2 Solution space showing constraints which reduce the number of alternative solutions available to the problem solver.

Some of the circles are stepping stones to better solutions, and chances are that the better solutions will be harder to find because of the constraints borne by tradition and usage. The number of fictitious and unnecessary constraints is often decreased in the team approach because the varied backgrounds possessed by team members assist in recognizing these constraints and in discovering what is technologically and economically possible. Equivalently, solution procedures developed by OR/MS analysts can assist individual problem solvers by providing proved decision routines.

The purging of unacceptable and unwanted solutions from the solution space should not be done until all unnecessary constraints have been removed. Free-wheeling ideas, no matter how ridiculous, should not be discounted during the team's brain-storming session because they often serve as associative links that are essential to the creative process. Rather, each constraint should be examined to see if it is actual or fictitious. Some of the more typical fictitious constraints include:

1. *Provincialism:* Creating artificial time and space restrictions to exclude taboo regions, e.g., short-range profiteerism, isolationism, and self-righteous thinking.

2. *Ivory-tower syndrome:* Lack of factual information on current data or techniques, because the researcher is too preoccupied with his own work.

3. *Laissez-faire thinking:* The doctrine of noninterference—if someone has an idea, why spoil it by proposing another?

4. *Perfectionism:* An insatiable demand for precision where an approximation would do.

5. *Traditionalism:* What our ancestors did ought to be the best.

Actual constraints, on the other hand, include the following:

1. *Technological constraints:* Lack of awareness that something is possible because methods are unknown and too advanced. Also, data that require unavailable instruments.

2. *Physical constraints:* Violating the laws of physics. (Sometimes, these constraints turn out to be technological constraints—like breaking the sound barrier.)

3. *Economic constraints:* When the problem solver must operate within an allotted resource. (This constraint could also be self-imposed or at least elastic.)

4. *Political constraints:* When the problem-solver's life (physical or professional) is endangered. (A self-imposed constraint may turn out to be real indeed.)

5. *Moral constraints:* When the problem-solver's moral or religious life is endangered (or felt to be endangered).

8   Introduction to Operations Research and Management Science

6. *Societal constraints:* When the problem-solver's family may suffer substantial inconvenience.

An acronym that is favored by data systems analysts is TAPE. A solution that satisfies TAPE is *t*echnically feasible, *a*dministratively convenient, *p*olitically expedient, and *e*conomically viable.

To demonstrate the existence of constraints, especially the fictitious constraints, some braintwisters are given next as *tune-ups*. These tune-ups are short exercises designed to illustrate what has been discussed in the previous section. They are used throughout the book. Answers to the tune-ups are given at the ends of chapters.

SECTION 1-3 TUNE-UP

The following tricky questions are of the type found in puzzle books that look so easy *after* you know the answer. The reason they are initially baffling is that their solutions call for creative or unconventional thinking. In business affairs better decisions may also be unavailable for lack of creative thinking. Creativity is developed by throwing off the yoke of conventional thinking, by purposely breaking through hypothetical constraints. As you ponder each puzzle (you might have encountered some of them before and therefore know the answer), consciously look for the different angle and the novel approach that may lead (or have led) to its solution. When you have reached a solution, recall and identify the constraints you had to overcome and how you overcame them.

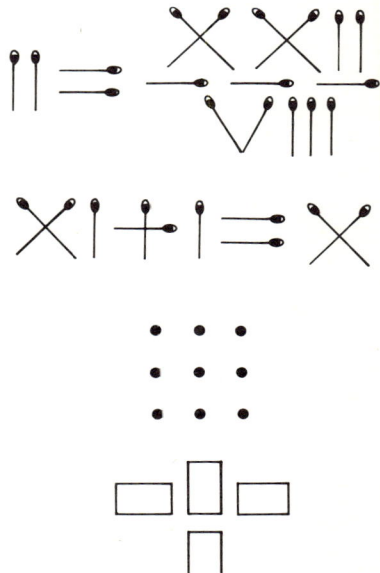

1. Matchsticks are laid out to form this incorrect equation. Form a correct equation by moving just one of the sticks.

2. Again matchsticks are arranged to form an incorrect equation. Make a correct equation but do not move any matchsticks.

3. The square contains nine dots. Connect all the dots with four straight lines without taking your pencil off the paper.

4. Four rectangular cards of identical size are placed as shown. Form a square by moving only one of the cards.

5. Divide the circle into as many parts as you can by drawing four straight lines.

1-4 Scientific approach

A scientific approach implies the use of a systematic methodology. Although there is no clear definition of what this methodology should encompass, it is usually understood that scientific experimentation of a sort must be included. In the case of an OR/MS study, this means that a mathematical or logical model of the problem must be created and various hypotheses must be tested against such a model. Since a model is an abstraction of a *system*, it also defines the system it is modeling by depicting its most salient features. Just as a statue or painting emphasizes the beauty of an object, an OR/MS model emphasizes the *objectives* and *controls* necessary to solve a problem. In other words, an OR/MS model must depict the *cause-and-effect* relationships for the problem it portrays.

PASCAL'S THEORY OF BETS Blaise Pascal, the French mathematician-philosopher (1623-1662), is well known for inventing the first successful mechanical calculator with a mechanism for automatic carries as well as for contributions to mathematics (e.g., Pascal's triangle) and literature (e.g., "The heart has its reasons which reason does not know..."). He was also a very religious person and should be credited with developing the first practical (?) application of what we now consider to be an OR technique, game theory. (What follows is a very *liberal* interpretation of his thoughts.)

In his essay "Pensées," Pascal proposes a logical argument to justify why it pays to be a good Christian. His *theory of bets* suggests that we have our choice of being either good Christians (good enough to go to heaven) or unscrupulously selfish playboys (bad enough to enjoy all the sinful pleasures on earth). Obviously, a Christian believes in the existence of God and eternal life, while an atheist denies the existence of both. If the atheist is right, all the earthly sacrifices of Christians would go unrewarded, and playboys would enjoy all the sinful pleasures without punishment in heaven. If the Christian is right on the other hand, eternal happiness would be granted to the good Christians and eternal damnation would await playboys. Pascal demonstrated candidly that as long as there is any possibility of God's existence, it would seem logically advantageous to be good Christians.

Without being sacrilegious, let us adopt some monetary measures for the outcomes Pascal discusses. (We should note, of course, that Pascal never placed monetary values on his outcomes.) Let us estimate that sacrifices and earthly pleasures are worth −$1 million and +$1 million respectively, and that eternal happiness and damnation are worth +$100 million and −$100 million, respectively. Then, depending on the decision-maker's beliefs as to whether God does or does not exist, outcomes may be selected from the following *payoff matrix*, a tabular representation of the solution space:

Possible states of Nature

	God does not exist	God exists
Good Christian	Earthly sacrifices = −$ 1 million	Earthly sacrifices = −$ 1 million Eternal happiness = $100 million ——————— $ 99 million
Unscrupulous playboy	Earthly pleasures = +$1 million	Earthly pleasures = +$ 1 million Eternal damnation = −$100 million ——————— Net payoff = −$ 99 million

Alternatives ← (left label)   Payoffs ← (bottom label)

MAXIMAX PRINCIPLE A person may be an optimist, a pessimist, or somewhere in between. A typical example of an optimist's philosophy is the motto attributed to the Jesuits: "One is justified in doing an action for which there is any probability, however small, of its being the best possible." Using this principle, we note that the biggest payoff of +$99 million occurs when we behave as good Christians. In other words, +$99 million was the maximum of the maxima of the rows (decision maker's choice). This idea of choosing the alternative with the biggest payoff is called the *maximax principle*.

MINIMAX PRINCIPLE A pessimist is a person who always expects the worst possible outcome regardless of his choice. Such a person, viewing the payoff matrix, would consider the worst outcome in each row and would then choose the alternative affording the best of the worst values. The maximum loss for being a good Christian is −$1 million while that of being an unscrupulous playboy is −$99 million. The minimum of the maximum loss is −$1 million. Thus, a pessimist should also strive to be a good Christian.

This idea of minimizing maximum losses or maximizing minimum gains is called either the *minimax principle* or the *maximin principle* and forms the basis for many OR/MS decision-making models.

DUALITY PRINCIPLE An important feature of a systems model is that there are usually two ways of looking at a problem. The fact that both pessimists and optimists could gain by behaving as good Christians presents the *primal* model of the problem that is illustrated graphically in Figure 1-3, which portrays the original two alternatives as two vertical axes. The horizontal axis represents all the intermediate levels between being a good Christian and an atheist playboy. Each point on this axis is considered a "mixed" strategy of being sometimes good and sometimes bad. The expected value of any mixed strategy depends on the proportion of the mix and the probability of each state of nature—in this case the existence of God. Since we have not undertaken the task of assigning a probability to the existence of God, the question is classified as a *decision under uncertainty*.

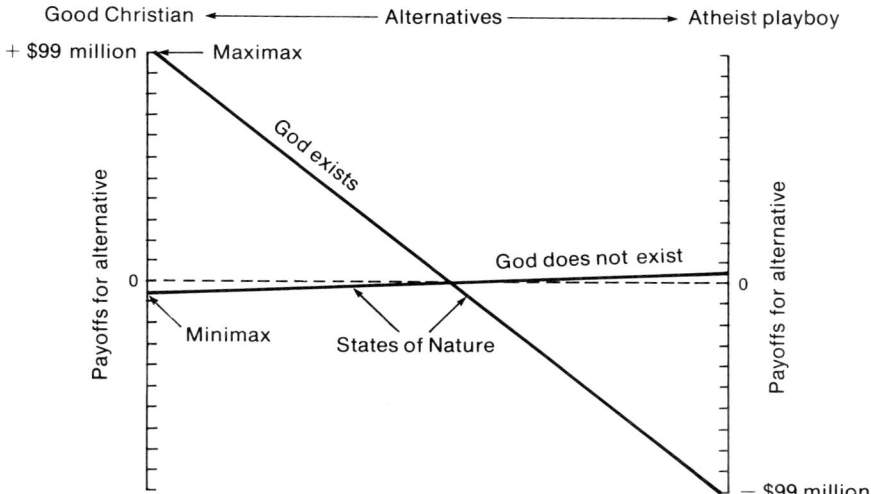

Figure 1-3 Primal model of Pascal's theory of bets (not to scale).

About all we can judge from the primal graph is that the payoff is zero for a mixed strategy of being half good and half bad, as indicated by the intersection of the crossing lines at the midpoint of the horizontal axis.

Another way to picture Pascal's theory of bets is to let vertical axes represent the payoffs associated with each state of nature, as shown in Figure 1-4. The two crossing lines now show the return to be expected from following either style of behavior. Again, it is apparent that the range of positive returns

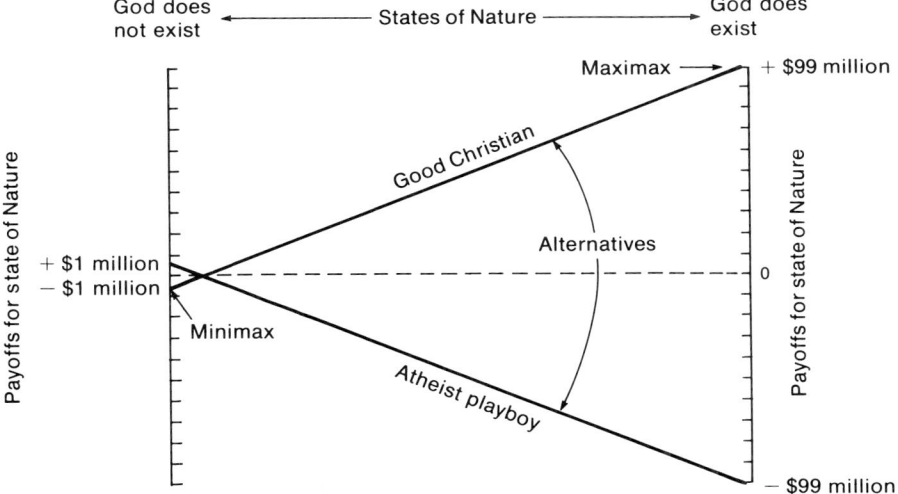

Figure 1-4 Dual model of Pascal's theory of bets (not to scale).

favors the good Christian alternative. This modified view of the same problem depicted in Figure 1-3 is called the *dual* model. From this dual graph, we see indeed that the probability that God does not exist must be extremely small before the atheist playboy policy starts to pay off.

Several important OR/MS concepts were included in this cursory discussion of Pascal's bets, a subject to which we shall return in Section 6-7. First we made the assumption that numbers can be used to measure abstractions such as eternal happiness and damnation, and then numbers were arranged in a payoff matrix and analyzed to determine the preferred alternative. This approach to finding the expected value of different courses of action is widely used for problems involving probabilities. Another concept, the potential of mixed strategy as used in game theory, was introduced. Finally, the idea of primal and dual perspectives was illustrated to indicate that there are usually two ways of looking at each problem. In later chapters on linear programming we shall observe how the two views, primal and dual, complement each other and contribute to making a more thorough evaluation.

SYSTEMS STUDY Operations researchers, management scientists, systems analysts, general systems researchers, systems engineers, and industrial engineers are all professional people engaged in some *systems-study* activities. They do not necessarily work in a multidisciplinary team, nor do they always advocate a minimax or maximax principle of optimality.[1] Nevertheless, there is a process, more or less equivalent among all systems problem solvers, that characterizes their profession. The following steps are necessary because of the complexity of the systems that are studied. The model that is constructed must be simple enough to permit the study but accurate enough to reflect the system it is portraying.

Step 1. Problem identification

Need analysis	We must know not only that the problem exists, but also that it is worth our efforts to solve it.
Cause-and-effect analysis	We must identify all the controls (causes) and their effects.
Pareto analysis	We must identify which controls and effects are worth modeling.

Step 2. Model construction

Data collection	A model is only as good as the data used to build it.

---

[1] More often than not, an OR/MS study tends to be conservative. The minimax principle is imbedded in many OR/MS tools, including linear programming and game theory.

Model design	We must assume most parameters to be constant; for example, all interactions between the system and the environment must be considered as *satisficing*[2] *constraints*, and only a few can be incorporated into *optimizing objective function*.
Model verification	The model should be tested to see if it is a reasonable replicate of the system under study.

Step 3. Experimentation

Feasibility analysis	Hypotheses are tested on the model to see if they are possible and do not violate any constraint (i.e., satisficing all constraints).
Optimality analysis	Decision variables are studied to find a set of values that gives the best performance.
Adaptivity analysis	Sensitivity of the proposed solution to changes in environment, learning effects, and other dynamic behaviors are checked.

Step 4. Implementation

Management approval	An official sanction is needed to obtain full cooperation in implementation.
Test operation	If possible, the proposed system should be implemented parallel to the existing system while being debugged. A small-scale pilot operation is recommended when the parallel operation is not possible.

---

[2]*Satisfice* is an OR/MS term that indicates having to meet a set of requirements without making an attempt to excel and maximize. The level accepted is feasible and satisfactory but is not necessarily ideal or exact. The original use of this word is credited to a social scientist, H. Simon, who used the theory of *bounded rationality* in 1961 to describe "the behavior of human beings who satisfice because they have not the wits to maximize." An OR/MS analyst confronted with multiple conflicting objectives will convert all but one of the objectives into satisficing constraints which must be met while maximizing the chosen objective. Another expression with an almost opposite meaning, *out of kilter*, is attributed to D. R. Fulkerson (1961).

14 Introduction to Operations Research and Management Science

        Full implementation   A system is incomplete if it does not have a control mechanism built into it to either take a corrective action or alert the management when its operation falls below a standard of performance.

Step 5. Evaluation

        Documentation   The system should be fully documented to enable others to learn it easily.

        Performance auditing   A periodic check should be conducted, especially to test the operation of the control and reporting mechanisms: No news is not necessarily good news.

        System updating   When new techniques, technologies, and equipment become available, the system should be checked to see if it could benefit from updating. If the needs for a system cease to exist, it should be discontinued.

Not all these steps are necessarily found in all systems studies, and modifications are needed depending on the particular application. However, these steps (which will be discussed in subsequent chapters) have been listed here to give a bearing on the implications of OR/MS studies. In this book we shall emphasize the first three steps: problem formulation, model construction, and experimentation.

SECTION 1-4 TUNE-UP

There are many problems where all the facts needed to identify a solution are known but are so disorganized that they seem useless. The following is an example of such a problem. Unless some form of systematic search is employed, the solution cannot be found.

    An OR/MS study team consists of five members having different occupations, and they are brought together to work on a difficult problem. They are temporarily housed in a row of five rooms, each with a different colored door. Each team member is an expert in a different OR/MS technique, and each has a unique mannerism. The following facts are known about the team members and where they dwell:

    1. The economist has a room with a red door.

2. The businessman likes to doodle.
3. Queueing theory is the specialty of the person in the room with the green door.
4. The engineer scratches his head when he is thinking.
5. The room with the green door is next to and on the right of the ivory-door room.
6. The mathematician in the room with a yellow door fidgets while she is sitting.
7. The economist has a room between the engineer and the businessman.
8. The administrator's primary specialty is neither game theory, linear programming, nor statistics.
9. The person who specializes in decision theory twitches.
10. The room with a blue door is not next to the room where the nose-puller lives.

Who is the nose-puller?

1-5 Foreword and forward

Hopefully this first chapter has served much the same purpose as a welcome mat in front of a home. A welcome mat invites you to come in but to wipe your feet first, and this introduction invites you to learn about OR/MS but to wipe away hesitations about what is involved. The subject is fascinating and worthwhile, but it is demanding. In this book a fresh approach is presented to make the subject easier to grasp through innovative pictorial aids. You will see abundant graphic representations of problems and solution procedures. In particular, RPM networks are utilized to portray key relationships to make situations more readily understood. Emphasis on a pictorial approach is endorsed by the ancient adage that "one picture is worth a thousand words." If the adage is correct, you have the equivalent of many thousands of words awaiting you.

The brief treatment of the origin of OR/MS in this chapter touched only a few of the highlights. Many acclaimed names and their associated methodologies were omitted; for example, Dantzig of linear programming, Bellman of dynamic programming, and Erlang of queueing theory. These and other important contributions will be discussed in subsequent chapters. The team-oriented approach of early operations-research studies may give the impression that current OR/MS activities always involve teams. Some do, but most do not. Few organizations are large enough to afford the luxury of standby specialists from several disciplines. Instead, individual management scientists are imbued with the importance of multidisciplinary considerations and are trained in the methodologies that were derived from and contribute to total systems analysis.

Practitioners in almost every profession can benefit from some exposure to OR/MS. Applications are evident in engineering, business, administration, medicine, government affairs, and health care. Maximin study goals for your introduc-

TUNE-UP SOLUTIONS

Section 1-3

Answers

1.

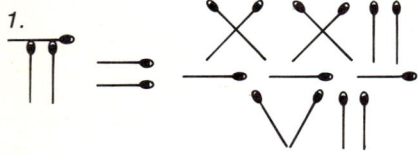

2. Turn the book around and then read the equation

3.

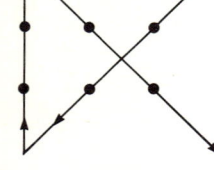

4.

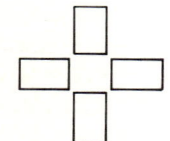

5.

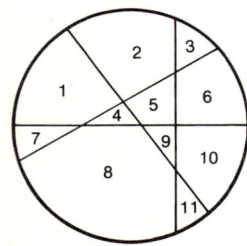

Discussion

1. Unless the problem solver knows that pi is approximately equal to $^{22}/_{7}$, he is blocked by a technological constraint.

2. Usually the first reaction to this puzzle is to assume that a misprint exists: "none" should read "one." Then it would be a simple matter to remove one stick from the plus sign to make it a minus sign. This would be an example of a fictitious constraint.

3. A mental block occurs if one assumes that the lines cannot extend outside the dotted pattern. When this artificial boundary is breached, the solution follows rather easily. (The region outside the dots constituted a *taboo* area.)

4. Just move the top card upward until the opened space forms a square. A person usually tries to make a space composed of rectangles instead of one formed by rectangles; habits can be fictitious constraints.

5. This exercise is widely used to demonstrate the importance of having an open mind while solving a problem. The conventional approach is to use four lines to divide the circle in eight equal parts, like cutting a pie. The assumptions that the lines have to be the same length and meet at the center are fictitious constraints

probably due to our cultural upbringing (traditionalism) or eagerness for symmetry (perfectionism). (To create an optimal solution, draw each line to intersect all previous lines at distinct points.)

Section 1-4

One way to organize the data is to make a matrix that matches descriptions with the team members. The clues (circled numbers) by which each cell was filled and a possible sequence of filling (boxed numbers) are shown below. Note that some of the locations are arbitrary, such as having the yellow door be in the first column instead of column 5 or assigning the engineer to the blue-door slot instead of the ivory-door slot. However, regardless of the interchangeable slots, the process finally narrows choices until the nose-puller is identified as the administrator.

Team Members

CLUES	1	2	3	4	5
Door color	[1] (7) Yellow	[10] (7) Blue	[4] (1)(7) Red	[2] (5) Ivory	[2] (5) Green
Discipline	[1] (7) Mathematician	[5] (7) Engineer	[4] (1)(7) Economist	[5] (7) Businessman	[8] (8) Administrator
Specialty			[9] (9)(10) Decision theory		[3] (3) Queueing theory
Mannerism	[1] Fidgets	(7)[7] (4) Scratches	[9] (9)(10) Twitches	[6] (2) Doodles	Nose puller

Another approach is to immediately eliminate the mathematician, businessman, and engineer as possible nose-pullers by clues 6, 2, and 4, respectively, which leaves the economist and the administrator. The economist has a room with a red door (clue 1), and so it can be deduced from clues 5 and 7 that the administrator's door is green. Then from clue 3, which states that the administrator's specialty is queueing theory, it is apparent (clue 9) that the only mannerism left for him is nose pulling.

EXERCISES

For each of the "teasers" in Exercises 1-1 to 1-3, try to find a solution and identify the constraints you had to overcome.

1-1 Moving only one matchstick, try to create an equality.

1-2 The matchstick picture of a cow is facing right. Moving only two matchsticks, have the cow face the opposite direction.

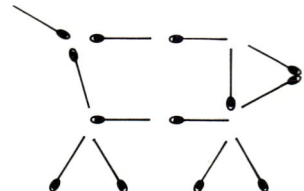

1-3 A triangle of 10 pennies points away from you. Moving only 3 pennies, make the triangle point toward you.

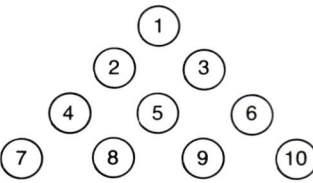

1-4 Think of several simple inventions (e.g., a bicycle, an airplane, and a transistorized color television) and identify the primary constraints that their inventors had to overcome.

1-5 Gray-Mare is a trucking company that is competing with the giant of the industry, Ham-Truck. The management of Gray-Mare decide to discount its fare to attract new customers, but the effectiveness of this strategy will depend greatly on what the competitor is planning to do. If Ham-Truck discounts its fare first, for example, Gray-Mare could lose a large share of its present market. Using the following payoff matrix, identify the strategy Gray-Mare should take if it were using (*a*) the maximax principle, (*b*) the minimax principle, and (*c*) you as its consultant.

		Market share to be gained by Gray-Mare	Ham-Truck	
			Discounts, fare first	Discounts, fare after
Gray-Mare		discount	−20%	+40%
		no discount	−10%	−5%

PROBLEM INVESTIGATION: Cause & Effect Diagrams

Chapter 2

2-1 Getting started

Frequently the toughest part of a project is to get started. Inertia is a physical law that seems to have a counterpart in mental motion. Once mental activity gets under way, things happen and it is relatively easy to keep them happening, but it is difficult to ignite that first spurt of activity.

There are always abundant excuses to postpone starting: it's not needed yet, things may change soon, someone else should do it, etc. The psychological aspects of being a self-starter are outside the province of OR/MS, but some assistance is available in the form of *cause-and-effect* (*C & E*) *diagrams*.[1] Diagramming aids in the initial investigation of a problem by providing a format which encourages the problem solver's first effort to get something on paper, organize thoughts, determine what is known and what is missing, collect data in a digestible form, and quickly see what needs yet to be done. Whether the diagram looks formal or resembles doodling, the simple expedient of putting marks on paper makes the first step seem downhill instead of uphill.

---

[1] M. S. Inoue and J. L. Riggs, "Describe Your System with Cause and Effect Diagrams," *Industrial Engineering*, pp. 26–31, April 1971.

2-2 Problem portrait

OR/MS studies are typically directed at solving a recognized problem. Sometimes the problem is a very evident obstacle, but more often it stems from a feeling that something can somehow be done better. In the former situation it is likely that the causes or roots of the problem are evident, while in the latter situation the emphasis is on the desired effects. But exclusive attention to either causes or effects may prejudice the options theorized for a solution.

A familiar model of a problem situation is a simple *black-box diagram.* As shown in Figure 2-1, inputs are converted to outputs by an undefined transformation that takes place in the black box. This representation delays consideration of *how* to implement a solution (what goes on in the black box) until *what* solution to implement has been investigated (examination of the inputs and outputs). In terms of TAPE, technical and economic feasibility are evaluated before administrative and political expediency are negotiated.

A C & E diagram is a natural extension of the black-box model. Comparison of Figures 2-1 and 2-2 shows that the transformation box of Figure 2-1 is replaced by a problem identification symbol in Figure 2-2. The interlocking arrows anchored to the hexagonal symbol provide additional details about input and output. The main shaft on the left indicates principal causes, and the one on the right indicates main effects. Smaller arrows directed toward the shafts relate control parameters, and those directed away detail the measure of effects.

In a typical application of a black-box model, visible inputs and outputs are investigated to reveal the effective workings of the system represented by the box. In this manner, the analyst is able to avoid involvement with the complex inner mechanism. A C & E model starts with the identification of the problem and expands to explore ways in which the operating mechanism of the problem affects or is affected by the environment. The objectives are to discover what can be done with the problem (controllable inputs) and how the effectiveness of control can be measured (observable outputs). To introduce the structure and procedures of a C & E diagram a sample application is provided in Example 2-1.

Example 2-1: *C & E diagram to improve product performance* Disappointing sales for a certain product led to an investigation of the reasons for its poor performance. Factors contributing to its production and marketing were entered on a C & E diagram, and the results are shown in Figure 2-3. A thorough investiga-

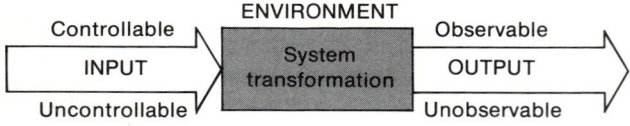

Figure 2-1 Black-box diagram focusing attention on input and output to reveal information about the transformation process.

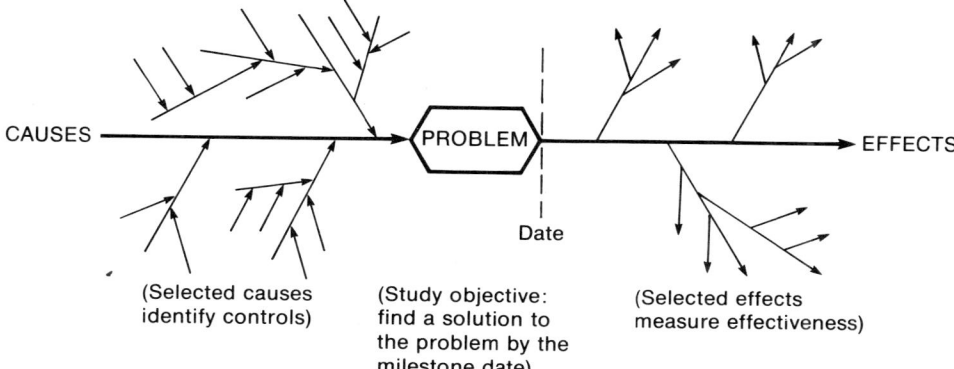

Figure 2-2 C & E diagram concentrating attention on the problem to be solved by displaying in detail its causes and the anticipated effects of its solution.

tion would likely yield many more factors than those recorded; however, Figure 2-3 provides a sample of their form and content. Note that the types and ranges of controls are entered for causes, as are measurement units for effects. These details should assist further investigation of the problem or even the implementation of a solution if one is suggested by the drawing.

The construction and development steps for the product acceptance problem are displayed in Figure 2-4. The final step is to study the completed diagram with the intention of identifying feasible solution alternatives. Diagramming cannot be expected to provide proof that a certain solution is the best, but it can be expected to suggest possibilities and the means by which they can be compared.

2-3 C & E analysis procedures

The mechanics of drawing a C & E diagram are elementary, but the thought processes that should precede the drawing are demanding. Eight steps are outlined in Figure 2-4 and will be elaborated upon in this section.

1. *Identify the problem* In *War and Peace*, Tolstoy's character Hume quipped: "The combination of causes or phenomena is beyond the grasps of the human intellect. But the impulse to seek causes is innate in the soul of man." There are many intriguing problems that challenge every manager. Some are routine and trivial and should be delegated to an assistant or a mechanized procedure; others are philosophical and not relevant to the administration of a program. Most problems for OR/MS studies result from conflicting interests involving the use of resources. A problem is a candidate for investigation when it is deemed that a solution is possible (feasible), that a better solution can be distinguished from inferior ones (measurable), and that the cost of solving it will be

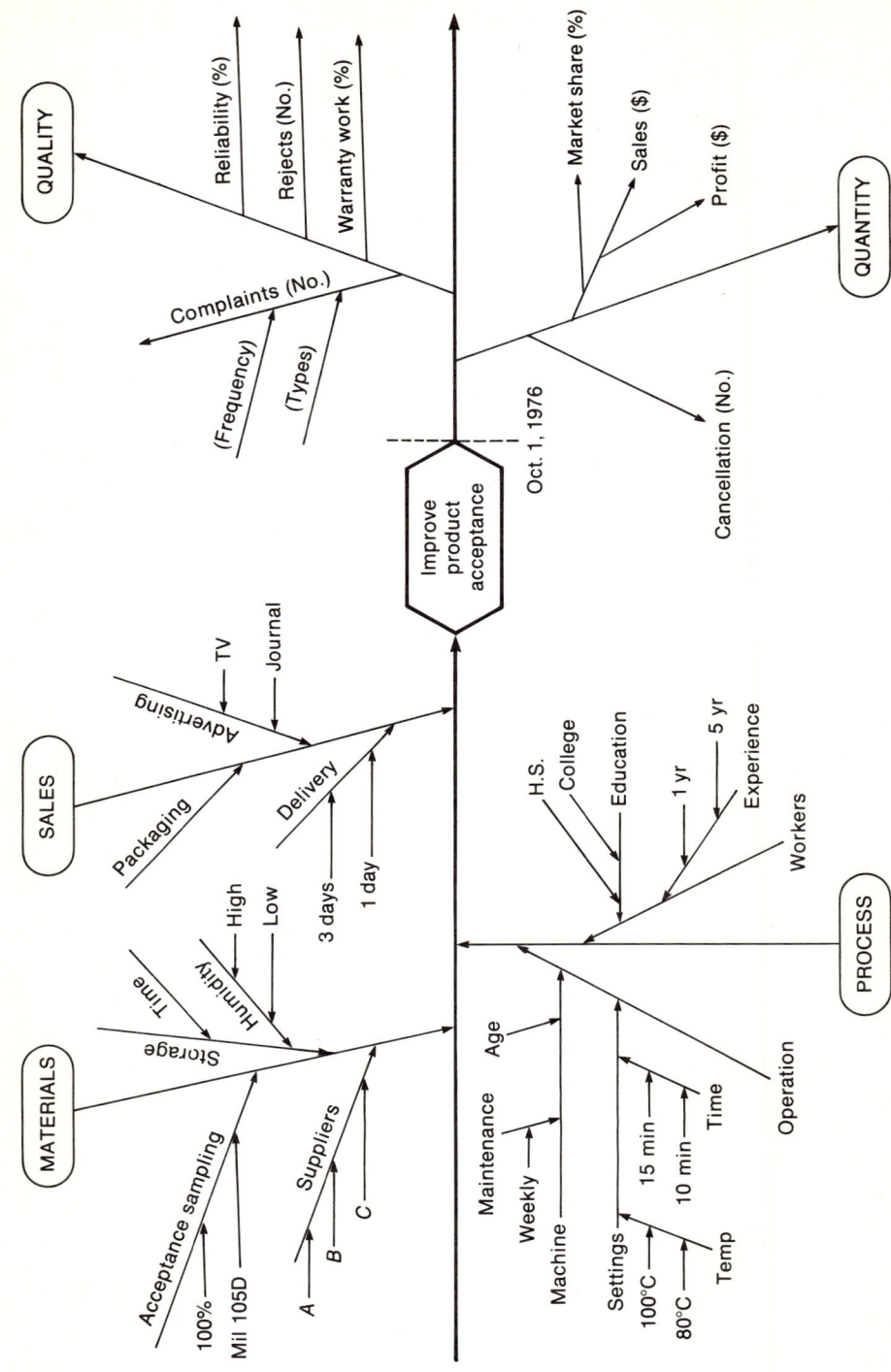

Figure 2-3 Factors contributing to product acceptance.

Problem Investigation: Cause & Effect Diagrams

Steps in developing a C & E diagram:

1. Identify the problem.
2. State the characteristic of the problem that can be expected to yield a solution.

Steps in constructing the diagram in Figure 2-3:

1. Disappointing sales for product
2.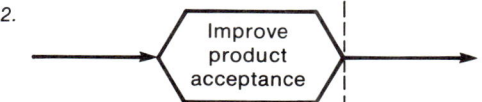

3. Specify the milestone date to separate inputs from outputs.
4. Identify the major evaluation factors as arrow shafts out of the horizontal effect line.

3. Implementation date of the solution is 10-1-76
4.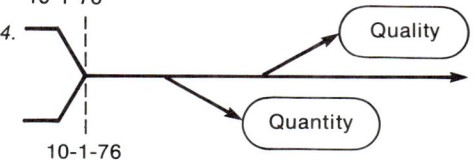

5. Identify the major controls as arrow shafts to the horizontal cause line.

5.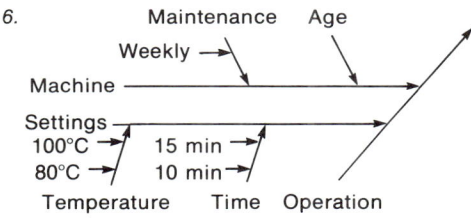

6. Identify types and ranges of controls available. Show them as sub-arrows to the major shafts.

6.
```
                    Maintenance   Age
           Weekly →
Machine ─────────────────────────────
Settings
100°C →     15 min →
 80°C →     10 min →
Temperature  Time   Operation
```

7. Identify measures and measurement units of the effects. Show them as sub-arrows from the major shafts.

7.
```
──────────────────────────────────→
           → Market share (%)
           → Sales ($)
           → Profit ($)
  Quantity
```

8. Identify a feasible solution for more study. Circle and connect the related factors.

8.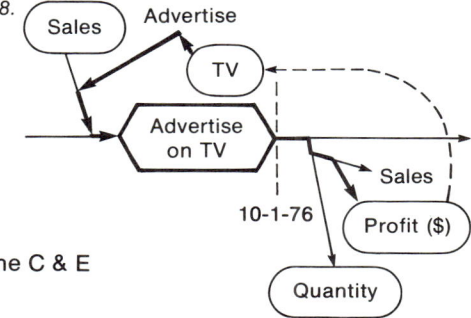

Figure 2-4 Steps followed in developing the C & E diagram for product acceptance.

exceeded by the benefits created from the solution (optimal). Equivalently, the problem must be worth solving at a certain time and at least partly controllable, and its solution must be at least partly observable.

2. *State an ideal solution* In order to find the best solution, the one that is feasible and optimal, it is usually advisable to start from an "ideal" solution rather than to investigate all potential solutions. There is typically one ideal (and usually not feasible) solution to a problem, while there are many feasible but not optimal solutions. A vehement proponent of the *ideal-system* approach states: "A better system and method design is achieved by actually using an ideal system design as a model from which the recommended design makes a minimum departure than by using the present system analysis model from which the 'bad' activities are removed."[1]

   In Figure 2-3 the ideal solution was to "improve product acceptance." Note that a verb is preferred in the statement of a solution when action is implied to solve a problem. An alternative use of C & E diagramming is to describe the sources and uses of a resource, in which case a noun is used for the investigation statement.

3. *Specify the milestone date* Time is the criterion that separates possible causes from effects. Though it is true that not everything that precedes a phenomenon is its cause, it is logically true that the effect cannot precede the cause. Identifying the milestone, or cutoff date, avoids confusion resulting from a shift in time frame during the analysis. In Example 2-1 the cutoff date was the implementation date of the solution. No factor following that date can be considered a cause, and no phenomenon observed prior to the cutoff date can be regarded as an effect. The precise date (October 1, 1976) need not be given at this stage, as long as the milestone's relation to the ideal solution is clearly slated (e.g., project initiation date).

4. *Identify major evaluation factors* It is often easier first to consider effects rather than causes associated with the solution. In Example 2-1 both the quality and quantity aspects of product acceptance are expected to be maximized by the ideal solution. These output characteristics are best described by nouns (in circles).

5. *Identify major control factors* On the cause side of a C & E diagram, resources are noted that contribute to the solution before the cutoff date even if the total availability of all such resources is not consistent or feasible. [Again, a noun (encircled) is the preferred form for an input resource description.] In Example 2-1, process, materials, and sales were the three control factors identified to improve product acceptance. It may not be financially, legally, or technically feasible to carry out efforts in all these areas, but in the ideal solution every factor is included. When idealism conflicts with reality, the analyst must reconcile differences to arrive at a feasible solution.

[1] G. Nadler, *Work Design*, Richard D. Irwin, Homewood, Ill., 1963, p. 37.

6. *Identify types and ranges of controls* At this stage of development the sample C & E diagram indicates that control over the process, materials, and sales should improve product acceptance, as will be seen by the quality and quantity of sales to be observed after the date of implementation of this ideal solution. Now definitions must be made more specific. Each shaft on the control (cause) side of the diagram must be subdivided until specific control ranges are itemized as subarrows. For example, materials can be controlled in quality by applying a 100 percent inspection plan or by adopting the military standard 105D sampling plan; similarly, the temperature settings for the process machines may vary from 100 to 80°C.

7. *Identify measures and measurement units* Evaluation factors for future effects should also be detailed. If available, data should include how the factors are to be measured and in what measurement units.

8. *Identify a feasible solution* Entries in a completed C & E diagram should reveal all the factors the analyst can envision. Some factors will have little bearing on the solution, and others will expose discouraging limitations or promising possibilities. The analyst must attempt to relate needs to the resources required for fulfillment. When a desired solution is determined to be nonfeasible due to resource constraints, the conflict is resolved by either lowering expectations or finding ways to relieve resource limitations. The most promising relationships are linked on the diagram. If an optimal feasible solution is identified, it replaces the ideal but nonfeasible solution originally entered on the diagram. However, in most cases C & E diagrams are used as a tool to help organize the search for a solution and are not expected to isolate an optimal solution.

SECTION 2-3 TUNE-UP

The C & E diagram is useful for recording data from group discussions. It has a unique capacity for assessing the problem-solving potential of a group and its leader. The logic and analytic abilities of a group will be apparent by the structure of the diagram, while the wealth of knowledge will show up as the details of entries. An unbalanced structure reveals the specific subject areas in which the group lacks expertise. The following are four patterns which might emerge from C & E records of group meetings. Each is described as an ailment. Prescribe the cures.

Symptom

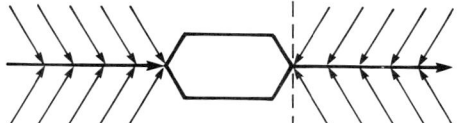

Ailment

1. *Malnutrition:* Not enough thought has gone into the diagram. Data are not sorted, classified, or ordered. Spacing is too crowded for entering additional details, and the wrong arrow direction indicates carelessness. Cure?

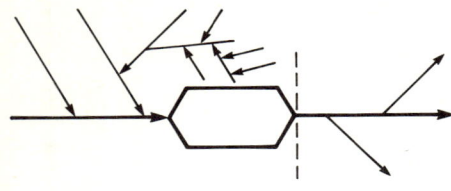

2. *Unbalanced diet:* Too much expertise in one area and not enough in others. Cure?

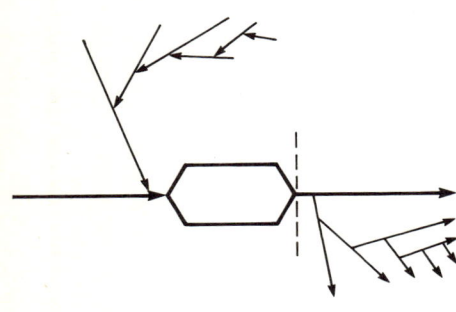

3. *Feverish:* Apparent singlemindedness yields exotic detailing, but breadth is obviously lacking. Any exhaustive classification has at least two branches at the same level. Cure?

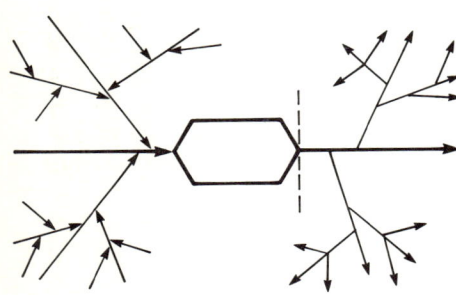

4. *Mental hiccups:* The classification is too mechanical (either/or) and seems to ignore other possibilities. Cure?

2-4 Variations of C & E diagrams

In the previous section, the basic analysis procedures used in developing C & E diagrams were discussed. Innumerable modifications can be made to suit the diagramming to the situation. This flexibility is demonstrated by the following variations of C & E diagrams.

SINGLE-SIDED PATTERN Often it is desired only to investigate the causes *or* effects of a problem. This situation occurs when either the input or the output of a question is predetermined and unalterable. A pattern that appears exclusively on the left side of a C & E diagram can serve as a diagnostic tool to identify major causes and the degrees of control appropriate to them. This type of diagram is called an *Ishikawa diagram* and is depicted in Figure 2-5. Similarly, a pattern appearing on the right side of a C & E diagram can be used to study the effects of a particular action such as raising the price of a product, the effects of a two-day strike in a factory, or the effects of installing a new machine. Such single-sided diagrams superficially resemble a decision tree with its branching format, but re-

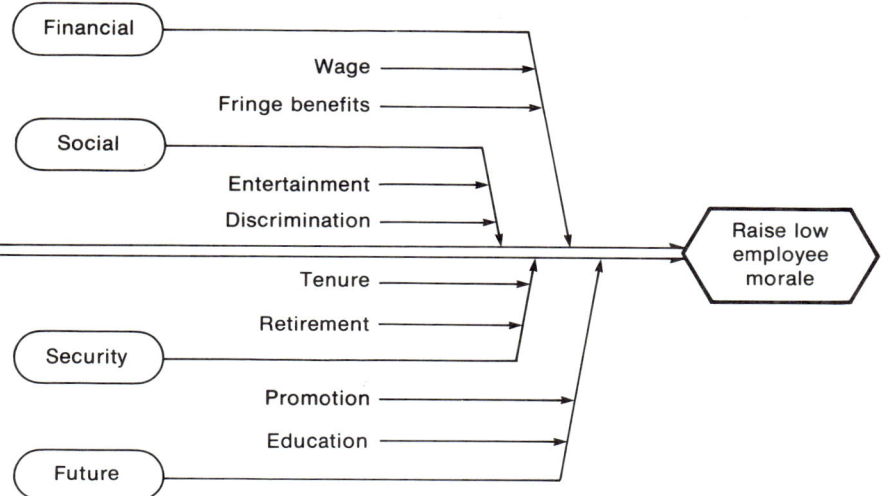

Figure 2-5 Single-sided diagram displaying the causes of low morale and assisting the diagnosis of the reasons behind the problem.

semblance in appearance does not extend to application. In drawing a decision tree, the objective is to identify decision points and to understand how future decisions will affect the present; conversely, in drawing a C & E diagram the objective is to better understand the present to solve a current problem in a way that optimizes future effects.

CLUSTER PATTERN It is sometimes easier to organize factors when the format depicting physical or organizational arrangements is familiar to an OR/MS team. A traditional process flowchart (Figure 2-6), assembly diagram, organizational

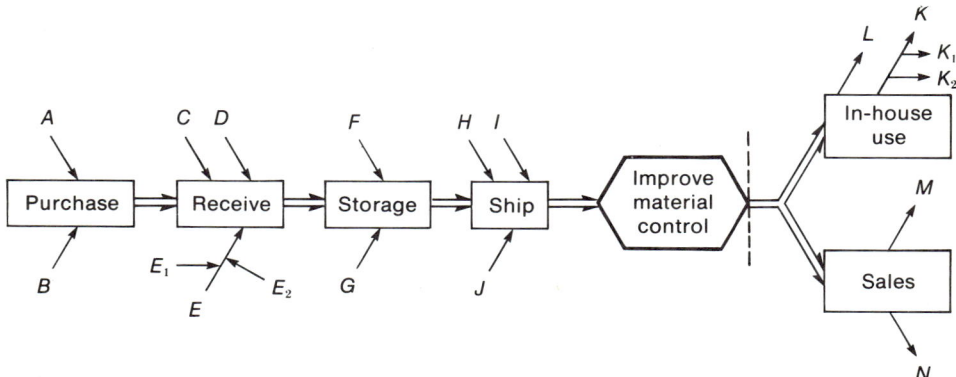

Figure 2-6 Cluster-patterned C & E diagram drawn to resemble the actual flow of a process.

chart, or other familiar format can be used as the basic frame upon which to build a C & E diagram. Related arrows of pertinent causes and effects are clustered around each division. The advantage of this approach is the familiarity of the format; the disadvantage is that it may elicit preconceptions which may limit the analysis to thinking within a traditional framework.

SCALED PATTERN Another structural variation of a C & E diagram is to scale its basic backbone. Using a time scale, for example, the process-flow condition displayed in Figure 2-6 can be redrawn as shown in Figure 2-7. The chronology and technological ordering of purchasing, receiving, storage, and shipping are indicated by the relative positions of their arrows on the time scale. Other useful sequential scales are *degree of technology* and *hierarchy of increasing responsibility*.

Example 2-2: Recognizing the obvious An industrial engineer volunteered to assist the management of a sheltered workshop overcome a production problem. The shop serves as a rehabilitation center for handicapped workers. It provides training and work for the handicapped in assembly operations and production of wood products such as pallets, packing cases, wishing wells, and picnic tables. The work is purposely designed to emphasize hand labor, and consequently the processes employ minimum mechanization.

A quality-control problem occurred when the center began work on a contract to produce berry boxes. The customer threatened to cancel the contract if sturdier boxes were not produced within a month. The first analysis of the problem identified the obvious causes and effects, as shown in Figure 2-8. An obvious solution appeared to be to add an inspection station for outgoing boxes to ensure the use of good wood and adequate fastening. Then it was noticed that attention was being focused strictly on effects, not causes. Maybe it would be better to have the workers inspect as they produced.

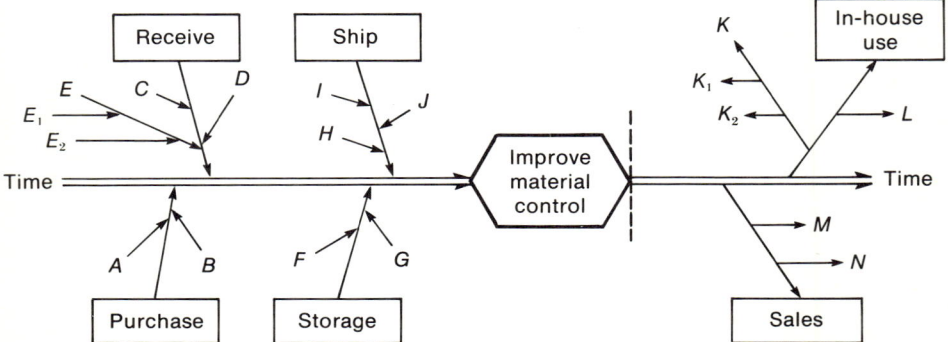

Figure 2-7 Time-scaled C & E diagram portraying the same process flow shown in Figure 2-6.

Problem Investigation: Cause & Effect Diagrams

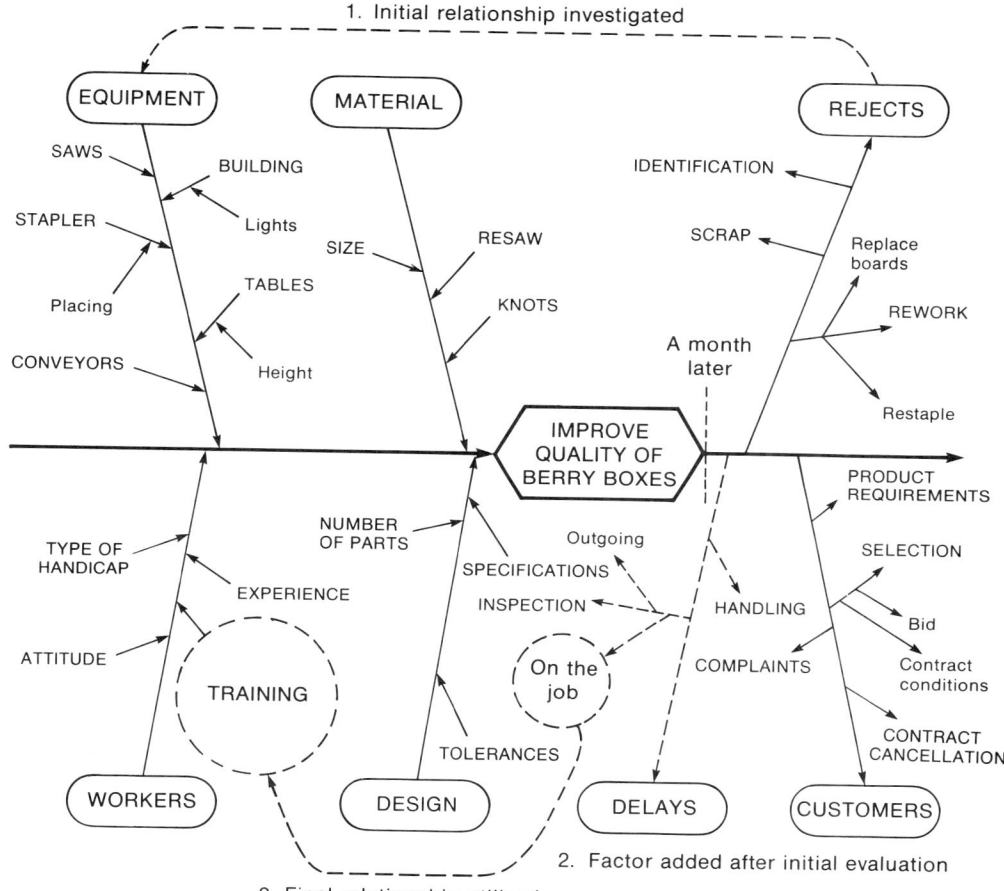

Figure 2-8 Initial and revised C & E diagram representing production of berry boxes in a rehabilitation center. Steps in the solution are numbered.

As a result of this internal inspection idea, attention was given to the need for better physical facilities, brighter lights, lower work tables for wheelchair workers, jigs for more accurate stapling, etc. These and other considerations led to the addition of a new effect, delays (shown in Figure 2-8 by dashed arrows). To minimize delays, a suggestion was made to improve the motion patterns of workers. Finally, the subject of training was considered, and it was then recognized that training was directed to general skills, but little effort was made to tell individual workers what was expected of them and what particularly should be watched in satisfying each production contract.

Thus, the berry-box problem was solved simply by informing the workers what was needed and how to do it with existing facilities. The optimal feasible solution is indicated by the connected and circled factors shown in the lower portion of Figure 2-8. Perhaps the answer may appear patently obvious, but how many times have sophisticated solutions been installed where a simple change could have produced the same results at lower cost and less loss of dignity?

2-5 History and theory

The C & E diagrams described in this chapter evolved from the one-sided cause analysis, or single-sided diagram developed and widely acclaimed in Japan. This diagram is called *Tokusei-Yoin Hyo*, or the *Ishikawa diagram*, in honor of Professor Kaoru Ishikawa of Tokyo University, who devised this form of analysis in 1953 while doing quality-control consulting for Kawasaki Steel Company. He used it to communicate with managers who felt the complexities of quality problems were overwhelming when explained orally. Today, hardly a quality-control textbook is written in Japan without a discussion of the Ishikawa diagram.

The principles of causality have interested philosophers and scientists for centuries. The famous Greek philosopher Aristotle (384–322 B.C.) taught that all science was the search for causes. He gave *cause* a far broader definition than is generally accepted today. To Aristotle a *cause* meant an answer to the question "Why are things as they are?" Furthermore, he proposed that all causes can be classified into one or more of the following four types:

1. *Material cause:* The resource of which a thing is made (the "nouns" in a C & E diagram)

2. *Formal cause:* The structure of the entity (the tree structure of a C & E diagram)

3. *Efficient cause:* The activity that transforms the resource (the "verbs" in a C & E diagram)

4. *Final cause:* The end purpose, or goal, as which the process of change aims and terminates (the center box in a C & E diagram)

CAUSALITY IN ASTRONOMY AND PHYSICS Aristotelian viewpoints persisted among the medieval philosophers. They regarded an *effect* as flowing from the nature of its cause, and they held that the following premises are indisputably true about the nature of causality:

Nothing can come from nothing.

Nothing can give what it does not have.

The cause must have at least as much detail (perfection) as its effects.

However, the pitfall of Aristotelian philosophy was its insistence on attributing *final cause*, or *intention*, to inanimate objects. It insisted on explaining *why* things behaved as they did instead of discovering the physical laws which would describe *how* they behaved.

Astronomers such as Nicolaus Copernicus (1473–1543), Johann Kepler (1571–1630), and Galileo Galilei (1564–1643) were the first to substitute *reasons* for causes, thus paving the way for Newtonian (Sir Isaac Newton, 1642–1727) physics. In Newtonian physics planets do not move in their orbits because of their own volition; rather, their orbits are a consequence of the laws of motion. The Scottish philosopher and historian David Hume (1711–1776) is usually credited with being the first to appreciate the full implications of the revolution in physics. He generalized that causality is merely the expectation, derived from past experience, that an effect is forthcoming just as physical laws are expectations that are borne of repeated observations.

It was not until the birth of quantum mechanics that the concept of strict determinism in causality was successfully challenged. Heisenberg's celebrated uncertainty principle (1925) established a limit to the certitude of any physical observation. The principles of classical mechanics are still being used today, but only as expected measures for predicting the macroscopic behavior of physical objects.

CAUSALITY IN OR/MS Aristotle's view of causality is compatible with the OR/MS viewpoint toward systems studies. Resources (material cause) are transformed by activities (efficient cause) of the system under investigation (formal cause) to produce a profit (final cause). Similarly, in accord with medieval philosophers, in systems studies it is recognized that a problem must have a cause, a solution cannot rely on unavailable resources, and the effects of a solution should match the causes of the problem. Though these views may appear too fundamental to be useful, they do advise against some practices that have troubled problem solvers, such as assuming that the end (profit) justifies the means (activities), relying on free advice (something for nothing), and prescribing simple cures for complex ailments.

The modern view of causality also carries a message for OR/MS practitioners. The uncertainty principle pertains to management problems as well as to quantum mechanics; that is, it is assumed that factors will occur at certain values even though OR/MS analysts are aware that these values are subject to variations and uncertainties. For instance, in solving a distribution problem, it is commonly assumed that supply and demand are known, that current cost figures are accurate, and that assets, goals, and other conditions will remain essentially unchanged in the future. These are big assumptions, but they are not unreasonable and they allow a problem solver to employ proven techniques. Otherwise, a whole spectrum of possible solutions would be required to account for all kinds of future conditions. Thus, deterministic solution methods are considered reputable and enjoy wide acceptance. However, their use should be accompanied by reservations that recognize they are based on approximations, and the solutions derived should be considered as guides (probably the best available) rather than inevitable consequences.

SECTION 2-5 TUNE-UP

1. You must decide what kind of flashlight to buy. Investigate the problem by constructing a C & E diagram to show the causes of illumination and the desired effects.

2. What assumptions of certainty did you make in developing the diagram? How can you defend them?

2-6 C & E benefits and applications

It should be apparent by now that a C & E diagram is not a precision tool for identifying a solution. Although a solution may be strongly suggested from appraising a diagram, the drawing exercise is primarily intended to guide an analyst toward the factors that will most likely yield a solution, not prove that a solution is optimal. The diagram's effectiveness thus depends on its completeness and on how well its contents are evaluated.

One of the most important benefits of a C & E evaluation should be obtained very early in the investigation: An agreement should be made among the OR/MS analysts and the people with the problem as to the true intent of the study. Too often an OR/MS study is launched on the basis of a short, cryptic problem statement that leaves many details in doubt. By exploding this statement into its component causes and effects, a mutual understanding should evolve about what controls are available and how the effectiveness of the solution will be evaluated. Without this agreement, even a well-conducted study may disappoint everyone. Additional benefits and applications for C & E analyses are summarized below.

CONCEPTUALIZATION The network of arrows in a C & E diagram constitutes a catalog of ideas. Additional inspirations tend to develop from association with factors already inserted in the diagram. The structured format may discourage innovative thinking, but important ideas are not likely to be overlooked owing to its systematic approach. Improved problem conceptualization can save a lot of time, money, and embarrassment.

CAPITULATION If the generation of free-wheeling ideas is considered preferable because it is more creative, the C & E diagram may be drawn by an observer of these brain-storming sessions. Some difficulty may arise, as randomly generated ideas tend to create parameters before the factors are identified. However, this difficulty may be alleviated by first tape-recording the brainstorming session and then having the team members themselves construct a C & E diagram. After the skeleton of the diagram has been drawn, the recording can be played back and pertinent ideas inserted in appropriate spots on the diagram.

SYSTEMATIZATION A formal questioning routine is created when the shafts of a C & E diagram are labeled with journalistic probes. This format is particularly useful when data are being collected through interviews. The following questions are derived:

Who?   (Activists involved with the causes and associated with the effects)
What?   (Materials, production, equipment, and other resources)
Where?   (Location and organizational relationships)
When?   (Time frame of actions and events)
Why?   (Behavior stemming from inter- and intrarelationships)
How?   (Methods, processes, training, and testing)

Answers to these questions tend to reveal factors which may seem trivial initially but which assume more substance as the investigation continues. Overlapping or related factors can be marked for regrouping when a pattern of key contributors emerges from the standard questions.

COMMUNICATION AND DOCUMENTATION Descriptions via connected lines have the advantages of simplicity, continuity, and cohesiveness. Unbelievers can point to a line and say no, or the unconvinced can finger their doubts to ask why. Group discussions can be diagrammed progressively in a controlled search for harmony, and then the results agreed upon can be capsulated as a dated C & E diagram for recordkeeping and review. A surprisingly large amount of information can be condensed in one C & E diagram with the advantage that all pertinent data are logically presented to the analyst on one single sheet of paper. A C & E diagram can be used to delegate to a manager both the authority and responsibility for undertaking a project, and the manager can use the completed diagram to report his findings to top management.

EXPERIMENTATION How many times has a great solution been developed for the wrong problem? Or worse, the wrong solution to the wrong problem? Problem definition helps pinpoint the true problem. It also helps detect the best solution method. Delineating the major factors concentrates effort in the most profitable solution area. Noting that certain factors are hazy or tend to interact with other factors may indicate a need for more or improved data. Distinguishing between directly controllable, selectable (e.g., time of the day or weather), and uncontrollable factors suggests designs for experiments.

INDIVIDUAL AND TEAM EVALUATION A C & E diagram developed by an individual provides an obvious appraisal of his knowledge of the subject. Most important, perhaps, is that a C & E diagram is one of the rare tools available for assessing the ability of a group to work as a team and the ability of an individual to act as a leader. C & E diagrams developed by different groups are usually so contrasting that it is easy to determine which group is best suited to handle a task.

34 Introduction to Operations Research and Management Science

The wealth of vocabulary is usually a good indication of the knowledge possessed by the team members, while the logical structure usually reveals the ability of the leader to organize the team effort in a constructive manner.

TUNE-UP SOLUTIONS

Section 2-3

1. Start over with a new leader and recorder. Check to see if all the main shafts actually represent principal causes and effects, and then get the recorder a larger sheet of paper.

2. First check to make sure that the construction has been logical so far. Bring in expert witnesses or resource persons to supply needed information. Check back later.

3. Select a more able discussion leader and shut off any bullies who want to monopolize the meeting. Then check for a balanced diet.

4. Check the pulses of the participants to see if you are dealing with people or computers. Bring in some refreshments and entertainment to enliven the action. Also put in a cutoff date to separate causes from effects.

Section 2-5

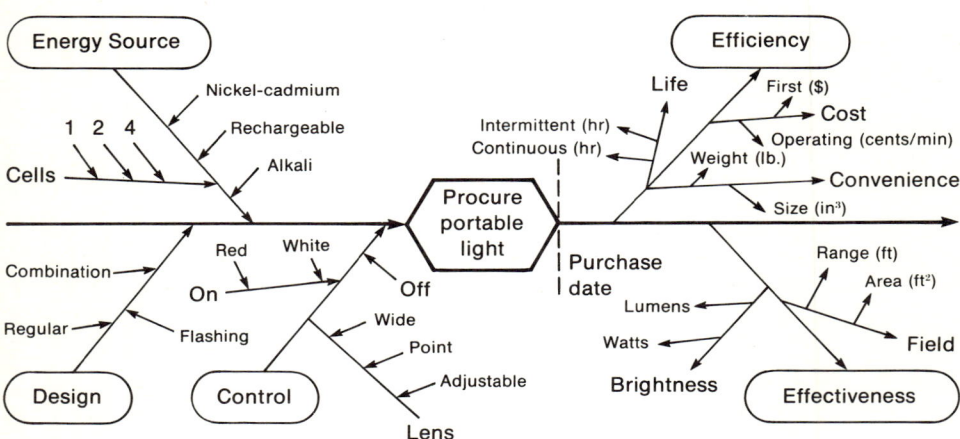

1. A sample solution is shown. Many different factors could have been recorded, but those given describe the types of flashlights available and what can be expected from them.

2. It is assumed that all types of flashlights will be available at the purchase date, and that future needs and expectations for the flashlight will remain the same. Both as-

sumptions are reasonable because the cutoff date and expected use are not far in the future; that is, the planning horizon is very short.

EXERCISES

2-1 In the discussion of C & E diagrams, several observations were made about precautions an OR/MS analyst should consider; for example, agreement should be obtained about what is expected from a study *before* commencing the study. List five additional precautions that apply to OR/MS studies.

2-2 Figure 2-9 represents the results of the initial phase of research undertaken by the National Marine Fisheries Service to investigate the feasibility of harvesting saury, a fish prized in the Far East as a delicacy but ignored by U.S. fishermen. Little was known about saury except that they could be harvested by taking advantage of their propensity to gather under a strong light source at night and that they school within range of West Coast fisheries.
   (a) Comment on the format and completeness of the C & E diagram in Figure 2-9.
   (b) Although you are not a saury expert, could you develop an outline for a research report from the causes and effects shown in the diagram? What would be the main section headings?

2-3 Your task is to provide a public address system for a regional meeting of your professional society. Develop a C & E diagram for the factors that should be considered. (At the time of drawing the diagram you do not know the rooms in which the meetings will be held; therefore, the drawing should reveal the options available and the decisions that must be made before the public address system is secured.)

2-4 Select a dangerous street intersection with which you are familiar and develop a C & E diagram to determine what might be done to reduce the number of accidents that occur at that intersection.

2-5 Based on the following definition of a *professional*, construct a C & E diagram to identify the main considerations in defining a professional. [*Hint:* Find the "true" problem behind the definition of a professional (the apparent problem) and try to construct a C & E diagram for its ideal solution.]

> The 1947 amendments to the labor law arose from the problem which existed under the 1935 Wagner Act whereby the desires of professional employees were lumped with those of nonprofessional employees, the result often being that the wishes of the professional employees were swamped by those of the numerically superior nonprofessional employees. Congress adopted the definition of "professional employee" to be: (a) any employee engaged in work (i) predominantly intellectual and varied in character as opposed to routine mental, manual, mechanical, or physical work; (ii) in-

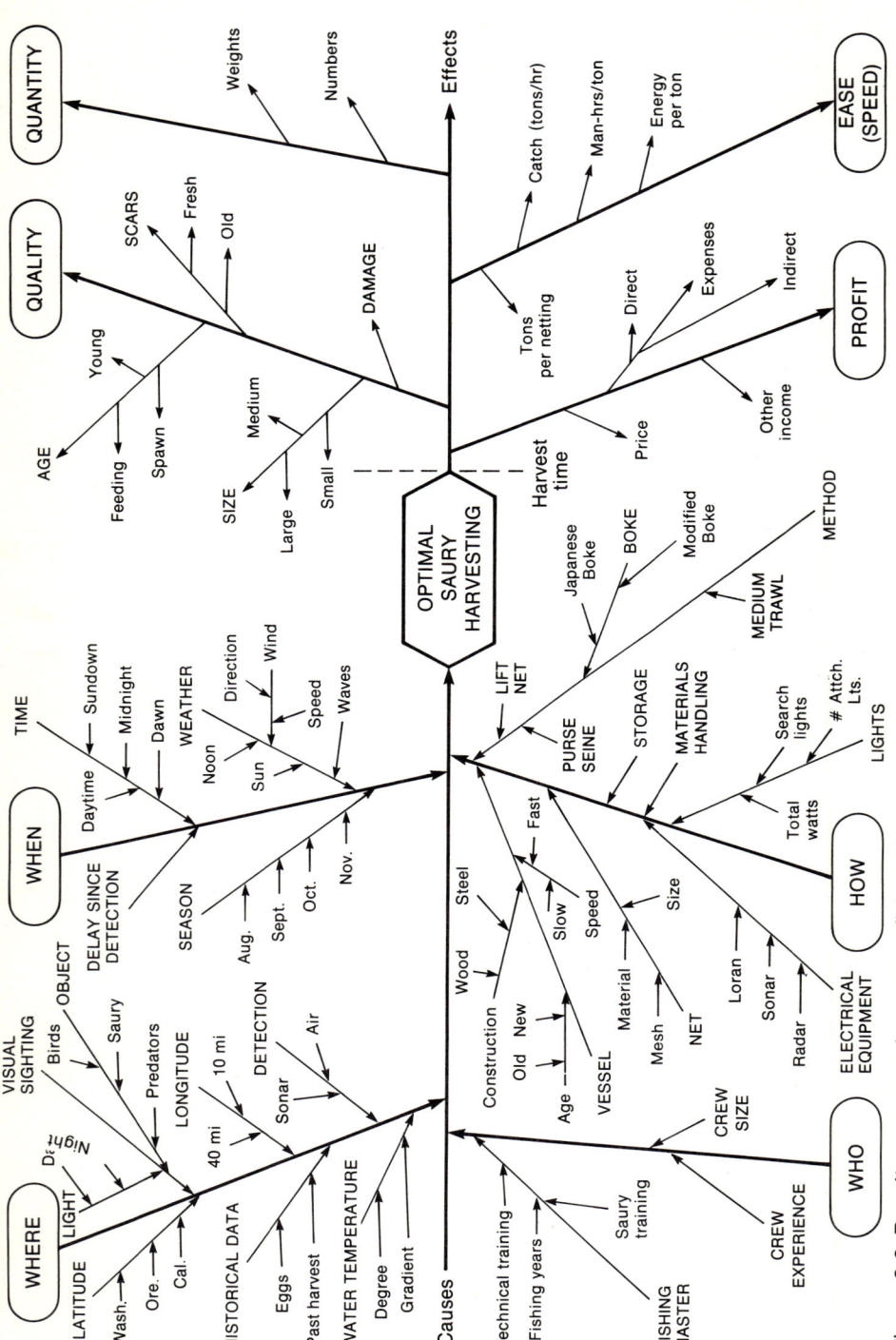

Figure 2-9 Results or research on saury fish performed by the National Maritime Fisheries Service. (Pacific saury is officially known as *Cololabis saira*.) (See M. S. Inoue and W. T. Pereyra, "Fisheries: Newest Frontier for Industrial Engineers," *Industrial Engineering*, pp. 40–45, Sept. 1971.)

volving the consistent exercise of discretion and judgement in its performance; (iii) of such a character that the output produced or the result accomplished cannot be standardized in relation to a given period of time; (iv) requiring knowledge of an advanced type in a field of science or learning customarily acquired by a prolonged course of specialized intellectual instruction and study in an institution of higher learning or in a hospital, as distinguished from a general academic education or from an apprenticeship or from training in the performance of routine mental, manual, or physical processes; or (b) any employee, who (i) has completed the courses of specialized intellectual instruction and study described in case (iv) of paragraph (a). and (ii) is performing related work under the supervision of a professional person to qualify himself to become a professional employee as defined in paragraph (a).[1]

2-6 Draw a C & E diagram to relate the following causes and effects noted by participants of a brainstorming session. *Hint:* First identify the problem and then identify the major factors.

Machines	Machines that are out of adjustment
Too much materials handling activity	Materials
Low productivity	Process
Lack of enthusiasm	Poor information system
Materials that are too brittle	No replacement parts
Obsolete model equipment	Nonexistent fringe benefits
Poorly prepared workers	Low educational level
Low wages	Workers
Lack of on-the-job training	

2-7 Draw a C & E diagram for the legislation and enactment of Social Security old-age benefits starting at age fifty-eight.

---

[1] NSPE *pub. No. 1007*, June 1973.

DATA ANALYSIS:
Pareto Pattern

Chapter 3

3-1 Data deluge

Experts postulate that by the middle of the eighteenth century, humanity's total fund of knowledge had doubled from what it was at the birth of Christ. Supposedly it doubled again by the year 1900 and again by 1950. Thus it took about 1,750 yr for the first doubling of knowledge, 150 yr for the second, and 50 for the next. What is more startling is that the next two doublings of humanity's knowledge took place in 1960 and 1968.

Today's wealth of knowledge is mind boggling. Even scientists have difficulty in keeping up with innovations in their fields of specialty, and a manager cannot possibly keep abreast of all the new developments that affect his broad interests. Ever faster machines with ever larger capacities are designed to store the data deluge, but it still takes time to retrieve the data and organize the information. Perhaps even more critical is knowing what data to extract and how to analyze it.

OR/MS techniques are nuggets in the expanding wealth of knowledge. Their value is owed in part to their capacity for incorporating abundant data into a systematic solution search. But utilization of OR/MS techniques depends first on being aware of their existence and then on gaining enough familiarity with them to decide if their use will be advantageous. When a technique is deemed suitable for solving a problem, pertinent data still are required before it can be applied. For these reasons, OR/MS users are concerned with two aspects of the data deluge: keeping up with recent technical developments and securing the data needed to implement them. Ways to treat both concerns are suggested from extensions of concepts proposed by Vilfredo Pareto.

3-2 Vilfredo Pareto

Few professionals have achieved as lasting fame as Vilfredo Pareto. And he did it in three professions: engineering, economics, and sociology. Pareto's lifetime can be roughly divided into segments corresponding to his three professional careers.

In 1869, at the age of 21, Pareto graduated with a Ph.D. in engineering from the Polytechnic Institute of Turin in Italy, achieving first position in the final examinations. He then became a consulting engineer for the Italian railways. Four years later he took a position as general superintendent of an iron works, and in this position his attention was drawn to problems of production, transportation, politics, and business. When his father died in 1882, Pareto's inheritance freed him from work obligations and he pursued the study of economics. Pareto's most productive years as an economist were from 1892 to 1912, during which he succeeded his teacher Leon Walras (1834-1910) to the chair of political economy at the University of Lausanne in Switzerland in 1892 and helped establish the foundations for modern demand and production analysis, new welfare economics, and econometrics. His name has been given to his concept of an ideal societal condition (*Paretian optimality*), a method for graphically portraying statistical distributions (*Pareto diagram*), and the income distribution he detected (*Pareto distribution,* or *Pareto's law*).

During his twilight years until he died in 1923, Pareto's interests switched from economics to sociology, and he brought to the field his earlier emphasis on scientific and rational methodology. Although the political aspects of his social theories have been criticized heavily, his contributions are acknowledged. In effect, Pareto was a one-man OR/MS team.

SECTION 3-2 TUNE-UP: Paretian optimality

A major difficulty in evaluating the outcome from a certain course of action is caused by the fact that different people place different values on the same outcome. For instance, acquiring a glass of water would have relatively little value for a person who has plenty of water available, but it would have a huge value for someone dying of thirst. Pareto suggested that society should seek a condition where each person has maximum satisfaction without decreasing the degree of achievement of any other person, and a situation where this condition has been achieved is known as a *Pareto optimum*. A lasting problem in promoting this condition has been to find a way to measure personal satisfaction.

Putting measurement difficulties aside, Paretian optimality is a worthy criterion for judging social actions, and it also implies criteria that can be used for general problem solving. For example, extensions of Pareto's reasoning could lead to the following two OR/MS guides. State how each guide can be considered related to Paretian optimality, what difficulties can be expected, and how each can assist in problem solving.

1. When a study has multiple objectives, the situation should be designed to satisfy each specific objective without adversely affecting any other objective. (*Hint:* Consider a situation where a course of action is desired that will maximize profit and employee morale but minimize damage to the environment.)
2. Resources which affect a problem but are not exhausted by competing activities are not constraints and need not be included in a study. Only those resource restrictions which are difficult to satisfice without causing an out-of-kilter condition need be included. (*Hint:* Consider the energy crisis and its repercussions.)

3-3 Pareto diagram

In his attempt to characterize the distribution of wealth, Pareto gathered statistical data from such diverse countries as England, Germany, Italy, and Peru. By ranking personal fortune in a decreasing order of magnitude, he observed that the greater the personal fortune, the smaller the number of persons who possess it. A histogram portraying this situation would have the tallest bar representing the majority of the population with the lowest income to the left, and the shortest bar representing the minority with great fortune (and thus income) to the right. To show the percentage of the total population below a given level of wealth, a cumulative distribution curve, or *ogive*, can be superimposed to represent the area of the histogram to the left of that level. Since the bars of the histogram are arranged in a nonincreasing order, the ogive would naturally form a concave curve. A composite graph of a histogram and its ogive is known today as a *Pareto diagram*, and we shall use the term *Pareto pattern* to describe the concave characteristics.

Example 3-1: *Graphic analysis of operating conditions for a 40-ft fishing vessel.* The factors affecting the economics of operating a commercial fishing vessel are displayed in Figure 3-1*a*.[1] The relative magnitude of the costs and revenues is more apparent when graphed as shown in Figure 3-1*b* and *c*. The two Pareto diagrams reveal that variable costs are most significant as they account for 63.2 percent of the total expenses, and variable plus fixed costs amount to 85.7 percent. Similarly, tuna accounts for 39.7 percent of the total revenue, and the combined revenue from tuna and crab accounts for 75 percent. Another more familiar way of displaying these data is by the breakeven chart shown in Figure 3-1*d*. All

---

[1]Data are from "Fishing Business Management," by F. J. Smith, *Oregon State University Sea Grant Publication No. 6*, revised June 1973.

(*a*) C & E diagram for the typical annual costs and catches for a 40-ft vessel

(*b*) Pareto diagram of expenses

(*c*) Pareto diagram of revenues

(*d*) Breakeven chart

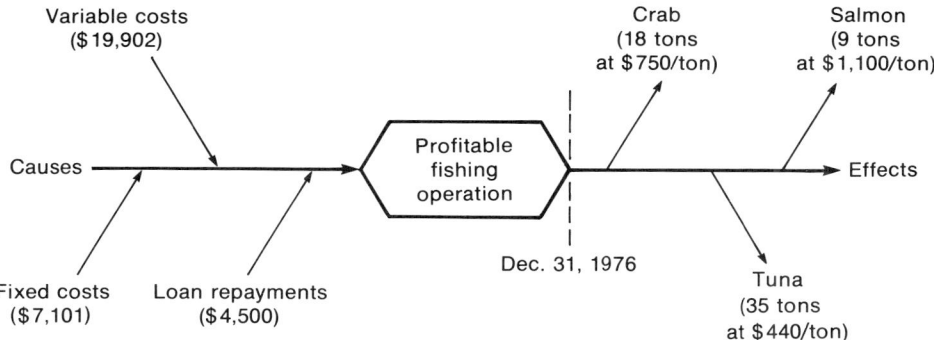

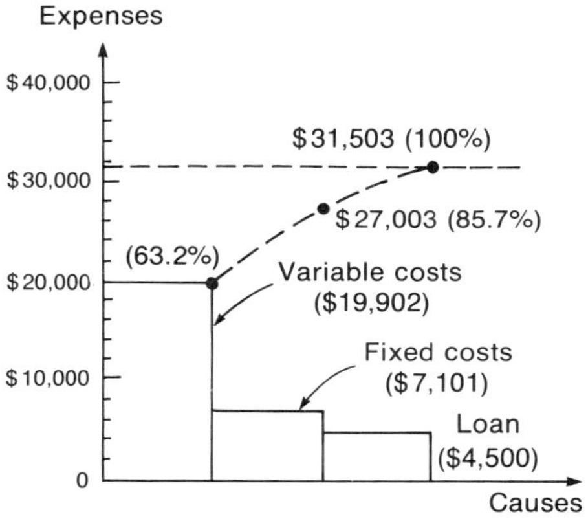

Figure 3-1 Operations analysis of a 40-ft fishing vessel.

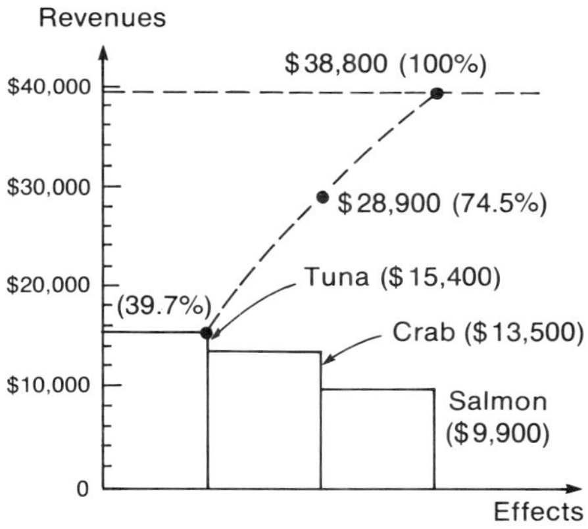

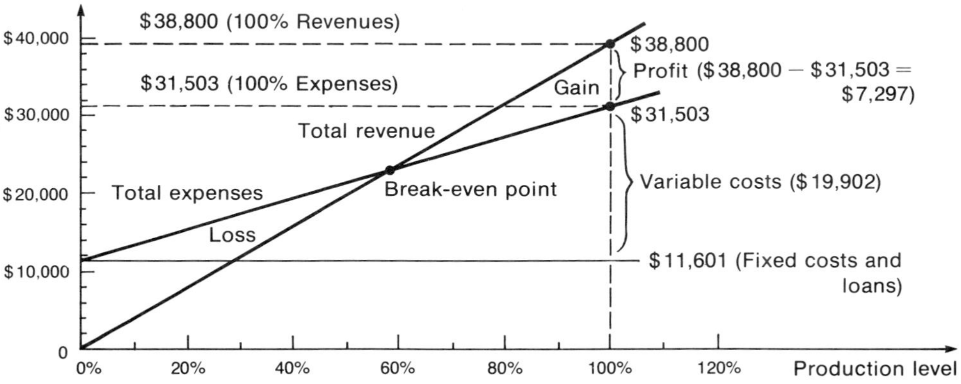

three versions have their unique values: The C & E diagram helps in the collection of data, the Pareto diagrams focus attention on the most significant factors, and the breakeven chart shows the (supposedly linear) relationship of the monetary values in terms of capacity utilization.

As an example, let us consider the effect that a ban on salmon fishing would have on this operation. The Pareto diagram (Figure 3-1c) shows the revenues will drop $9,900 to 74.5 percent of the present level. The breakeven chart (Figure 3-1d) shows that the operation will be barely breaking even at the 74.5 percent level. Assuming that it is not possible to increase revenues, an OR/MS study may be needed to reduce the expenditures and restore the $9,900 loss in profit. The Pareto diagram (Figure 3-1b) shows that it is fruitless to focus our attention to the reduction of loans ($4,500) or fixed costs ($7,101) unless the variable costs ($19,902) can also be cut down. It is then time to go back to our C & E diagram (Figure 3-1a) to find more details on items included within the variable costs.

3-4 Pareto patterns

Pareto diagrams offer interesting possibilities for OR/MS analysts, but their values can be enhanced by a statistical insight into the Pareto pattern.

PARETO DISTRIBUTION Pareto's study of income distribution leads to a family of ogives that can be characterized by the continuous function

$$F(X) = 1 - X^{-\alpha}$$

where $F(X)$ is the proportion of the total population living on an income of X or less, and α is a parametric constant. Figure 3-2 is obtained by assuming $\alpha = 0.5$.

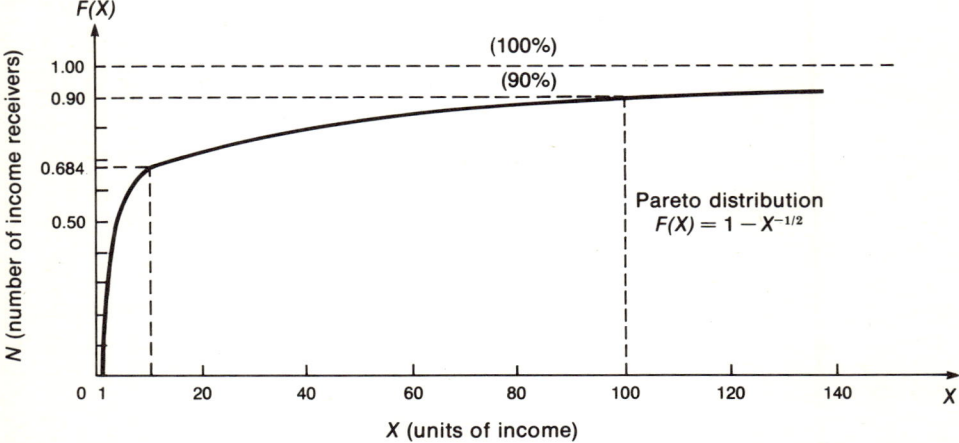

Figure 3-2 Pareto income-distribution ogive based on the formula $F(X) = 1 - X^{\alpha}$ where $\alpha = 0.5$.

It is seen that while 68.4 percent of the population exists with an income of 10 units of X or less, 10 percent of the population enjoys the affluence of 100 units of X or more.

Though sometimes labeled *Pareto's law*, the universality of this function is questionable. Figure 3-2 shows a negative population $F(X) \leq 0$ for income levels of X between 0 and 1, and illustrates that the very rich must be infinitely wealthy $[X = \infty$ to attain $F(X) = 1.0]$. In fact, Pareto wrote:

This law being empirical, it may not always remain true, especially not for all mankind. At present, however, the statistics which we have present no exception to the law; it may, therefore, provisionally be accepted as universal. But exceptions may be found, and I should not be greatly surprised if some day a well authenticated exception were discovered.[1]

Nonetheless, having a mathematical model to characterize the income distribution contributed greatly to furthering advances in economic theories. Extending Pareto patterns outside economic theory is even more impugnable, but some credence can be awarded to the general nature of Pareto's distribution through the consideration of statistical properties.

TCHEBYCHEV'S INEQUALITY Statistical distributions have an infinite variety of shapes. Yet, if only the mean and standard deviation of a distribution can be determined, *Tchebychev's inequality* guarantees that the probability of the variable deviating from its mean by more than k times its standard deviation is equal to or less than $1/k^2$. Furthermore, if the distribution is known to be *unimodal* (having only one peak and the distribution is monotonically decreasing on both sides of its peak), then the *Camp-Meidel extension* to Tchebychev's inequality maintains that the probability will be less than or equal to $1/2.25k^2$. By virtue of the histogram's declining shape on its right, a Pareto diagram always has a unimodal distribution; therefore, the Camp-Meidel extension is applicable to any Pareto diagram.

CENTRAL LIMIT THEOREM Since an OR/MS study is concerned with the behavior of complex systems, each identifiable factor in a study is likely to reflect the composite effects of several variables. In general, if a continuous variable is the sum of several independent contributing variables, then it tends to have a *normal distribution* (also known as a *bell-shaped*, or *Gaussian*, distribution). A more formal statement of this principle is known as the *central limit theorem*.

NEGATIVE-EXPONENTIAL DISTRIBUTION The general formula for a negative-exponential density function is

$f(X) = Ae^{-AX}$

where $0 \leq A \leq 1.0$ is a parameter and $e = 2.71828\ldots$. If we were to plot the

---

[1] *J. Polit. Econ.*, vol. 5, p. 501, September 1897.

cumulative area under this curve to the left of X, we would obtain an ogive with the form

$$F(X) = 1 - e^{-AX}$$

Note the resemblance of this formula to Pareto's income distribution $F(X) = 1 - X^{-\alpha}$. Both have similar shapes, but the negative-exponential distribution has the advantage of remaining nonnegative for $0 \leq X \leq 1$. Both the mean and standard deviation of the negative-exponential density function are equal to $1/A$.

The cumulative distribution values tabulated in Figure 3-3 for the negative-exponential distribution compare favorably with estimates obtained from Tchebychev's inequality, Camp-Meidel's extension, and the normal distribution. Using $f(X)/A$ and $k = AX$, the cumulative distribution value of $1 - e^{-k}$ is easily obtained by knowing the relative height of the histogram e^{-k}. The relative height of the histogram bar will indicate the proportion of the total area to the right of the k value.

It is equally easy to identify the value of k from $f(X)$, $K = -\ln f(X)$, or from $F(X)$, $k = -\ln[1 - F(X)]$. The table in Figure 3-3 may also be used for approximation. Figure 3-3 portrays two graphs, one for $A = 1/2$, and another where the curves have been normalized using $k = AX$.

MANAGEMENT IMPLICATIONS The foregoing extension of the Pareto pattern is not a binding rule for data analysis, but rather it suggests the possibilities for examining data in ways that render them more useful. We should recognize that all data do not follow the negative-exponential distribution exactly, but many activities have the general Pareto pattern. Lacking further insight, a negative-exponential distribution helps us estimate the magnitude of the overall problem and focuses our attention on the area where the need is the greatest.

One of the most famous management credos is implied from the shape of the ogive: "Devote primary attention to the few activities where most of the action is concentrated." This advice is raised to the status of a rule in inventory control where the *ABC rule* divides supplies into three categories. The *A* category accounts for only about 20 percent of the types of items in storage but almost 80 percent of the total dollar value. As shown in Figure 3-4, the proportions are reversed in passing from class *A* to *C* items. This recognition of the more active items in a population directs attention to areas where analysis effort will be most beneficial. In inventory control, *ABC* analysis effectively "buys" time for control of *A* items by overstocking *C* items.

A negative-exponential distribution is most likely to occur naturally rather than artificially. In Chapter 12, its well-accepted use in queuing situations will be described. In information theory, the frequency of occurrence of certain messages tends to be distributed negative exponentially. In reliability models, defects tend to occur similarly. If a distribution differs markedly from a negative-exponential pattern, it is a good indication that there is an artificial factor causing the imbalance to occur. An OR/MS study may be facilitated when such an imbalance

(a) Comparison of statistical distribution assumptions

Type of distribution		Any	Unimodal	Normal	Negative exponential	
Principle		Tchebychev	Camp–Meidel	Central limit	Cumulative area $(1 - e^{-k})$	Relative height (e^{-k})
Area within $\mu \pm k/A$ where $1/A$ is the standard deviation	$k = 0$	0^a	0^a	0^a	0^a	100^a
	$k = 1$	0	55.6	68.27	63.21	36.79
	$k = 2$	75	88.9	95.45	86.47	13.59
	$k = 3$	88.9	95.05	99.73	95.02	4.98
	$k = 4$	93.75	97.22	100	98.17	1.83
	$k = 5$	96	98.22	100	99.33	0.67

⟵ Always add up to 100% ⟶

[a] These values are in percents.

(b) Integration of Ae^{-AX} where $A = 1/2$

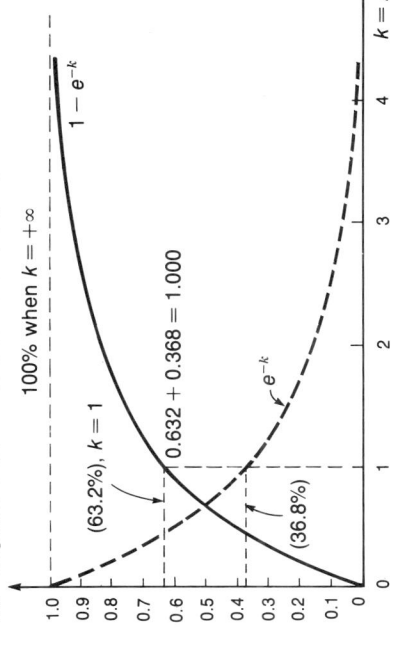

(c) Negative exponential distribution, $f(k) = e^{-k}$

Figure 3-3 Negative-exponential histogram, its ogive, and comparison with other distributions.

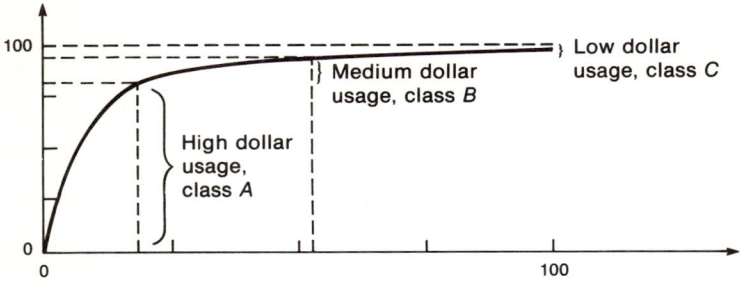

Figure 3-4 Pareto pattern of dollar transactions with respect to types of items held in inventory.

is observed on the Pareto diagram. "Management by exception" is another management credo that can benefit from a Pareto analysis.

SECTION 3-4 TUNE-UP: Paretian "guesstimates"—when all else fails!
Let us assume that you are put on a spot to make an educated (?) guess at the following answers with no further knowledge or data. State your guess and your reasoning.

1. From August 1973 through April 1974, Japan imported roughly 2 million 20-kg bags of onions from the United States and 1 million from Taiwan. If these countries were the leading exporters of onions to Japan, what would be the total number of 20-kg bags of onions imported by Japan during that period?

2. In Example 3-1, you have decided to analyze the variable costs further, and you have found the following leading items:

Crewshare	$9,605
Vessel repairs	$2,990
Gear repairs	$2,486
Galley	$1,525

   Estimate how many more items you should investigate in order to uncover at least 95 percent of all variable costs.

3. A study of California's ocean-related needs by James L. Sullivan of the University of Santa Barbara (1972) revealed that the five top-priority items identified in an inquiry through 71 interviews (7 representing members of a chamber of commerce, 9 conservationists, 10 regional and local governments, 5 universities and colleges, 6 industries, 5 citizens and consultants, and 29 state and federal governments) were as follows:

Categories	Votes
Planning and management	40
Recreation	38

Preservation and conservation   27
Living marine resource use   18
Pollution control   16

If multiple votes were possible, estimate the total number of votes received for all categories.

4. In the study in question 3, estimate the number of categories needed to cover 95 percent of all responding votes.

The following example describes a study where the general tools we have discussed previously are applied in an OR/MS setting. In addition, a general solution procedure for a particular type of problem is introduced.

Example 3-2: Cable-TV planning Assume that you have an investment opportunity to set up a community cable-TV operation in a region inhabited by 40,000 people. A market survey indicates 5,000 households are willing to pay $5/mo for the TV service. You are willing to invest in this venture provided that the operation becomes profitable within 5 yr, requiring that the equipment, cable, and other expenses be paid off by that time. The major factors for this operation are shown by the C & E diagram in Figure 3-5, and a rough estimate of expenditures reveals the following cost figures:

Personnel

1 manager at $2,000/mo	$24,000
1 bookkeeper-receptionist at $1,000/mo	12,000
2 technicians-repairmen at $14,000/yr each	28,000
2 operators at $13,000/yr each	26,000
Total	$90,000/yr

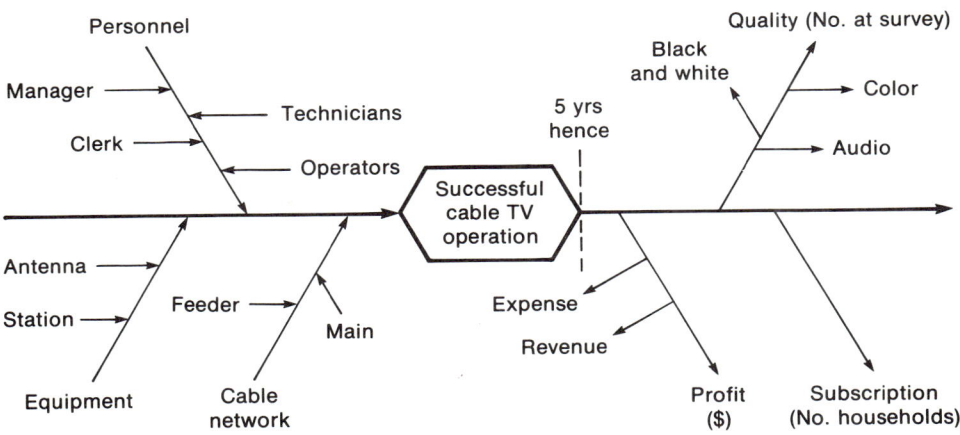

Figure 3-5 C & E diagram for establishing a cable-TV company.

Equipment
Antenna, station, electronic gear, etc. $200,000, or $40,000/yr

Operating Costs
Electricity, utilities, administration, etc. $24,000/yr

Local taxes and licenses $18,000/yr

Other expenses $ 8,000/yr

Cable-connection costs
Main-line cable $3/ft, or $15,000/mi
Feeder line to individual houses   25 cents/ft

A map of the area to be served by the cable-TV company is shown in Figure 3-6. Installing main cables at $15,000/mi quickly becomes expensive. Separate cable lines radiating from the antenna and main-station location indicate a need for about 53 mi of cable at an approximate total cost of $795,000: over a 5-yr amortization period the annual cost is $159,000 (not including interest expenses).

Cost categories are displayed in Figure 3-7. It is apparent that the total annual cost of $339,000 will not be recovered by charging 5,000 customers $60/yr. Also, the Pareto pattern suggests that there may be additional expense items yet to be

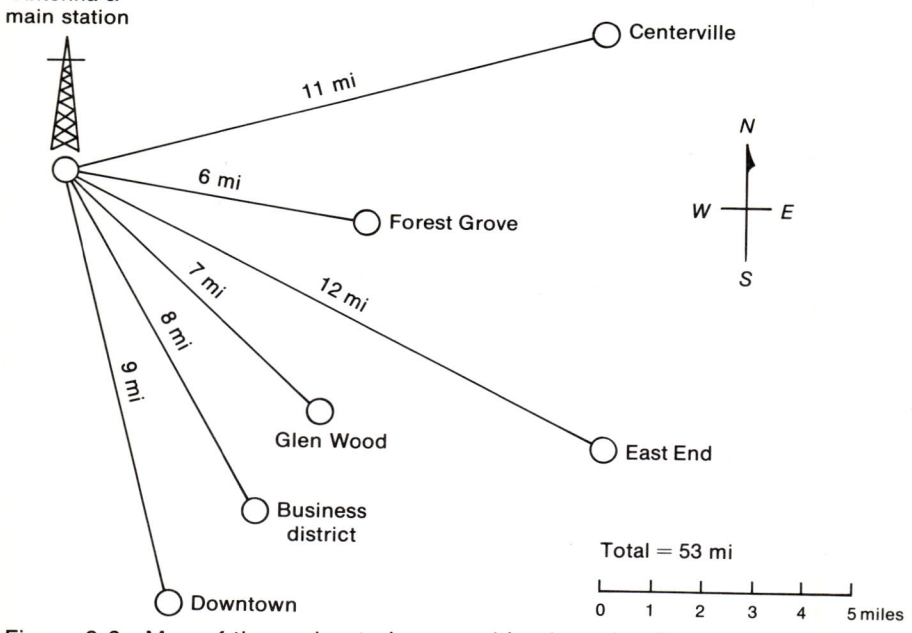

Figure 3-6   Map of the region to be served by the cable-TV company.

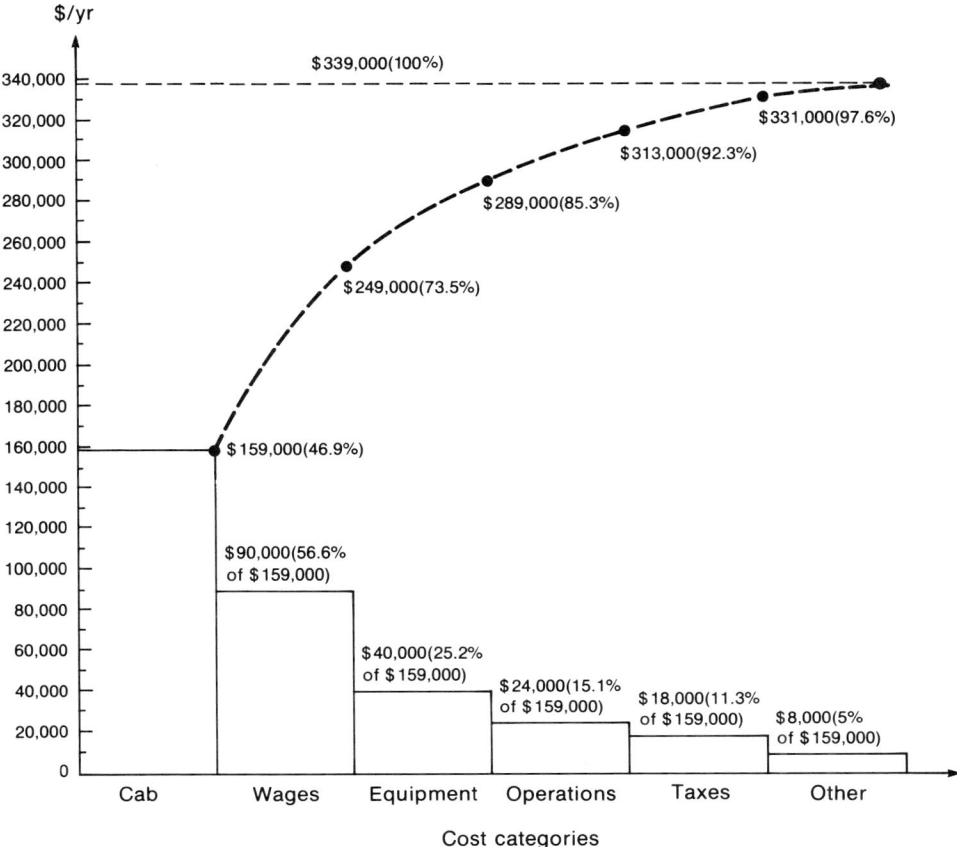

Figure 3-7 Pareto pattern of annual costs for the cable-TV company assuming the installation costs are not passed on to the customers. The histogram of bars represents cost categories, and the cumulative costs are shown by dashed lines.

identified. After further investigating the subscription experiences of cable-TV operations in other regions, it appears feasible to charge a one-time-only hookup cost, but it must be as low as possible.

An alternative proposal to the pattern shown in Figure 3-6 is to relocate the main cables. The cost per mile is approximately the same whether one or more cables are buried together; the major cost components are excavation and right-of-way acquisition, not the cost of cables or the amount of electrical signals to be transmitted (size of cables). The problem is to find the most economical network configuration.

NETWORK ALGORITHM It is possible to list all the ways of connecting the areas to be served by the cable-TV company and then select the shortest network;

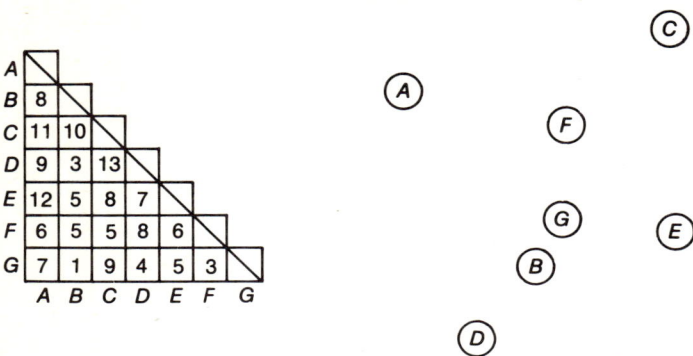

Figure 3-8 Distance matrix showing links between areas to be served by the cable and a map of the region showing the same relative positions of the service areas.

however, it would take an exorbitant amount of effort to do so. A systematic solution procedure is needed. A procedure that guarantees a feasible solution (usually the optimal solution) for a general class of problems is called an *algorithm*. For example, the fact that you may never have carried out the division of one particular number, say, 10, 365, 987, 590, 134 by another specified number, 98, 978, 354, 012.02, does not stop you from being confident that you can carry out that operation. This is because the process of long division is an algorithm you have learned to apply to any set of two numbers.[1]

There is a simple algorithm, the network algorithm, that neatly solves the problem of finding the shortest path connecting the areas to be served by cable TV. First construct a table of distances between all points; Figure 3-8 represents such a matrix. With the given matrix the algorithm can be applied as follows:

Step 1. Find the smallest number in the matrix (in case of a tie, select one arbitrarily). Circle that number.

Step 2. Draw a line across the columns and rows corresponding to the column and the row label of the number selected.

Step 3. Select the smallest number in the row or the column that has one and only one line through it (break ties arbitrarily). Circle that number.

Step 4. Draw a line through the column and/or the row corresponding to the number selected in step 3. Repeat steps 3 and 4 until all points have been connected; every cell should be crossed through both vertically (columnwise) and horizontally (rowwise). There should be one less circle than the

---

[1]The word *algorithm* comes from the surname of a ninth century Persian mathematician, *Al-Khuwarizmi*, which means "from the region of Khuwarazam," known today as *Khiva* in the Soviet Union. This scholar wrote a book entitled *Kitab al jabr w'almuquabala* in Baghdad (A. D. 825) which can be translated to mean "A Book on the Rules of Restoration and Reductions." His full name, as far as it can be traced, seems to have been Mohammed ibn-Musa al-Kuhwarizmi, and the book is more simply known as *Liber Algorism*.

number of points (number of rows or columns), and the set of circles identifies the solution.

Figure 3-9 shows how the network algorithm can be applied to the cable-TV data. The following steps were used:

Step 1. B-G connection was found to have the smallest number (1).

Step 2. Either G-F or B-D could have been selected (both 3); G-F was chosen arbitrarily.

Step 3. B-D (3) is the smallest number eligible; we now have F-G-B-D for 7 mi total.

Step 4. B-E, C-F, or E-G could have been selected; B-E was selected arbitrarily.

Step 5. C-F was connected.

Step 6. A-F completes the minimum length network of 23 mi. Other choices (where an arbitrary choice was made) would have yielded the same total length.

An alternative optimal solution is to use the G-E connection as shown in Figure 3-10.

Note that a cell having both vertical and horizontal lines going through it cannot be selected, even if it happens to contain the smallest number, because such a connection would create a closed loop. For example, the G-D connection in step 5 contains the number 4; but using that connection would create a needless loop B-D-G-B. Similarly, a cell having neither a horizontal nor a vertical line going through it cannot be selected because such a connection would create a disconnected branch, which may or may not be an optimal connection. For example, choosing the connection E-F in step 1 would have added the value 6, which is not optimal since the correct solution would connect E to either B or G but not F.

Conclusion The linkage developed with the aid of the network algorithm saved 30 mi of cable from the original estimate. Over a 5-yr period this saving translates to a dollar reduction of $30 \times \$15{,}000 = \$450{,}000$ to make the annual cost of the cable network just

$$\frac{23 \text{ mi} \times \$15{,}000/\text{mi}}{5 \text{ yr}} = \$69{,}000/\text{yr}$$

When this figure is included with the other annual costs, the sum is $249,000, which is comfortably below the expected subscription receipts of $300,000/yr; therefore, it appears advisable to charge prospective customers only for the cost of the feeder lines.

Although Example 3-2 is oversimplified, it still illustrates the systematic OR/MS approach to problem solving. It also illustrates the power of a simple algorithm to organize data and lead the solution search. The answer could have been discovered intuitively, but in a more complex problem, say, involving 100

52 Introduction to Operations Research and Management Science

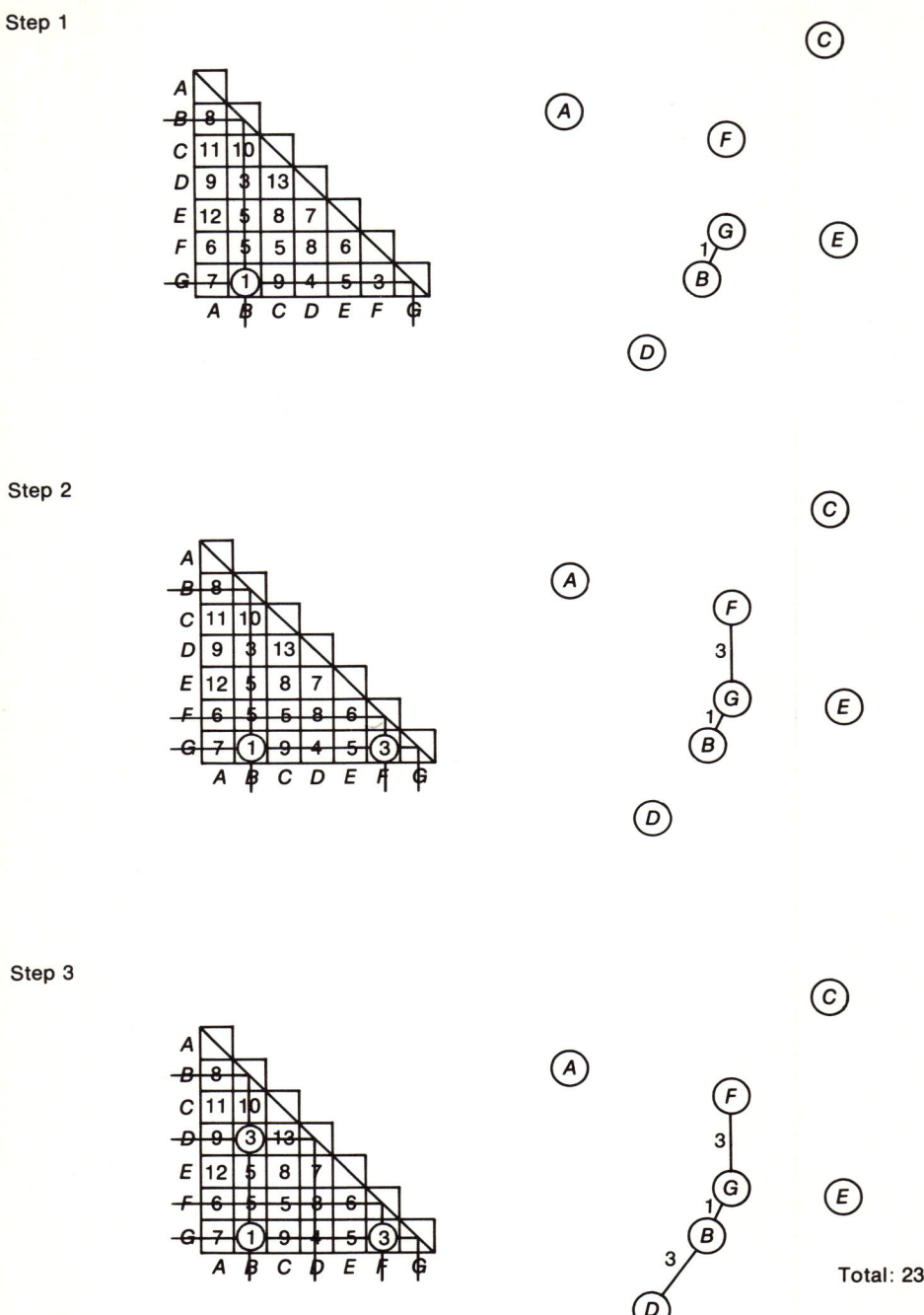

Figure 3-9 Application of the network algorithm to the cable-TV data.

Data Analysis: Pareto Pattern   53

Step 4

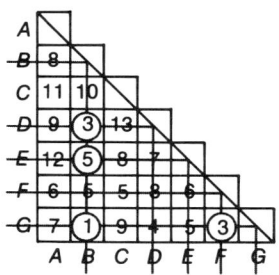 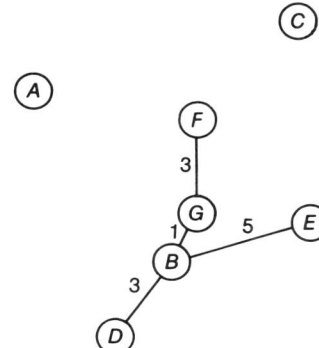

Step 5

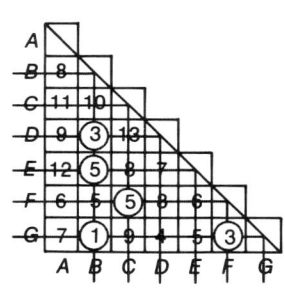 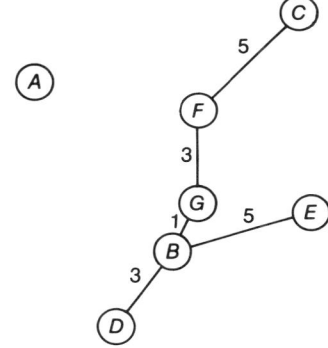

Step 6

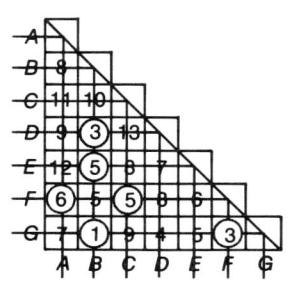 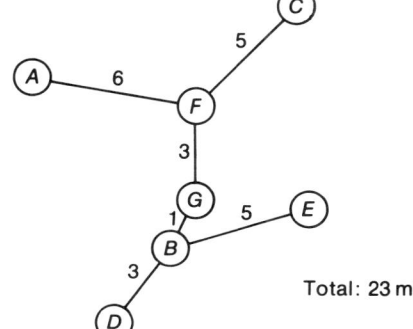

Total: 23 mi

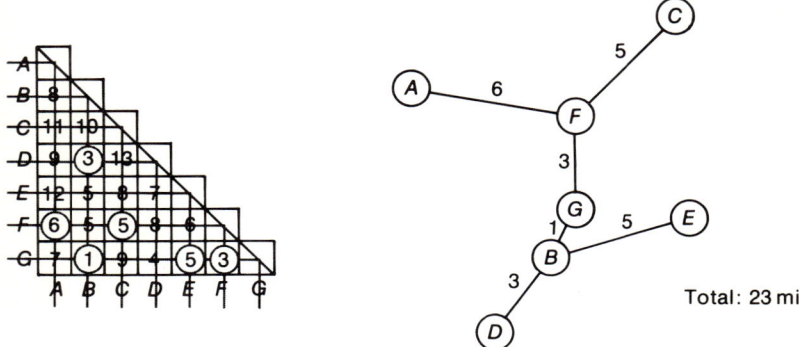

Figure 3-10 Alternative optimal solution to the cable-TV problem.

sites, an intuitive approach becomes absurd. For situations such as this and many others where proven solution procedures have already been developed, it is obviously worthwhile to know what they are and how to use them.

TUNE-UP SOLUTIONS

Section 3-2

1. *Relationship:* Multiple objectives represent a population, and a solution is an attempt to achieve Paretian optimality.
   Difficulties: Different objectives are likely to have different units of measurements, which create difficulty in comparing one with the other.
   Assistance: An acceptable solution provides at least some degree of satisfaction for all objectives; it should not maximize one objective at the expense of the others.

2. *Relationship:* If the supply of a resource is adequate and no extra portions are needed to provide full satisfaction, then that resource is no longer a factor in achieving Paretian optimality.
   Difficulties: A resource that is not an influencing condition today may become a factor in the future owing to a dwindling supply or an increasing demand.
   Assistance: Being able to recognize factors that are not influential reduces the size of the problem to be analyzed.

Section 3-4

1. In going from the 2 million kg bags of onions for the United States to 1 million for Taiwan, we have decreased the relative height of the histogram by 50 percent. If the exponential decay were to persist, the 50 percent would occur each time: 2, 1, ½, ¼, etc. The remaining area can be estimated as being close to the lowest histogram bar, in this case the 1 million bags from Taiwan. The total Japanese import must then be $2 + 1 + $ (remainder $= 1) = 4$ million bags. The actual statistics show that the total was 3.9 million bags, including ½ million bags from Spain and almost the same amount from the remaining countries such as Australia and New Zealand. (*Source:* Oregon Dept. of Agriculture, *Trade Notes,* No. 64, July 9, 1974.)

Data Analysis: Pareto Pattern   55

An alternative method is to compute the relative height of the Taiwan export to Japan

$$\frac{1 \text{ million}}{2 \text{ million}} = 0.5 = e^{-k}$$

and subtract it from 1 to obtain the cumulative value for the first bar: $1 - e^{-k} = 0.5$. Thus, if 2 million bags is 50 percent, 100 percent must be 4 million bags. A third approach is to compute the k value:

$$k = -\ln(e^{-k}) = -\ln(0.5) = 0.693 \ldots$$

From Figure 3-3, we know that we would need 3 standard deviations to cover 95 percent. Thus, four countries $e^{-.693} + e^{-1.386} + e^{-2.079} + e^{-2.7725}$ would make up $0.5 + 0.25 + 0.125 + 0.0625 = 0.9375$, or roughly 94 percent, of which the first two account for 75 percent (1.5 million bags).

2. A rough estimate can be made by taking the galley over the crewshare

$$\frac{1,525}{9,605} = 0.15877$$

and computing k:

$$k = -\log_e(0.15877) = 1.84$$

corresponding to three intervals between the four histogram bars. To obtain 95 percent, we need $k = 3$, either from Figure 3-3 or by computation: $-\log_e(1 - 0.95) = 2.9960$, that is,

$$\left(\frac{3}{1.84}\right) \times 3 = 4.89 \text{ intervals}$$

or two more items. The actual figures given by Smith (1973)[1] are as follows:

Crewshare	$9,605				
Vessel repairs	$2,990	Actual	Estimated	Actual	Estimated
Gear repairs	$2,486				
Galley	$1,525	83.44% ≈ 1 − 0.15877 = 0.8423%		94.98% = 95%	
Fuel	$1,196				
Transportation	$1,100				
Bait	$ 789				
Ice, miscellaneous	$ 211				
Total	$19,902				

3. The sum of the first five items $40 + 38 + 27 + 18 + 16 = 139$ must correspond to $1 - e^{-k} \approx 1 - {}^{16}/_{40} = 60$ percent of the total. Thus, $^{139}/_{.6} = 231$ votes would be the estimate for the total number of votes received in the survey.

4. k for the 5 items can be computed as $k = -\log_e({}^{16}/_{40}) = 0.916$. Since we need $k = 3$ to obtain the 95 percent coverage, a total of $5 \times {}^{3}/_{0.916} = 16.37$ items will be needed.

These data do *not* prove the validity of negative-exponential approximation to other data. It is always possible to regroup data in such a way as to make this method completely inappropriate. However, as a "rule of thumb" to estimate the

[1] Op. cit.

scope of an OR/MS project when there are no other data or methods available, the negative-exponential distribution seems to be an expedient procedure that deserves its place among other *fudge factor* estimators.

EXERCISES

3-1 Once upon a time a great king attempted to locate the very finest man in the kingdom to marry his only daughter. Being a wise king, he knew he could not have an athletic contest, a beauty contest, or a mental quiz to select the best suitor because he sought the best all-everything man, and so he turned to his wizards for advice. The wizards reasoned that to find the best man in the whole kingdom, they would have to collect data on all the men. Since this information-gathering process would be very expensive, they figured they might as well obtain data about everyone in the kingdom at the same time and use it for tax purposes as well.

Census-takers were sent out all over the kingdom. Later they returned with their data, and the files in the castle grew and grew. Unfortunately, computers had not been invented yet, and the scribes could not organize the data as fast as they were accumulated. The disgusted king fired his wizards, hired a batch of consultants, and gave them the same assignment. The consultants were very scientific. They immediately saw that they did not need to collect data on every male because some were too old, some were too young, some were already married, and so on. Thus they decided to develop a questionnaire and send it to all eligible men. But all this took a lot of time because printing presses had not been invented yet.

Meanwhile the poor princess wasn't getting younger. As the completed questionnaires piled up waiting to be evaluated, she grew despondent. Finally she wandered down to the local lily pond, pulled out a promising frog, kissed it, and naturally it turned into a handsome prince. She married him, of course, and they lived happily ever after.

Every fairy tale should have a moral. Identify four morals from this tale that illustrate the use of the handling of information for problem-solving.

3-2 Are research administrators people who always wanted to become administrators, or are they scientists who reluctantly became administrators because it is the way of promotion to greater rewards? Eugene S. Uyeki[1] made a study of this question. He obtained 214 responses by contacting federal government scientist-administrators. The three most frequent responses are listed below:

Reason for becoming an administrator	Percent of 214 responses
Necessary for advancement	49.5
Wanted to administer	21.1
Doing administrative and scientific work	7.0

[1] M. C. Yovits et al. (eds.), *1965 Proceedings of Conference on Research Program Effectiveness*, Office of Naval Research, Washington, D. C., 1966.

(a) Assuming a Pareto pattern exists, how many other categories should have been included to give a 95 percent confidence level?

(b) After you have answered (a), compare your categories with those reported by Uyeki:

Reason for becoming an administrator	Percent of 214 responses
Doing scientific work with some supervision	5.6
Started in administration	2.3
Not doing any administration or supervision	3.7
Not ascertained	4.6

According to your analysis, should the last miscellaneous category be subdivided to provide a more meaningful analysis? If so, how many items should it contain?

3-3 The 20 largest United States companies, based on market value January 1, 1973, are listed in the following table. Under the assumption that the distribution follows a Pareto pattern, calculate the number of companies that account for 63.21 percent ($k = 1$) and 86.47 percent ($k = 2$) of the total market value of all companies. How do you account for the differences in the number of companies within each standard deviation range? What estimate would you give for the number of companies needed to account for 95 percent of the total market value in the United States? Why?

Company	Market value (in hundreds of thousands of dollars)
IBM	46,792
AT & T	29,208
Eastman Kodak	23,933
General Motors	23,195
Exxon	19,623
Sears, Roebuck	18,212
General Electric	13,288
Xerox	11,715
Texaco	10,201
Minnesota Mining	9,680
Proctor & Gamble	9,149
Coca-Cola	8,872
DuPont	8,447
Ford	8,017
Avon	7,910
Mobil	8,529
Johnson & Johnson	7,363
Standard of California	6,749
Merck	6,614
American Home Products	6,378
	282,875

3-4 Marquis and Straight (in Yovits et al., op. cit., pp. 441-458) identified the following indicators of project authority. Obviously, there may be many other similar indicators. Using the Pareto pattern, estimate how many similar indicators can be found to cover the 95 percent confidence range. Discuss.

Indicators of project authority	Percent of respondents agreeing
Initiate work in supporting areas	92
Change schedules for project subactivities	92
Create additional concurrent schedules	84
Assign priority of work in supporting areas	73
Relax performance requirements (e.g., omit tests)	73
Authorize total overtime budget	68
Contract change in technical scope of content	65
Authorize subcontractors to reduce technical content	65
Authorize subcontractors to exceed cost or schedule	60
Contract change in schedule or cost	57
Make versus buy	51
Select sources of supply for off-shelf items	51
Hire additional people	51
Exceed personnel ceiling for crashing project	51
Bring subcontracted work in-house	49
Select subcontractors	43
Authorize exceeding company funding	8

3-5 Using a map of your state, plan a communication net that would link all of your major population centers.

3-6 Assume that you are planning a teletype network to join points A, B, C, D, E, F, G, and H. The cost of joining each pair of points is shown below. Identify all optimal networks that are possible. (NA indicates connections which are not possible owing to legal restrictions.)

```
A
B   2
C   5    6
D   3    9    8
E   NA   2   10    5
F   11   4   12    6    7
G   5    3    7    8    8    6
H   8    9    8    9   10   12   NA
    A    B    C    D    E    F    G
```

3-7 Find the shortest network connecting the following major cities:

a Atlanta, Ga.
b Boise, Idaho
c Chicago, Ill.
d Denver, Col.
e El Paso, Tex.
f Los Angeles, Calif.
g New Orleans, La.
h New York, N.Y.
i Portland, Ore.
j Salt Lake City, Utah
k San Francisco, Calif.
l Seattle, Wash.
m Washington, D.C.

Distance

2,361											
758	1,755										
1,407	853	1,026									
1,423	951	1,558	653								
2,221	901	2,110	1,184	840							
516	2,167	957	1,314	1,106	1,969						
936	2,602	847	1,849	2,218	2,897	1,324					
2,684	404	2,103	1,277	1,396	928	2,491	2,950				
1,911	349	1,494	504	879	704	1,718	2,303	764			
2,519	651	2,246	1,277	1,287	397	2,279	3,093	698	748		
2,709	503	2,070	1,402	1,770	1,101	2,709	2,917	173	809	802	
703	2,483	728	1,627	1,991	2,664	1,143	206	2,831	2,142	2,730	2,886
a	b	c	d	e	f	g	h	i	j	k	l	m

PROBLEM FORMULATION: Resource Planning & Management System

Chapter 4

4-1 Value of resources

An old adage in industrial engineering says:

>To manage, we must control
>To control, we must measure
>To measure, we must define
>In defining, we must quantify

Operations research and management science become meaningful only if they can provide models that are useful in the management of our resources. These resources are called *factors of production* in economics and are precious because of their scarcity and multiple uses. Land, labor, and capital goods (use of equipment, for instance) are among our traditional resources; energy, information, ecology, and technology are also important resources. These resources are considered scarce when the demand for them is at a higher rate than the supply can make them available, a condition we identify by measuring. Thus, we *impute* values to resources according to their competing uses. The highest bidder determines the market value that the others must pay, and the value of an activity may be determined by the resources it consumes and creates. A practical model in OR/MS must clearly indicate the relationships which exist between resources and activities.

SAINT THOMAS AQUINAS This concept of *imputed value* was known to Saint Thomas Aquinas (1225–1274), an Italian monk of the Dominican order. Convinced that there could be no real conflict between *revealed* and *rational* truth, he undertook the task of interpreting pagan science theories by subjecting them to Christian theology. In the section entitled "Of Cheating and of the Sin of Usury" of his famed work *Summa Theologica*, he justifies making profits on goods sold:

> ...for instance, when a man has great need of a certain thing, while another man will suffer if he be without it. In such a case the just price will depend not only on the thing sold, but on the loss which the sale brings on the seller. And thus it will be lawful to sell a thing for more than it is worth in itself, though the price paid be not more than it is worth to the owner.

As we shall see throughout this book, the levels of activities and values of resources are interdependent and are best analyzed by looking at their *primal-dual* relationship. A *resource planning and management system* (RPMS) is a procedure that has been designed explicitly to emphasize the interactions between activities and resources. In the next section we shall undertake the actual task of model construction.

SECTION 4-1 TUNE-UP

Not all items considered as resources in this section are conservative. For example, information can be duplicated without losing its meaning. Can you think of artificial means that cause essentially abundant resources to be conserved?

4-2 Model construction

In Chapters 1 to 3 we studied three aspects of problem formulation: need analysis, cause-and-effect analysis, and Paretian data analysis. In Chapter 1 we were warned about fictitious constraints and were provided with two tools to combat them: the multidisciplinary team approach and the scientific approach. In Chapter 2 we were taught how to use C & E diagrams to pin down a problem, and in Chapter 3 we were given a rule of thumb for estimating the relative wealth of information gathered versus what remains uninvestigated.

As we may recall from Section 1-4, there are three phases of model construction: data collection, model design, and model evaluation. These phases are succeeded by three phases of experimentation: feasibility analysis, optimality analysis, and adaptivity analysis. Figure 4-1 is an RPMS flowchart that shows the roles that these phases occupy in a typical systems study.

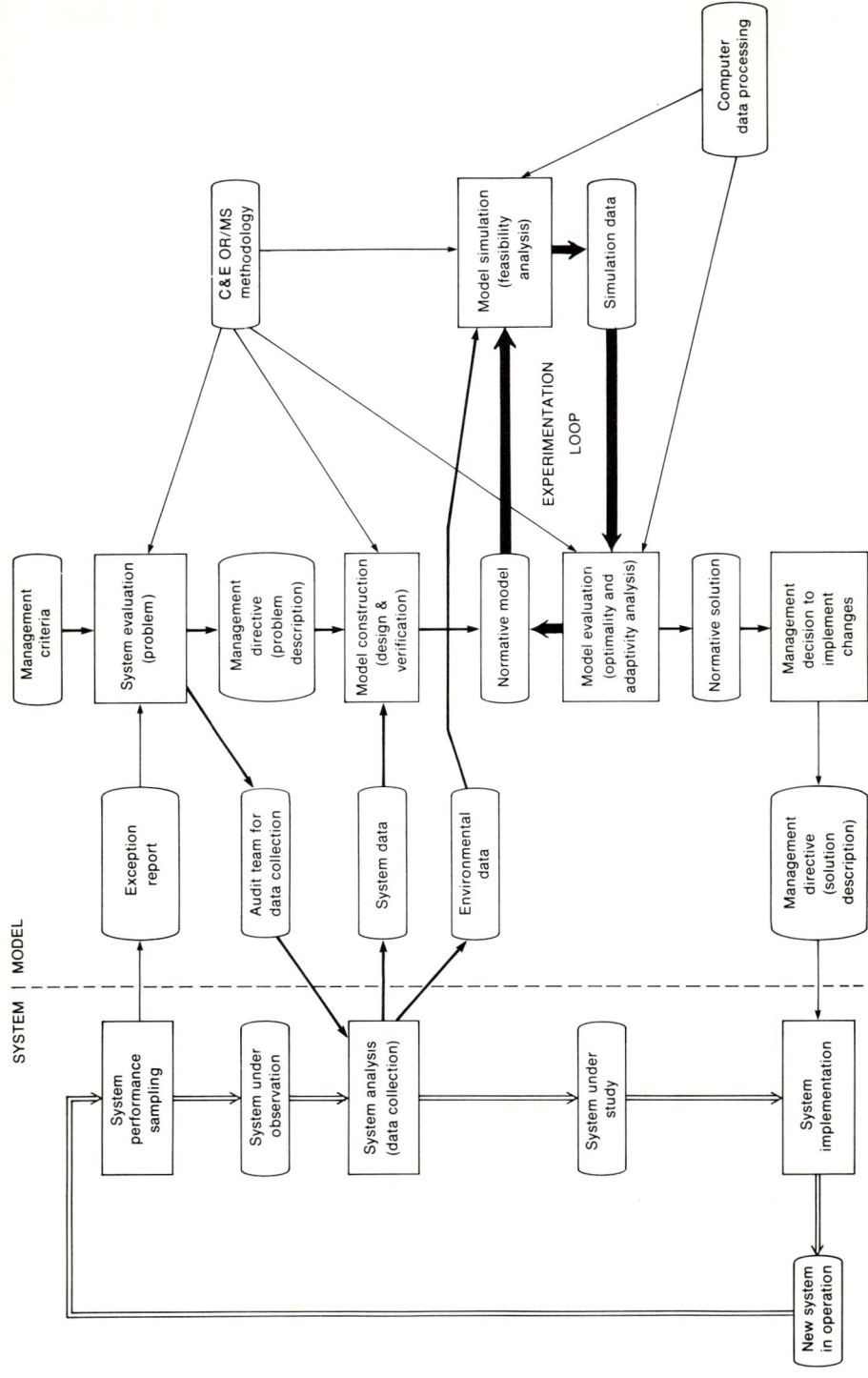

Figure 4-1 RPMS flowchart for systems study. (Oval shapes are used here instead of circles to facilitate the artwork.)

DATA COLLECTION The identification of major resources and activities must precede any model-design effort. Only resources that are scarce and therefore that constitute a restriction on the solution space need be considered. Similarly, we are interested only in activities that affect the scarcity of such resources. If the C & E study and the data analysis have been conducted properly, there should be little left to do except to sort out the data and quantify them. Quantified data must be obtained for each factor and activity in order to build a mathematical model. "Garbage-in-garbage-out" (GIGO, pronounced "guy-go") is a common saying in any data processing task and is especially appropriate in OR/MS modelbuilding. Only objective, timely, pertinent, and accurate data are useful. If data collected reveal nonquantifiable insights into the problem, they should be added to the C & E diagram.

Objective and pertinent data can be obtained through cooperative efforts of all concerned personnel, which means obtaining not only management authorization but also agreement with individuals who work directly on the system. This is a unique opportunity to gain or lose the support of operating personnel, and this is where many projects are predestined to succeed or fail even before they are started. A "problem" exists in the minds of people, and so do its solutions. Regardless of the scientific merits of a proposed solution a problem remains unsolved until people are convinced that the proposed solution is correct. It is likely that the operating personnel know more about a specific problem and may even have found their own solution, and trespassing in their domain could create a bigger problem than the one being investigated. Good OR/MS analysts are learners who are willing to "intern" within a system; they are not fault-finders who criticize and ridicule from the outside.

A problem exists when we are alerted of an impending disaster and when we still have some choice of what to do about it. The warning may have been precipitated by a crisis, but there is no problem unless a bigger one is anticipated. Thus, a problem exists only in the mind of the beholder—the universe has no problem, only its destiny.

MODEL DESIGN To find solutions to a problem, an individual should make the problem known to all concerned. Unless the same image of the problem is seen by all, there cannot be a solution that satisfies everyone. Minor personal differences must be resolved in order to create a common image of a problem before a solution procedure can be sought and applied. Thus, one of the major reasons for using a model in an OR/MS study is to clearly identify and communicate a problem. Then, when a solution has finally been found, the team has an objective way of evaluating its merits.

Frequently, one model must be created from another to serve a particular need. In general, we can distinguish two types of models: *descriptive models*, which are used in "describing" or communicating either a problem or its solution, and *normative models*, which are used in "solving" a problem.

The use of descriptive models, such as C & E or Pareto diagrams, can bridge the communication gap between the users (management) and OR/MS analysts.

The use of a *mathematical model* facilitates internal communication among OR/MS team members, and the use of a *computer model* facilitates "communication" with a computer in a manner that is meaningful to both humans and the machine. The information communicated by a model makes it useful also as a documentation record and a subject for OR/MS experimentation.

MODEL EVALUATION A model should be evaluated in terms of its effectiveness as a documentation, communication, and experimentation tool. We might ask the following questions:

1. Is the model truly representative of the problem as it appears to people who need the problem solved?

2. Is the model simple and clear enough for people to understand and use?

3. Will the model lead to a solution that will be acceptable, feasible, optimal, and also adaptive to expected changes without undue effort or delay?

SECTION 4-2 TUNE-UP
Sometimes one model can be used to describe a problem, solve it, and describe its solution. In Chapter 2, the berry-box problem of Example 2-2 illustrates such a case. Using Figure 4-1, identify all nodes (boxes and circles) in terms of the berry-box problem.

4-3 General systems theory

The term *system* is commonly used to describe an entity being modeled for an OR/MS study. No two OR/MS studies are completely alike (or they won't be worthy of the names operations *research* and management *science*), and new applications are being found everywhere, from agriculture and fisheries to hospitals and social programs. To move freely from one type of application to another, an analyst needs models and a methodology that can be used in all branches of science, industries, and business.

Operations researchers, management scientists, and engineers are not alone in seeking these generalized models and a methodology. Biologists, social scientists, geographers, and researchers from other disciplines are also trying to bring together an interdisciplinary science of systems modeling. The contributions of one biologist, in particular, should be acknowledged.

LUDWIG VON BERTALANFFY (1901–1972) The idea of general systems theory is generally credited to Ludwig von Bertalanffy, who was born near Vienna, Austria, in 1901. He received a Ph.D. in biology from the University of Vienna at the age of twenty-five, and became professor at his alma mater where he stayed until 1948. During the 1930s, von Bertalanffy tried to apply the classical systems concepts from engineering sciences to biological systems, but he found them unsatisfactory because of their *closedness*, which isolated the systems from their environments. Since biological systems must interact with the environment, von Bertalanffy produced *open system models* whose structures are maintained through the exchanges of information and energy with their environment. He then generalized these open system models to other fields.

Von Bertalanffy's first oral presentation of his models took place in Chicago in 1937. Shortly thereafter he became Professor and Director of Biological Research at the University of Ottawa, Canada. In 1955, he founded the Society for General Systems Research (SGSR) and became the coeditor of the Society's yearbook, *General Systems*. Von Bertalanffy applied his general system theory to psychiatry (1959), behavioral sciences (1960), physics (1950), robotics (1967), social systems (1968), and many other fields. In the fall of 1969, he became Faculty Professor at the State University of New York at Buffalo, where he stayed until his death in 1972.

In the first volume of *General Systems*, von Bertalanffy writes:

> ... there exist models, principles, and laws that apply to generalized systems or their subclasses, irrespective of their particular kind, the nature of their component elements, and the relations of "forces" between them. It seems legitimate to ask for a theory, not of systems of a more or less special kind, but of universal principles applying to systems in general.
>
> In this way we come to postulate a new discipline, called General System Theory. Its subject matter is the formulation and derivation of those principles which are valid for "systems" in general.[1]

RESOURCE PLANNING AND MANAGEMENT SYSTEM A resource planning and management system (RPMS) is a general system tool, which encompasses four types of systems models:

1. *R*elational models, such as C & E diagrams and network models, which depict any causal relationship among members of the system
2. *P*recedence models, such as models used in critical path method (CPM) and project evaluation and review technique (PERT), which depict the chronological and technological relationships among elements of the system
3. *M*athematical models, such as optimization models, which have an objective for the system that can be portrayed mathematically
4. *S*tochastic models, such as simulation models, which are used in experimentation

---

[1]Ludwig von Bertalanffy, and Anatol Rapaport, eds., "General Systems Theory," *General Systems*, vol. 1, no. 1, 1956.

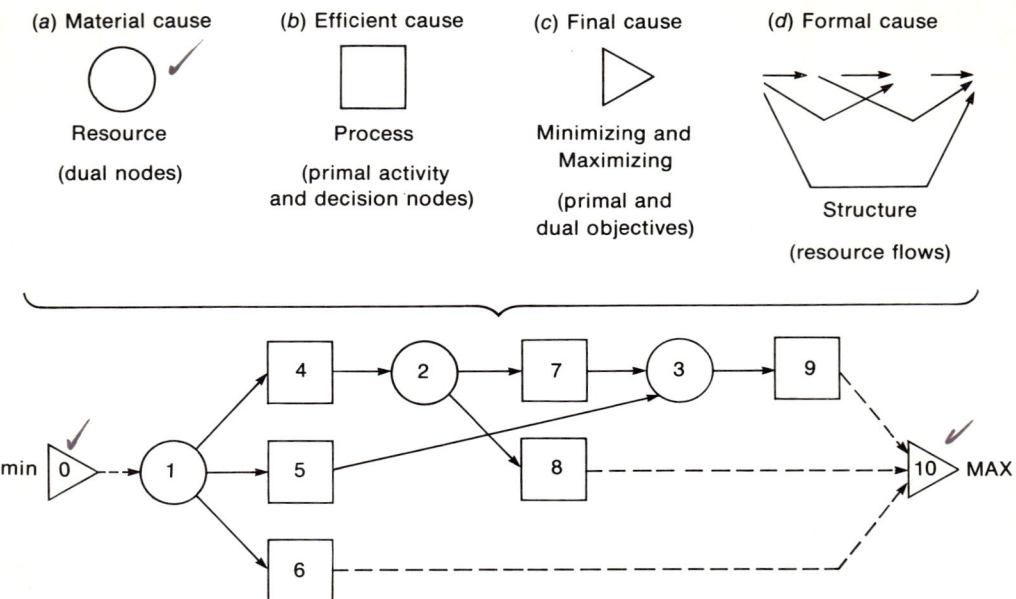

Figure 4-2 Aristotelian interpretation of an RPMS network.

An RPM[1] network is a graphic model used in an RPMS study. It has four components, which correspond to the four causes of Aristotle (see Chapter 2, Section 2-5).

1. *Resource* nodes (material cause), symbolized by circles
2. *Process* nodes (efficient cause) representing activities transforming resources from one form to another, symbolized by squares
3. *Minimizing* source and *maximizing* sink node (final cause) representing the system's environment, symbolized by triangles pointing right
4. Structure (formal cause) representing interrelationships among nodes by arrows indicating the technological constraints

Figure 4-2 is an Aristotelian interpretation of a general systems model using the RPMS conventions. It is general because it can be used to represent a variety of problems (systems).

Example 4-1: Education- and career-paths plan for high school graduates One interpretation of the RPM network of Figure 4-2 is to regard it as a plan for a high school graduate entering the society (1) [the system entered from the source

[1] M. S. Inoue, and J. L. Riggs, "Resource Planning and Management Network," *Proceedings of the International Symposium on Systems Engineering and Analysis*, Purdue Univ., Lafayette, Indiana, 1972.

0 via exogenous flow (dotted arrow from 0 to 1)] and wishing to choose the career (6, 8, or 9) that is most rewarding [dotted arrows from 6, 8, and 9 to 10 indicate career contributions to the objective (10)]. Figure 4-3 illustrates this education-and-career-paths representation. There are four alternatives:

1. Going to a 2-yr junior college (4) to obtain an A.S. or A.A. degree (2) and to move on to a university (7) to obtain a B.A. or B.S. degree (3). This should qualify the student to enter a professional career (9) with a corresponding life satisfaction (arrow 9 to 10).

2. Joining a technical career (8) upon graduation from a 2-yr junior college (4) with a corresponding life satisfaction (arrow 8 to 10).

3. Going directly to a 4-yr college (5) and joining a professional career (9).

4. Going to work directly after high school graduation (path 0-1-6-10).

In Figure 4-3 note that dotted arrows are used wherever the open system (comprising elements 1, 2, 3, 4, . . . , 9) interacts with its environment (comprising the source node 0 and the sink node 10). The primal objective of the student (who has controls over the choice of activities) is to maximize the total life satisfaction (node 10) given a high school diploma (resource 1). The corollary is a dual objective of the environment (the society with control over resources to be made available to the system) which may be interpreted as minimizing the high school graduation requirement (the value of node 1) while still meeting the given level of a student's aspiration (value of node 10).

The network in Figure 4-2 illustrates causal relations among nodes. In Figure 4-3, *time* is used as the causal relationship. Thus, event 1 (high school graduation) must precede processes 4, 5, and 6; similarly, process 4 (2-yr education) is a

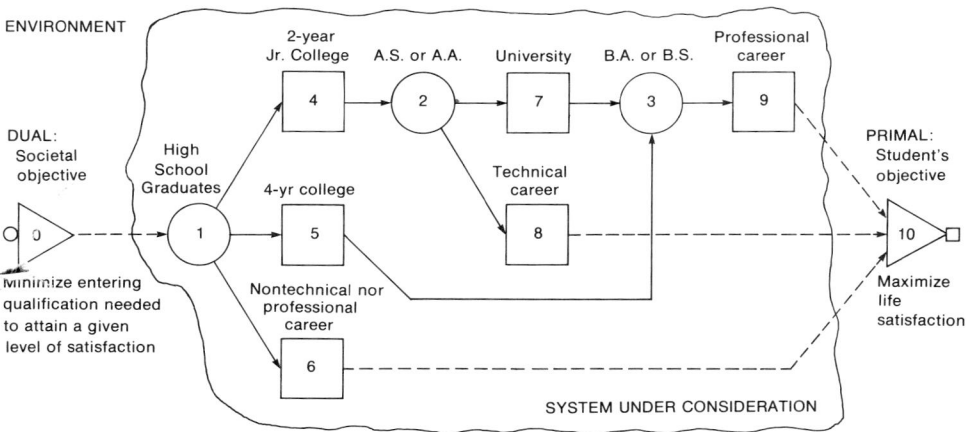

Figure 4-3   Education- and career-paths plan for the RPMS network of Figure 4-2.

prerequisite to event 2 (A.S. or A.A. degree), and the path 0-1-4-2-7-3-9-10 is chronologically ordered in the direction of the arrowheads. Such a network is called a *precedence network,* or simply a *P network.* A P network is necessarily an R network, but a P network may or may not be a mathematical network (M network) or a stochastic network (S network). If probabilities could have been assigned to the transitions from one event to another (resources), Figure 4-3 could have been interpreted as a stochastic model called a *Markov chain.* If statistical distributions could have been given to durations of activities (processes), the same network could have represented a computer-simulation model flowchart, such as the ones used in the computer-simulation language GPSS (*general-purpose simulation system*).

Example 4-2: *M network for an investment portfolio* Figure 4-4 presents another interpretation of Figure 4-2; it depicts a P network which is also an M network. Let us assume that you are a retirement-fund manager who has $1 million to invest for a 3-yr period. You must find the best investment portfolio that will return the largest dividend (and principal) at the end of the 3-yr investment period. Let us assume that you have investigated all possible and viable investment opportu-

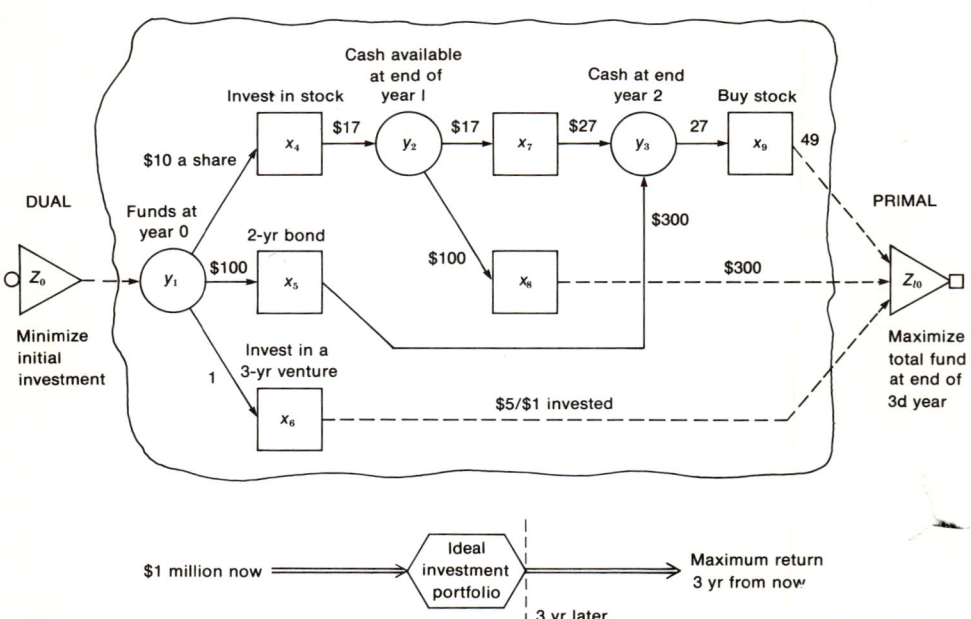

Figure 4-4   RPMS network of Figure 4-2 interpreted as an investment model (M network).

nities and have selected three possible processes: a stock that can be purchased or liquidated at any time; a 2-yr bond that can be purchased now or in 1 yr and that will yield $300 for each $100 invested; and a venture project that needs the full 3 yr but that will return $5 for every dollar invested. The projected stock-value growth per share is estimated as follows:

Year	Growth, $/share
Year 0 (now)	10
1	17
2	27
3	49

The interpretation of Figure 4-4 should be easy. For instance, x_4 is the number of shares bought at $10 per share now, yielding $17 per share if cashed at the end of 1 yr; thus, there will be $x_4 \times \$17$ potentially available cash on hand at the end of the first year. This fund will have an imputed value of y_2 per unit resource ($1) and can be used to buy more stock (x_7) or to purchase 2-yr bonds at $100 per issue ($x_8$). The cash at the end of the second year is the sum of stock investments $x_7 \times \$27$ and bond investments $x_5 \times \$300$ and will have an imputed value of y_3 per unit resource ($1). The final accounting will come at the end of the third year when all stocks (x_9), 2-yr bonds (x_8), and 3-yr investments (x_6) are liquidated to pay back the retirement fund.

The solution procedure is almost intuitive, and you may wish to identify the optimal investment portfolio by using a trial-and-error method or even by inventing your own algorithm. In Chapter 10 this problem will be solved using two different techniques: linear programming and dynamic programming.

SECTION 4-3 TUNE-UP

System is a word that is often misused because it has no universally accepted rigorous definition. Yet, if RPMS professes to be a general systems modeling tool, it must be compatible with popularly accepted definitions of *systems* and be able to represent them graphically using its own convention. We shall now state our basic premise, give a definition of RPMS and a corollary, and illustrate their examples graphically. We shall then state other commonly accepted definitions and ask you to sketch their appropriate illustrative examples using RPMS symbols.

Basic premise: A system is whatever is intended to be represented by a model.

Definition of RPMS: RPMS is the effective planning and management of limited resources by a collection of activities that share in their transformation to achieve a defined purpose (maximizing primal).

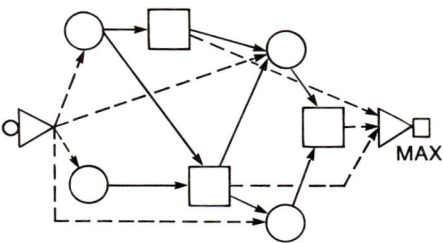

Corollary: RPMS is the effective planning and management of activities that will produce resources with the highest total utility to the cause of the defined purpose (minimizing primal).

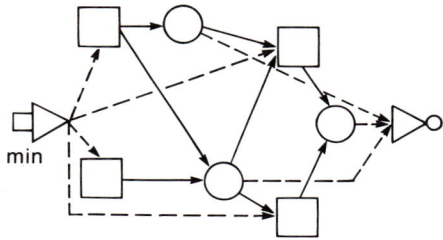

Definition 1: A system is any group of items considered as an entity.[1]

Definition 2: A system is any large collection of interacting functional units that together achieve a defined purpose.[2]

Definition 3: Most systems are open, meaning they exchange energy with their environments. A system is closed if there is no import or export of information, heat, or physical materials, and therefore no change of components.[3]

Definition 4: A system is a collection of activities which share in transformation of resources to achieve a defined purpose.

---

[1] Masano Toda, and Emir H. Shufford, "The Logic of Systems: An Introduction to a formal Theory of Structure," *General Systems*, vol. 10, p. 8, 1965.
Peter H. Roosan-Runge, "Toward a Theory of Parts and Wholes: An Algebraic Approach," *General Systems*, vol. 11, p. 13, 1966.
[2] W. D. Rowe (ed.), *Transactions: Systems Theory and Cybernetics* (new name: *Systems, Men, and Cybernetics*), vol. 1, 1965.
[3] Arthur D. Hall, *A Methodology for Systems Engineering*, p. 69, Nostrand, New York, 1962.

4-4 RPMS postulates

The activity level of a process is obviously constrained by the amount of resources made available to and/or required of it. The quantitative data put on an RPMS M network (which we shall refer to simply as an *RPM network*) take on mathematical relevance when subjected to fundamental systems principles.[1]

RPMS CONSERVATION-OF-RESOURCES POSTULATE The simple observation that the output of an RPM network cannot be increased when available resources have been exhausted leads to the age-old concept of *conservation of resources* and the modern mathematical programming concept of *nonnegativity of variables and residues*.

As we have seen in Chapter 2 (Section 2-5), the idea of conservation of resources dates back to Aristotle and has been the central theme of various branches of science, especially physics. Conservation of energy (the first law of thermodynamics), conservation of mass, and conservation of momentum are three basic principles upon which the classical physics developed. They are the modern versions of the first two laws of Aristotelian causality: Nothing can come from nothing, and nothing can give what it does not have.

We now understand (thanks especially to Albert Einstein, who showed that $E = mc^2$) that the conservation of energy, mass, and momentum are not independent. More recently, efforts have made to integrate those principles. For example, Howard T. Odum has restated the first law of thermodynamics as "the first law of energetics: energy in processes not involving appreciable conversion of energy and matter is neither created nor destroyed."[2]

We shall state our conservation-of-resources postulates simply as follows:

First postulate of RPMS (*conservation of resources*)*:* The total inflow at a process or resource node cannot be smaller than the sum of the outflows from the same node:

Total input $\geq$ total output
Total input = total output + residue

where residue ≥ 0

The flow from a *process node* is defined as the flow of resource computed as a function of the process rate (activity level) and the transmittance indicated in the direction of the arrow. The flow from a *resource node* is defined as the flow of the value of resource computed as a function of the resource value (imputed price) and the transmittance indicated in the direction of the arrow. *Exogenous flows* (dotted arrows) are directly added to the balance equation. In Figure 4-5 we note that the direction of the arrowheads corresponds to the direction of the inequality

---

[1] Inasmuch as linear models are the easiest to understand, we shall assume linearity in examples used in this chapter; however, RPMS is not limited to linear models.
[2] Howard T. Odum, *Environment, Power, and Society*, Wiley, New York, 1971.

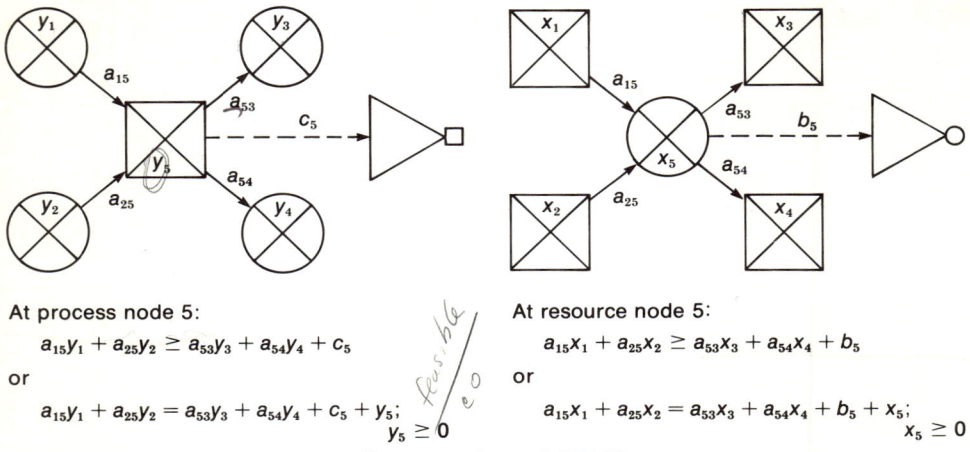

Figure 4-5 Application of the first postulate of RPMS.

($\rightarrow$ meaning $\geq$), and that the real variable values (values of resources and levels of activities) are shown on top of the X's in the nodes while the residues are shown below. The direction of an arrow can be reversed by changing the sign of the transmittance ($\underleftarrow{c_5}$ is the same as $\underrightarrow{-c_5}$; $\underrightarrow{a_{15}}$ is the same as $\underleftarrow{-a_{15}}$).

When the first postulate applies to a node, we shall say that the nodal condition has been *satisficed* (see Chapter 1, Section 1-4). When the node is satisficed and saturated (i.e., there is no residue), we say that the variable corresponding to that node is *basic*. Such a node may have a double circle (if it is a resource node) or a double-square enclosure (if it is a process node) and have a 0 entered in the residue cell. A path joining only the basic nodes is called a *basic path* and is usually illustrated by double arrows, as shown in Figure 4-6.

RPMS OPTIMIZATION POSTULATE The second law of thermodynamics tells us that energy flows from a high potential source to a lower potential sink in order to perform work. A similar phenomenon was observed by George Kingsley Zipf.[1] Zipf's law says that individuals work to minimize their expected expenditure of ef-

---

[1]George Kingsley Zipf, *Human Behavior and the Principle of Least Effort*, Hafner Publishing Co., New York, 1949,

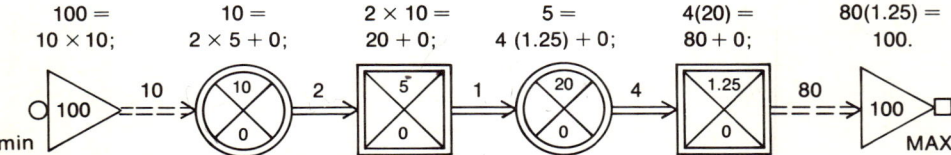

Figure 4-6 Basic path passing through basic nodes.

forts. However, it was Charles Robert Darwin (1809-1882), son of a small-town British physician, who introduced the idea of the *maximization of power* (i.e., flow of energy) for a useful purpose as being the criterion for *natural selection* (a theory first described in Darwin's *The Origin of Species*, published in 1855).

We should hasten to add that the word *purpose* is being used here (as in the definitions of Section 4-3 Tune-up) to mean not an intention (or cause) imbedded in inanimate or animate objects in the Aristotelian sense, but an apparent and a convenient description of the process to be modeled. In other words, the intention is in the mind of the analyst, not in the system itself. The solar system is not aware of belonging to a system, no more than the children from a ghetto have consciously joined such a social subculture; astrophysicists and sociologists are responsible for having labeled those "purposes" for their convenience in conceptualizing. Darwin tried to explain that the apparent *purposeness* is due to a natural tendency for randomness coupled with a pruning process that destroys those that are not appropriately equipped for the changing environment. In short, the term *purpose* provides us with a convenient way of describing the interaction of a system with its environment, as illustrated graphically in RPM network models. Herbert Spencer (1820–1903) is a British philosopher who helped extend Darwin's concept of purpose to social systems. He is given credit for inventing the expression "the survival of the fittest" and remarking, "Progress, therefore, is not an accident, but a necessity. It is a part of nature."[1]

Second postulate of RPMS (optimization): The productivity of an RPM network is to be optimized either by maximizing the net effective output while holding the exogenous input constant or by minimizing the input while maintaining the output at the given level.

A stable, *steady-state* system in one that has a net inflow equal to the net outflow; and when all entries are nonnegative (i.e., meeting the first postulate) we say that the system is both feasible and optimal. The basic paths in such a model represent natural selection, and the nonbasic nodes could be deleted without affecting the solution. These concepts will be elaborated in the following chapters.

Figure 4-7 illustrates examples of objective functions generated by the optimization postulate. Note that all resources (circles) belong to one terminal node and all processes (squares) belong to another. The right-hand terminal is the sink that is to be maximized, while the left-hand terminal is the source that is to be minimized. The small square or circle attached to the triangle symbolizes the type of nodes to which the terminal belongs.

SECTION 4-4 TUNE-UP

1. Gustav Robert Kirchhoff (1824–1887), a German physicist, postulated what is today known as *Kirchhoff's current law:* The algebraic sum of the instantaneous currents entering a node is zero. Portray this electrical engineering principle as an RPM network.

---

[1]Herbert Spencer, *Social Statics*, part i, chapter 2, D. Appleton and Company, New York, 1888.

(a) Maximizing primal; minimizing dual

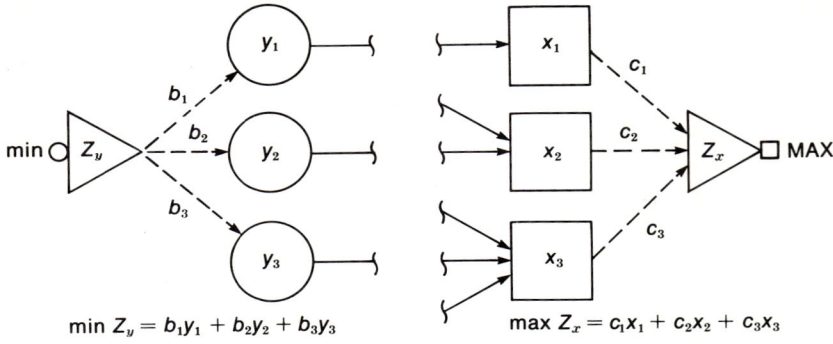

$$\min Z_y = b_1 y_1 + b_2 y_2 + b_3 y_3 \qquad \max Z_x = c_1 x_1 + c_2 x_2 + c_3 x_3$$

(b) Minimizing primal; maximizing dual

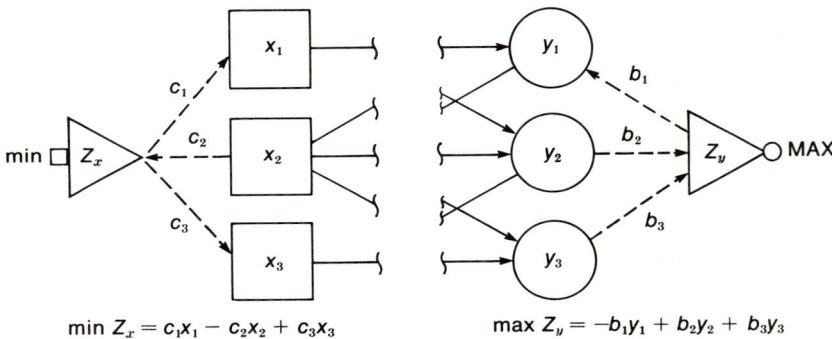

$$\min Z_x = c_1 x_1 - c_2 x_2 + c_3 x_3 \qquad \max Z_y = -b_1 y_1 + b_2 y_2 + b_3 y_3$$

Figure 4-7 Objective functions (purposes) ascribed to by the RPMS optimization postulate.

2. The basic accounting equation says: assets = liabilities + owners' equity. To what RPMS configuration would this equation correspond? Assume that the following figures are given on a balance sheet:

Balance Sheet for General Research and Development Services, Inc., October 31, 1980

Assets		Liabilities and owners' equity	
		Liabilities	
Cash	$10,500	Accounts payable	$ 89,000
Accounts receivable	100,600	Owners' equity	
Land	30,000	Capital stock	200,000
Building	60,000	Retained earnings	12,100
Computer equipment	100,000		
	$301,100		$301,100

4-5 RPM network construction procedure

Gerhard L. Hollander, in his keynote address at the Operations Research Society of America Joint National Conference on Major Systems (1971) identified the *fundamental task* shared by all systems-oriented specialists: "To organize resources into a configuration of men, machines, and procedures that has the highest expected payoff or results." The organization of resources is important because of their scarcity which makes their ineffective utilization a social crime. It is obviously not enough just to *plan* an effective configuration; we must also *manage* its operation and adapt it to a changing environment (i.e., changing both the availability of resources and the purpose of their use).

Since we have chosen RPMS as a vehicle that will help us accomplish this task, we should take time to review the procedure we have used to construct RPM network models. We shall assume that the initial phase of identifying the problem, conducting a C & E analysis, and selecting major C & E factors have all been accomplished. The following steps outline procedures to be followed throughout this text for constructing linear RPM network models of a problem, including selection of activities, resources, and objectives.

Step 1: Identify the process-activity set. From the controllable causes in the original C & E diagram, we must select actual decision variables that transform our resources into more useful states. For each such process, represented by a rectangular box in an RPM network, we must identify the unit by which we shall control the rate of transformation (level of activity) and another unit, common to all processes in the system, by which we shall measure its effect upon our objective. [When you have few resources and several possible ways of processing them, it is often easier to state the resources first (step 2) and then try to identify all possible ways of interacting them through activities (step 1).]

Step 2: Identify the resource-state set. From the set of processes, we can now identify the set of state variables describing the values of resources which are consumed or produced by each activity. A resource may need several state variables, depending upon time, location, and other conditions under which it is being made available. For example, in a transportation model, rice in China may be regarded as being a different resource than rice delivered to Bangladesh although they may be the same item; also, in an investment model (such as Example 4-2), $1 invested today is different from $1 received 3 yr hence. The utility of such a resource will be measured in terms of the effects and by the same unit we have chosen in step 1. The availability of a resource will be measured in whatever unit is convenient.

Step 3: Identify the C & E links between the two sets. Each process node may be regarded as a miniature C & E diagram relating causal resources to effect resources. Each resource node may also be regarded as a C & E diagram relating causal activities producing the resource to effectuated activities consuming it. The transmittance must be determined to convert the actual flow of resources from the unit used in the resource node to the unit used in the process node. The coefficient of the transmittance is *always* the ratio of one unit of resource over one unit of process regardless of the direction of the arrow connecting the resource and the process nodes. If the flow is exogenous, that is, relating the system to its environment, a dotted (or dashed) arrow must be used to connect the node to a source or sink terminal node.

Step 4: Construct the network. We must now draw a general structure of the problem using some logical or chronological ordering (left to right and/or top to bottom). The miniature C & E diagrams from step 3 should now be connected together, taking care that resource and process nodes are alternated. No direct connection from one resource node to another or from one process node to another is permitted. Each terminal connects to either the resource-node set or the process-node set, but never to both. The source node should be placed at the left or top of the diagram and marked "min" within the appropriate node symbol, and the sink node should be placed at the right or bottom of the diagram and marked "max" within its appropriate node symbol.

Step 5: Interpret the RPM network mathematically. By applying the two RPMS postulates to either the process-node set (plus its terminal) or the resource-node set (plus its terminal), we may obtain a dual or primal mathematical statement of the problem.

This problem of minimizing or maximizing a linear objective function subject to a set of linear constraints is known as *Linear Programming* (LP). All variables in such a model must remain nonnegative (positive or zero, but not negative) and linear (additive and proportional). Although RPMS models are not limited to linear models, LP problems are most easily constructed with the aid of RPM networks, and many such examples will be presented in subsequent chapters (especially Chapter 6).

In this chapter we have outlined the philosophical background of RPMS methodology and its development. Although the details of RPM network construction will be discussed later, let us discuss one important point now.

LOGICAL RELATIONSHIPS IN AN RPM NETWORK MODEL A resource node in an RPM network has the logical OR (union) characteristic, while a process node has the AND (intersection) characteristic. Thus, a resource can be realized as an output of any or all of its preceding activities and can be shared by all processes to which it is an input; on the other hand, a process cannot be started until all its input resources are available, and, once started, it will neces-

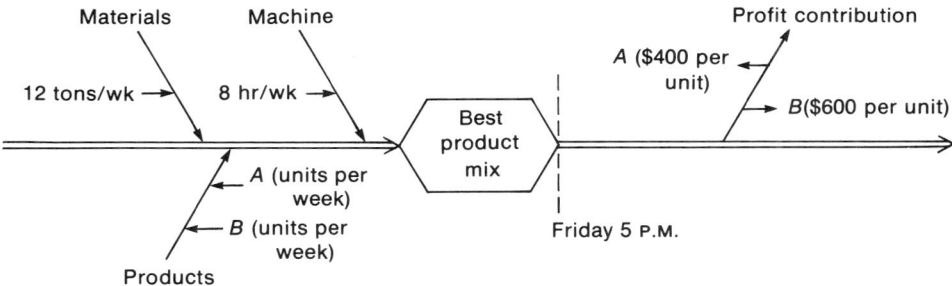
Figure 4-8 C & E diagram for a simple product mix.

sarily produce all of its output resources. This distinction, though simple, must be kept in mind during the network construction.

SECTION 4-5 TUNE-UP

You are the production manager for a plant that manufactures two products A and B. Each A requires 1 hr of machine time and 1 ton of raw material, and each B requires 2 hr of machine time and 4 tons of raw material. You foresee 8 machine-hr and 12 tons of material available during the next week, and you wish to maximize the total profit contribution knowing that each A and B will bring $400 and $600 respectively. The C & E diagram is given in Figure 4-8. Construct the RPM network and interpret its mathematical model.

TUNE-UP SOLUTIONS

Section 4-1

Patents, copyrights, and trademarks are examples of artificial means used to render information more valuable through scarcity. It is also true that energy is always required in transmitting any information, and that there is scarcity of energy, which makes information valuable. A piece of information concerns an unusual distribution of some resource, be it a flood, a presidential message of high information content, an airplane accident, or a strike. It takes resources to create a news item, and those resources could affect a series of activities.

Section 4-2

See Figure 4-9.

Section 4-3

See Figure 4-10.

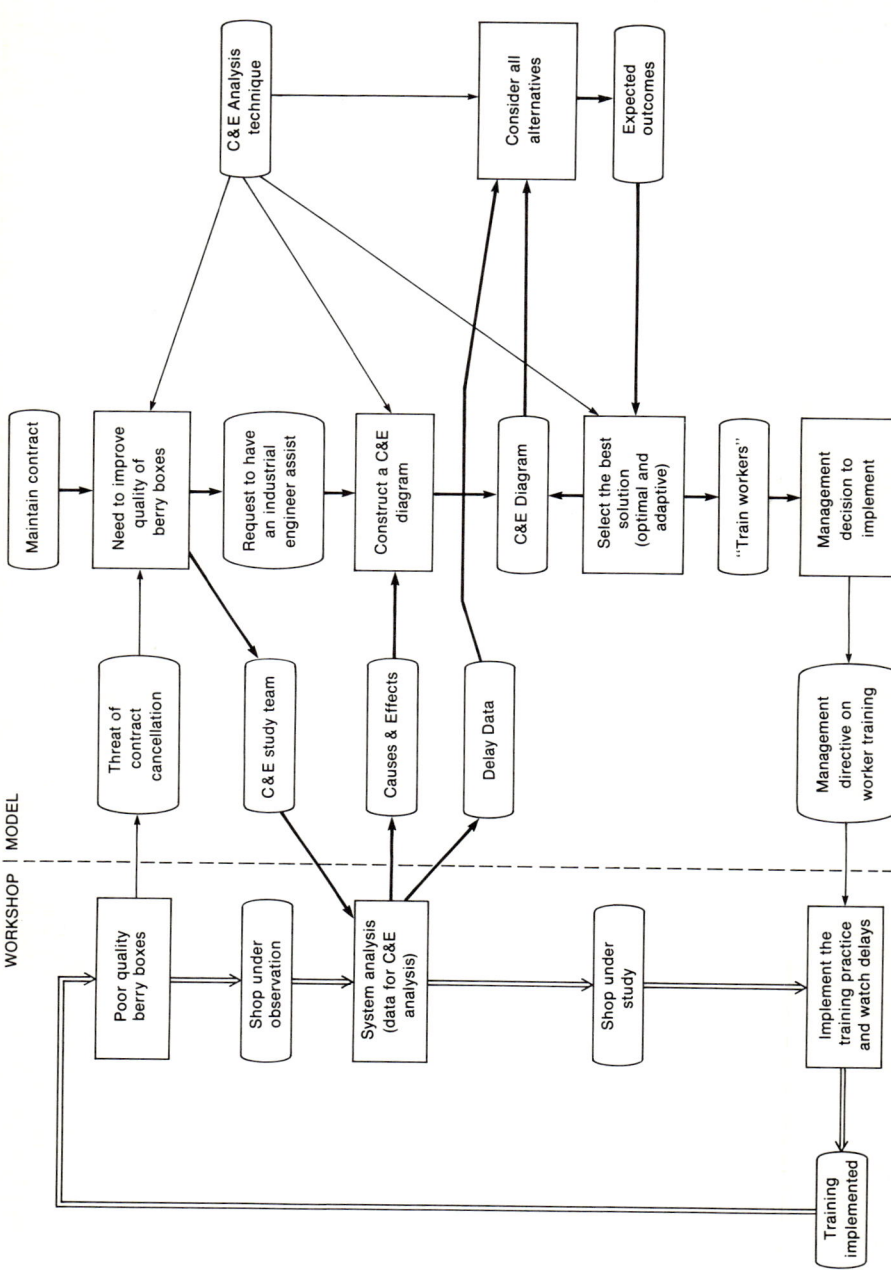

Figure 4-9 Section 4-2 Tune-up solution. (Oval shapes used here instead of circles to facilitate the artwork.)

Problem Formulation: Resource Planning & Management System

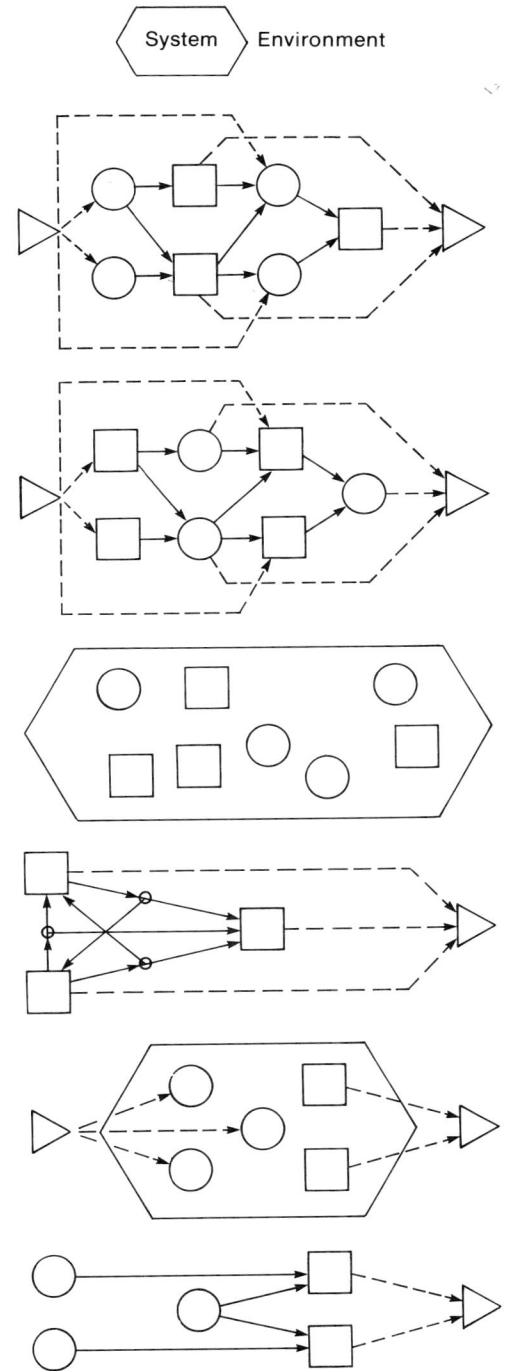

Basic Premise: A system is whatever is intended to be represented by a model.

Definition of RPMS: RPMS is the effective planning and management of limited resources by a collection of activities that share in their transformation to achieve a defined purpose.

Corollary: RPMS is the effective planning and management of activities that will produce resources with the highest total utility to the cause of the defined purpose.

Definition 1: A system is any group of items considered as an entity.
  This is a basic definition advocated by many systems theorists, engineers, and analysts, including Toda and Shuford (1965), Roosen and Runge (1966), etc.

Definition 2: A system is any large collection of interacting functional units that together achieve a defined purpose.
  This definition was first advanced by W. D. Rowe in 1965.

Definition 3: Most systems are open, meaning they exchange energy with their environments. A system is closed if there is no import or export of information, heat, or physical materials, and therefore no change of components. (Arthur D. Hall, 1962.)

Definition 4: A system is a collection of activities which share in transformation of resources to achieve a defined purpose.

Figure 4-10 Section 4-3 Tune-up solution.

Section 4-4

1. If we interpret the *node* to be a constraint (a resource), then we cannot allow it to have any residue:

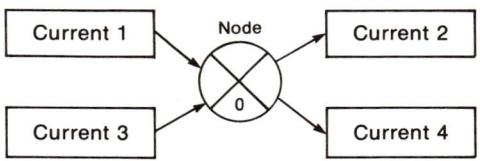

2. The computation of owners' equity is usually performed from our knowledge of assets and liabilities; thus, we could interpret it as the residue:

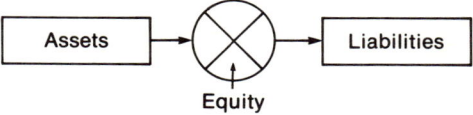

On the other hand, if we wish to maximize the retained earnings as a measure of the company's activity (say, a fixed percentage of it), we may show this as

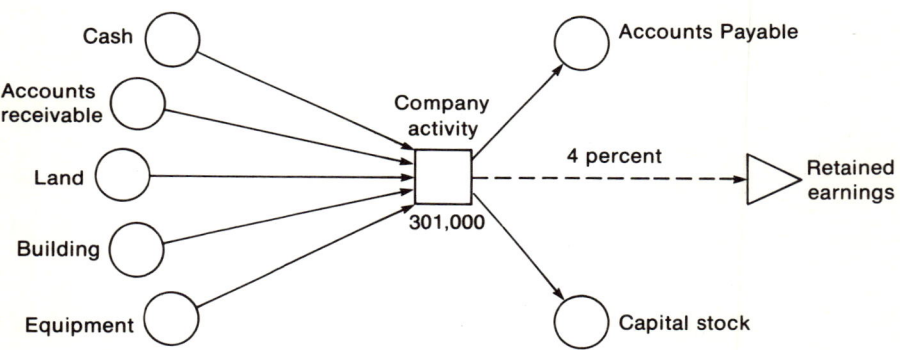

Section 4-5

Step 1: *Process-Activity set.* Produce X_1 units of A and X_2 units of B per week.

Step 2: *Resource-state set.* 12 tons of raw materials and 8 machine-hr are available per wk.

Problem Formulation: Resource Planning & Management System

Step 3: C & E links.

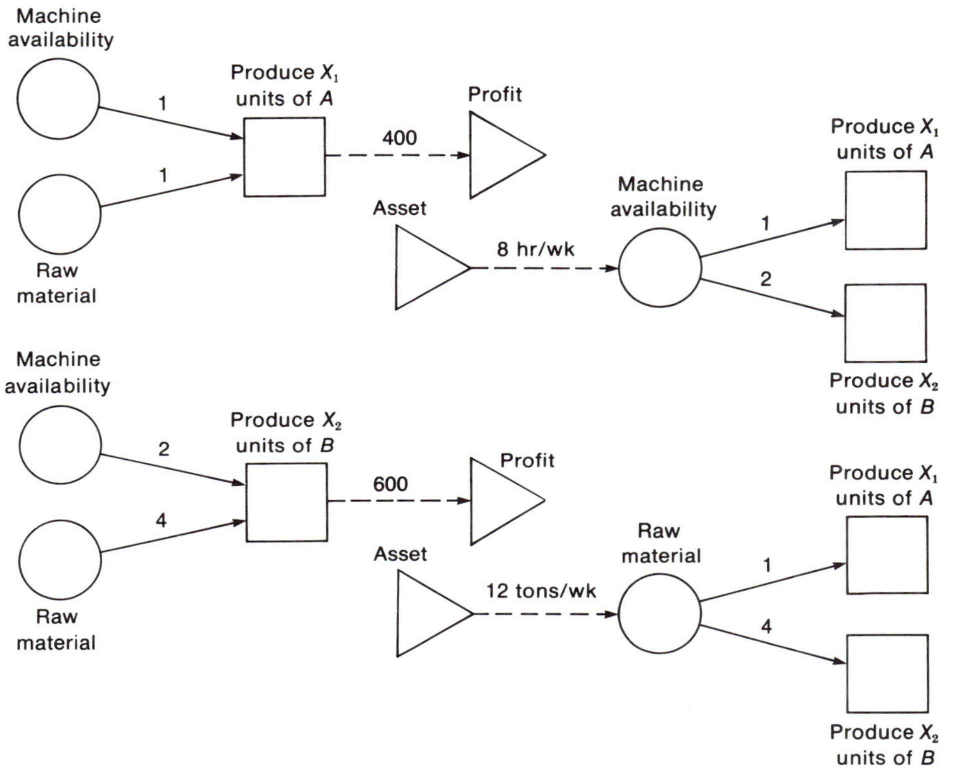

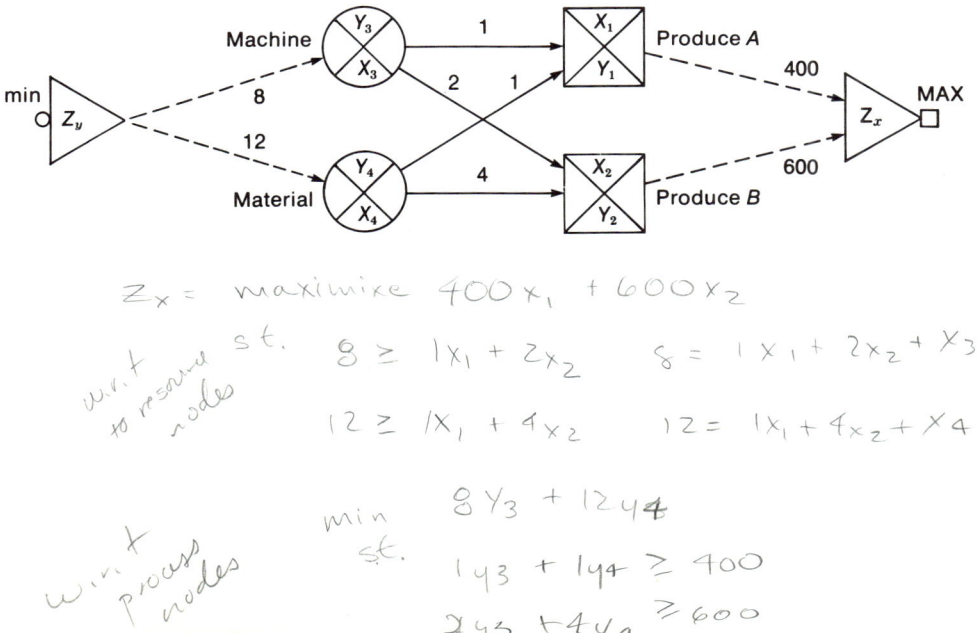

Step 4: Construct the network.

$Z_x = $ maximize $400 x_1 + 600 x_2$

w.r.t. to resource nodes s.t. $8 \geq 1 x_1 + 2 x_2$ $8 = 1 x_1 + 2 x_2 + x_3$

$12 \geq 1 x_1 + 4 x_2$ $12 = 1 x_1 + 4 x_2 + x_4$

w.r.t. process nodes min s.t. $8 y_3 + 12 y_4$

$1 y_3 + 1 y_4 \geq 400$

$2 y_3 + 4 y_4 \geq 600$

Step 5: Interpret the network mathematically.

max $Z_x = 400X_1 + 600X_2$
subject to $\quad 8 \geq X_1 + 2X_2 \quad$ at $Y_3 \quad$ or $\quad 8 = X_1 + 2X_2 + X_3$
$\qquad\qquad 12 \geq X_1 + 4X_2 \quad$ at $Y_4 \quad$ or $\quad 12 = X_1 + 4X_2 + X_4$
min $Z_y = 8Y_3 + 12Y_4$
subject to $\quad Y_3 + \ Y_4 \geq 400$ at $X_1 \qquad Y_3 + \ Y\ = 400 + Y_1$
$\qquad\qquad 2Y_3 + 4Y_4 \geq 600$ at $X_2 \qquad 2Y_3 + 4Y_4 = 600 + Y_3$
all variables nonnegative.

EXERCISES

4-1 The word *system* is used today in many professional fields. Here are some excerpts. Comment on them in terms of the RPMS concepts discussed in this chapter.

(a) *In its structure and function, nature consists of animals, plants, microorganisms, and human societies. These living parts are in turn joined by invisible pathways over which pass chemical materials that cycle round and round being used and reused and over which flow potential energies that cannot be reused. The network of these pathways forms an organized system for the parts.*[1]

(b) *All systems are implicitly dynamic, a fact too often forgotten in the preoccupation with equilibrium models of real systems. . . . Any such system can be characterized by:*

   1. *A rule which determines whether any particular object is to be considered a part of the system or of the environment (the system boundary).*

   2. *A statement of the input and output interactions with the environment.*

   3. *A statement of the interrelationships between the elements of the system, the inputs and the outputs, including any external interaction between output and input (feedback).*[2]

(c) *Industrial Engineering is concerned with the design, improvement, and installation of integrated systems of men, materials and equipment. It draws upon specialized knowledge and skill in mathematical, physical, and social sciences together with the principles and methods of engineering analysis and design, to specify, predict, and evaluate the results to be obtained from such systems.* (Official definition of industrial engineering adopted by American Institute of Industrial Engineers.)

---

[1] Howard T. Odum, *Environment, Power, and Society*, p. 1, Wiley, New York, 1971.
[2] Warren A. Hall and John A. Dracup, *Water Resource Systems Engineering*, McGraw-Hill Book Company, 1970.

(d) *Although the same basic accounting principles are applicable to all types of businesses, each enterprise requires an individually tailored set of accounting forms, records, and reports to fit its particular needs. Designing an accounting system and putting it into operations is thus a special phase of accounting. With the advent of various accounting machines and electronic data-processing equipment, the problems that arise in creating an effective accounting system have become increasingly complex. On the other hand, once the system is devised and working, machines take much of the drudgery out of the bookkeeping process.*[1]

(e) *There are three recent efforts to apply systems analysis (in these cases linear programming) to educational planning, and all use at least some of both cost-benefit and manpower planning methods. ... The Bernard and Adelman models apply to the total economy, though working out the education sector in special detail. Bowle's model is for the educational sector only, taking inputs into that sector from elsewhere as exogenous variables or constraints.*[2]

4-2 Find three definitions of *system* in your field and compare them with the definitions cited in this chapter.

4-3 Interpret the cable-TV example of Chapter 3, Example 3-2, in terms of the flowchart given in Figure 4-1.

4-4 You are planning a family get-together for Thanksgiving. Your uncle Joe and aunt Donna will be arriving with their only child on Monday and will be staying with you until Sunday. Your uncle Mike and aunt Mary will be bringing their twins and triplets from Wednesday to Friday. Your cousins Ken and Betty will arrive with their two babies and stay from Tuesday to Thursday; and your cousins Tom and Diana will bring their only child and stay on Thursday only. Assuming that these children are all babies and toddlers needing 10 diapers per day each, you wish to provide them with sufficient diapers during their visit. You have the choice of buying disposable diapers at 20 cents each, buying reusable cloth diapers, at 30 cents each, washing soiled diapers at home for 5 cents each, or sending them out (it will take 24 hr) to be washed at 15 cents each. Construct a model (an RPM network) showing all the alternatives that are open to you.

---

[1] Walter B. Meigs and Charles E. Johnson, *Accounting*, p. 5, McGraw-Hill Book Company, 1962.
[2] M. J. Bowman, "The Human Investment Revolution in Economic Thought," *Soc. Ed.*, vol. 39, pp. 111–38, 1966.

MODEL EXPERIMENTATION: Graphic Introduction to Linear Programming

Chapter 5

5-1 OR/MS experimentation

In a *science* knowledge is obtained through systematic experiments, that is, investigations utilizing physical or conceptual models to prove or refute hypotheses. Having defined OR/MS as a science in Chapter 1, and having proposed RPMS as a modeling methodology for OR/MS in Chapter 4, we are now in the position to demonstrate the utility of RPM network models when subjected to OR/MS experimentation. Three stages of an OR/MS experimentation have been defined in Section 1-4.

✓ 1. *Feasibility analysis:* First, we need to identify all feasible solutions to our problem. We do this by creating a feasible solution space (FSS), as in Figure 1-2. The boundary of an FSS is made of *uncontrollable inputs* and *unobservable outputs* (Figure 2-1) interpreted as resource-satisficing constraints.

✓ 2. *Optimality analysis:* From the FSS, we must select the best alternative by identifying one observable output to be used as a measure of relative worth of all alternatives in the FSS. Graphically, we portray this as an objective function vector upon which we project the FSS.

3. *Adaptivity analysis:* Finally, we must ascertain the sensitivity of our proposed solution to changes in environment: exogenous changes in the direction of the objective.

FEASIBLE SOLUTION SPACE A feasible solution space is a convenient abstract concept. As in Figure 1-2, we imagine all solutions to a problem to be stars (points) in space where coordinates are *controllable variables* for our spacecraft. Knowing the direction and the magnitude of our trajectory is a prerequisite to reaching that star from our present location. The graphical method for solving a linear programming problem visually portrays a typical OR/MS experimentation procedure. This is also a practical solution procedure for problems limited to either two or three variables or two or three constraints where we can deal with a three-dimensional world.

When we have more variables or constraints than can be portrayed visually, we must rely on mathematical abstraction to create a conceptual space with more than three dimensions, still obeying laws similar to those we accept about the three-dimensional universe. Such a space is called *Euclidean space,* after the Greek philosopher Euclid [330–275 B.C. (?)], who wrote "The Elements," the first treatise on geometry.

ANALYTICAL GEOMETRY. The word *geometry* comes from the Greek word *geometria: geo* means "earth," and *metria*, "to measure." It is the branch of mathematics that is concerned with the properties, measurement, and relations among lines, surfaces, and solids, and, as a branch of mathematics, it has its own rules.

> *A given set of mathematical objects is sometimes like the parts of a game. Symbols, pictorial or abstract, are supplied the contestant. He is then provided with a strict set of rules for manipulating the symbols. The important aspect of the game is that once the rules have been set they can never be violated at any extension of the game. Very often it is difficult to decide just how to represent a situation in nature by a mathematical object. The choice of the mathematical object is never unique, and the usefulness of a given choice depends largely upon the skill and insight of the scientist.*[1]

In "The Elements," Euclid included a number of definitions, five postulates, and nine axioms, which were considered to be *self-evident truths* and were drawn from physical experiences. In Euclidean space, for example, the shortest distance between two points of a space is a straight line (or the line-of-sight), which is unique and can be extended indefinitely.

[1] George E. Owen, *Fundamentals of Scientific Mathematics*, p. 2, Harper and Row, Publishers, Inc., New York, 1964.

René Descartes (1596–1650), a French philosopher and mathematician, invented the *Cartesian coordinate system*, which related geometry to algebra and created what is known today as *analytic geometry*. His study of space by means of algebraic equations and equalities was published in 1637 under the title "La Geometrie." There are two reasons why our discussion of this Cartesian description of Euclidean space is important. First, today there are many non-Euclidean geometries that discard one or more of Euclid's self-evident truths, all serving useful purposes but not appropriate to linear programming representation. Second, the seemingly trivial and limited procedure of using analytic geometry serves as a basis for understanding the *simplex* (meaning a single geometric figure) method used to solve linear programming problems with computers.

5-2 Construction of E^2 FSS and its role in optimization

Figure 5-1 illustrates a procedure for constructing a two-dimensional Euclidean-space (E^2) model of a feasible solution space. This simple problem involves two controllable decision variables (processes X_1 and X_2), which are used as the Cartesian coordinates, two input-resource limitations (less than or equal to b_1 and b_2), and two output-resource requirements (greater than or equal to b_3 and b_4). The FSS is then a *simplex* geometric figure with a piecewise linear boundary. The optimization procedure (step 4) consists of expressing the primal objective function as a vector in E^2 with the arrowhead pointing toward the direction of higher preference and having the FSS orthogonally projected upon it. The shadow of the FSS upon the vector will show the range of objective-function values corresponding to all feasible solutions. The silhouette shows the extreme values (minimum and maximum) and identifies the least and the most preferred solution. This fact that the silhouette of the FSS's shadow upon the objective-function arrow must correspond to a corner (or two) of the FSS simplex is known as the *extreme-point* or *corner-point* theorem of linear programming.

Extreme-point (or corner-point) theorem: *If a linear programming problem possesses a finite feasible and optimal solution, then there is at least one extremum (corner point) of the FSS which is the feasible and optimal solution.*

The adaptivity analysis usually pertains to the sensitivity analysis of the optimal solution when the boundary or the direction of the objective-function vector is perturbed. These concepts are illustrated in the following example.

Example 5-1: *The tale of a cabinetmaker* Let us assume that you are the sole proprietor of a small woodworking shop specializing in the manufacture and sale of bookcases (Figure 5-2). In order to increase your income, you are contemplating a contract with a local discount store that wishes to purchase low-cost ready-to-finish bookcases. Under the proposed terms of contract, the store will supply you

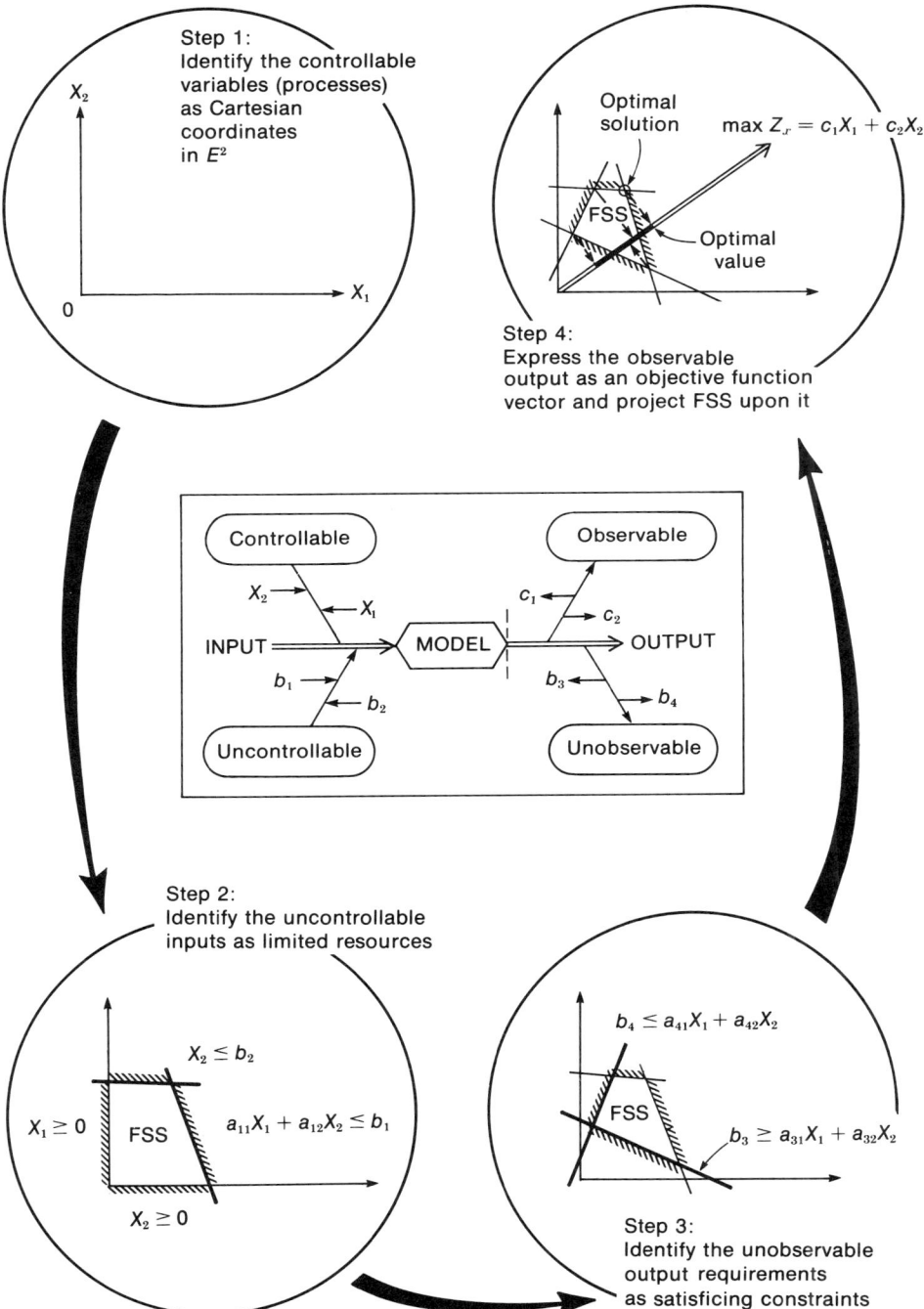

Figure 5-1 Construction of a graphic optimization model.

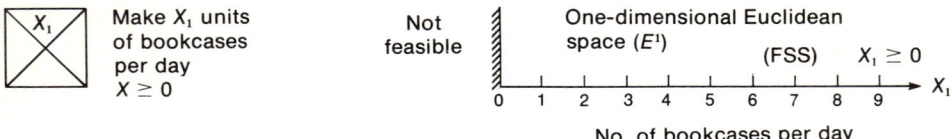

Figure 5-2 Single nonnegative decision with an unbounded FSS.

180 bdft[1] of lumber per day (Figure 5-3). With this lumber supply, you may make X_1 number of bookcases per day, each requiring 30 bdft. The maximum number of bookcases that can be manufactured per day would then be $^{180}/_{30} = 6$ units per day. The graph in Figure 5-4 illustrates the new feasible solution space ($0 \leq X_1 \leq 6$) and the shaded nonfeasible solution spaces ($X_1 < 0$ and $X_1 > 6$).

Upon conferring with the manager of the discount store, you find out that the store is also interested in purchasing ready-to-finish desks, each requiring 20 bdft of the same lumber. The 180-bdft supply may be used to make either X_1 bookcases or X_2 desks, or any linear combination of both. The new solution space can be expressed as

$$180 \geq 30X_1 + 20X_2 \text{ with } X_1 \geq 0 \text{ and } X_2 \geq 0$$

which is shown graphically in Figure 5-5.

Let us assume that you have enough idle production capacity to absorb the task of manufacturing either or both of these products. However, since the workshop is small, you have a storage problem. The discount store is willing to use their truck to haul your products away once daily but not more often. You have 60 ft² of storage floorspace, and you estimate that each bookcase will take up to 6 ft² and each desk will occupy 12 ft²; Figure 5-6 illustrates the new solution space. Should you sign the contract with the discount store to make either bookcases or desks, or both?

✓ **FEASIBILITY ANALYSIS** The "scarce" resources that have been identified so far are the limited lumber supply and storage space. They are considered uncontrollable and therefore exogenous to the problem. To determine whether or not

---

[1] 1 board foot (bdft) is a measure of lumber volume based on one foot square piece of one inch thickness.

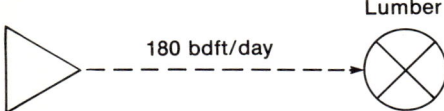

Figure 5-3 Resource node for 180 bdft/day of lumber.

Model Experimentation: Graphic Introduction to Linear Programming   89

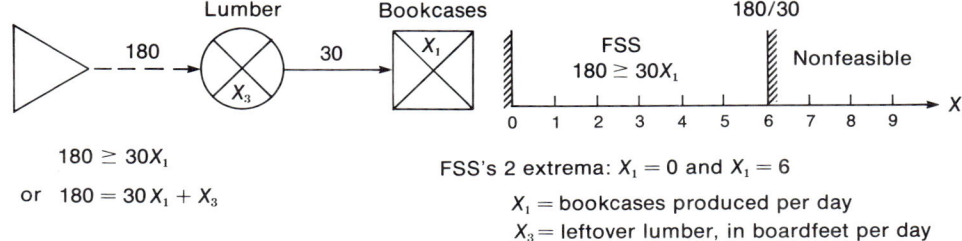

$180 \geq 30X_1$

or $180 = 30X_1 + X_3$

FSS's 2 extrema: $X_1 = 0$ and $X_1 = 6$

X_1 = bookcases produced per day
X_3 = leftover lumber, in boardfeet per day

Figure 5-4 E^1 FSS for bookcases.

you should sign the contract with the discount store, you may wish to consider the additional revenue to be generated by this venture. There are two approaches for evaluating such an output. You may use the revenue either as an *observable output* (to be made into the objective function) or as an *unobservable constraint* (to be satisfied internally). Thus, the terms *observable* and *unobservable* refer to the output being *endogenous*, that is, generated within the system and flowing out to the environment (dotted arrow out to the *sink* node) or being *internal* to the system. The former has an objective function; the latter is only a constraint.

A feasibility analysis is simply a test of the hypothesis that there is at least one possible solution. It has only constraints and no objective function. To conduct a feasibility analysis on your new furniture sales venture, you must set up a minimum requirement for product's output. The discount store is willing to pay $9 per unit for either bookcases or desks in addition to the free supply of lumber and free pickup service. Let us assume that you have decided that the new venture will not be worth your while unless you receive a revenue of at least $27/day. This condition gives a minimum constraint (greater than or equal to 27,

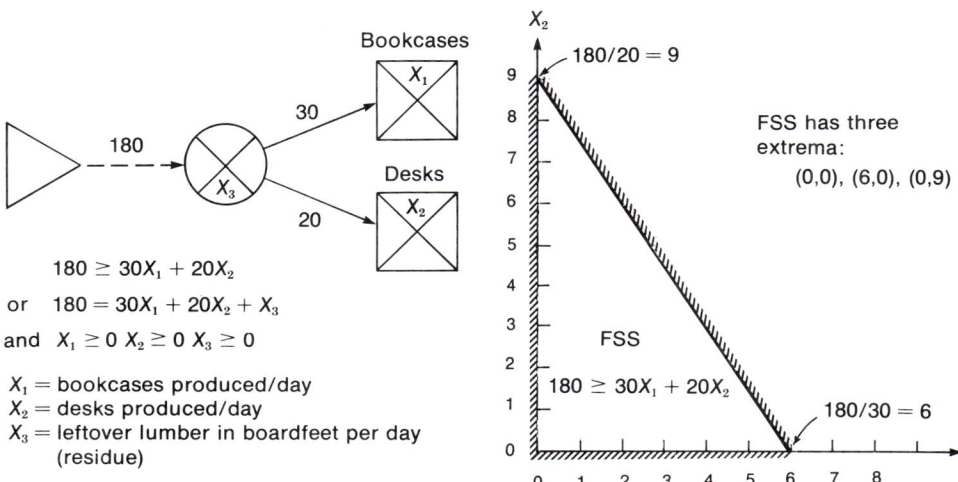

$180 \geq 30X_1 + 20X_2$

or $180 = 30X_1 + 20X_2 + X_3$

and $X_1 \geq 0 \ X_2 \geq 0 \ X_3 \geq 0$

X_1 = bookcases produced/day
X_2 = desks produced/day
X_3 = leftover lumber in boardfeet per day
       (residue)

Figure 5-5 E^2 FSS for bookcases and desks.

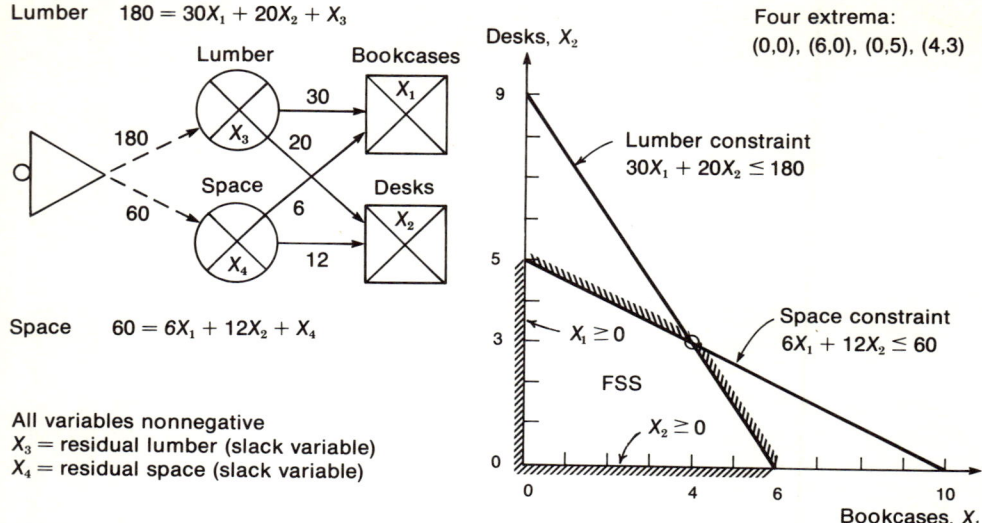

Figure 5-6 E^2 FSS with two constraints and two variables.

abbreviated as ≥ 27) which can now be incorporated to see if any FSS still remains. Other constraints originating, say, from TAPE (Chapter 1, Section 1-2) should also be added at this time to make certain that the FSS provides viable solutions.

Figure 5-7 shows that some FSS still remains. The alternative solutions that satisfice all three constraints (lumber, space, and revenue) include the five extrema (corner points), any point on the boundary, and any point interior to the FSS. Extrema solutions are called *basic feasible solutions* (BFS). Solutions for these two decision variables and three constraints can be expressed in E^2 (using coordinates X_1, X_2) or in a five-dimensional Euclidean space E^5 (using coordinates

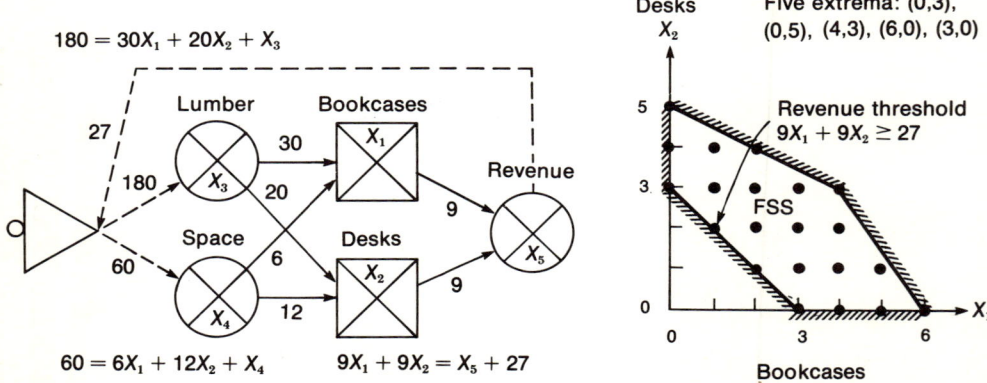

Figure 5-7 Feasibility analysis for the cabinetmaker.

$(X_1, X_2, X_3, X_4, X_5)$. Some of the alternative solutions are:

Make X_1 bookcases and X_2 desks		$E^2(X_1,X_2)$	$E^5(X_1,X_2,X_3,X_4,X_5)$	
6	0	(6,0)	(6,0,0,24,27)	BFS
3	3	(3,3)	(3,3,30,6,27)	Interior
2	1	(2,1)	(2,1,100,36,0)	Boundary
0	3	(0,3)	(0,3,120,24,0)	BFS
5	1.5	(5,1.5)	(5,1.5,0,12,21.5)	Boundary

Note that there are two zeros in the E^5 notation of any BFS and one zero in those solutions that happen to be on the boundary. Also note that making the revenue requirement high enough, say $9X_1 + 9X_2 \geq 65$ would eliminate the entire FSS and make the problem impossible to solve.

OPTIMALITY ANALYSIS In order to determine which of the alternative solutions in the FSS should be chosen, all feasible solutions must be ranked in an order of preference. An objective function is a *vector* that serves as an automatic ranking device. We shall project the shadow of the FSS upon it to determine which solution corresponds to the farthest (if maximizing) or the nearest (if minimizing) end of the shadow. See Figure 5-8.

In E^2, an objective function may have the form of a vector with an angle $\tan^{-1}(c_2/c_1)$:

$$\max Z_x = c_1 X_1 + c_2 X_2 \text{ or } \min Z'_x = -c_1 X_1 - c_2 X_2 \text{ where } Z'_x = -Z_x$$

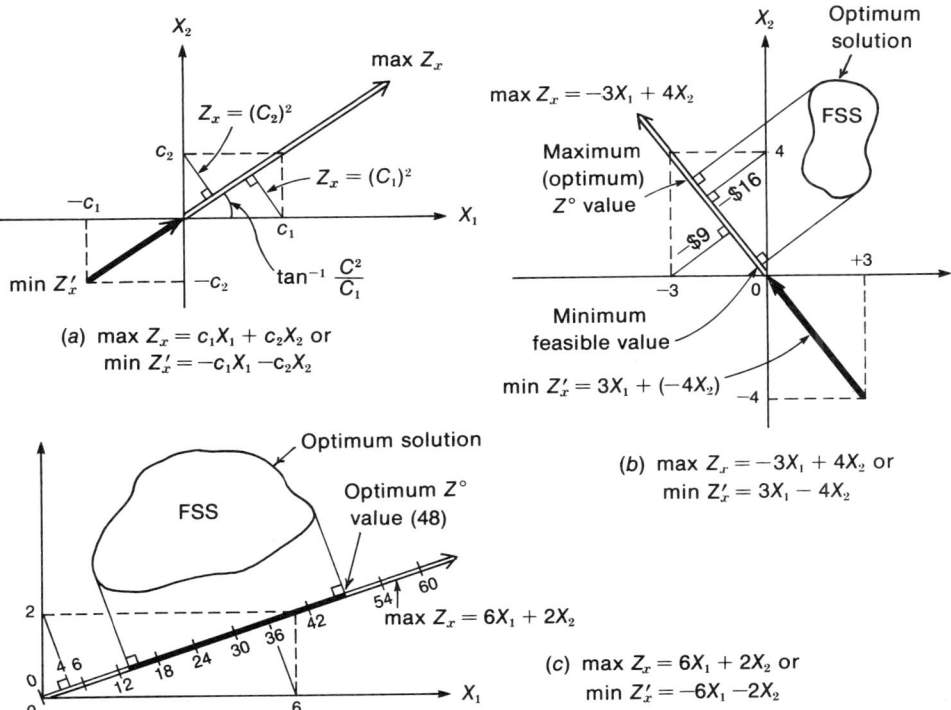

Figure 5-8 Examples of objective functions interpreted as vectors.

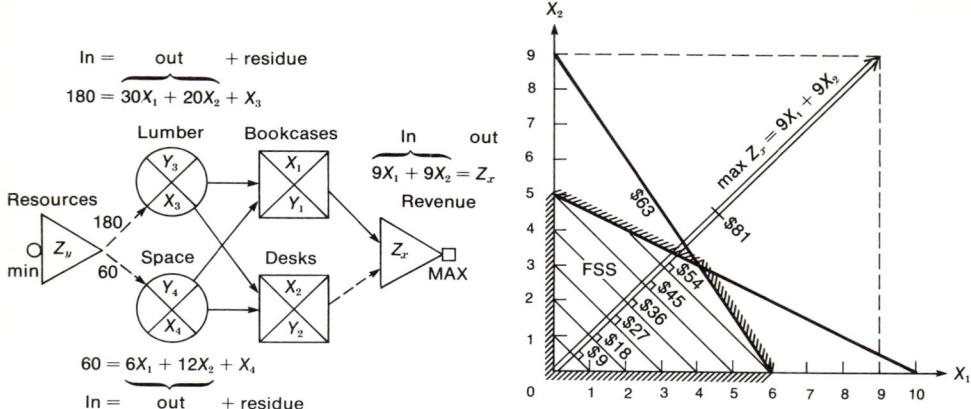

Figure 5-9 Woodworking shop optimality analysis.

To construct this vector, simply locate c_1 on X_1 and c_2 on X_2 and draw the vector as a diagonal to the rectangle $[(0,0), (c_1,0), (c_1,c_2), (0,c_2)]$. Orthogonal projections of $(c_1,0)$ and $(0,c_2)$ on the vector can be used to scale the vector values at c_1^2 and c_2^2; $Z_x = 0$ at the origin $(0,0)$ also helps interpolate other values.

Any satisficing constraint used to create the FSS may be made observable by making it an objective function. Thus, any one of the resources, revenue, lumber, or space, can be converted into an objective function.[1] This primal objective function may either be maximizing or minimizing, but it should be the opposite of whatever the terminal node for the resources is.

Let us illustrate the maximizing primal case. The most obvious choice for an objective function is the maximization of revenue. Thus, instead of setting the minimum satisficing level of revenue as $27, we try to maximize the revenue within the feasible limits. To state it mathematically, we are moving from the feasibility analysis problem to an optimality analysis problem:

1. *Feasibility analysis*

   Identify the FSS subject to the following constraints:

   $9X_1 + 9X_2 \geq 27$ Satisficing minimum revenue
   $30X_1 + 20X_2 \leq 180$ Satisficing lumber-supply limitation
   $6X_1 + 12X_2 \leq 60$ Satisficing space limitation
   $X_1 \geq 0$ Nonnegativity constraints (allowing solutions in the first quadrant of E^2 only)
   $X_2 \geq 0$

---

[1] Goal programming is a formal extension of linear programming that converts each goal, originally stated as an objective function, into a constraint before applying the next goal of a lower priority. See Sang M. Lee, *Goal Programming for Decision Analysis*, Auerback Publishers, Inc., Philadelphia, 1972.

2. Optimality analysis

$$\max Z_x = 9X_1 + 9X_2 \quad \text{Objective function}$$

subject to

$$\left.\begin{array}{r}30X_1 + 20X_2 \le 180 \\ 6X_1 + 12X_2 \le 60\end{array}\right\} \text{Resource constraints}$$

$$\left.\begin{array}{r}X_1 \ge 0 \\ X_2 \ge 0\end{array}\right\} \text{Nonnegativity constraints}$$

Figure 5-7 for the feasibility analysis now appears as Figure 5-9 for the optimality analysis with an objective function vector Z_x at 45° ($\tan^{-1} \frac{9}{9} = 45°$) in the first quadrant.

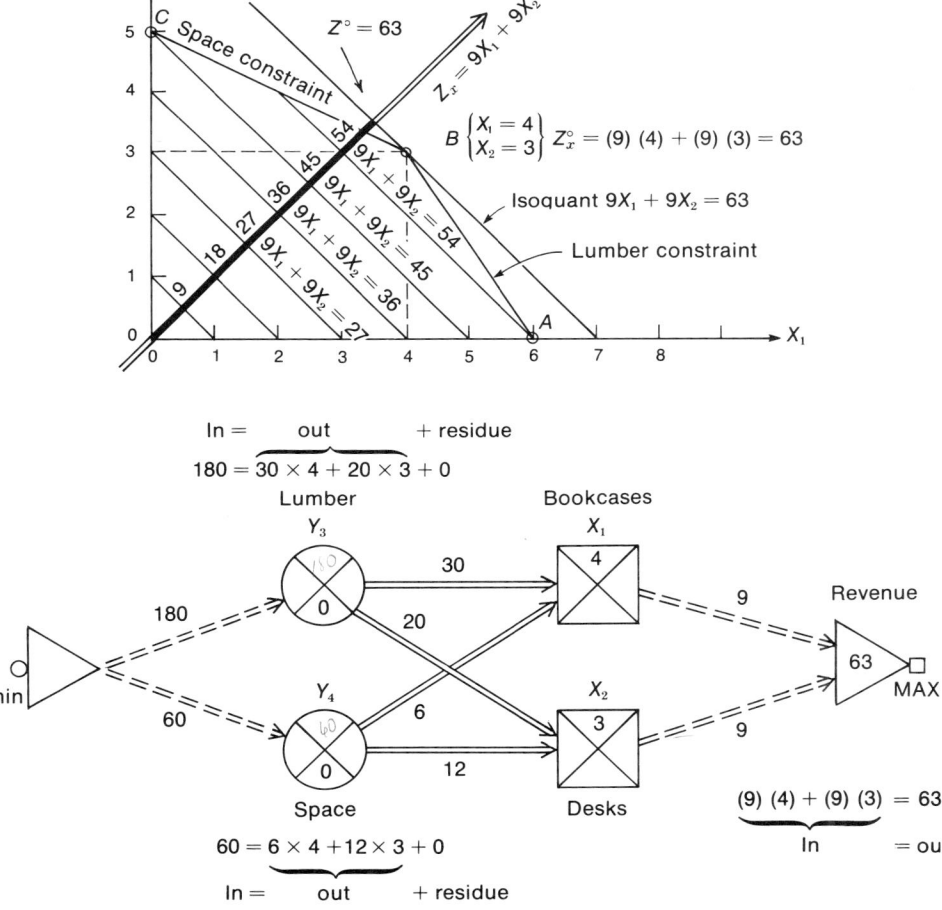

Figure 5-10 Optimal solution for the woodworking shop example.

The objective function vector indicates the direction perpendicular to a series of *isoquants* (lines of equal profit, sometimes known as *isoprofit lines*), which are really no more than the revenue threshold of Figure 5-7, as we change the value of Z_x in $9X_1 + 9X_2 \geq Z_x$ from 0 to 27 and on to infinity. Since the value of the isoquant $Z_x = 9X_1 + 9X_2$ increases in the direction of the arrowhead, the largest revenue Z_x° will be obtained when the isoquant is barely touching the boundary and is about to leave the FSS. This point corresponds to the tip end of the shadow cast by the FSS upon the objective function vector. In Figure 5-10, we have $X_1^\circ = 4$, $X_2^\circ = 3$, and $Z_x^\circ = \$63$, as shown both in the E^2 graph and in the accompanying RPM network.

SECTION 5-2 TUNE-UP

A company makes two products: electric motors (X_1) and alternators (X_2). Each motor contributes \$4 profit per unit, and each alternator contributes \$1. The objective to maximize profit can be written as max $Z_x = $ _____. Draw the objective function vector in E^2 as vector Z_x:

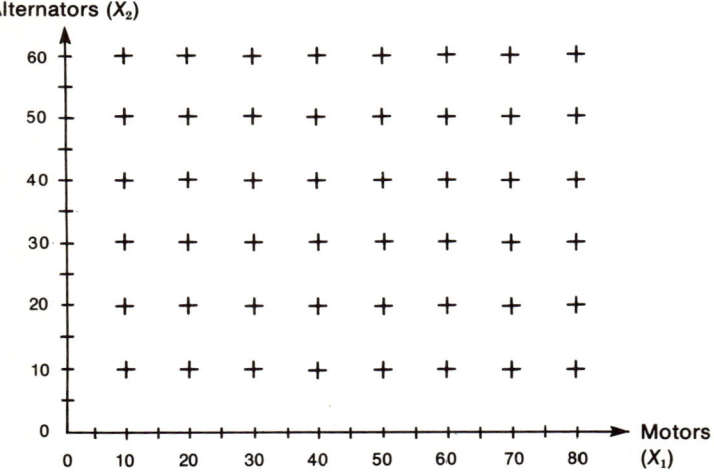

The winding department has nine workers (360 man-hr/wk) available. Each motor takes 6 man-hr, and each alternator takes 6 man-hr. Draw this as resource constraint A on the E^2 graph. This constraint and the objective function tell us that the optimum product mix is _____ units of motors and _____ units of alternators for the total profit of \$_____/wk. Draw an RPM network to illustrate this situation:

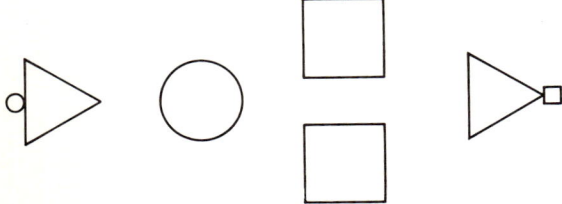

Because of the shortage of commutators, only 50 motors can be made weekly, this imposes an additional constraint B. Add B to your RPM network. The node-balance equation around the node B can be written as an inequality _____ which is drawn on the E^2 graph as constraint B. Similarly, because of the limited supply of rectifiers, only 40 alternators can be made weekly. Show this constraint as resource C on the E^2 graph and on your RPM network. Now the optimum solution is to make _____ units of motors and _____ units of alternators. The new profit is $_____.

The management has decided that it is not a good policy to make less than 20 alternators weekly because of customer relations. Show this as constraint D on the E^2 graph and on your RPM network. This constraint, _____, gives us a new optimum solution of _____ motors and _____ alternators for $_____ profit contribution per week. Redraw your final RPM network as shown below and insert all primal variable values and their residues as well as the objective function value. State your final problem mathematically.

(B) Commutators

(A) Winding department

min

Motors (X_1)

Alternators (X_2)

(C) Diodes

(D) Customers

Profit contribution

MAX

max $Z_x =$ _____

subject to

A _____
B _____
C _____
D _____

and nonnegativity constraints _____ and _____.

5-3 Adaptivity analysis

An OR/MS study should not be just a feasibility and optimality analysis. Valuable information can be obtained by an in-depth study of the proposed solution.

96   Introduction to Operations Research and Management Science

The study of the environmental effects upon the system is variously called *adaptivity analysis*, *sensitivity analysis*, and *postoptimality analysis*. In computer processing such a printout is known as a *range report*.

SENSITIVITY (POSTOPTIMALITY) ANALYSIS Let us return to our woodworking example. Thus far the optimality analysis seems to indicate that it would be most profitable to make a contract with the discount store to manufacture four bookcases and three desks daily for an additional revenue of $63. A wise investor, however, must foresee any potential difficulties and plan for contingencies.

Let us assume that in signing a contract your main concern with the store is the sensitivity of your solution to changing discount prices (discount stores are known to cut the sales price of any item that is not moving fast). The present price of $9 per piece for either a desk or bookcase results in a 45° slope (gradient = arctan c_2/c_1 = $\tan^{-1} 1 = 45°$). When the furniture is actually displayed in the discount store, it is conceivable that one type of furniture will become more popular and sell faster. Their respective prices may then be adjusted to take advantage of higher demand or to make up for the lack of popularity. The ratio of c_2/c_1 will affect the optimality of product mix, while the magnitude of c_1 and c_2, by making $c_1 X_1 + c_2 X_2 < 27$, may render the solution undesirable.

Figure 5-11 shows how the product mix varies with the ratio of c_2 to c_1. We should keep in our mind that a solution may be optimal but not feasible if price and demand drop too low. On the other hand, keeping the same product mix while prices are rising may result in a feasible but nonoptimal solution. In Figure 5-11 note that the basic paths pass through nonzero primal process nodes and resource nodes with no residue. These basic resource nodes correspond to the constraints that are binding at that time.

A shift in production policy occurs when the objective function has a slope corresponding to one of the limiting constraints. Thus, we are advised to manufacture bookcases ($X_1 = 6$) only as long as the profit from a desk is less than two-thirds of that from a bookcase (Figure 5-11a); manufacture both bookcases ($X_1 = 4$) and desks ($X_2 = 3$) if the ratio of c_2/c_1 is between $2/3$ to 2 (Figure 5-11b); and manufacture only desks ($X_2 = 5$) if the ratio is greater than 2 (Figure 5-11c).

DEGENERACY The condition in which there is more than one optimal solution is called *degeneracy*, as shown in Figure 5-11 (ii) and (iii). When $c_2/c_1 = 2/3$, we may make either bookcases only ($X_1 = 6$) or a combination of bookcases ($X_1 = 4$) and desks ($X_2 = 3$) for the same revenue of $Z_x = 4c_1 + 3c_2 = 6c_1$. In fact, any linear combination of these two solutions is also acceptable as an optimum solution. For example, one-half of each solution would give us $X_1 = 5$ and $X_2 = 1.5$ for the total revenue of $5c_1 + 1.5c_2$; but since $c_2/c_1 = 2/3$, this is the same as $5c_1 + 1.5(2c_1/3) = 6c_1$. Thus, the line segment AB corresponds to all feasible and optimal solutions under condition (ii). Similarly, (iii) has degenerate solutions between B and C: $\overline{BC}$.

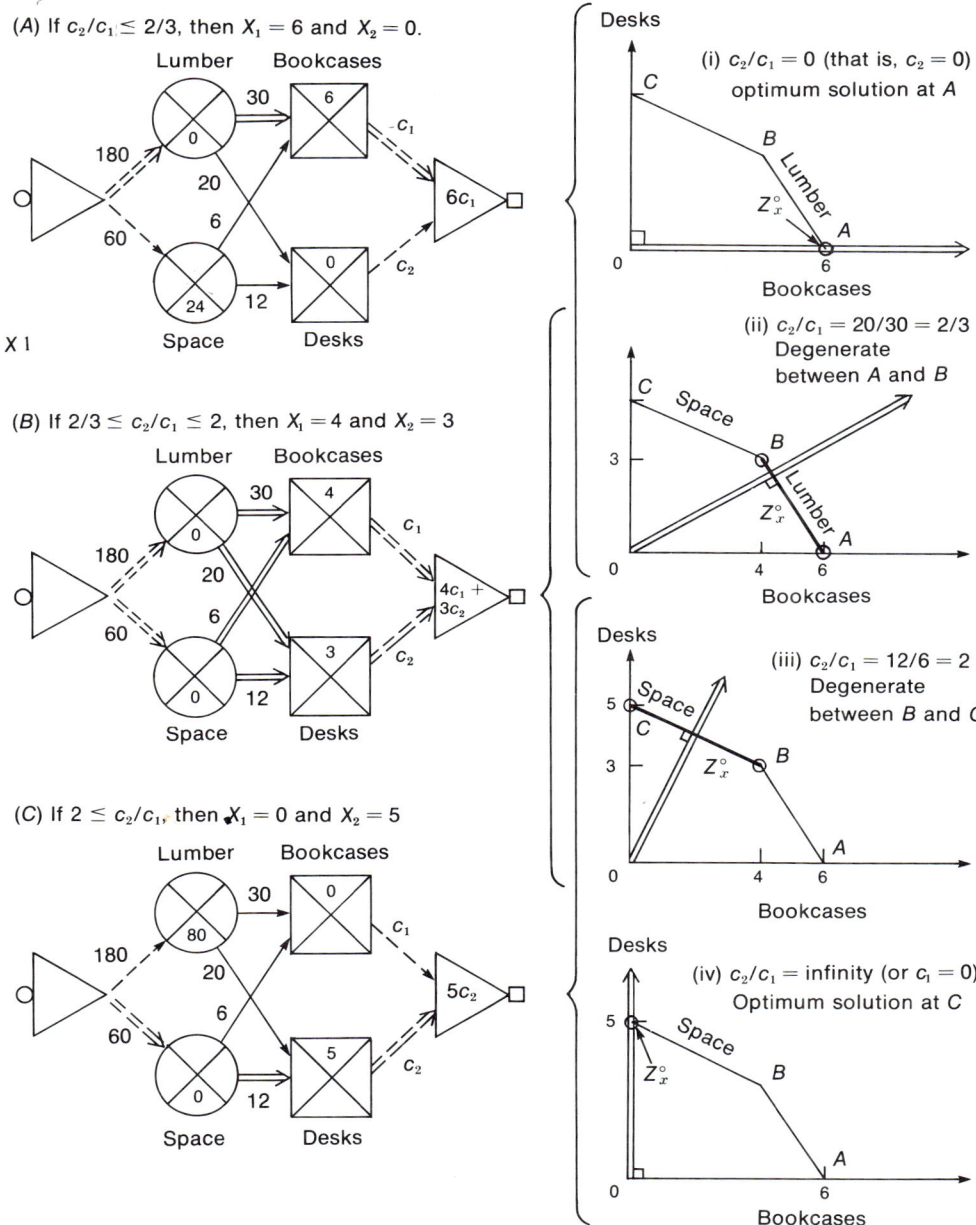

Figure 5-11 Changing gradient of an objective function.

98 Introduction to Operations Research and Management Science

EXHAUSTIVE SEARCH Note that the extreme-point theorem (Section 5-1) holds true even in the case of degeneracy. For each degenerate solution, there exist two extrema [A and B for condition (ii); B and C for condition (iii)] which have the same objective function value as the degenerate solution.

In a simple problem such as the one we have been discussing, it is easy to find all extrema (corner points), substitute their values into the objective function, and identify whichever set of Cartesian coordinate values achieves the optimum value. Unfortunately, there are two pitfalls to this simplistic reasoning. First, not all intersections of constraint boundaries are feasible: for example, ($X_1 = 10$, $X_2 = 0$) is an intersection of the boundary lines for $X_2 = 0$ and $6X_1 + 12X_2 = 60$, but is not a part of the FSS since it violates the other constraints as seen in Figure 5-6. Second, the number of intersections grows rapidly as more variables and constraints are considered. In general, with m resources and n processes (that is, n nonnegative constraints), we have $m + n$ total constraints in either E^n (primal) or E^m (dual) spaces. Since a corner in E^k is an intersection of k constraints (for example, E^2's corners are intersections of two lines;

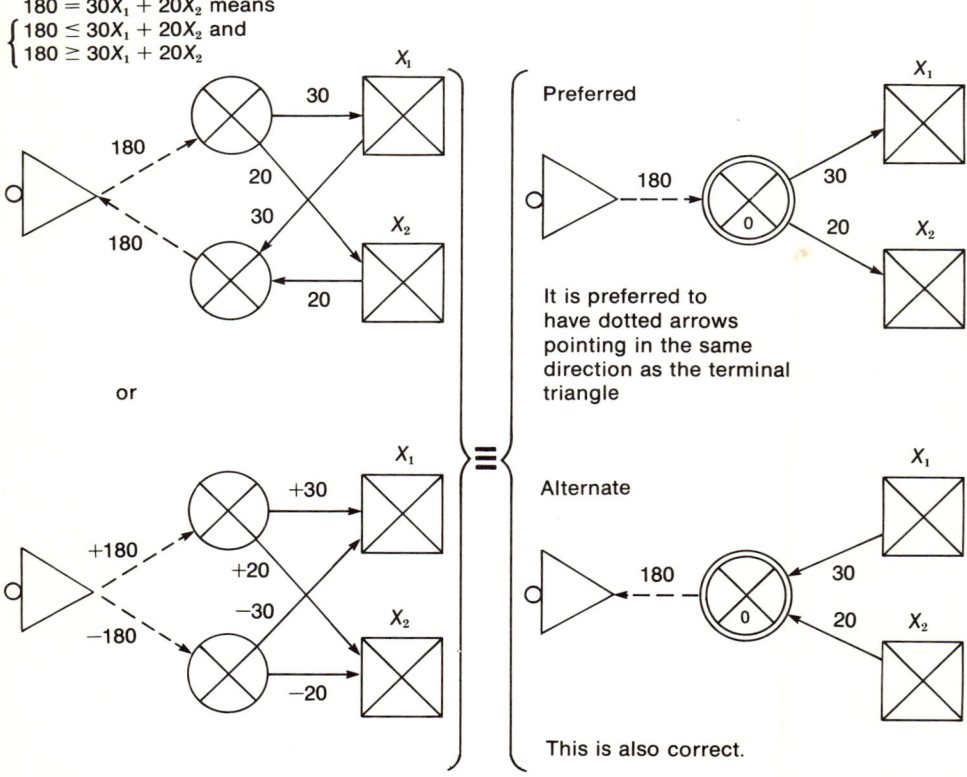

Figure 5-12 Four ways of representing $180 = 30X_1 + 20X_2$.

E^3's corners are intersections of three planes), we have $\binom{n\ +\ m}{n}$ or $\binom{n\ +\ m}{m}$ corners in E^n and E^m, where the combinations ( ) are defined in terms of factorials $n!$, $m!$, and $(n + m)!$:

$$\binom{n+m}{n} = \frac{(n+m)!}{n!m!} = \binom{n+m}{m}$$

In our example, $n = 2$, $m = 2$, $n! = 2 \times 1$, $m! = 2 \times 1$, $(n + m)! = 4! = 4 \times 3 \times 2 \times 1$, and $\binom{4}{2} = (4 \times 3 \times 2 \times 1)/(2 \times 1)(2 \times 1) = 6$ corners in E^2. For a modest problem of 20 resources and 10 constraints, we have $\binom{30}{20} = \binom{30}{10} = 6{,}609{,}903{,}299$ extrema to investigate. This disturbing phenomenon is commonly called *the curse of dimensionality*, an expression attributed to Richard Bellman.[1]

EQUALITY An *equality* can be expressed as two opposing inequalities $\geq$ and $\leq$. To exhaust the lumber supply, we write 180 ($\geq$ and $\leq$) $30X_1 + 20X_2$ and express this as a double circle with zero residue (Figure 5-12). The direction of the arrow is arbitrary, as arrows are used to separate the two sides of the equation. In E^2, the FSS is now reduced to a line.

SECTION 5-3 TUNE-UP

Refer to Section 5-2 Tune-up. Suppose that the President's Office of Price and Production Surveillance (PPS) imposed the restriction that exactly 30 motors must be produced by your company. How will this appear on your E^2 graph and in your RPM network? Identify your new solution.

5-4 Minimization

In our woodworking shop example we have been assuming that only the revenue will vary and that all other resources will be fixed and satisficed by the feasible solutions. Is it possible that a resource other than revenue can vary and act as the objective function? Certainly! The only difference is that the other constraints are *inputs* to processes, not outputs. Thus, the objective function must be minimizing instead of maximizing and the resource terminal will have to be changed to maximizing instead of minimizing.[2] Figure 5-13 shows examples.

DUALITY Just as our primal mathematical model has been obtained by applying RPMS postulates to the resource nodes and the primal objective terminal, a dual model can be obtained by applying these postulates to the process nodes and the dual objective node. For example, in our woodworking shop, with maximizing

---

[1]Richard Bellman, *Dynamic Programming*, Princeton University Press, Princeton, N. J., 1957.
[2]See footnote 1, p. 92.

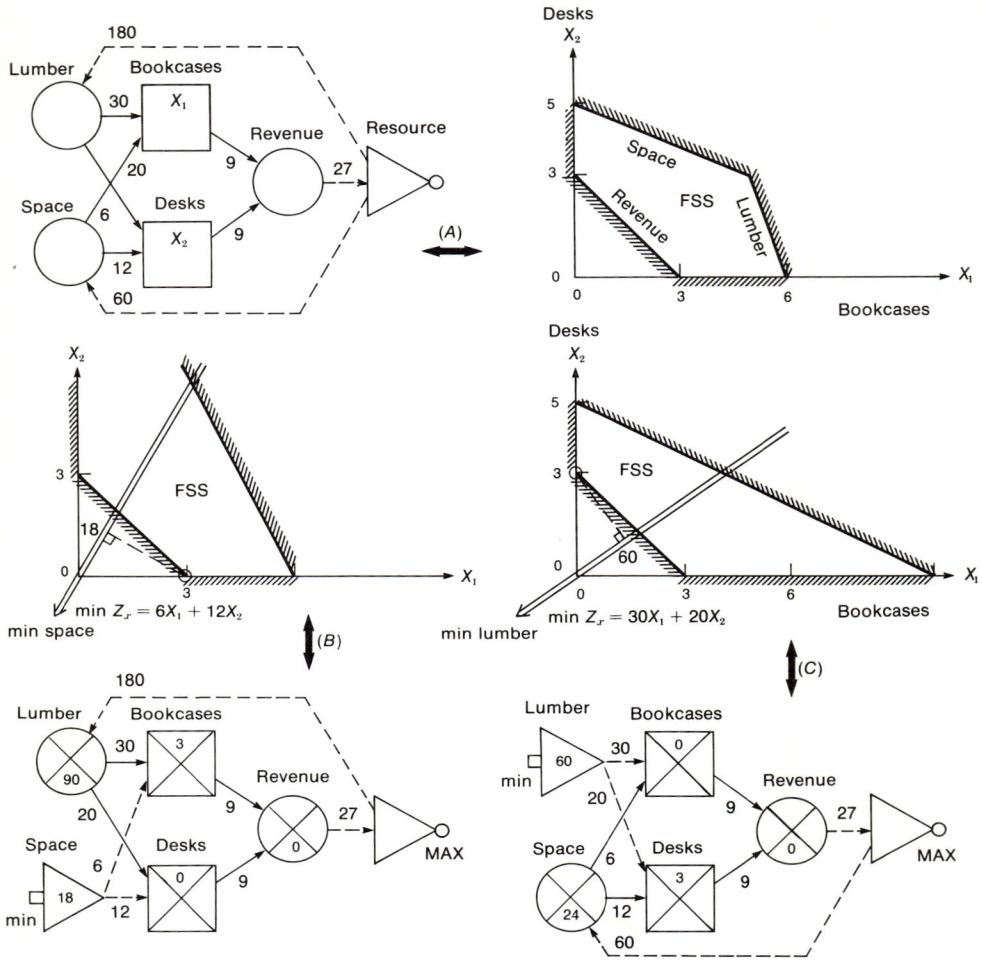

Figure 5-13 Converting resources into an objective function.

revenue, we would have

$$\min Z_y = 180Y_3 + 60Y_4$$ (Summing around Z_y and applying the second postulate)

subject to

$$30Y_3 + 6Y_4 \geq 9$$ (Summing around X_1 and applying the first postulate)

$$20Y_3 + 12Y_4 \geq 9$$ (Summing around X_2 and applying the first postulate)

$$Y_3 \geq 0 \text{ and } Y_4 \geq 0$$ (Nonnegativity assumption)

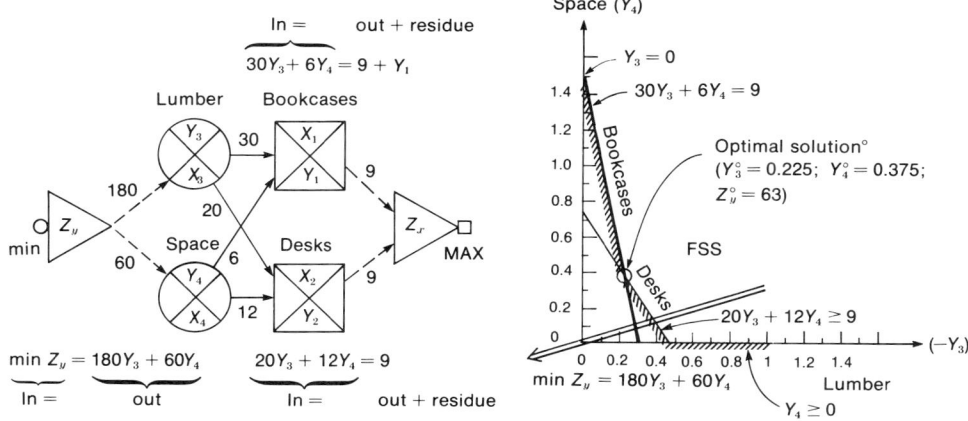

Figure 5-14 Graphic analysis of a dual model for Example 5-1.

Assuming linearity and nonnegativity, a similar graphic analysis can be performed for minimization. In Figure 5-14 the optimum (°) value of $63 is obtained for $Y_3^\circ = 0.225$ and $Y_4^\circ = 0.375$.

Figure 5-15 incorporates both the primal and the dual results for the optimal solution. We note that $Z_x^\circ = Z_y^\circ = \$63$ and that each node contains at least one zero. The paths through basic nodes (nodes with zero residue) constitute basic paths through the RPM network. In this case all paths are found to be basic. These basic paths can be identified from our knowledge of the primal solution alone. They pass through the primal basic variable nodes and also through resource

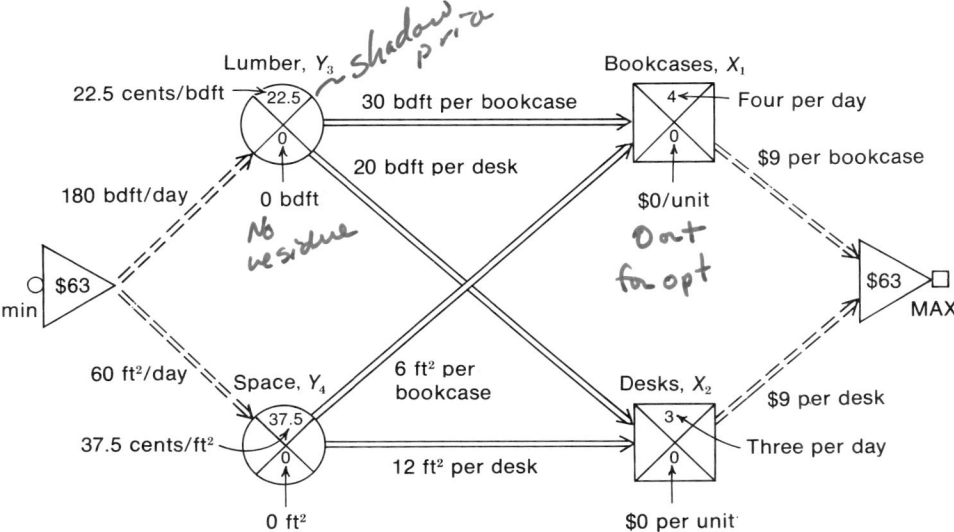

Figure 5-15 RPMS interpretation of Example 5-1 (primal and dual models).

nodes whose residues are depleted by the basic processes. Since equality must hold for nodes with zero residue, we may write

$30Y_3 + 6Y_4 = 9$ (balancing around X_1)

$20Y_3 + 12Y_4 = 9$ (balancing around X_2)

Solving these equations simultaneously, we obtain the correct values for the dual variables: $Y_3 = 0.225$ and $Y_4 = 0.375$. The units of these dual variables are dollars per unit of the particular resource, and the computed values are called *shadow prices*, or *imputed costs*. We can check these values by computing, for example,

Z_x° = ($9 per bookcase)(4 bookcases) + ($9 per desk)(3 desks)

  = $63

Z_y° = ($0.225/bdft) (180 bdft) + ($0.375/ft²) (60 ft²)

  = $63

And also internally

($0.225/bdft)(30 bdft per bookcase)(4 bookcases) + ($0.225/bdft)(20 bdft per desk) (3 desks) + ($0.375/ft²) (6 ft² per bookcase) (4 bookcases) + ($0.375/ft²) (12 ft² per desk) (3 desks) = $63

Shadow prices are useful in computing the sensitivity of the solution to perturbation in resource supplies: Figure 5-16 illustrates the effects of varying lumber and space resources. The significance of Figure 5-16 can be studied to appreciate the utility of the concept of shadow price.

1. Let us suppose that there is a possibility of a decrease in lumber supply from 180 to 140 bdft/day. Knowing the shadow price of lumber $Y_3 = \$0.225$, it is easy to compute the decrease in profit: $(140 - 180)(\$0.225) = -\$9$; thus, the new profit will be $63 - $9 = $54. (See Figure 5-16a.)

2. Let us assume that you can clear some junk out of your warehouse to create 24 ft² of additional storage space. Since the shadow price of storage is $0.375, this act will contribute $24 \times \$0.375 = \$9$. From the original condition, you have increased the revenue to $63 + $9 = $72. (See Figure 5-16b.)

3. Thus, you can feel at ease in knowing that should a decrease in lumber supply occur, you can compensate for the potential decrease in profit by creating additional storage space and changing your product mix from four bookcases and three desks a day to seven desks and zero bookcases a day. (See Figure 5-16c.)

Of course, a shadow price is meaningful only when the basic nodes remain unchanged; as soon as the basic path shifts its course, new shadow prices must be computed. In other words, the preceding discussion remains valid only for Figure 5-11b, not Figure 5-11a or c. If the lumber supply had decreased further in Figure 5-16c, our arguments would not have applied.

(a) Decrease lumber supply from 180 to 140
$(-40)(0.225) = -\$9 \quad \$63 - 9 = \$54$

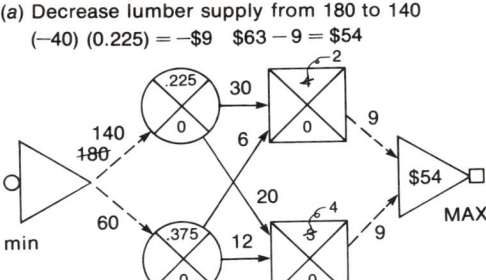
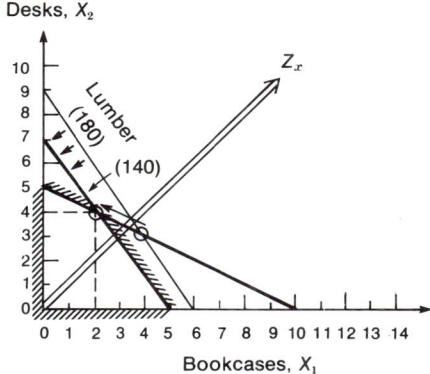

(b) Increase space from 60 to 84
$(+24)(0.375) = \$9 \quad \$63 + 9 = \$72$

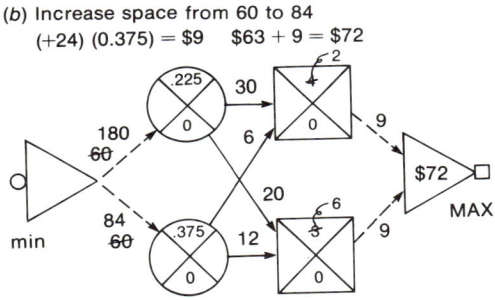
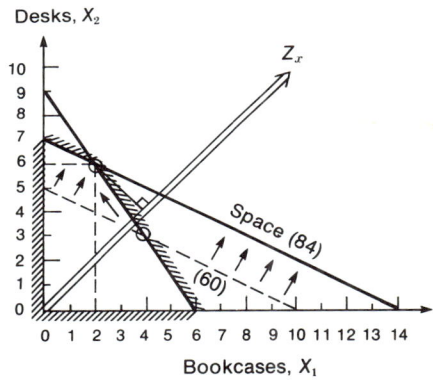

(c) Decrease lumber and increase space

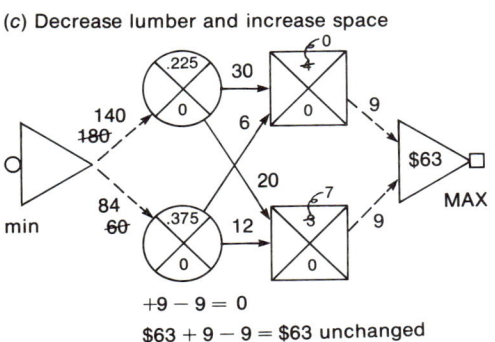
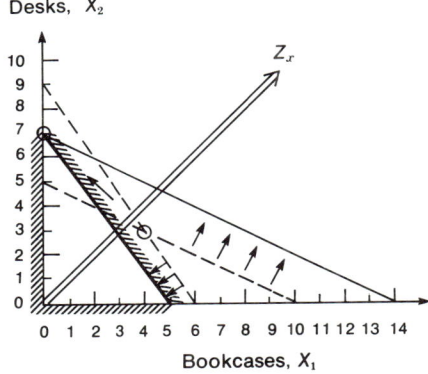

$+9 - 9 = 0$
$\$63 + 9 - 9 = \$63$ unchanged

Figure 5-16 Sensitivity analysis when resources are perturbed.

5-5 RPM network interpretation

Since we assume that all variables are nonnegative in linear programming, we should examine how the relationships between the primal and dual representations of the same problem can be utilized. Figure 5-17 illustrates both the primal and dual graphic E^2 models of our woodworking shop, together with RPM networks that correspond to each of the six possible corners. The extrema A, B, and C were discussed in Section 5-3 (Figure 5-11). The corner O corresponds to the origin of the graph and to the trivial solution that no bookcase and no desk is made for an expected profit increase of $0. Corners D and E violate one of the two resource constraints (space or lumber) and are therefore nonfeasible. With the original objective function vector $Z_x = 9X_1 + 9X_2$, the extremum B is optimal and C and A are suboptimal with profits ($45 and $54) that are less than the optimal profit ($63).

From the dual E^2 graph, we see that the *nonoptimal* primal solutions (A and C) correspond to nonfeasible dual solutions (also marked A and C) that are outside of the dual FSS. The *nonfeasible* primal solutions (D and E), on the other hand, correspond to nonoptimal dual solutions. Applying the first postulate to all nodes in RPM networks, we find that the nonfeasibility and nonoptimality conditions correspond to negative values or negative residues. Figure 5-18 summarizes those conditions which can be ascertained from Figure 5-19. In subsequent chapters we shall make use of these "symptoms" to spot possible improvements.

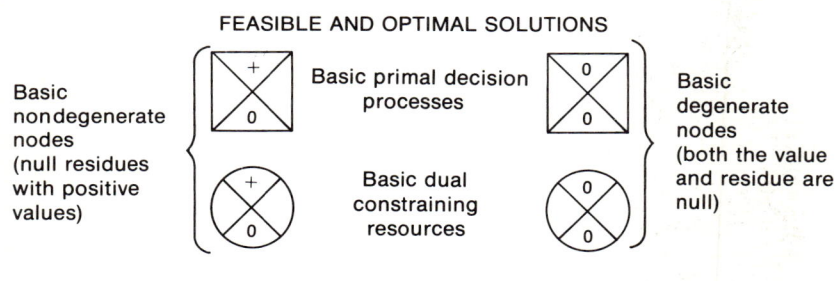

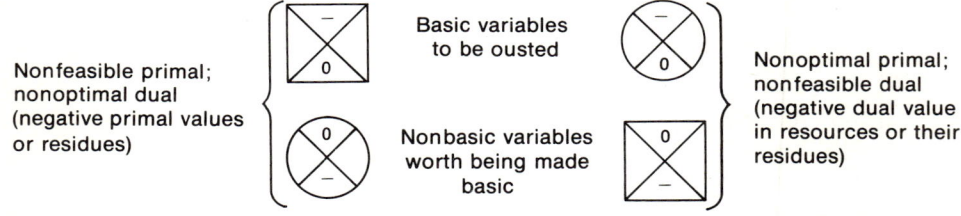

Figure 5-17 Feasibility and optimality interpretation of the woodworking shop RPMS.

Model Experimentation: Graphic Introduction to Linear Programming

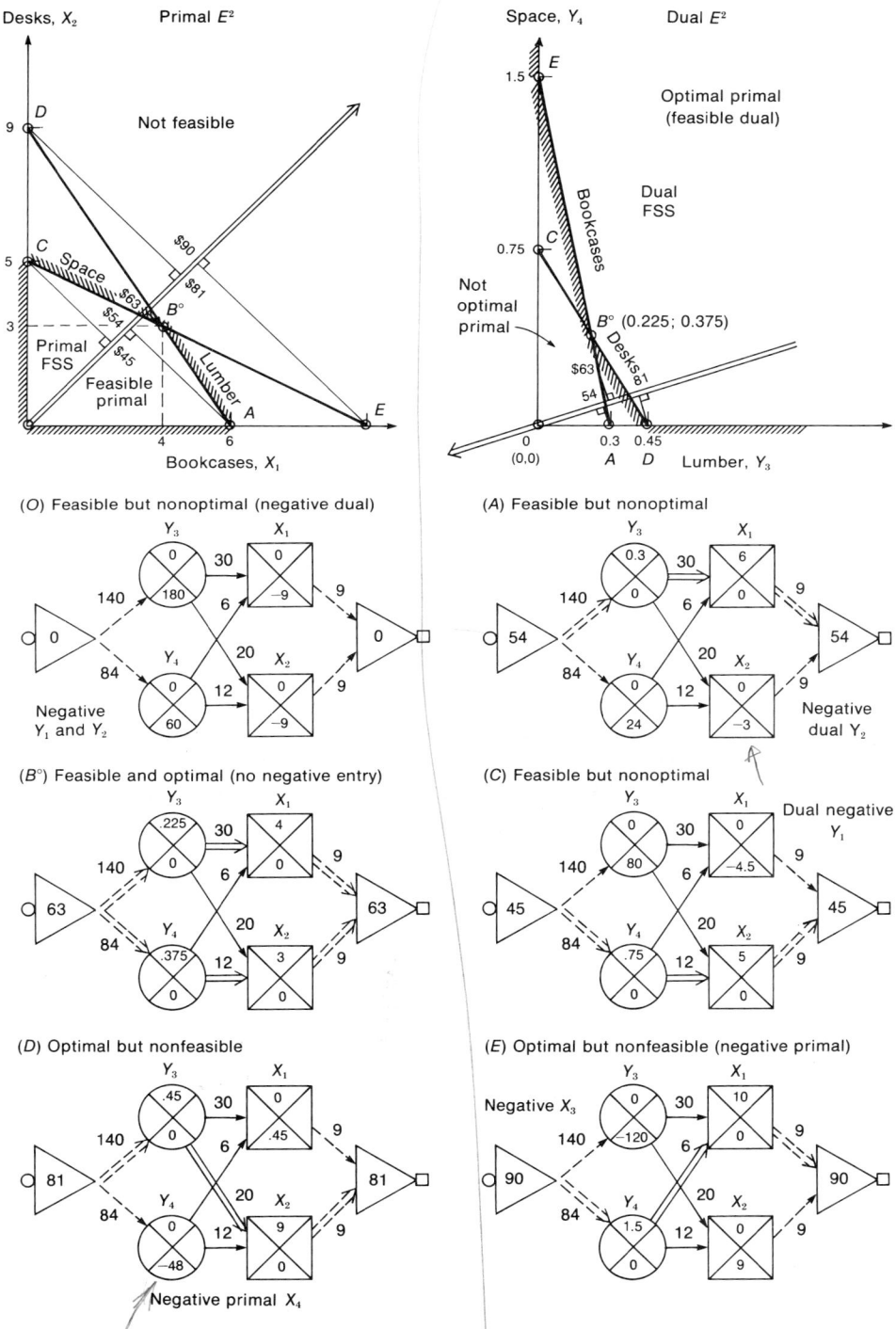

Figure 5-18 RPM interpretation of feasibility and optimality.

SECTION 5-4 TUNE-UP

Since the objective function value is the same in both the primal and the dual model under optimality, and since variables can easily be computed once the basic path has been identified, we can solve a problem with many variables as long as it has only two constraints and its dual can be represented on an E^2. Let us assume that you have just inherited a Chinese restaurant from your Dutch uncle. He left you the premises with 60 chairs and 16 tables but no money to remodel or purchase additional furniture. Being a faithful OR/MS practioner, you have computed the average profit per hour per table from various possible arrangements of the tables and chairs; the results are shown in Figure 5-19. Using the RPM network and the E^2 layout in Figure 5-19, solve the problem of op-

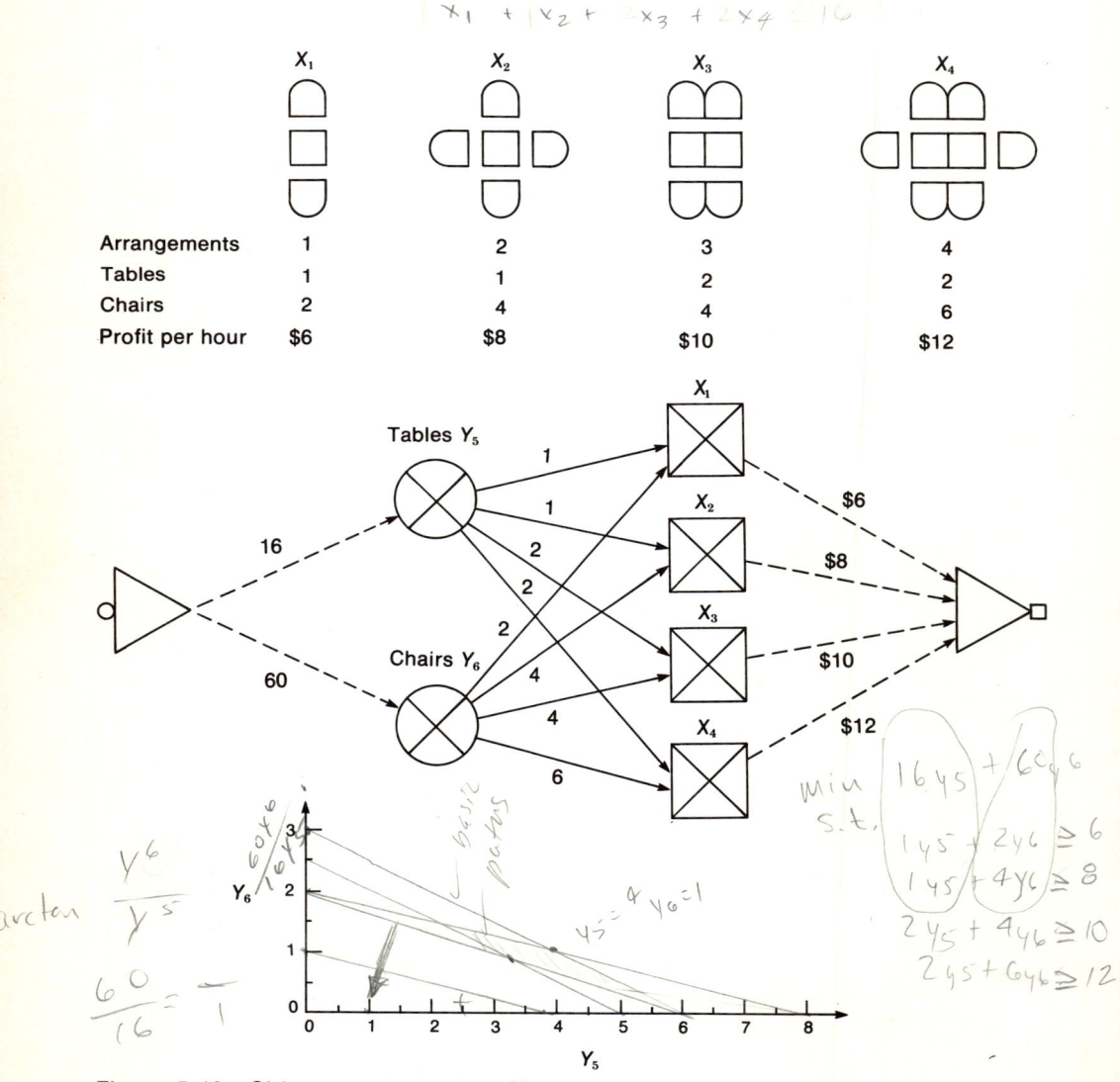

Figure 5-19 Chinese restaurant problem.

timally allocating chairs and tables to maximize your expected profit. First find Y_5 and Y_6, and then compute the values of X's.

TUNE-UP SOLUTIONS

Section 5-2

max $Z_x = 4X_1 + X_2$
subject to

(A) $360 \geq 6X_1 = 6X_2$

$X_1^\circ = 60$ motors

$X_2^\circ = 0$

$Z_x^\circ = \$240/\text{wk}$

(B) $50 \geq X_1$

$X_1^\circ = 50$ motors

$X_2^\circ = 10$ alternators

$Z_x^\circ = \$210/\text{wk}$

(C) $40 \geq X_2$

$X_1^\circ = 50$ motors

$X_2^\circ = 10$ alternators

$Z_x^\circ = \$210/\text{wk}$

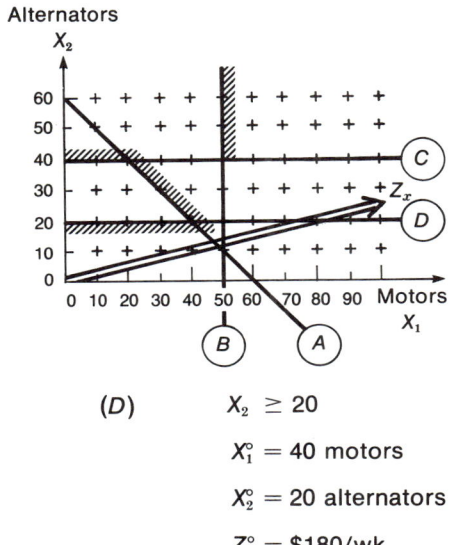

(D) $X_2 \geq 20$

$X_1^\circ = 40$ motors

$X_2^\circ = 20$ alternators

$Z_x^\circ = \$180/\text{wk}$

and nonnegativity constraints $X_1 \geq 0$ and $X_2 \geq 0$.

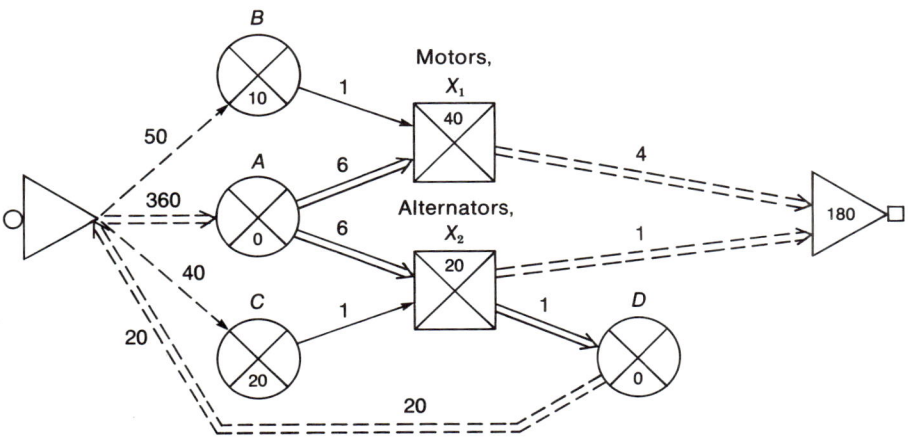

Section 5-3

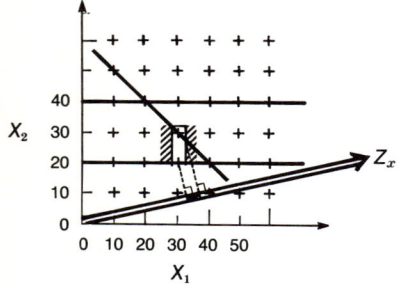

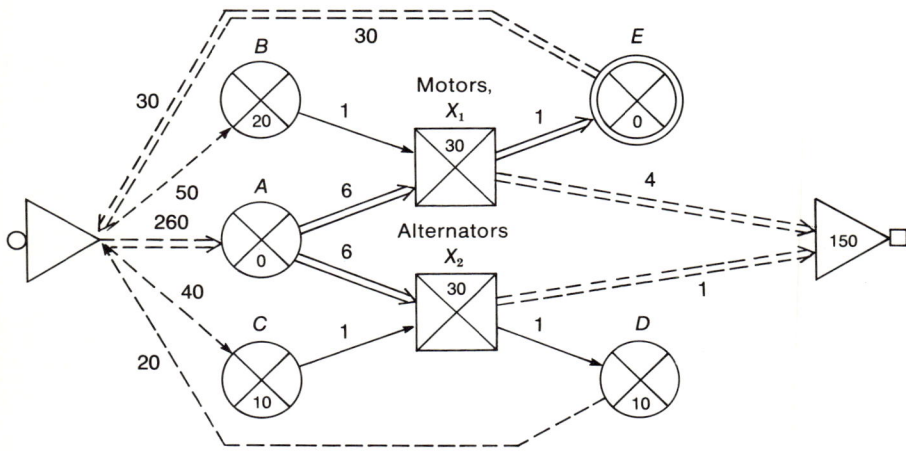

Section 5-5

The primal model is

$$\max Z_x = 6X_1 + 8X_2 + 10X_3 + 12X_4$$

subject to
$16 \geq X_1 + X_2 + 2X_3 + 2X_4$ around the Y_5 node
$60 \geq 2X_1 + 4X_2 + 4X_3 + 6X_4$ around the Y_6 node (all X's ≥ 0)

The dual model is
$\min Z_y = 16Y_5 + 60\ Y_6$
$Y_5 + 2Y_6 \geq 6$ at X_1
$Y_5 + 4Y_6 \geq 8$ at X_2
$2Y_5 + 4Y_6 \geq 10$ at X_3
$2Y_5 + 6Y_6 \geq 12$ at X_4 (all Y's ≥ 0)

Solving graphically, we find

$Y_5^\circ = 4 \qquad Y_6^\circ = 1 \qquad Z_y^\circ = \$124 = Z_x^\circ$

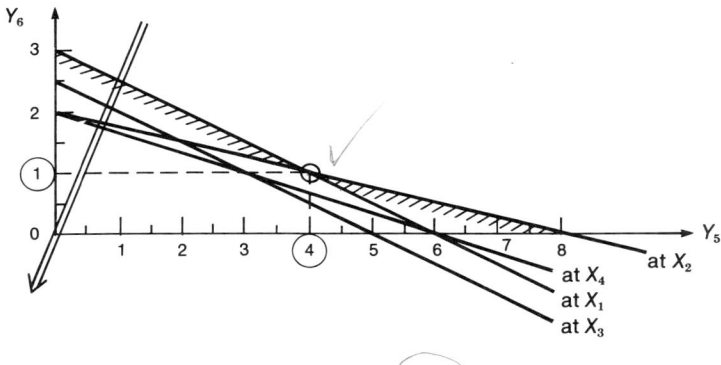

From the basic paths, we obtain

$16 = X_1 + X_2 \qquad \text{and} \qquad 60 = 2X_1 + 4X_2$

Solving them simultaneously we find

$X_1^\circ = 2 \qquad X_2^\circ = 14 \qquad Z_x^\circ = 124$

All other X's must be zero; otherwise, we shall lose $2 for each X_3 or X_4 arrangement.

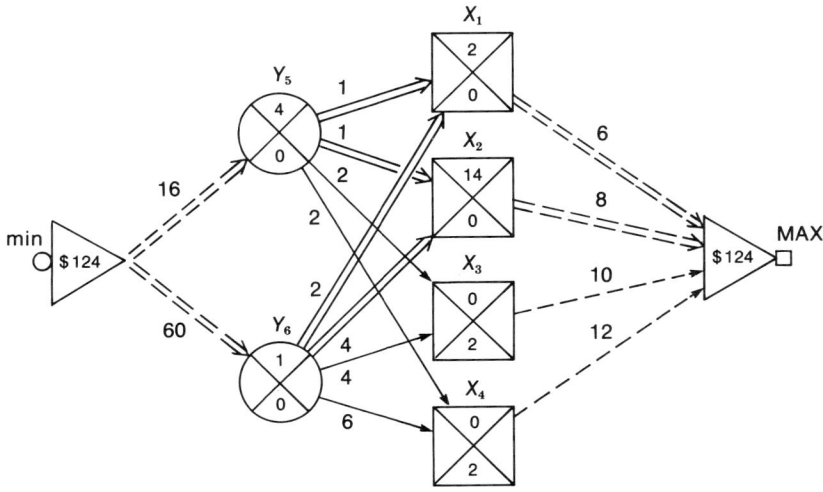

EXERCISES

5-1 Compute all the dual-variable values in Figure 5-13 (B) and (C).

5-2 Compute all the dual-variable values in the Tune-up Solutions for Sections 5-2 (page 107) and 5-3 (page 108).

5-3 Compute all values for the RPM network of Figure 5-11 (A) and (B), assuming $c_1 = 15$ and $c_2 = 10$.

5-4 Your restaurant business is causing you to put on weight and you have decided to go on a diet. A "quick-pounds-loss" diet by your favorite dietician, Dr. Stallman, recommends that you eat only two types of foods: pulverized dried skin of boa constrictor and condensed milk of alpaca. Each ounce of alpaca milk (A) and boa constrictor skin (B) costs $16 and $60, respectively, and have the following nutritional values:

Nutrients	Alpaca milk (A), units/oz	Boa constrictor skin (B), units/oz	Minimum daily requirement (MDR), units/day
Type 1	1	2	6
Type 2	1	4	8
Type 3	2	4	10
Type 4	2	6	12
Cost, dollars/oz	16	60	

Stallman recommends that you take a minimum of 6, 8, 10, and 12 units of the respective nutrients per day. Minimize the cost of your diet.

5-5 You are working for a company that produces two types of chemicals A and B. For each of the following situations draw an RPM network, interpret the primal model mathematically, identify the E^2 FSS and an optimal solution, and insert the primal and dual values back into your RPM network.

    a The Department of Environment Quality (DEQ) of your state permits no more than 16 ppm (1 ppm = 1.15 mg/m^3) emission of carbon monoxide (CO). Your processes emit 1 and 2 ppm, respectively, for each ton of A or B. Each ton of A and B also contributes $1,000 and $2,000, respectively, to the company's profit. You wish to maximize the total profit contribution.

    b You have decided to help your community by minimizing CO emission as long as your profit contribution does not fall below $18,000.

    c The governor of your state has declared an energy crisis. You now wish to minimize your total power consumption, given that each ton of A needs 100 kwhr versus 400 kwhr for each ton of B, but you would still like to maintain the pollution and profit standards.

d The OPEC nations have curtailed oil production. Your government is limiting the supply of crude oil needed for processing *A* and *B*. Your company is told that it will receive exactly 10 tons/mo which is adequate to produce 5 tons of *A* or *B* or a combination thereof.

NORMATIVE MODEL FORMULATION: Programming LP Problems

Chapter 6

6-1 Origin of programming

The Greek word *programma* means "public written notice." This form of public proclamation lasted into the seventeenth century, when associated ideas of *descriptive notice* and *plan of intended proceedings* emerged. The *plan to be followed* concept became military terminology for war strategists as early as 1917.

The Air Staff (predecessor to U.S. Air Force) created a *program monitoring* function early in World War II, and the term came to mean the formulation of a *war plan* to achieve wartime objectives using wartime resources. Training programs for pilots, production programs for weapons, deployment programs for combat personnel, and programs for maintenance and procurement all had to share the limited resources, follow detailed schedules, and exchange information and transform resources to achieve the end objective—win the war.

It is ironic that a discipline placing so much emphasis on overall system performance (global optimization, we even call it) owes its origin to the decidedly suboptimal game of nations destroying other nations. The irony is overwhelming when we consider how little we have learned from our history. Nonetheless, many technological advances were made as a result of the United States war efforts. Project SCOOP (scientific computation of optimum programs) was initiated in 1947 under the auspices of the United States Air Force. Its objective was to provide a solution procedure, using existing methods and calculating machines, to optimize the resource allocation problems within the Air Force. Scientists were skeptical of their SCOOP assignment from the beginning. The computational difficulties of even the smallest allocation problem taxed any actually or potentially available computer beyond its physical limitations; the team discovered the *curse of dimensionality* (see Chapter 5, Section 5-3) of exhaustive search procedures. In 1948, SCOOP modified its mission and proposed the development of an efficient computational scheme called *triangular models* of linear programming. The goal was to find a general solution procedure for systems of linear equations with many degrees of freedom.

Earlier, Tjalling C. Koopmans (1944) and Frank L. Hitchcock (1941) independently formulated transportation models of linear programming. These models came to the attention of George B. Dantzig, who conceived a special algorithm for such models in 1950. Furthering his research in 1951, Dantzig subsequently generalized the algorithm to apply to all linear programming problems. M. Montalbano and C. Diehm prepared simplex codes to solve triangular models in 1950. All of these algorithms were programmed on computers available at that time: the SEAC (sequentially encoded automatic computer), which was installed in Washington, D.C., in May 1950; UNIVAC-I also installed in Washington, D.C., in 1951; and IBM 602A, 604, 701, and 704 computers. We may note in passing that there was also a computer named ORACLE installed in June 1953, not at the temple of Apollo, but in Oak Ridge, Tennessee.

Thus, it is not by coincidence that today we find two uses of the word *programming*: *mathematical programming* indicates the computational algorithm for resource allocation, and *computer programming* indicates the complex coding that is needed to implement such an algorithm on a computer. The purpose of this chapter and the next is to present several sample problems of linear programming using RPM network representations and to explain the preparation of input to computer programs. We have purposely delayed the discussion of the simplex algorithm (a systematic procedure for solving LP problems) until Chapter 9 so that we can first discover the wide variety of applications that exists for linear programming. Our approach is not unlike that of a travel agent who first tries to show prospective customers all the fun places to visit before discussing the details of how the trips are going to be financed. RPM examples serve as maps to entice your appetite for applications: then we shall be ready to explore the mysteries of algorithms and the wonder of mathematical reasoning, the mechanism which supports the application.[1]

---

[1]If you have not already done so, read through Appendixes A and B (or at least A) while you are studying this chapter because computer printouts will be used to illustrate problem solutions and the Appendixes explain their details.

6-2 Standard forms of LP problems

Linear programming is mathematically defined as the maximization or minimization of a linear function of nonnegative variables subject to a set of linear constraints. We can write this algebraically as

$$\max Z_x = \sum_{j=1}^{n} c_j x_j$$

subject to

$$\sum_{j=1}^{n} a_{ij} x_j \leq b_i \qquad \text{for } i = 1, \ldots, m \text{ and } x_j \geq 0, j = 1, \ldots, n$$

or,

$$\min Z_y = \sum_{i=1}^{m} b_i y_i$$

subject to

$$\sum_{i=1}^{m} a_{ij} y_i \geq c_j \qquad \text{for } j = 1, \ldots, n \text{ and } y_i \geq 0, i = 1, \ldots, m$$

When the two above models describe the same problem (that is, when a_{ij}, b_i, and c_j in both models have the same values), we say that one is the *dual* of the other.

TUCKER DIAGRAM A tabular representation of this primal-dual relationship is called a *Tucker diagram*, or *Tucker tableau*, after A. W. Tucker. The original idea of duality is attributed to John von Neumann and to George B. Dantzig who discussed it as early as 1947. Tucker, together with his associates David H. Gale and H. W. Kuhn, was able to formally establish the *duality theorem* in 1951. Figure 6-1 illustrates a Tucker diagram with a corresponding RPM network.

STANDARD RPM FORMAT[1] The Tucker diagram representation of an LP problem assumes that all primal constraints are .LE. ($\leq$) type, which means that any .GE. ($\geq$) constraint must be changed into an .LE. constraint by multiplying both sides of the inequality by -1. Similarly, each .EQ. ($=$) constraint must be made into .LE. *and* .GE. constraints, with the latter converted into another .LE. constraint through negation. Equivalently, all dual constraints must be represented as .GE. restrictions. The outcome of this transformation is that b_i's and c_j's may be mixtures of positive and negative values.

The standard RPM network represents an adaptation of the Tucker diagram which allows three types of constraints in both the primal and dual models, but permits only positive constants (exogenous and endogenous flows). An equality ($=$) constraint which would have been represented by two dual variables in a Tucker

---

[1] .LE., .GE., and .EQ. stand for less-than-or-equal-to, greater-than-or-equal-to, and equal-to, respectively.

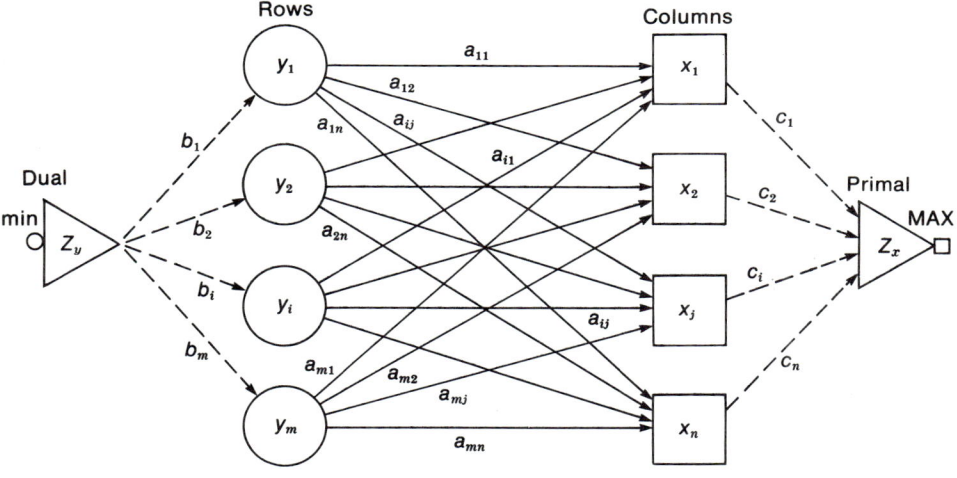

Variables	$x_1 \geq 0$	...	$x_2 \geq 0$	...	$x_j \geq 0$	...	$x_n \geq 0$	(L)	Constants (RHS)
$y_1 \geq 0$	a_{11}		a_{12}	...	a_{ij}	...	a_{1n}	$\leq$	b_1
$y_2 \geq 0$	a_{21}		a_{22}	...	a_{2j}	...	a_{2n}	$\leq$	b_2
⋮	⋮		⋮		⋮		⋮	⋮	⋮
$y_i \geq 0$	a_{i1}		a_{i2}	...	a_{ij}	...	a_{in}	$\leq$	b_i
⋮	⋮		⋮		⋮		⋮	⋮	⋮
$y_m \geq 0$	a_{m1}		a_{m2}	...	a_{mj}	...	a_{mn}	$\leq$	b_m
(G)	IV		IV		IV		IV		min Z_y
Constants (N)	C_1		C_2		C_j		C_n	max Z_x	

Columns give primal values.
Rows give dual values.

Figure 6-1 Tucker diagram and a standard maximizing RPM network. Inside ( )'s are terms used by computer programs (see Appendixes A and B).

diagram (corresponding to the two opposing inequality constraints) is represented by a *free* variable[1] in the RPM network. Such a free variable may assume either a positive or a negative value, depending on the direction in which the constraint is binding (.LE. or .GE.). Then, a *frozen* variable (.EQ.) in a primal would correspond to a free variable in its dual, and a frozen variable in a dual would correspond to a free variable in its primal. Figure 6-2 illustrates a simple RPM network of a Tucker diagram.

---

[1] A double circle with fixed primal residue (= 0) is used to represent a free dual node.

Original problem
max $Z_x = -c_1 x_1 + c_2 x_2$
subject to $a_{11} x_1 + a_{12} x_2 \geq b_1$
$a_{21} x_1 + a_{22} x_2 = b_2$
$a_{31} x_1 + a_{32} x_2 \leq b_3$

All x's are nonnegative.

max $Z_x = -c_1 x_1 + c_2 x_2$
subject to $-a_{11} x_1 - a_{12} x_2 \leq -b_1$
$a_{21} x_1 + a_{22} x_2 \leq b_2$
$-a_{21} x_1 - a_{22} x_2 \leq -b_2$
$a_{31} x_1 + a_{32} x_2 \leq b_3$

RPM diagram	$x_1 \geq 0$	$x_2 \geq 0$	
$y_1 \geq 0$	a_{11}	a_{12}	$\geq b_1$
Free $(y_2 - y_3)$	a_{21}	a_{22}	$= b_2$
$y_4 \geq 0$	a_{31}	a_{32}	$\leq b_3$
	IV	IV	
	c_1	c_2	

Tucker diagram	$x_1 \geq 0$	$x_2 \geq 0$	
$y_1 \geq 0$	$-a_{11}$	$-a_{12}$	$\leq -b_1$
$y_2 \geq 0$	a_{21}	a_{22}	$\leq b_2$
$y_3 \geq 0$	$-a_{21}$	$-a_{22}$	$\leq -b_2$
$y_4 \geq 0$	a_{31}	a_{32}	$\leq b_3$
	IV	IV	min Z_y
	$-c_1$	c_2	max Z_x

Standard RPM network

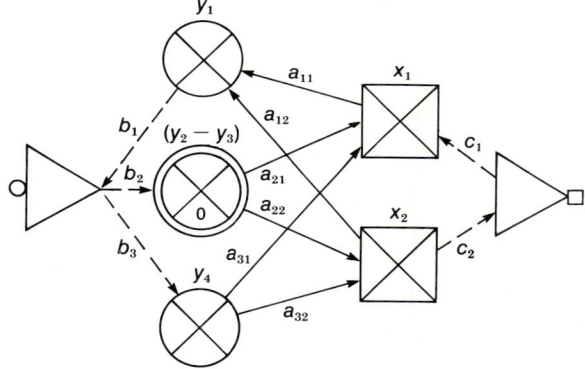

Figure 6-2 Standard RPM representation.

SECTION 6-2 TUNE-UP

In Section 5-3 Tune-up, we had the problem of a manager trying to set up a production schedule for motors and alternators:

max $Z_x = 4x_1 + x_2$

subject to

$6x_1 + 6x_2 \leq 360$

$x_1 \qquad \leq 50$

$\qquad x_2 \leq 40$

$$x_2 \geq 20$$
$$x_1 = 30$$

with all x's nonnegative. Set this problem up both as a Tucker diagram and as an RPM version of the Tucker diagram (as shown in Figure 6-2).

6-3 Diet problem

In Chapter 4, Section 4-5, we introduced a procedure for creating an RPM network model, and in Problem 5-4, we interpreted the dual of the Chinese restaurant problem as a diet problem (Section 5-4 Tune-up). Now we want to consider several typical linear programming prototype problems—paradigms, if you wish—to illustrate and elaborate on the RPM system of normative model construction.

For many years, mass starvation due to a population explosion has been a major concern of scientists. Although the "green revolution" seems to have delayed actual worldwide famine, many advocates of zero population growth still cite food supply as a major issue for the future. "The Cost of Subsistence" is a famous article by G. J. Stigler that treats an operations research model of a diet problem. This article appeared in 1945[1] and preceded Dantzig's discovery of the simplex algorithm. Stigler used a heuristic method to find a combination of 77 food items that would be the most economical source of minimum daily adult requirements (MDAR) for 15 vitamins, minerals, proteins, and fats. After identifying a solution that would cost less than $39.93/yr to feed an adult (1939 prices), Stigler commented: "The procedure is experimental because there does not appear to be any direct method of finding the minimum of a linear function subject to linear constraints." According to S. Vajda,[2] Dantzig reworked the problem later using his simplex algorithm and found the optimum to be $39.639.

We may be consoled that we can live so inexpensively provided that we survive the monotony of a daily diet consisting of enriched wheat flour, evaporated milk (or beef liver in Dantzig's version), cabbage, potatoes, and spinach. Fortunately, the major concern of our affluent society seems to be that of minimizing our caloric intake while satisfying our Epicurean palates.

The *diet problem* is one of the linear programming paradigms and is a popular application among feed-mix suppliers (for cattle and pets) as well as for dieticians, cereal makers, and pharmaceutical companies.

Example 6-1 *The case of undernourished teenagers* Let us assume that you are a parent who is concerned about feeding your teenage children, who have developed the eating habits of typical adolescents—all junk and no nutrition. Fortu-

---

[1] *Journal of Farm Economics*, vol. 27, pp. 303–314.
[2] S. Vajda, *Readings in Mathematical Programming*, John Wiley, New York, 1962, p. 55.

nately, you know their weakness, which happens to be three brands of morning breakfast cereals that they do not mind eating: Alfa-bets, Bravo-balls, and Charlie-treats. You wish to provide all the MDAR of vitamins and minerals with their breakfast menu in three cereals and skim milk, while minimizing their caloric intake.

By checking the labels of the three cereals, you find that all meet the MDARs for vitamin B2 (1.2 mg of riboflavin), vitamin D (400 USP units), niacin (10 mg), phosphorus (750 mg), and other nutrients. However, you have found them inadequate in vitamins A, B1, and C, and in iron and calcium unless more than one type of cereal is consumed. You have a budget of 20 cents/child to buy the cereals, but enough skim milk is delivered to your house daily to meet all potential demand. The information in Figure 6-3 was obtained from the cereal-box labels.

Steps 1 and 2: Identify all activities and resources. The objective function to be minimized: calories (CALO)

The resources: budget (BDGT), vitamin A (VA), vitamin B1 (VB), vitamin C (VC), iron (FE), and calcium (CA)

The process activities: Serve

ALFA helpings of Alfa-bets

BRAVO helpings of Bravo-balls

CHARL helpings of Charlie-treats

Step 3: C & E analyses of nodes (see Figures 6-4 and 6-5). If we were to use an MPS-type computer program (Appendix B), the input data file could be prepared directly from our C & E diagrams. The easiest convention is to use only .LE. constraints and write all inputs as positive and all outputs as

Cereal brand	Nutrients per ½-oz serving with ½-cup (4 oz) skim milk						Cost per 10-oz box (cents)
	A (USP)	B-1 (mg)	C (mg)	Iron (mg)	Calcium (mg)	Calories (mg)	
Alfa-bets	1000	0.5	10	0	200	100	60
Bravo-balls	2000	1.0	10	2	20	200	40
Charlie-treats	1000	0	20	5	100	300	50
MDAR	4000	1.0	30	10	730		

Figure 6-3 Cereal-box labels.

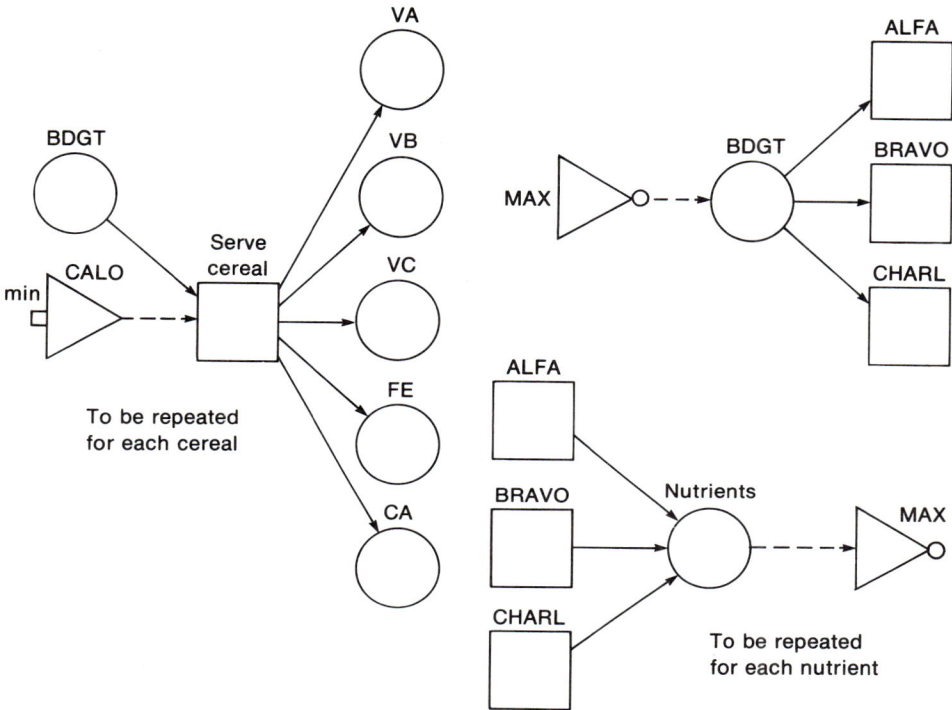

Figure 6-4   C & E analysis of the cereal problem (Example 6-1).

negative,[1] for identifying processes (COLUMNS). Diagrams are shown for ALFA and RESOURCE together with a complete input file for this problem on *REX.

Step 4: Construct an RPM network (see Figure 6-6). The integration of all C & E diagrams results in an RPM network, as shown in Figure 6-6. This is also the time to conduct a dimensional analysis to make sure that all units match between resources, processes, terminals, and transmittances. The objective function can have just one dimension, such as dollars or calories, but the resource terminal (the dual objective) may be joined with flows with different units (for example, dollars for the budget, USP units for vitamin A, and milligrams for vitamins B1 and C). We must also verify that all flows into a resource node have a single dimension because the

---

[1] When only .LE. and .EQ. constraints are specified in ROWS, COLUMN entries are positive for solid arrows coming into the box and negative if flowing out. In a MINIMIZE problem, the dotted arrows follow the same convention. In a MAXIMIZE problem, the dotted arrows are interpreted as negative coming in and positive going out. In either case, the RHS section lists dotted arrows into the dual RESOURCE terminal as negative and dotted arrows out of the terminal as positive.

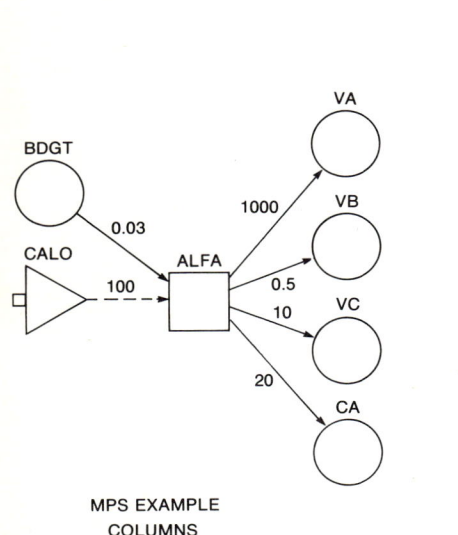
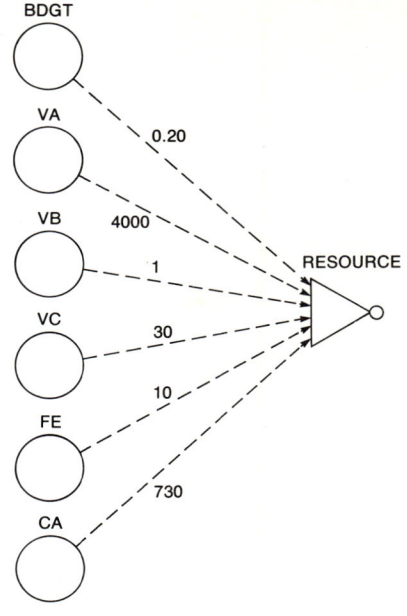

MPS EXAMPLE
```
   COLUMNS
       ALFA     CALO     100.
       ALFA     BDGT      .03
       ALFA     VA     −1000.
       ALFA     VB        −.5
       ALFA     VC        −10.
       ALFA     CA        −20.
   RHS
       RESOURCE  BDGT      .20
       RESOURCE  VA     −4000.
       RESOURCE  VB        −1.
       RESOURCE  VC        −30.
       RESOURCE  FE        −10.
       RESOURCE  CA       −730.
   ENDATA
```

TUCKER DIAGRAM

Columns Rows	ALFA	BRAVO	CHARL		RHS
$ CALO	100	200	300	min	
< BDGT	.03	.02	.025	≤	.20
< VA	−1000	−2000	−1000	≤	−4000
< VB	−.5	−1	0	≤	−1
< VC	−10	−10	−20	≤	−30
< FE	0	−2	−5	≤	−10
< CA	−200	−20	−100	≤	−730

Note that the Tucker Diagram is read column-wise for MPS or *REX, and row-wise for *LINPRO.

*REX EXAMPLE
```
00001:ROWS
00002:$CALO <BDGT <VA <VB <VC <FE <CA
00003:COLUMNS
00004:ALFA CALO 100 VA −1000 VB −.5 VC −10 CA −200 BDGT .03
00005:BRAVO CALO 200 VA −2000 VB −1 VC −10 FE −2 CA −20 BDGT .02
00006:CHARL CALO 300 VA −1000 VC −20 FE −5 CA −100 BDGT .025
00007:RHS
00008:RESOURCE BDGT .20 VA −4000 VB −1 VC −30 FE −10 CA −730
00009:EOF

)OUT,*YOURNAME
```

Figure 6-5   MPS and *REX input example.

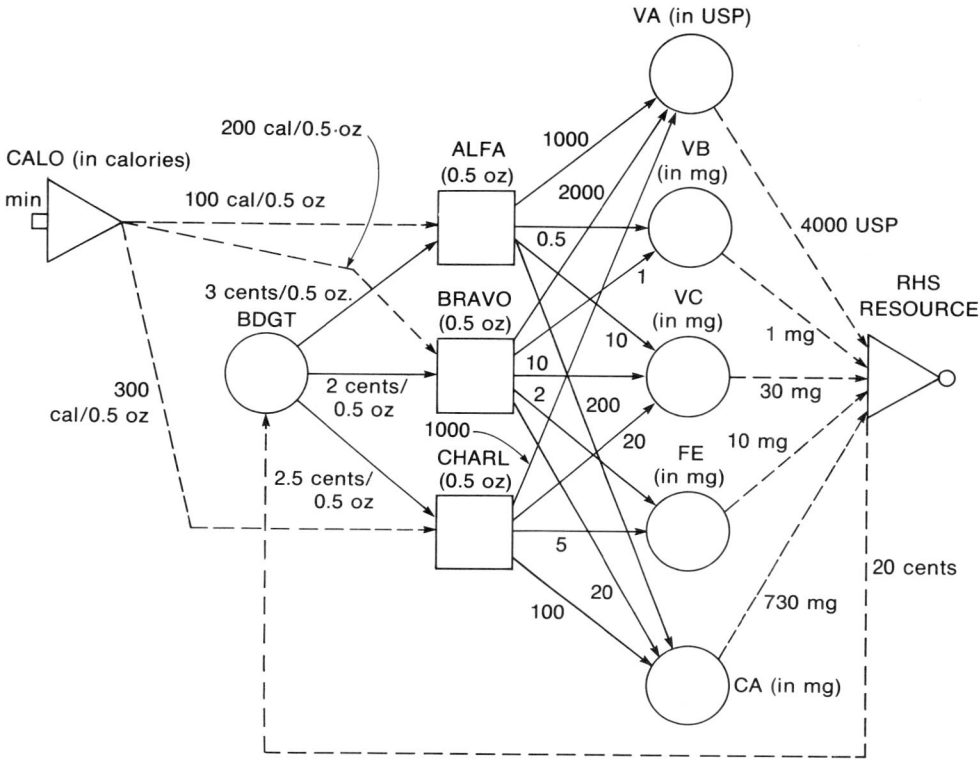

Figure 6-6 RPM network for Example 6-1.

OR condition implies interchangeability of flows. Conversely, the *AND condition* for a process enables us to stipulate conditions with different dimensions (e.g., a serving of ALFA requires a 3 cent budget *and* 100-cal allocations) to produce outputs with varied dimensions (for example, 1,000 USP of vitamin A, and 0.5 mg of vitamin B1—all per unit of activity, that is, a $\frac{1}{2}$-oz serving). Figure 6-6 illustrates the RPM network and indicates the dimensional units used for each resource and activity.

Step 5: Interpret the model mathematically. The primal model can be written from the RPM network as:

[min] CALO = 100 ALFA + 200 BRAVO + 300 CHARL

or alternatively

[max] − CALO = − 100 ALFA − 200 BRAVO − 300 CHARL

subject to

$$0.20 \geq 0.03 \text{ ALFA} + 0.02 \text{ BRAVO} + 0.025 \text{ CHARL} \qquad \text{at BDGT}$$
$$1{,}000 \text{ ALFA} + 2{,}000 \text{ BRAVO} + 1{,}000 \text{ CHARL} \geq 4{,}000 \qquad \text{at VA}$$
$$0.5 \text{ ALFA} + 1 \text{ BRAVO} + \phantom{20 \text{ CHARL }} \geq 1 \qquad \text{at VB}$$
$$10 \text{ ALFA} + 10 \text{ BRAVO} + 20 \text{ CHARL} \geq 30 \qquad \text{at VC}$$
$$2 \text{ BRAVO} + 5 \text{ CHARL} \geq 10 \qquad \text{at FE}$$
$$200 \text{ ALFA} + 20 \text{ BRAVO} + 100 \text{ CHARL} \geq 730 \qquad \text{at CA}$$

with all variables nonnegative. The dual model can be formulated in a similar manner. This step is optional in MPS but is needed to prepare input for a computer program of the *LINPRO type; Figure 6-7 is an

```
*LINPRO
THIS LINEAR PROGRAMMING MODEL WILL HANDLE UP TO 25 VARIABLES
AND 20 CONSTRAINT EQUATIONS. PLEASE TERMINATE ALL RESPONSES
WITH A CARRIAGE RETURN. THANK YOU.

DO YOU WANT A TABLEAU FOR EACH ITERATION (TYPE 1)
OR ONLY THE FINAL TABLEAU AND SOLUTION (TYPE 2)?       2

HOW MANY VARIABLES ARE IN YOUR OBJECTIVE FUNCTION?     3
PLEASE TYPE IN THE COEFFICIENTS.
-100 -200 -300
THANK YOU.

YOUR OBJECTIVE FUNCTION IS:                    ←*LINPRO Maximizes.
 -    100.00A  -    200.00B  -    300.00C
CORRECT?    YES

HOW MANY OF YOUR CONSTRAINT EQUATIONS USE LESS THANS AS OPERATORS?
1
PLEASE TYPE IN THE COEFFICIENTS AND THE CONSTRAINT CONSTANT FOR
EACH.
.03  .02  .025   .20

HOW MANY USE EQUAL SIGNS AS OPERATORS?     0

HOW MANY USE GREATER THANS AS OPERATORS?    5
PLEASE TYPE IN THE COEFFICIENTS AND THE CONSTRAINT CONSTANT FOR
EACH.
1000 2000 1000 4000
.5 1 0 1
10 10 20 30
0 2 5 10
200 20 100 730
THANK YOU.

YOUR CONSTRAINT EQUATIONS ARE:        note the effect of rounding
  1)
  +        .03A   +       .02B   +         .03C   <      .20
  2)
  +    1000.00A   +    2000.00B  +     1000.00C   >    4000.00
  3)
  +        .50A   +      1.00B   +         0C     >       1.00
  4)
  +      10.00A   +     10.00B   +        20.00C  >      30.00
  5)
  +          0A   +      2.00B   +         5.00C  >      10.00
  6)
  +     200.00A   +     20.00B   +       100.00C  >     730.00
CORRECT?    YES
```

Figure 6-7 *LINPRO used for Example 6-1.

Normative Model Formulation: Programming LP Problems   123

```
YOUR VARIABLES    A  THROUGH    C                           (a) *LINPRO
SLACK VARIABLES      S1  THROUGH  S6                            OUTPUT
ARTIFICIAL VARIABLES     A1  THROUGH  A5

TABLEAU NUMBER    7
                      A           B           C          S1         S2         S3
OBJ FNCTN         -100.00     -200.00     -300.00        0          0          0
    S6               0           .01         0           0          0          0
    S2               0         -1.05         0           0        1.00         0
    C                0           .40        1.00         0          0          0
    A              1.00        -0.10         0           0          0          0
    S1               0       -1700.00        0          1.00         0          0
    S3               0         -3.00         0           0          0        1.00
SIMPLEX CR         -0         -90.00        -0          -0         -0         -0

                      S4          S5          S6         A1         A2         A3
OBJ FNCTN            0           0           0           0          0          0
    S6             .00          .00        1.00          0          0          0
    S2             .05         -0.00         0           0        -1.00        0
    C             -0.20          0           0           0          0          0
    A              .10         -0.00         0           0          0          0
    S1           -100.00       -5.00         0         -1.00        0          0
    S3            -3.00        -0.05         0           0          0        -1.00
SIMPLEX CR        -50.00        -0.50       -0          -0         -0         -0

                      A4          A5     CONSTANTS
OBJ FNCTN            0           0
    S6            -0.00        -0.00        .07
    S2            -0.05         .00         .33
    C              .20          0          2.00
    A             -0.10         .00        2.65
    S1           100.00        5.00       650.00
    S3             3.00         .05        36.50
SIMPLEX CR        50.00         .50       865.00

VALUE OF OBJECTIVE FUNCTION =           -865.0000
```

```
                            (b) *REX OUTPUT
ANSWERS:                    TITLE ***CEREAL DIET FOR DAUGHTERS***
                            OBJ = CALO
                            RHS = RESOURCE
                            MINIMUM   =        865.000000
    VARIABLES               ROWS                         PRIMAL (RESIDUE)        DUAL
    IN SOLUTION   UNITS     CALO      Z        865.000000    -865.000000        1.000
        S6        .0705     BDGT      B           .129500       .070500         -0.000
        S2        .3250     VA        B      -4649.999999    649.999999
        C        2.0000     VB        B         -1.325000       .325000
        A        2.6500     VC        B        -66.500000     36.500000
        S1     650.0000     FE        U        -10.000000         0           50.000
        S3      36.5000     CA        U       -730.000000         0             .500
                            COLUMNS             PRIMAL                         DUAL
                            ALFA      B          2.650000    100.000000
                            BRAVO     L               0      200.000000       90.000
                            CHARL     B          2.000000    300.000000
```

Figure 6-8   (a) *LINPRO and (b) *REX printouts for Example 6-1.

example of the maximizing *LINPRO used for the primal model. Another approach would be to use the dual of our minimizing primal and still obtain the same answer in much the same way as we treated the Chinese restaurant problem in Chapter 5 (Section 5-4 Tune-up).

Step 6: Interpret the results of the optimization. Figure 6-8 shows how the computer printout might look for *LINPRO and *REX programs. The solu-

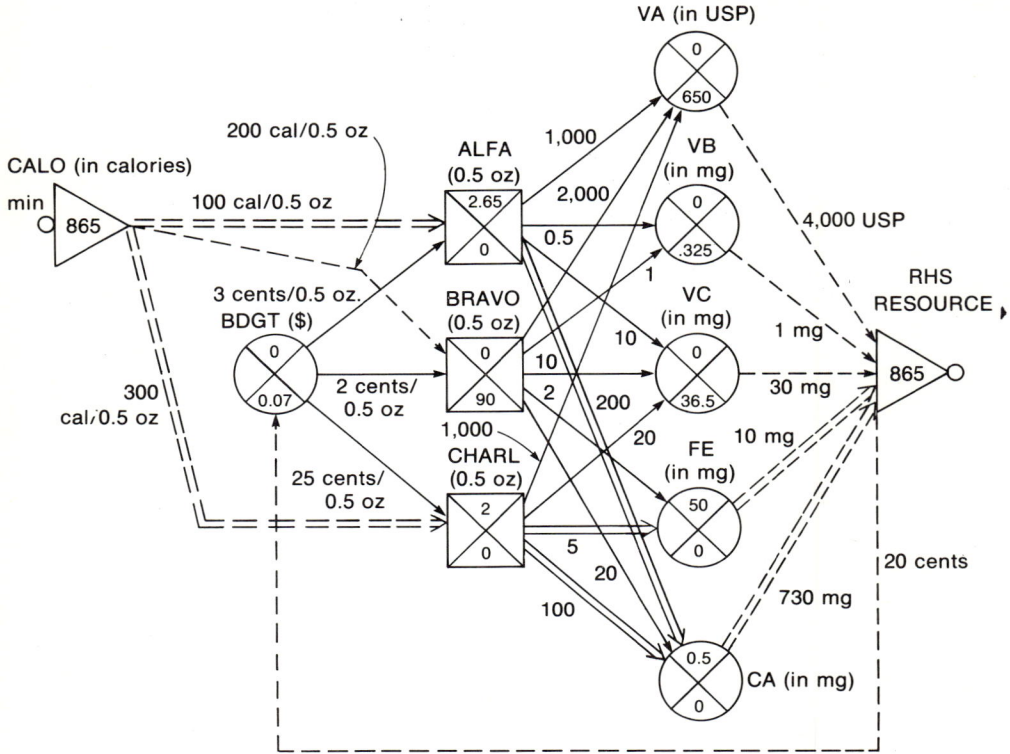

Figure 6-9 RPM network illustrating the solution to Example 6-1.

tion as illustrated in Figure 6-9 indicates that we should serve 2 helpings of Charlie-treats and 2.65 helpings of Alfa-bets. Assuming that your teenagers are willing to eat that much cereal in the morning, they will be ensured of consuming surplus vitamins and MDAR of iron and calcium. The total daily caloric intake is 865 calories, which could be reduced by buying iron pills and calcium tablets. Since there is 7 cents per person left in the budget, iron pills are recommended to produce a 50-cal saving for each 1 mg of iron provided. The solution also shows that using Bravo-balls would add 90 cal per serving even if such a serving is to decrease the use of other cereals.

The double arrows in Figure 6-9 join all nodes with zero residue and represent basic paths for the solution. In other words, the problem will yield the same solution even if other arrows and nodes were discarded. These unused constraints and processes are "dominated" by the basic resources and activities.

SECTION 6-3 TUNE-UP

Suppose that you have found a new cereal called *DELI* with the following label:

Nutrients per ½-oz serving with ½ cup skim milk	
Vitamin A	3,000 USP
Vitamin B1	2.0 mg
Vitamin C	30 mg
Iron	1.0 mg
Calcium	10 mg
Calories	400

The cost of this cereal is 20 cents per 10-oz box. Would this cereal improve your children's diet? Estimate the effects of its inclusion without rerunning the linear programming program.

6-4 Using dominance to simplify an LP model

When an RPM model is used as a descriptive tool to communicate with managers and administrators, it is often desirable to include details that encourage greater understanding. Excessive amounts of detail do not usually enhance the value of normative models; simplification is a virtue. Some analysts take pride in the size of their problems by citing the number of activities and constraints; however, if these same problems can be solved with fewer variables and inequalities, their boasts are unjustified. We shall study two methods for limiting the size of LP models to be formulated out of RPM network models: by utilizing dominance and by identifying nonresidue nodes. Let us present an example of how the first approach works.

Example 6-2: Staffing the Wonderland Hospital Assume that you are the President of the new Republic of Wonderland. Because it is a small country, you serve many concurrent positions in addition to your presidency. One such job happens to be chief administrator of the Wonderland National Hospital, the only all-night emergency hospital in the capital city of Micropolis.

The law requires that two nurses always be on duty at the hospital, but the demand for their service varies according to the hour of day or night. The demand is heavy during the day and in the evening when you have a monopoly on accident services, and is light in the early morning. You have six overlapping shifts and are trying to economize on your staffing needs, especially the extra cost for the moonlight shifts. The accounting department has collected the following cost data:

Team	A	B	C	D	E	F
Shift	1 A.M.-9 A.M.	5 A.M.-1 P.M.	9 A.M.-5 P.M.	1 P.M.-9 P.M.	5 P.M.-1 A.M.	9 P.M.-5 A.M.
Cost, $/man-hr	$6	$5	$4	$5	$6	$7

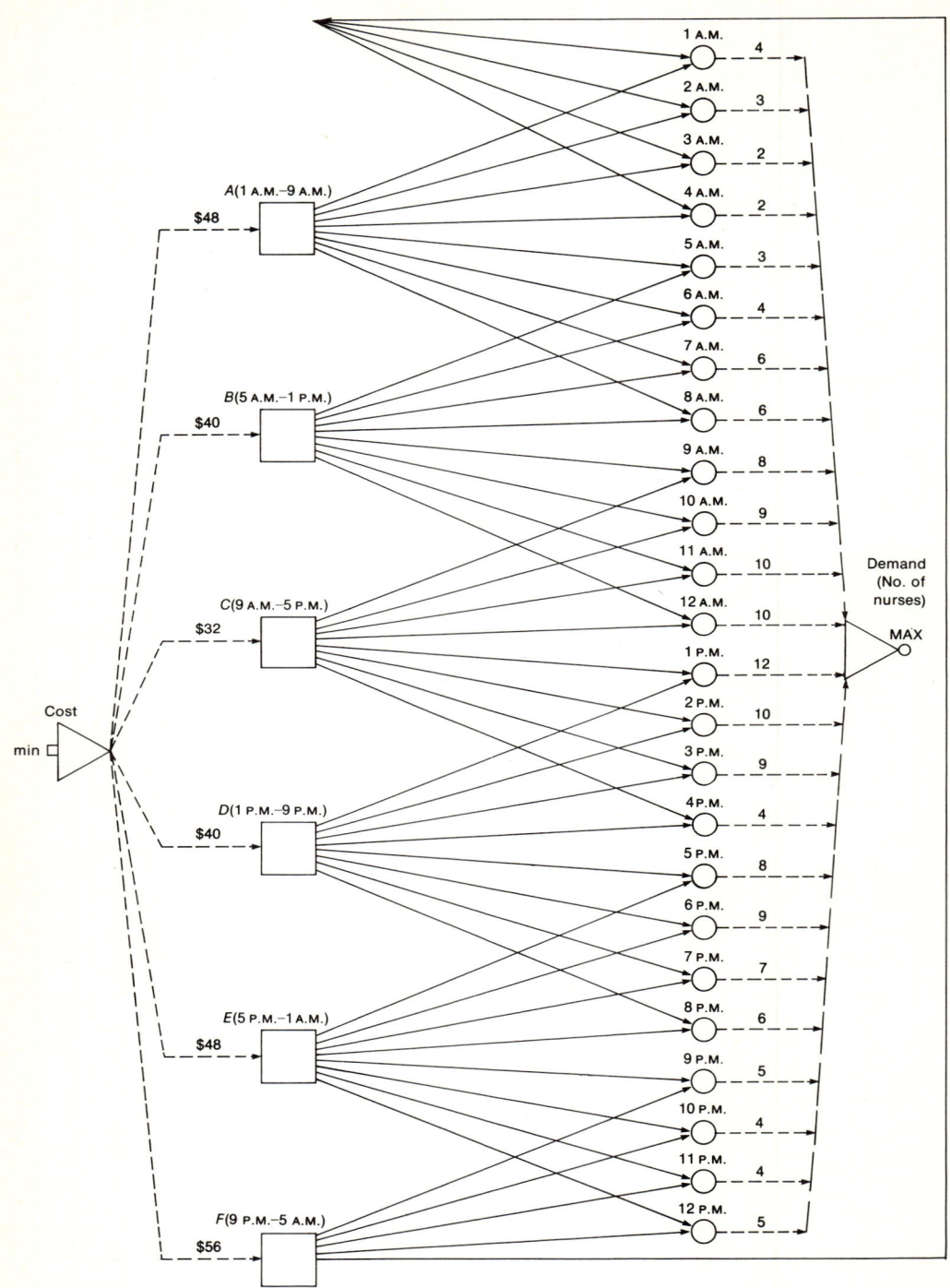

Figure 6-10 Scheduling nurses at the Wonderland Hospital (brute-force model).

The hospital industrial engineer has tabulated the following statistics for the number of nurses required to handle all emergencies adequately 99 percent of the time:

Hour, A.M.	1	2	3	4	5	6	7	8	9	10	11	12
Staff	4	3	2	2	3	4	6	6	8	9	10	10

Hour, P.M.	1	2	3	4	5	6	7	8	9	10	11	12
Staff	12	10	9	4	8	9	7	6	5	4	4	5

A "brute force" approach would have created the RPM network shown in Figure 6-10.

But is it really necessary to include all these constraints? From 1 A.M. to 4 A.M., when the staffing is shared by teams A and F, for example, we have four constraints:

$A + F \geq 4$ at 1 A.M. $A + F \geq 3$ at 2 A.M.
$A + F \geq 2$ at 3 A.M. $A + F \geq 2$ at 4 A.M.

It is then obvious that the requirement at 1 A.M. dominates all other constraints, and that this is the only one that needs to be considered for A and F. Similarly, we select 6 for A and B (there are 2 hr when this is the requirement—7 and 8 A.M.), 10 for B and C, 12 for C and D, 9 for D and E, and 5 for E and F. The new RPM network reduces to the simple pattern shown in Figure 6-11.

Figure 6-11 looks so simple that we may be tempted to hazard a common-sense

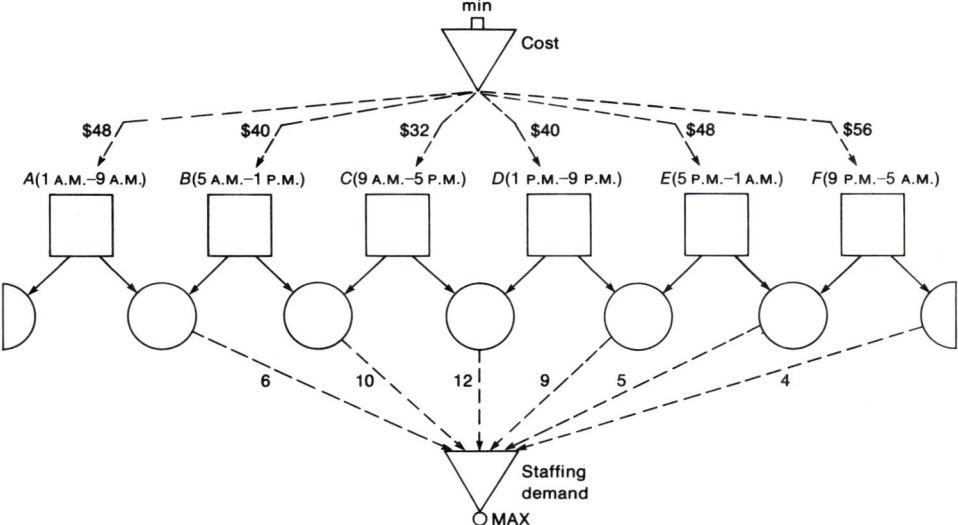

Figure 6-11   Hospital RPM showing dominating constraints only.

solution to this staffing problem which now reads

min $Z_x = 48A + 40B + 32C + 40D + 48E + 56F$

subject to
$$A + B \geq 6$$
$$B + C \geq 10$$
$$C + D \geq 12$$
$$D + E \geq 9$$
$$E + F \geq 5$$
$$A + F \geq 4$$

One common-sense solution is to staff most nurses when the hospital is the busiest and the expense is the lightest. Setting $C = 12$, we can automatically solve for others: $B = 0$; $A = 6$; $F = 0$; $E = 5$; and $D = 4$.

SECTION 6-4 TUNE-UP

The actual optimal solution for this hospital problem turns out to be $928/day. *LINPRO's answer is shown below. Construct an RPM network using the optimal values and compare them with the solution in Figure 6-12. Note how the allocations have changed at B, where the dual value of -8 indicates an economic opportunity of gaining $8 per staff. Why do you think that the actual gain in optimality was considerably higher than $2 \times \$8$? Indicate all basic paths in your network.

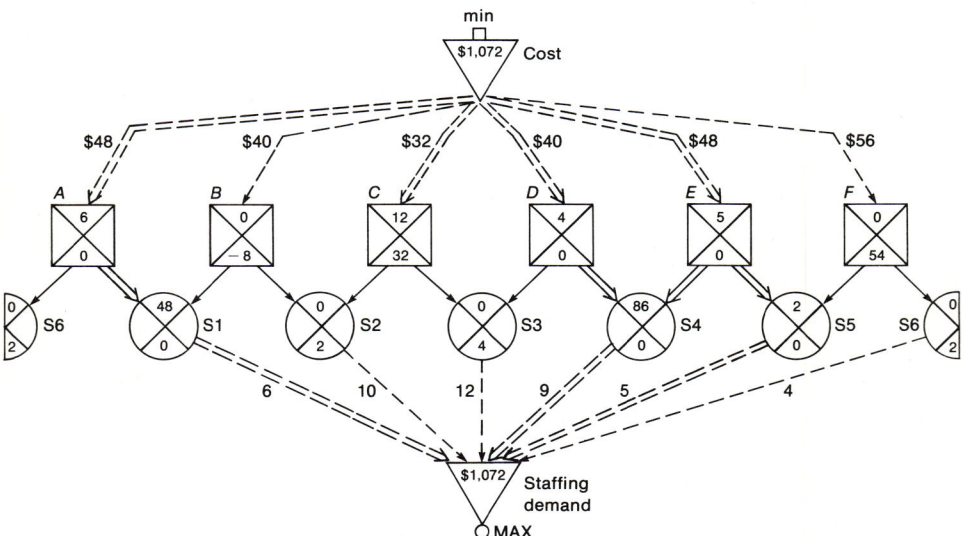

Figure 6-12 Common-sense solution to Example 6-2.

VARIABLES IN SOLUTION	UNITS
S2	0
B	2.0000
C	8.0000
D	4.0000
E	5.0000
A	4.0000

VARIABLES NOT IN SOLUTION	SIMPLEX CRITERIA
F	8.0000
S1	40.0000
S3	32.0000
S4	8.0000
S5	40.0000
S6	8.0000

6-5 Using basic nodes to simplify LP models

A good descriptive model is not necessarily a good normative model, and an efficient normative model is not always easily understood. Most LP models presented in operations research or management science textbooks appear deceptively simple, yet trying to construct such streamlined versions in actual practice often seems to be an overwhelming chore. We shall now introduce two additional techniques for simplifying models: using dual basic nodes and combining parallel flows.

BASIC NODES Whenever a node has null residue, it is a *basic variable*; and whenever a node is basic, it implies an equality. Then, when we have an equation, we can use it to substitute one set of variables for another. A resource node with no residue is basic in its dual sense. It ties one set of primal variables to another set, equating the input set to the output set. A process node with no residue acts as a *short circuit*, fusing two sets of constraints into one. Two examples are shown in Figure 6-13, and other examples can be constructed and easily checked out by using algebraic substitutions.

Identifying resource nodes with null residues can be done intuitively. We simply ask the question "Would we ever want to have something left there?" If the answer is negative, then the node must be dual basic. This instinctive identification of basic nodes directly simplifies the RPM network. As long as our logic is valid, our solution will be valid also. The equalities thus used eliminate variables that do not interest us and minimize our LP problem to the essentials.

PARALLEL FLOWS In the course of network contraction we may have the opportunity to combine parallel flows. If two or more arrows join the same pair of

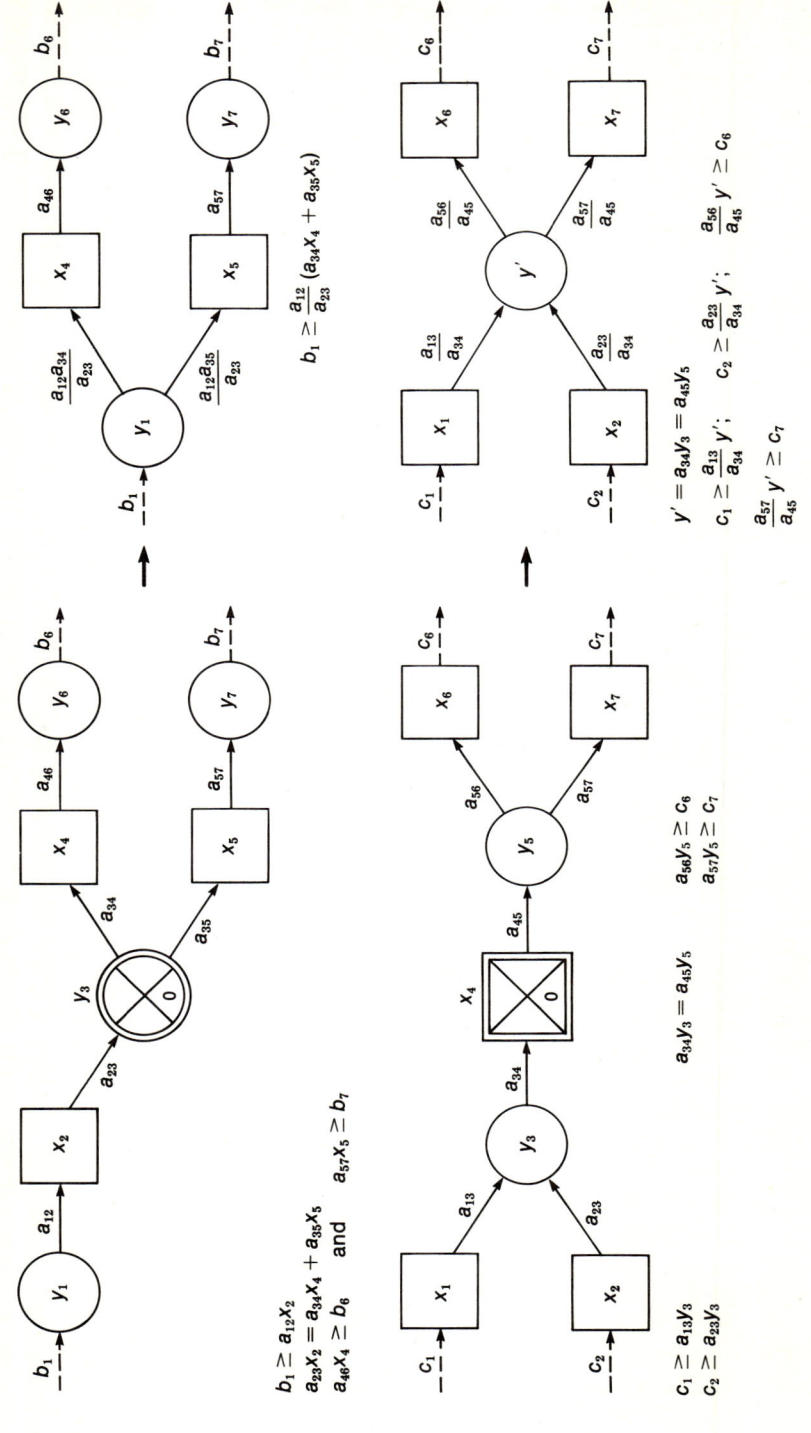

Figure 6-13 Examples of basic contractions.

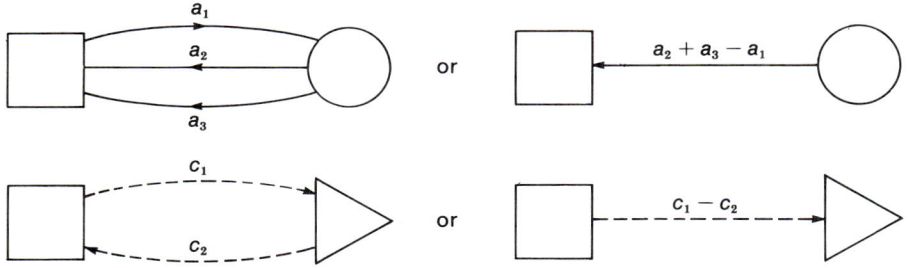

Figure 6-14 Simple examples of additive flows.

nodes, they can be made into a single arrow, and in LP models this amounts to adding them algebraically. Figure 6-14 illustrates several examples.

Example 6-3: ABC Manufacturing Company—What ado about a simple product mix! The ABC Manufacturing Company is a wonderland industrial firm that specializes in leisure and sporting goods. In one plant it manufactures three products: Aloha surfboards, Bambi sleds, and Crysty skis, each wholesaling at $60, $72, and $192, respectively. These products are processed through three machine centers (shops 1 to 3) where 1, 2, and 1 production machines can be made available. A flow diagram (Figure 6-15) has been acquired from the plant industrial engineer, and the following cost information has been provided by the corporate accountant to help determine the optimum product mix:

Product	Aloha	Bambi	Crysty
Raw material, $/unit	10	14	17
Factory overheat, $/unit	10	12	32

Machine costs are computed at $102/hr of operation for each machine center, and labor cost is computed at $18/hr. The time data and costs obtained for the three shops are as follows:

Shop No.	Time, machine-min	Cost, $	Time, operators-min	Cost, $
1: A1	3	5.1	3	.90
B1	10	17.0	10	3.00
C1	12	20.4	12	3.60
2: A2	10	17.0	10	3.00
C2	40	68.0	40	12.00
3: A3	2	3.4	2	.60
B3	10	17.0	10	3.00

In order to operate a machine, it is assumed that an operator must oversee its operation. Engaging personnel, operating machines, and purchasing raw materials are all prerequisites to producing finished goods. Figure 6-16 is an RPM network model of the ABC Manufacturing Company's operations. An LP model with 17

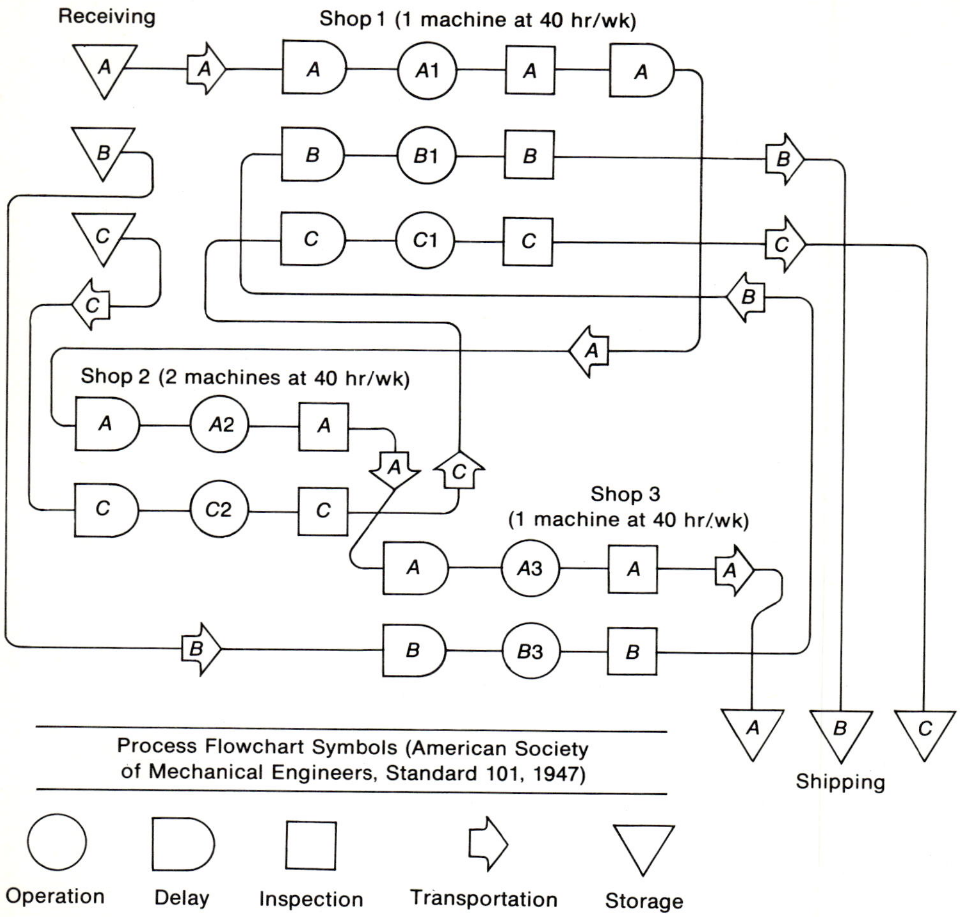

132 Introduction to Operations Research and Management Science

Figure 6-15 Flow diagram for the ABC Manufacturing Company (Example 6-3).

max $PROFIT $= -10A0 - 14B0 - 17C0 - 18HW - 17M1 - 17M2 - 17M3 + (60 - 10)A4 + (72 - 12)B4 + (192 - 32)C4$

subject to
$60HW \geq M1 + M2 + M3$ at hm
$40 \geq M1/60$ at h_1
$80 \geq M2/60$ at h_2
$40 \geq M3/60$ at h_3
$A0 \geq A1$ at a_0
$B0 \geq B3$ at b_0
$C0 \geq C2$ at c_0
$M1 \geq 3A1 + 10B1 + 12C1$ at m_1
$M2 \geq 10A2 + 40C2$ at m_2
$M3 \geq 2A3 + 10B3$ at m_3

17 primal variables (processes)
17 constraints (resources)

$A1 \geq A2$ at a_1
$B1 \geq B4$ at b_1
$C1 \geq C4$ at c_1
$A2 \geq A3$ at a_2
$C2 \geq C1$ at c_2
$A3 \geq A4$ at a_3
$B3 \geq B1$ at b_3

and all variables nonnegative

Figure 6-16a Linear programming interpretation of Figure 6-16b.

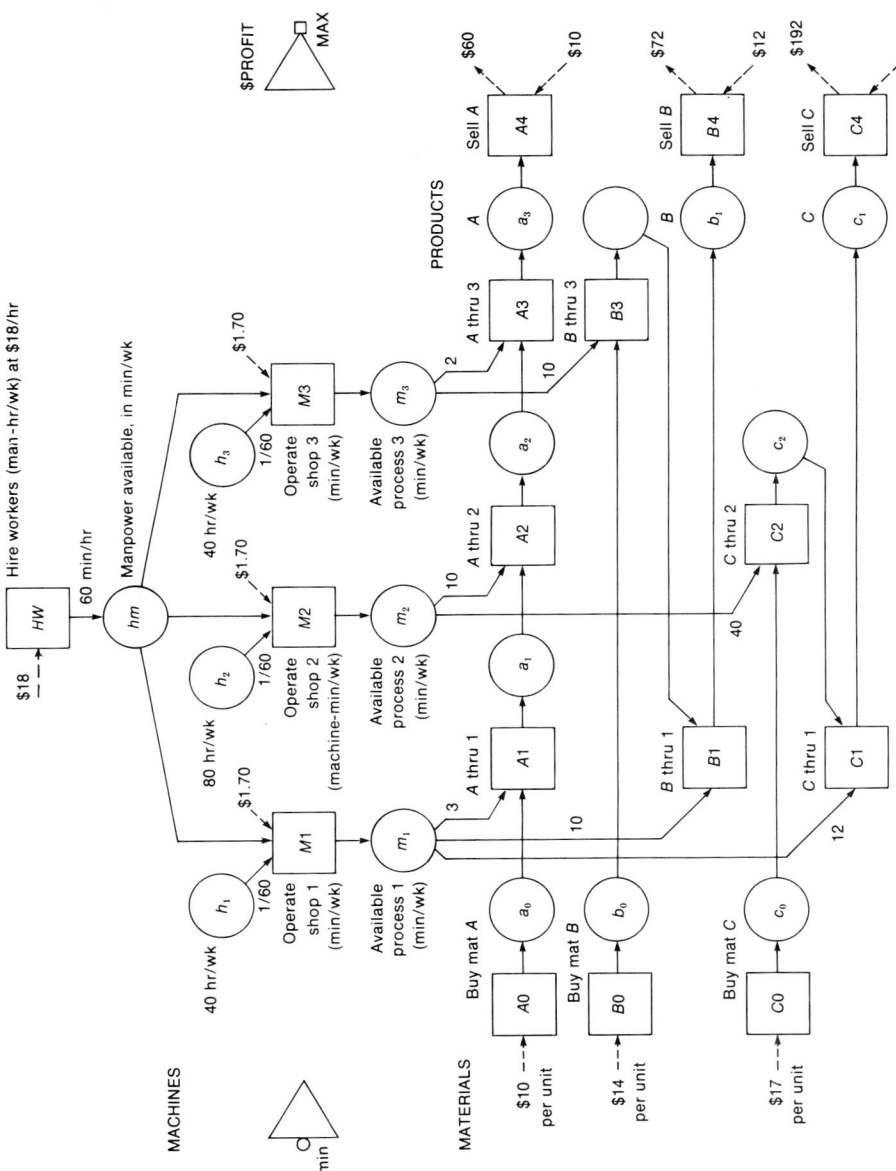

Figure 6-16b RPM network model of the ABC Manufacturing Company's operations.

variables and 17 constraints is not a very large problem. The data from Fig. 6-16 could be fed to either *LINPRO or MPS directly, and solutions would quickly follow. But since we are illustrating simplifying techniques, let us proceed to identify all basic resource nodes. (See Figure 6-17.)

The resource hm represents workers engaged to operate machines. It is unlikely that we would hire more operators than we need; thus, we may assume no residue for this node. Thereby the \$18/hr resource is used by the three shops $M1$, $M2$, and $M3$. Then the \$1.70 and \$0.30[1] exogenous flows can be combined into a single flow of \$2/min. By a similar reasoning, we conclude that no raw material will be purchased for $A(A0)$ unless it is expected to be used in $A1$ (that is, a_0 is basic), and that we will not process A through shop 1 ($A1$) unless it can also be processed

[1] \$18/hr = \$0.30/min

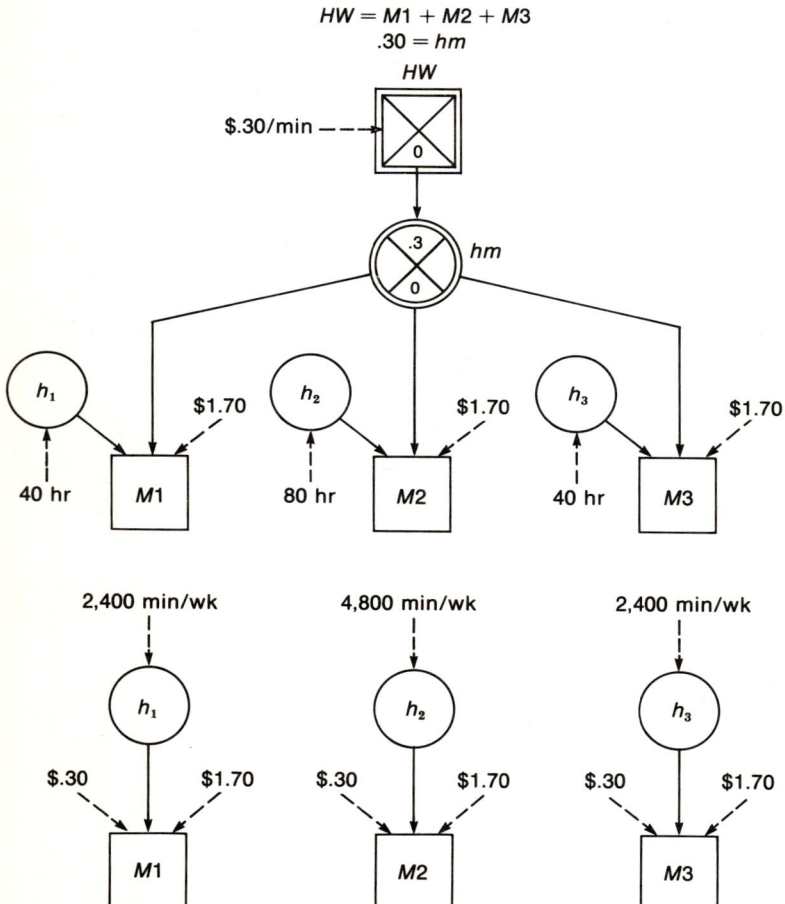

Figure 6-17 Elimination of nodes HW and hm.

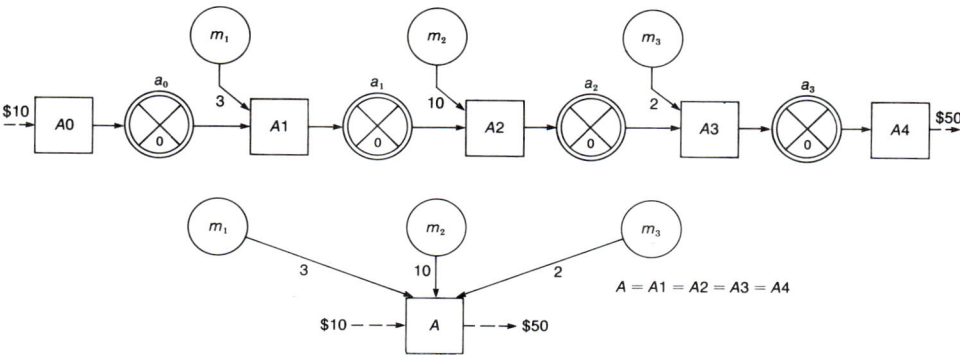

Figure 6-18 Horizontal condensation.

through shops 2 and 3 (that is, a_1 and a_2 are also basic). Of course, there is no sense doing all this unless we intend to sell the product ($A4$) and make a profit from the $60 price minus the overhead cost of $10 (that is, a_3 is also basic). Figure 6-18 illustrates this contraction.

Realizing that m_1, m_2, and m_3 must also be basic, the entire problem collapses to a neat package of three variables and three constraints. After combining parallel flows and transferring exogenous flows to the main variables, our problem takes the form shown in Figure 6-19. The end result turns out to be a very simple product-mix problem, and yet the simplicity is deceiving. We must be cautious to avoid incorrect interpretations and conclusions. For example, looking at Figures 6-19 and 6-20, we may be tempted to venture a guess at the optimum product mix, as shown in Figure 6-20. We observe that Crysty has the highest return ($39/192 = 20.3$ percent) in terms of profit generated by sales; Bambi, on the other hand, gives only $6/72 = 8.33$ percent; and Aloha, 16.7 percent. Thus, ABC Manufacturing Company should make as many Crysty's as possible. However, the LP solution (Figure 6-21) reveals that the optimum solution consists of Aloha and Bambi but excludes Crysty.

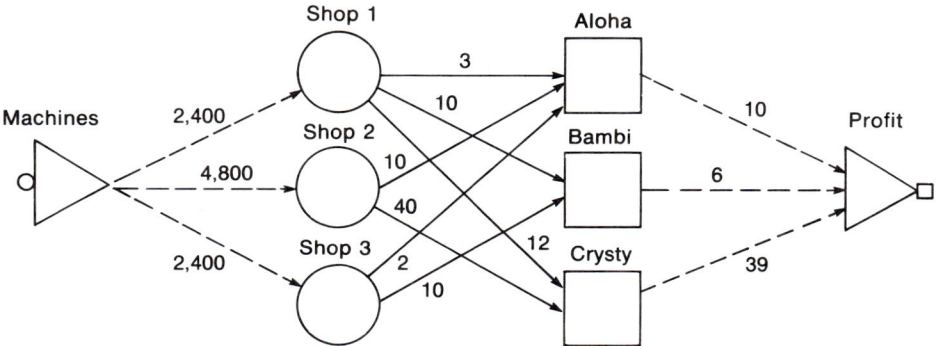

Figure 6-19 Simpler RPM for Example 6-3.

	Product		
	Aloha	Bambi	Crysty
Material cost	$10	$14	$17
Labor cost	3	4	10.4
Machine cost	27	36	93.6
Overhead	10	12	32
Profit	10	6	39
Wholesale price	60	72	192

Figure 6-20   ABC Manufacturing Company cost breakdown.

In Figure 6-21 two points are worth emphasizing. First, our rule for plus input and minus output holds for all data entries *except* the objective function. The signs of objective coefficients (Cj's) will be as you wish to have them appear on the objective function whether you are minimizing or maximizing. *B* in the column section indicates a basic primal variable with a zero residue. *B* in the row section indicates that the primal residue is basic but not the dual value. Thus, *B* for shop 3 indicates that the residue for shop 3 is basic and therefore the resource is *not* dual basic. Shops 1 and 2 at the upperbound *U*, on the other hand, are dual basic and are to be used in constructing our basic paths.

SECTION 6-5 TUNE-UP

Using the preceding RPM network and the computer output from Figure 6-21, compute all nodal values for the original ABC Manufacturing Company problem and enter them on the RPM network on page 138. Afterward, answer the following questions:

1. How many man-hours per week of worker time are you engaging?

2. How much would you have to raise the price of Crysty to make it competitive with the other two products?

3. You have been approached by a lease company, which offers to furnish unlimited process time in shop 2, m_2, for $150/hr, including both equipment and personnel. Will you accept or decline the offer?

4. Your engineer tells you that the machine in shop 3 can be modified to assist shop 1 or 2 operations, but it will cost $20/hr more to operate it in that manner. What will you do?

6-6   Value of Leftovers

A constraint is not basic in a dual sense when it is dominated by some other constraint. In a trivial case, the dominating constraint may be simply the nonnega-

Normative Model Formulation: Programming LP Problems

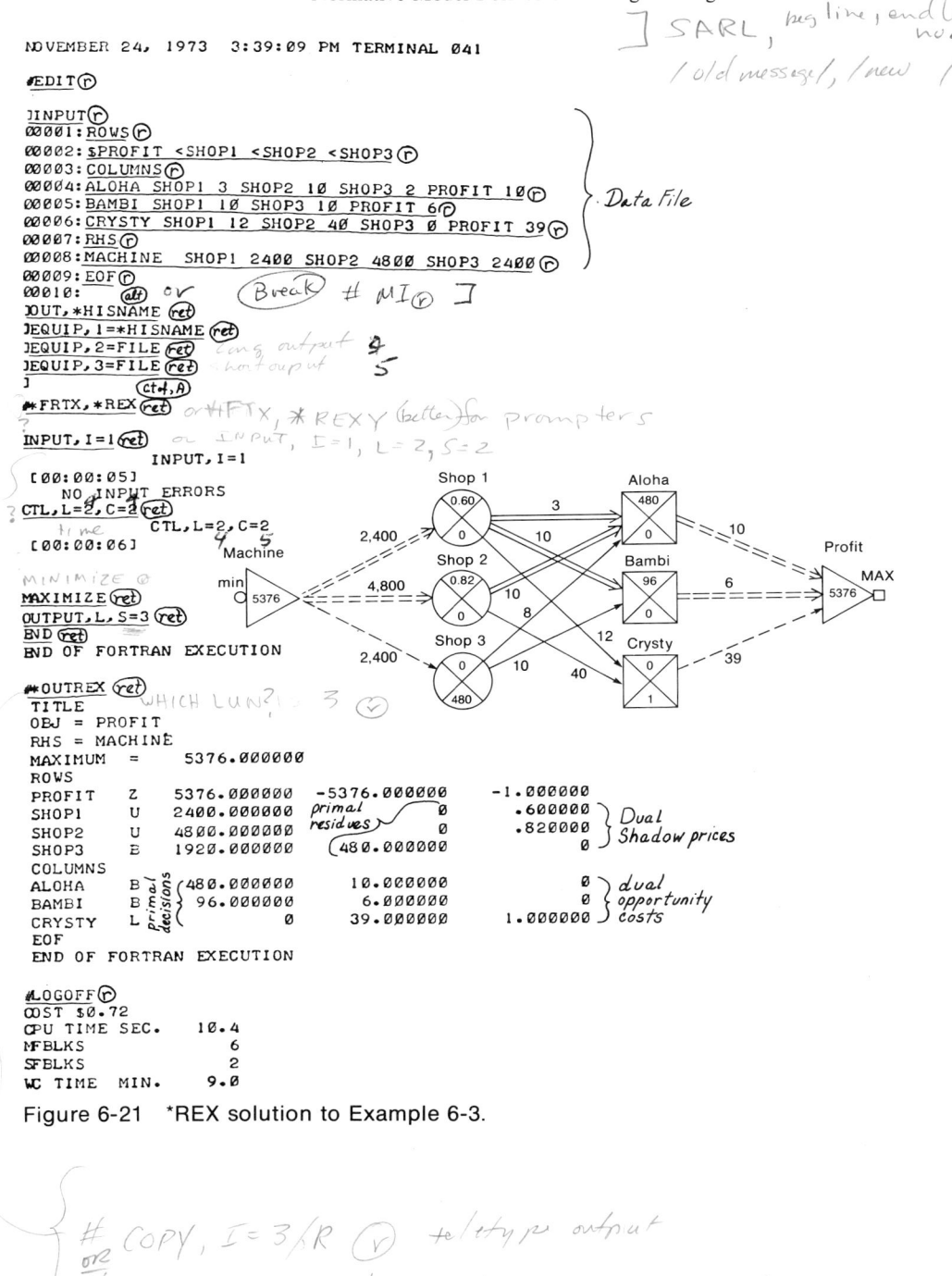

Figure 6-21 *REX solution to Example 6-3.

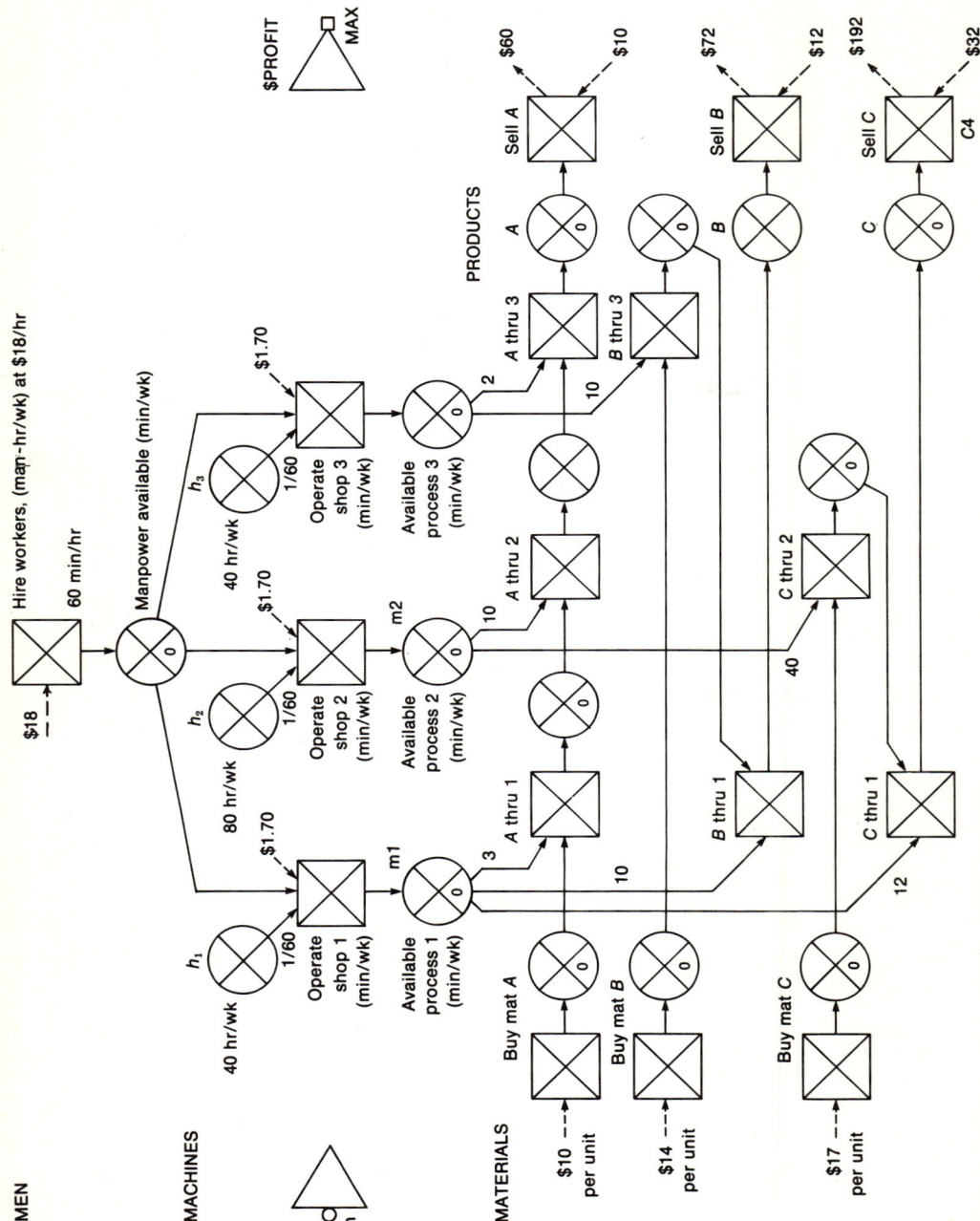

tivity constraint giving a zero value to a pertinent primal variable. If a constraint is not dominated, it will be basic and binding and will have a recognized value. Thus, for a resource to be valuable, it cannot have any *leftover* (residue); similarly, for a process to be in force, its economic value (residue) with respect to the system's present performance must be zero. Consequently every node of an RPM network representing a basic solution must have at least one zero entry. This condition is illustrated graphically in Chapter 5, Figure 5-18, and we shall now establish it formally as the complementary-slackness theorem of linear programming. The two postulates of RPMS (Chapter 4, Section 4-4), the extreme-point theorem (Chapter 5, Section 5-2), and the complementary-slackness theorem are four vital concepts that must always be kept in mind while constructing, solving, and interpreting RPMS models.

Complementary-slackness theorem: In any node i of an RPM network representing a basic (corner-point) solution, either the primal or dual value (or both) must be zero: $x_i y_i = 0$.

The concept is evident if we go back to the definition of a basic solution. An LP problem with m resources and n processes can be described geometrically as a simplex FSS in primal E^n or dual E^m (Chapter 5, Section 5-3). There are

$$\binom{m+n}{m} = \frac{(m+n)!}{m!\,n!} = \binom{m+n}{n}$$

corners in either representation, each corner point corresponding to a basic solution. A basic primal solution is intersected by n hyperplanes representing resource constraints, resulting in at least n number of zero primal values out of $m + n$ process values and resource residues. In E^m of the resource space, this point corresponds to an intersection of m hyperplanes representing the m remaining nonzero (therefore active) primal variables. Thus, each basic solution has m nonzero primal values corresponding to m zero dual values and n nonzero dual values corresponding to n zero primal values. Figure 5-19 may help you visualize the situation. If the concept is still difficult to grasp, the simplex and transportation algorithms described in subsequent chapters should improve your understanding. Meanwhile, let us remember that leftovers have no value and anything worthwhile has no leftovers.

SECTION 6-6 TUNE-UP

In each basic solution of an LP problem there should be as many primal basic values as there are resource nodes and as many dual values as there are process nodes. Identify all primal and dual basic nodes in:

1. Figure 6-21

2. Figure 6-9

6-7 When nature is hostile

At the beginning of this chapter we noted some military implications of programming. Since then we have observed how linear programming is used to determine the most efficient allocation of resources. The difference between the two aspects is mostly situational: Military programming often operates in a short-term competitive situation where economics is a secondary consideration; management science applications are typically made in a long-range peaceful situation where the supply-and-demand mechanism acts as the referee. By assuming economics to be impartial, we focus attention on ways to best utilize resources rather than strategies to protect our resources from competitors. Sometimes, however, it is worthwhile to recognize that nature, too, is a partner with a stake in our game, playing the role of competitor in charge of the dual model. It is a faithful, intelligent partner that would play any role that may be assigned, including that of a hostile competitor.

GAME THEORY Game theory is the foundation for analyzing actions in competitive situations. We shall introduce the subject here to show how it is related to linear programming and how it can help us understand the role of duality in programming. It will not only reinforce the concept of dominance, but also give us a new perspective in appreciating the critical role nature plays in our decision-making. In Chapter 13 we shall consider it again as a device to aid our planning for the future.

In the jargon of game theory a *game* is a confrontation between players with opposing objectives but equal knowledge. A *zero-sum two-person* game means just two players are involved and any gain made by one player equals the loss by the other. The value of the game, or its worth W, is the average gain per play over a long series of plays under identical conditions.

LP INTERPRETATION OF A ZERO-SUM TWO-PERSON GAME The fact that such a game can be described by an LP model is seen easily by examining a simple 3×3 (each player has three alternatives) payoff matrix (Figure 6-22). First let us look at X's position. X is interested in maximizing the minimum gain that can be

X's strategy (X_i)	Y's strategy (Y_j)		
	Y_1	Y_2	Y_3
X_1	a_{11}	a_{12}	a_{13}
X_2	a_{21}	a_{22}	a_{23}
X_3	a_{31}	a_{32}	a_{33}

Figure 6-22 3×3 zero-sum, two-person-game-payoff table.

obtained from playing this game. The objective is to maximize the minimum worth of the game, say, W, subject to the constraint that regardless of the alternative Y chooses, the expected payoff will at least equal W. We can write this as

max W maximize minimum worth W

subject to

$a_{11}X_1 + a_{21}X_2 + a_{31}X_3 \geq W$ in case Y plays alternative Y_1
$a_{12}X_1 + a_{22}X_2 + a_{32}X_3 \geq W$ in case Y plays alternative Y_2
$a_{13}X_1 + a_{23}X_2 + a_{33}X_3 \geq W$ in case Y plays alternative Y_3
$X_1 + X_2 + X_3 = 1$ since X is forced to play one of three available alternatives

The classical approach is to divide all constraints by W and attempt to minimize $1/W$ instead of W. This is a valid procedure, provided that W is not negative or zero, and can be guaranteed if all outcomes a_{ij}'s are positive. Thus, when we do have a negative entry, we add an equivalent constraint to all entries, which will artificially raise the value of the game by that much; the true answer can be obtained later by subtracting that amount from the computed result. Thus, assuming all a_{ij}'s are positive, we can define a new variable set $U_i = X_i/W$. Then, combining the last equality into the objective function, we have

$$\min \frac{1}{W} = U_1 + U_2 + U_3$$

subject to

$a_{11}U_1 + a_{21}U_2 + a_{31}U_3 \geq 1$
$a_{12}U_1 + a_{22}U_2 + a_{32}U_3 \geq 1$
$a_{13}U_1 + a_{23}U_2 + a_{33}U_3 \geq 1$

where all U's are nonnegative. Similarly, the Y's problem can be interpreted as the dual to the LP model by defining $V_i = Y_i/W$. The resulting Tucker diagram appears in Figure 6-23.

	$V_1 \geq 0$	$V_2 \geq 0$	$V_3 \geq 0$	
$U_1 \geq 0$	a_{11}	a_{12}	a_{13}	≤ 1
$U_2 \geq 0$	a_{21}	a_{22}	a_{23}	≤ 1
$U_3 \geq 0$	a_{31}	a_{32}	a_{33}	≤ 1
	IV 1	IV 1	IV 1	min / max

Figure 6-23 Tucker diagram for 3 × 3 zero-sum, two-person game.

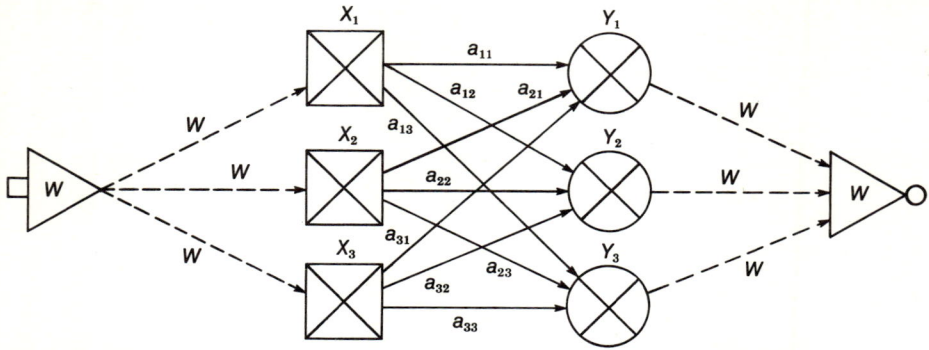

Figure 6-24 RPMS representation of a 3 × 3 zero-sum, two-person game.

RPMS INTERPRETATION OF A ZERO-SUM TWO-PERSON GAME. The objective function for the preceding LP problem used $1/W$. Although it was treated as a variable, we also know that it has a specific optimal value, say, $1/W°$. There is no harm in multiplying U's and V's by $W°$ if $W° > 0$, and this must be done to recapture answers to the original problem. We can go a step further and multiply our objective function by $(W°)^2$ to give us back the original $W°$ worth of our game. Thus, for the optimal (and feasible) solution values of $W = W°$, we can write

$$\min W° = W°X_1° + W°X_2° + W°X_3°$$

and

$$a_{11}X_1° + a_{21}X_2° + a_{31}X_3° \geq W°$$
$$a_{12}X_1° + a_{22}X_2° + a_{32}X_3° \geq W°$$
$$a_{13}X_1° + a_{23}X_2° + a_{33}X_3° \geq W°$$

Dropping the cumbersome ° superscript, we can construct an RPM network as shown in Figure 6-24. It turns out that the RPMS configuration is a valid tool for representing games with negative or zero game values W as well as positive ones. All RPMS conventions hold true for Fig. 6-24, and residues indicate losses that would be incurred should the player decide to take that alternative. Process-node values indicate player X's strategy, while resource-node values indicate player Y's strategy. Several numerical examples are presented in Figure 6-25.

PASCAL'S THEORY OF BETS REVISITED Game theory has given us an opportunity to apply RPMS to a different type of LP problem and to observe the game theory counterpart of simplification through dominance. All games can be represented by LP models, and all LP models can be interpreted as games. In effect, we are constantly competing with nature (RPMS postulate 2). As a further example, let us revisit Pascal's theory of bets.

(a) Pure strategy: a minimum of the row is also the maximum of the column.
    In RPM: a minimum flow out of X is the maximum into a Y: the value of that
    flow is W.

	Y_1	Y_2
X_1	3	2
X_2	4	③

$W = 3$; strategies: X_2 and Y_2.
NOTE: The mini-max point (3)
is also called a "saddle point."

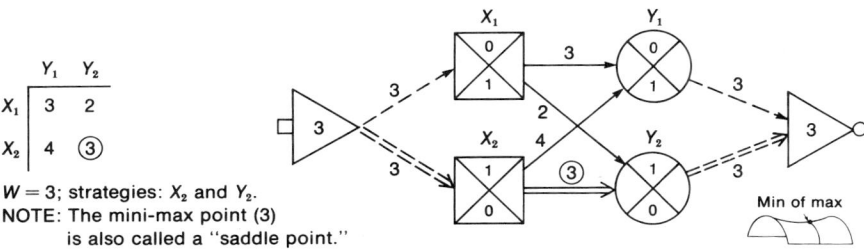

Min of max

(b) Dominance for X: all entries in a row are lower than corresponding entries of one or a
    combination of other rows: ignore that row.
    In RPM: a process with lower contributions to resources than another process
    or a combination of processes is not basic.

	Y_1	Y_2
X_1	-1	0
X_2	4	1
X_3	1	4
X_4	2	2

X_1 is dominated by all.
X_4 is dominated by $0.5(X_2 + X_3)$.
$W = 5/2$; strategies: $1/2$ of X_2 and X_3; $1/2$ of Y_1
and Y_2. (See (c) below to get values.)

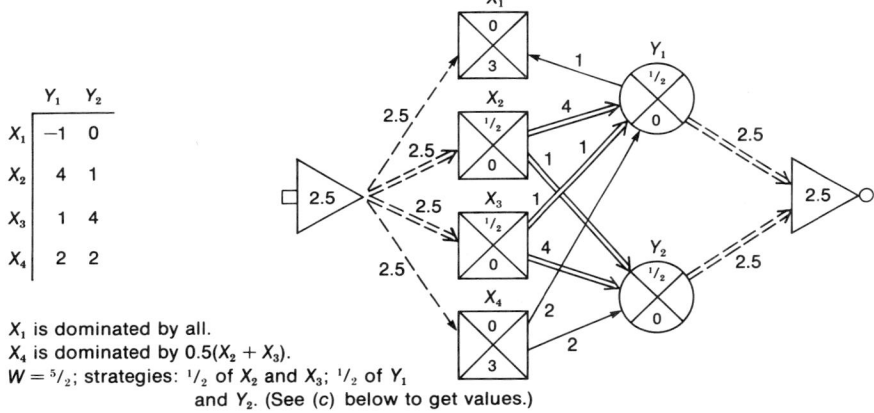

(c) Mixed strategy for 2 × 2: Take the row (or column) difference and assign it to
    the other row (or column); add the differences and divide
    each by the sum.
    In RPM: take the differences between solid flows from one node and
    assign it to the other node; add the differences and divide
    each by the sum to get the value of the nodes.

	Y_1	Y_2	
X_1	5	1	$4 - 2 = 2$ $2/6$
X_2	2	4	$5 - 1 = 4$ $4/6$

$4 - 1 = 3$ $2 + 4 = 6$
$5 - 2 = 3$
$3 + 3 = 6$
$3/6$ $3/6$

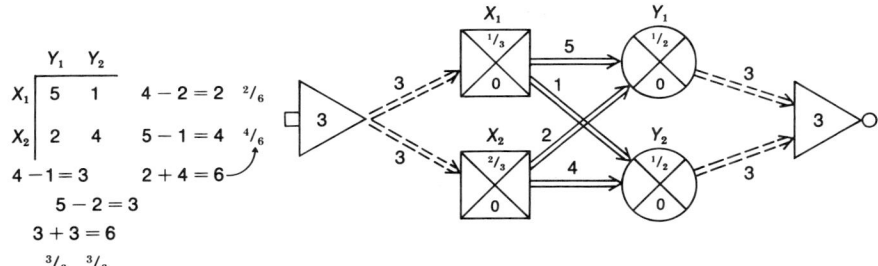

$W = 5X_1 + 2X_2 = 1/3(5) + 2/3 2 = 3$ at Y_1; W can be obtained at any node
by balancing the inputs with the outputs. Also, the total internal products
must equal W: $(X_1 \times 5 \times Y_1) + (X_1 \times 1 \times Y_2) + (X_2 \times 2 \times Y_1) + (X_2 \times 4 \times Y_2) = W = 3$

Figure 6-25A Examples of RPMS representations of zero-sum, two-person games.

(d) **Dominance for Y**: All entries in a column are larger than corresponding entries on another or a combination of other columns.
   In RPM: A resource with higher inflows from processes when compared against other resources or a combination of other resources cannot be basic.

	Y_1	Y_2	Y_3	Y_4
X_1	1	2	3	10
X_2	1	1	2	5
X_3	0	2	1	3

Y_4 is dominated by Y_3;
Y_3 is dominated by $1/2\,(Y_1 + Y_2)$;
in the remaining cells, X_2 and X_3 are dominated by X_1; and in X_1, Y would choose Y_1. In fact, the a_{11} cell is a saddle point.
[See Figure 6-25A(a).]

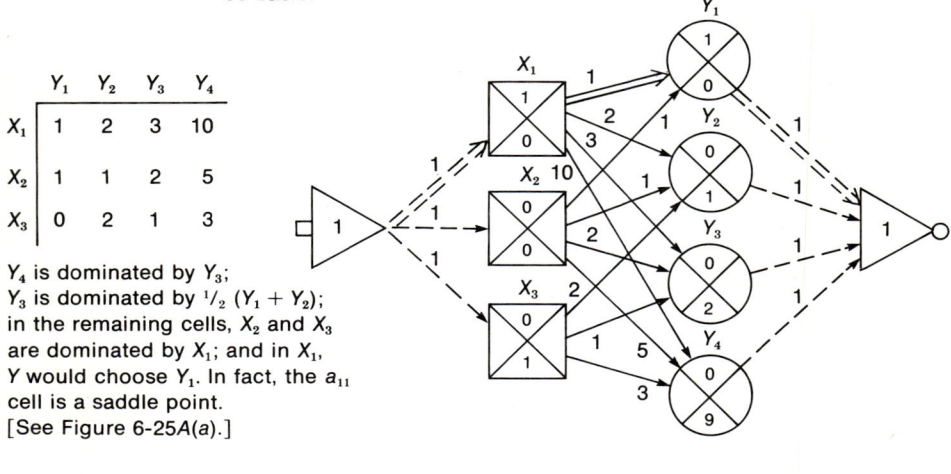

(e) **Negative W**: To be treated similarly.

	Y_1	Y_2	
X_1	-2	-5	$3/6$
X_2	-6	-3	$3/6$
	$2/6$	$4/6$	

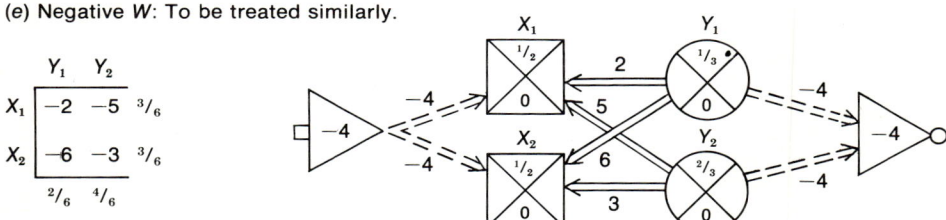

Figure 6-25B Additional examples of RPMS representations of zero-sum, two-person games.

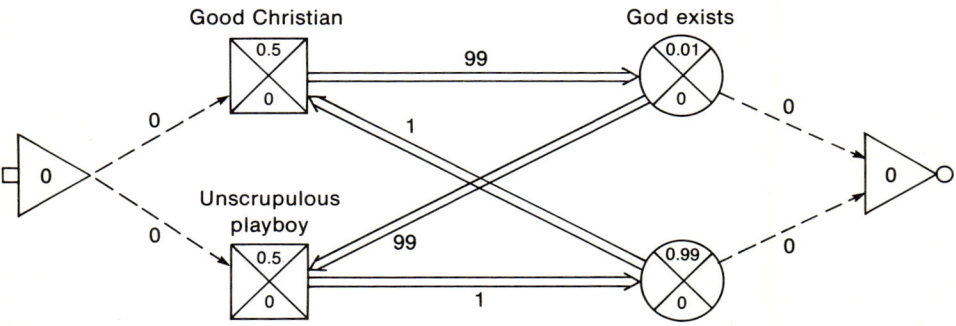

Figure 6-26 Pascal's game.

Figure 6-26 illustrates an **RPMS** representation of the situation. We see that Pascal's game has a value of zero. $W = 0$ does not affect our **RPMS** representation. What is striking, however, is the strategy chosen by the model.

1. The square process nodes identify humanity's strategy to maximize life's worth: 50 percent good behavior and 50 percent naughty behavior.
2. The circle resource nodes identify God's strategy to minimize W (or maximize $1/W$): 1 percent existence and 99 percent nonexistence.

What are the meanings of these two observations?! The second assumes that God is free to exist or not to exist on his own free will and that God's objective is to minimize humanity's happiness, a case that would be true only if God were vengeful. God's strategy is to exist 1 percent of the time to reward $99 million to a good Christian and to disappear 99 percent of the time, with a penalty of $1 million; thus, the payoff to a good Christian equals that to an unscrupulous playboy. Such a malicious pretense of the part of God is, of course, unthinkable to a Christian whose definition of God is "good" itself. God is not capable of "bad," and Pascal's theory is eminently plausible to a believer.

A nonbeliever, for whom the argument was designed, however, may or may not believe in the all-goodness of God. Instead a nonbeliever might take the strategy (1) of hedging against the odds that God may not have humanity's best interest in mind. Strategy (2) will confuse God, so that the nonbeliever won't be hurt regardless of God's decision. Thus, the nonbeliever has made the payoffs appear to be even to God.

We don't claim to be theologians, and this discussion is best left to those that are better qualified, but we cannot resist the temptation to conjecture a word of warning to devil-worshippers whose "god" is evil by their definition. According to game theory, those followers had better be at least "half good" or they could get burnt for being too sincere!

SECTION 6-7 TUNE-UP

Consider the case of a company which seeks competition with the ABC Manufacturing Company. It has heard the rumor that the ABC Manufacturing Company has hired a new OR/MS analyst who is recommending the discontinuation of product C. The company wishes to build competing models A', B', or C', but their expected revenue will be greatly influenced by what ABC is going to do. Using the following payoff table, construct an RPM network. Can you use dominance to find the answer?

	Competitor's revenue* for selling		
ABC Manufacturing Co.	A'	B'	C'
Discontinues C	100	120	200
Continues to produce C	150	200	120

*$1,000s/year.

TUNE-UP SOLUTIONS

Section 6-2

Tucker diagram

	$X_1 \geq 0$	$X_2 \geq 0$	
$Y_1 \geq 0$	6	6	≤ 360
$Y_2 \geq 0$	1	0	≤ 50
$Y_3 \geq 0$	0	1	≤ 40
$Y_4 \geq 0$	0	−1	≤ -20
$Y_5 \geq 0$	1	0	≤ 30
$Y_6 \geq 0$	−1	0	≤ -30
	IV	IV	
	4	1	

RPMS version

	$X_1 \geq 0$	$X_2 \geq 0$	
$Y_1 \geq 0$	6	6	≤ 360
$Y_2 \geq 0$	1	0	≤ 50
$Y_3 \geq 0$	0	1	≤ 40
Y_4 free	1	0	$= 30$
$Y_5 \geq 0$	0	1	≤ 20
	IV	IV	
	4	1	

Section 6-3

Σ inflow = Σ outflows + residue
0.01 + 400 = 3,000(0) + 2(0) + 30(0) + 1(50) + 10(15) + residue
Residue = +345

which means that your teenagers would gain 345 calories more per serving from including Deli in the menu.

Section 6-4

We need to take into account not only the increase in B of 2 [2x(−8) = −16], but also the decrease of C from 12 to 8 [−4x(32) = −128] for the total improvement of −16 − 128 = −144, 1072 − 144 = 928. [Note that Figure 6-12 does not represent a BFS. C can be 10 instead of 12 and still satisfy the constraints (then we would have had a BFS).]

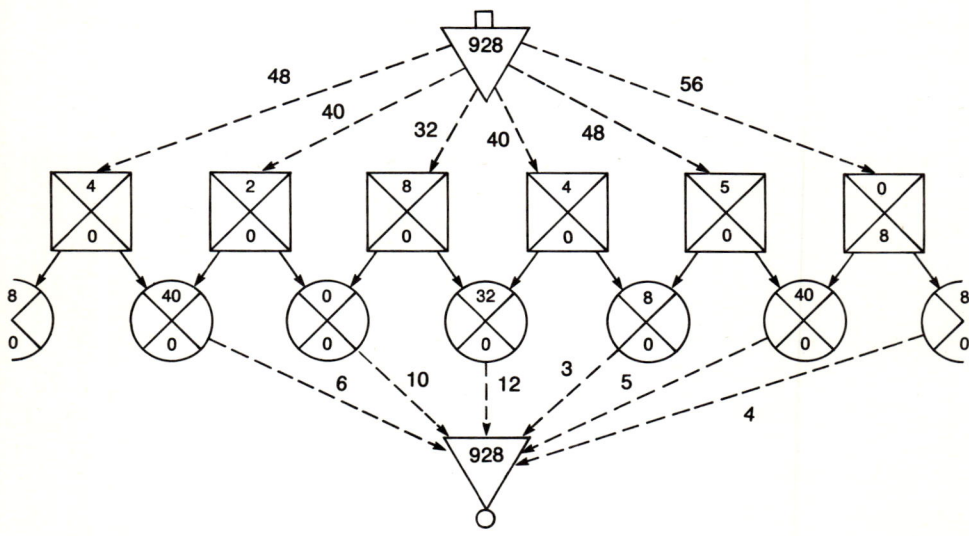

Section 6-5 (see page 148)

1. 152 man-hr, as indicated in node HW.
2. Raise it $1 and it is degenerate (see the dual residue in node C4); raise it more and Crysty will improve the total profit by that much.
3. The shadow price of m_2 is $2.82/min of process, or $169.20/hr. Do lease it for $150 and you would gain $19.20 for each hour leased.
4. The shadow prices for m_1 and m_3 are $2.60/min and $0/min respectively, or $156/hr and $0/hr, but these figures include labor. We use h_1, and h_2, and h_3 ($36/hr, $49.20/hr, and $0/hr) instead. Since h_1 and h_2 are worth more than $h_3 + \$20 = \$20$/hr, we opt to convert h_3's residue of 8 hr into h_2 (first) and h_1.

Section 6-6

1. Basic primals: ALOHA, BAMBI, SHOP 3 ($m = 3$)
   Basic duals: SHOP 1, SHOP 2, CRYSTY ($n = 3$)
2. Basic primal: ALFA, CHARL, VA, VB, VC, BDGT ($m = 6$)
   Basic duals: BRAVO, FE, CA ($n = 3$)

Section 6-7

A' is always inferior to B' ($100 < 120$; $150 < 200$) and is dominated by B'. Discarding A', we find that B' and C' are symmetrical. The answer is to mix strategies B' and C' evenly to confuse ABC (that is, even out the risk for the newcomer regardless of what ABC does). ABC Manufacturing Company can also retaliate by evening out its strategy (i.e., cut Crysty's production halfway).

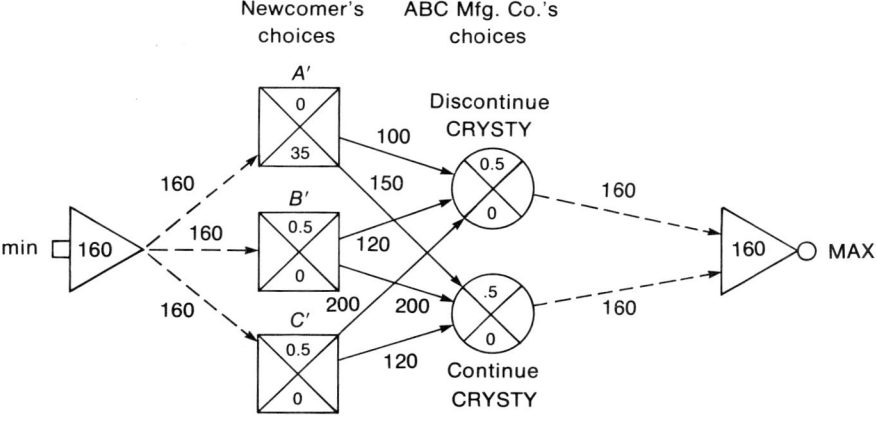

148

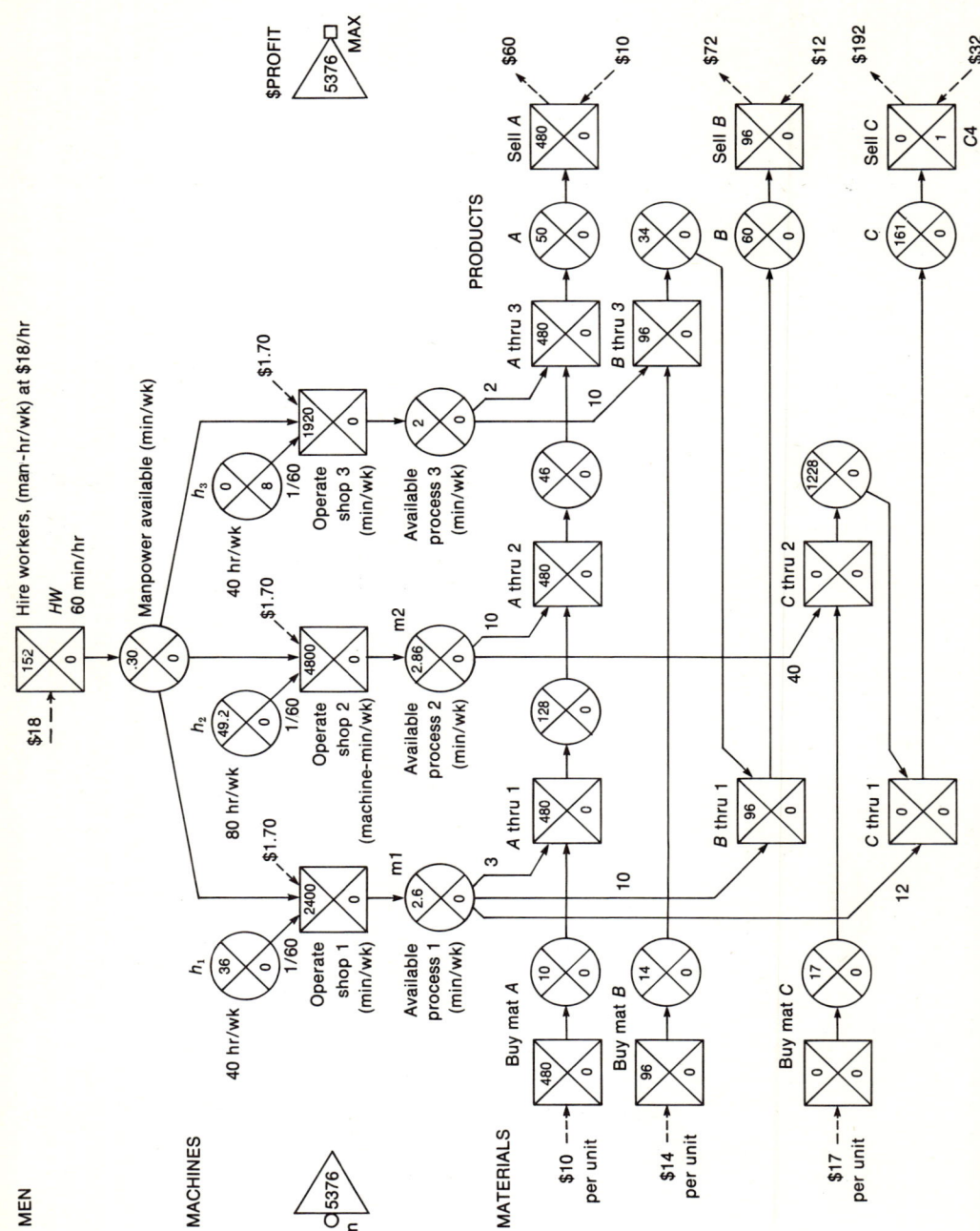

EXERCISES

6-1 Let us suppose that the Wonder Valley region will need 200 MWhr of electricity during the coming winter and that the Micropolis metropolitan area will need 300 MWhr. You have a thermonuclear plant that is capable of generating 300 MWhr. while creating an effective pollution of 2 ppm carbon monoxide over the area, a hydraulic plant with a maximum output of 100 MWhr. at 1 ppm, and a conventional thermal power plant with a capacity of 200 MWhr. at 20 ppm. The transmission losses are as follows:

From (plant)	To (destination)	Losses, percent
Nuclear	Wonder Valley	10
Nuclear	Micropolis	5
Hydraulic	Wonder Valley	20
Hydraulic	Micropolis	15
Thermal	Wonder Valley	10
Thermal	Micropolis	15

Draw an RPM network, condense it using the basic node approach, and prepare a Tucker diagram. If you have access to a computer, try to run the problem.

6-2 The LP results for Pascal's theory of bets can be obtained graphically from Figures 1-3 and 1-4 directly without computation. Identify where the following items appear on those graphs: (1) strategy for humanity; (2) strategy for God; (3) game value $W°$.

6-3 It's time to mow the lawns of your estate again. Your mansion has a front lawn of 1.2 acres and a back lawn of 2.4 acres. For this task, you have available 2.5 gal of gasoline, one fully charged battery, and three different mowers. You are told that you should choose the equipment that would maximize your calorie loss to keep your figure trim (along with the diet described in this chapter). Draw an RPM network and state the primal and dual problems mathematically.

Equipment	Fuel Usage	Calorie Loss from Exercise, k/cal/acre	Lawn Location
Electric riding mower	1 acre/charge	1	Front
	1 acre/charge	1	Back
Self-propelled reel mower	0.5 gal/acre	1.5	Front
	1.5 gal/acre	2.0	Back
Hand-pushed rotary mower	0.8 gal/acre	2.0	Front
	0.9 gal/acre	8.0	Back

6-4 Solve the following two-person zero-sum games:

$$\begin{bmatrix} 1 & 2 \\ 3 & 4 \end{bmatrix} \qquad \begin{bmatrix} 1 & 3 \\ 4 & 2 \\ 0 & 1 \end{bmatrix} \qquad \begin{bmatrix} 1 & -1 \\ -1 & 1 \end{bmatrix}$$

$$\begin{bmatrix} 1 & 2 & 3 & 4 \\ 5 & 6 & 7 & 8 \\ 3 & 2 & 1 & 0 \end{bmatrix} \qquad \begin{bmatrix} -1 & 2 & 3 & 0 \\ 4 & -1 & 2 & -7 \\ -4 & -1 & -1 & 0 \\ -1 & 1 & 1 & -4 \end{bmatrix}$$

APPLIED NORMATIVE MODELS: Linear Programming Paradigms

Chapter 7

7-1 Golden rules of RPMS linear programming

The good old rule
Sufficeth them, the simple plan,
That they should take, who have the power,
And they should keep who can.
(William Wordsworth, 1803)

The rules we have established for RPMS are few and intuitively plausible, but because they are so basic, they are important to remember. Using the acronym RPMS in Figure 7-1 we have brought together four "golden rules" of RPMS as applied to linear programming. In this chapter we shall utilize these four rules in developing, experimenting, analyzing, and interpreting various linear programming models. Several LP problems have already been formulated and discussed in Chapters 5 and 6. We are now ready to look at other interesting applications that explore RPMS normative model formulation in preparation for our studies of the mechanisms behind optimization techniques.

(R) Resource conservation postulate (Sec. 4.4): First posptulate of RPMS

Σ input ≥ Σ output or Σ input = Σ output + residue
(You can't get something for nothing!)

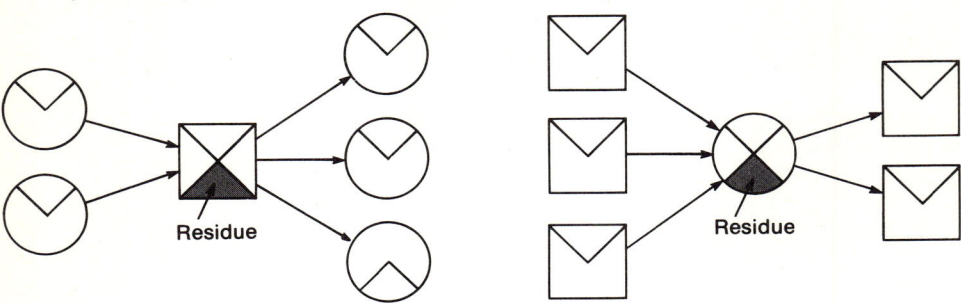

(P) Positive or zero requirement (Sec. 6.6): Complementary-slackness theorem

A primal entry must be positive or zero to be feasible; a dual entry must be positive or zero to be optimal. Moreover, either or both entries in a node of an RPM network representing a basic feasible solution must be zero.

(We take for granted what we've got plenty of, and value only what we lack!)

(M) Maximizing or minimizing objective (Sec. 4.4): Second postulate of RPMS

Maximize output, when given input; or minimize input, when requested output.

[Get most out of what we've got, or do as little as possible to get by! (Zipf's law)]

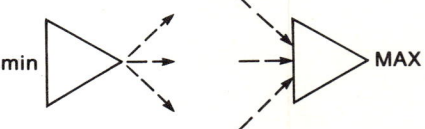

(S) Solution criterion (Sec. 5.2): Extreme-point theorem

If a feasible, optimal solution exists, there is a corresponding basic feasible colution.

(When all entries on an RPM network are positive or zero, we have an optimal and feasible solution.)

Figure 7-1 Four "golden rules" of RPMS as applied to linear programming.

The four golden rules of RPMS linear programming should be supplemented by other conventions and practices we have already established. Some of the more important items are:

1. Never connect a circle to another circle or a square to another square directly.

2. Use solid arrows for internal flows and dotted arrows for exogenous or endogenous flows.

3. All squares are explicitly or implicitly (with zero objective-function value) connected to one terminal, and all circles are explicitly or implicitly connected to the other terminal; no mixing of terminals is allowed.

4. The dimension of the arrow coefficient is always resource-unit/process-unit regardless of the direction of the flow.

5. A resource node implies an OR relationship among flows; none, any, or all flows may be realized at the same time and all must have the same resource unit of measurement.

6. A process node implies an AND relationship among flows; all flows must be realized when the process is basic primal. If one input is missing, the process cannot be realized; and if the process is realized, all outputs will be generated. The units of these flows may be in different measurement units since the function of a process is to convert a set of input resources into a more useful set of output resources.

7. It is advisable to set the RPM network in a more or less chronological order, flowing from left to right or from top to bottom, and label the date whenever possible. A resource at one time is different from the same resource at another time.

8. The dimensional units of resources and processes may be changed to suit the convenience of the analyst and/or user. (The details of scaling are discussed in Chapter 9, Section 9-2.)

9. The double circle implies an equality constraint where residue must be zero. The dual value of the resource may then be either positive or negative, and the dual variable is said to be "free" while the connected process may be "frozen" because of the equality.

10. A double square may be used in a similar manner to imply a free decision (primal) variable, which may be either positive or negative but which will always be basic (i.e., no residual value). Such a process can always be represented by two parallel processes with opposing arrows.

7-2 Basic RPM network patterns

Let us now tabulate the various basic RPM network patterns we have discussed so far.

SHARING A LIMITED RESOURCE Often one resource must be shared by several processes, as was the case for lumber in a woodworking shop (Example 5-1), a budget for a diet (Example 6-1), and man-hours in a product mix model (Example 6-3). Figure 7-2 illustrates a typical pattern with the corresponding MPS

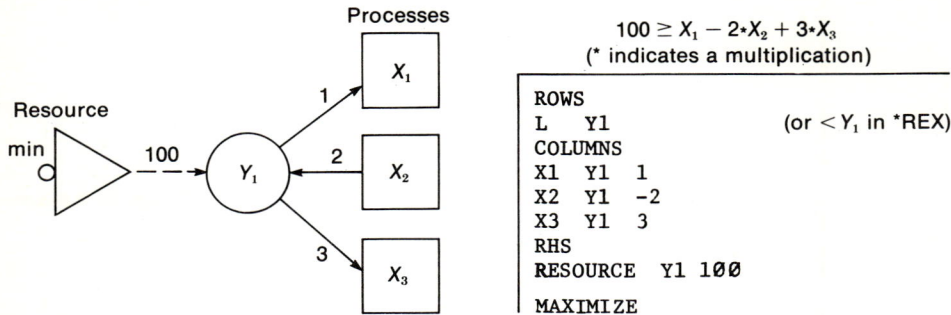

Figure 7-2 RPM network pattern for the sharing of a resource. A maximizing primal problem is shown with a mathematical programming system (MPS) computer program data file.

entry for primal maximization; Figure 7-3 illustrates the same pattern for primal minimization.

TRANSFORMATION OF RESOURCES The function of a process is to transform a set of input resources into a more valuable set of output resources. Input resources comprise not only raw materials, labor, and equipment, and other physical resources, but also allowances for possible wastes from production, information needed to start the process, and other intangible factors of production. (See Figure 7-4.) The question one might ask is "Would I be sorry later, if I went ahead with my decision to process now?" If you are not sure that you can use the output of your process, perhaps you should wait for feedback from the user who is requesting the production. (In Section 7-3, we shall elaborate further on this idea.)

CAPACITATED FLOWS When there is an upper limit to a process (primal) value, we can use either the standard .LE. constraint or a shortcut method of bind-

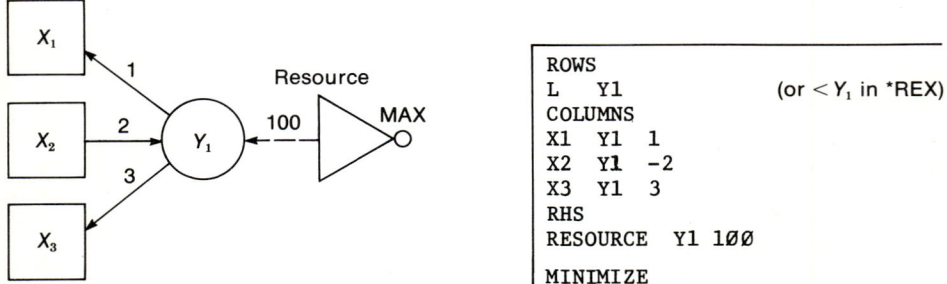

Figure 7-3 RPM network pattern for the sharing of a resource. A minimization for the primal problem is shown with a corresponding MPS data file.

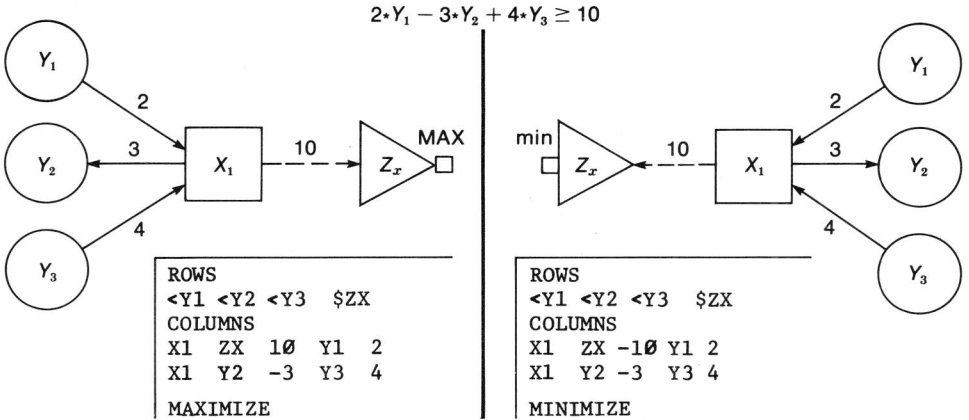

Figure 7-4   Transformation of resources patterns. Note that *REX notation is used for conciseness. For MPS, the second statement (card) must be replaced by L Y1, L Y2, L Y3 and N ZX, each on a separate card. (See Appendix B for details.)

ing the variable. In MPS, all binding statements must be grouped under the BOUNDS section of the data file using symbols such as LO (lower bound), UP (upper bound), FX (fixed value), FR (free variable), MI (minus infinity), and PL (plus infinity). In *REX, it suffices to add *BOUND* and state the lower-bound (positive) or upper-bound (negative) value following it in the COLUMN section. The advantage of using the .LE. conventional method is that you will obtain the shadow price for the constraint which will not be given by the BOUND. Since the transmittance coefficient is always 1 in a binding statement, we can directly attach the circle to the process on the RPM configuration. Figure 7-5 illustrates both MPS and *REX examples. In LINPRO no shortcut method is available.

BOUNDED FLOWS   A natural extension of the capacitated flow concept is the bounding of the flow using both the upper and lower limits. Again, it is possible either to use the traditional method of utilizing two constraints, with the advantage of obtaining the dual resource value for each limit, or to use the BOUNDS notation available on MPS or *REX (see Figure 7-6).

FROZEN VARIABLE   The extreme case of bounding is when the upper and lower limits have the same value, a condition that is equivalent to having an equality constraint. Again, the use of the equality constraint is recommended if the dual constraint value needs to be obtained, but a special command is also available on MPS and *REX. A frozen variable can be substituted using equality (see Figure 7-7).

FREE VARIABLE   An equality constraint used in *freezing* a process can be considered as two parallel constraints, of which only one can be basic dual at

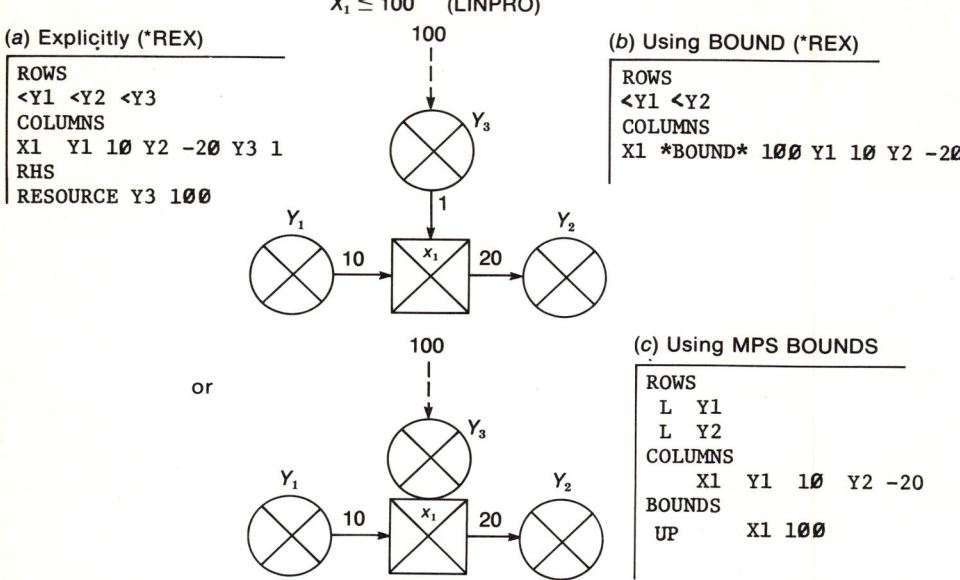

Figure 7-5 Capacitated flow, and computer data file examples.

any one time. Since the arrows on such constraints would be opposing and only one constraint is binding at a time, we can make one free dual variable perform double duty, i.e., take on a positive dual value when the binding action is in the direction of the arrows and a negative dual value when it is opposite to the direction of the arrow (Section 5-3).

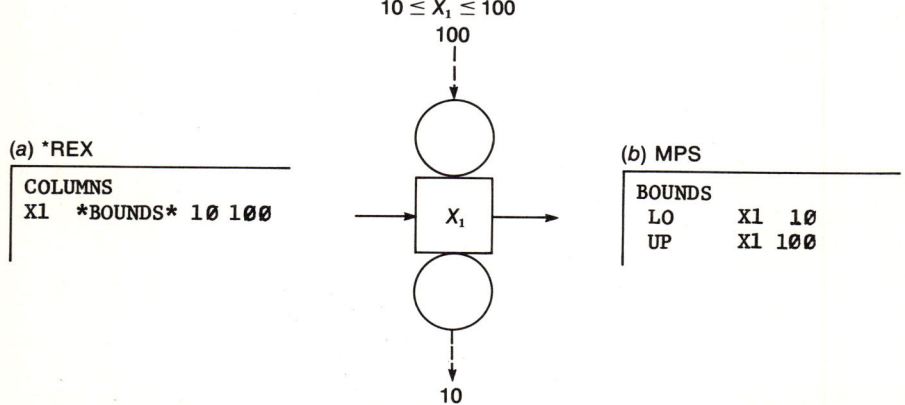

Figure 7-6 Bounded flow using BOUNDS. (It is also possible to use RANGE.)

Applied Normative Models: Linear Programming Paradigms   157

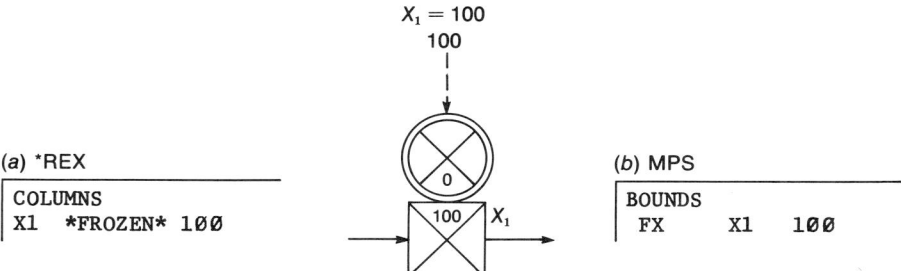

(a) *REX

COLUMNS		
X1	*FROZEN*	100

(b) MPS

BOUNDS		
FX	X1	100

Figure 7-7 Frozen variable. (It is also possible to use an E (=) constraint instead.)

A process activity can also be made to perform double duty by specifying it as a free variable. Such a variable would appear to defy the nonnegativity constraint of the linear programming when, in fact, it is a shorthand for two opposing nonnegative primal variables. The corresponding dual value is then frozen at zero. We shall use a double box to represent such a process (Figure 7-8).

SECTION 7-2 TUNE-UP: Capacitated transshipment

Figure 7-9 illustrates the monthly trucking capability of a seafood processing company between two processing plants and to three destinations. Describe the meaning of all flows, including the possible discrepancy for the trucking charge at the double square. How would you remedy the problem? (All units are in tons per month or dollars, and all solid arrows have a unit coefficient.)

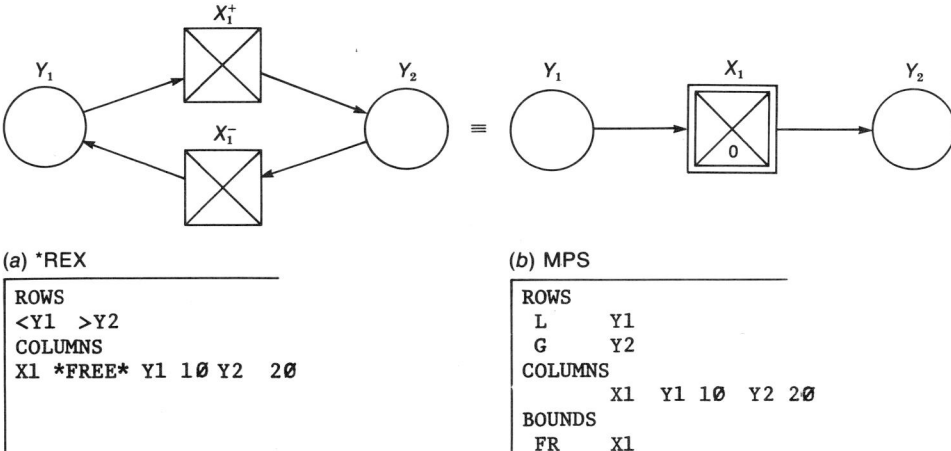

(a) *REX

ROWS				
<Y1	>Y2			
COLUMNS				
X1	*FREE*	Y1	10	Y2	20

(b) MPS

ROWS				
L	Y1			
G	Y2			
COLUMNS				
	X1	Y1	10	Y2	20
BOUNDS				
FR	X1			

Figure 7-8 Free process variable. Note the use of .GE. (>) constraint, which could have been written as .LE. (<) with negative values as in Figure 7-5.

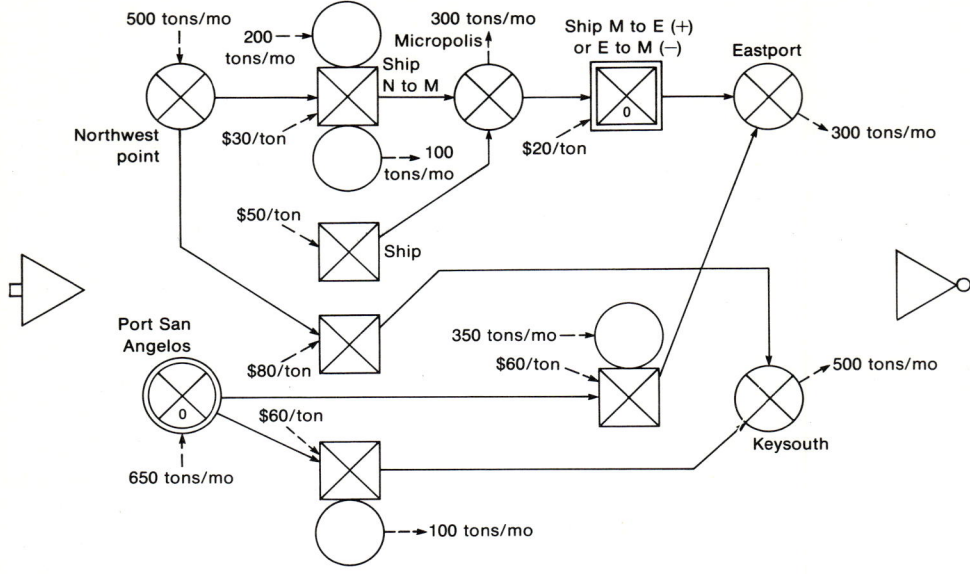

Figure 7-9 Section 7-2 Tune-up network.

7-3 Technological constraints

Whether an OR/MS solution is practical or academic often depends upon whether the model includes or omits those technological "know-hows" that are the trade secrets of the industry. It is typical of management to tell an OR/MS analyst to maximize profit and then find the solution objectionable: "Of course we want to optimize our profit. But you've got to keep some balance between A and B, or the product won't coagulate. And, you could not just discontinue C without finding a suitable substitute for our customers to use. . . ." It would be helpful to OR/MS analysts if management would state its problem originally as: "Optimize our profit subject to the condition that A should not be less than 30 percent of B, and that at least 10 percent of the total output should come from D or E." Technological constraints usually take the form of ratios between processes and/or resources, which can be added to the original normative model.

RATIOS BETWEEN PROCESSES Ratios between processes are easy to implement; a simple .LE.O or .EQ.O constraint can be used to connect the appropriate processes. For instance, in the preceding paragraph if A, B, C, and D represent processes, Figure 7-10 would be the corresponding RPM network.

SIMPLIFYING RATIOS BETWEEN PROCESSES In Figure 7-10b, an equality node was created to sum all outputs (A, B, C, D, and E) into an *output total*

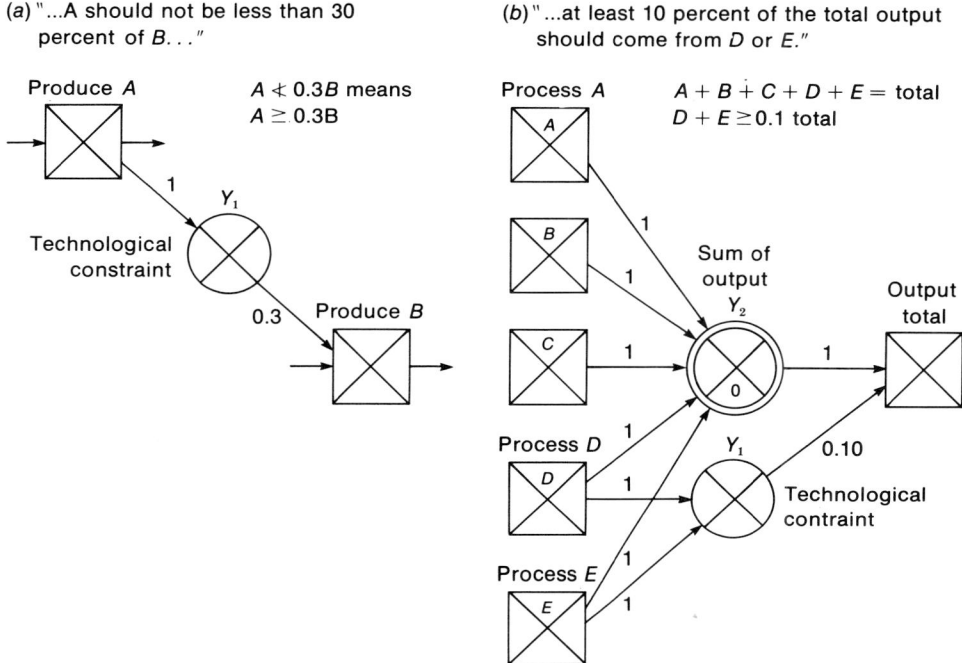

Figure 7-10 Technological constraints.

process, which was then used to tie the ratio of ten percent (0.1) of D and E to 1.0 of A, B, C, D, and E. The inclusion of this equality constraint implies that we can use the method of Chapter 6, Section 6-5, to reduce the RPM network. We can perceive this process visually by first reversing the arrow direction of equality (Figure 7-11a) and then substituting the equality into the technological constraint (Figure 7-11b). Although Figure 7-11b is a more elegant normative model, Figure 7-11a is perhaps more descriptive of the meaning of the constraint.

It is nonetheless possible to interpret Figure 7-11b meaningfully if we consider the technological constraint as *information* created by one process to authorize another. For example, each unit of D or E would create a 0.9 allowance, which authorizes A, B, or C to increase production by nine units. Or, putting it another way, production of A, B, or C should not proceed unless there is an assurance that D or E could match its production 1:9. It is permissible for D and E to start production without knowing what A, B, and C are doing, but the reverse is not true. To A, B, and C, the technological constraint is as much a factor of production as any physical resource such as labor, machine-hours, and materials may be, and the RPM network makes no distinction between the physical and informational resources.

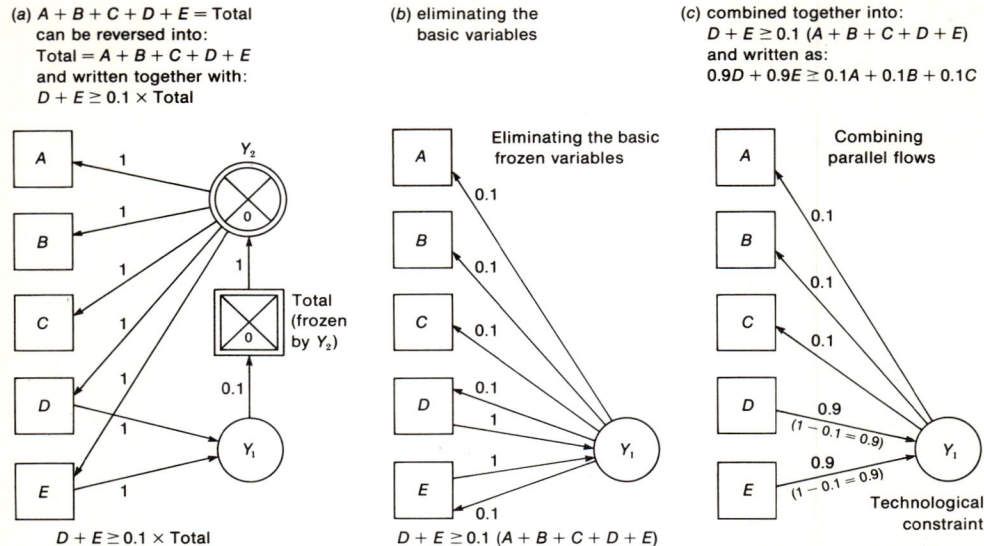

Figure 7-11 Further condensation of Figure 7-10 b: (a) reversing direction on .EQ.; (b) eliminating basic variables; (c) simplifying.

RATIOS BETWEEN RESOURCES Comparing the networks (*a*) and (*c*) in Figure 7-11, we see that the ratio of 0.1:1 relates two resources in (*a*) while the ratio of 0.9:0.1 relates two sets of processes in (*b*). Thus, ratios between resources can always be expressed as ratios between processes. We must take into account that a process relates all inputs and outputs using an AND relationship, in contrast with a resource that has an OR relationship. Thus, if we want a technological constraint to be binding in addition to all other constraints, such information must be conveyed to a process rather than to a resource. One *or* more processes may provide or utilize a resource, but all input resources must be present before a process can replace a resource. By the same token, once a process is activated, all its outputs are produced simultaneously. A judicious use of these AND and OR conditions, together with the reversal of arrows (negation), can simulate any logical situation that fits within the framework of linear programming.

SECTION 7-3 TUNE-UP: A personal investment portfolio

You have decided to set up an investment portfolio that would ensure a comfortable retirement plan when you reach 60. Your children have all joined communes, and you have grown tired of having to mow the lawns of your large estate. By selling your mansion and moving into a small condominium you have acquired $40,000, which you now wish to invest. You have narrowed down your choice of investments to the following:

Invest in	At least, %	But not more than, %	For the expected dividend of, % yr
Life insurance	10	—	3
Corporate bond	—	—	8
Municipal bond	20	40	10
Growth stock	—	10	15
Blue-chip stock	—	—	7
Utility stock	—	50	6

Construct an RPM network that represents this situation for maximizing the total annual dividend. Then, using your common sense, identify what you think is a feasible and optimal plan. Check your solution by inserting it back in your RPM network and computing the respective dual values.

7-4 Blending problems

A popular application of linear programming that incorporates ratio constraints is a *blending problem*. A blending problem is similar to a diet, or product-mix, problem in that amounts of ingredients must be selected that satisfy final requirements, but it is different in that many technological constraints must be met. In a diet problem we may be required simply to select an adequate amount of certain nutrients under the least cost (or calorie) criterion. If we are careless, we could conceivably end up with a ridiculous solution, such as a diet in which one consumes an enormous amount of low-cost low-nutrient food, say 1 ton of whey per day. Common sense should prevail in solving such mundane problems. In a blending problem, however, technological constraints must be built into the model or the solution may not be valid at all. For example, 2 gallons of 70-octane gasoline may not do the job of 1 gallon of 100-octane gasoline.

Blending problems occur frequently in the petroleum industry. "Blending Aviation Gasolines—A Study in Programming Interdependent Activities in an Integrated Oil Company" was published in *Econometrica* in 1954.[1] At one time the petroleum industry was the largest user of linear programming.[2] A typical petroleum application involves 400 to 600 processes and 200 or more resource variables. Without the use of linear programming, our recent fuel shortage could have been more severe.

Blending problems also occur outside of the petroleum industry, for example, in chemical, pharmaceutical, or metallurgical processing plants. As noted previously, the main difference between a diet, or product-mix, problem and a blending model is that in the latter minimum or maximum requirements for all con-

---

[1] A. Charnes, W. W. Cooper, and B. Mellon, "Blending Aviation Gasolines—A Study in Programming Interdependent Activities in an Integrated Oil Company," *Econometrica*, vol. 22, pp. 193–217, 1954.

[2] *An Introduction to Linear Programming*, Data Processing Application E20-8171, IBM, p. 14, 1964.

stituents must be met but with certain constraints (for example, volumes or weights). In other words, the internal ratios of constituents must be balanced. The following example illustrates such a situation.

Example 7-1: Wonderland whisky industry. The government of Wonderland controls its alcoholic beverage production through a government-operated monopoly. Part of the income is derived through sales of three brands of whisky, Mad Hatter Classic, Nevermore Prime, and Old Pete, which retail for $13.50, $11.98, and $9.99 a fifth, respectively. Since it does not have its own distillery, the government imports three grades of whisky, Ace, Better, and Cheap, and mixes these as shown in the following table. The table also gives the monthly availability of imported whiskies, together with their prices.

Brand of whisky	Grade of Whisky			Retail Price, dollars
	Ace	Better	Cheap	
Mad Hatter	At least 50%	Any	No more than 20%	13.50
Nevermore	Any	At least 35%	No more than 60%	11.98
Old Pete	Any	Any	No more than 30%	9.99
Purchase price, $/fifth	14	10	7	
Availability, fifths/mo.	2,000	3,000	5,000	

The resulting RPM network and optimal solution are shown in Figure 7-12.

COMMENTS ON EXAMPLE 7-1 SOLUTION The solution shown in Figure 7-12 deserves a careful review. Looking at the data in the table, we see that Ace whisky costs $14 a fifth while the top-notch Mad Hatter sells for only $13.50 a fifth. Yet, it turns out that Mad Hatter is a profitable brand to produce; its quality is far superior to the specification, containing 80 percent Ace ($D/M = {}^{2,000}/_{2,500} = 0.8$) instead of the marginal 50 percent specified by Y_7. The Old Pete, selling for $9.99 a fifth, would seem like a profitable item when compared with its specification (30 percent of Cheap at $7, with the remaining 70 percent coming from, say, Better at $10, for a total cost of $9.10 a fifth); but LP tells us not to produce any Old Pete. The O process (sell Old Pete) contains two zeros and is degenerate; but in trying to make O, we need Y_{13}, which now has no residue. J, K, or L may be used to create Y_{13}, but the penalties are $4.26 for J and K, and $0.49 for L. Thus, each Old Pete we happen to produce will cost (30% × $0.49) + (70% × $4.26) = $3.129 a fifth. We can say that the Old Pete must be priced at $13.12 a fifth, or $1.14 more than Nevermore, before we can profitably consider including it in our product mix.

It is also significant to find that both Ace (Y_4) and Better (Y_5) are worth the

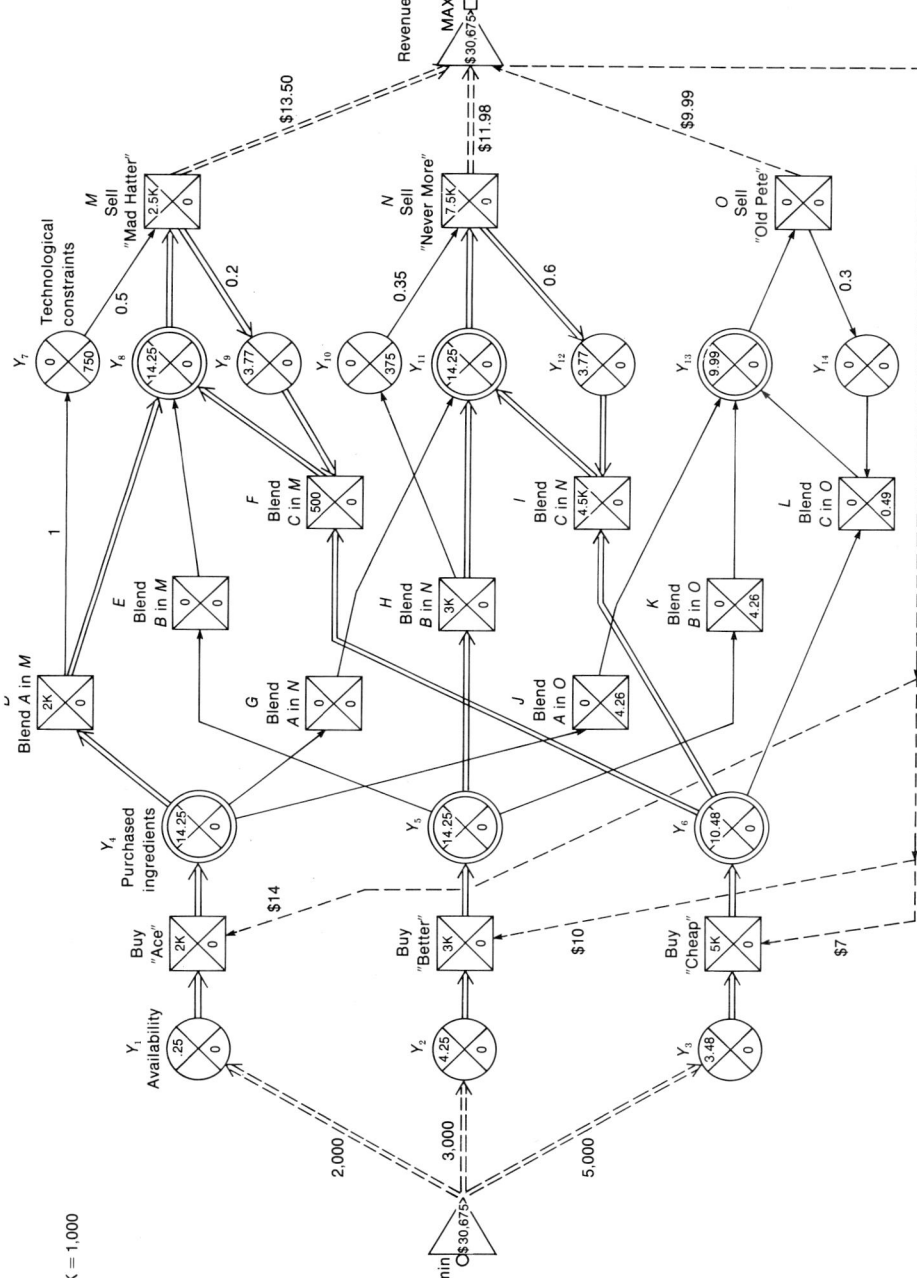

Figure 7-12 Wonderland whisky production schedule. K = 1,000.

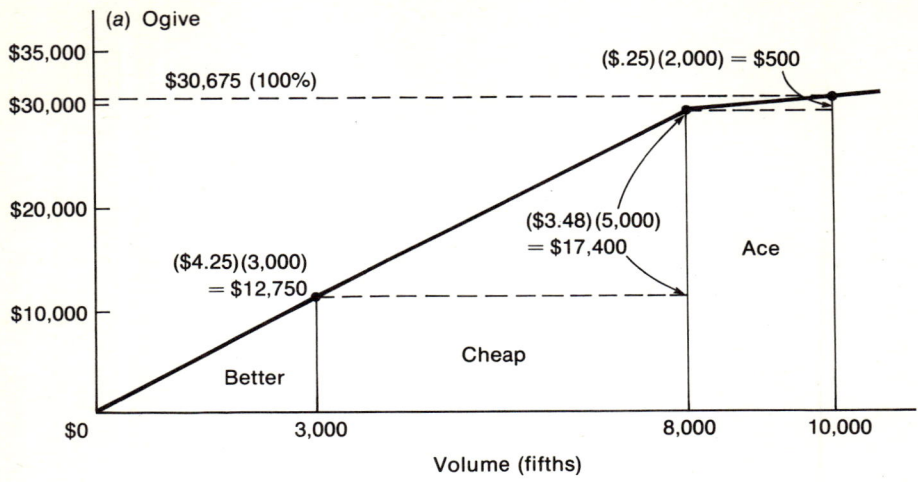

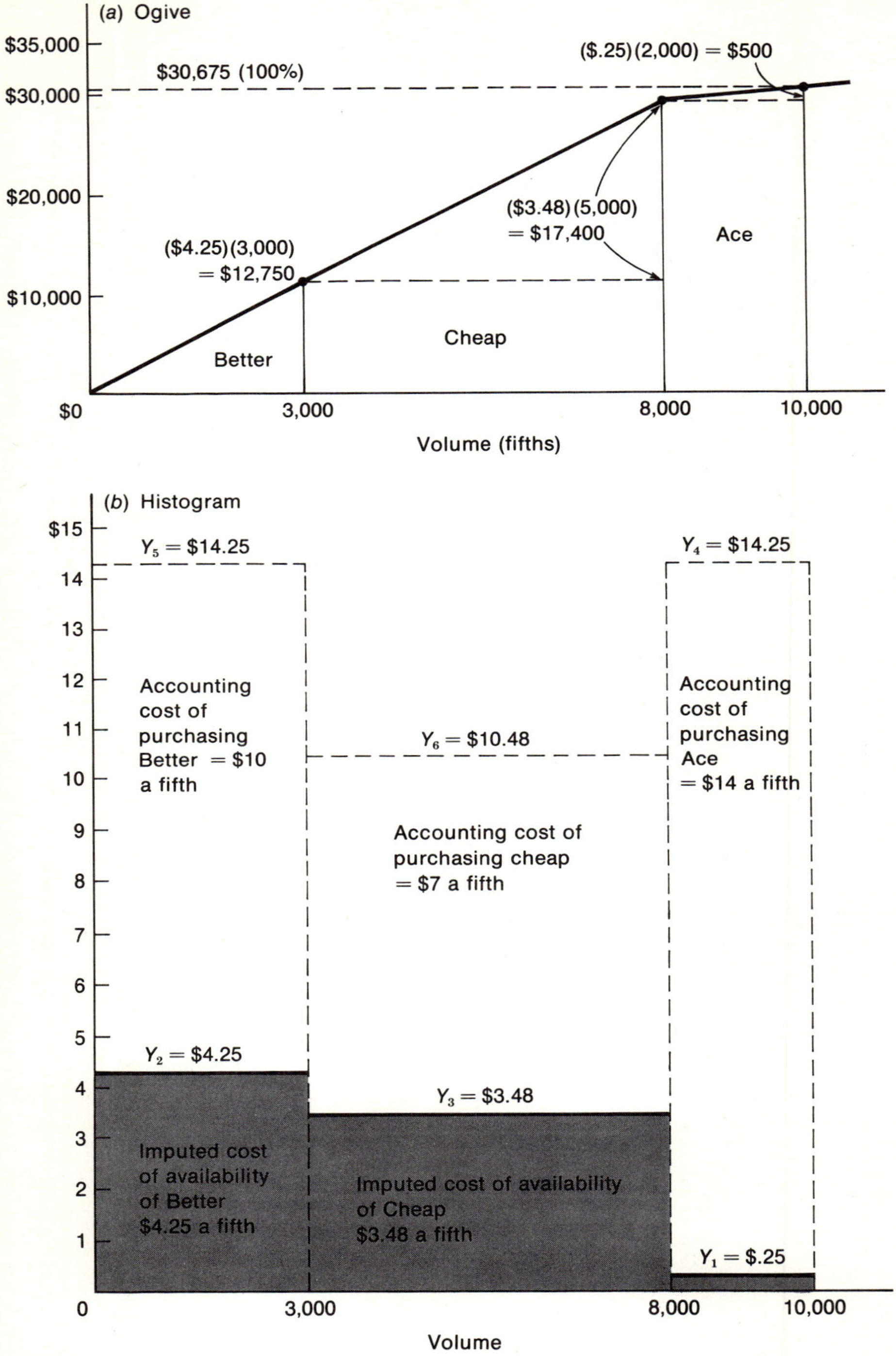

Figure 7-13 Pareto analysis of input resources. (a) Ogive; (b) histogram.

same ($14.25 a fifth) in the LP model. In other words, given an option of increasing the availability of raw whiskies, we would prefer to increase first Better ($Y_2 = \$4.25$ per availability of a fifth), then Cheap ($Y_3 = \$3.48$), and lastly Ace ($Y_1 = \$0.25$). This kind of analysis can be portrayed graphically using Pareto diagrams.

PARETO ANALYSIS OF EXAMPLE 7-1 The significance of imputed resource values for Y_1, Y_2, and Y_3 can be portrayed visually in an adaptation of a Pareto diagram, where the horizontal abscissa indicates the volumes of the resources and the ordinate is used to show the dollar values. Because of the scaling problem, we shall use two graphs to portray the histogram and the ogive separately.

Figure 7-13 shows the input-resource analysis, demonstrating how the imputed resource values Y_1, Y_2, and Y_3 contribute to the total revenue of $30,675 and how they make up the nonaccounting portions of the resource values Y_4, Y_5, and Y_6. Figure 7-14 performs a similar analysis on the output products Nevermore and Mad Hatter and is a graphic representation of how linear programming automatically assigns portions of revenues to each basic resource. It is interesting to note that the imputed resource values, $Y_{11} = Y_8 = \$14.25$ a fifth include the imputed costs of technological constraints Y_9 and Y_{12}. Similar Pareto analyses can be performed on any portion of RPM network; often they reveal insights to the problem that are otherwise hard to grasp.

SECTION 7-4 TUNE-UP

Figure 7-12 includes several technological constraints which can be interpreted in the manner of Section 7-3. For example, Y_7 indicates that the use of Ace in Mad Hatter (process D) enables more Mad Hatter (process M) to be sold, but the blending of Cheap into M (process F) should not take place until we have been given authorization (Y_9) so that we do not overdilute our Mad Hatter with the Cheap ingredient. Unfortunately, no such information flow is apparent in the case of E (mixing Better into Mad Hatter), although the consequence of pouring too much Better might be that we would dilute the Mad Hatter beyond the availability of Ace. In other words, if we were to dump the entire 3,000 fifths of Better into the tank, the total amount of Ace available (2,000 fifths) would not be able to return the dilution mix to the allowable 50 percent. By reducing the RPM network in Figure 7-12 through elimination of equality nodes and forced variables, create a condensed RPM network (see Figure 7-11) and illustrate how the technological information was actually fed back to hold process E down. Insert and check the validity of all primal and dual values on the reduced network. How would this reduction affect the Pareto analysis of resource values?

7-5 Cyclic scheduling

Thus far we have been concerned with problems that have had definite beginnings and endings; that is, if we started out from a source terminal, we could trace our-

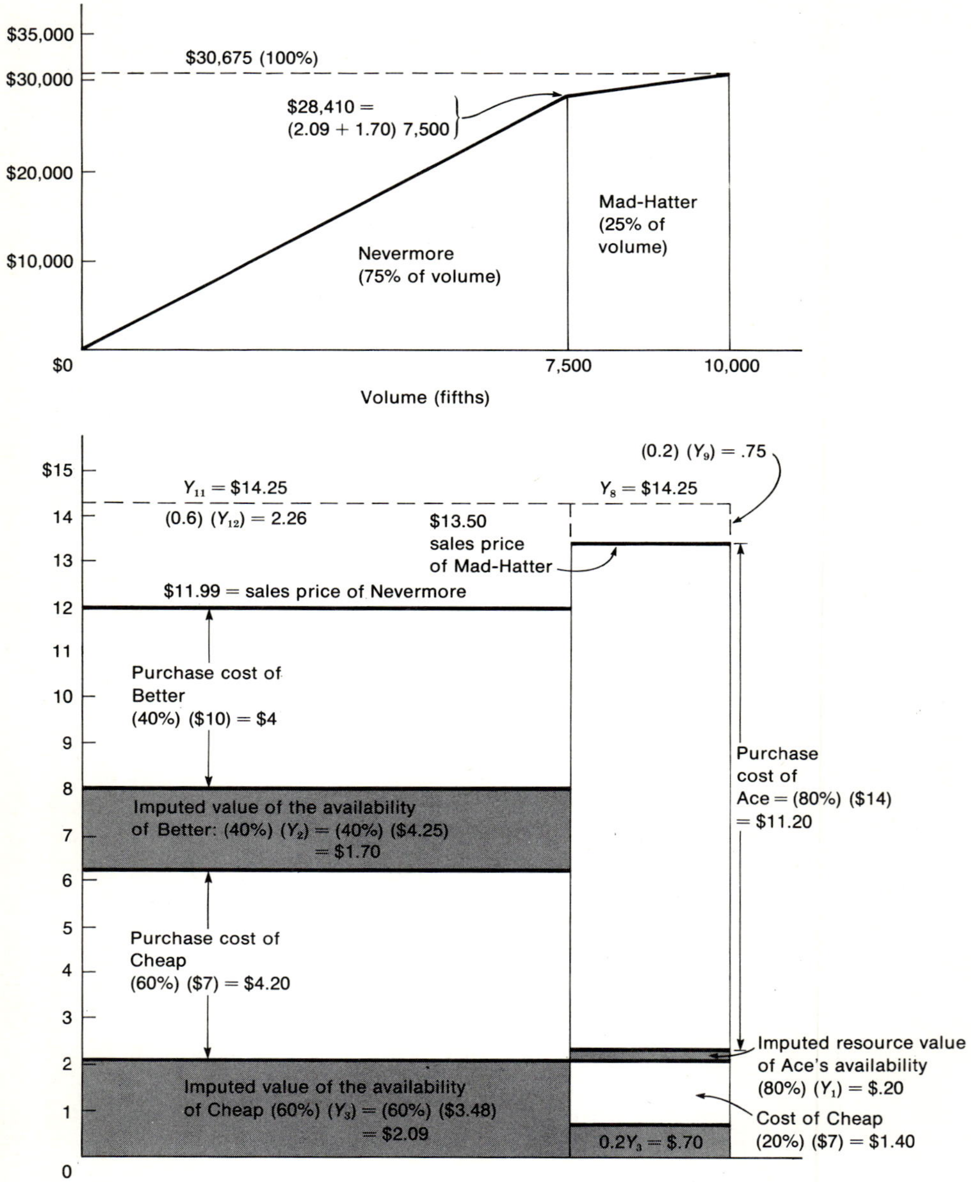

Figure 7-14 Pareto analysis of whiskey. (*a*) Ogive; (*b*) histogram.

selves safely to the sink terminal. But what about solving problems that do not have definite beginnings or endings? Can we still use our modeling approach? Example 6-2 was one such problem; now let us look at others.

POSITIVE FEEDBACK We have already dealt with problems that have endless loops incorporated into them. Figure 7-11a includes loops around $D-Y_1$-total-Y_2-D and $E-Y_1$-total-Y_2-E. In Figure 7-12 there are three such loops: one around Mad Hatter ($M-Y_9-F-Y_8-M$), one around Nevermore ($N-Y_{12}-I-Y_{11}-N$), and one around Old Pete ($O-Y_{14}-L-Y_{13}-O$). Fortunately, all those feedback loops had loop gains that were less than unity: 0.1 in Figure 7-11; and 0.2, 0.6, and 0.3 in Figure 7-12. If the flows were to grow as they went around the loop, we would have an ever-growing self-perpetuating system that would no longer allow us to use linear programming to find an optimal solution. It is like a monster who can feed on its own tail and keep growing—the only way to control such growth is to chop off its tail and break the never-ending loop.

In mathematical programming, a model that can grow indefinitely is said to be *unbounded*. Such a model cannot be optimized within the present framework of mathematical programming, but we come close to such a situation by optimizing a steady-state condition of a loop where neither a gain nor a loss is incurred. In other words, it is permissible for us to model a situation where the ending state of the system is the same as the beginning state of the system, and to find such a state that would optimize our objective function.

DUMMY-NODE NOTATION Before we illustrate our procedure, let us refresh our memories and formalize the introduction of dummy nodes (Section 6-4) used to represent cyclic systems. A dummy node is a **D**-shaped resource node that indicates that the other half of the same node is to be found elsewhere on the diagram by a complementing dummy node ◖ bearing the same label. This connector-type notation greatly simplifies a diagram by enabling us to avoid criss-crossing paths that are common to cyclic problems. A dummy node is used in the following example as well as in Section 7-5 Tune-up.

Example 7-12 The Wonder Widget Company The Wonder Widget Company, Inc., manufactures Widgets, which are used by children and adults alike in Wonderland's national pastime of outdoor widgeting games. The production manager is interested in scheduling plant production over four quarters ($j = 1, 2, 3, 4$) to meet the seasonal demands of 5,000 for the fall ($j = 3$), and 20,000 for the summer quarter ($j = 4$). Each quarter, there are 10,000 hr of regular production time RA_j and another 10,000 hr of overtime available at the respective expenses of $4 per unit at 1 unit per hr (RT_j), and $6 per unit also at 1 unit per hr (OT_j). Inventory is possible for $4 per unit-quarter, and the warehouse has unlimited storage space.

RPM SOLUTION OF EXAMPLE 7-2 This is a cyclic scheduling problem with a minimizing primal objective function. Figure 7-15 shows the RPM network which gives an optimal solution. The solution indicates that overtime production is warranted during the spring ($j = 3$) and summer ($j = 4$) quarters only, and that regular production should be cut in half during the fall quarter. The storage space is used from winter to spring ($ST2$) only. $D1$ has been split into two dummy nodes.

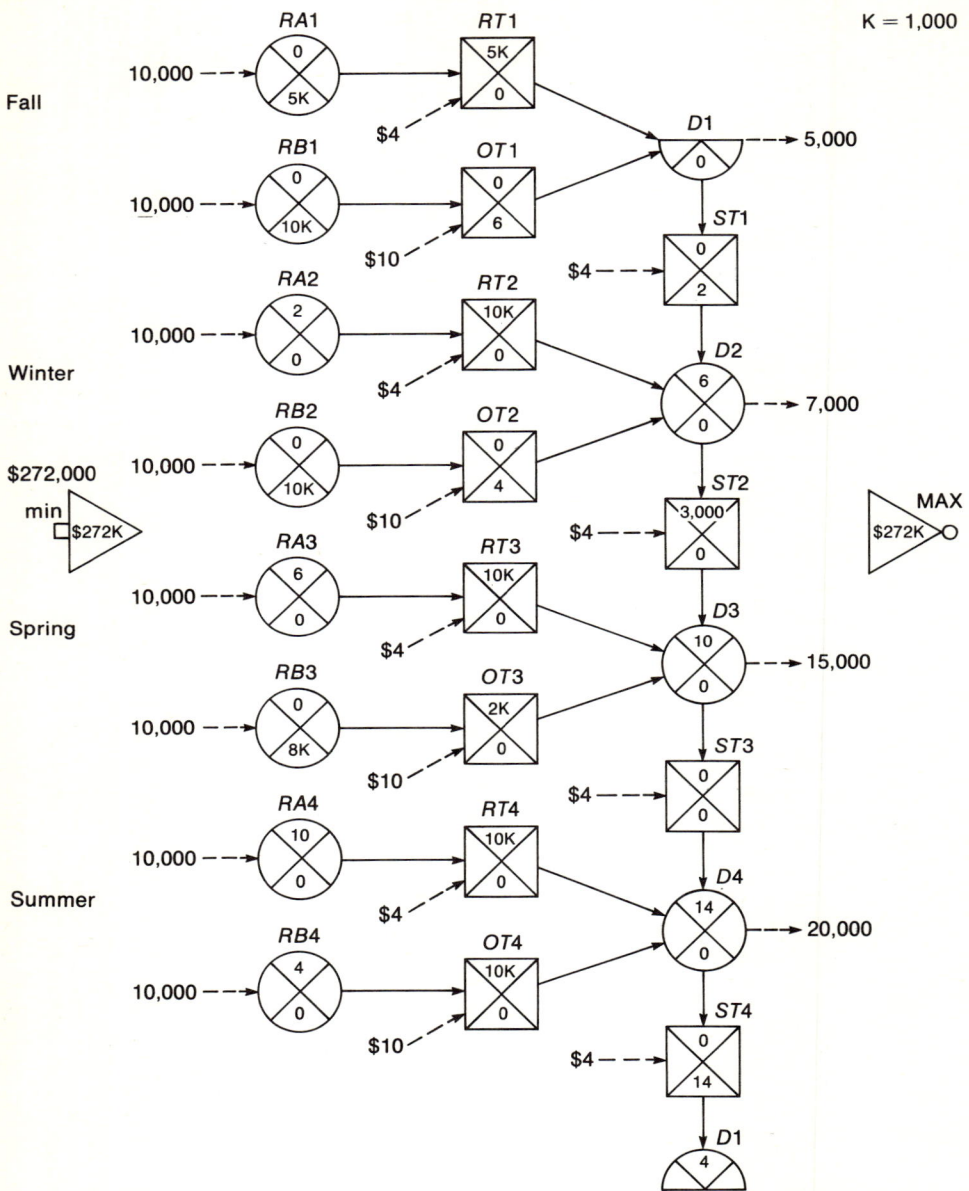

Figure 7-15 RPM network showing an optimal solution for Wonder Widget Company, Inc. K = 1,000.

DISCONTINUATION OF WAREHOUSING Since the warehouse is used only during one quarter, it is natural to ask if we may eliminate storage altogether and save on the cost of maintaining a large warehouse. This is indeed possible if we

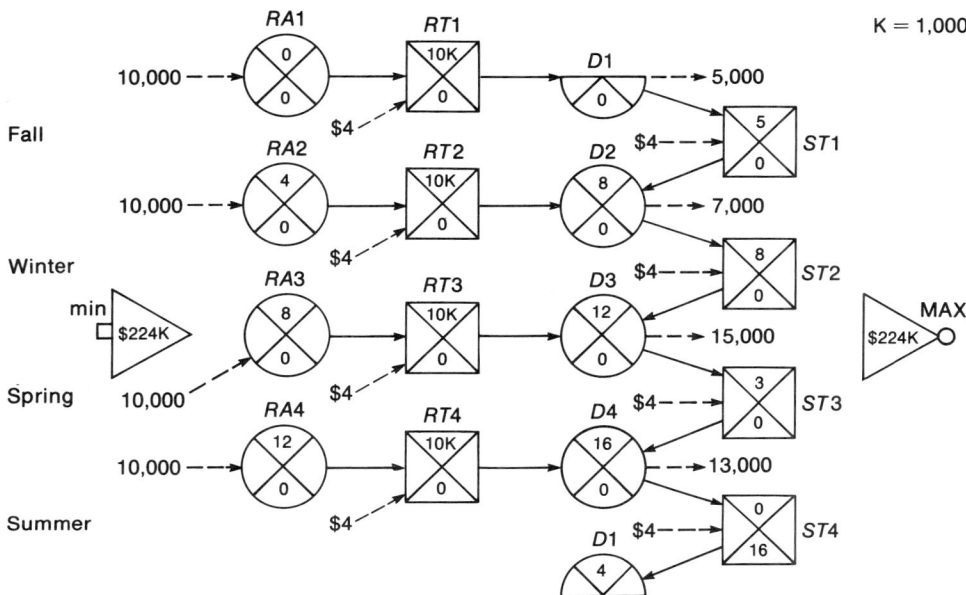

Figure 7-16 Revised optimal solution for Wonder Widget Company, Inc. K = 1,000.

increased $OT3$ from 2,000 to 5,000 and reduced $RT2$ from 10,000 to 7,000 units. The increase in expenditure can be calculated by noting that $RA2$ has a resource value of $2 per unit while $RB3$ is $0. Thus, exchanging the two would cost $2 per unit, and for a change of 3,000 units we need an additional $6,000.

AVOIDING OVERTIME PRODUCTION Instead of discontinuing storage space, we might consider leveling the production schedule by eliminating overtime and concentrating on regular production time only. However, quick calculation will show that if we made such a cutback in production time we could not possibly meet the total demand: we could produce only 40,000 units (the total demand is 47,000 units).

Where shall we cut back? Again, it suffices to look at dual values. In Figure 7-15 the highest penalty for storage occurs at $ST4$ for $14 per unit. It would seem wise to forego 7,000 units of the 20,000-unit demand for summer and to try to meet the demand for 13,000 by making use of all storage except $ST4$. This turns out to be the optimal solution, and it is given in complete form in Figure 7-16.

SECTION 7-5 TUNE-UP Sales personnel scheduling problem

A company that produces and markets seasonal and perishable products *FA, FB, RC,* and *FC* has three divisions and a sales organization. The Atlas division processes raw

170

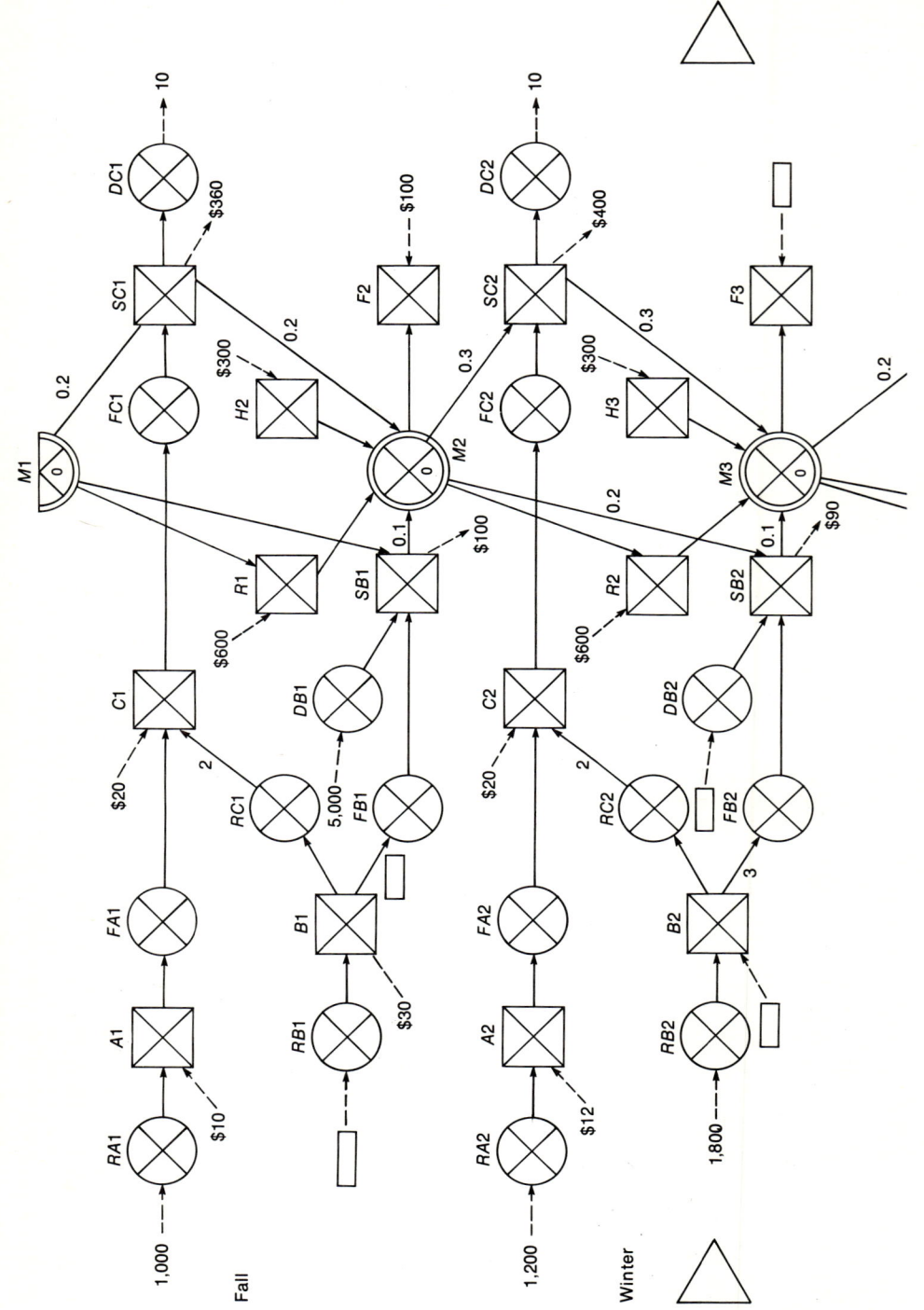

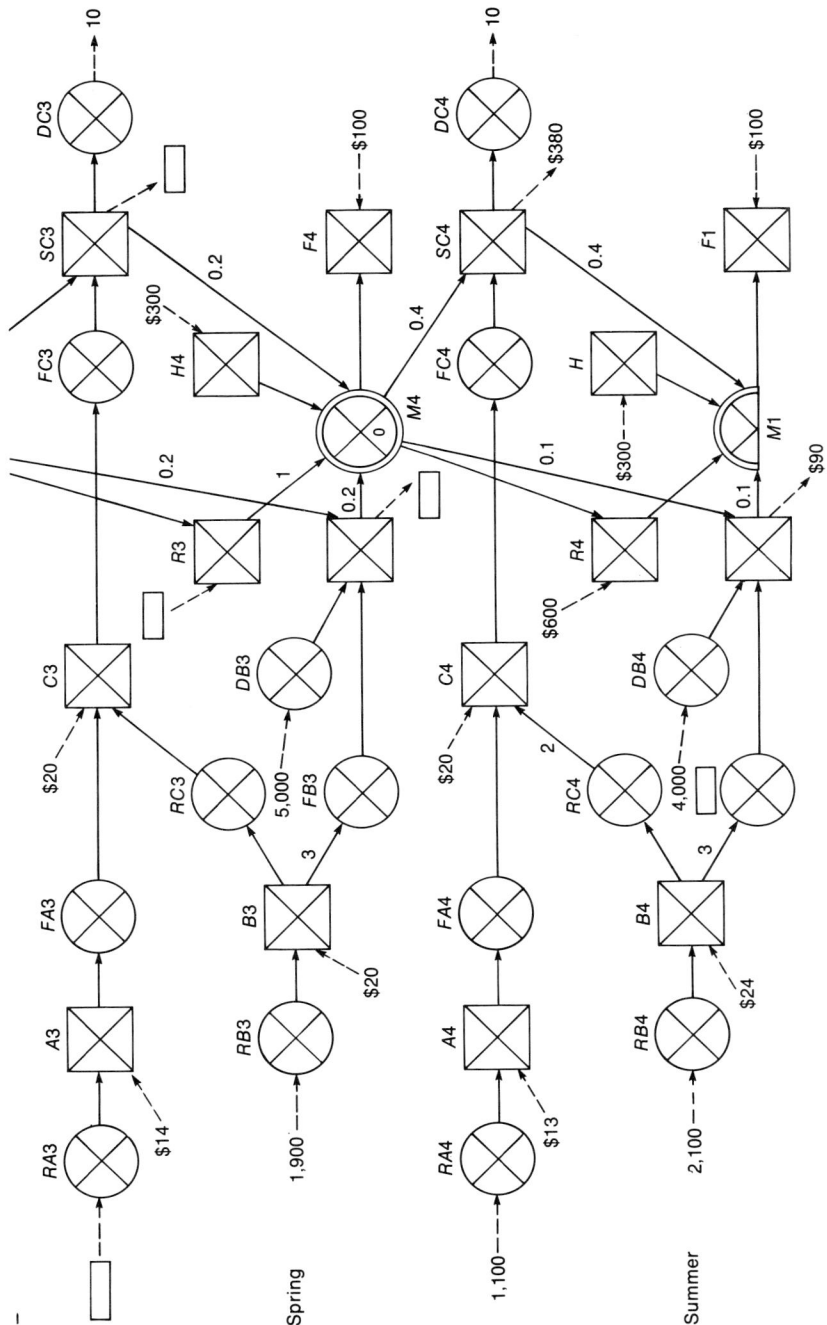

Figure 7-17 Partially filled R RPM network for Section 7-5 Tune-up.

materials *RA* into semifinished products *FA*; the Bonanza division transforms each ton of *RB* into three units of *FB*, which is marketed directly, and one unit of *RC*, which is used by the Colombo division; and the Colombo division uses one unit of *FA* and two units of *RC* to produce one unit of *FC*.

As an OR/MS analyst, you have been asked to analyze the scheduling of sales personnel engaged to market *FB* and *FC* for this vertically integrated company. Your predecessor, who was originally assigned this same task, collected data, partially formulated an RPM network (Figure 7-17), created a data file (Figure 7-18), and even obtained the results from a computer run (Figure 7-19). However, your predecessor

```
#COPY,I=1/R
    ROWS
    $PROFIT
    <RA1  <RA2  <RA3  <RA4  <RB1  <RB2  <RB3  <RB4  <RC1  <RC2  <RC3  <RC4
    =M1   =M2   =M3   =M4   <FC1  <FC2  <FC3  <FC4  <DB1  <DB2  <DB3  <DB4
    <FA1  <FA2  <FA3  <FA4  <FB1  <FB2  <FB3  <FB4  <DC1  <DC2  <DC3  <DC4
    COLUMNS
    A1  PROFIT  -10  RA1  1  FA1  -1
    A2  PROFIT  -12  RA2  1  FA2  -1
    A3  PROFIT  -14  RA3  1  FA3  -1
    A4  PROFIT  -13  RA4  1  FA4  -1
    B1  PROFIT  -30  RB1  1  RC1  -1  FB1  -3
    B2  PROFIT  -26  RB2  1  RC2  -1  FB2  -3
    B3  PROFIT  -20  RB3  1  RC3  -1  FB3  -3
    B4  PROFIT  -24  RB4  1  RC4  -1  FB4  -3
    C1  PROFIT  -20  FA1  1  RC1  2  FC1  -1
    C2  PROFIT  -20  FA2  1  RC2  2  FC2  -1
    C3  PROFIT  -20  FA3  1  RC3  2  FC3  -1
    C4  PROFIT  -20  FA4  1  RC4  2  FC4  -1
    SC1 PROFIT  360  FC1  1  M1  .2  M2  -.2  DC1 -1
    SC2 PROFIT  400  FC2  1  M2  .3  M3  -.3  DC2 -1
    SC3 PROFIT  400  FC3  1  M3  .2  M4  -.2  DC3 -1
    SC4 PROFIT  380  FC4  1  M4  .4  M1  -.4  DC4 -1
    SB1 PROFIT  100  FB1  1  M1  .1  M2  -.1  DB1 1
    SB2 PROFIT  90   FB2  1  M2  .1  M3  -.1  DB2 1
    SB3 PROFIT  100  FB3  1  M3  .2  M4  -.2  DB3 1
    SB4 PROFIT  90   FB4  1  M4  .1  M1  -.1  DB4 1
    H1  PROFIT  -300 M1  -1
    H2  PROFIT  -300 M2  -1
    H3  PROFIT  -300 M3  -1
    H4  PROFIT  -300 M4  -1
    F1  PROFIT  -100 M1  1
    F2  PROFIT  -100 M2  1
    F3  PROFIT  -100 M3  1
    F4  PROFIT  -100 M4  1
    R1  M1  1  M2  -1  PROFIT  -600
    R2  M2  1  M3  -1  PROFIT  -600
    R3  M3  1  M4  -1  PROFIT  -600
    R4  M4  1  M1  -1  PROFIT  -600
    RHS
    RESOURCE  RA1  1000  RB1  2000  DB1  5000
    RESOURCE  RA2  1200  RB2  1800  DB2  6000
    RESOURCE  RA3  1400  RB3  1900  DB3  5000
    RESOURCE  RA4  1100  RB4  2100  DB4  4000
    RESOURCE  DC1  -10   DC2  -10   DC3  -10  DC4 -10
    EOF
```

Figure 7-18 *REX input data file for Section 7-5 Tune-up.

```
**OU TREX
TITLE ==2-PHASE 3-PRODUCT MFG &SALES===
OBJ = PROFIT
RHS = RESOURCE
MAXIMUM = 2828050.000000
ROWS
PROFIT    72828050.0000002828050.000000*         -1.000000
RA1     B    1000.000000                         0
RA2     B     900.000000      300.000000         0
RA3     B     950.000000      450.000000         0
RA4     U    1050.000000       50.000000         0
RB1     B    2000.000000                         0       175.000000
RB2     U    1800.000000                         0       428.000000
RB3     U    1900.000000                         0       123.000000
RB4     U    2100.000000                         0       149.500000
RC1     U                                        0       205.000000
RC2     U                                        0       184.000000
RC3     U                                        0       143.000000
TIME OUT
#TIME                                                           } System
TIME 179.9 SECONDS   CFBLKS 12   MFBLKLIM 35                    } Interrupt
#TIME= 200
#GO
RC                        0                      0       173.500000
RA      U                 0                      0      -100.000000
M1      F                 0                      0       300.000000
M2      F                 0                      0       300.000000
M3      F                 0                      0      -100.000000
M4      F                 0                      0       440.000000
FC1     U                 0                      0       400.000000
FC2     U                 0                      0       320.000000
FC3     U                 0                      0       380.000000
FC4     U                 0                      0       140.000000
DB1     U   5000.000000   0                      0
DB2     B   5400.000000              600.000000  0
DB3     U   5000.000000   0                      0        20.000000
DB4     U   4000.000000   0                      0        90.000000
FA1     U                 0                      0        10.000000
FA2     U                 0                      0        12.000000
FA3     U                 0                      0        14.000000
FA4     U                 0                      0        13.000000
```

FB1	B	-1000.000000| 1000.000000	0
FB2	U	0	90.000000
FB3	B	-700.000000| 700.000000	0
FB4	B	-2300.000000| 2300.000000	0
DC1	B	-1000.000000| 990.000000	0
DC2	B	-900.000000| 890.000000	0
DC3	B	-950.000000| 940.000000	0
DC4	B	-1050.000000| 1040.000000	0
COLUMNS
A1	B	1000.000000	-10.000000	0
A2	B	900.000000	-12.000000	0
A3	B	950.000000	-14.000000	0
A4	B	1050.000000	-13.000000	0
B1	B	2000.000000	-30.000000	0
B2	B	1800.000000	-26.000000	0
B3	B	1900.000000	-20.000000	0
B4	B	2100.000000	-24.000000	0
C1	B	900.000000	-20.000000	0
C2	B	950.000000	-20.000000	0
C3	B	1050.000000	360.000000	0
C4	B	1000.000000	400.000000	0
SC1	B	950.000000	400.000000	0
SC2	B	1050.000000	380.000000	0
SC3	B	5000.000000	100.000000	0
SC4	B	5400.000000	90.000000	0
SB1	B	5000.000000	90.000000	0
SB2	B	4000.000000	-300.000000	0
SB3	L		-300.000000	0
SB4	B	110.000000	-300.000000	0
H1	B	380.000000	-100.000000 |400.000000	0
H2	L		-100.000000
H3	B	120.000000	-100.000000 |400.000000	0
H4	L		-100.000000 |400.000000	0
F1	B	370.000000	-600.000000 |200.000000	0
F2	L		-600.000000 |600.000000	0
F3	L		-600.000000 |1000.000000	0
F4	L		-600.000000 |600.000000	0
EOF
```

Figure 7-19   *REX output for Section 7-5 Tune-up.
```

was transferred to the South Pole and is now assigned to a crash program to discover untapped oil and mineral sources deep under the ice. You have been cautioned against bothering your predecessor, lest you wish to end up in the Antarctic expedition also.

You know that the availability of raw materials RA and RB is seasonal, and so are the costs of processing them. The selling prices for FB and FC are also seasonal and require different amounts of sales personnel time (ranging from 0.1 man-quarter to 0.4 man-quarter per unit product). The wages of the sales personnel have already been deducted from the sales revenues for selling C (SC) and B (SB), but it will cost $600 per quarter to retain a sales person R who is not needed for marketing. A sales person M can be hired H or fired F at the beginning of each quarter for the added costs of $300 and $100, respectively. No inventory is allowed because of the perishable nature of the products, and the company is committed to supplying 10 units (DC) of FC every quarter to the government at the prevailing market price. Otherwise, there is no limit on the market potential of FC. FB, on the other hand, competes with other companies' products, and the sales limits have been forecasted for the four seasons to 5,000 (fall), 6,000 (winter), 5,000 (spring), and 4,000 (summer); $DB =$ limits on SB. All items are expressed in units or dollars, except M, H, F, and R, which are in man-quarters and RB and B which are in tons. A, B, and C refer to the activity levels of the three divisions, and the numerals 1, 2, 3, 4 refer to fall, winter, spring, and summer quarters.

1. Using the data file printout (Figure 7-18), fill in any missing entries in the RPM network (Figure 7-17). (Missing coefficients, constants, and node labels are indicated, and you can assume that the data file is correct.)

2. Using the *REX printout (Figure 7-19), enter all primal and dual values in your network (Figure 7-17), and identify basic paths with a colored pencil.

3. Complete the following table for the sales organization:

	Fall (1)	Winter (2)	Spring (3)	Summer (4)
Newly hired sales personnel				
Newly fired sales personnel				
Total sales force during quarter				
Sales personnel marketing B				
Sales personnel marketing C				
Sales personnel idle				

4. (a) If a salesperson quits voluntarily (without incurring the cost of firing of $100) at the beginning of a quarter, what action should the company take and how much would it cost? (Give answers for all four seasons.)

   (b) Another company is interested in purchasing your product FA at $100 per unit. Should your company sell it? For which seasons?

   (c) The company fears that unionization will stop its hiring and firing practices and force it to retain sales personnel even when they are idle. What would this cost the company per salesperson?

(d) If it were possible to keep one of the products *FA*, *FB*, *RC*, or *FC* over one quarter in inventory, which product and which season would you choose?

7-6 Potpourri: traditional LP paradigms

Product mix, blending, diet, games, personnel staffing, and scheduling are among the applications of linear programming we have already studied. These applications are *paradigms*, or typical LP prototype models, which are often used by OR/MS analysts to build modeling skills and to illustrate the versatility of linear programming for solving a wide variety of practical problems. Many other applications will be treated in subsequent chapters, as we examine the various algorithms that are available for solving RPMS models. But the primary objective of this book is to help the reader become a confident OR/MS model-builder who can turn actual problematic situations into OR/MS models, solve them manually or using a computer, and interpret the solutions thoroughly by utilizing all pertinent information that is available. If you have not already done so, we strongly encourage you to pick a problem (either from your own experience or from reading or talking with people) and begin building your own C & E diagrams and RPM networks.

To encourage such endeavors, several more LP paradigms are presented in Examples 7-3 to 7-5 to widen the scope of LP and RPMS applications. In each example the paradigm is explained briefly and is accompanied by an RPM network that already includes a solution from a computer run of LINPRO or *REX. Many solutions are degenerate, which means that you may find alternative optimal and feasible solutions that are equally valid, most of which can be derived by juggling a few flows in the solution that is given. The optimal objective-function value should be the same for all degenerate solutions.

Example 7-3: Trim loss at the Jabberwocky Company Steel mills, pulp and paper plants, and aluminum sheet manufacturers usually have one problem in common: They produce long continuous sheets of a standard width that are made into rolls of a standard size. These standard-rolls must be cut into rolls of different widths as required by the customers. It is not uncommon for a plant to have to deliver its products in hundreds of different specifications as orders vary from day to day. Since most combinations of desired widths produce trim loss, it is customary for many plants to make use of linear programming to create optimal cutting schedules every morning. Some companies have customized programs while others use standard, or "canned," programs such as LINPRO and MPS. The objective is to minimize trim loss.

Let us consider the case of Jabberwocky Company, which specializes in the production of gift-wrapping paper. The paper is produced in rolls 60 in wide and weighing 120 lb, which are cut into rolls of 40-in, 25-in, and 14-in widths, weighing 80, 50, and 28 lb, respectively. Let us say that on one particular day there are orders for 1,600 rolls of 40-in width, 1,500 rolls of 25-in width, and 3,000 rolls of

(a) Four combinations for cutting rolls.

	Combinations				Demand	
	A	B	C	D	(lbs)	(rolls)
40 in rolls	1	0	0	0	128,000	1,600
25 in rolls	0	2	1	0	79,000	1,500
14 in rolls	1	0	2	4	84,000	3,000
Total width cut (in)	54	50	53	56		
Original width (in)	60	60	60	60		
Trim loss (in)	6	10	7	4		

(b) Combination C illustrated.

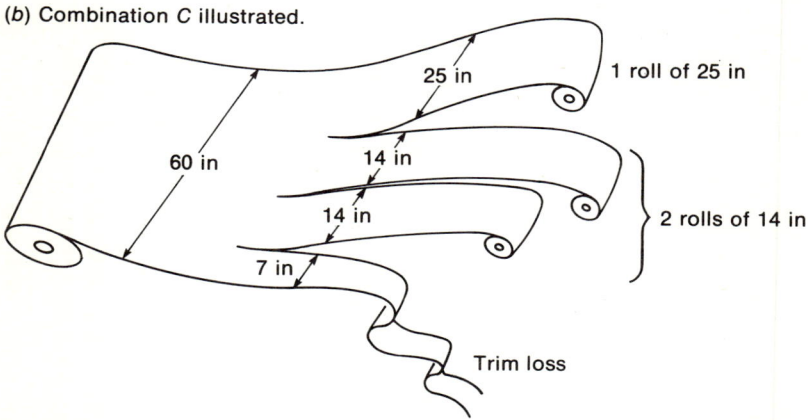

Figure 7-20 Cutting paper rolls to yield one day's orders at the Jabberwocky Company.

14-in width. There are four different combinations yielding these three rolls, and they are tabulated in Figure 7-20a; combination C is shown pictorially in Figure 7-20b.

Figure 7-21 is an RPM network representing the optimum cutting schedule for this particular day's orders. We cut 2,700 standard rolls 60 in wide; 1,600 rolls according to combination A, yielding 1,600 rolls 40 in wide and 1,600 rolls 14 in wide; 750 rolls according to combination B, yielding 3,000 rolls 25 in wide; and 350 rolls according to combination D, yielding 1,400 rolls 14 in wide. The respective trim losses are 1,600 rolls 6 in wide, 750 rolls 10 in wide, and 350 rolls 4 in wide, the total equivalent of 18,500 1-in rolls. Another schedule could have increased the trim loss, and no other schedule would reduce it.

The dual values in this RPM network are given in terms of trim loss. The 40-in rolls are charged with 5 in out of the 6-in trim loss for combination A, the remaining 1 in being charged to 14-in rolls. Each 25-in roll is charged 5 in trim loss, giving $2 \times 5 = 10$ in total trim loss for combination B. The double zeros in C indicate that that variable is degenerate and that the combination C could have been brought into the solution without increasing the total trim loss. These dual values can help the management decide how much of the trim loss should be charged to each product. For example, a customer buying a 40-in roll could be charged for the cost of discarding an additional 5 in while a customer buying a 14-in roll could be charged only for a 1-in trim loss.

Example 7-4: Humpty Dumpty Trading Company: a case of arbitrage Arbitrage is the business of profiting from unequal prices and availability of securities, commodities, money, or other resources in different markets by simultaneously buying, selling, or exchanging the goods and currencies. The goods that are traded don't even have to exist yet. For example, agricultural products are commonly traded in "futures" with notes promising delivery when a commodity is harvested; some grains and feeds have had their futures sold several years in advance. However, the scarcity of energy and resources tends to aggravate market conditions, and some petroleum products, for example, may no longer be bought with money alone but must be exchanged with other scarce resources.

Examples of such international trading practices are plentiful. For instance, if you know that a certain type of plastic resin costs more in one country than in another, you could transact simultaneous purchase and sales, and profit from your arbitrage, provided that you have enough margin to absorb the transportation, taxes, and other incidental expenses. The simultaneous purchase of foreign currencies, such as Hong Kong dollars, British pounds, German deutsche marks, and Japanese yens, may have a similar effect. Sometimes, an arbitrator may be forced to purchase or trade several commodities, both for spot and future deliveries, all at once in a package deal. For example, one may buy silk in China,

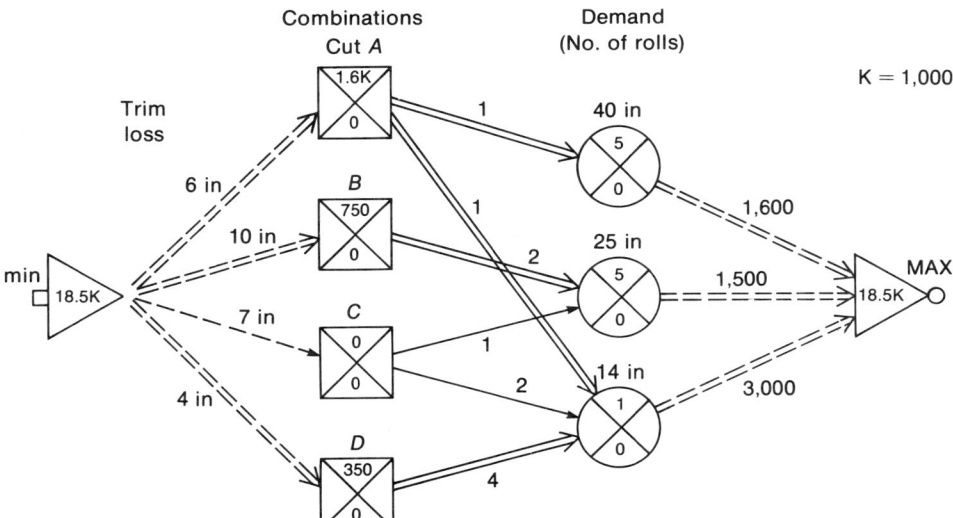

Figure 7-21 Optimal cutting schedule for the Jabberwocky Company. K = 1,000.

sell wheat there, trade silk and United States dollars for crude oil and naphtha in Saudi Arabia, sell crude oil in Europe and buy wine there, and sell wine and naptha in Canada for cash plus wheat.

Humpty Dumpty Trading Company is an arbitrator. On one particular day, it receives information for the following possible transactions. There are four commodities I, II, III, and IV which can be sold for $40, $10, $5, and $20/ton, respectively. The company has in possession rights to 100 tons of commodities of III and IV, and there is an offer to trade (at no cost) 1 ton of commodity IV into 1.1 tons of commodity II and 2 tons of I. The company has also been approached by another trading firm that wants to sell 1.2 tons of commodity I and 1 ton of III in exchange for 1 ton of commodity II, 2 tons of IV, and $10. These offers are unlimited in quantities, and the company must decide what to sell and how much, and what to trade. The transactions can be summarized in a table:

Resource	Transaction						Amount on hand
	A	B	C	D	E	F	
U. S. dollars	40	10	5	20	0	−10	We can borrow any amount
Commodity I, tons	−1	0	0	0	2	1.2	0
Commodity II, tons	0	−1	0	0	1.1	−1	0
Commodity III, tons	0	0	−1	0	0	1	100
Commodity IV, tons	0	0	0	−1	−1	−2	100

Figure 7-22 illustrates these arbitrage transactions in an RPM network. The solution indicates a profit of $4,725.8065 from four simultaneous transactions:

F: Pay $322.581, 64.6 tons of commodity IV (on hand), and 32.2581 tons of commodity II (not on hand but which can be obtained from *E*) for 38.70972 tons of commodity I and 32.2581 tons of III.

E: Exchange the entire remaining commodity IV (35.4893 tons) for 70.9678 tons of commodity I and 39.03229 tons of II.

A: Sell 109.6774 tons of commodity I for $4,387.096.

C: Sell 132.2581 tons of commodity III for $661.2905.

Net profit = $4,387.096 + $661.2905 − $322.581 minus the cost of commodities III and IV on hand.

The numerical values should be rounded off to significant digits that are practical, as in Figure 7-22, but the exact figures are given here to facilitate comparison with solutions obtained from another computer or another program.

Figure 7-22 is significant in that linear programming has imputed the values of resources that can be used in future management decision-making. It may be obvious that 1 ton of commodity I is worth $40 since that is the trading value, but commodity II is worth $37.70/ton instead of the $10/ton price tag. In other words, if transaction *B* were reversible, the Humpty Dumpty Trading Company should

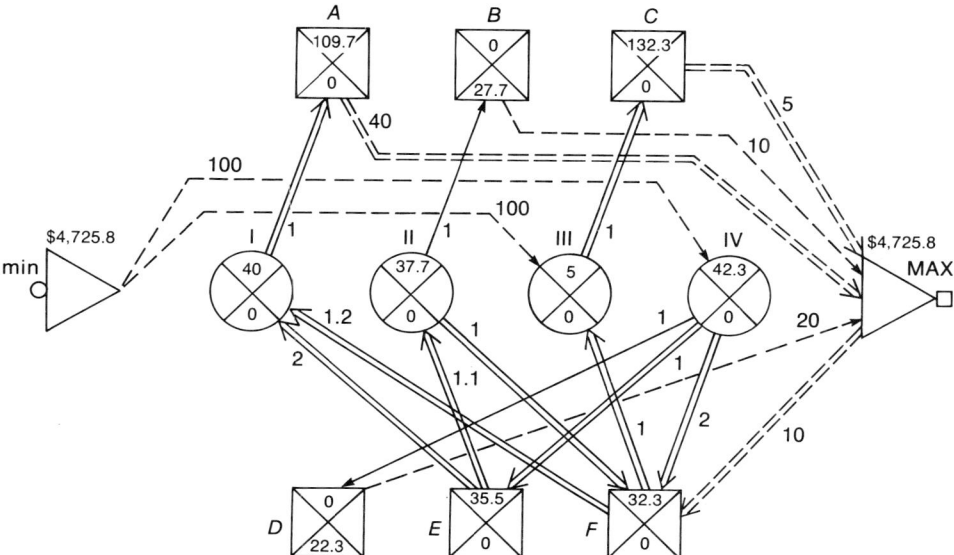

Figure 7-22 RPM network showing arbitrage by the Humpty Dumpty Trading Company. (Numerical values have been rounded off.)

buy commodity II at $10/ton and gain $27.74 for each ton of transaction. Putting it another way, we can use this program to assess the values of resources at hand and the insurance values that should be carried on the goods. Each ton of commodity III is worth $5, and we have 100 tons of it, or $500 total value; each ton of commodity IV is worth $42.2581, and we also have 100 tons, or $4,225.81 total value. Summing the two values, we obtain $4,725.81, the same revenue figure computed from the primal values. If more money than this was originally spent to acquire these resources, the company may have lost money; otherwise it will profit by the transactions.

Example 7-5 Wonder River sewage-treatment program Wonder Valley is crisscrossed by Wonder River and its two tributaries, Tweedledum and Tweedledee. Five cities are located on this tributary system; Aurora, Baker, Cornvallis, Dallas, and Eastport. These communities discharge wastes into the river system but are now being asked by the Wonderland government to submit a consolidated plan for building sewage-treatment plants. Because of the distance involved, it is necessary to build a plant in each community and/or discharge the waste into the river. Individual cities must cooperate to satisfy specific biochemical oxygen demand (BOD) levels at minimum cost. Neglecting waste decomposition in the river, the following data were obtained. See Figure 7-23.

Assuming that each plant, if built, will be able to handle 100 percent of BOD that it processes, and that the waste may be discharged into the river system as

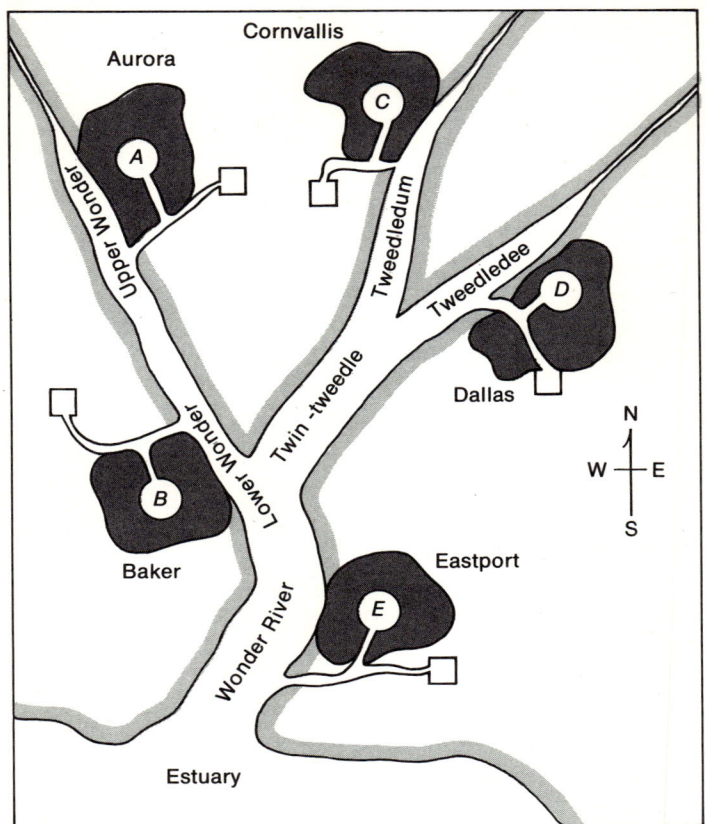

City	BOD load waste discharged by the community, lb/day	Sewage plant treatment cost, $/lb of BOD	Streamflow at the city, ft³/sec	Maximum BOD in stream, lb/ft³	Maximum BOD pounds allowed in the river, lb/day
Aurora	2,200	.18	3.2	0.0012	332
Baker	800	.22	3.6	0.0012	373
Cornvallis	2,000	.16	4.5	0.0010	389
Dallas	500	.25	5.0	0.0015	648
Eastport	1,200	.20	13.1	0.0013	1,452

Maximum allowable Twin-tweedle river BOD is 829 lb/day.

Figure 7-23 Wonder Valley river system.

long as the maximum tolerable BOD is not violated in each segment of the system, the five cities wish to find the optimum construction and operation schedule. (At the present time Cornvallis is the only city committed to building a sewage plant, but this commitment is for a plant that would process 1000 lb/day of BOD.)

Figure 7-24 is an RPM network depicting this situation. The solution indicates that Aurora and Cornvallis should process all their wastes and not dump any into the river; Dallas should dump the entire 500 lb/day of BOD into Tweedledee; and Baker and Eastport should process portions of their wastes and dump the rest into Wonder River. Note that equality nodes were used to avoid having residue pile up without flowing downstream. Because of the equality constraints, we find many negative dual values that are legitimate. (This use of equality also means that the normative model could have been simplified considerably; doing so, however, would have greatly impaired the visual appeal of the network.)

Linear programs similar to the one in Example 7-5 can be written to design the loads of air-conditioning, heating, and ventilating equipment for a large building. Such a building may have different heating and cooling requirements depending on the time of the day, the weather, and whether or not the machinery inside the building (say, a large computer or an array of keypunchers) is working.

Similar LP models can be designed to solve traffic problems. For example, the Meihanshin Expressway in Japan has gates that control inputs of traffic onto its expressway system. The gates monitor the traffic continuously and forecast expressway occupancy rates using a linear programming model. From the occupancy rates at various points on the expressway system, it is possible to predict the time it will take for a vehicle entering any ramp to reach its destination. When the expressway is congested, motorists are discouraged from entering the expressway by seeing on an indicator panel that it will probably take longer to reach their destination on the expressway than by using the regular highways. (The linear programming model used in this system was formulated in the late 1960's by H. Mine and T. Hasegawa, professors at Kyoto University.)

7-7 Double Trouble: Common Problems and Cures

A linear programming model must be *linear* and *programmable*. Although it is a very versatile and powerful tool, it also has limitations. When we violate these limitations, we shall either fail to obtain a solution or obtain a solution that is not appropriate.

LINEARITY ASSUMPTION Four major limitations of LP models result from the linearity assumption: continuity, proportionality, additivity, and linearity of the objective function. *Continuity* implies that a variable may assume any nonnegative fractional value between zero and positive infinity (and even this nonnegativity may be relaxed by using a free variable). Thus, it is possible for the solution to indicate that 1.333 persons should be hired and 0.01 unit of some product should be produced. When linear programming is modified to encourage variables to assume discrete values only, it is called *discrete programming*; when the values are restricted to integers (0, 1, 2, . . .), it is called *integer programming;* finally, when only 0 and 1 are allowed as possible values, it is called *0–1* (*zero-one*) *programming*.

Proportionality means that all relations are linear when plotted on a graph; nonlinear relationships must be approximated by piecewise linear relationships,

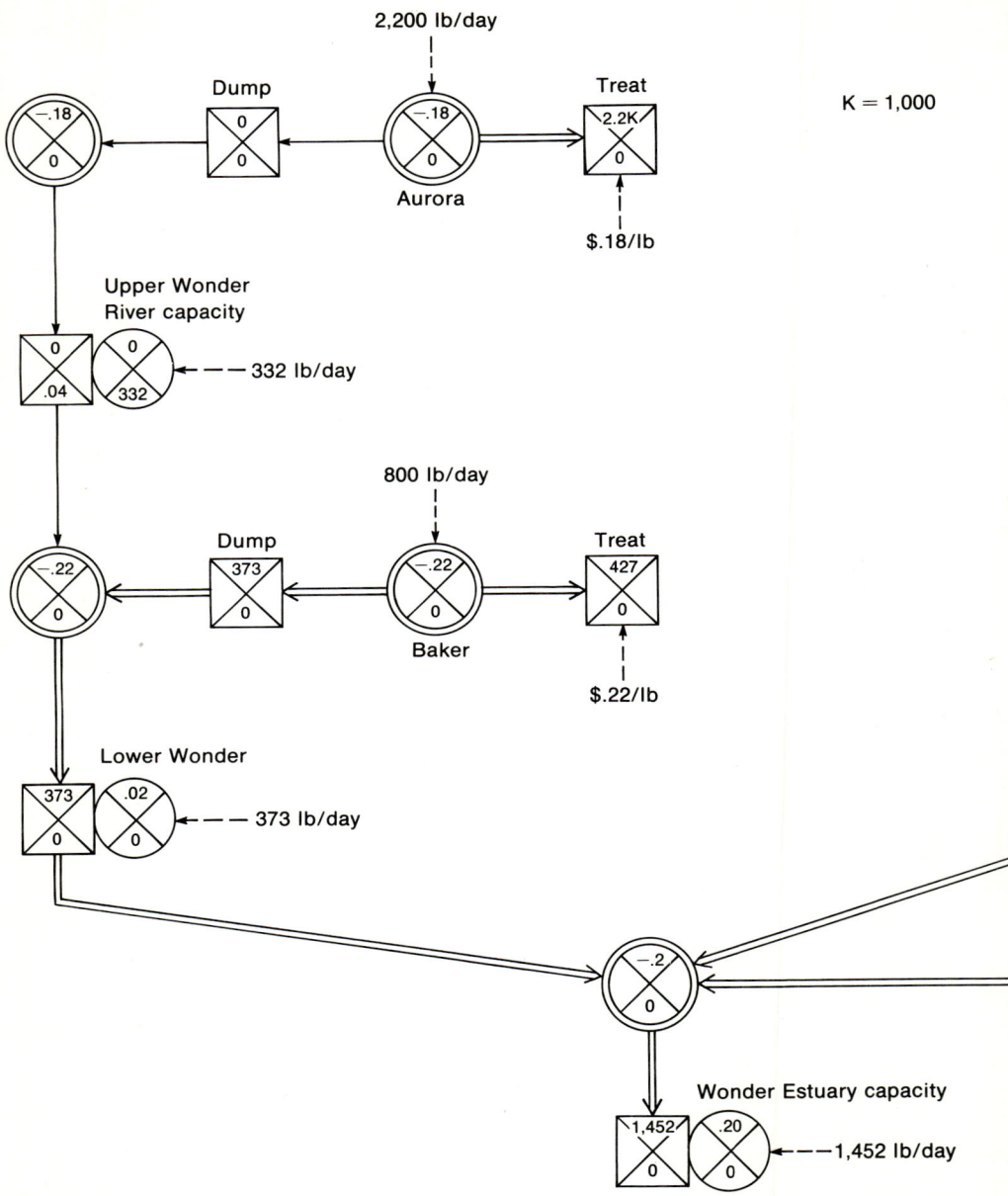

Figure 7-24 RPM network for the Wonder River sewage treatment program. K = 1,000.

Applied Normative Models: Linear Programming Paradigms 183

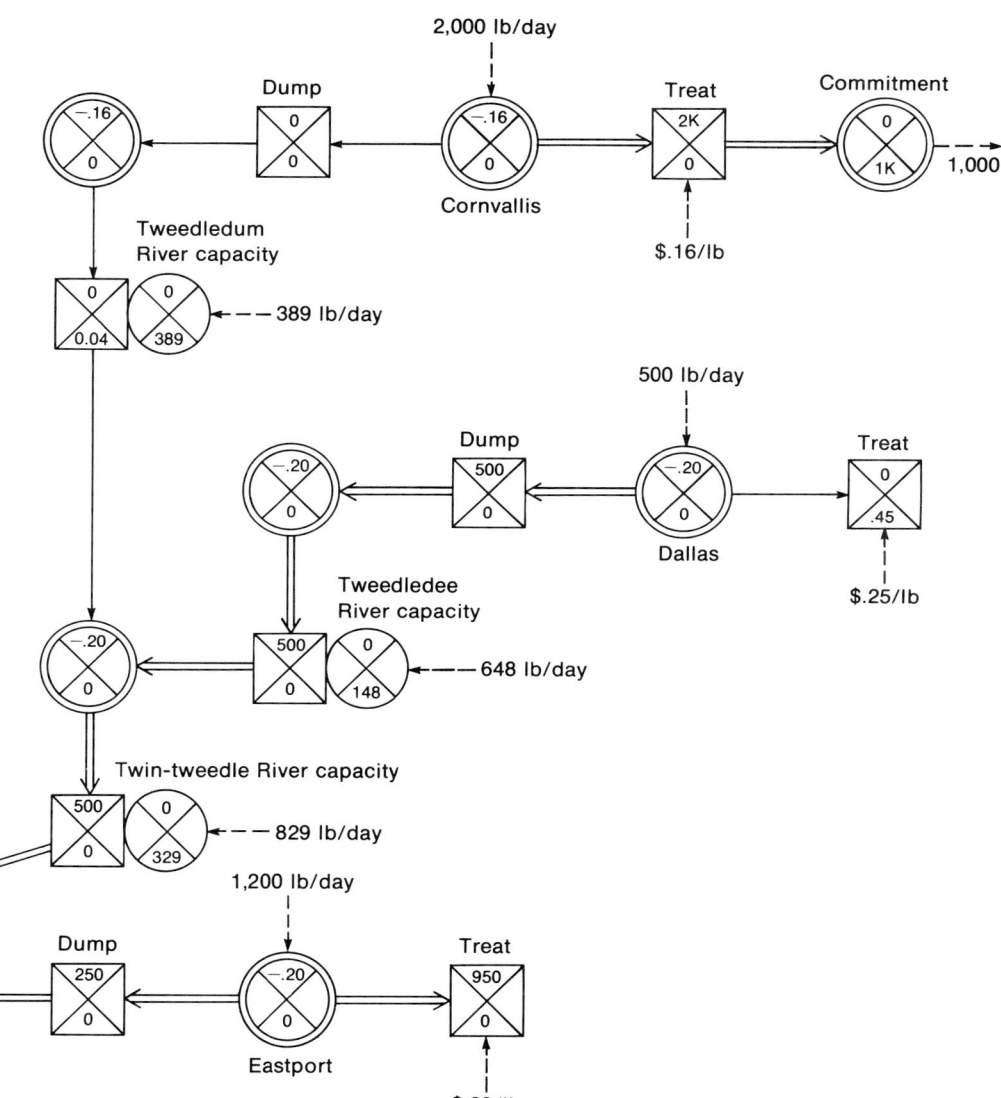

or a set of overlapping constraints and processes. These relationships must all be deterministic; that is, once a process has assumed a positive value, all input and output flows must be realized at the rates indicated on the arrows—no more and no less.

Additivity implies that all flows into a resource node must be homogeneous and indistinguishable. If two different resources, times, or locations are involved, these must be indicated by two different resource nodes.

Linearity of the objective function assumes that tradeoffs are possible among processes as to their contribution to the objective function. If two processes have two irreconcilable types of contributions, we must make one into a constraint and keep the other as the objective function, or follow the Goal Programming approach of optimizing one objective at a time.[1] Paretian optimality is a nice ideal, but it is not necessarily feasible. To realize Paretian optimality, we must set the minimum requirement for all resources to some low values so that there are surplus resources to be allocated according to merits beyond the basic needs. Moreover, we must also have a scheme that would evaluate each individual's merits fairly, and try to satisfy each one's desire equally and impartially. The existence of such a mathematical expression is precisely the requirement of the objective function. In order to be modeled by a linear program, such an expression must also be linear.

PROGRAMMABILITY ASSUMPTION Unfortunately OR/MS novices tend to build gigantic models before mastering the basics completely, then they become frustrated when the computer indicates either an *unbounded* or a *nonfeasible* solution.

Unbounded solutions occur when a model is allowed to grow indefinitely. This could occur in two ways: by missing .LE. constraints in a maximization program or by having positive feedback that is not capacitated. Figure 7-25 shows an extreme case of each and how it can be remedied.

Nonfeasible solutions occur when we request the RPMS to model an impossible situation. This can occur either by not giving an adequate amount of exogenous input to meet the demand imposed by the endogenous output or by inadvertently reversing the arrow direction along the path, discontinuing the flow between the input to the required output. In a primal maximization problem, an inclusion of a .GE. or .EQ. constraint is usually the cause; in a primal minimization problem, an inclusion of an .LE. or .EQ. constraint is usually the cause. The remedy is simple: Include only .LE. constraints in the first run of a primal maximization problem and only .GE. constraints in the first run of a primal minimization problem. These conditions are also portrayed in Figure 7-25.

Max-flow min-cut theorem We began this chapter by reviewing old rules for RPMS, and we shall conclude it by introducing a well-known theorem in OR/MS, *the max-flow min-cut theorem*.[2]

[1] Sang M. Lee, *Goal Programming*, Auerbach, N.Y., 1972.
[2] L. R. Ford, Jr., and D. R. Fulkerson, *Flows in Networks*, Princeton Univ. Press, New Jersey, 1962, p. 11.

(a) Unbounded B will keep increasing Y_1 to A also. No limit to Z_x.

(b) Growth of B attested by Y_3. Z_x is now finite.

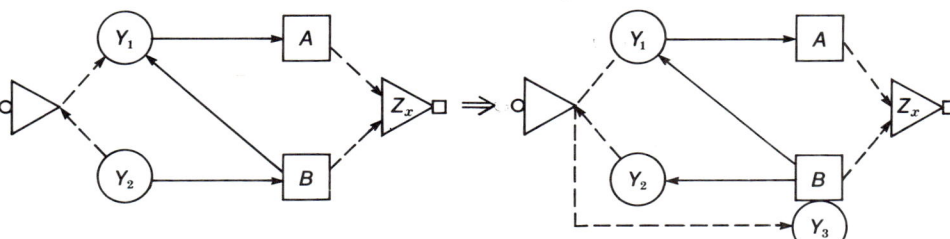

(c) Unbounded due to positive feedback that is not capacitated.

(d) Growth attested by the capacitation of the feedback. Y_3 could be at A instead of B.

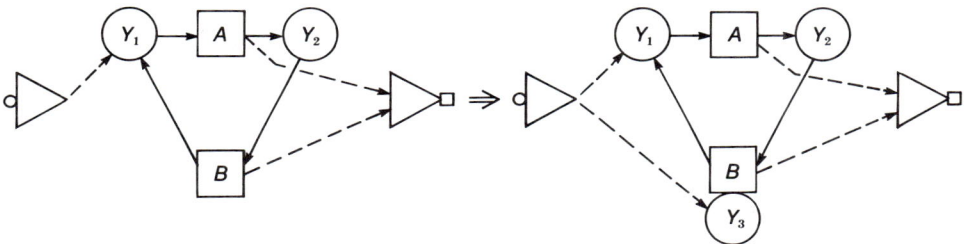

(e) No feasible solution. A nonnegative A cannot satisfy need at Y_2.

(f) Feasibility restored. A can now meet needs at Y_2.

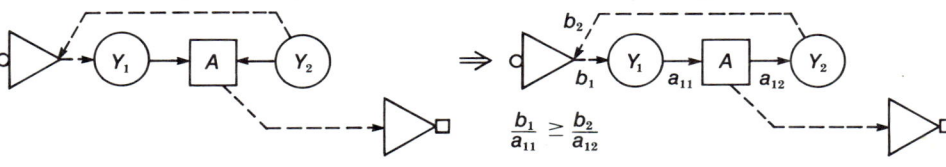

$$\frac{b_1}{a_{11}} \geq \frac{b_2}{a_{12}}$$

(g) No feasible solution. A nonnegative C cannot satisfy demand at Y_2.

(h) Feasibility restored.

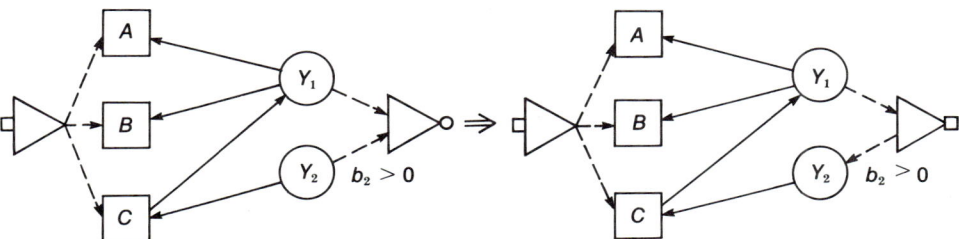

Figure 7-25 Examples of unbounded and nonfeasible solutions.

186 Introduction to Operations Research and Management Science

Max-flow min-cut theorem: For any network the maximal flow value from its source terminal to the sink terminal is equal to the minimal cut capacity of all cuts separating the two terminals.

This theorem provides a tool for quickly checking unbounded or nonfeasible-solution problems. In the case of a planar graph, that is, a network where arrows do not crisscross, the set of cuts can be found easily, forming a new network, the *cut-set* network (called the *dual network* by electrical engineers). This network is created by identifying each spatial division by a node and connecting it with other similar nodes by arrows that cross arrows on the original network. Corresponding to the two terminals on the original network, we also have two nodes on each half of the environment as we would have it divided by connecting the two original terminals together. The direction of the new arrows must relate to the direction of the arrow it is crossing. These conventions are illustrated in Figure 7-26.

It is interesting to observe that cut-set networks made from inherently unbounded or nonfeasible-solution RPM networks contain feedback loops. The efforts made to regain bounds or feasibility result in networks that have minimum cuts. Figure 7-27 illustrates cut-set networks created from the four RPM networks of Figure 7-25. Figure 7-27*a*, which contains an unrestricted flow path in Figure 7-25*a*, becomes a cut-set network with a feedback loop (4-3-2-4) resembling the unbounded feedback of the original Figure 7-25*c*. The attempt (Figure 7-25*b*) to restore an upper bound (Y_3) is translated to the cut-set network (Figure 7-27*b*) by the breaking of the loop. Similar observations can be made for other cases.[1]

The max-flow min-cut theorem can be used directly to solve capacitated-flow problems where all coefficients are unity and no conversion is needed to compare one cut path with another. What is more important, however, is to learn a formalized way of looking at our intuitive reasoning approach. Tracing the primal path through the original network to identify a feasible solution is really an application of what Ford and Fulkerson called *labeling*, and this approach is sometimes used as the starting point in dynamic programming. Although the primal flows are being determined in these situations, we must constantly keep track of the cut-set structure by asking the question "How can we circumvent our bottlenecks (i.e., capacitating cuts) and improve the overall flows?"

TUNE-UP SOLUTIONS

Section 7-2

Shipping from North-West point to Micropolis is capacitated between 100 to 200 tons/mo at a cost of $30/ton. From Port San Angelos to Eastport, we can ship any

---

[1]The actual computation of a min-cut value must be delayed until all coefficients in the model are determined, but it has been helpful to show that some structures are inherently unbounded or nonfeasible regardless of what coefficient values may be assigned to the arrows.

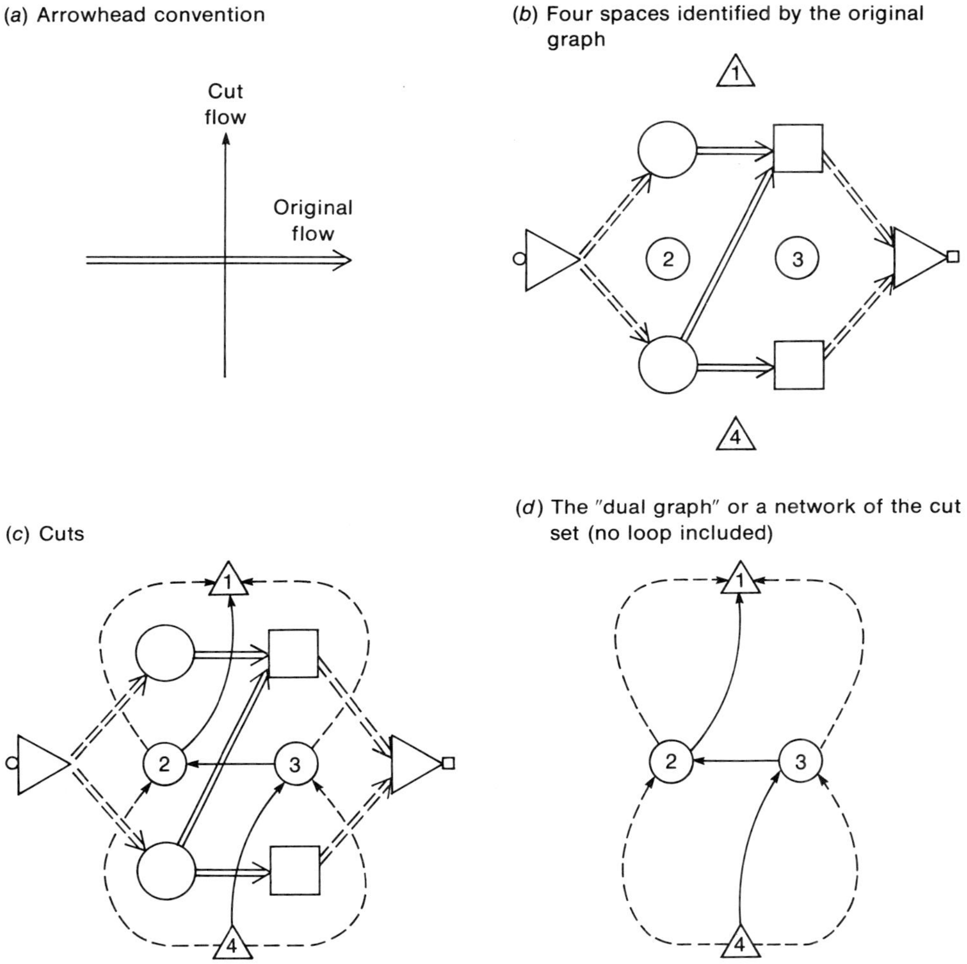
(a) Arrowhead convention
Cut flow
Original flow
(b) Four spaces identified by the original graph
1
2
3
4
(c) Cuts
1
2
3
4
(d) The "dual graph" or a network of the cut set (no loop included)
1
2
3
4

Figure 7-26 Developing the cut-set network from an original RPM network.

amount up to 350 tons/mo at $60/ton, and we are obligated to ship at least 100 tons/mo from Port San Angelos to Keysouth at $60/ton. From Micropolis to Eastport, we can ship any amount at $20/ton, and the flow can be reversed by letting goods flow from Eastport to Micropolis at an *income* of $20/ton. This income is the result of having to reverse *all* arrowheads when using a negative value for a free variable. We were not asked to solve this problem, but a solution is easily obtained by trial and error as shown in Figure 7-28.

Section 7-3

(See Figure 7-29.)

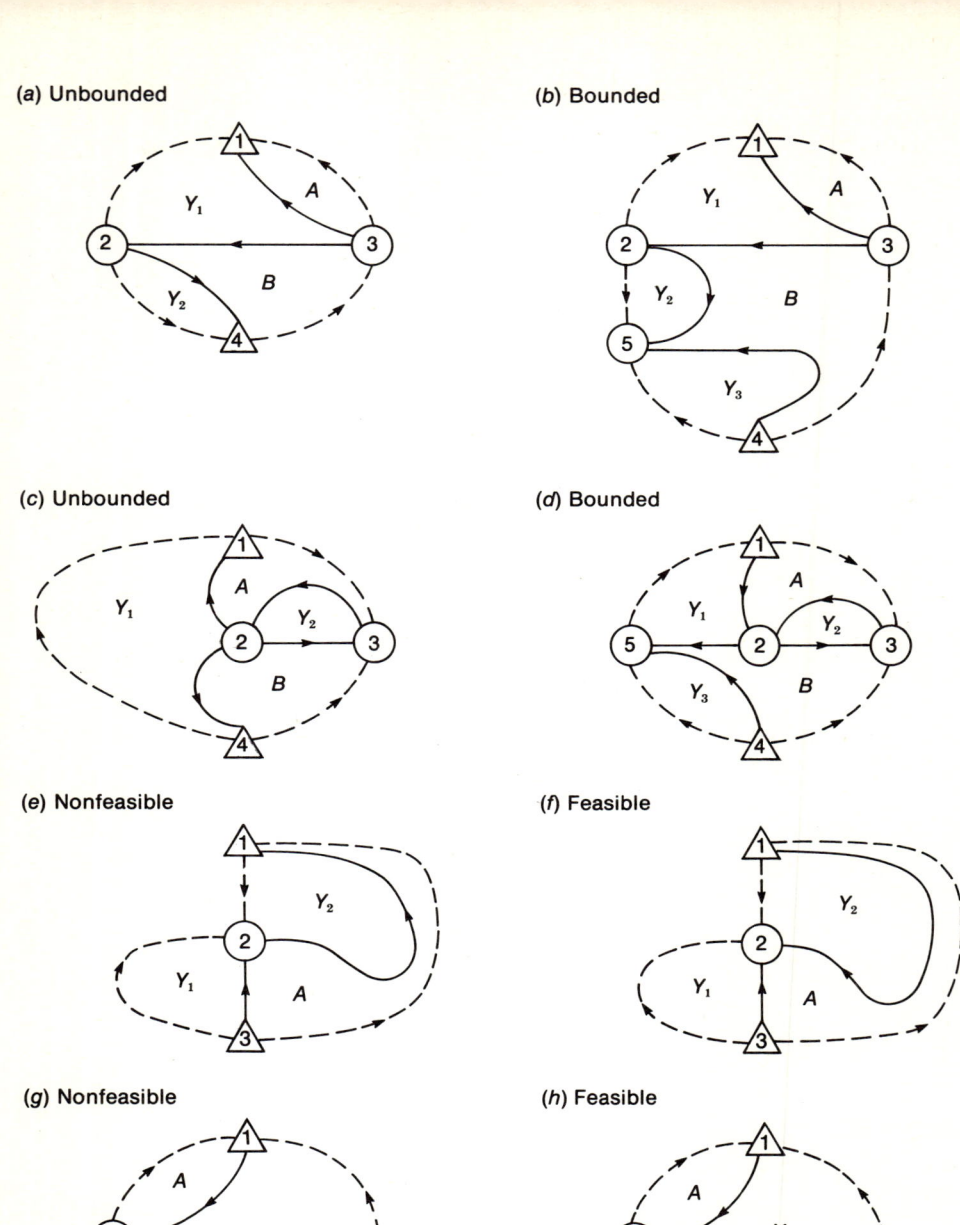

Figure 7-27 Cut-set networks for the unbounded and nonfeasible networks of Figure 7-25.

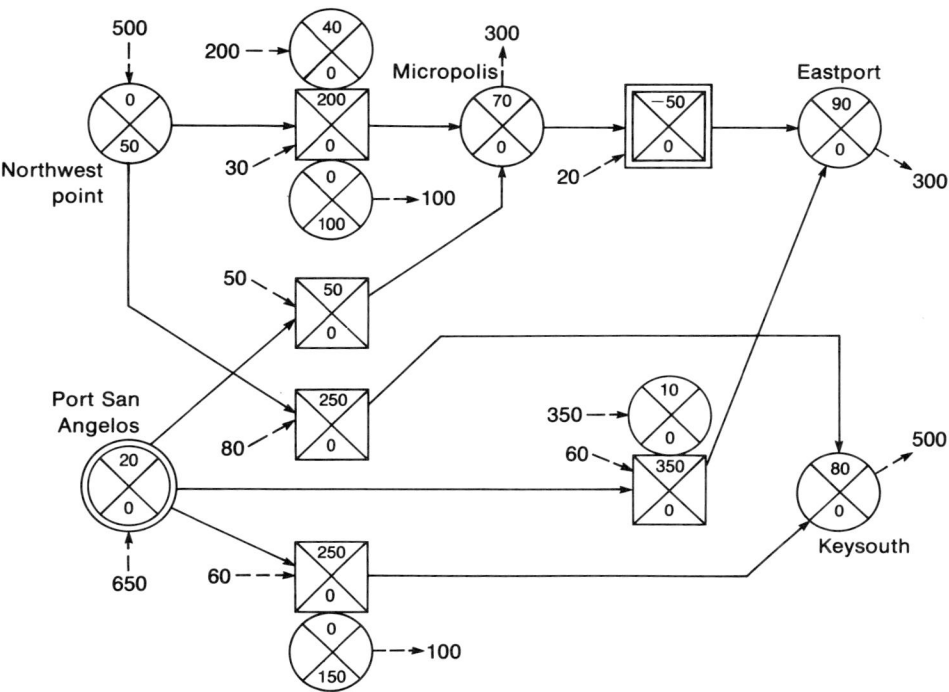

Figure 7-28 RPM network solution for Section 7-2 Tune-up.

Section 7-4

(Note that E now has a technological constraint Y_7 attached to it in Figure 7-30.)

Section 7-5

1 and 2.

3.

	Fall ($j = 1$)	Winter ($j = 2$)	Spring ($j = 3$)	Summer ($j = 4$)
Newly hired sales personnel (H_j)	0	110	380	0
Newly fired sales personnel (F_j)	120	0	0	370
Total sales force during quarter $= SB_j + SC_j + R_j$	$820 - 120 = 700$	$700 + 110 = 810$	$810 + 380 = 1{,}190$	$1{,}190 - 370 = 820$
Sales personnel marketing B [(SB_j) × coefficient]	$5{,}000 \times 0.1$	$5{,}400 \times 0.1$	$5{,}000 \times 0.2$	$4{,}000 \times 0.1$
Sales personnel marketing C [(SC_j) × coefficient]	$1{,}000 \times 0.2$	900×0.3	950×0.2	$1{,}050 \times 0.4$
Sales personnel idle (R_j)	0	0	0	0

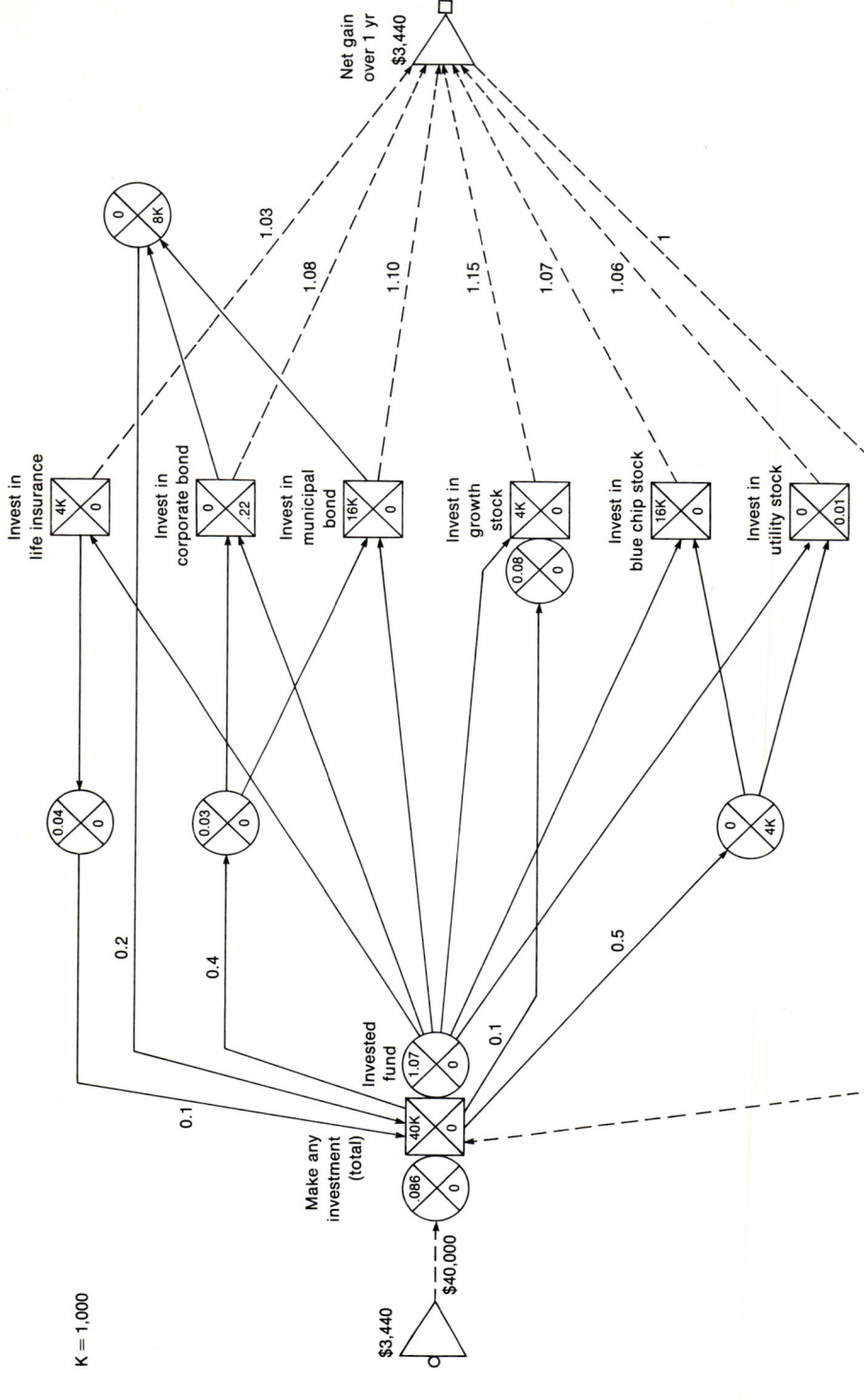

Figure 7-29 RPM network solution for Section 7-3 Tune-up. K = 1,000.

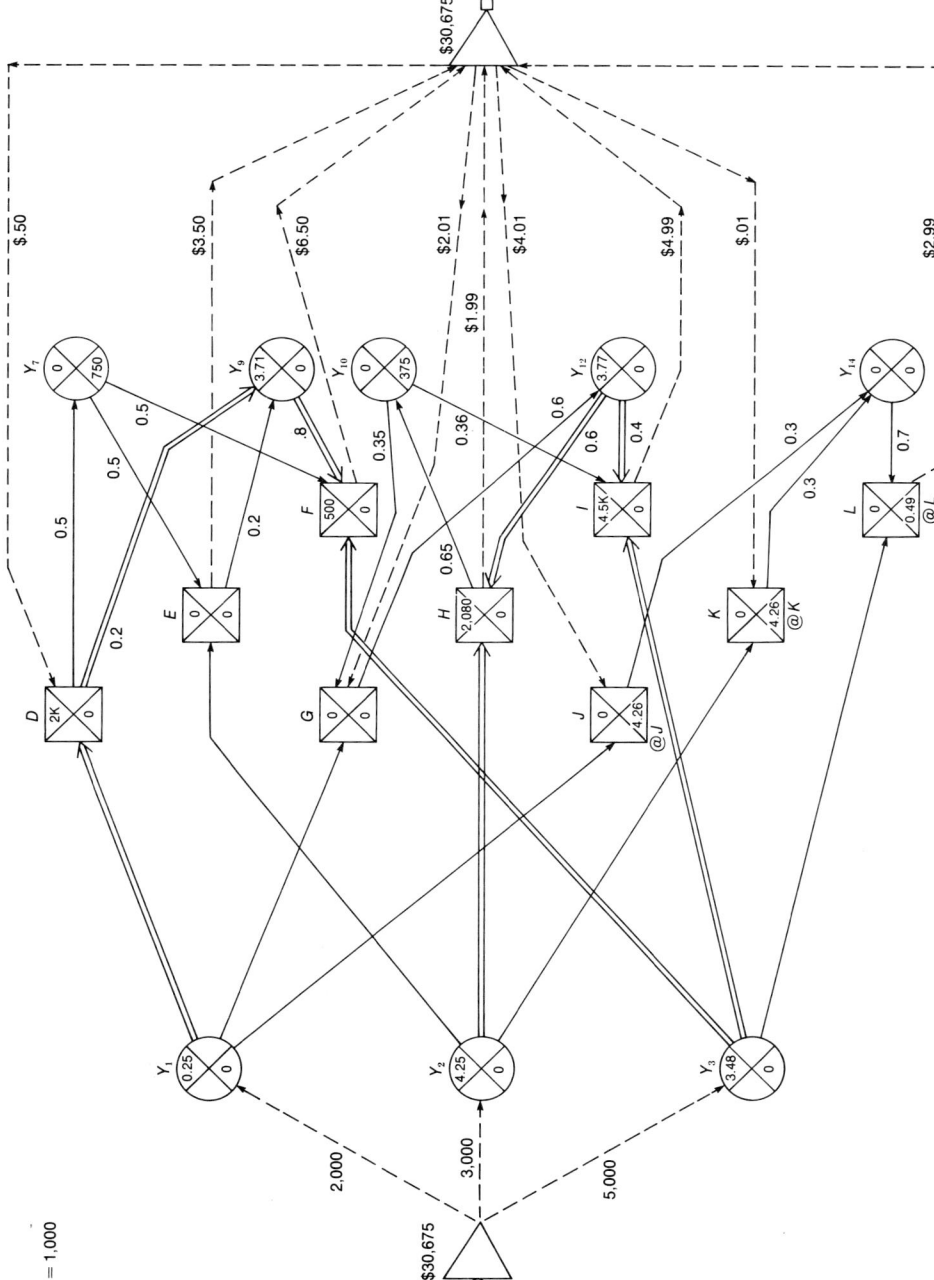

Figure 7-30 RPM condensation for Section 7-4 Tune-up. K = 1,000.

192

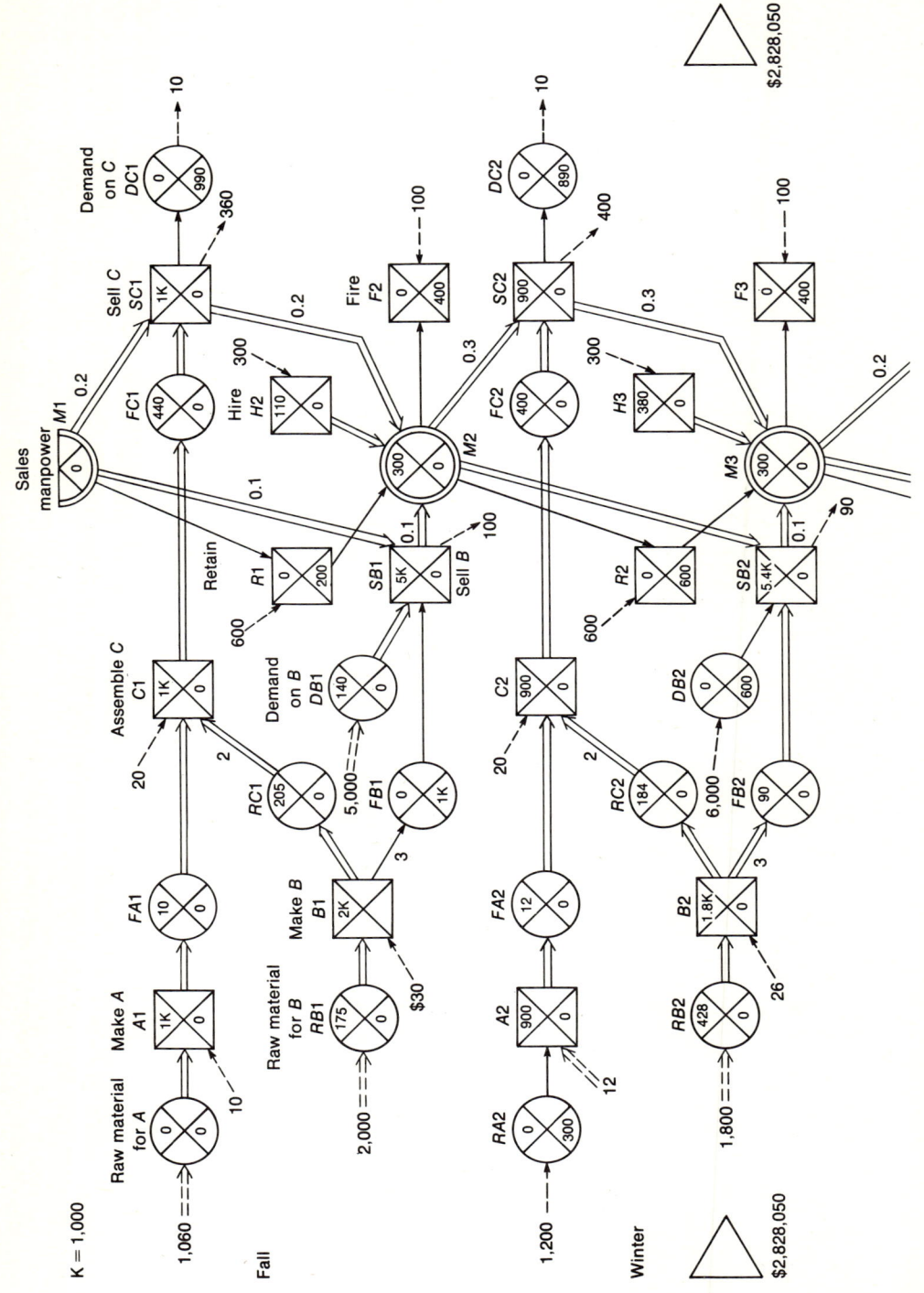

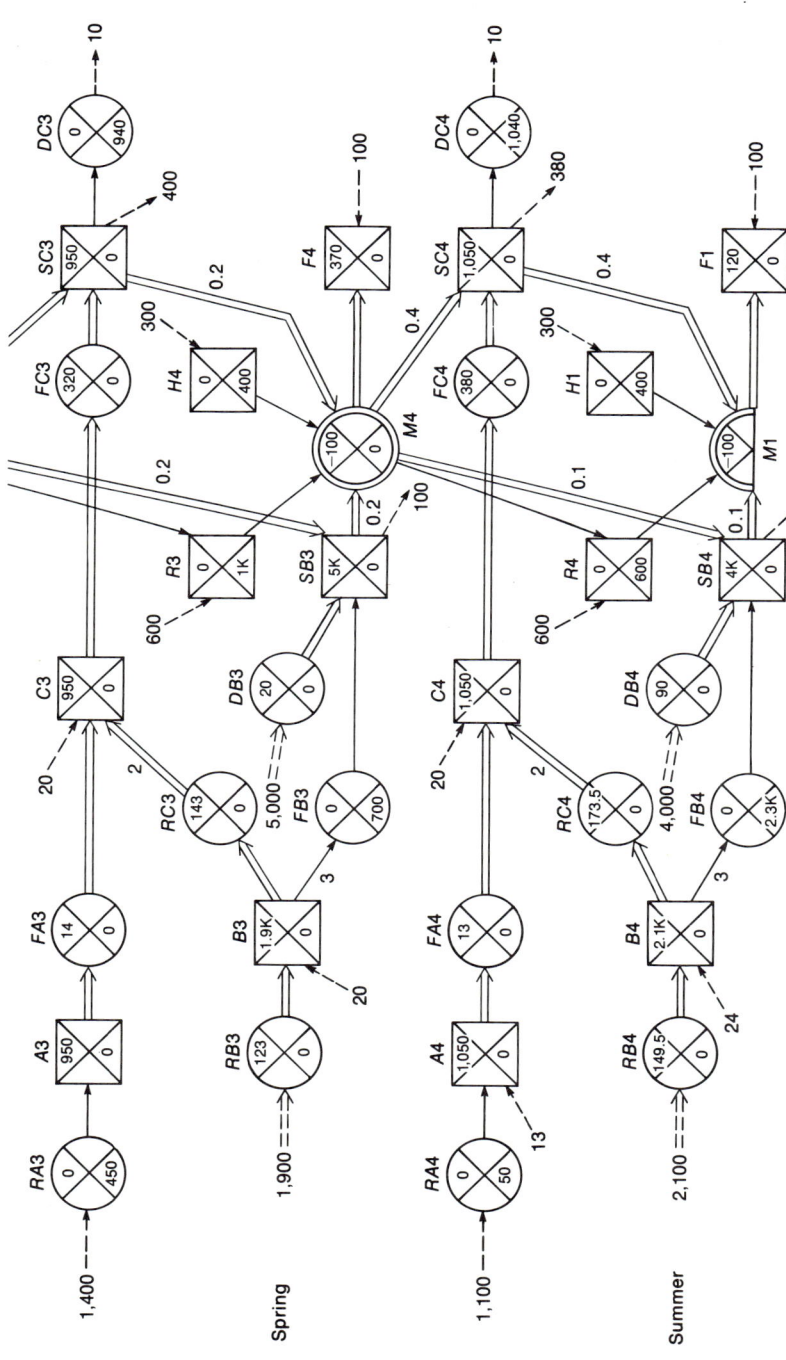

Figure 7-31 Section 7-5 Tune-up solution. K = 1,000.

Note that personnel adjustment occurs at the beginning of each quarter. The total sales force can be computed as: old force + hired − fired = new force.

4. *a* If he quits at the beginning of

	Fall	Winter	Spring	Summer
Do	Fire one less $F1 = 119$	Hire one more $H2 = 111$	Hire one more $H3 = 381$	Fire one less $F4 = 369$
Save (−) or add cost (+)	$M1 = -100$	$M2 = +300$	$M3 = +300$	$M4 = -100$

  b It seems plausible to sell all FA's all four quarters since the shadow prices are all below $100. But we cannot sell what we do not have, and we need to check the feasibility as well as the optimality of our actions. $FA1$ is $10 per unit, but $A1$ is at full capacity with no residue at $RA1$. To sell $FA\ 1$, we need to cut down $C1$; and if we do that, we would lose $FC1 - RC1 - FA1 = \$440 - 205 - 10 = \$225$ per unit, which is more than our meager $100 per unit offer. In winter, spring, and summer, on the other hand, we would be justified in increasing our production of $A2$, $A3$, and $A4$ by 300, 450, and 50, respectively, and selling the excess at $100, making a profit of $88, $86, and $87 per unit, respectively, for a total increase in profit of $69,450. The improved profit figure will then be $2,897,500.

  c We shall have to maintain a sales staff of 1,190 to avoid having to hire and fire sales personnel. $R1$, $R2$, $R3$, and $R4$ have dual values of 200, 600, 1,000, and 600, respectively, and we would have to keep 490, 380, 0, and 370 sales people on retainer for the total cost of $548,000 reducing the profit to $2,280,050. The extra revenue resulting from (*b*) is not included.

  d The largest shadow-price difference for keeping each product for one quarter is $2/$FA$, $90/$FB$, $30.50/$RC$, and $60/$FC$. Thus, we would want to keep $FB1$ ($0) to $FB2$ ($90) from fall to winter.

EXERCISES

7-1 You are the personnel manager for a Wonderland government agency which must comply with the new equal-opportunity affirmative-action guidelines. Presently your staff includes 100 white males, 40 white females and 20 minority males, but no minority females. You wish to increase your staff as much as 300 percent (to as many as 480) but are allowed to do so only if you can comply with the following regulations: (*a*) At least 20 percent of the newly hired personnel must be from a minority group; (*b*) the total work force must be equally divided between males and females within a 10 percent tolerance range (that is, between 40 percent and 60 percent). Construct an RPM network for this project assuming that each employee's average service period in the government is worth $10,000, and that the hiring expenses are $150 for white males, $200 for white females, $250 for minority males, and $400 for minority females. There are no limitations on the availability of suitable volunteers as long as these recruiting expenses are incurred.

7-2 Wonderland is facing a critical shortage of crude oil. It has negotiated two sources of new supplies: an Alaskan broker, who wants to charge as much as $100 per barrel ($100/bbl), and a Beirut broker, who wants to charge $80/bbl. Wonderland needs 50,000 bbl of aviation fuel but can live without automotive fuel if it is absolutely necessary. The profit contribution has been computed using the newly quoted charges, shipping costs, and refining expenses. Using the following data, construct an RPM network and translate your model into mathematical expressions for input into a computer.

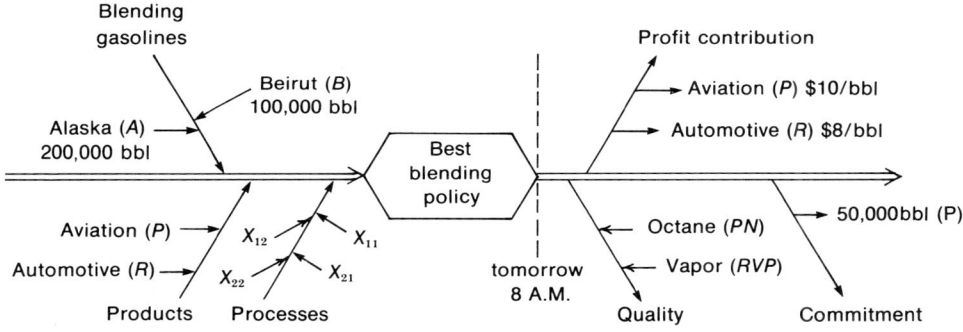

A C&E diagram for the gasoline-blending problem.

Blending gasoline data

Brand	Performance number, PN (octane rating)	Reid-vapor pressure, RVP	Amount available, bbl
Alaska, A	110	4	200,000
Beirut, B	90	10	100,000

Marketable gasoline data

Product	Minimum PN rating	Maximum RVP	Profit contribution $/bbl	Committed minimum, bbl
Aviation, P	105	6	10	50,000
Automotive, R	95	8	8	None

7-3 *Farming cooperative.* A farming cooperative comprises three major farms with limited acreage and water supply which share the 1,000-ton supply of fertilizer. Each farm can grow one or more of the three types of crops, and it has been agreed that each farm will cultivate an equal portion of its arable land. Using other pertinent data which follow, construct an RPM network that maximizes the cooperative's total return.

	Farm		
	1	2	3
Arable land, acres	1,000	1,000	500
Water supply, acre-ft	1,500	2,000	3,000
Labor available, (man-days)	300	600	900

The three types of crops must satisfy the commitments each farm has made but should not exceed the maximum acreage allowed per quota. The objective is to maximize the profit expected from the total operation.

	Crop		
	I	II	III
Promised acreage	10	200	300
Maximum acreage	800	900	500
Water consumption, acre-ft/acre	10	5	8
Expected labor need per acre, man-days	1	2	1
Profit per acre, $	1,000	500	800
Fertilizer per acre, lb	0.5	1	0.2

7-4 In 1954 a Japanese mining company used LP models to optimize the copper and sulfur production from its three mines.[1] The following is a simplified and fictitious version:

ABC mining company has three mines, A, B, and C with respective maximum production capacities of 1,000, 2,000 and 3,000 tons/mo. The ores extracted from these mines have the following constituencies:

Ore from	Percent of elements of				Excavation cost, $/ton	Capacity, tons/mo
	1	2	3	4		
Mine A	10	0	20	0	100	1,000
Mine B	20	10	10	5	200	2,000
Mine C	0	30	0	10	300	3,000

Three alloys P, Q, and R are to be produced from the elements extracted from the ores. The requirements for these alloys are:

[1] S. Moriguchi, *Introduction to Linear Programming* (in Japanese), Japanese Union of Scientists and Engineers, Tokyo, Japan, 1957, p. 141.

Alloys	Constituents	Minimum, %	Maximum, %	Sales price/ton, $
P	1	10	Any	500
	2	None	20	
	3	30	Any	
	4	None	Any	
Q	1	None	None	600
	2	10	80	
	3	30	Any	
	4	None	None	
R	1	10	10	700
	2	None	None	
	3	None	None	
	4	30	Any	

The company has only $500,000/mo operating capital. Plan its operation to maximize profit, assuming that it can sell up to, but no more than, 2,000 tons/mo of combined alloys.

7-5 A plant has received a short-term contract to produce special equipment for the government. The delivery schedule is as follows:

During Month, t	1	2	3	4	5
No. of Units	50	200	100	200	50

This project requires a special type of manufacturing process which must be taught to workers. Presently, the plant has only five workers who can be put to work on this process. Each worker can produce 10 units of this product each month, or be used as an instructor to teach four other new workers to learn this skill in 1 mo. It is also possible to hire workers already trained in this skill at the cost of $1,000 per worker in addition to their monthly wage. Each unit of product promised but not delivered on schedule requires a penalty of $1,000 per unit per mo until the product is delivered. Any product produced ahead of schedule must be stored at the cost of $100 per unit per mo. All products must be delivered at the end of the fifth month, and overproduction has no salvage value. All idle workers must be paid the regular wage of $1,500/mo, and any worker put on overtime may double his production (from 10 to 20 units per mo) and must be paid a triple wage ($4,500/mo). It will cost the management $2,000 to remove a worker from this production (either firing or transferring), and all workers must be removed at the end of the fifth month. A worker under training must be paid a wage of $800/mo, and the instructor is paid a total wage of $1,800/mo. No hiring cost is involved in recruiting unskilled workers, but only eight unskilled workers can be transferred into this production each month. All skilled workers are paid $1,500/mo. Find the minimum-cost hiring, training, production, and storage schedule.

7-6 A company manufactures three products *A*, *B*, and *C*, and the quarterly demands for these are 1,000, 2,000, and 3,000 respectively. *A* and *B* can be produced independently, but each *C* requires one unit of *A* and two units of *B* as components. Plant I can produce either *A* or *B* at $100 or $200 per unit, respectively; plant II can either produce *B* or assemble *C* at $100 or $300 per unit, respectively. Each unit of *A*, *B*, and *C* brings in a revenue of $1,000, $2,000, and $5,000 per unit, respectively. Plant I has a production capacity of 5,000 units per quarter regardless of whether *A* or *B* is made; plant II has a regular production capacity of 6,000 units per quarter for *B*, and 2,000 units per quarter of *C*, and an equal amount of overtime production capacity at double the cost of production. Find the optimal production schedule for all three quarters.

7-7 Two seafood canneries located in Portland and San Francisco must ship their products to warehouses in Chicago, Houston, and New York. Their plant capacities per month are 350 tons at Portland and 650 tons at San Francisco. The requirements per month are 300 tons at Chicago, 300 tons at New York, and 300 tons in Houston. The shipping routes are limited to: Portland to Chicago at $30/ton; Portland to Houston at $80/ton; San Francisco to Chicago at $40/ton; San Francisco to New York at $60/ton; San Francisco to Houston at $60/ton; and Chicago to New York at $20/ton. Find the cheapest shipping schedule.

NETWORK PROGRAMMING: Transportation and Transshipment

Chapter 8

8-1 Hitchcock-Koopmans transportation problem

The principal drive of worldwide industrial activity is to increase the value of resources. Raw materials are converted into finished products. Low-grade resources are combined with higher-quality resources to produce a net quality gain for a mix. Subtle transformations such as those based on time increase the value of investments and antiques; more conspicuous maneuvers such as transportation increase values by making resources more accessible. OR/MS studies assist the value-increase process by identifying the most effective allocations and movements.

Ways to determine the most economical routes for matching supply with demand have been studied for centuries. This type of problem is a showcase for linear programming. Early efforts to solve transportation problems were made by F. L. Hitchcock in 1941 and T. C. Koopmans in 1947, who worked independently but now share the honor of having this class of solution methods named after them. A more inclusive linear programming formulation was developed later by G. B. Danzig (1963).

In this chapter we shall consider the traditional transportation model, methods of solution, and associated RPMS analysis. The model structure is introduced first. Two methods of obtaining an initial feasible solution method are explored: the *northwest-corner rule* and *Vogel's approximation method* (VAM).[1] MODI, the *modified distribution method* studied by scholars such as Dantzig, Koopmans, Henderson, and Schlaifer since 1951, is used to find the optimal solution. RPM networks are presented to assist the problem formulation and to reveal the intent of the calculation procedures.

8-2 Relating supplies to transfer costs to demands

A traditional transportation model is a minimization problem. It seeks the most economical assignments of routes between m sources (e.g., manufacturing plants) and n destinations (e.g., warehouses) while assuming costs are linear and the total demand at the destinations equals the total supply available at the sources. These conditions are expressed mathematically as follows:

$$\min Z_x = \sum_{i=1}^{m} \sum_{j=1}^{n} c_{ij} X_{ij} \qquad c_{ij} = \text{transfer costs}$$

$$X_{ij} = \text{amount transferred from source } i \text{ to destination } j$$

subject to

$$\sum_{j=1}^{n} X_{ij} = a_i \qquad a_i = \text{amount of supplies available at source } i$$

$$\sum_{i=1}^{m} X_{ij} = b_j \qquad b_j = \text{amount required at destination } j$$

$$\sum_{i=1}^{m} a_i = \sum_{j=1}^{n} b_j \qquad \text{sum of the supplies} = \text{sum of the demands}$$

where $i = 1, \ldots, m$; $j = 1, \ldots, n$; and all parameters are positive or zero.

Due to the last condition there are only $n + m - 1$ independent equations. This means that $n + m - 1$ X's will be solved and the other X's will be zero.

A pictorial interpretation of the mathematical description is available through a *transportation tableau* (Figure 8-1) and an RPM network (Figure 8-2). The transportation tableau is a matrix with m rows (representing sources of supply) and n columns (representing destinations to satisfy demands). Therefore, each cell in the matrix represents a unique routing for shipments from sources to destinations. The cost to ship one unit by each route is given by the unit charge c_{ij} entered in the top-right corner of the cell. Rim conditions on the right and bottom sides of the

---

[1] Named after W. R. Vogel, who developed it in 1958.

Network Programming: Transportation and Transshipment   201

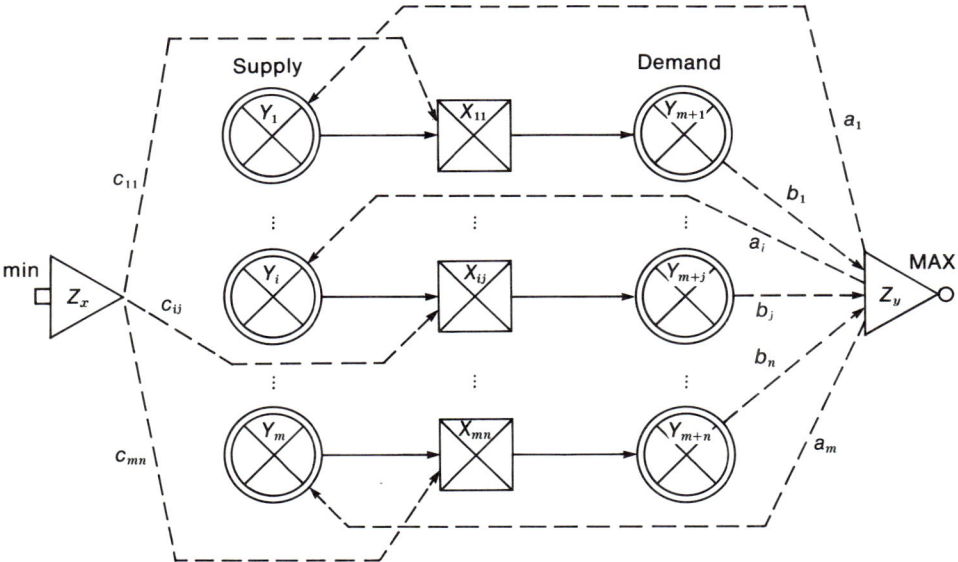

Figure 8-1   Transportation tableau.

matrix show, respectively, the amount of supplies a_i available at each source i and the amount required b_j at each destination j. The objective of the problem is to identify the amount X_{ij} to ship from each source to satisfy demands with minimum transportation costs.

Figure 8-2   Initial RPM network for a traditional transportation problem. (A complete network would have a process node for each supply-to-demand route with the associated cost c_{ij}.)

In the RPM network that corresponds to the transportation tableau (Figure 8-2) resource nodes indicate supply sources and destination demands. They are numbered consecutively from 1 to $m + n$. Rim conditions of the tableau appear as original entries in the resource nodes derived from the dotted arrows. Since transmittances are on a per unit basis, there is no need to insert values for the solid arrows. Per unit transportation costs c_{ij} are shown by initial entries to the process nodes.

Comparing the tableau and RPM network, it should be apparent that both formats display the same data and can be used to compute a solution. The tableau is the more compact of the two formats, and yet it provides adequate working space to manually solve most transportation problems. Large problems are better handled by using the *simplex method* (which is explained in Chapter 9). The RPM network is most useful in setting up the transportation problem and reducing it to essentials, but it also can be used to develop a solution by utilizing the methods described in previous chapters, as will be demonstrated in Example 8-1.

Example 8-1: Procurement of Wonderland uniforms A government agency is usually obligated to allow open bidding on all its purchases. When bids are received, the price bid, quality of offering, availability of services, and numerous other factors must be considered in selecting the best bid; and this must be done impartially and objectively. Linear programming has been used to construct an optimization model to select offers which minimize taxpayers' dollars while meeting the requirements of the public agency.

As the president of the Republic of Wonderland and its purchasing agent, you need 3,000 red uniforms for the fire department, 5,000 purple uniforms for the post office department, and 4,000 black uniforms for the police department. In response to your announcement, you have received three offers. An African firm offers to sell up to 6,000 surplus white police uniforms at the cost of $40 per set; a British firm says that it can find 6,000 blue Bobby uniforms at $60 per set; and a Canadian firm says that it has 2,000 slightly used red Mountie uniforms for $50 per set. The transportation costs to Wonderland are found to be $10, $5, and $15 per set from Africa, Britain, and Canada, respectively. You must find the cheapest way of providing the uniforms needed by Wonderland.

The foreign uniforms must first be dyed to the proper colors and then altered to meet regulations for styles. These costs can be tabulated as follows:

Dyeing costs, dollars

From	To		
	Red	Purple	Black
White	10	10	10
Blue	NA	5	10
Red	0	15	10

Alteration costs, dollars

From	To		
	Fire	Post	Police
African Police	20	10	0
British Bobbies	NA	10	5
Canadian Mounties	5	10	5

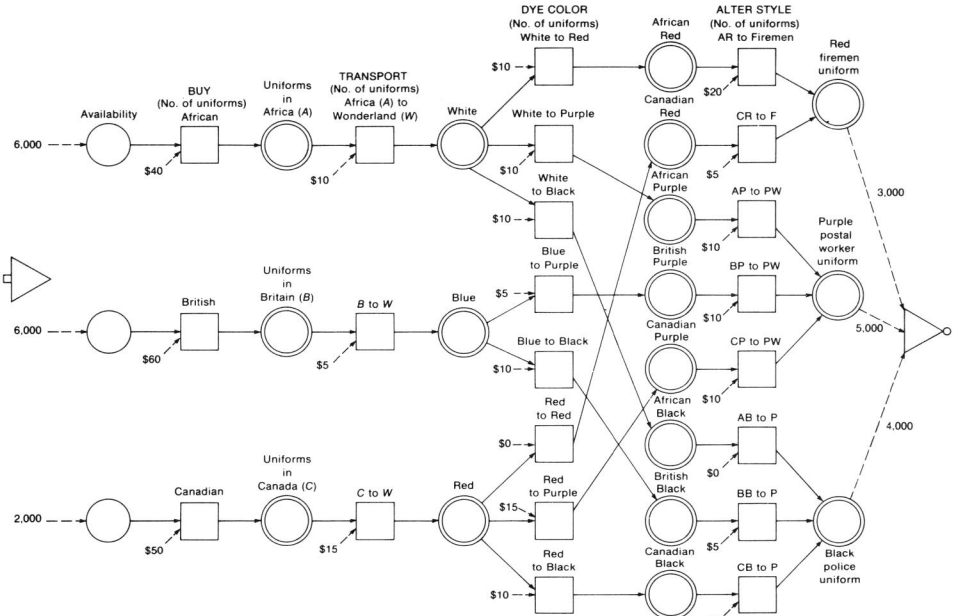

Figure 8-3 Uniform procurement by the Wonderland government.

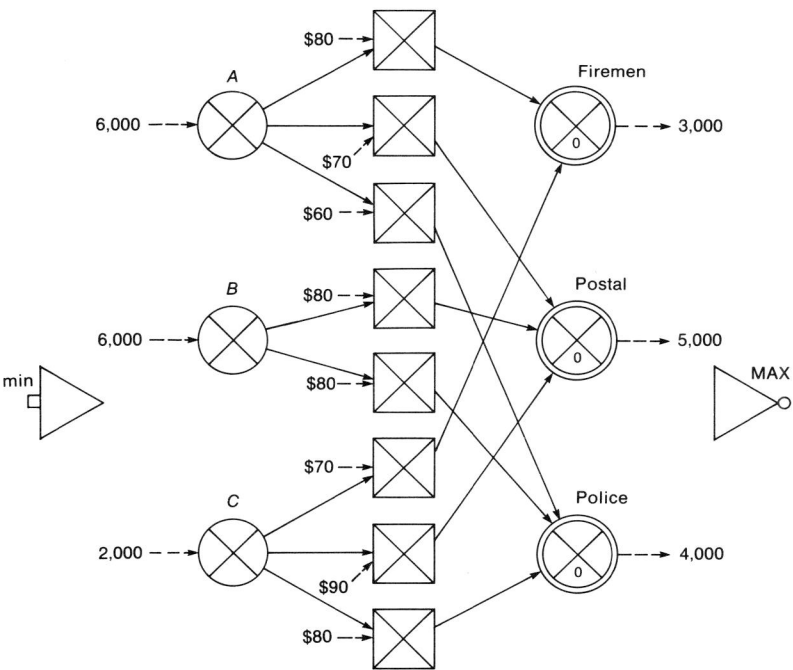

Figure 8-4 Condensed RPM network for uniforms.

204 Introduction to Operations Research and Management Science

Figure 8-3 shows an RPM network constructed according to these data. Note that there are many equality constraints and that the method of Chapter 6, Section 6-5, can be used to condense the network. Figure 8-4 is an outcome of such a contraction where each cost figure is the sum of all expenses incurred along the contracted path. For example, the cost of $80 for going from A (Africa) to the fire department is the sum of the purchase ($40), transportation ($10), dyeing ($10), and alteration ($20) costs.

Figure 8-5 shows that the cheapest way to obtain uniforms for the fire department is to convert the uniforms of the Canadian Mounties at $70 each; thus, we may decide to send the entire 2,000 uniforms of C to the fire department. Since there is only one other way to provide uniforms for the fire department, we have no choice but to use 1,000 uniforms of A at $80 to fill the 3,000 quota. There are now 5,000 uniforms remaining at A which may be sent to the post office or police department. Since $60 is less than $70, we may decide to send 4,000 uniforms to the police department (Figure 8-6). By filling the post office needs by the cheaper A uniforms and the remaining 4,000 by B uniforms, we obtain Figure 8-7.

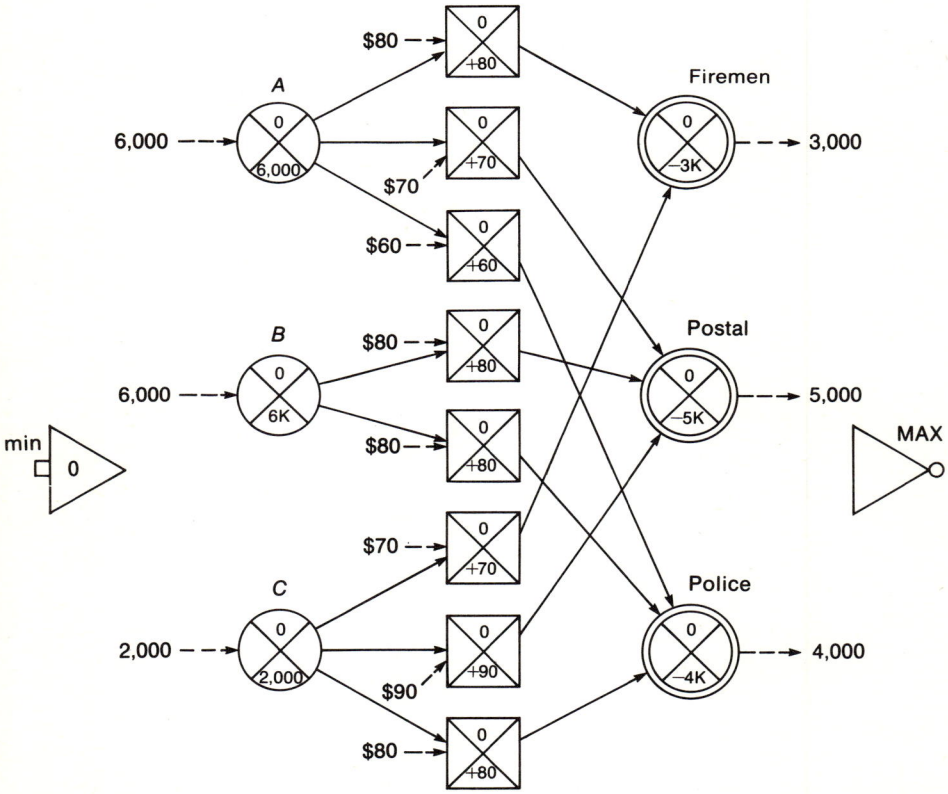

Figure 8-5 Nonshipment schedule.

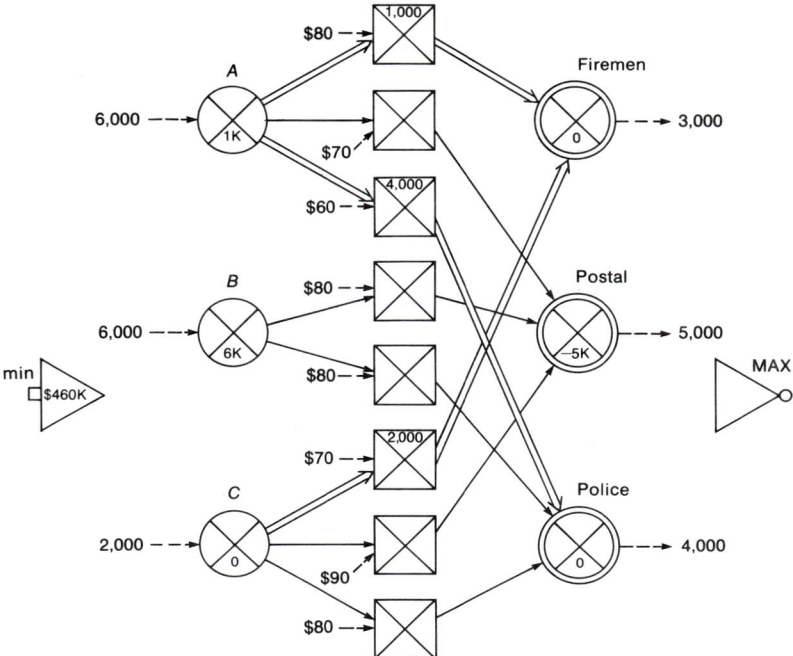

Figure 8-6 Partial shipment schedule.

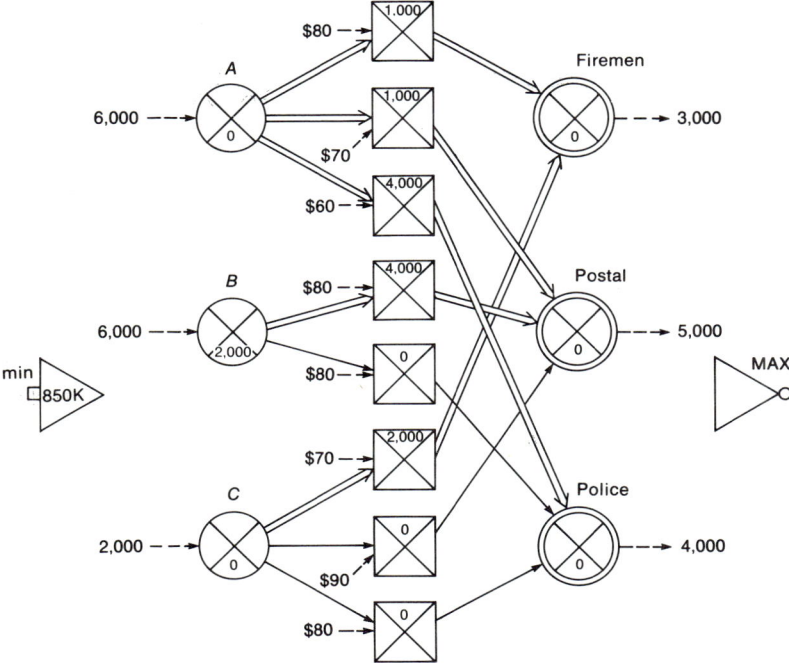

Figure 8-7 Full shipment schedule.

Now that we have a feasible solution, let us check for its optimality. Figure 8-8 shows the result of applying the complementary slackness theorem. Noting that B is the only known resource value, we use this to compute the resource value at the post office $(0 + 80 = 80)$. Following the basic path back to A, we have $80 - 70 = 10$, which can be used to compute the values for the fire department $(10 + 80 = 90)$ and police department $(10 + 60 = 70)$, and then C $(90 - 70 = 20)$ (Figure 8-9). Nonbasic dual values are computed as residue = input − output, and none is found to be negative (Figure 8-10). The objective-function value of 850k is checked both by the primal values $(80 \times 1k + 70 \times 1k + 60 \times 4k + 80 \times 4k + 70 \times 2k = 850{,}000)$ and by its dual values $(90 \times 3k + 80 \times 5k + 70 \times 4k - 6k \times 10 - 2k \times 20 = 850{,}000)$.

The resulting solution can now be transcribed upon the original network (Figure 8-11) to provide the necessary information for purchasing, transportation, dyeing, and altering the uniforms.

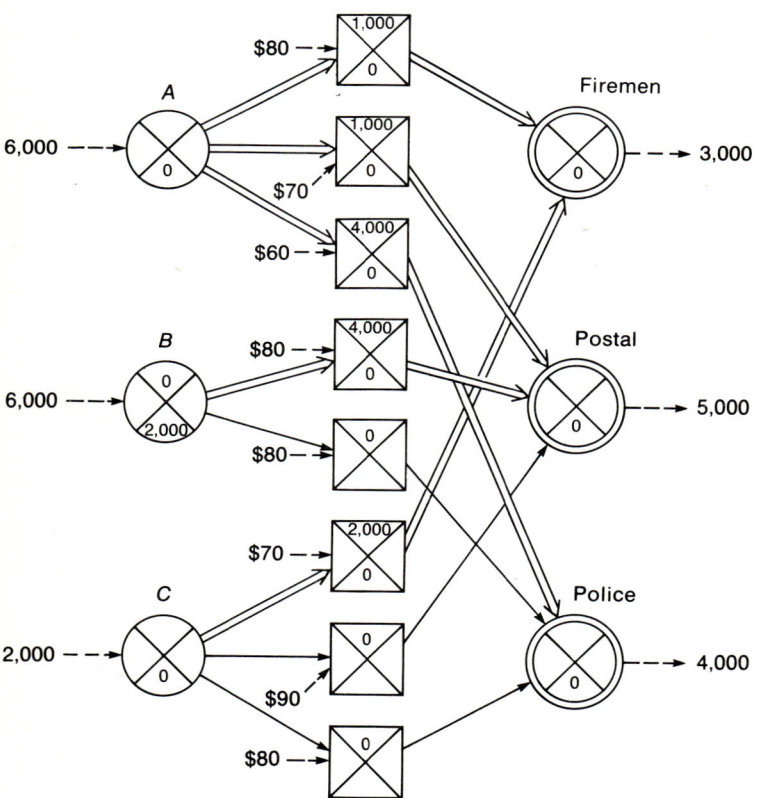

Figure 8-8 Complementary-slackness theorem applied to the full shipment schedule.

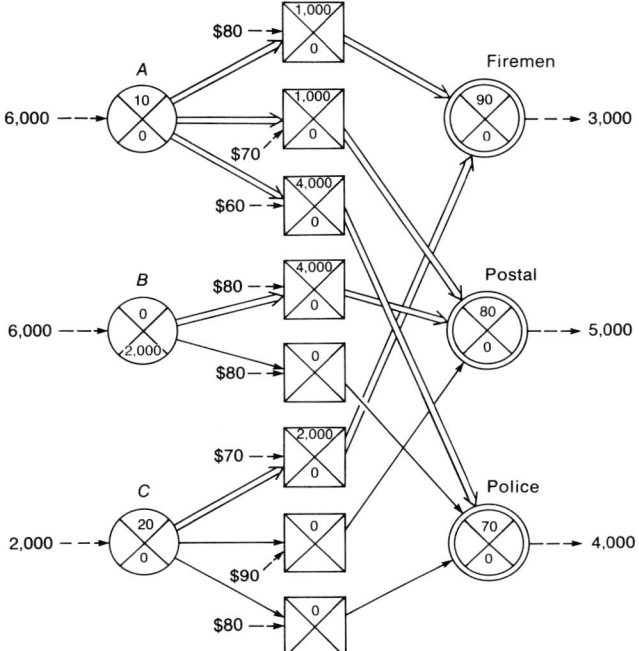

Figure 8-9 Basic dual values computed.

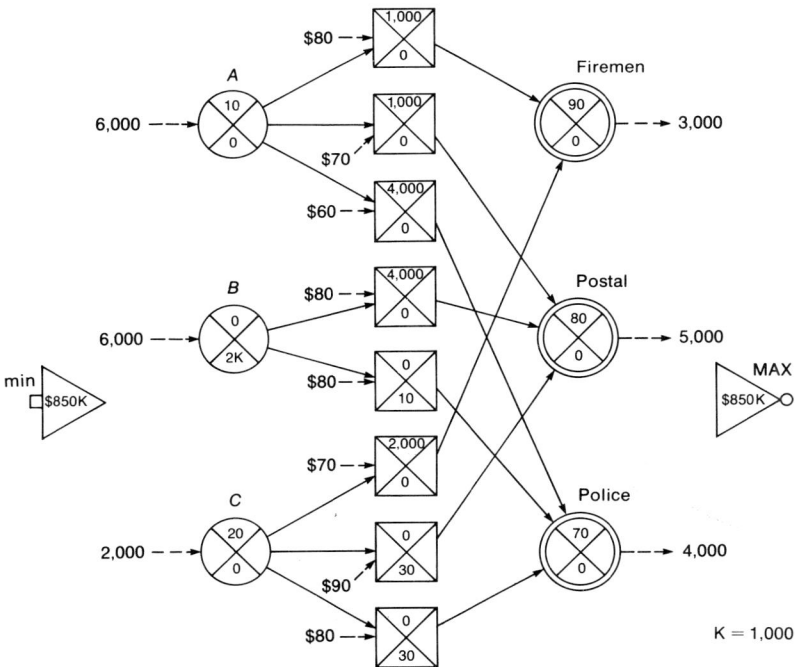

Figure 8-10 Optimal solution.

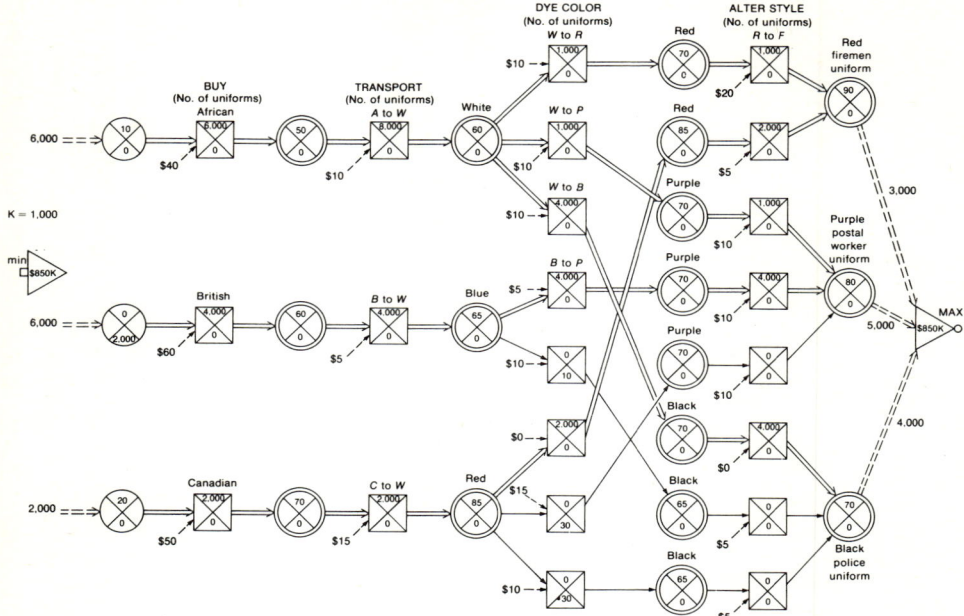

Figure 8-11   Optimal solution for Example 8-1.

SECTION 8-2 TUNE-UP

Supplies at *U* and *S* are needed at *D*, *E*, and *M*, and the conditions for their transfer are shown in the RPM network of Figure 8-12.

1. What are the rim conditions for a transportation tableau?
2. Determine the most economical shipping routes by inspection. What is the minimum-cost routing procedure?

Hint: When Σ supply $= \Sigma$ demand, there will be no residue at any resource node. An arbitrary assignment of 0, at the NW corner (node *U*) can start off your dual value computation and will yield correct regrets and shadow prices.

8-3   Feasibility analysis

In Example 8-1 we observed how transportation problems can be solved intuitively via RPM networks. Traditional solution methods utilize numerical manipulations based on the transportation tableau. This tableau solution procedure starts with the development of a feasible, but not necessarily optimal, solution. In this section we shall investigate two methods for identifying feasible transfer routes:

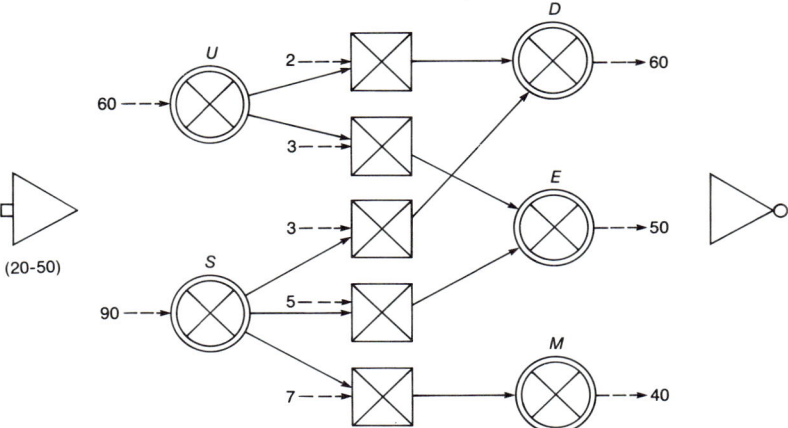

Figure 8-12 RPM network display for Section 8-2 Tune-up.

the northwest-corner rule and Vogel's approximation method (VAM). The following situation illustrates these methods.

Three plants, $S1$, $S2$, and $S3$ each produce 100 units per week, which are shipped to three warehouses $D1$, $D2$, and $D3$. The number of units required at the warehouses varies from week to week, but the current demand is 80 at $D1$, 70 at $D2$, and 150 at $D3$. The transportation costs are tabulated as follows:

Transportation costs per unit, dollars

From plant	(To warehouse)		
	D1	D2	D3
S1	30	M*	10
S2	M*	20	30
S3	20	50	60

*M indicates routes prohibited by legal, physical, or economic reasons: thus M amounts to an infinite cost.

NORTHWEST-CORNER RULE A simple way to make initial allocations is to start at the upper-left (northwest) corner of the tableau. Allocate the supplies available in the first row to the column demands until the first source is exhausted, and then repeat the process for the other rows while being careful not to violate the rim conditions. As shown in the tableau of Figure 8-13, the first allocation from $S1$ is 80 units to satisfy the demand at $D1$; the remaining 20 units at $S1$ are assigned to $D3$, which exhausts $S1$, satisfies $D1$, and partially meets $D3$. Then turning our attention to $S2$, the first unsatisfied demand is at $D2$ (no units were assigned from $S1$ to $D2$ because the route was blocked by the M transfer cost). After 70 units go to $D2$ to satisfy that demand, the 30 remaining units at $S2$ are assigned to $D3$. Finally, the 100 units at $S3$ are designated for $D3$, the only remaining unsatisfied demand. Since supply and demand are balanced in the problem, the final allocation satisfies all the rim conditions.

	D1	D2	D3	
S1	30 80	M 20	10	100
S2	M	20 70	30 30	100
S3	20	50 100	60	100
	80	70	150	300

Transportation tableau for the given situation with initial assignments that satisfy the rim conditions

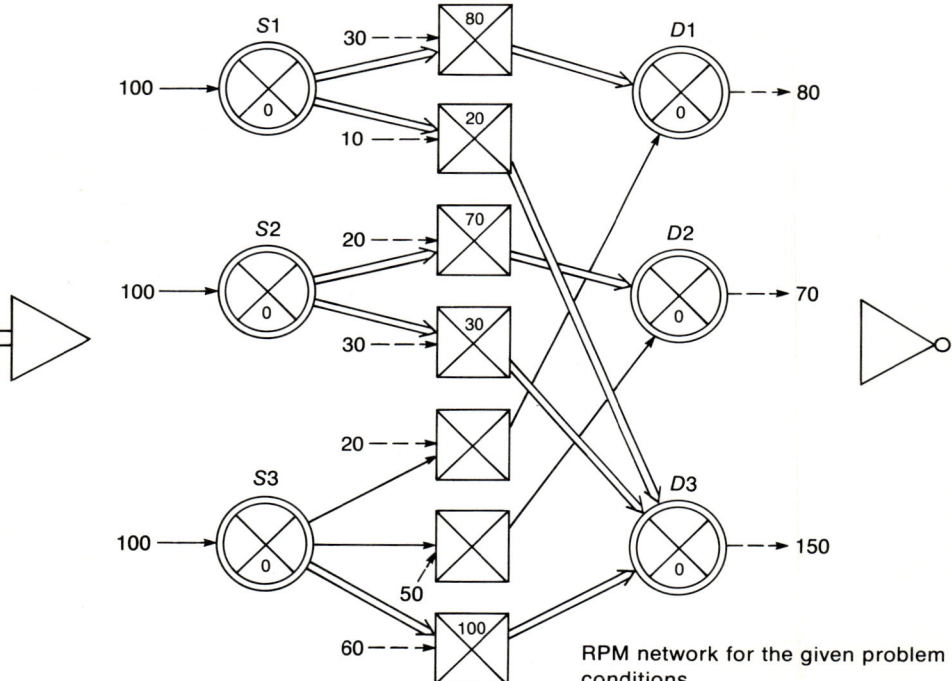

RPM network for the given problem conditions

Figure 8-13 Initial feasible solution for a transportation problem developed by use of the northwest-corner rule.

An RPM network for the same problem is also given in Figure 8-13. The RPM procedure equivalent to the northwest-corner rule is to start at the top process node and make assignments to successively exhaust each lower supply source (resource nodes on the left). Thus the first assignment from $S1$ is to the top process node where it satisfies the demand at $D1$. Entries in the top four process nodes complete the allocations from $S1$ and $S2$. After all assignments have been made, every resource node contains a zero, which confirms that no residues remain, a pattern that is equivalent to checking rim conditions.

The systematic procedures just described do not *have* to be used. In Example 8-1 we demonstrated how initial allocations can be made by inspection. However, a logical, automatic procedure such as the northwest-corner rule has obvious application in computer programming where a set routine is required to start the solution process. A more elaborate method designed for manual applications to produce an optimal or near optimal initial solution is described next.

VAM—VOGEL'S APPROXIMATION METHOD VAM does not yield an initial solution as quickly as the northwest-corner rule, but its initial allocations are likely to be closer to the optimal solution. It achieves this optimality approach through calculations of *regret*, or the extra expense incurred from not selecting the lowest possible cost routes. In VAM regret is defined as the difference between the lowest-cost route and the next lowest-cost route available. The objective is to make allocations that minimize total regret. This is accomplished by calculating the regret for each supply and demand, making an assignment that overcomes the worst regret of those calculated, and then repeating the process until the rim conditions are satisfied.

A detailed application of VAM to the problem conditions just described is given in Figure 8-14. The transportation tableau is set up in the usual form, and VAM calculations are conducted around the rim of the tableau. The first regret computation reveals the greatest regret is -30 at row $S3$ and column $D2$. Since it is arbitrary which one of the equal regrets is avoided by an assignment, we shall first allocate to $S3$ where an assignment of 80 at $D1$ cancels one of the starred regrets (-30^*). As shown in the middle tableau of Figure 8-14, regrets are recalculated to account for the allocation that satisfied the demand at $D1$. The rim conditions are also altered to show the effect of this assignment by crossing off 80 at $D1$ and replacing 100 by 20 at $S3$. Now the -30 regret at $D2$ is avoided by an allocation of 70 from $S2$. A third regret recalculation is shown in the bottom tableau, but it is not really necessary because all the remaining supplies must be allocated to $D3$ in order to meet rim conditions. These allocations complete the initial feasible solution.

VAM calculations equivalent to those just performed on the tableau can be conducted on an RPM network. Regrets are calculated for each supply and demand node, and these calculations are shown in Figure 8-15. Also shown is the first allocation from $S3$ to $D1$. After this assignment, regrets are recalculated and the remaining assignments are made in the same order and amounts as detailed for the tableau. The resulting feasible solution is then ready to be checked for optimality.

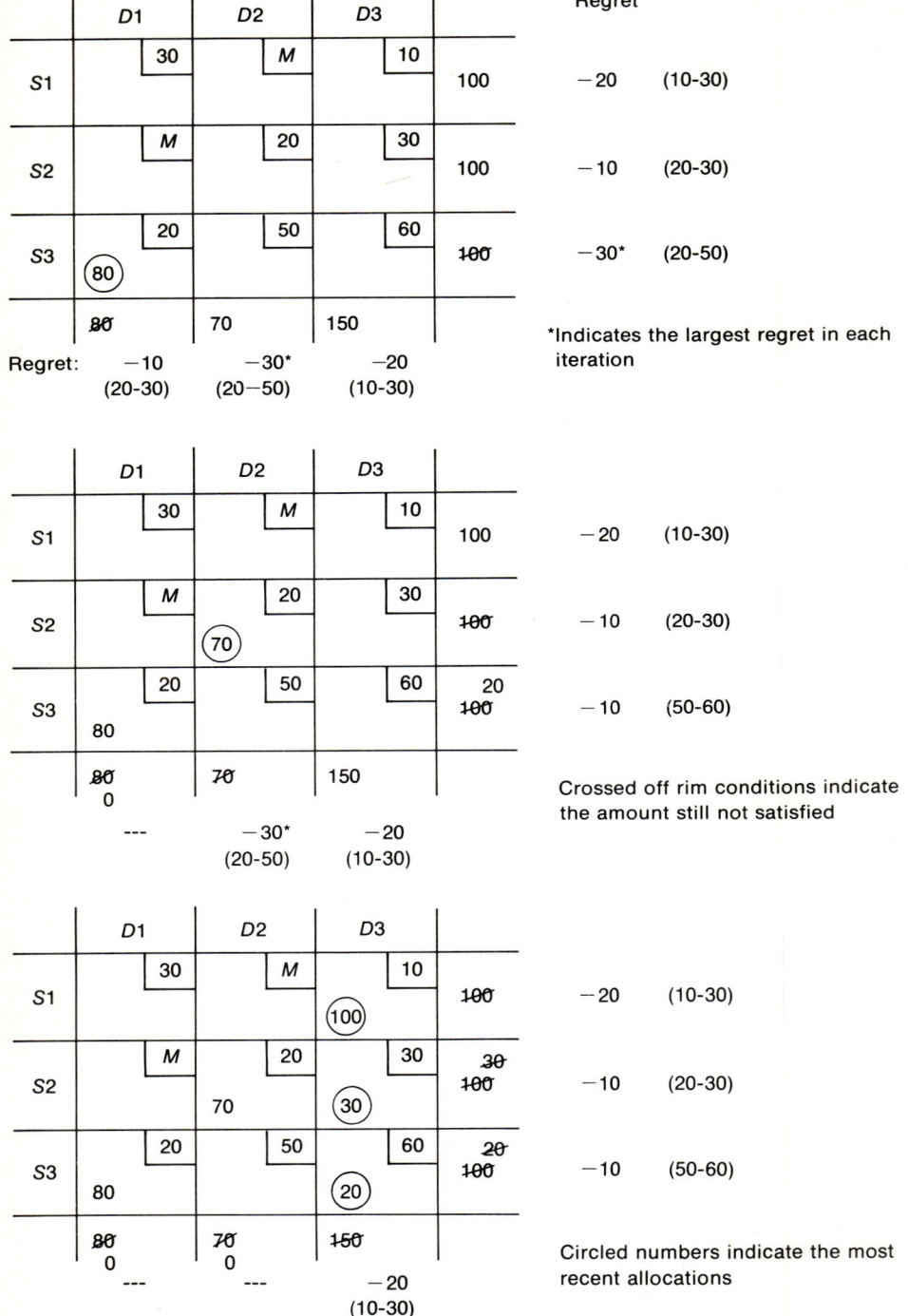

Figure 8-14 VAM applied to a transportation tableau based on the problem conditions of Figure 8-12.

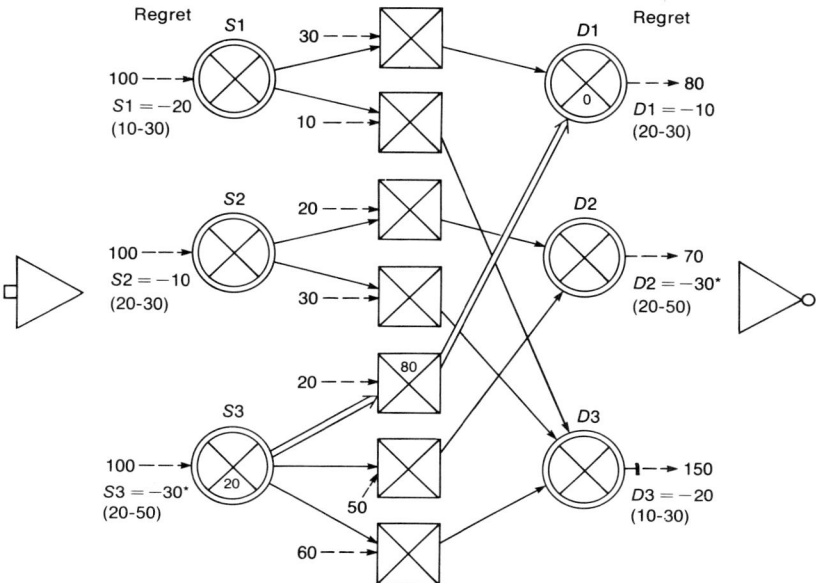

Figure 8-15 VAM applied to an RPM network based on the problem conditions of Figure 8-14. (Only the first assignment is shown.)

*Indicates the largest regret in this iteration

Example 8-2: *The assignment method, or crossoffs on a collapsed tableau* A special case of transportation problems involves the assignment of single units of supply to single-unit demands. The solution procedure is called the *assignment method*, Flood's technique, or the Hungarian method. The procedure is computationally more efficient than the simplex and transportation methods in situations where it is applicable.

	Machine 1	Machine 2	Machine 3	Job supply
Job 1	26	23	29	1
Job 2	20	19	30	1
Job 3	24	29	27	1
Machine demand	1	1	1	

The transportation tableau shows the cost of performing each job on each machine. The objective is to match job and machine assignments to minimize the total cost of doing one job on each machine.

Figure 8-16 Transportation tableau for a problem that can be solved by the assignment method.

214   Introduction to Operations Research and Management Science

(A)	M1	M2	M3
J1	26	23	29
J2	20	19	30
J3	24	29	27

(a) *Original matrix*: The number of columns equal the number of rows. Cell entries are the assignment costs.

(B)	M1	M2	M3
J1	3	0	6
J2	1	0	11
J3	0	5	3

(b) *Row regret*: Subtract the lowest entry in each row of Matrix A from all entries in that row. The result is the "regret" for not choosing the lowest row cost.

row reduction 66
LB

(C)	M1	M2	M3
J1	3	0	3
J2	1	0	8
J3	0	5	0

(c) *Total regret*: Subtract the lowest number in each column of Matrix B from all numbers in that column. The result is the total job-machine regret.

column reduction $66+3=69$
LB = 66+3 = 69

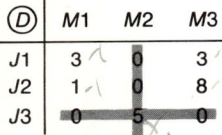

(D)	M1	M2	M3
J1	3	0	3
J2	1	0	8
J3	0	5	0

feasibility

(d) *Optimality check*: Draw the minimum number of straight lines (vertical or horizontal) to cover all zeros. If all zeros are covered by fewer lines than there are rows or columns, an optimal solution has *not* been discovered.

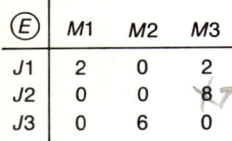

(E)	M1	M2	M3
J1	2	0	2
J2	0	0	8
J3	0	6	0

(e) *Revised regret*: Select the smallest number in Matrix D not covered by a drawn line (1). Subtract this number from all uncovered numbers and add it to all numbers at drawn line intersections (5 + 1 = 6).

changes the matrix
69+1 = 70

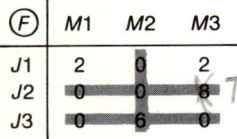

(F)	M1	M2	M3
J1	2	0	2
J2	0	0	8
J3	0	6	0

(f) *Optimality check*: Again draw straight lines to cover all zeros. When the number of lines required equals the number of rows or columns, an optimal solution is identified. If not, return to (d).

(G)	M1	M2	M3
J1	2	(0)	2
J2	(0)	0	8
J3	0	6	(0)

(g) *Assignment*: Make assignments where regret is zero. There may be more than one set of assignments that produce the same minimum cost. In our example there is only one optimal assignment. The total cost is 23 + 20 + 27 = 70.

Job 1 to Machine 2 at $23
Job 2 to Machine 1 at $20
Job 3 to Machine 3 at $27

Figure 8-17   Solution procedures for the assignment method.

The transportion tableau in Figure 8-16 displays a situation where there are three jobs, each to be completed on one of the three available machines (rim conditions are all equal to 1). With the cost of each job on each machine given, the problem can be treated as a regular transportation or linear programming problem. However, after collapsing the tableau to contain just the job-machine costs, as shown in part a of Figure 8-17, we can follow the steps shown in Figure 8-17b to g to obtain the optimal assignments. The steps are essentially a routine to minimize regret.

SECTION 8-3 TUNE-UP

1. Apply VAM and the northwest-corner rule to the assignment problem in Example 8-2.

2. Construct a transportation tableau and apply VAM to the situation described by the RPM network in Section 8-2 Tune-up.

8-4 Optimality analysis

Two different initial feasible solutions resulted from the application of the northwest-corner rule and VAM in Section 8-3. At least one of them is obviously not an optimal solution, and perhaps neither is. To check the optimality of a solution we determine whether a saving in transportation cost can be secured by including an unused route. This means that each unused cell in a tableau or unused path in a network represents a possible saving and must be checked. There are two checking procedures: the *stepping-stone* and *MODI* methods. We shall explore these checking procedures by applying them to the sample problem discussed in Section 8-3.

STEPPING-STONE METHOD The stepping-stone method for checking optimality draws its name from comparing a tableau to a pond; the occupied cells are considered to be stepping stones, and a path is sought from an unoccupied cell to the stepping stones in the pond and back. By comparing costs along this roundtrip path we can determine whether the starting point should be in the minimum-cost solution.

The transportation routes obtained in Figure 8-13 by applying the northwest-corner rule are shown in Figure 8-18; also included is a closed path from cell $S3,D1$. By considering the transportation costs of the occupied stones along the path, we can see whether $S3,D1$ should be part of the solution in place of one of the other assignments. A starting point for the path is selected by observing the unit costs c_{ij} of the unoccupied cells. Lower costs are obviously better candidates for an improved solution, but all reasonably priced routes should be checked. In our example there are only two cells to check because the other unoccupied cells are blocked by big M costs. The closed path from the cell selected for checking is

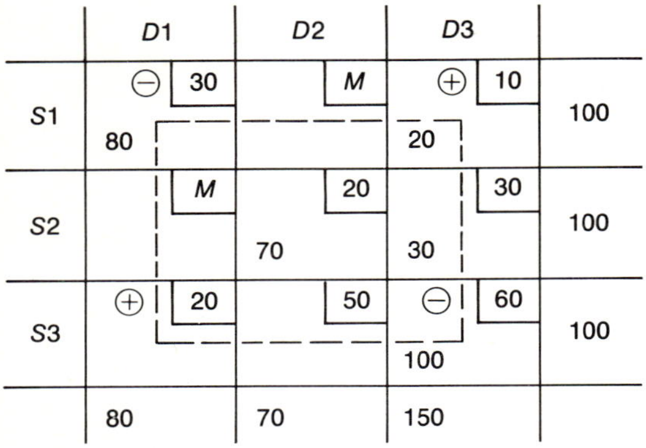

	D1	D2	D3	
S1	⊖ 30 80	M	⊕ 10 20	100
S2	M	20 70	30 30	100
S3	⊕ 20	50	⊖ 60 100	100
	80	70	150	

Dotted lines show the closed path required to check the desirability of changing the transportation pattern to include the unused route S3, D1.

Figure 8-18 Stepping-stone check for a lower-cost transportation route.

composed of horizontal and vertical lines. Corners occur only at occupied cells and may be separated by either occupied or unoccupied cells. Only the most direct route is used.

To find the value of the starting cell we alternately assign minus and plus signs to the unit costs of the occupied cells. It makes no difference whether you travel clockwise or counterclockwise around the path, but the first *cornerstone* on the path must be assigned as minus. Then the value of the cell being checked is calculated by adding the unit costs for plus cornerstones and subtracting unit costs for minus cornerstones. In Figure 8-18, $S1, D1$ and $S3, D3$ are minus stones while $S1, D3$ is a plus stone; thus the value of the route is

$$S3, D1 = -30 + 10 - 60 + 20 = -60$$

What we have found is that we are losing $60 for each unit that is *not* shipped from $S3$ to $D1$. Our regret is $-\$60$ per unit for $S3, D1$. As in all RPM models, any

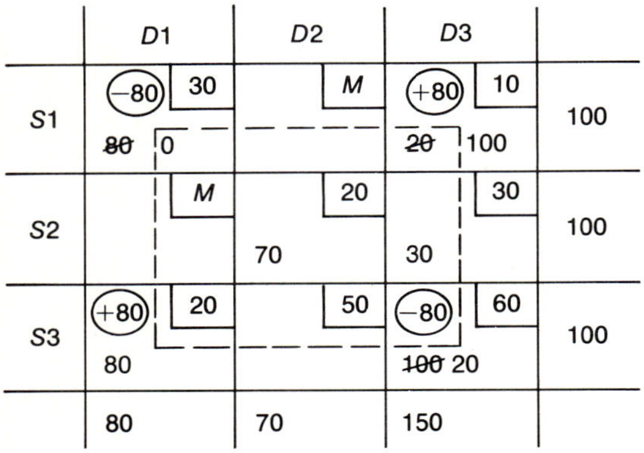

	D1	D2	D3	
S1	⊖80 30 ~~80~~ 0	M	⊕80 10 ~~20~~ 100	100
S2	M	20 70	30 30	100
S3	⊕80 20 80	50	⊖80 60 ~~100~~ 20	100
	80	70	150	

Circled numbers show the reallocations indicated by the stepping-stone path used in Figure 8-18. Previous entries are crossed off to show the revisions. The given changes produce an optimal solution.

Figure 8-19 Reassignment of transportation amounts and routes.

unused cell with a minus residue means the solution can be improved; in an optimal solution all empty cells have a plus or zero residue.

The closed path that reveals a route that should be included in the solution also reveals how to make reassignments. The minimum number of units in any negative cell on the path should be transferred to the empty cell. As shown in Figure 8-19, 80 units are in the minus cell at $S1,D1$ (the other minus cell at $S3,D3$ has 100 units, and so 80 is the minimum), and these are transferred to $S3,D1$. Then the other cells on the path are balanced by corresponding transfers: 80 units are added to $S1,D3$, and 80 units are subtracted from $S3,D3$. Thus the rim conditions are maintained. The relationship of the regret calculation and the reassignment are as follows:

Closed path	From $S3,D1$ to $S1,D1$ to $S1,D3$ to $S3,D3$
Regret	$+$ Cost at $S3,D1$; $-$ cost at $S1,D1$; $+$ cost at $S1,D3$; $-$ cost at $S3,D3$
Reassignment	$+$ 80 at $S3,D1$; $-$ 80 at $S1,D1$; $+$ 80 at $S1,D3$; $-$ 80 at $S3,D3$

The other empty cell ($S3,D2$ in the original solution should now be checked by the closed path $S3,D2$; $S2,D2$; $S2,D3$; and $S3,D3$. Regret at $S3,D2 = +50 - 20 + 30 - 60 = 0$; therefore, no savings would result from transferring units to $S3,D2$. However, since no additional cost is involved in such a transfer, a zero-cost cell offers an alternative optimal shipping pattern as demonstrated in the following table:

Optimal assignment and total cost from Figure 8-19				Alternative optimal assignment including route $S3,D2$			
Units		Cost per unit, $	Total	Units		Cost per unit, $	Total
S1 to D3:	100	×	10 = 1,000	S1 to D3:	100	×	10 = 1,000
S2 to D2:	70	×	20 = 1,400	S2 to D2:	50	×	20 = 1,000
S2 to D3:	30	×	30 = 900	S2 to D3:	50	×	30 = 1,500
S3 to D1:	80	×	20 = 1,600	S3 to D1:	80	×	20 = 1,600
S3 to D3:	20	×	60 = 1,200	S3 to D2:	20	×	50 = 1,000
Total transportation cost			$6,100	Total transportation cost			$6,100

MODI METHOD The *modified distribution* (MODI) method is a streamlined version of the stepping-stone method. Both methods share the same objective—to identify the unused routes that will improve a solution—and both use the same closed-path reallocation procedure to make the indicated improvements. The effective difference is that the MODI method avoids going through the stepping-stone paths to check the value of empty cells. We shall first consider the application of MODI to RPM networks and then show the same procedure on a tableau.

Calculating dual variable values in a network is equivalent to making cell checks on a tableau. Both methods reveal the same numbers for empty cells.

218 Introduction to Operations Research and Management Science

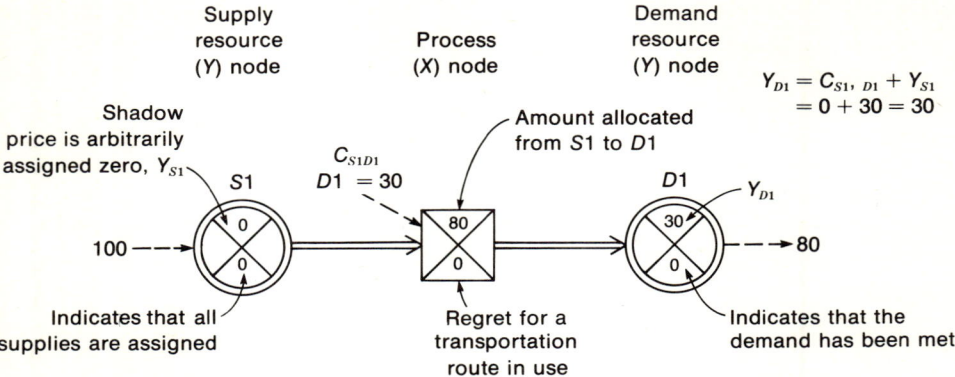

Figure 8-20 Balancing X-node flows to calculate resource shadow prices. (In MODI, all arrowheads around supply resource nodes will be reversed.)

These numbers are the shadow prices that indicate the gain or loss which results from altering a solution. As we check for an optimal solution we are looking for negative numbers which reveal how much can be gained by switching transportation routes. Since Σ supply $= \Sigma$ demand, we could start the dual calculations by assigning a zero to any Y node, but for conformity we shall follow the practice of giving the zero to the top supply node. In the sample problem, this practice sets a zero shadow price for the resource node Y_{S1}. With Y_{S1} and the transfer cost $C_{S1,D1}$ given, we can apply the RPMS postulate to node $X_{S1,D1}$ as shown in Figure 8-20. Shadow prices for the other resource nodes are determined by balancing the flows around each X node. For instance, by following a basic path (a used transportation route) from Y_{S1} to Y_{D3}, we find $Y_{S1} + C_{S1,D3} = Y_{D3}$ or $Y_{D3} = 0 + 10 = 10$. By using the calculated value of Y_{D3} to solve for Y_{S3} and Y_{S2}, and then Y_{S2} to yield Y_{D3}, the resource shadow prices are completed as shown in Figure 8-21.

After the resource shadow prices are entered in the network, the dual value for each X node on an unused route is equal to the given input minus output. Using the paths in Figure 8-22, we find the regret:

$Y_{S3,D1} = $ input $-$ output

$= Y_{S3} + C_{S3,D1} - Y_{D1}$

$= -50 + 20 - 30$

$= 60$

$Y_{S3,D2} = Y_{S3} + C_{S3,D2} - Y_{D2}$

$= -50 + 50 - 0$

$= 0$

which are the same values obtained by the stepping-stone method. Therefore,

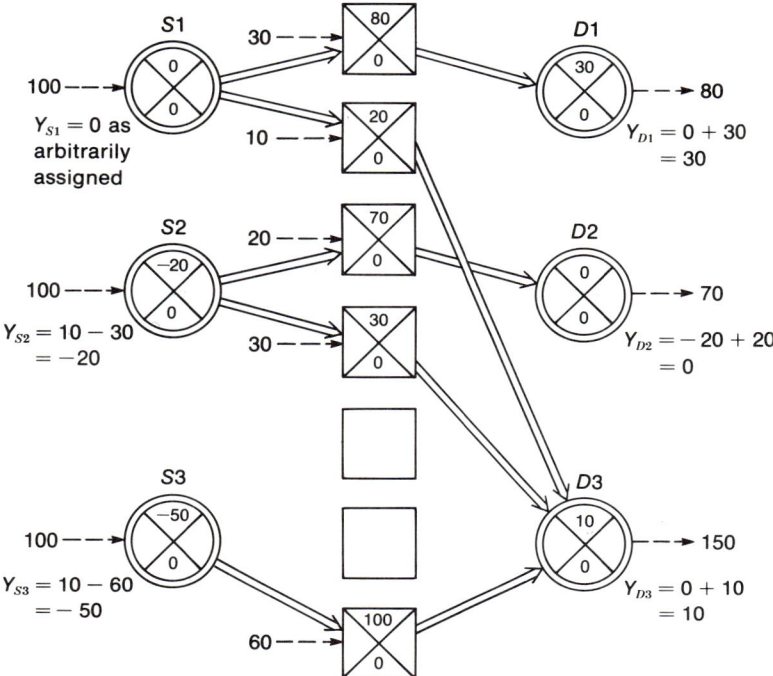

Figure 8-21 Computation of resource shadow prices for the initial feasible solution of Figure 8-13. (Only the basic paths are shown in the network.)

units should be transported from $S3$ to $D1$ to save $60 per unit, but no gain is achieved by utilizing route $S3,D2$.

To take advantage of the discovered savings for route $X_{S3,D1}$ we must transfer units from $X_{S3,D3}$, increase $X_{S1,D3}$ to compensate for the decrease at $D3$, and decrease $X_{S1,D1}$ to balance the supply at $S1$. Consequently, the largest allocation that can be made for $X_{S3,D1}$ is the smallest of $X_{S1,D1}$ and $X_{S3,D3}$, which is 80 units.

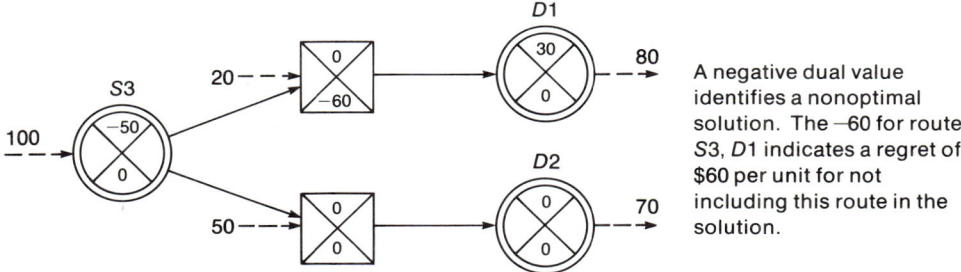

A negative dual value identifies a nonoptimal solution. The –60 for route $S3, D1$ indicates a regret of $60 per unit for not including this route in the solution.

Figure 8-22 Calculation of dual values for X nodes on the unused paths of the sample transportation problem.

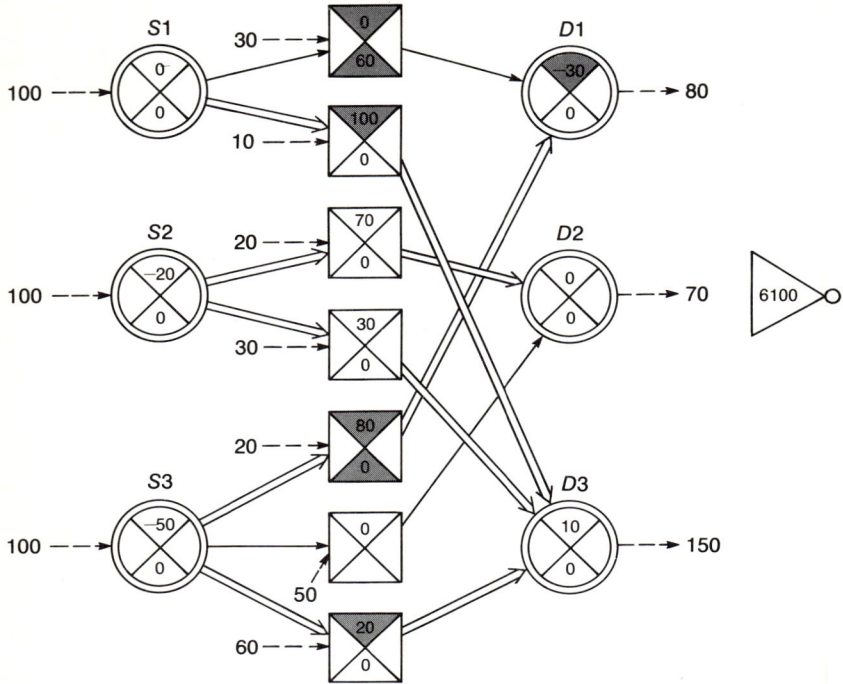

Figure 8-23 Routing reassignments produce an optimal solution as indicated by the zero or positive regret values.

Making these 80-unit transfers produces the improved solution. Allocation changes and revised dual values for the X nodes are shaded in Figure 8-23. Since all the new X-node dual values are zero or positive, the solution is optimal.

Before leaving the RPM solution, we should be alerted to the information available from the dual calculations. We have always seen how the process-node dual values reveal which unused routes should be included in the final solution. The resource shadow prices point out how much the value of units has increased by transporting them. For example, the difference between the shadow prices at $D3$ and $S3$ is \$10 − (\$−50) = \$60, which equals the transportation cost from $D3$ to $S3$; similarly, output minus input for the $S3,D1$ route is \$−30 − (\$−50) = \$20. By such Y-node calculations, which recognize the increased value of the output over the input, we can calculate the total transportation cost. The total charges are identical to those computed by using X-node values:

For an optimal solution
Resource input value + transportation cost
= resource output value (since regret = 0 for occupied cells)

which leads to
total transportation cost = total output value − total input value

where

Total output value
= ($−30 × 80) + ($0 × 70) + ($10 × 150)
= $−900

Total input value
= ($0 × 100) + ($−20 × 100) + (−50 × 100)
= $−7,000

Total transportation cost
= $−900 − ($−7,000) = $6,100

Essentially the same techniques followed in applying the MODI method to an RPM network are appropriate for a transportation tableau. Although the input/output relationships are not as apparent in MODI calculations on a tableau, they are still the basis for determining regret costs. The only difference is that MODI effectively reverses all arrow directions around the source nodes. Such reversals are shown in Figure 8-27 in Example 8-3 where an RPM network is adapted to represent the MODI convention. This representation is permissible only when the resource node represents an equality condition, that is, supply equals demand. Then, compared to the RPM calculation of $Y_{D3,S1} = Y_{D3} + C_{D3,S1} - Y_{S1}$, MODI would have $R_{D3,S1} = -V_{D3} + C_{D3,S1} - U_{S1}$, where R is the MODI regret and V and U are MODI shadow prices.

Applying the MODI method to a tableau starts with the calculation of row and column reference values, designated U and V, respectively. The first row reference value U_1 is arbitrarily set equal to zero as was the first Y value on the RPM network, and then a U and a V value are computed for each row i and column j from the relationship

$$U_i + V_j = C_{ij}$$ when $R_{ij} = 0$ if occupied

applied to each occupied cell where $R_{ij} \equiv 0$. The procedure is described in the following equations, and the results are shown for the sample problem tableau in Figure 8-24.

$U_1 \quad = 0$ by arbitrary assignment
$U_1 + V_1 = C_{11}$ from the transportation cost at the occupied cell $S1,D1$
$V_1 \quad = C_{11} - U_1$
$\quad = 30$
$V_3 \quad = C_{13} - U_1$
$\quad = 10$ by similarly using U_1 and the transportation cost at $S1,D3$
$U_2 \quad = C_{23} - V_3$ from knowing V_3 and the transportation cost at the occupied cell $S2,D3$
$\quad = 30 - 10$
$\quad = 20$
$U_3 \quad = C_{33} - V_3$
$\quad = 50$ from the same V_3 and the transportation cost at $S3,D1$

222 Introduction to Operations Research and Management Science

		$V_1 = 30$		$V_2 = 0$		$V_3 = 10$	
Reference values		D1		D2		D3	
		30		M		10	
$U_1 = 0$	S1						100
		80				20	
		M		20		30	
$U_2 = 20$	S2						100
				70		30	
		20		50		60	
$U_3 = 50$	S3						100
				100			
		80		70		150	300

Figure 8-24 Row and column reference values for the application of the MODI method to the initial feasible solution of Figure 8-13.

$$V_2 = C_{22} - U_2 \text{ by using } U_2 \text{ and transportation cost at } S2, D2$$
$$= 20 - 20$$
$$= 0$$

After a little practice, these calculations can be conducted mentally.

Once the row and column reference values are known, the next step is to evaluate each unused cell, that is, to calculate the regret for all routes not included in the present solution. This is accomplished by applying the following formula to the empty cells:

Regret $= C_{ij} - U_i - V_j$

If the result is negative, the indicated amount can be saved for each unit transferred to that route. As applied to the unused routes in our sample problem,

Regret for $S3, D1 = C_{31} - U_3 - V_1 = 20 - 50 - 30 = -60$

Regret for $S3, D2 = C_{32} - U_3 - V_2 = 50 - 50 - 0 = 0$

These regrets agree with those calculated by the stepping-stone method and with the RPM network.

In the MODI method the reassignment procedure on a tableau at this point is the same as previously described. The procedure is briefly summarized in the following four steps:

1. Trace a closed path from the unused cell with the most regret (the largest negative number).

2. Place a plus sign in the cell selected and alternately place minus and plus signs at each corner of the closed path composed of vertical and horizontal connecting lines.

Network Programming: Transportation and Transshipment 223

Reference values

		$V_1 = 30$	$V_2 = 0$	$V_3 = 10$	
		D1	D2	D3	
$U_1 = 0$	S1	30	M	10	100
			100		
$U_2 = 20$	S2	M	20	30	100
			70	30	
$U_3 = 50$	S3	20	50	60	100
		80		20	
		80	70	150	300

The final reference values are indicated, only V_1 has changed. Revised regret values are calculated as

Regret at S1, D1 = 30 − 30 = 0
Regret at S3, D2 = 50 − 50 = 0

Since the regrets are positive or zero, the solution is optimal as shown.

Figure 8-25 Optimal solution obtained by the MODI method.

3. Identify the smallest allocation among all cells marked negative on the path. Add this amount to all plus cells and subtract it from all minus cells.
4. Check the improved solution to see if any unoccupied cells still show regret; if not, total transportation costs for the optimal solution can be calculated.

A tableau checked for an optimal solution to the sample transportation problem is shown in Figure 8-25.

Example 8-3: Wonderwhere Rental Car Company redistributes its fleet A map of Wonder Valley was given in Figure 7-23. Owing to business activities, rental cars tend to accumulate in Aurora and Baker. The Wonderwhere Rental Car Company maintains offices in all five cities in the valley and currently has the bulk of its fleet stranded in Aurora and Baker. Since the company lacks any piggy-back car carriers, college students are hired to drive the cars to desired locations. Consequently, the cost of transportation is directly proportional to the distance. A mileage chart between the cities and the surplus or shortage of cars for each city are given in the following table:

From	To (distance in miles)			Surplus cars
	Cornvallis (C)	Dallas (D)	Eastport (E)	
Aurora (A)	44	70	92	36
Baker (B)	88	75	53	49
				85
Car shortage	29	28	38	95

Since the shortage of cars is 10 greater than the supply, Wonderwhere has decided to buy additional cars. The bid price for an order of 10 cars is the same at Dallas and Eastport, and these two cities are 40 mi apart. Cornvallis is 38 mi from Dallas and 116 mi from Eastport. Now the company must decide where to buy cars and what transportation routes to use after the purchase.

First Tableau (VAM)

	Cornvallis	Dallas	Eastport	
Aurora	② 44 29	④ 70 7	92 ~~36~~ 7	
Baker	88 ④ 11	75 ③ 38	53 ~~49~~ 11	
Dallas	38 ① 10	0	40 ~~10~~	
	~~29~~	~~26~~ ~~18~~ ~~11~~	~~36~~	95

Regret iterations (top right):
①	②	③	④
−36	−36	−22	−22
−22	−22	−22	−13
−38			

Regret iterations (bottom):
① −6, −70, −13
② −6, −5, −13
③ , −5, −13
④ , −5,

Circled numbers indicate the order in which allocations were entered in the tableau. Crossoffs show stages by which rim conditions were met.

Second Tableau (MODI)

		$V_1 = 44$ Cornvallis	$V_2 = 70$ Dallas	$V_3 = 48$ Eastport	
$U_1 = 0$	Aurora	44 29	70 7	92 36	36
$U_2 = 5$	Baker	88 11	75 38	53 49	49
$U_3 = -70$	Dallas	38 10	0	40 10	10
		29	28	38	95

Regret for unused routes
A to E = 92 − 48 = 44
B to C = 88 − 49 = 39
D to C = 38 − (−26) = 64
D to E = 40 − (−22) = 62

Total transportation mileage
A to C: 29 × 44 = 1276
A to D: 7 × 70 = 490
B to D: 11 × 75 = 825
B to E: 38 × 53 = 2014
D to D: 10 × 0 =   0
                  ─────
                  4605

Figure 8-26 VAM and MODI applied to a tableau depicting the Wonderwhere Rental Car allocation problem when 10 new cars are purchased at Dallas.

One way to analyze the problem is to solve it twice, once with Dallas as a supplier and once with Eastport a supplier. The first solution is conducted on a transportation tableau. The initial feasible solution is conducted by applying VAM, and the regret values obtained for each VAM iteration are shown in the first tableau of Figure 8-26. In the second tableau the MODI method is used to check the solution; since all regret values are positive, the total transportation distance is calculated as 4605 mi. The second way of solving Wonderwhere's problem, based on buying cars in Eastport, is shown in Figure 8-27, where the MODI condition is de-

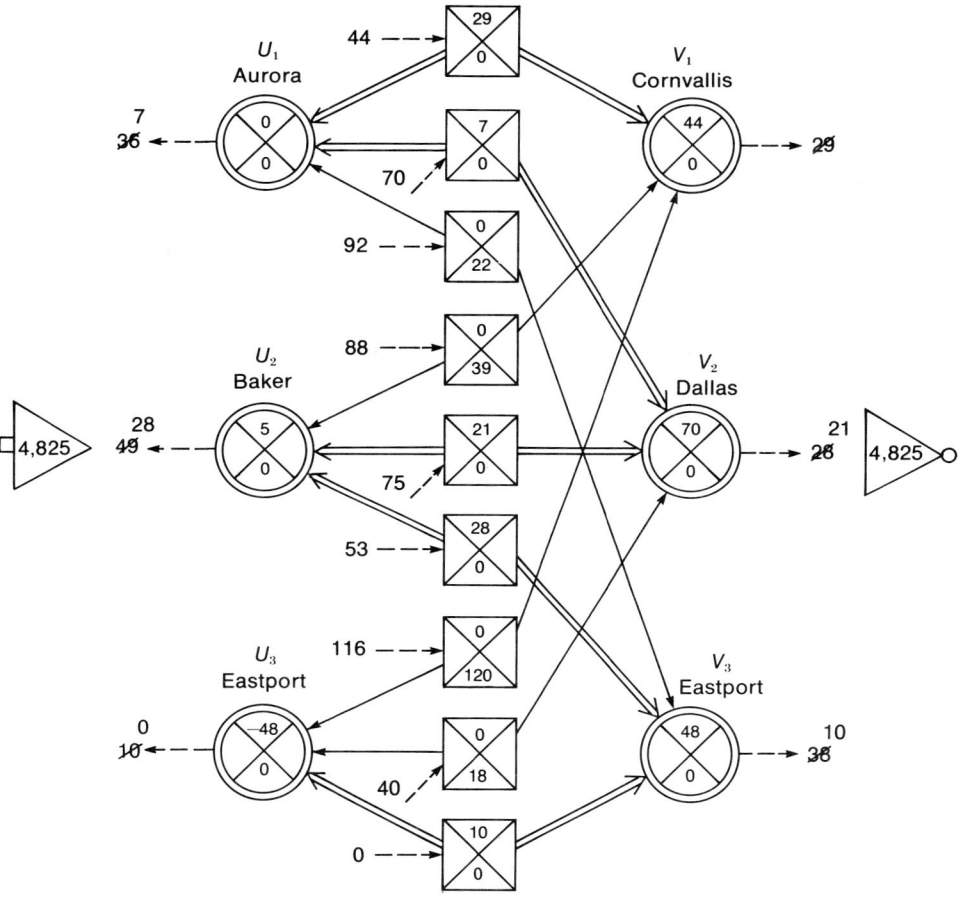

Total transportation mileage: $(44 \times 29 = 1276) + (70 \times 7 = 490)$
$+ (75 \times 21 = 1575) + (53 \times 28 = 1,484)$
$+ (0 \times 10 = 0) = 4825$ mi

Figure 8-27 RPM network solution of the Wonderwhere Rental Car reassignment problem which conforms to sign conventions of the MODI method.

veloped on an RPM network. The positive regret values at the X nodes indicate the solution is optimal. Comparing the total mileage for two alternative locations to purchase the new cars indicates that the Dallas source is preferable to the Eastport source.

SECTION 8-4 TUNE-UP Transshipment as a transportation problem

In Section 7-2 Tune-up, we encountered a capacitated transshipment problem. It is possible to formulate a noncapacitated transshipment problem in the form of a transportation model, the only difference from the standard model being that a transshipment model includes points of transshipment which act as both supplier and consumer of resources. In Example 8-3 we demonstrated how either a tableau or an RPM network can be used to solve such a model.

Assume there are five points in an organization's network: 1, 2, 3, 4, and 5. Points 1 and 2 are suppliers with capacities of 60 and 40 units, respectively; conversely, points 4 and 5 are consumers with demands of 50 units each. The costs of transporting 1 unit over each available linkage are as follows:

To From	1	2	3	4	5
1	0	2	4	10	NA*
2	3	0	2	NA	20
3	NA	NA	0	2	1
4	NA	10	10	0	NA
5	NA	NA	6	NA	0

*Not available.

In setting up the transportation model, we must first identify the total supply and demand. In this problem, total supply = 60 + 40 = 100, which is the same as the total demand 50 + 50 = 100; therefore, the reference value of supply and demand for each point is 100. To this reference value we add amounts that set the actual condition of each point. For example, point 1 has a supply of 100 + 60 = 160 while its demand is 100; similarly, Point 5 has a supply of 100 and a demand of 100 + 50 = 150. Construct a tableau and RPM network to represent the transportation model of transshipment.

8-5 Extensions of transportation models

Because the transportation model can be conveniently solved by manual methods, its use is extended by adaptations that expand its area of applicability. In this section we shall consider how the conditions of degeneracy and unequal supply and demand are treated when the MODI method is employed.

DEGENERACY IN TRANSPORTATION MODELS A degenerate condition exists in a transportation model when the number of occupied cells in a tableau is less than $n + m - 1$; thus, in a tableau with three rows and four columns, exactly $3 + 4 - 1 = 6$ allocations must be entered to avoid degeneracy. With fewer than this number of occupied cells it is not possible to check the solution for optimality. The stepping-stone method cannot be used because it is impossible to complete closed paths from some of the empty cells. Similarly, the MODI method does not work because a degenerate solution does not allow all the row and column reference values to be calculated. More than $n + m - 1$ allocations lead to contradictions.

Degeneracy can cause trouble in an initial feasible solution and in any revised solutions. As an example, consider the problem given in Section 8-2 Tune-up; a tableau showing the conditions given in its RPM network is provided in Figure

	D	E	M	
U	2	3	M	
	60			60
S	3	5	7	
		50	40	90
	60	50	40	

The given allocations were made according to the northwest corner rule. Rim conditions are satisfied, but the solution is degenerate.

Figure 8-28 Tableau for the RPM network in Section 8-2 Tune-up.

8-28. The initial feasible solution developed by the northwest-corner rule is entered in the tableau. However, since there are only three allocations and $2 + 3 - 1 = 4$ cells have to be occupied to avoid degeneracy, this initial solution cannot be checked for optimality (as a proof, try to calculate the regret for any unused path or try to develop the MODI reference values for any rows or columns except the first). Therefore, an additional technique is required to overcome this occasionally unavoidable difficulty.

The device used to overcome degeneracy is to add an infinitesimally small amount to an occupied cell. This amount, called *epsilon* (ϵ), is so small that it does not violate rim conditions but is still large enough for the cell in which it occurs to be considered occupied. The epsilon assignment is comparable to assigning an arbitrary exchange rate between two isolated economic systems as a prelude to future trade agreements. Although there is no rigid rule for guiding the placement of an epsilon, it is generally positioned to maintain an unbroken chain of occupied cells.

Once the epsilon is in place, the usual routine is followed to check the solution. In Figure 8-29, the epsilon is placed in cell U,E; then the MODI method is applied to reveal a -1 regret for the route S to D. The closed path required for the reassignment includes the epsilon-occupied cell. The smallest number (50) in a negative cell on the path is transferred, and the resulting solution is optimal. Equivalent procedures involving epsilon placements are conducted for degenerate solutions in RPM representations of transportation problems; epsilon is placed in an X node to allow the calculation of shadow prices (see Figure 8-30).

UNEQUAL SUPPLY AND DEMAND One of the conditions for applying MODI to solve a transportation model is that demand is balanced by supply. Unfortunately, most real problems are unbalanced; that is, the rim conditions for the rows and columns are not equal. To solve such problems by MODI we establish an artificial source of destination and then assign our surplus or shortage to this fictitious entity.

When demand is greater than supply, a fictitious source of resources is created, which is assumed to possess sufficient units to meet the demand. It is concep-

228 Introduction to Operations Research and Management Science

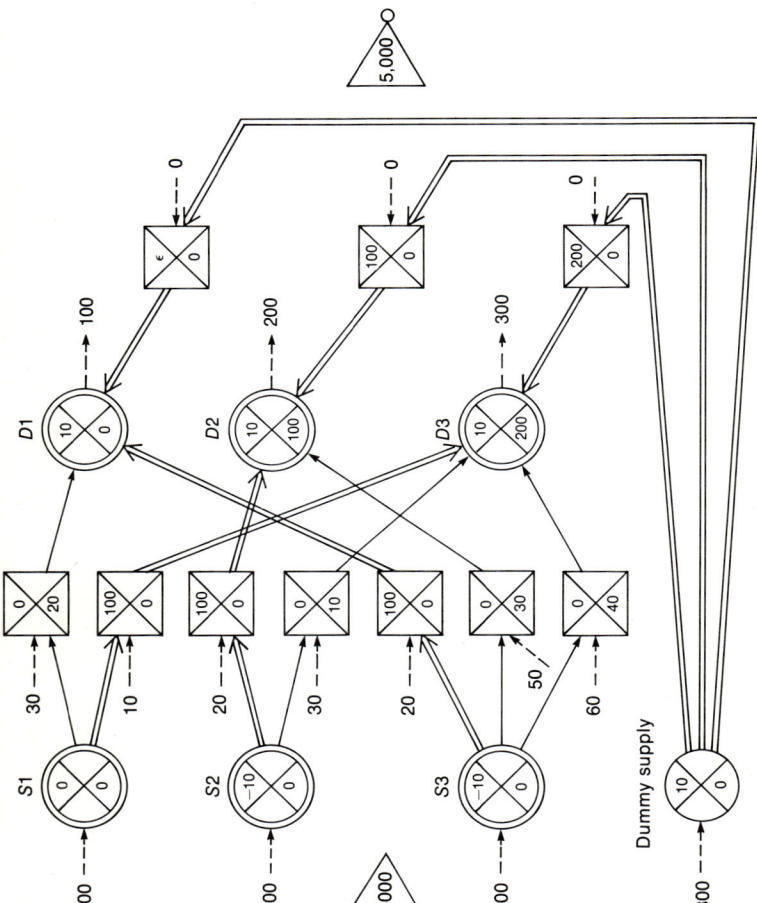

The dummy supply is assigned 300 units to balance demand. The optimal solution indicates these 300 fictitious units are allocated to D2 and D3. This routing provides the least expensive way to transport the 300 actual units to destinations.

Figure 8-30 RPM network with a dummy supply.

	$V_1 = 2$	$V_2 = 3$	$V_3 = 5$	
	D	E	M	
$U_1 = 0$ U	2 ⊖---⊕ 160 ε	3	M 60	60
$U_2 = 2$ S	3 ⊕------⊖ 50	5 40	7	90
	60	50	40	

	D	E	M	
U	2 10	3 50	M	60
S	3 50	5	7 40	90
	60	50	40	

Optimality check: Regret at
S, D = 3 − 2 − 2 = −1

Revised solution: 50 units
transferred. Solution is optimal.

Figure 8-29 Use of the infinitesimal ε value to overcome degeneracy in the initial feasible solution.

tualized on a tableau by an additional row, and on an RPM network by an extra resource supply node. The number of units assigned to the "dummy" supply is exactly the difference between actual supply and demand. Transportation costs from the dummy supply to any destination is naturally zero because no actual transfers can take place.

Figure 8-30 illustrates how excess demand is handled on an RPM network. The problem illustrated is the same as the one in Figure 8-13, with the exception that the demand is increased at every destination. The number of units assigned to the dummy supply is consequently 600 − 300 = 300, and the transfer costs for the associated X nodes are all equal to zero. The optimal allocation pattern assigns 100 units to each destination, leaving an unsatisfied demand of 100 units at D2 and 200 units at D3.

The procedures used to account for excess supply are very similar to those discussed for excess demand, and they are illustrated in Figure 8-31 on a transportation tableau. Again, the problem is an adaptation of the one in Figure 8-13; this time the supply is doubled at each source. An extra column with zero transfer costs is added to show the dummy demand. An RPM example for excess supply has already been studied in detail (Example 8-1, p. 202).

MAXIMIZATION Solution methods for transportation problems are designed to identify the allocations that minimize total cost. Occasionally a problem is most naturally stated in terms of expected profit instead of cost. This situation is accommodated for the transportation method by treating profits as negative losses and then applying regular minimizing techniques.

A convenient procedure for converting a profit statement into cost relationships is to subtract all stated profits from the highest profit; the resulting numbers are *relative costs* and are treated as regular costs in solving the problem. For example, if the largest profit possible in any resource transfer is 10, all

		$V_1 = 20$	$V_2 = 20$	$V_3 = 10$	$V_D = 0$	
		D1	D2	D3	Dummy	
$U_1 = 0$	S1	⑩ 30	M 150	10 50	0	200
$U_2 = 0$	S2	M 70	20	⑳ 30 130	0	200
$U_3 = 0$	S3	20 80	㉚ 50	㊿ 60 120	0	200
		80	70	150	300	600

Figure 8-31 Transportation tableau with an extra column added to account for excess supply.

transfer profits would be subtracted from 10; this policy gives $10 - 10 = 0$ relative cost for the most profitable route, which, of course, makes it the most attractive route for cost minimization. Similarly, the lowest profit route would have the highest relative cost. After all source-to-destination transfer charges are calculated, any of the methods previously described for a tableau or RPM network can be used to develop the solution. From the preferred routes indicated in the solution, the total profit can be calculated by using the original profit figures.

An application of the maximization policy to an assignment problem of the type introduced in Figure 8-17 is given in the following example.

Example 8-4: *Unbalanced assignment problem to maximize profit* The Wonderland talent agency handles most of the bookings for visiting entertainers. For a particular weekend the agency has booked four groups, each of which will be available for only a single performance before going on to another engagement. In each of the major cities of Wonderland (Aurora, Baker, Cornvallis, Dallas, and Eastport) a different audience size for each group can be expected owing to local preferences. Estimates of ticket sales in thousands of dollars for each group at each city are tabulated as follows:

City Group	A	B	C	D	E
1	112	132	101	140	103
2	46	64	48	55	45
3	69	74	60	94	66
4	88	86	51	80	75

Since the groups already have signed contracts to appear somewhere in Wonderland on the given date, the agency must decide which group to send where.

Network Programming: Transportation and Transshipment

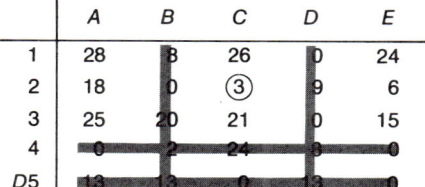

Figure 8-32 Six solution steps for the assignment method to solve in Example 8-4.

The step-by-step solution is shown in Figure 8-32. After altering the assignment matrix to include relative costs and a dummy row, three iterations are required to discover the most profitable assignments: 1 to Baker, 2 to Cornvallis, 3 to Dallas, 4 to Aurora, and 0 to Eastport. The maximum ticket revenue is $132 + 48 + 94 + 88 = 362$ ($362,000 from the original profit matrix). The circled numbers in the matrices in Figure 8-32 indicate the lowest entry not covered by a line that was used in the revision, and boxed numbers show the optimal assignment.

8-6 Branch-and-bound method

The assignment problem is a simple combinatorial riddle that is effectively solved by the Hungarian method. Unfortunately, most combinatorial problems are more complex and are not amenable to such a straight-forward approach. A notable problem is known as the *traveling-salesman problem*, which requires the determination of the shortest route connecting all given cities in an itinerary without visiting a same city twice. Until the last decade, this problem was considered unsolvable by many OR/MS researchers, and even a cash prize was offered to the first individual presenting a workable algorithm. In fact, Eliezer Naddor wrote in 1960:

> *No general method has yet been found to solve Travelling Salesman problems. One can always try the method of reduced matrices of the Assignment Problem. This may sometimes lead to a solution provided that the Assignment Problem is a feasible solution of the Travelling Salesman Problem. But if the solution is not feasible, there is no way of getting a solution to the Travelling Salesman Problem. This problem, as the* m × n *Sequencing Problem, has been tackled by some of our best mathematicians, but so far they have not succeeded in solving it.*

Today, there is a simple algorithmic solution procedure based on the creation of a decision tree. This procedure, broadly known as the *branch-and-bound (B & B) method*, is applicable to many OR/MS problems including that of creating an optimal integer solution to a mathematical programming problem. To introduce this method, let us return to the simple assignment problem of Example 8-3 and construct the B & B decision tree. Figure 8-33 illustrates the process.

The B & B method utilizes the reduction of the matrix to find a *promising move* and a decision tree to keep track of its trials. If at any time a previously foregone option appears to become desirable, the *back-tracking* is simplified by the bookkeeping of the lower (and upper if necessary) bounds at the nodes along the way. The flexibility of the B & B procedure is derived from the OR/MS analyst's ability to foreclose any undesirable option and obey whatever rules are appropriate. In the case of the traveling salesman, for example, the rule is not to let him visit the same city twice, but to return to the home base after he has visited all his clients. Each time the salesman takes on a new city, the matrix should be changed to make it impossible or extremely costly for him to return to the cities he has already visited. The procedure can be easily modified to account for other types of situations, and the branch-and-bound method is commonly used in job-shop scheduling, integer programming, and other OR/MS problems of a combinatorial nature.

Example 8-5: *Microbus routing* The Micropolis Inter-Metropolis Improvement Council (MIMIC) has decided that the city of Micropolis should have a bus route to connect its five major business and shopping districts (Figure 8-34). The route will be operated by one microbus on a minimal budget. In order to provide frequent trips while conserving fuel, it is imperative to find the shortest route connecting these five points.

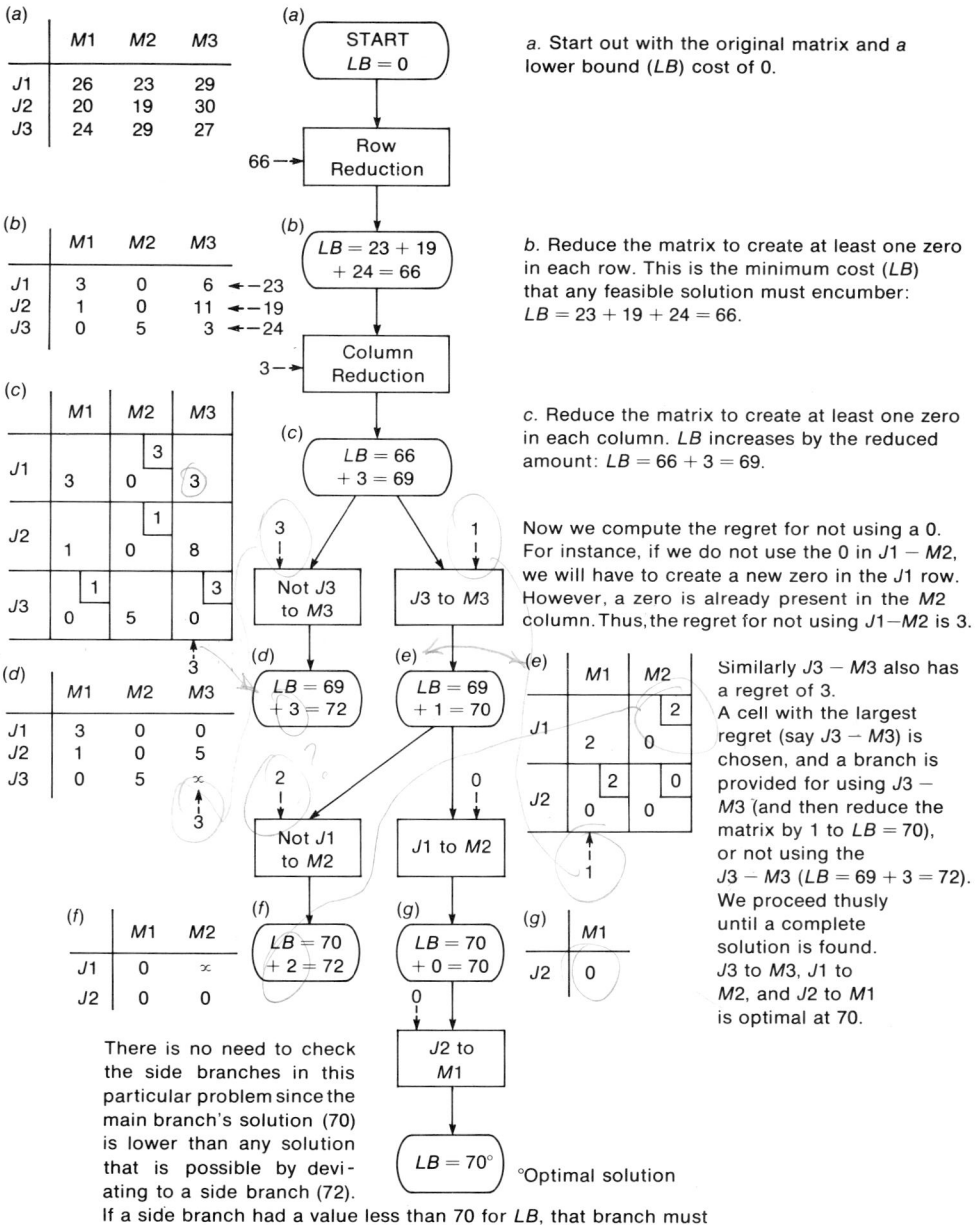

Figure 8-33 Example 8-3 revisited using branch-and-bound method.

234 Introduction to Operations Research and Management Science

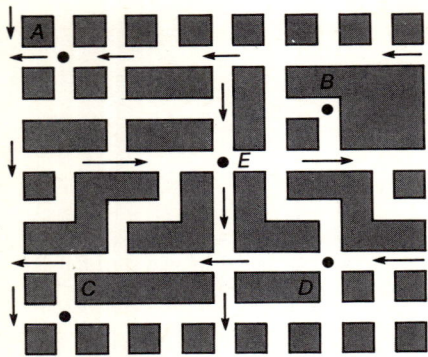

Figure 8-34 Downtown Micropolis.

The first task is to create a distance matrix similar to the one in Chapter 3 for Example 3-2. However, the matrix in this problem is asymmetric due to the one-way streets, and a full matrix must be constructed. Taking the number of city blocks as the measure, the distance matrix and their reduced matrices are obtained:

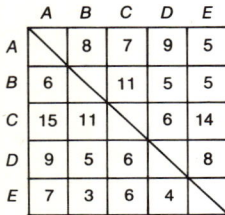

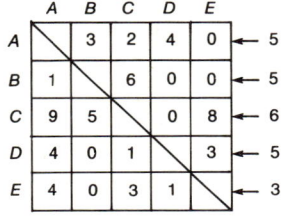

Total row reduction = 24

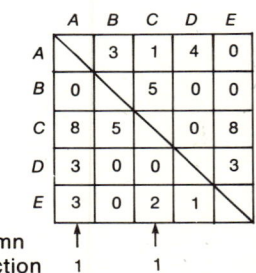

Column reduction 1 1

Total reduction = 24 + 2 = 26

For each zero in the reduced matrix, we need to compute the regret value in case that zero is not used. This regret is the sum of the smallest number in the row and the smallest number in the column corresponding to the zero. In our case, all regrets are zero, except 1 for *AE*, 3 for *BA*, 4 for $\overline{CD}$, 1 for *DC*, and 2 for *EB*. Since *C* to *D* has the largest regret *4*, the decision tree (Figure 8-35) shows the regret of 4 as being the cost for *not* choosing *CD* (the decision $\bar{C}\bar{D}$). Because of its extreme flexibility, the B & B method is gaining popularity as an important OR/MS tool. As seen in Figure 8-35, the procedure is intuitively obvious; it is necessary only to identify the cost of each decision and to foreclose any undesirable alternative by assigning a high cost (for example *D* to *C* in matrix *CD* has an infinite cost to prevent the loop *C-D-C* from forming).

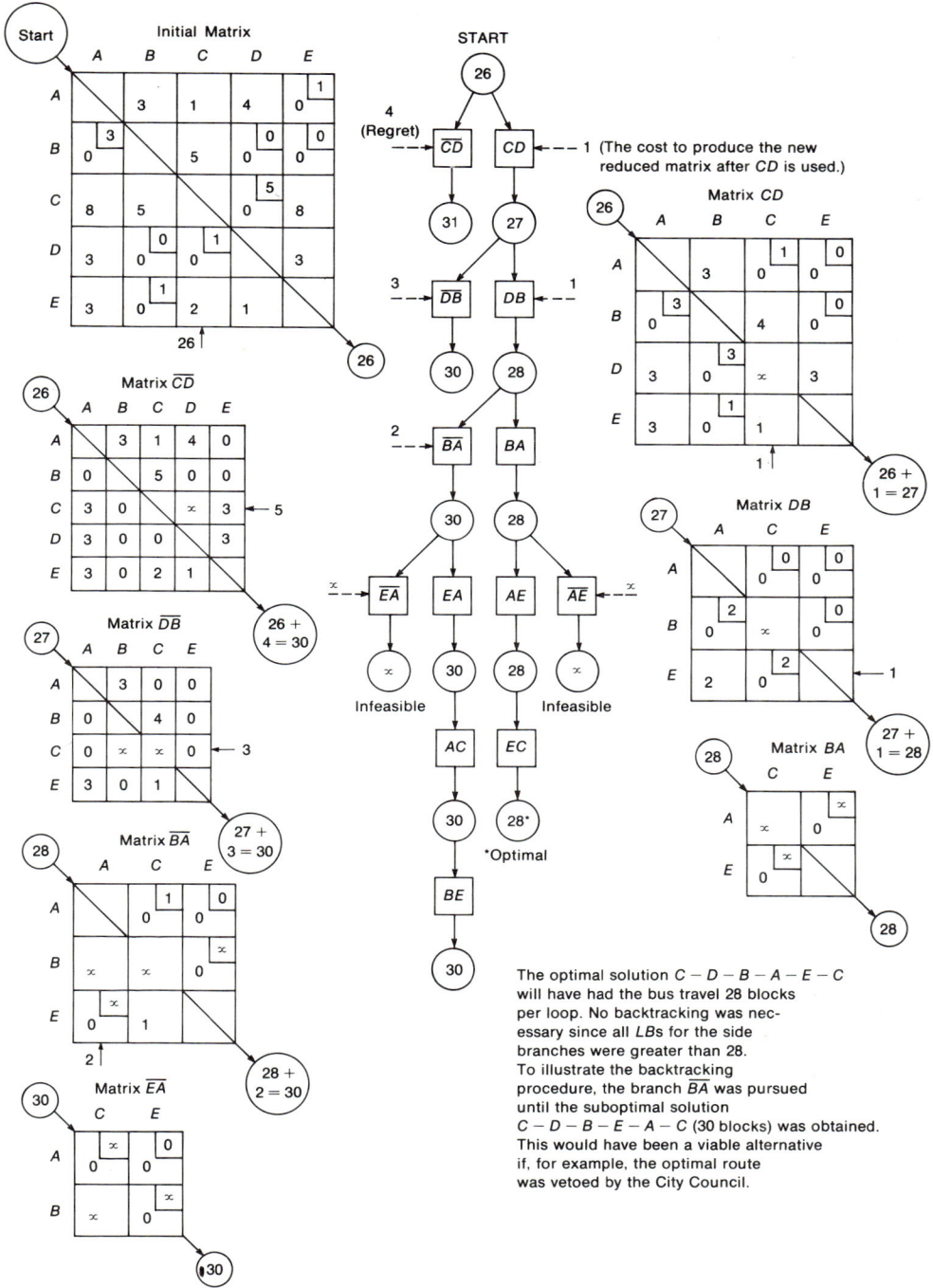

Figure 8-35 B & B method applied to the traveling-salesman problem of Example 8-6 (MIMIC bus route).

TUNE-UP SOLUTIONS

Section 8-2

1. *Rim conditions* refer to the data that define the supply-demand relationship. From Figure 8-12, the two supply sources contain 60 and 90 units while the three demand destinations contain 60, 50, and 40; thus total demand equals total supply. Please note this equality is a necessary condition for the application of MODI (Section 8-4).
2. After a small problem is adequately visualized, a solution can usually be obtained by inspection. From the network in Figure 8-12 it is obvious that demand M can be satisfied only from supply S; however, a little scrutiny shows it is less expensive to satisfy demand E from supply U. Following these observations produces the allocation pattern shown in Figure 8-36, where the process dual values confirm that the solution is optimal. (A tableau representing the same problem and solution is shown in Figure 8-29.) The negative entry, -1 in S, is due to the arbitrary assignment of 0 to U. It would not have occurred had 0 been assigned to S instead of U.

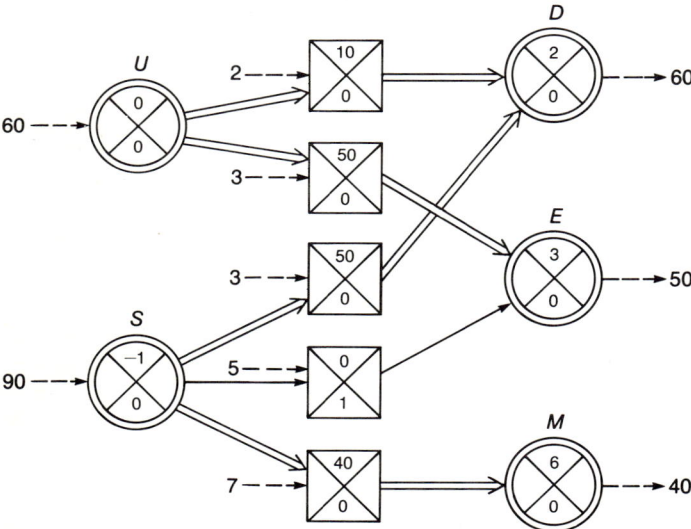

Figure 8-36 RPM network checked for optimality.

	*M*1	*M*2	*M*3	
*J*1	[26] 1	[23]	[29]	1
*J*2	[20]	[19] 1	[30]	1
*J*3	[24]	[29]	[27] 1	1
	1	1	1	

Northwest corner rule applied

VAM	*M*1	*M*2	*M*3		Regret
*J*1	[26]	[23] 1	[29]	1	−3
*J*2	[20] 1	[19]	[30]	1	−1
*J*3	[24]	[29]	[27] 1	1	−2
	1	1	1		
Regret	−4	−4	−3		

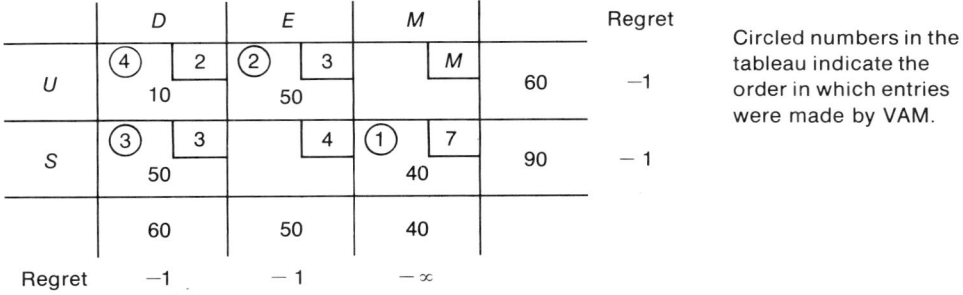

Figure 8-37 Initial feasible solutions for the assignment problem in Example 8-2.

	D	*E*	*M*		Regret
U	(4) [2] 10	(2) [3] 50	[*M*]	60	−1
S	(3) [3] 50	[4]	(1) [7] 40	90	− 1
	60	50	40		
Regret	−1	− 1	− ∞		

Circled numbers in the tableau indicate the order in which entries were made by VAM.

Figure 8-38 VAM applied to the problem also solved in Figure 8-36.

Section 8-3

1. VAM and the northwest-corner rule are applied to the assignment problem in Figure 8-37. VAM produces the same solution developed by the assignment method in Example 8-2.
2. The circled numbers in the tableau in Figure 8-38 indicate the order in which entries were made according to VAM.

238 Introduction to Operations Research and Management Science

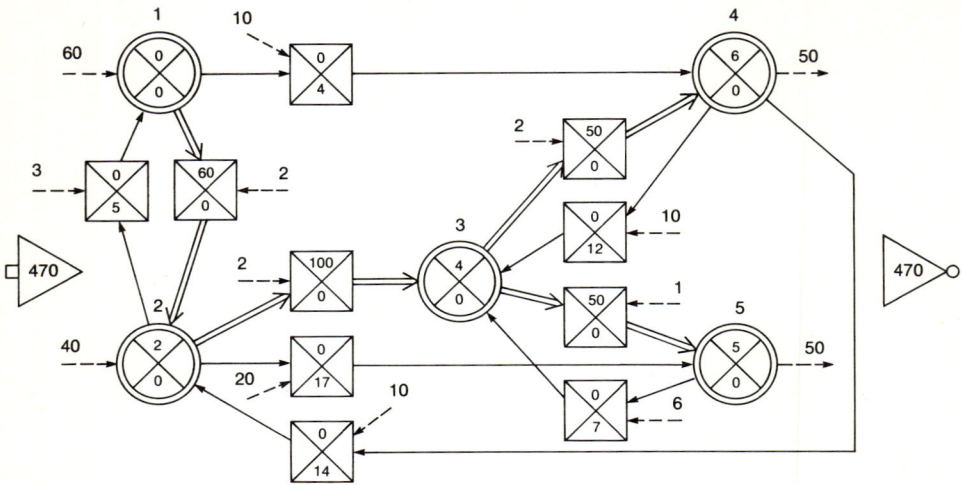

Figure 8-39 RPM network revealing the lowest-cost route for transshipment: 60 from 1 to 2; 100 from 2 to 3; and 50 from 3 to 4 and 5.

From \ To	1	2	3	4	5		Regret
1	⑤ 0 100	⑥ 2 60	4	10	M	160	−2
2	3	⑦ 0 40	⑧ 2 100	M	20	140	−2
3	M	M	0	② 2 50	④ 1 50	100	−1
4	M	10	10	① 0 100	M	100	−10
5	M	M	6	M	③ 0 100	100	−6
	100	100	100	150	150		
Regret	−3	−2	−2	−2	−1		

Figure 8-40 VAM applied to the transshipment problem. (Circled numbers indicate the order in which the entries are made.)

Network Programming: Transportation and Transshipment 239

MODI reference values		$V_1 = 0$	$V_2 = 2$	$V_3 = 4$	$V_4 = 6$	$V_5 = 5$	
		1	2	3	4	5	
$U_1 = 0$	1	0 100	2 60	0 4	4 4	10 M	M 160
$U_2 = -2$	2	⑤ 3 5	0 40	2 100	M M	⑰ 20 17	140
$U_3 = -4$	3	M M	M M ε	0 50	2 50	1 100	
$U_4 = -6$	4	M M	⑭ 10 14	⑫ 10 12	0 100	M M 100	
$U_5 = -5$	5	M M	M M	⑦ 6 7	M M 100	0 100	
		100	100	100	150	150	

Figure 8-41 MODI check for optimality of the transshipment solution.

Section 8-4

1. A transshipment model resembles actual physical proportions when it is laid out on an RPM network drawn like a map. As shown in Figure 8-39, the usual format for a transportation problem is abandoned in favor of the maplike representation, but all the calculation procedures are still applicable. Using the rim conditions suggested in the tune-up, a tableau for the transshipment problem can be constructed as shown in Figure 8-40 where VAM is applied to develop an initial solution. Figure 8-41 shows the MODI check for optimality.

EXERCISES

8-1 Solve the following transportation problems.

(a) Minimize the cost for the given routes:

							Supply
75	82	46	65	38	77	70	18
46	49	55	40	60	52	50	38
65	77	71	59	68	80	66	49
97	92	84	75	91	90	80	26
60	58	72	65	50	49	55	32
Demand							
24	12	36	40	16	17	18	163

(b) Maximize the profits:

					Supply
	15	51	42	33	23
	80	42	26	81	44
	90	40	66	60	33
Demand	23	31	16	30	100

(c) Minimize the cost:

							Supply
	90	41	88	30	32	40	100
	83	80	62	70	50	62	100
	49	40	70	88	40	40	100
	35	40	65	35	65	40	100
Demand	75	75	75	75	75	75	

8-2 A beef wholesaler ships carcasses from cold storage to retailers in different cities. The present routes are shown in the RPM network in Figure 8-42, together with the new shipping rates ($/lb) and costs for alternative routes. Determine whether the present routes should be changed.

8-3 Six new aides have been hired, and each will be assigned to work with a senior scientist. After brief interviews, all the scientists listed their preferences for the aides; a rating of 1 means the first choice of a scientist for that aide, and, naturally, a 6 indicates the least desirable matching. The ratings are listed in the following table. Select the assignments that will produce the best matchings for total satisfaction.

Scientists						
Aides	S1	S2	S3	S4	S5	S6
A1	3	1	2	2	3	4
A2	1	2	3	1	5	5
A3	5	6	4	3	1	6
A4	2	5	1	6	6	1
A5	6	4	5	5	2	2
A6	4	3	6	4	4	3

8-4 The Wonderworks machine shop has received four orders which can be completed at different machine centers in the shop. The hourly variable cost for each center for the type of work required on each order is available from accounting records, and the unit selling price is set by agreements with each purchaser. The amounts of time available in each center before the orders have to be delivered are also known from the master production schedule. An order can be divided among machine centers. Obtain the assignment that will maximize profit for the four orders.

Job number	Order size units	Unit price	Machine center	Capacity, units	Variable cost per unit, dollars			
					Job 1	Job 2	Job 3	Job 4
1	2,000	$3.75	1	3,900	1.85	1.70	2.10	1.85
2	1,500	4.00	2	500	1.10	1.45	1.35	1.50
3	900	4.15	3	1,100	1.55	1.60	1.40	1.60
4	2,600	3.50	4	2,300	2.05	1.95	2.00	1.75

8-5 Shipments of perishable items can be transported directly to a destination at a generally higher cost, or they can be transshipped after intermediate storage to preserve the freshness. The available routes and the linkage costs are shown in the following table. Units shipped from points A, B, and C must reach destinations F and G.

From	To (cost per unit, dollars)							Available
	A	B	C	D	E	F	G	
A	0	8	10	14	6		42	70
B		0	4		19		24	130
C	6	3	0	15	6	22	19	120
D				0	7	17		
E			5	7	0	12		
F						0		
G		20					0	
Required						180	140	

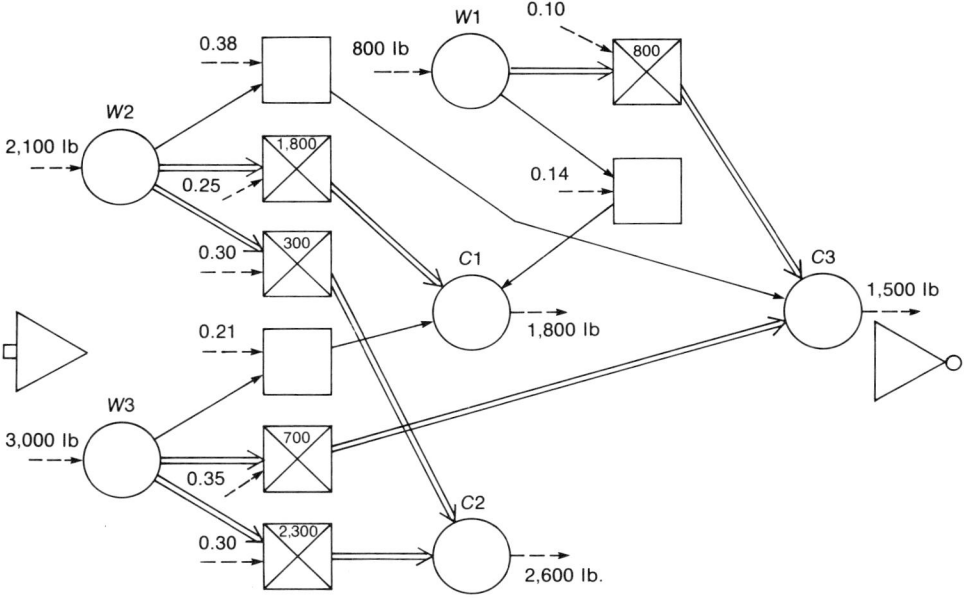

Figure 8-42 Current transportation routes to be checked for optimality.

8-6 Five artists have submitted bids to complete 4 sets of plates and the costs are given in the following table. One set of plates will be commissioned per artist. Which artist will not receive a commission? What is the minimum total cost?

Artist	Cost per plate, dollars			
	P1	P2	P3	P4
AA	2,450	2,950	2,100	3,600
AB	2,200	3,000	1,550	3,000
AC	2,500	2,200	1,900	3,200
AD	2,400	2,500	1,800	3,900
AE	2,350	2,450	2,000	3,700

SIMPLEX TABLEAU: A Table for Resource Exchange

Chapter 9

"But it's no use now," thought poor Alice,
"to pretend to be two people! Why,
there's hardly enough of me left to make
one respectable person!" (Lewis Carroll, 1865)

9-1 Climbing a convex hull

Linear programming has been the focus of our discussion in the last four chapters. In Chapter 5 we studied the basic concepts by means of two-dimensional graphic models and learned to identify the optimum solution by examining all extrema of the feasible solution space. In Chapters 6 and 7, applications were presented that could no longer be portrayed by two-dimensional FSS; computer programs were used to solve these problems, and dual values were used to check optimality of RPM networks. In Chapter 8, the role of dual values was formalized and the MODI method was introduced as an algorithm to solve transportation problems.

Let us now utilize what we have learned to understand the most popular method of solving linear programming problems: the use of *simplex algorithms*.

The word *simplex* implies a single body, as opposed to duplex, triplex, or multiplex. Simplex algorithms make use of *simplex tableaux;* a tableau is a picture. A two-dimensional *graphic* picture was used in Chapter 5; the simplex method uses a *mathematical* picture of a single-bodied FSS in an *n*-dimensional hyperspace E^n. In fact, a line segment is a simplex picture in E^1; a triangular patch is a pictorial representation of an FSS in E^2; a cube is a simplex FSS in E^3; and an FSS of a linear programming problem with *n* processes can be represented by a convex hull in E^n. *Convex* means that in going from one point to another inside a simplex body, the shortest path (a line of sight) between the two points is entirely contained within the body.

The extreme-point theorem (Chapter 5, Section 5-2) guarantees that the optimum solution occurs at one of the corners of the FSS, and a simplex algorithm finds it by moving from one corner to another in direct lines along an edge using the objective function as a "compass." Simplex procedures guarantee that each iteration (i.e., a straight-line move from one corner to an adjacent corner) is at least as profitable as the last one. This guarantee of nondecreasing optimality (*monotonicity*) is an effective weapon for combating the *curse of dimensionality* that would result if all extreme points were attacked indiscriminately. Dantzig (1963, p. 160) reports that the actual number of iterations required to achieve an optimal solution is usually close to the number of basic variables in the final set that were not present in the initial set, and rarely more than three times as many. For instance, a model with 10 processes and 20 resources has $\binom{10+20}{10} = 6{,}609{,}903{,}299$ intersections of hyperplanes (corners), including both feasible and nonfeasible solutions. By identifying and investigating only those corners that are feasible and by monotonically improving on its solution, a simplex procedure may require only 10 to 30 iterations before reaching the final solution. The economy would have been even greater if we had exercised common sense initially to identify some of the variables which enter the final solution.

SECTION 9-1 TUNE-UP

At the northwest corner of Micropolis stands Old Baldy, a hill with a steep and slimy slope on the city side, rising some 840 ft. This slope belongs to the State of Aliceka and forms the Foggy and Slimy State Park (FSS). Every year, on New Year's day, there is a race to the top of Old Baldy. The contestant is free to choose any method of transportation available, including automobiles, motorcycles, jeeps, and snowmobiles.

On your first visit to Micropolis, your friends (?) volunteer you as a contestant for this race and you find yourself at the starting point 0 with an old jalopy. You have no map and no directions, and it is so foggy that you cannot even see the summit. You do know, however, that the FSS is bordered by roads and trails and that they are all straight and uniformly ascending. Furthermore, there is no interior trail or road, and

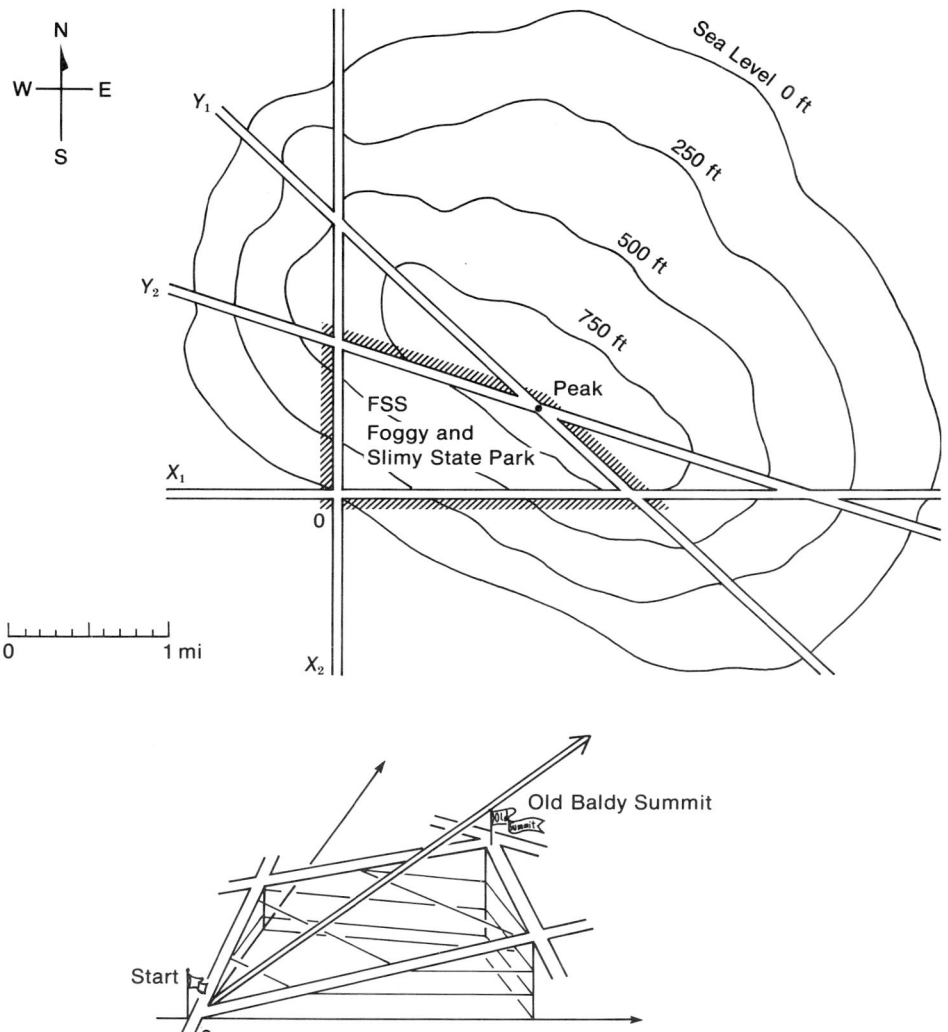

Figure 9-1 Trek to the top of Old Baldy.

the summit is found at an intersection of two such bordering trails. The map *which you do not have* is shown in Figure 9-1.

1. Formulate this problem as a linear programming problem.

2. Formulate a set of decision rules that would lead you to the summit without using the map. Interpret your rules and assumptions in terms of the theorems, principles, and logic you have learned thus far in OR/MS.

9-2 Economic interpretation of the dual flows in RPM networks

The unique advantage of using an RPM network to describe a linear programming problem, when compared with all other network models, stems from its ability to represent two types of flows in the same network model. Almost any network configuration can be used to describe the *physical* flows of resources through a system. But to portray, in addition, the flows of the values of resources through the same system requires that the model have a structure that automatically interrelates the availability, value, and transformation of resources. A system may be simulated by a model describing the primal flows, but the values of resources and processes must be known before the system can be optimized. Indeed, we need a naturally self-adjusting model.

For centuries, human beings have been trying to copy the inner workings of nature. From the religious beliefs that good will be rewarded and bad will be punished to the discovery in physics that every action is countered by an equal and opposite reaction, humanity has been in continual awe of the self-adjusting nature of the universe. The rudder on a rowboat is an early example of a man-made self-adjusting system; the 1790 invention of the Watt governor to keep the steam engine rotating at a constant speed is another example. And many other similar mechanisms are now classified as *negative-feedback devices* by scientists who specialize in *servomechanisms*, that is, mechanical devices with self-adjusting controls. The word *cybernetics* was created by Norbert Wiener in 1947 to designate the interdisciplinary science where the study of communication and control encompasses both biology and engineering. Today ecologists study nature's reactions to human civilization and apply the term *pollution* to those responses that are considered harmful to our well being.

But of all the human efforts to imitate nature's tendency to return to a state of *normalcy* (the universal equilibrium of complete randomness, or *maximum entropy*), no attempt has had as great an effect as the free economic system based on the concept of *money*. As it is used in most countries today, money is merely a piece of information that assigns a value to a resource as a function of its availability and demand. Scarce resources in great demand command higher prices than those in abundance or in less demand. As resources multiply, their unit values decline; for example, an abundant total harvest could make an individual farmer poorer and a fuel shortage could increase profits for an oil company. Our economic system acts as a natural deterrent to the wasteful use of our limited resources and as an incentive for converting resources of low values to resources of higher values, with increased utility to society. Every flow of a physical resource or a service is essentially accompanied by an opposite flow of money that establishes feedback.

The wonder of the free economy is that the system is self-adjusting and self-optimizing without any obvious control from a central agency. Each individual or corporation is free to set a price for the merchandise it markets, and without any price or production control, the market will automatically find the optimal price level for each commodity. To be certain, there are temporary fluctuations and deviations from the optimal values, and an individual who can spot them can take advantage of a situation and profit from such insights, but doing so will cause the situation to be reversed and return to normalcy. A business which charges too much for its services will eventually be driven out of the market by more reasonable competitors. A shortage of a resource will entice prospectors and inventors to create alternative sources, but a surplus, on the other hand, lowers the price, brings down the profit, and drives inefficient operators out of business.

In a free economic society each business firm receives information concerning the availability and value of resources and decides what and how much resources to buy, convert, store, and/or sell. Money is usually the criterion for such decisions, but not exclusively so. In fact, economics has been defined as:

> ...*the study of how men and society* choose, *with or without the use of money, to employ* scarce *productive resources to produce various commodities over time and distribute them for consumption, now and in the future, among various people and groups in society* (Samuelson, 1961).

If an OR/MS model is to emulate such a process, each decision node must be given information, not only on the feasibility of such a decision, but also on its optimality. Then each decision node can be acted on individually while achieving the collective objective for the entire system.

A simple assumption that to each action there is an equal and opposite reaction makes it easy for an RPM network to model this duality concept. In a linear programming model, the coefficient of conversion is shown as a constant parameter on each branch joining a process node to a resource node. In Figure 9-2, for example, the resource node y_i is connected to the process node x_j with a coefficient a_{ij}. Yet this same coefficient performs exactly the opposite function when evaluating the primal value as when evaluating the dual value. The coefficient acts as a multiplier for the flow out of a node and also as a divider for the flow into the node. Thus, when a process multiplies a resource, it dilutes the unit value; when it combines several resources into one product, the value of the product is at least as great as the sum of ingredients plus the processing cost.

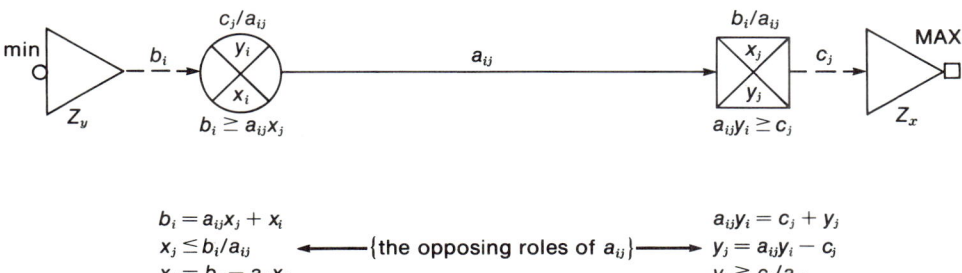

Figure 9-2 Dual flows through a sample network.

The inverse relationships are obvious in the simple one-resource–one-process case of Figure 9-2: from the balance equation around y_i, we have $x_j \leq b_j/a_{ij}$; and from around x_j, $y_j = a_{ij}y_i - c_j$.

These opposing roles of a_{ij} stem from the alternating process and resource nodes and the location of arrowheads identifying the inequalities and are automatic consequences of the construction of an RPM network. Its counterpart in a tabular notation is the familiar Tucker diagram, an example of which is shown in Figure 9-3b, where the reversal of the inequality symbols between rows and columns is easily seen. The primal-row interpretation is a maximization problem with all .LE. constraints, while the dual-column interpretation leads to a minimization problem with all .GE. constraints.

9-3 Simplex tableau format

Mathematics evolved around the use of *equations*. Thus the transportation problems given in Chapter 8 were the first LP problems to be solved analytically because the demands and supplies were exactly balanced to create equations for constraints. The development of transportation models by F. L. Hitchcock[1] predates the development of the simplex method for solving more general linear programming problems, and the origin of the Simplex method itself can be traced to Dantzig's attempt (1950) to optimize only the transportation problems. As mentioned in Chapter 6, Section 6-1, the first effort by project SCOOP was to represent resource allocation problems as systems of equations to be solved simultaneously. Thus, it is not surprising that the simplex procedure became available as soon as means were found to convert inequalities into equations. A simplex tableau is really the counterpart of a Tucker diagram using equations.

CANONICAL FORM When a system of inequalities is changed into a system of equations, we say that the new form is a *canonical representation* of the original problem. Then the original variables are referred to as the *structural*, or *real*, *variables* (LINPRO calls them YOUR variables), and the variables that have been added to take up the residual slack are called *logical variables*. Simple *residues* in RPMS are classified into three logical variables in traditional linear programming.

1. *Slack variables*, which are added to convert the .LE. (less than or equal to a constant) constraints into equations. For example,

    $a_{11}x_1 + a_{12}x_2 \leq b_1$

    may be written as

    $a_{11}x_1 + a_{12}x_2 + x_3 = b_1$

---

[1] F. L. Hitchcock, "Distribution of a Product from Several Sources to Numerous Localities," J. Math. Phys., vol. 20, pp. 224–230, 1941.

Simplex Tableau: A Table for Resource Exchange

(a) Standard LP form

$$\max Z_x = 9x_1 + 9x_2$$
$$\text{subject to: } 30x_1 + 20x_2 \leq 180$$
$$6x_1 + 12x_2 \leq 60$$
$$x_1 \geq 0$$
$$x_2 \geq 0$$

(b) Tucker diagram

Variables	$x_1 \geq 0$	$x_2 \geq 0$	Constants (RHS)
$y_3 \geq 0$	30	20	$\leq$ 180
$y_4 \geq 0$	6	12	$\leq$ 60
Constants	VI 9	VI 9	MAX Z_x / min Z_y

(c) Canonical LP form

$$\max Z_x - 9x_1 - 9x_2 = 0$$
$$30x_1 + 20x_2 + x_3 = 180$$
$$6x_1 + 12x_2 + x_4 = 60$$

Structural variables / Logical variables (residues)

All variables are nonnegative

(d) One form of simplex tableau

Base	x_1	x_2	x_3	x_4	RHS
x_3	30	20	1	0	180
x_4	6	12	0	1	60
Simplex* criteria	-9	-9	0	0	0

(e) RPM Network Form

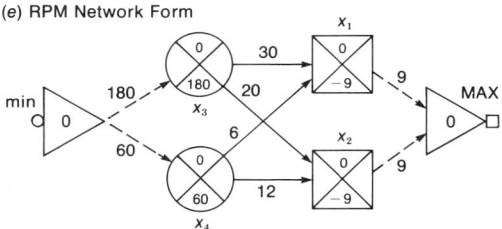

(f) Simplex tableau format adopted

Base	Primal value (X)	Z_x	x_1	x_2	x_3	x_4
Dual value (Y)		0	1	-9	-9	0	0
x_3	180	0	30	20	1	0
x_4	60	0	6	12	0	1

(g) Symbolic RPM network format

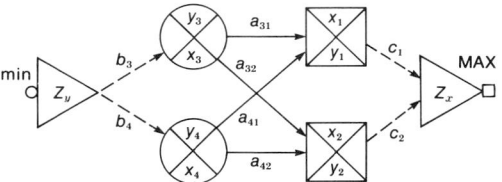

(h) Symbolic tableau format

Base	Primal value (X)	Z_x	x_1	x_2	x_3	x_4
Dual value (Y)	Z	1	y_1	y_2	y_3	y_4
x_3	x_3	0	a_{31}	a_{32}	1	0
x_4	x_4	0	a_{41}	a_{42}	0	1

Figure 9-3 Various representations of the Example 5-1. On many representations, simplex criteria are defined as the negative of the dual values. In LINPRO, for example, this row would have read: $+9 \quad +9 \quad 0 \quad 0 \quad 0$.

where x_3 is a slack variable, and x_1 and x_2 are structural variables.

2. *Surplus variables*, which are used to convert the .GE. (greater than or equal to a constant) constraints into equations. For example,

$$a_{21}x_1 + a_{22}x_2 \geq b_2$$

may be written as

$$a_{21}x_1 + a_{22}x_2 - x_4 = b_2$$

where x_4 is a surplus variable, and x_1 and x_2 are structural variables.

3. *Artificial variables*, which are not allowed in the final solution but are introduced artificially to relax a constraint momentarily for the convenience of the algorithm. These are used by the *big-M* and *two-phase* methods described in Section 9-6. For example,

$$a_{31}x_1 + a_{32}x_2 = b_3$$

may be written as

$$a_{31}x_1 + a_{32}x_2 + (\text{or } -)\, x_5 = b_3$$

where x_5 is an artificial variable. This permits a temporal inequality with an artificial residue of x_5. This inequality may either be .LE. or .GE., and it may not always be known which way the deviation occurs. Artificial variables are also used in .GE. constraints. For example,

$$a_{21}x_1 + a_{22}x_2 = b_2$$

is written as

$$a_{21}x_1 + a_{22}x_2 - x_4 + x_7 = b_2$$

where x_7 is an artificial variable that is required for this problem to be solved by the *big M* or *two-phase* method.

Example 5-1 was stated as

$$\max Z_x = 9x_1 + 9x_2 \qquad \text{for revenue } Z_x \text{ in dollars}$$

subject to

$$30x_1 + 20x_2 \leq 180 \qquad \text{for lumber limitations, bdft}$$
$$6x_1 + 12x_2 \leq 60 \qquad \text{for space limitation, ft}^2$$
$$x_1, x_2 \geq 0$$

Rewritten in canonical form, this problem becomes

$$\max Z_x - 9x_1 - 9x_2 - 0x_3 - 0x_4 = 0$$

subject to

$$30x_1 + 20x_2 + 1x_3 + 0x_4 = 180$$
$$6x_1 + 12x_2 + 0x_3 + 1x_4 = 60$$
$$x_1, x_2, x_3, x_4 \geq 0$$

Note that the objective function is now written in the form of a resource (a free constraint). Also note that x_1 and x_2 are structural variables while both x_3 and x_4 are slack logic variables. (See Figure 9-3 for the various representations of Example 5-1.)

SIMPLEX TABLEAU A simplex tableau is essentially a Tucker diagram built around the canonical representation of a linear programming problem. There are several different versions of simplex tableaux, and at present there is no one standard format that is used by all OR/MS practitioners. Figure 9-3d shows one common formation which has the advantage of being very close to a Tucker diagram representation (Figure 9-3b). It does have the handicap, unfortunately, that the right-hand-side (RHS) column representing the primal values is away from the base column where variables are identified; similarly, the simplex criteria row representing the dual values is the furthest down from the top row where the variable names are identified. When the tableau is large, it is easy to misread the columns and rows and therefore to obtain incorrect interpretations of a correct tableau. Also, when a computer program prints out the solution in this format (which LINPRO does, unfortunately), the entire tableau must be printed before the solution is given. In a conversational time-sharing system, the speed of the teletypewriter terminal limits the rate at which the tableau is composed. To a hurried user, this format can be frustrating.

Thus, we have come to adopt the simplex tableau format that appears in Figure 9-3. In this format, we label the RHS column as "primal value" and the simplex criteria row as "dual value." The primal values for variables whose names do not appear in the base column are zero. Accordingly, from the first two columns, we can easily read: $x_1 = 0$; $x_2 = 0$; $x_3 = 180$; $x_4 = 60$; similarly, from the first two rows, we read: $y_1 = -9$; $y_2 = -9$; $y_3 = 0$; $y_4 = 0$. At the intersection of the primal and dual values, we have $Z = Z_x = Z_y = 0$.

These values are included in the RPM network nodes, as shown in Figure 9-3e. When all structural variables are set to zero, the residues (logical variables) correspond to whatever exogenous inputs (+) or endogenous outputs (−) are required by the environment: $x_3 = b_3 = 180$; $x_4 = b_4 = 60$; $y_1 = -c_1 = -9$; $y_2 = -c_2 = -9$.

Symbolic models are presented in Figure 9-3g and k to facilitate the understanding of these equivalences. Note that the first row should be labeled y_1, y_2, y_3, y_4 instead of x_1, x_2, x_3, and x_4. Here we are bowing to traditional usage of identifying everything in terms of primal variables rather than dual variables. Dual values are thought of as simplex criteria *for* the primal variables, rather than being treated as dual variables with rights that are equal to those of the primal variables.

SECTION 9-3 TUNE-UP

Construct a simplex tableau for each of the following RPM networks and identify all logical variables.

252   Introduction to Operations Research and Management Science

1.
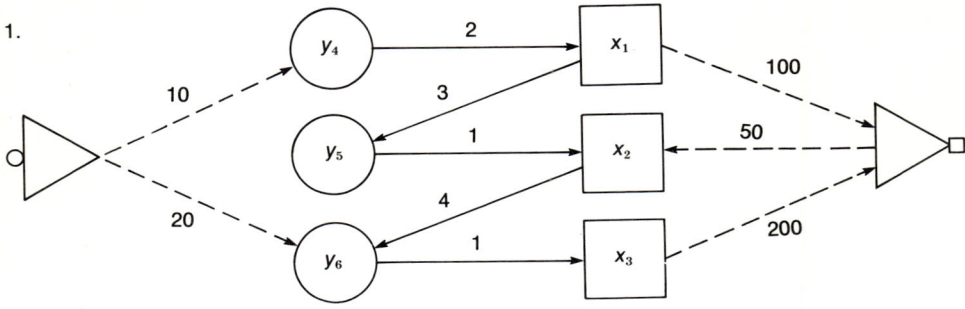

2.
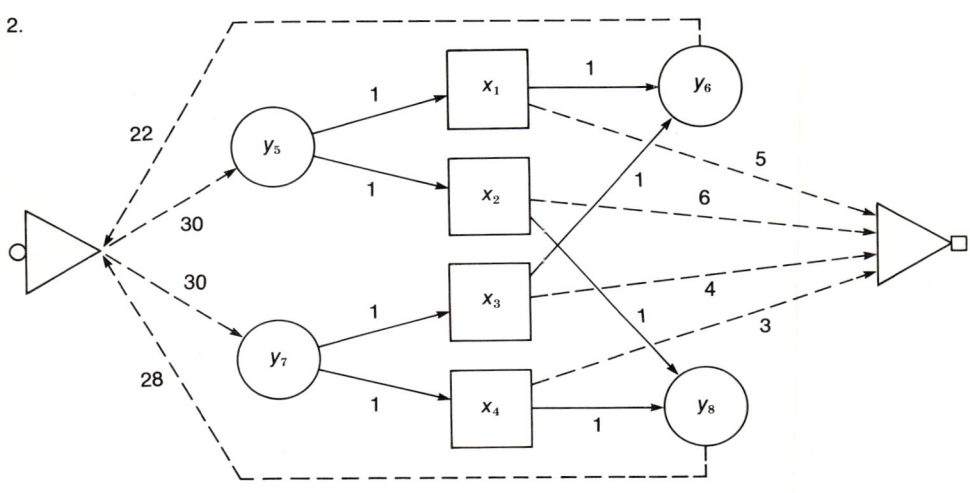

3.
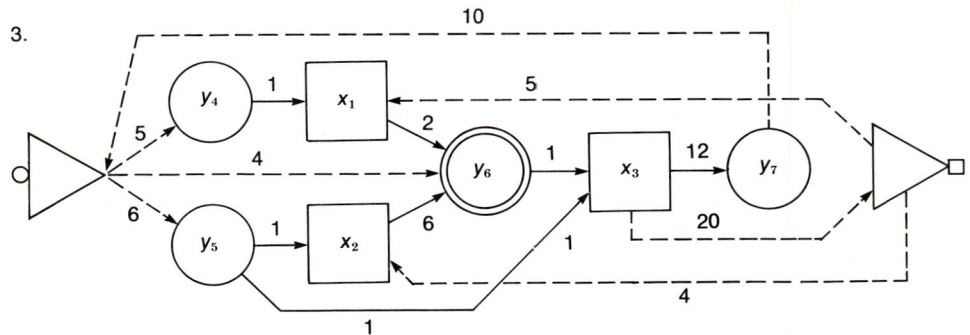

9-4 Dimensional scaling

An important and useful tool that should be introduced at this time is the practice of scaling. Returning to Example 5-1, we have:

$$\max Z_x = 9x_1 + 9x_2 \quad \text{for revenue } Z_x, \text{ in dollars}$$

subject to

$$30x_1 + 20x_2 \leq 180 \quad \text{for lumber limitation, bdft}$$
$$6x_1 + 12x_2 \leq 60 \quad \text{for space limitation, ft}^2$$
$$x_1, x_2 \geq 0$$

In creating a simplex tableau, we note that the logical variables always have coefficients of 1. If coefficients for the real structural variables are either very large or very small, it is conceivable that the unbalanced magnitude would be a source of inaccurate computation by computers. If the tableau computation is to be performed manually, it is even more important that the numbers be simple to manipulate. Scaling allows us to simplify our calculations.

SCALING THE OBJECTIVE FUNCTION In Example 5-1, to simplify our writing, we could scale the objective function to be evaluated, say, in millions of dollars, and the LP solution would not be influenced by this arbitrary, but consistent, change in units. The objective function could also be evaluated in another currency. An optimal solution evaluated in U. S. dollars should remain the same when evaluated in German marks or British pounds. Supposing that the exchange rate between the Wonderland currency (say Wonders) and the U. S. dollar were 1 Wonder = 75 cents, we can rewrite the objective function for Example 5-1 as:

$$\max Z_x = 12x_1 + 12x_2 \quad \text{for revenue } Z_x, \text{ in Wonders}$$

SCALING THE RESOURCES By the same token, the resource units can be scaled to simplify equations. For example, we can choose 10 bdft (1,440 in^3) and 2 ft^2 to state our resource constraints:

$$\max Z_x = 12x_1 + 12x_2 \quad \text{for revenue } Z_x, \text{ in Wonders}$$

subject to

$$3x_1 + 2x_2 \leq 18 \quad \text{for lumber limitation, in 10 bdft units}$$
$$3x_1 + 6x_2 \leq 30 \quad \text{for space limitation, in 2 ft}^2 \text{ units}$$

with the nonnegative constraints as before.

SCALING THE PROCESSES Finally, we can also scale our processing units by multiplying each column of the simplex tableau by a constant. Counting book-

(a) The original tableaux

Base	Dual	Primal	Z_x	x_1	x_2	x_3	x_4
	0	0	1	−9	−9	0	0
x_3		180	0	30	20	1	0
x_4		60	0	6	12	0	1

≡

Base	Dual	Primal	Z_x	x_1	x_2	x_3	x_4
	0	0	1	−4	−6	0	0
x_3		18	0	1	1	1	0
x_4		30	0	1	3	0	1

(b) RPM networks displaying an optimal solution to the original problem

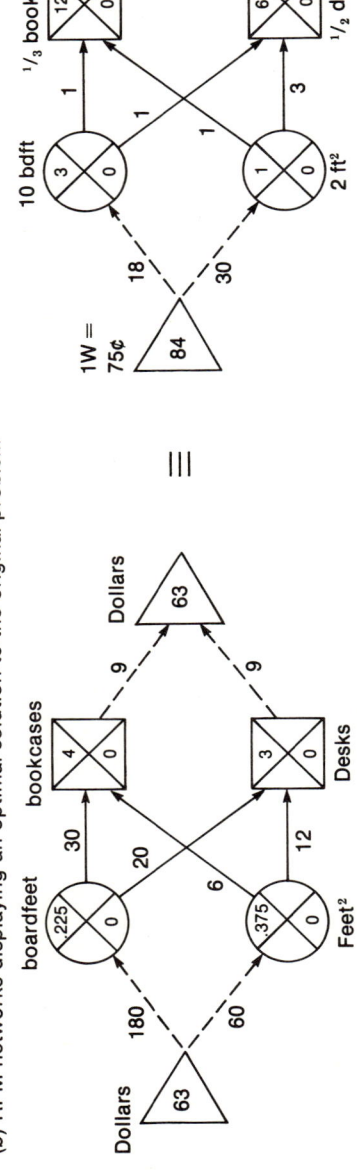

Figure 9-4 Two equivalent representations of Example 5-1 before (left) and after (right) scaling.

cases by $\frac{1}{3}$ and desks by $\frac{1}{2}$, we now have

$$\max Z_x = 4x_1 + 6x_2$$

subject to

$$x_1 + x_2 \leq 18$$
$$x_1 + 3x_2 \leq 30$$

where Z_x is in W's, $x_1 = \frac{1}{3}$ bookcases, and $x_2 = \frac{1}{2}$ desks.

Figure 9-4 shows the initial tableau and final RPM network of Example 5-1 before and after scaling. There is no doubt that scaling simplifies the entries on the tableau and potentially contributes to the reduction of computational efforts and errors.

NORMALIZING Scaling through an equation by a constant to yield a unit coefficient for a particular variable is called *normalizing*. Thus, $30 = x_1 + 3x_2 + x_4$ can be normalized for x_2 if we divide through by 3:

$$10 = 0.33x_1 + x_2 + 0.33x_4$$

ELIMINATING In a system of linear equations, it is permissible to substitute one equation into another or subtract one equation from another. Thus, a variable can be eliminated if we use one equation to substitute for that variable in all equations. For example to eliminate x_1, $18 = x_1 + x_2 + x_3$ can be subtracted once from $30 = x_1 + 3x_2 + x_4$ to yield

$$30 - 18 = (1-1)x_1 + (3-1)x_2 - x_3 + x_4 \quad \text{or} \quad 12 = 2x_2 - x_3 + x_4$$

PIVOTING When all entries in a column have been eliminated except for the normalized equation used in subtraction, we say that a *pivoting* has occurred. The simplex procedure evolved from the so-called triangularization and diagonalization procedure for solving a system of linear equations. Figure 9-5 illustrates how the triangular and diagonal structures emerge. In a simplex tableau, the diagonal form is being maintained while the pivoting occurs to move from one solution to another. Each pivoting is also called a *cycle* or an *iteration*.

9-5 Standard simplex procedure

The standard simplex procedure is an algorithm that will gradually and steadily improve upon a feasible initial solution until an optimum solution is attained. It is an iterative process that pivots from one solution (extreme point) to another through normalization and elimination. Each tableau represents a feasible and usually nonoptimal solution. The simplex experimentation goes through an optimality analysis, and if it is nonoptimal, through a pivot to another feasible solution. The tableau serves as a table of exchange for both the primal and dual val-

(a) Original form

$x_0 - 9x_1 - 9x_2 = 0$ (row 1)
$30x_1 + 20x_2 = 180$ (row 2)
$6x_1 + 12x_2 = 60$ (row 3)

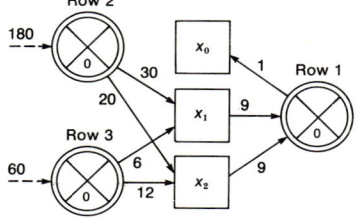

Total	x_0	x_1	x_2	Row
0	1	−9	−9	1
180	0	30	20	2
60	0	6	12	3

(b) Multiplying row 3 by 5

$x_0 - 9x_1 - 9x_2 = 0$
$30x_1 + 20x_2 = 180$
$30x_1 + 60x_2 = 300$

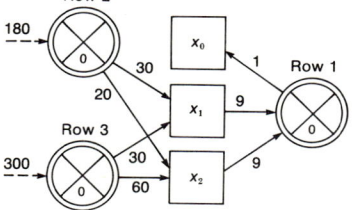

Total	x_0	x_1	x_2	Row
0	1	−9	−9	1
180	0	30	20	2
300	0	30	60	3

(c) Subtracting row 2 from 3

$x_0 - 9x_1 - 9x_2 = 0$
$30x_1 + 20x_2 = 180$
$40x_2 = 120$

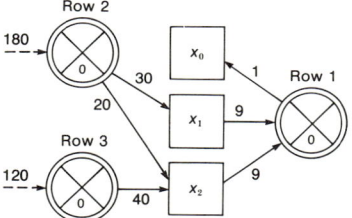

Total	x_0	x_1	x_2	Row
0	1	−9	−9	1
180	0	30	20	2
120	0	0	40	3

(d) Triangular form

$x_0 - 9x_1 - 9x_2 = 0$
$30x_1 + 20x_2 = 180$
$x_2 = 3$

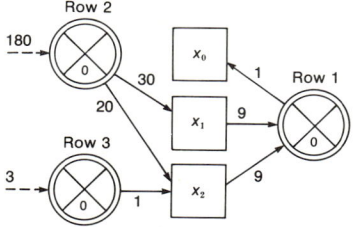

Total	x_0	x_1	x_2	Row
0	1	−9	−9	1
180	0	30	20	2
3	0	0	1	3

Figure 9-5 Solving a system of linear equations.

Simplex Tableau: A Table for Resource Exchange   257

(e) Substituting row 3 into 1 and 2

$x_0 - 9x_1 = 27$
$30x_1 = 120$
$x_2 = 3$

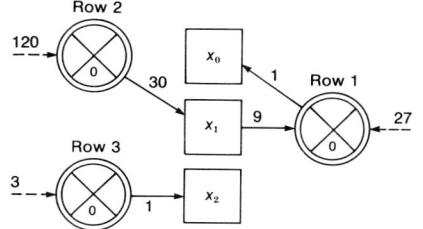

Total	x_0	x_1	x_2	Row
27	1	-9	0	1
120	0	30	0	2
3	0	0	1	3

(f) Dividing row 2 by 30

$x_0 - 9x_1 = 27$
$x_1 = 4$
$x_2 = 3$

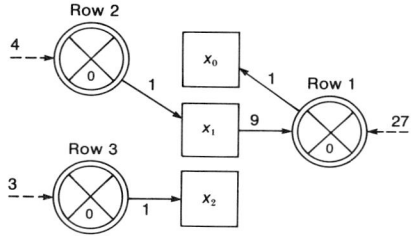

Total	x_0	x_1	x_2	Row
27	1	-9	0	1
4	0	1	0	2
3	0	0	1	3

(g) Diagonal form

$x_0 = 63$
$x_1 = 4$
$x_2 = 3$

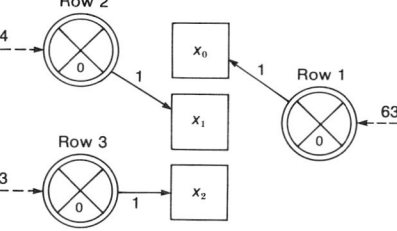

Total	x_0	x_1	x_2	Row
63	1	0	0	1
4	0	1	0	2
3	0	0	1	3

(h) Representing the solution (g) on the original RPM network.

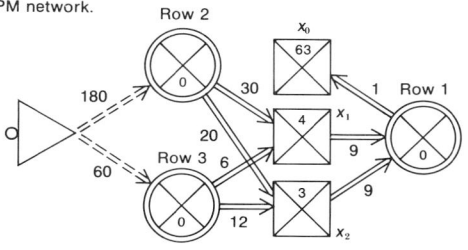

Pivoting = normalizing + eliminating
(d) and (f)   (c) and (e)

ues. The primal resource conversion is seen from rows to columns, while the dual value exchange is found by searching from columns to rows.

In order to illustrate the standard simplex procedure and appreciate the significance of the simplex tableau, we shall study a series of examples with a cumulative set of conditions.

Example 9-1: *One-resource case* Huge Wonder Aircraft Company is a Wonderland manufacturer of commercial airplanes. It is planning to augment its production of jumbojets and/or SSTs. The net profit per plane is $2 million per plane for the jumbojets and $1 million per plane for the SSTs. The assembly plants have adequate capacity to handle 100 more planes of either or both types. You have been asked to maximize the company's profit.

This trivial problem has one resource (the production capacity) and two decisions (how many jumbojets? How many SSTs?) with a linear objective function that can be scaled to millions of dollars:

$$\max Z_x = 2x_1 + 1x_2 \qquad \text{profit to be maximized}$$

subject to

$$1x_1 + 1x_2 \leq 100 \qquad \text{production constraint}$$
$$x_1, x_2 \geq 0 \qquad \text{nonnegativity constraints}$$

The problem can be written in a canonical form as

$$0 = Z_x - 2x_1 - 1x_2$$
$$100 = 1x_1 + 1x_2 + 1x_3$$

where x_3 is the slack variable. The corresponding tableau, the E^2 FSS, and the RPM network are shown in Figure 9-6, where columns that contain one 1 and 0s elsewhere (Z_x and x_3) may form an identity matrix like the diagonal form of Figure 9-5g. They identify the basis and show that the row primal value corresponds to the column primal variable.

Since all primal values are nonnegative but there are negative dual values, the initial solution is feasible but not optimal. To improve the solution, it would be reasonable to attempt to include the alternative with the largest regret: $y_1 = -2$ indicates that we are losing $2 million for each jumbojet that is not being made. How many jumbojets can be made is a question that is answered by looking at the intersection of x_3 row (resource to be used) and x_1 column (resource to be made). The coefficient 1 indicates that 1 jumbojet can be made for each unit of capacity available in residue x_3. Thus, dividing the primal residue $x_3 = 100$ by the conversion rate 1, we obtain $x_3/a_{31} = 100/1 = 100$. Since the coefficient $a_{31} = 1$, the normalization does not change the row entry except to label it x_1 instead of x_3. The complementary slackness theorem says, however, that if x_1 is nonzero, its dual value must be zero. To set $y_1 = 0$ where we now have -2, the RPM network shows that we need to increase the value of y_3 from 0 to $2a_{31} = 2$. In the tableau, this operation can be performed by noting that the second row can be multiplied

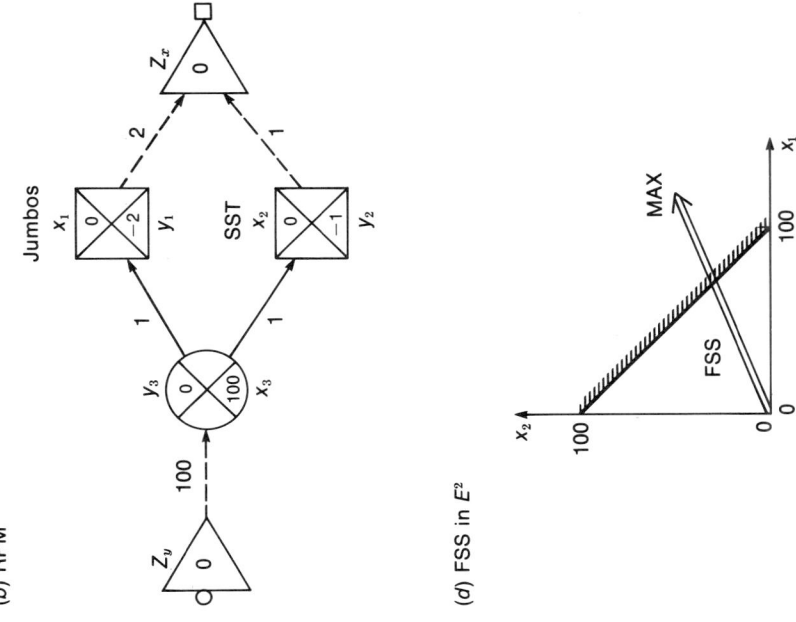

Figure 9-6 Initial solution for Example 9-1.

by 2 and added to the first row to produce 0 at y_1; in other words, one unit value of y_1 can be traded for one unit value of x_3. Figure 9-7 shows the result of the iteration with the new basis x_1 replacing the old basis x_3. The solution is both feasible and optimal since all primal and dual values are nonnegative.

Example 9-2: Two-resource case The Huge Aircraft Company has adequate supplies of SST engines to produce 100 or more SST planes per year, but the supplier can furnish only 480 engines yearly for the jumbojets. Each jumbojet needs three engines, and the FAA and CAB require that there be one spare engine for each engine on the plane. Estimate the effect that the addition of this constant will have on the previous solutions.

The new LP problem can be written as

$$\max Z_x = 2x_1 + 1x_2 \qquad 0 = Z_x - 2x_1 - 1x_2$$

subject to

$$x_1 + x_2 \leq 100 \qquad\qquad 100 = 1x_1 + 1x_2 + 1x_3 \quad \text{(for plant)}$$
$$6x_1 \qquad\quad \leq 480 \quad \text{or} \quad 480 = 6x_1 \qquad\qquad + 1x_4 \quad \text{(for engines)}$$
$$x_1, \; x_2 \geq 0 \qquad\qquad\qquad x_1, x_2, x_3, x_4 \geq 0$$

INITIAL TABLEAU In our standard simplex procedure, the starting point must be found within the FSS. The usual approach is to set all real variables to zero and assign all residues to the logical variables. In a simplex tableau, as in an RPM network, a solution is feasible if no negative value is included. Thus, the feasibility analysis of the initial tableau is simply to:

1. Make sure that there is an identity matrix corresponding to the intended bases. If not, some entries must be eliminated to create zeros and all diagonal elements normalized to give ones.

2. Then check to see if any entry in the primal value X column is negative. (Any negative entry must be eliminated by one of the methods discussed in Section 9-6.)

In Figure 9-8a, as in all maximizing LP problems with .LE. constraints only, the initial solution is found to be trivial but feasible.

OPTIMALITY CHECK A negative entry in the dual value row indicates a regret for not having an optimal solution. The largest regret, that is, the most negative dual value, is chosen to identify the alternative to be brought into the basis. Since -2 is more drastic than -1, we choose the column x_1 as the *pivot column* (pc) for the new variable. This -2 is really the marginal increase in the objective function when x_1 is increased by one unit; it is the "shadow" of one unit of x_1 cast upon the objective-function vector in the E^2 space. That x_1 has a higher regret than x_2 in-

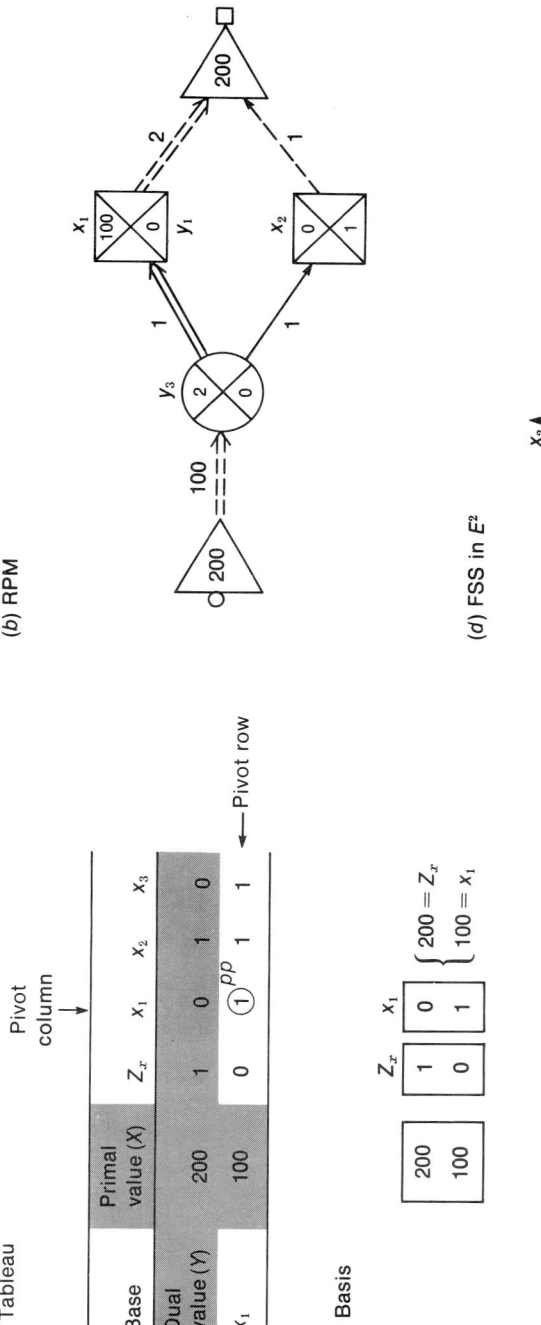

Figure 9-7 Second and optimal solution for Example 9-1.

262

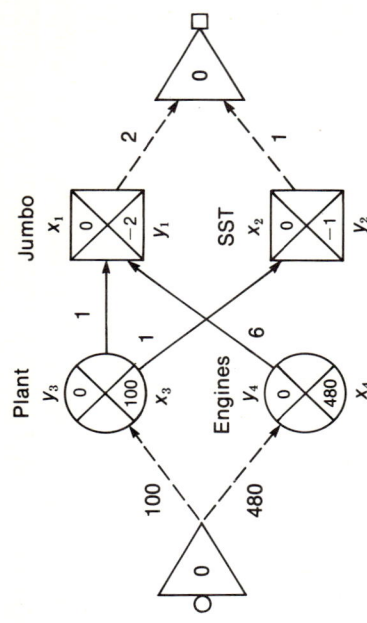

(a) Initial solution: $x_1 = 0$ $x_2 = 0$ $x_3 = 100$ $x_4 = 480$
$Z = Z_x = Z_y = 0$ $y_1 = -2$ $y_2 = -1$ $y_3 = 0$ $y_4 = 0$

Base	Primal value (X)	Z_x	Real		Logical		
			x_1	x_2	x_3	x_4	
	0	1	−2	−1	0	0	
x_3	100	0	1	1	1	0	$^{100}/_1$ ← pr
x_4	480	0	⑥	1	0	1	$^{480}/_6$
Dual value (Y)			↑ pc	↑ pp			

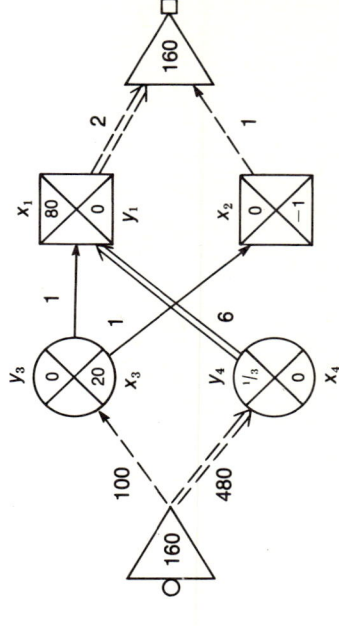

(b) Second solution: $x_1 = 80$ $x_2 = 0$ $x_3 = 20$ $x_4 = 0$
$Z = 160$ $y_1 = 0$ $y_2 = −1$ $y_3 = 0$ $y_4 = ^1/_3$

Base	Primal value	Z_x	x_1	x_2	x_3	x_4	
	160	1	0	−1	0	1/3	
x_3	20	0	0	①	1	−1/6	$^{20}/_1$ ← pr
x_1	80	0	1	0	0	1/6	$^{80}/_0$
Dual value				↑ pp		↑ pc	

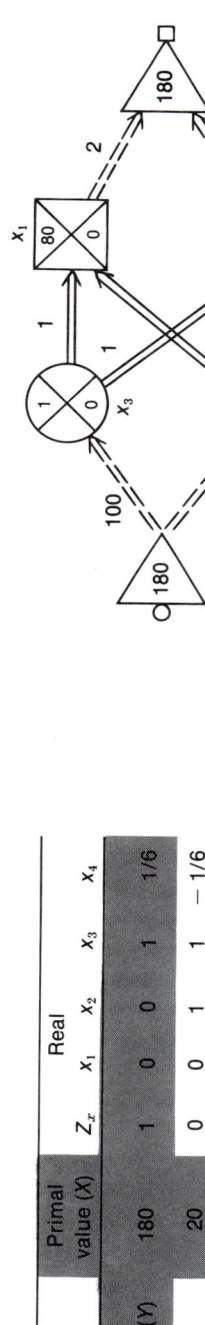

(c) Optimal solution: $x_1 = 80$ $x_2 = 20$ $x_3 = 0$ $x_4 = 0$
$Z = 180$ $y_1 = 0$ $y_2 = 0$ $y_3 = 1$ $y_4 = 1/6$

Base	Primal value (X)	Z_x	Real x_1	x_2	x_3	x_4
		180	1	0	0	1/6
x_2	20	0	0	1	1	−1/6
x_1	80	0	1	0	0	1/6
	Dual value (Y)					

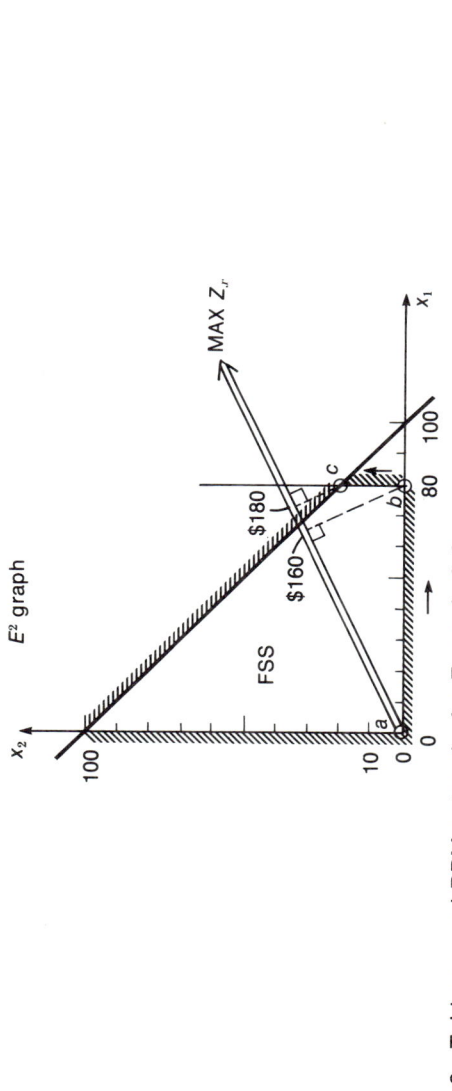

Figure 9-8 Tableaux and RPM networks for Example 9-2.

dicates that the objective-function vector makes a smaller angle with x_1 than it does with x_2 and that the Z_x vector is more in the direction of x_2.

FEASIBILITY CHECK In the first simplex tableau (Figure 9-8*a*), looking down column x_1 to be *pivoted in*, we note that the -2 regret can be reduced to zero if 1 times y_3 and/or 6 times y_4 values are increased by that much. In other words, the value of y_1 could affect y_3 at the same rate (1) and y_4 at one-sixth (1/6) of the marginal rate of y_1. But in order to create these values at y_3 and/or y_4, the resource must be made scarce. There are 100 units of x_3 and 480 units of x_4, and the rate of usage is 1 for x_3 and 6 for x_4. Since $480/6 = 80$ is smaller than $100/1 = 100$, x_4 will be exhausted before x_3, and y_4 will have the resource value of $2 \times 1/6$, or $1/3$. The resource whose primal value is exhausted x_4 is called the *pivot row* (*pr*) variable. The exchange rate that was used at the intersection of the pivot row and the pivot column (6) is called the *pivot point* (*pp*).

The mechanics of tableau iteration are easy. After having identified the *pc* in the optimality check, the entries in the primal value (PV) column are divided by the corresponding terms in *pc*. The base with the smallest positive ratio of PV/*pc* is the *pivot row* (*pr*). This smallest positive value indicates the first intersection of the x_1 axis with the constraint $6x_1 = 480$, and violating this boundary will put the solution in the region outside the FSS.

NORMALIZING To obtain the second tableau from the first, all entries in the *pr* are divided by the *pp*. Then, we relabel the row by the new variable name x_1. The old *pp* is now equal to 1 and sits at the intersection of column x_1 and row x_1, illustrating that the exchange rate between x_1 and x_1 (or y_1 and y_1) is equal to 1. As shown in Figure 9-8*b*, the row now reads x_1 80 0 1 0 0 $1/6$.

ELIMINATING If x_1 is the new basic variable, then y_1 must be zero. To create a zero at the dual value row in the x_1 column, the entire *pr* row must be subtracted from the dual value row as many times as necessary to create a zero at the cell. Either one-third of the old x_4 row or twice the new x_1 row can be added to the dual value row to accomplish this. Mathematically, the new diagonal element for the identity matrix is created. Optimizationwise, the resource values are reassigned by shifting the dual residue from the new basic variable to other nonbasic variables, using the input/output relationships of the basis. The new dual value row reads 160 1 0 -1 0 $1/3$, confirming our previous reasoning about $y_4 = 1/3$.

We still have the task of creating another zero at row x_3 and column x_1 so that the diagonal element of the identity matrix will correspond to x_1. We can follow the same procedure used with the dual value row, subtracting the x_1 row as many times as necessary from the x_3 row to reduce the content of the cell from 1 to 0. In this particular case, it suffices to subtract the new x_1 row just once from row x_3. We now have the second tableau (Figure 9-8*b*).

INTERPRETATION OF FIGURE 9-8*b* The primal value column and the dual value row are called the *rim conditions* (as in the transportation tableau), or more simply the *stub*. These values are shown in the RPM network and indicate that we are now at point B of the E^2 graph of Figure 9-8b, with a profit of $160 million.

The dual value row indicates how effectively the jumbojet engines at $y_4 = 1/3$ million dollars are being used and how the profit could be improved by introducing x_2. The row x_3 indicates that there are 20 units of x_3 available and that each unit of x_3 can be exchanged for 1 unit of x_2, 1 unit of x_3 itself, or $-1/6$ unit of x_4. The value of $-1/6$ signifies that $1/6$ unit of x_3 will be gained by an attempt to create 1 unit of x_4. Since x_4 is now 0, the only way to create a residue at x_4 is to make less x_1. One unit at x_4 means reducing x_1 by $1/6$, which will of course save $1/6$ unit of x_3 also.

Similarly the x_4 column can provide information on both the primal and dual flows. An additional unit of x_4 would create $1/6$ unit of x_1, use up $1/6$ unit of x_3, and also add $1/3$ million to the profit. Conversely, $1 increase in value of y_1 will increase the value of y_4 by $$1/6$, while $1 increase in y_3 will cut down the value of y_4 by $1/6. This information could be obtained from the RPM network, but the tableau makes the arithmetic computation unnecessary.

OPTIMAL SOLUTION The optimal solution in the third tableau (Figure 9-2c) is obtained by pivoting in x_2 and pivoting out x_3. Since the pivot point is 1, no normalizing is needed. Adding row x_3 to the dual value row, we obtain the final optimal tableau.

THE COOKBOOK FORMULA After *pc*, *pr*, and *pp* have been identified, the elimination stage can be performed automatically by applying the formula:

$$\text{New} = \text{Old} - \frac{(pc)(pr)}{pp}$$

where *pc* is the entry in the pivot column at the row of the cell in consideration, and *pr* is the entry in the pivot row at the column of the cell. For example, the cell y_4 at the dual value row and x_4 column for the tableau in Figure 9-8b can be computed from Figure 9-8a knowing that x_4 is *pr*.

$$\text{New} = \text{Old} - \frac{(pc)(pr)}{pp} = 0 - \frac{-2 \times 1}{6} = +1/3$$

Going from Figure 9-8b to the optimal tableau (Figure 9-8c), the same cell may be computed using x_2 as *pc* and x_3 as *pr*:

$$\text{New} = 1/3 - \frac{(-1) \times (-1/6)}{1} = +1/6$$

This procedure applies to all cells in the tableau, except for the pivot row, which needs to be normalized simply by dividing it by the *pp* value.

CHECK When the computation is performed manually, it is easy to make arithmetic mistakes, but these can be minimized by performing a simple check of the computation. An extra column can be created on the side of the tableau where the sum of all entries in the row is indicated for each row. For example, in Figure 9-8a the dual value row 0 1 −2 −1 0 0 can have $0 + 1 - 2 - 1 + 0 + 0 = -2$ as the check digit; the second row would have 103; and the third, 487. These values can be operated by the same simplex procedure to yield $163^{1}/_{3}$, 21, and $^{5}/_{6}$ for the first tableau, and 81 and $^{1}/_{6}$ for the second. These figures can be checked by again adding the elements in the rows: $160 + 1 + 0 - 1 + 0 + 0.333 = 160.333$, and so on. If the sums do not match, we suspect an error in computation. (The cookbook formula applies also to the check digits.)

MANUAL COMPUTATION PROCEDURE Although a computer program can easily perform equivalent computations, manual computations can also be facilitated by the use of a calculator. Figure 9-9 illustrates a procedure for performing the simplex computations using a calculator.

SECTION 9-5 TUNE-UP

Construct and iterate a simplex tableau for the following problem. Explain all terms and display the solution graphically.

max $Z_x = 4x_1 + 6x_2$

subject to

$x_1 + 2x_2 \leq 12$

$x_1 + x_2 \leq 8$

$x_1, x_2 \geq 0$

9-6 Nonfeasible initial solution

In Section 9-5, we assumed that setting all real variables to zero automatically created a feasible starting solution. This is usually true in problems that contain only .LE. constant constraints, but unfortunately many LP problems contain both .GE. and .EQ. constraints in addition to the .LE. constraints. Three approaches are possible in the latter case. We can use either the dual of the problem (as in Chapter 5) or the big-*M* or two-phase method. It is not necessary to actually find the dual tableau for applying the duality concept, and a special algorithm has been found to operate the dual approach directly on the primal tableau; such a method is known as the *dual simplex algorithm*. Although the dual method is more popular among computer programs, the big-*M* and two-phase methods are introduced for the pedagogic reasons. Let us use Example 9-2 with a new twist.

Example 9-3: *The .GE. Constraint* The Huge Aircraft Company (see Example 9-2) is owned by the Trans Wonderland Airways, which is threatening to liquidate

(1) Check-digit computation
    *For each row, add up all entries
    and enter (or check against the figure
    already entered) as the check digit.
(2) Pivot Point (*pp*) identification
    (a) Choose the most negative "dual"
        entry on the top row—this is
        the new pivot column (*pc*).
    (b) For each entry (except the dual
        row entry) in the "primal" column
        entry, divide the entry by the
        corresponding value in the *pc* column.
    (c) Compare all ratios computed in step (b)
        above, identify the row with the smallest
        ratio—this is the new pivot row (*pr*).
    (d) Store the figure in the cell where *pc* and *pr*
        intersect—this is the new pivot point (*pp*).
(3) New pivot row computation
    (a) For each entry in *pr*, divide the figure by
        the stored constant *pp*, and record the result
        in the corresponding box of the new tableau.
    (b) Do this for all figures in *pr* including the
        check digit.
(4) Computation of other entries in the new tableau
    (a) For each row (except *pr*), identify the entry
        in *pc*, divide it by *pp* and store *pc/pp* as the
        constant.
    (b) Recall *pc/pp*, multiply it by an entry in *pr*
    (c) Subtract from (*pc* × *pr*)/*pp*, the corresponding entry
        from the row of step 1, then enter the *negative*
        of the result in the new tableau.
    (d) Repeat steps *b* and *c* for all entries in the row
        including the check digit.
    (e) Repeat steps *a* through *d* for all entries needed on
        the new tableau.

Figure 9-9 Computation procedure for Example 9-2 using a calculator.

the aircraft company unless it shows an additional profit of more than $100 million/yr. Evaluate the effects of adding this constraint.

It is obvious that the addition of this constraint does not change our optimal solution. But let us assume that we have no such knowledge and that we need to start from the beginning. The problem is now stated as

$$\max Z_x = 2x_1 + 1x_2$$

subject to

$1x_1 + 1x_2 \leq 100$ plant capacity

$6x_1 \quad\quad\;\; \leq 480$ jumbojet engines

$$2x_1 + 1x_2 \geq 100 \quad \text{corporate requirement}$$

$$x_1, x_2, x_3 \geq 0$$

The addition of the slack variables x_3 and x_4, the surplus variable x_5, and the artificial variable x_6 transforms the problem into

$$\max Z_x = 2x_1 + 1x_2$$

subject to

$$1x_1 + 1x_2 + 1x_3 = 100$$
$$6x_1 + 1x_4 = 480$$
$$2x_1 + 1x_2 - 1x_5 + 1x_6 = 100$$

(Since $-x_6 = x_5$, x_5 and $-x_6$ are combined into a free variable in MPS and other advanced computer programs.)

BIG-M METHOD The original solution for Example 9-3 is illustrated in Figure 9-10. The graphic display shows that $x_1 = x_2 = 0$ is no longer inside the FSS, and the RPM network O confirms the solution to be infeasible on account of negative x_5. The addition of the variable x_6 forces the residue x_5 to become zero and render the solution feasible, but x_6 is an "artificial" variable which is not a part of the original problem. No harm is done as long as x_6 does not remain basic in the final solution. In the big-M method we simply assign a very large M penalty to the use of x_6 (thus the name big M) and hope that it will not appear in the final solution.

In Figure 9-10, pivot points are indicated by circles in the tableaux. It is noted that tableaux O and A' are not in a proper form because they lack the diagonal structure for an identity matrix. Tableau O is nonfeasible because of the negative primal value PV (-100) at x_5. In Tableau A' the inclusion of x_6 added the dual value DV of M, which ruined the identity matrix; this was corrected by subtracting row x_6 from DV M times. Note that x_6 is no longer used after it becomes nonbasic.

TWO-PHASE METHOD The two-phase method is really the big-M method where the M values have been sorted out. In the first phase we take only the M coefficients and find the initial feasible solution; in the second phase we improve the feasible solution. In Figure 9-11 note that a minimization problem is actually solved in Phase 1: min $W = 1x_6$ was changed into max $-W = -x_6$. Also, checks were incorporated into the computation to illustrate their applications. If there is more than one artificial variable, all of the coefficients would be included in the W function. An equality may be solved either as a pair of .LE. and .GE. constraints or simply by adding the artificial variable which is driven to zero.

SECTION 9-6 TUNE-UP

In Example 9-3, assume that the federal government is now requiring that exactly 40 SSTs be produced yearly by the aircraft company. Solve this problem from the beginning using the two-phase method.

9-7 Complications in simplex tableaux

Various complications must be detected in our examination of simplex tableaux. Not all linear programming models are feasible, and some have unbounded solutions. Still others have a degeneracy, which may or may not be harmful. Simple examples are presented in Figures 9-12 and 9-13 to explain these conditions and help us discern similar conditions in more complex models.

NO FSS All maximization LP problems that have only .LE. constraints possess a valid FSS. When a model has a .GE. or an .EQ. constraint in addition, it is possible that no feasible solution exists because of contradicting constraints. Figure 9-12*a* illustrates such a situation. In a two-phase model, the nonfeasibility is easily detected by the W value not becoming zero when all other DV entries in phase 1 have become nonnegative. The .LE. negative constant constraint is really a .GE. constraint and could lead to nonfeasible solution space.

UNBOUNDED FSS BUT A BOUNDED SOLUTION Depending on the direction of the objective-function vector, it is possible to have a bounded finite solution even when the FSS is unbounded. An extreme example is: min x_1 subject to $x_1 \geq 0$, with its optimal solution at $x_1 = 0$; a more reasonable example is presented in Figure 9-12*b*.

UNBOUNDED FSS AND UNBOUNDED SOLUTION Linear programming is not suited for modeling a growing system. An LP problem has a bounded solution only when the system is stable and has a steady-state condition. Figure 9-12*c* shows a model that can keep growing indefinitely by increasing x_1. In the simplex tableau, the condition is easily detected by not having any limit when a new base is to be introduced. In Figure 9-12*c* x_1 is obviously the next pc; however, in dividing the respective elements of PV by pc, we obtain $2/_{-1}$, $4/_0$, which are both interpreted as being infinity.

DEGENERACY A degeneracy occurs whenever an RPM network node has zeros entered on both the top and the bottom. In a simplex tableau, the condition can be recognized by the same variable having a zero value in both PV and DV. A degeneracy can occur when the objective-function vector is perpendicular to a binding constraint. In Figure 9-13*a*, the constraint that is perpendicular to the objective-function vector Z is not binding but is dominated by a nonorthogonal con-

270

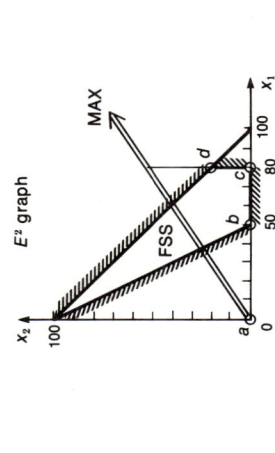

RPM network for (0) and (a')

E^2 graph

RPM network for (a")

(0) Nonfeasible solution without x_6

Base	Primal value	Z_x	x_1	x_2	x_3	x_4	x_5
Dual value	0	1	−2	−1	0	0	0
x_3	100	0	1	1	1	0	0
x_4	480	0	6	0	0	1	0
x_5	−100	0	2	1	0	0	−1

(a')

Base	Primal value	Z_x	x_1	x_2	x_3	x_4	x_5	x_6
Dual value	0	1	−2	−1	0	0	0	M
x_3	100	0	1	1	1	0	0	0
x_4	480	0	6	0	0	1	0	0
x_6	100	0	2	1	0	0	−1	1

(a") Cleaned-up starting tableau

Base	Primal value	Z_x	x_1	x_2	x_3	x_4	x_5	x_6
Dual value	−100M	1	(−2−2M)	(−M−1)	0	0	M	0
x_3	100	0	1	1	1	0	0	0
x_4	480	0	6	0	0	1	0	0
x_6	100	0	②	1	0	0	−1	1

271

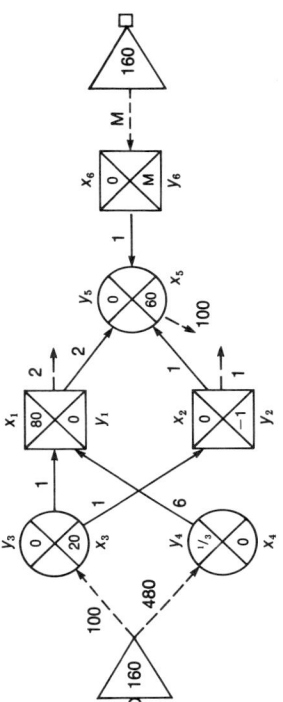

(b) Second tableau

Base	Primal value	Z_x	x_1	x_2	x_3	x_4	x_5	x_6
Dual value	100	1	0	0	0	0	−1	1+M
x_3	50	0	0	1/2	1	0	1/2	−1/2
x_4	180	0	0	−3	0	1	③	−3
x_1	50	0	1	1/2	0	0	−1/2	1/2

(c) Third tableau

Base	Primal value	Z_x	x_1	x_2	x_3	x_4	x_5	x_6
Dual value	160	1	0	−1	0	1/3	0	M
x_3	20	0	0	①	1	−1/6	0	0
x_5	60	0	0	−1	0	1/3	1	−1
x_1	80	0	1	0	0	1/6	0	0

(d) Final tableau

Base	Primal value	Z_x	x_1	x_2	x_3	x_4	x_5	x_6
Dual value	180	1	0	0	1	1/6	0	M
x_2	20	0	0	1	1	−1/6	0	0
x_5	80	0	0	0	1	1/6	1	−1
x_1	80	0	1	0	0	1/6	0	0

Figure 9-10 Big-M application to Example 9-3.

272

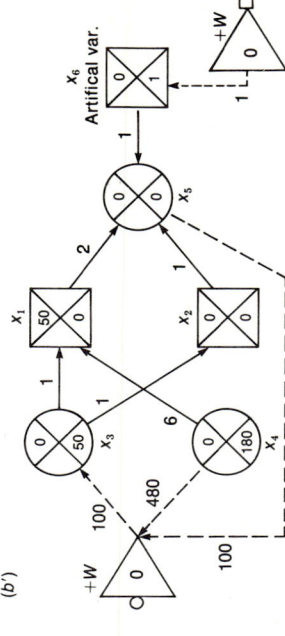

PHASE 1
(0) Minimizing W (or maximizing $-W$)

Base	Primal value	$-W$	x_1	x_2	x_3	x_4	x_5	x_6	Check
Dual value	0	1	0	0	0	0	0	1	2
x_3	100	0	1	1	1	0	0	0	103
x_4	480	0	6	0	0	1	0	0	487
x_6	100	0	2	1	0	0	−1	1	103

(a) Cleaned up tableau for phase 1

Base	Primal value	$-W$	x_1	x_2	x_3	x_4	x_5	x_6	Check
Dual value	−100	1	−2	−1	0	0	1	0	−101
x_3	100	0	1	1	1	0	0	0	103
x_4	480	0	6	0	0	1	0	0	487
x_6	100	0	2	1	0	0	−1	1	103

(b′) Phase 1 completed.

Base	Primal value	$-W$	x_1	x_2	x_3	x_4	x_5	x_6	Check
Dual value	0	1	0	0	0	0	0	1	2
x_3	50	0	0	1/2	1	0	1/2	−.5	51.5
x_4	180	0	0	−3	0	1	3	−3	178
x_6	50	0	1	1/2	0	0	−.5	.5	51.5

(a) Phase 1

(b′)

PHASE 2
(b') Copying from phase 1

Base	Primal value	Dual value	Z_r	x_1	x_2	x_3	x_4	x_5	Check
		0	1	−2	−1	0	0	0	−2
x_3	50		0	0	.5	1	0	.5	52
x_4	180		0	0	−3	0	1	3	181
x_1	50		0	1	.5	0	0	−.5	51

(b) Cleaned up tableau for phase 2

Base	Primal value	Dual value	Z_r	x_1	x_2	x_3	x_4	x_5	Check
		100	1	0	0	0	0	−1	100
x_3	50		0	0	.5	1	0	.5	52
x_4	180		0	0	−3	0	1	3	181
x_1	50		0	1	.5	0	0	−.5	51

(b) Phase 2

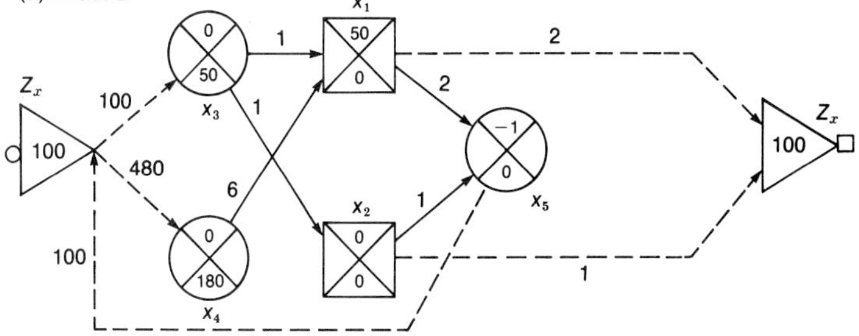

(c)

Base	Primal value	Dual value	Z_r	x_1	x_2	x_3	x_4	x_5	Check
		160	1	0	−1	0	1/3	0	161 1/3
x_3	20		0	0	1	1	−1/6	0	21 5/6
x_5	60		0	0	−1	0	1/3	1	60 1/3
x_1	80		0	1	0	0	1/6	0	21 1/6

The final optimal tableau is the same as in Figure 9-10 (d).

Figure 9-11 Two-phase method applied to Example 9-3.

(a) No FSS

Base	Primal value	$-W$	x_1	x_2	x_3	x_4	x_5
Dual value	-7	1	-1	-1	0	1	0
x_3	12	0	2	3	1	0	0
x_5	7	0	1	1	0	-1	1
Dual value	-1	1	0	1/2	1/2	1	0
x_1	6	0	1	3/2	1/2	0	0
x_5	1	0	0	$-1/2$	$-1/2$	1	1

No feasible solution out of phase 1

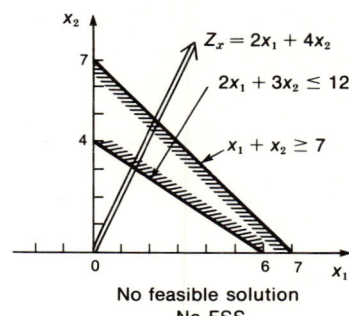

No feasible solution
No FSS

Phase 1 network for the second tableau fails to reduce W to 0.

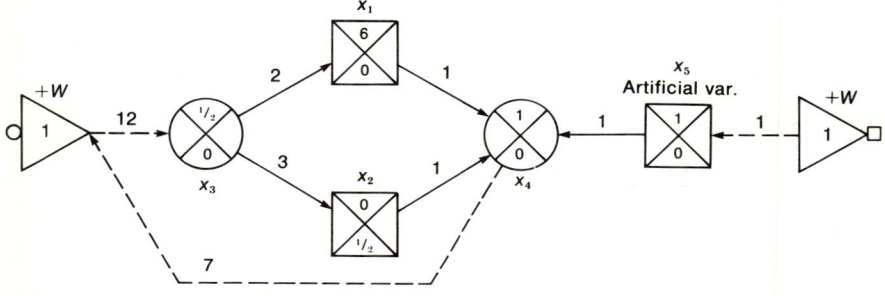

(b) Unbounded FSS with a bounded solution

Base	Primal value	Z_x	x_1	x_2	x_3	x_4
Dual value	4	1	1	0	2	0
x_2	2	0	-1	1	1	0
x_4	2	0	1	0	1	1

Feasible and optimal tableau

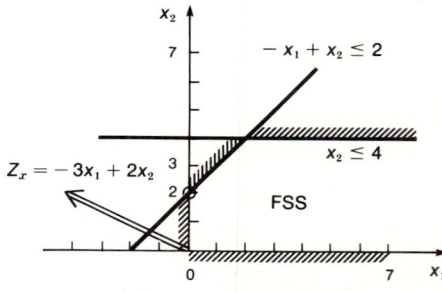

A feasible and optimal BFS
in spite of unbounded FSS

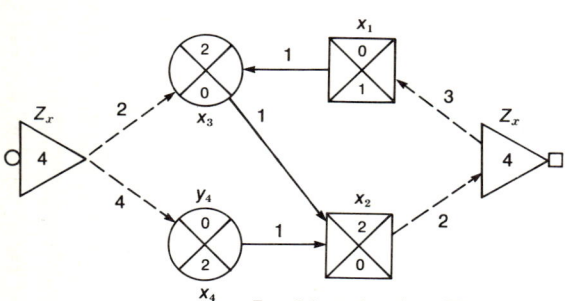

Feasible and optimal RPM network

(c) Unbounded solution. x_1 can be pivoted in by an unrestricted amount

Base	Primal value	Z_x	x_1	x_2	x_3	x_4
Dual value	0	1	−3	−2	0	0
x_3	2	0	−1	1	1	0
x_4	4	0	0	1	0	1

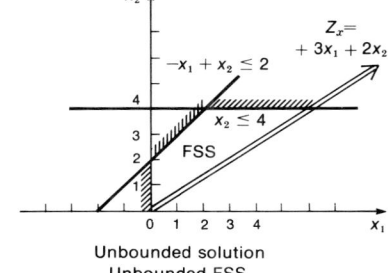

Unbounded solution
Unbounded FSS

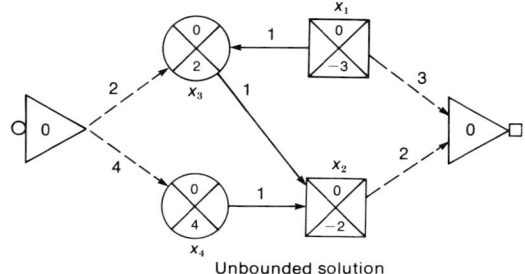

Unbounded solution

Figure 9-12 Effects of solution space FSS.

straint, and therefore the solution is not degenerate. In Figure 9-13b, on the other hand, the objective-function vector is orthogonal to the binding constraint, and the solution is degenerate, which implies that any linear combination of ($x_1 = 0$, $x_2 = 4$) and ($x_1 = 6$, $x_2 = 0$) is an optimal condition. A degeneracy occurs also when several constraints intersect at an extreme point (Figure 9-13c).

A degeneracy may be temporary, but it may also cause the simplex algorithm to *cycle*, or *circle*, endlessly without ever reaching an optimal solution. Fortunately, although degeneracy is a common occurrence, cycling is not; and remedies exist whereby a computer can automatically break the cycle. E. L. Beale proposed a simple example of cycling,[1] and the example adopted in Figure 9-14 is based on her original work. Actual cycling can be observed on most LINPRO type programs, although the order of constraints may have to be changed. The starting problem is

$$\max Z_x = -150x_1 + 0.02x_2 - 6.0x_3 + 0.75x_4$$

subject to

$$-90x_1 - 0.02x_2 + 3.0x_3 + 0.50x_4 \leq 0$$
$$-60x_1 + 0.04x_2 + 9.0x_3 + 0.25x_4 \leq 0$$
$$1.0x_3 \leq 1.0$$

---

[1] E. M. L. Beale, "Cycling on the Dual Simplex Algorithm," *Naval Res. Logist. Quart.*, p. 269–276, vol. 2, no. 4, Dec. 1955.

(a)

Base	Primal value	Z_x	x_1	x_2	x_3	x_4
Dual value	6	1	0	1/2	1/2	0
x_1	6	0	1	3/2	1/2	0
x_4	1	0	0	−1/2	−1/2	1

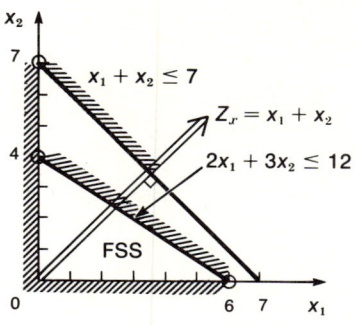

Feasible and optimal
The dominating constraint is nondegenerate

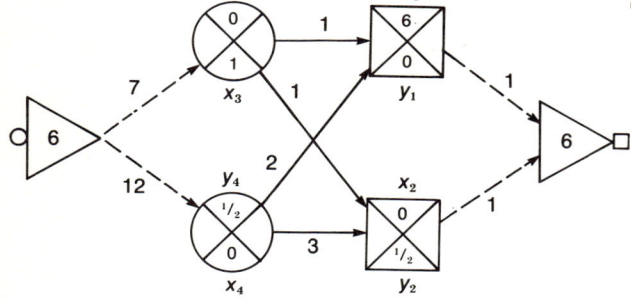

(b)

Base	Primal value	Z_x	x_1	x_2	x_3	x_4
Dual value	12	1	0	0	0	0
x_3	3	0	1/3	0	1	−1/3
x_2	4	0	2/3	1	0	1/3

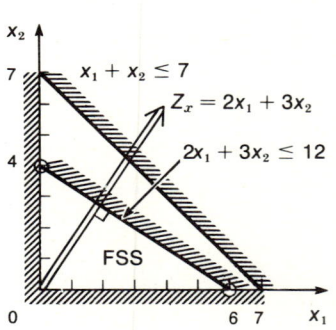

Dominated constraint degeneracy

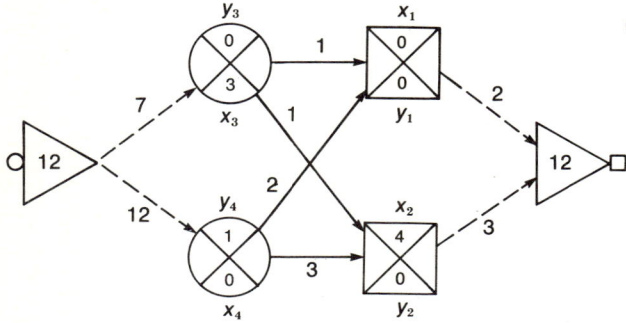

(c)

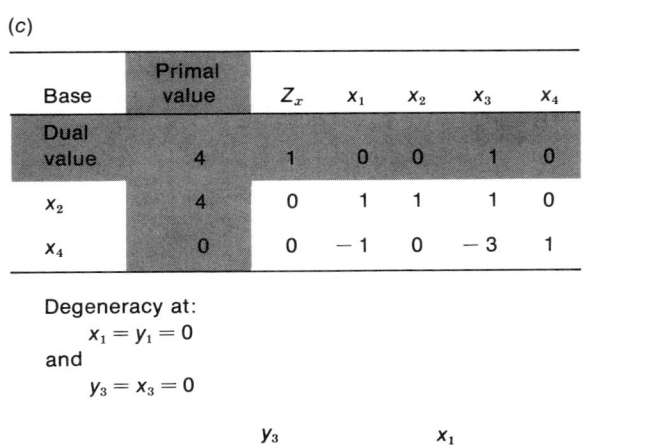

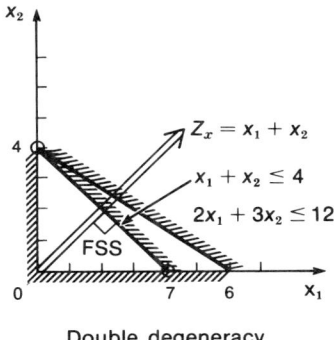

Degeneracy at:
$x_1 = y_1 = 0$
and
$y_3 = x_3 = 0$

Double degeneracy

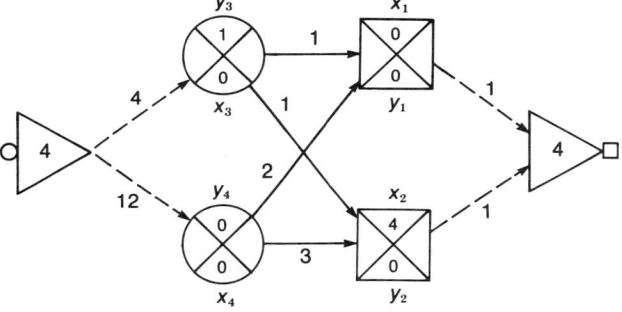

Figure 9-13 Various cases of degeneracy.

with all x's nonnegative. From the RPM network it is apparent that the problem is unbounded since the objective-function value can be increased indefinitely by assigning an arbitrarily large x_2. But because of the arrangement of columns and rows, this never does happen. Altering rows or columns can easily destroy the cycling, and the problem may not cycle when used with another computer program. However, most computer programs are not equipped with a special algorithm to break the cycling.

PARAMETRIC PROGRAMMING It is not necessary that all entries in a simplex tableau be constants. We may use parameters instead of constants and evaluate the effects of changing them. The RPM nodal values will then also be a function of these parameters and will visually illustrate the changes in a solution when the parametric values are altered. Such a procedure is called *parametric programming*.

(a)

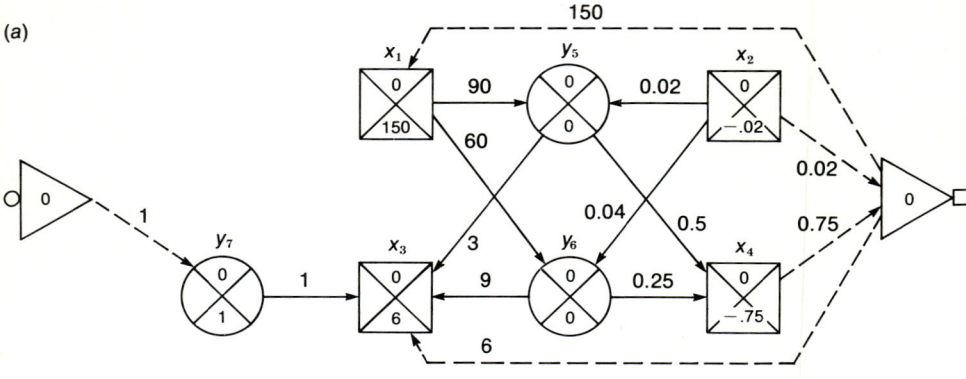

(b)

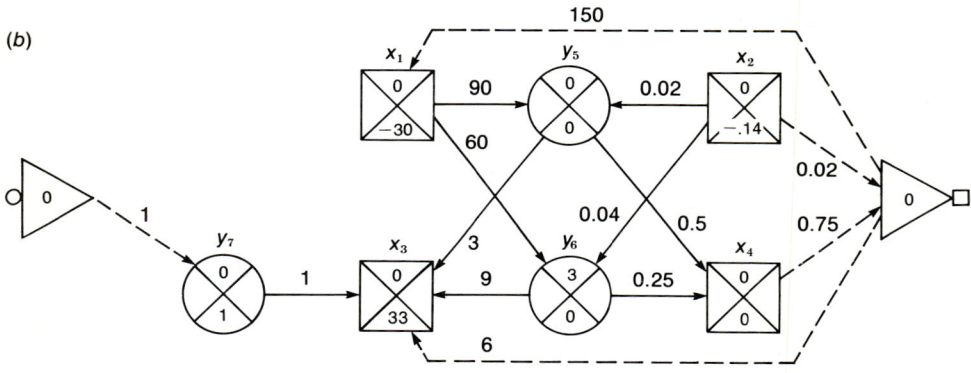

(c)

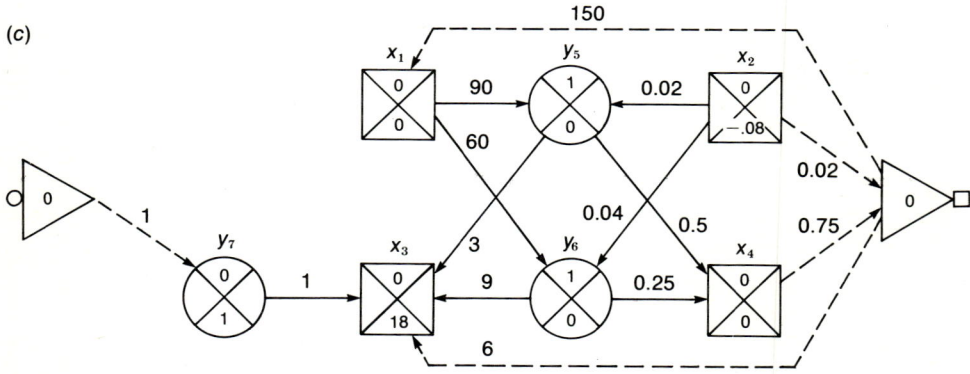

Figure 9-14 Example of cycling.

Simplex Tableau: A Table for Resource Exchange 279

(d)
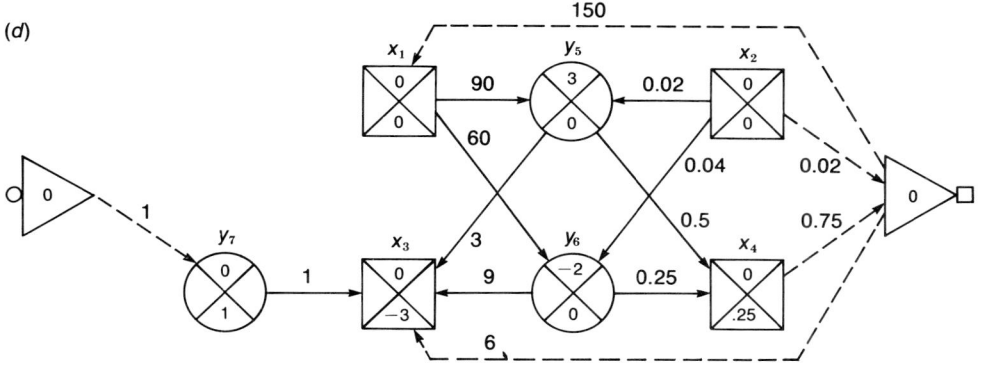

(e)
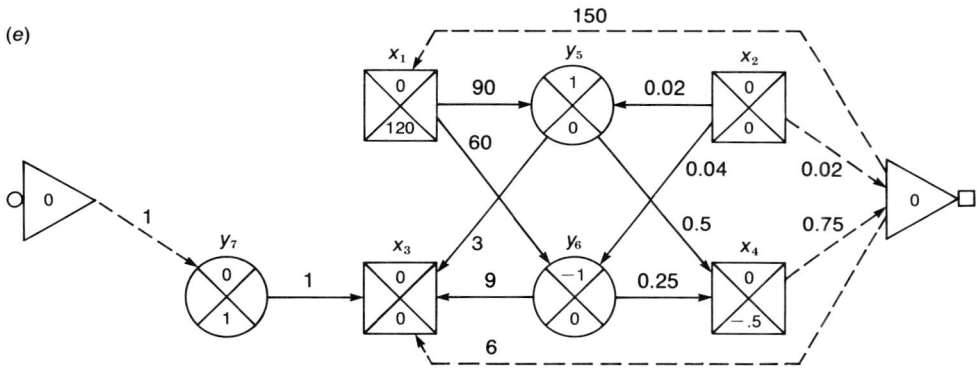

(f)
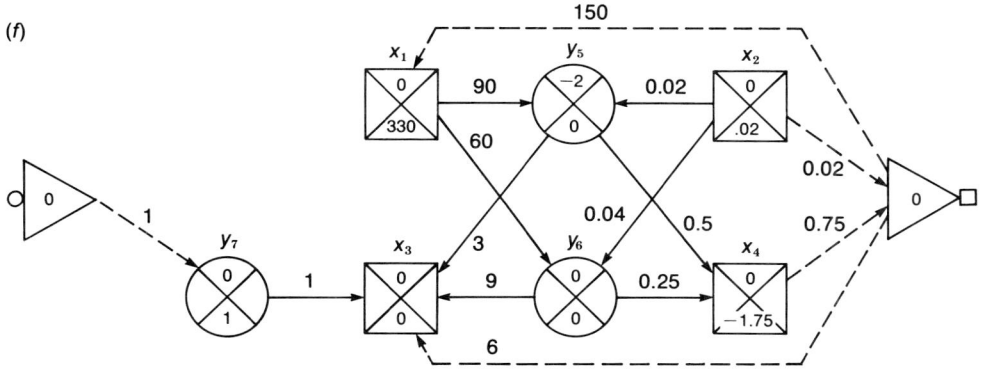

The cycling now repeats (a), (b), ... ad infinitum.

9-8 Incorporating a tableau within an RPM network

Being a table for resource exchange, a simplex tableau is easily incorporated within the structure of an RPM network. When the tableau is sparse (i.e., having many zero entries), a network is the preferred mode of representing a problem; on the other hand, when the tableau is dense, a corresponding network could be rather involved and unsightly. For example, in Figure 6-9 an RPM network of a diet problem shows 12 arrows among 3 activities ALFA, BRAVO, and CHARL and 5 resources VA, VB, VC, FE, and CA. Since the columns of a simplex tableau represent primal variables and the rows correspond to resource constraints, such a tableau can replace the crowded arrows, as shown in Figure 9-15. Several such tableaux can be included within an RPM network and have been found useful in many large-scale industrial applications where LP programs are already constructed and require conversion to RPM networks.

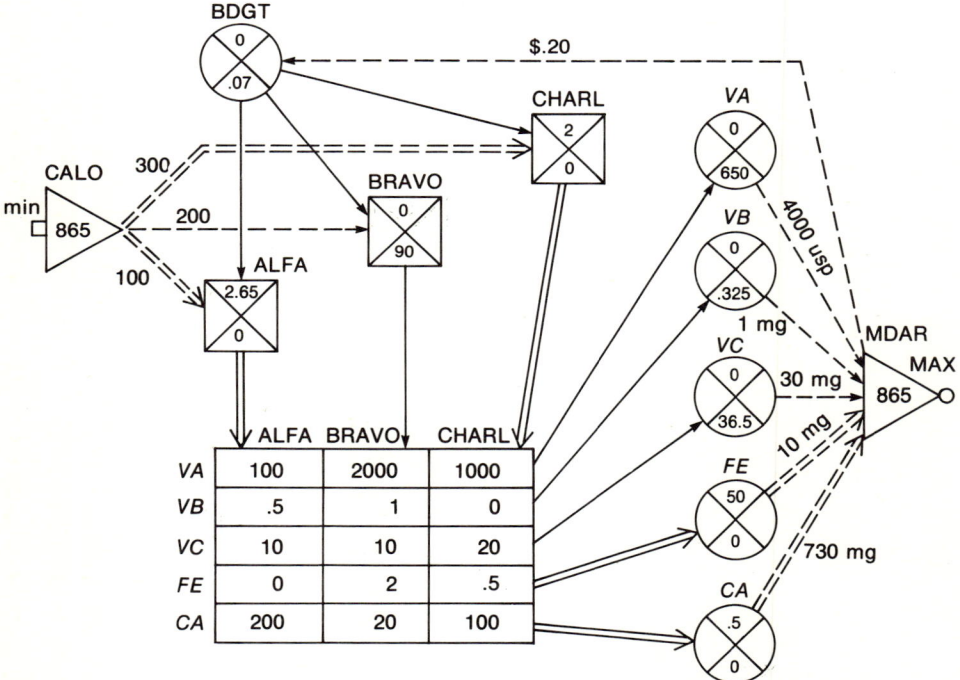

Figure 9-15 Incorporating a tableau within an RPM network (Figure 6-9 revisited).

TUNE-UP SOLUTIONS

Section 9-1

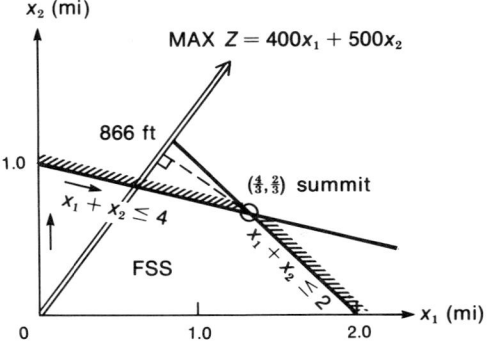

1. max $\quad Z_x = 400x_1 + 500x_2$
   $x_1 + 4x_2 \leq 4$
   $x_1 + x_2 \leq 2$
   $x_1, x_2 \geq 0$

2. The rule: Start at the foot of the park, $x_1 = x_2 = 0$:

   At an intersection, always take a path with the steepest ascent.

   Continue on a path until a new intersection is encountered.

   Never cross another path.

   Stop when neither the path to your right nor to your left is ascending.

   The conditions necessary for this scheme to work are exactly those that are provided by the assumption of a feasible LP problem. First, your starting point must be inside the FSS. You must have one finite summit (i.e., a bounded solution), and each path segment bordering the park must be straight and of a uniform slope (i.e., linear constraints and a linear objective function) and entirely remain within the allowed confine of FSS (i.e., the convexity assumption). The roads should connect to form a boundary containing the FSS (i.e., a simplex body), and the slope to the top must be uniformly ascending (i.e., a monotonically increasing objective function).

Also, you must be able to evaluate your bearings—location and altitude (basic primal values and dual simplex criteria must be evaluated at each intersection)—so that you may choose the steepest ascending trail (i.e., the most negative regret) and know when you have reached the summit (no negative primal or dual value). Above all, you must also have faith in your friends who have told you the summit is at an intersection (extreme-point theorem) and that an ascending path will eventually get you to the top.

Section 9-3

1.

Base	PV	Z_x	x_1	x_2	x_3	x_4	x_5	x_6
DV	0	1	100	−50	200	0	0	0
x_4	10	0	−2	0	0	1	0	0
x_5	0	0	−3	1	0	0	1	0
x_6	20	0	0	−4	1	0	0	1

2.

Base	PV	Z_x	x_1	x_2	x_3	x_4	x_5	x_6	x_7	x_8
DV	0	1	−5	−6	−4	−3	0	0	0	0
x_5	30	0	1	1	0	0	1	0	0	0
x_6	−22	0	−1	0	−1	0	0	1	0	0
x_7	30	0	0	0	1	1	0	0	1	0
x_8	−28	0	0	−1	0	−1	0	0	0	1

Negative values in PV must be changed by multiplying the row by −1 and adding the necessary artificial variable.

3.

Base	PV	Z_x	x_1	x_2	x_3	x_4	x_5	x_6	x_7
DV	0	1	−5	−4	20	0	0	0	0
x_4	5	0	1	0	0	1	0	0	0
x_5	6	0	0	1	1	0	1	0	0
x_6	4	0	−2	−6	1	0	0	−1	0
x_7	−10	0	0	0	−12	0	0	0	1

Section 9-5

	Primal value	Z_x	Structural		Logical	
Base			x_1	x_2	x_3	x_4
Dual value	$Z = 0$	1	$y_1 = -4$	$y_2 = -6$	$y_3 = 0$	$y_4 = 0$
x_3	12	0	$a_{31} = 1$	$a_{32} = 2$	1	0
x_4	8	0	$a_{41} = 1$	$a_{42} = 1$	0	1

Primal value

	Z_x	x_3	x_3
Z_x	0	1	0	0
x_3	12	0	1	0
x_4	8	0	0	1

Identity matrix

meaning

Primal
Base (row) = value = Columns

Z (dual) = 0 = Z_x
x_3 = 12 = x_3
x_4 = 8 = x_4

The dual values for all variables are

$y_1 =$ shadow price for $x_1 = -4$ ($4 opportunity lost by not making x_1)

$y_2 =$ shadow price for $x_2 = -6$ ($6 opportunity lost by not making x_2)

$y_3 =$ shadow price for resource 1 = $0 (resource 1 is not scarce; $0 for the 12 units left over)

$y_4 =$ shadow price for resource 1 = $0 (resource 2 is not scarce; $0 for the 8 units left over)

The primal values of the nonbasic variables are equal to zero; that is:

$x_1 = 0$ (do not make any x_1) $x_2 = 0$ (do not make any x_2)

The simplex iterations are shown in Figure 9-16, page 284.

Section 9-6

A simple way of handling this problem is to replace x_2 by 40 and solve the remaining unknowns. This procedure is not recommended, however, because you can no longer monitor the variable eliminated and because you may succumb to a physically unrealizable solution. The simplex procedure for handling an equality is either to replace it by a combination of one .GE. and one .LE. constraint or simply to add an artificial variable which is driven to zero during the first phase.

max $Z_x = 2x_1 + x_2$

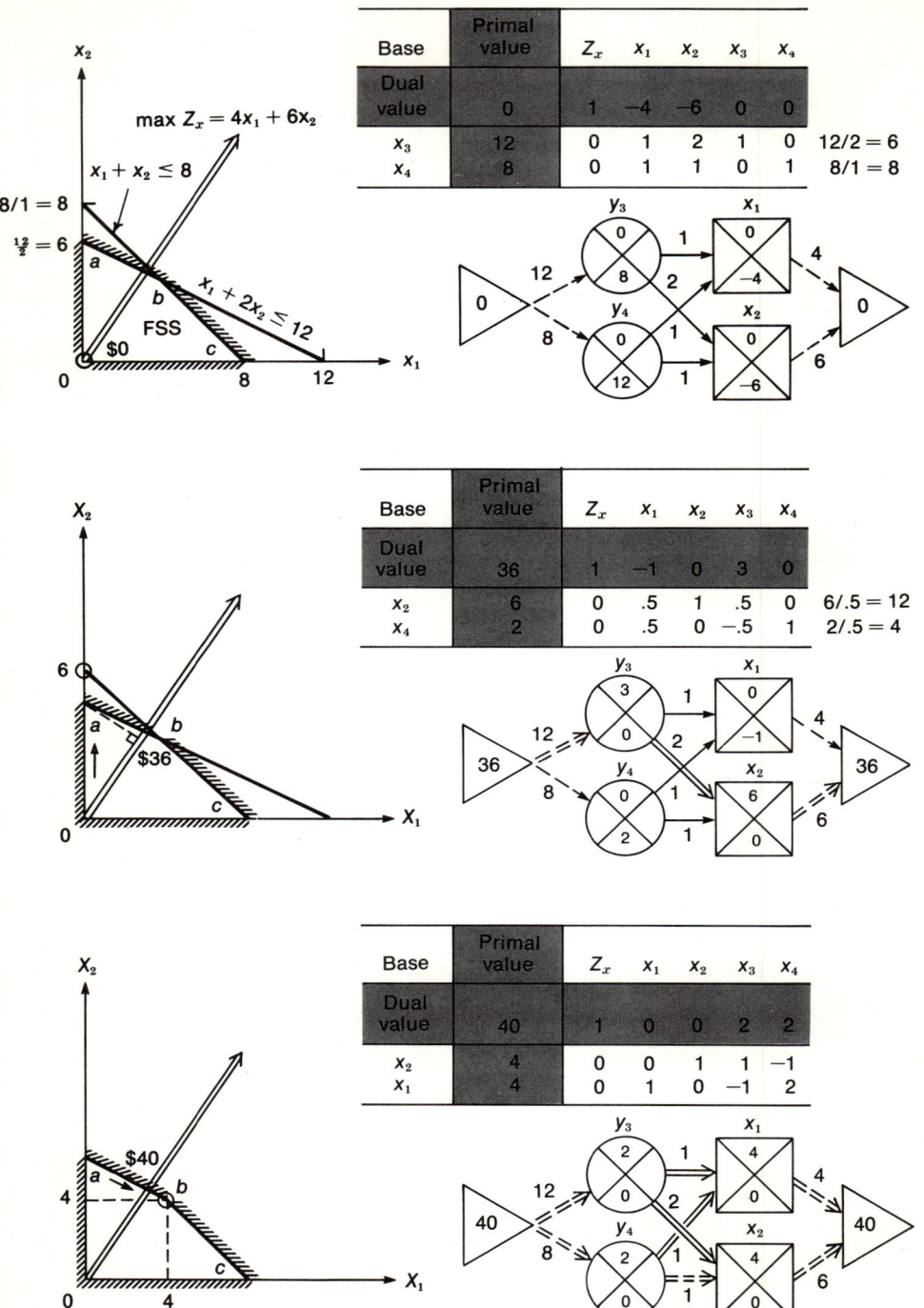

Figure 9-16 Section 9-5 Tune-Up solution.

Simplex Tableau: A Table for Resource Exchange

subject to

$$x_1 + x_2 \leq 100$$
$$6x_1 \leq 480$$
$$2x_1 + x_2 \geq 100$$
$$x_2 = 40$$

By elimination, we have $x_2 = 40$:

$$\max Z_x = 2x_1 + 40$$

subject to

$$x_1 \leq 60$$
$$6x_1 \leq 480$$
$$2x_1 \geq 60$$

The answer is obviously

$$x_1 = 60 \quad \text{and} \quad Z_{dx} = 2(60) + 40 = 160$$

By conversion,

$$x_2 = 40$$

can be written as

$$x_2 \leq 40 \quad \text{and} \quad x_2 \geq 40$$

Using the artificial variable approach, we can write

	PV	−W	x_1	x_2	x_3	x_4	x_5	x_6	x_7	PV/a	Check
−W	0	1	0	0	0	0	0	1	1	XXX	3
x_3	100	0	1	1	1	0	0	0	0		103
x_4	480	0	6	0	0	1	0	0	0		487
x_6	100	0	2	1	0	0	−1	1	0		103
x_7	40	0	0	1	0	0	0	0	1		42

Cleaning up, we obtain

	PV	−W	x_1	x_2	x_3	x_4	x_5	x_6	x_7	PV/a	Check
−W	−140	1	−2	−2	0	0	+1	0	0	XXX	−142
x_3	100	0	1	1	1	0	0	0	0	100	103
x_4	480	0	6	0	0	1	0	0	0		487
x_6	100	0	2	1	0	0	−1	1	0	100	103
x_7	40	0	0	1	0	0	0	0	1	40	42

	PV	−W	x_1	x_2	x_3	x_4	x_5	x_6	x_7	PV/a	Check
−W	−60	1	−2	0	0	0	1	0	2	XXX	−58
x_3	60	0	1	0	1	0	0	0	−1	60	61
x_4	480	0	6	0	0	1	0	0	0	80	487
x_6	60	0	2	0	0	0	−1	1	−1	30	61
x_2	40	0	0	1	0	0	0	0	1		42

	PV	−W	x_1	x_2	x_3	x_4	x_5	x_6	x_7	PV/a	Check
−W	0	1	0	0	0	0	0	1	1	XXX	3
x_3	30	0	0	0	1	0	$1/2$	$-1/2$	$-1/2$		$30^{1}/_{2}$
x_4	300	0	0	0	0	1	3	−3	3		304
x_1	30	0	1	0	0	0	$-1/2$	$1/2$	$-1/2$		$30^{1}/_{2}$
x_2	40	0	0	1	0	0	0	0	1		42

Phase 2

	PV	Z_x	x_1	x_2	x_3	x_4	x_5	PV/a	Check
Z_x	0	1	−2	−1	0	0	0	XXX	−2
x_3	30	0	0	0	1	0	$1/2$		$31^{1}/_{2}$
x_4	300	0	0	0	0	1	3		304
x_1	30	0	1	0	0	0	$-1/2$		$30^{1}/_{2}$
x_2	40	0	0	1	0	0	0		41

Cleaning this up, we obtain

	PV	Z_x	x_1	x_2	x_3	x_4	x_5	PV/a	Check
Z_x	100	1	0	0	0	0	−1	XXX	100
x_3	30	0	0	0	1	0	$1/2$	60	$31^{1}/_{2}$
x_4	300	0	0	0	0	1	3	100	304
x_1	30	0	1	0	0	0	$-1/2$	−60	$30^{1}/_{2}$
x_2	40	0	0	1	0	0	0		41

	PV	Z_x	x_1	x_2	x_3	x_4	x_5	PV/a	Check
Z_x	160	1	0	0	2	0	0	XXX	163
x_5	60	0	0	0	2	0	1		63
x_4	120	0	0	0	−6	1	0		115
x_1	60	0	1	0	1	0	0		62
x_2	40	0	0	1	0	0	0		41

Answer: Build 60 air buses and 40 SSTs for a profit of $160 million/yr.

EXERCISES

9-1 Solve the following LP problem by the standard simplex method.
$$\max Z_x = 50x_1 + 30x_2$$
subject to
$$10x_1 + 50x_2 \leq 250$$
$$25x_1 + 5x_2 \leq 100$$
where all variables are nonnegative.

9-2 For the cycling problem in Figure 9-14, construct simplex tableaux and follow through six iterations.

9-3 Solve the dual problem of Example 9-1.

9-4 Solve the dual problem of Example 9-2.

9-5 In Example 9-3 and Section 9-6 Tune-up, imagine that the Huge Tool Company decides that aircraft manufacturing be used to claim losses for tax purposes. It now wishes to minimize instead of maximize its profit. Solve this minimization problem by the simplex method. (Maintain all other conditions, including the minimum profit requirement of $100 million/yr.)

SEQUENTIAL DECISION PROCESS: Dynamic Programming

Chapter 10

10-1 One thing at a time

The simplex methods introduced in Chapter 9 are powerful tools for solving linear optimization models by a computer. But they have the handicaps of being rather tedious for manual computation and of being bound by the same linearity conditions that prevent application of linear models to discrete models and nonlinear cost functions. Also, simplex procedures solve all variables at once and make no attempt to guarantee that the value of a variable introduced during an iteration be meaningful in the final solution.

    RPMS provides a way of thinking that decomposes a large problem into processes and resources. Each process or resource can then be treated as a hub for a cause-and-effect analysis. By looking at a problem as a series of smaller decision-making opportunities and making use of our "common sense," we are often able to identify the optimal or near optimal solution intuitively. A more formalized OR/MS technique that makes use of this step-by-step decision process is known as *dynamic programming* (DP), a name given to the process by its originator

Richard E. Bellman (1957). Its gist is contained in the statement of the principle of optimality:

An optimal policy has the property that whatever the initial state and initial decision are, the remaining decisions must constitute an optimal policy with regard to the state resulting from the first decision.[1]

Harvey M. Wagner has supplied a simpler version of the principle:

An optimal policy must have the property that regardless of the route taken to enter a particular state, the remaining decisions must constitute an optimal policy for leaving that state.[2]

A layman's version of the principle may simply state: "if you don't do your best with what you've got, you will never do better later than if you would have done your best now."

Example 10-1: *A simple investment scheme* The city of Micropolis raised $2 million on a bond issue and wants to invest it for 3 yr until the fund is needed for a major construction project. Mayor Haigha has asked you to compile a portfolio, and you have identified three plans (and their combinations): (1) an annual deposit at 10 percent compounded yearly (i.e., returning 110 percent after 1 yr); (2) a bi-annual investment returning 120 percent at maturity (10 percent/yr simple interest); and (3) a 3-yr certificate returning 132.1 percent at the end of the third year. There are distinct advantages to each plan, and you feel that the mayor should decide which one to adopt. How would you recommend each investment opportunity from the financial point of view?

This problem requires no formal OR/MS tool for its solution; but if you were to draw the problem out in an RPM network format (Figure 10-1), you would recognize this to be essentially the same as in Example 4-2 in Chapter 4. Solving the problem intuitively and filling in all primal and dual values would produce the RPM network in Figure 10-1. Thus, if all investments were equally appealing to the mayor, the investment should be made in three consecutive yearly deposits, earning $662,000 in dividends.

Looking at the dual values, it does appear that an investment in the 2-yr program is the least favorable during the first year ($y_B = 0.011$) and not much more favorable during the second year ($y_E = 0.01$); in fact, the latter appears only as good as the 3-yr investment program ($y_C = 0.01$). Before we embark on a discussion of the accuracy of these observations, let us focus our attention on heuristic methods for solving this problem.

---

[1] Richard E. Bellman and Stuart E. Dreyfus, *Applied Dynamic Programming*, Princeton Univ. Press, Princeton, N.J., 1962, p. 15.
[2] Harvey M. Wagner, *Principles of Operations Research*, Prentice-Hall, Inc., Englewood Cliffs, N.J., 1969, p. 257.

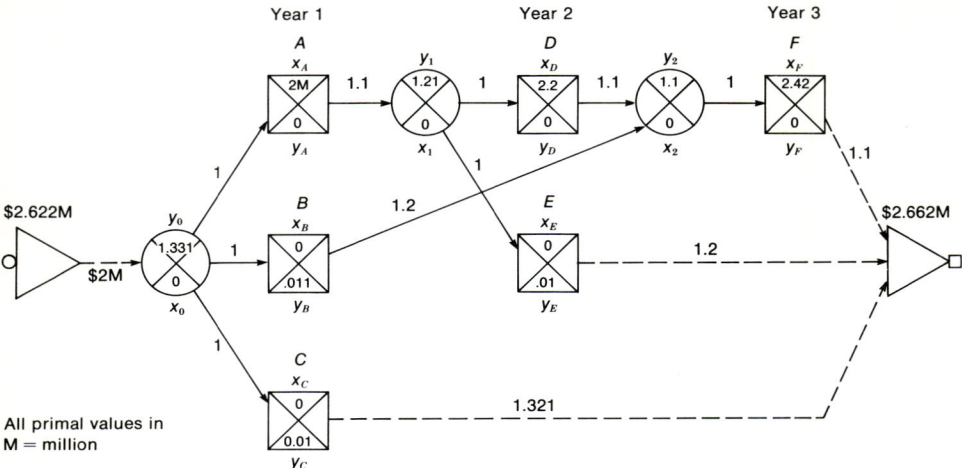

Figure 10-1 Example 4-2 revisited (LP solution).

RESOURCE FLOWS One salient feature of dual values in linear programming is that they are always considered on a "per unit" basis. For example, the Y values in Figure 10-1 are marginal costs per dollar invested. How much resource is actually flowing through a resource node, say, Y_2, is not obvious. A flow through resource node y_2 must be computed from its residue ($x_2 = 0$), input process nodes ($x_d = \$2.2$ million and $x_B = 0$) and their coefficients (1.1 and 1.2), and output process nodes and their coefficients. In this case, the flow through node y_2 is the value of x_F, or $\$2,420,000$.

Each node in RPMS is divided into four quadrants, and so far we have used only the top and the bottom entries. Two side cells have been reserved specifically for identifying total flows through the nodes. This features is especially attractive when interpreting an RPMS model using dynamic programming or critical-path scheduling method (Chapter 11).

In both dynamic programming and project scheduling (CPM and PERT), there are two flow computations, one moves forward in search of the *final state*, and the other moves backward in search of the *initial* state. In the case of dynamic programming, these are known as the *forward* and *backward* analyses, or *final state* and *initial state* computational procedures; in critical-path scheduling they are known as the *earliest* and *latest time computations*.

FORWARD ANALYSIS There are three decision stages in our problem:

1. At the beginning of year 1 (y_0) when $2 million is given, we must decide between the 1-yr (A), 2-yr (B), and 3-yr (C) investments
2. At the end of year 1, x_A needs to be redistributed between x_D and x_E

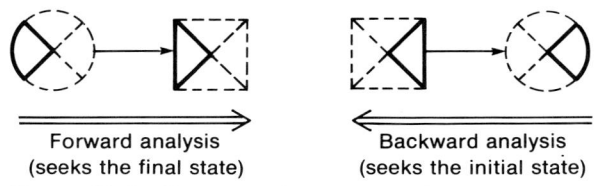

Forward analysis
(seeks the final state)

Backward analysis
(seeks the initial state)

Figure 10-2 Resource flow conventions.

3. At the end of year 2, we must decide how much to put into x_F. At each stage, our investment success can be measured by our total amount of assets, including both the principal $2 million and the accumulated dividends. Passing through an investment process, we have picked up the dividend which is compounded into the resource flow. To distinguish between the forward and the backward analyses, we have adopted the convention of using side cells as shown in Figure 10-2.

During forward and backward analyses, we shall attempt all resource flows until paths merge at a resource node (a logical OR condition), and then choose the best route(s). Which path will be selected depends on the decision rule that is applicable to the particular dynamic programming problem. In the case of the *longest-path* problem, we select the heavier resource flow; in the case of the *shortest-path* problem, we select the lighter resource flow. Other rules, such as first-in-first-out and two-out-of-three, are also possible.

We shall begin the forward analysis with our $2 million and proceed down the three alternatives available at the first stage. At this time, our RPM network would look like Figure 10-3.

The bag hanging at the end of each arrow indicates the resource flow out of that path: $2 million × 1.1 = $2.2 million for x_A; $2 million × 1.2 = $2.4 million for

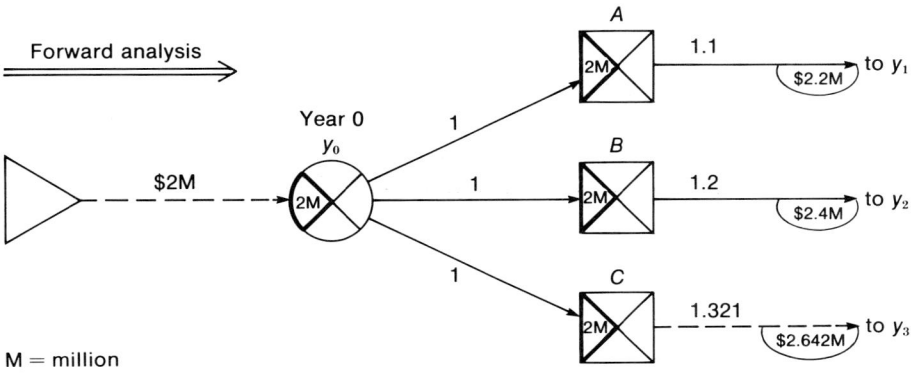

M = million

Figure 10-3 First-stage forward flows.

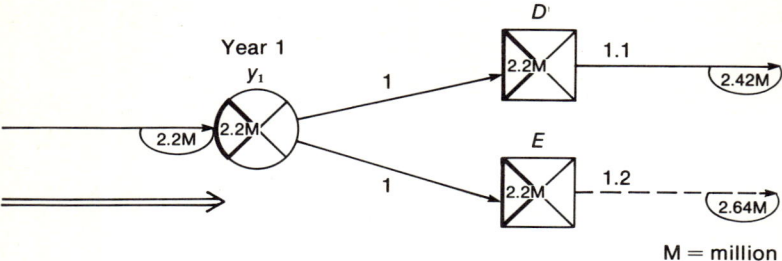

Figure 10-4 Second-stage forward flows.

x_B; and $2.642 million out of x_C. Knowing all the possible flows into y_1, we can proceed with our second-stage analysis (Figure 10-4).

We continue our forward analysis and reach the third stage at the end of year 2. Our resource could come either from x_D ($2.42 million) or x_B ($2.40 million). Since this is a standard LP model, the resource node has a simple *logical OR* rule: Either or both inflows are allowed. Obviously x_D is a better deal, and we decide to invest $2.42 million in F for the final return of $2.662 million (Figure 10-5). As the three paths merge together at the end of the third year, it is easy to pick the basic path through F (2.662 million) over those through E ($2.64 million) or C ($2.642 million). We note that the 3-yr investment x_C ($2.642 million) seems preferable to the investment path through E ($2.640 million) in spite of our earlier observation, but before discussing this, let us conduct the backward analysis.

BACKWARD ANALYSIS The backward analysis is conducted in a similar manner but in reverse. The first decision stage is to identify the resources needed by

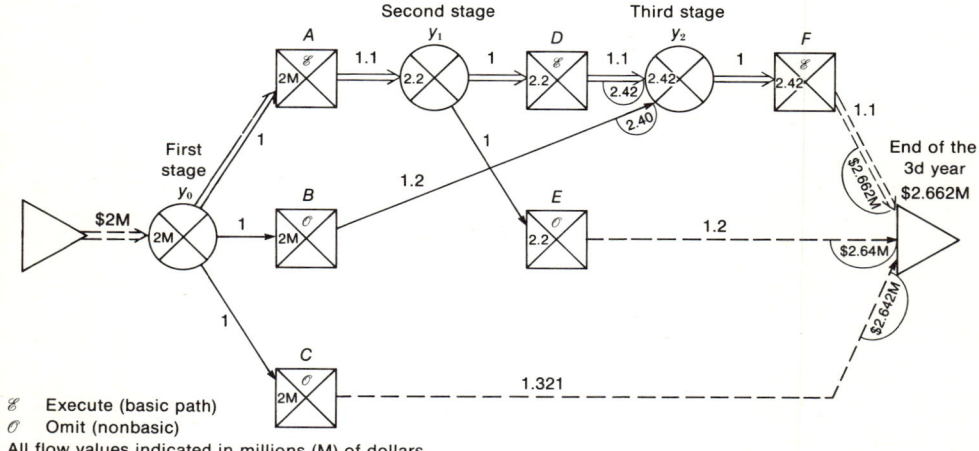

𝒪   Execute (basic path)
𝒪   Omit (nonbasic)
All flow values indicated in millions (M) of dollars

Figure 10-5 Forward analysis completed (third stage).

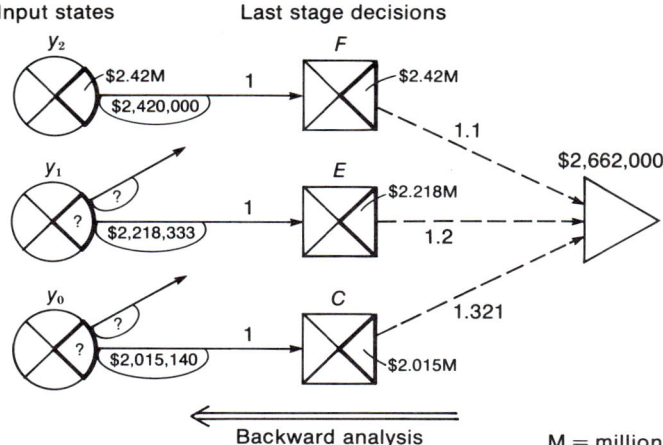

Figure 10-6 Beginning of backward analysis.

the three investment processes F, E, and C to achieve the $2.662 million (see Figure 10-6). The next decision stage is at y_2, the end of year 2, where we must compare the resource flow through D ($2.2 million at y_1) against the flow through B ($2,016,667) to achieve the same $2.4 million observed going through y_2. Backing up another step, we can observe that the path through D (2.2 million) is cheaper than the path through E ($2.218333 million), and therefore $x_D = $2.2 million is chosen over $x_E = $2.218333 million. This *decision* is marked by $\mathscr{E}$ in the node D and $\mathscr{O}$ in the node E. Proceeding in this manner, the entire backward analysis can be conducted, and Figure 10-7 shows the completed backward analysis. The basic path can be identified by this backward analysis alone, just as it is possible to

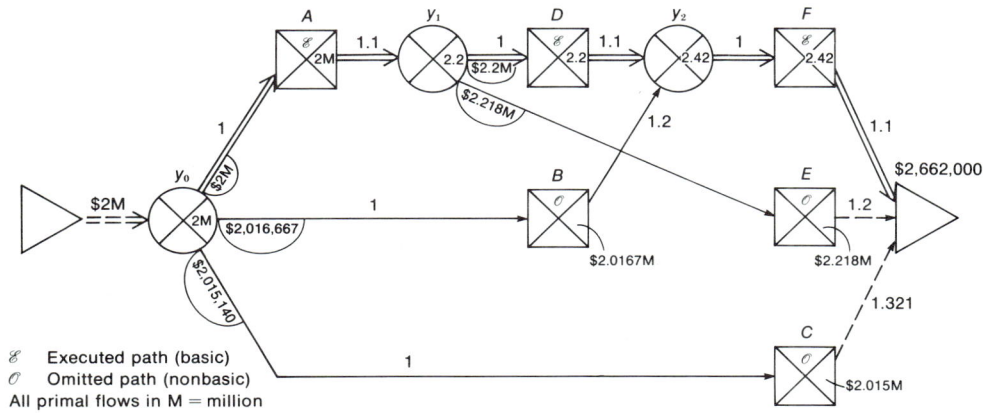

$\mathscr{E}$ Executed path (basic)
$\mathscr{O}$ Omitted path (nonbasic)
All primal flows in M = million

Figure 10-7 Completed backward analysis.

do so from the forward analysis alone. All we need is to keep track of the paths we choose.

In the forward analysis, we invoke the *maximization of the output* from the second postulate of RPMS; in the backward analysis, we use the *minimization of the input* part of the second postulate of RPMS. Therefore, at the resource node y_1, we choose the path with the least required flow out of the node ($x_D = \$2.2$ million is less than $x_E = \$2.218$ million). Similarly, at y_0 the endowment of $2 million should be funneled into the path requiring the least input, that is, investment A, since min $(x_A = 2M; x_B = 2,016,667; x_C = 2,015,140) = x_A$.

TOTAL-SLACK COMPUTATION Let us combine the forward and backward analyses. Each node now contains a value from the forward analysis and another value from the backward analysis. The difference between the two values is entered as the residue for that node. As in LP problems, the zero residue is an indication of a basic node. A nonzero residue indicates the additional input needed to make the nonbasic path as attractive as the basic path. But unlike LP problems, the opportunity cost is computed as a total rather than marginal value. Figure 10-8 illustrates the completed RPM network.

Using the complementary slackness theorem, we can now fill in a zero wherever the residue is nonzero. We could have also included the actual flow value as the primal variable in the processes, but instead we chose to indicate our *decision* simply by using $\mathscr{E}$.

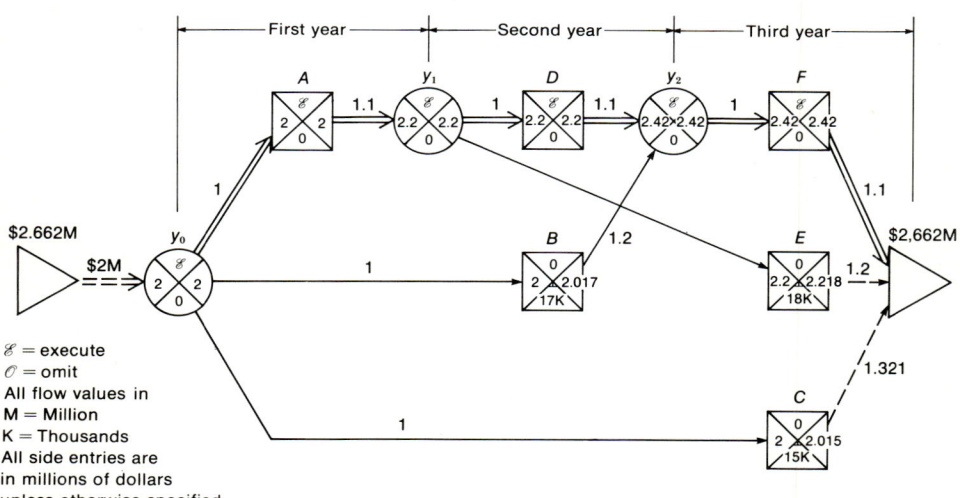

Figure 10-8 Completed RPM network with forward and backward analyses.

RECONCILING TOTAL FLOWS (DP) WITH MARGINAL VALUES (LP)
Unfortunately, we are still left with the task of reconciling Figure 10-8 with Figure 10-1. To facilitate our discussion, let us take the pertinent data from both figures:

	\multicolumn{6}{c}{Process}	
	A	B	C	D	E	F	
Marginal residue (LP)	0	0.011	0.01	0	0.01	0	Figure 10-1
Total residue (DP), dollars	0	16,667	15,140	0	18,333	0	Figure 10-8

Comparing the two 2-yr investment opportunities, we note that the total slack is $16,667 for B and $18,333 for E, which seems to contradict our observation in the marginal dual value analysis where E's 0.01 is obviously less than B's 0.011. Also, you may have difficulty reconciling what $16,667 for B is 0.011 of, or how 0.01 for C relates to $15,140, and why C and E, which have the same 0.01 in the marginal analysis, have such a large difference in the total slack analysis.

A little plodding, however, should clarify the situation and dissipate our uneasy feeling that linear programming and dynamic programming might be at odds with each other! The investment flow x_B reaches its maturity at the end of the second year, while the investment flow x_E does not mature until the end of the third year. The objective function was set up in terms of the money value at the completion of the project. The $16,667 invested in B can still be reinvested at 10 percent interest for another year: $16,667 × 1.10 = $18,333 at the end of the third year, putting the investment opportunity B on equal footing with E. In fact, 0.011 is 0.01 × 1.1 also, and, as our common sense tells us, investing $2 million at 10 percent for 1 yr and then at 10 percent simple interest for 2 yr (120 percent) is equivalent of investing $2 million at 10 percent simple interest for the first 2 yr and then at 10 percent for the last year.

Now it is clear that C is a preferred investment over either B or E, though less than A-D-F. In case Mayor Haigha does not wish to use the optimal route A-D-F, plan C should be recommended from the remaining three alternatives. To convert a total slack into a marginal value, it suffices to take the flow to the sink and then divide by the base of $2 million. Thus, for B

$$\frac{\$16{,}667 \times 1.2 \times 1.1}{\$2 \text{ million}} = 0.011$$

(as it should be). Similarly for C, we have

$$\frac{\$15{,}140 \times 1.321}{\$2 \text{ million}} = 0.01$$

SECTION 10-1 TUNE-UP
Solve the investment problem originally given in Example 4-2 using the dynamic programming approach (Figure 10-9).

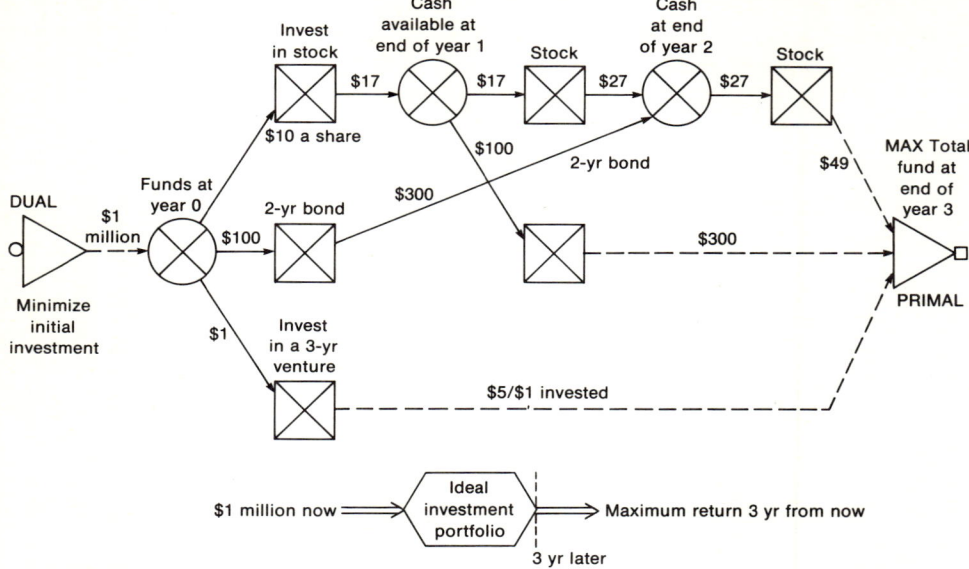

Figure 10-9 RPMS network of Figure 4-4 interpreted as a dynamic programming model.

10-2 Characteristics of DP models

A linear programming model can always be stated as a problem of maximizing (or minimizing) a linear functional subject to a set of linear constraints. Dynamic programming, on the other hand, has no such set format; it derives its strength and weakness from its complete flexibility.

The only requirement for a problem to be treated by dynamic programming is that it must accept the principle of optimality; that is, it must be decomposable into stages, and a recursive relation must be applicable at each stage. The nature of this decomposition and the resulting recursive functional relation will vary from one problem to another, and there is no one set model that can be used for all DP models. This explains the lack of a "canned" universal DP algorithm that parallels the simplex method for linear programming. It takes some creative thinking to identify a recursive function that is amenable to the solution of the problem without an undue hardship from the curse of dimensionality. This is probably the reason why dynamic programming is not as widely used in industry as linear programming. However, we note that it is this flexibility that enables dynamic programming to solve a wide variety of problems for which there is no correct LP formulation. Discrete, integer, nonlinear, and stochastic programming models can all be solved by dynamic programming.

DECOMPOSITION PRINCIPLE The entire RPMS methodology is devoted to the idea of decomposing a large problem into interacting processes and resources.

If a problem can be formulated as an RPM network, then it has already been decomposed. Every linear programming problem can be represented by an RPM network and, therefore, theoretically can be solved by dynamic programming. Several other typical problems will be represented by RPM network models and solved by dynamic programming in this chapter, and CPM and PERT models will be solved similarly in Chapter 11. A typical expression for decomposition is written as

$$f_N(x_N) = r_N(x_N, d_N) \oplus f_{N-1}(x_{N-1})$$

where $\oplus$ indicates a decomposable relation such as an addition, subtraction, or multiplication. f_N is the function being decomposed at the Nth stage between an immediate return function r_N (which depends on the available flow of resource x_N through the stage N and the decision d_N), and the cumulative function f_{N-1} at the previous stage where the flow of resource was x_{N-1}. In the case of a simple cash-investment problem, the saving at year N, f_N, can be computed in terms of the initial investment P and the interest rate r as

$$f_N = P \oplus (1 + r)^N$$

or in terms of the previous year's saving f_{N-1} as

$$f_N = (1 + r) \oplus f_{N-1} \quad \text{where } f_{N-1} = P \oplus (1 + r)^{N-1}$$

or in terms of the saving the year before f_{N-2} as

$$f_N = (1 + r) \oplus f_{N-1} = (1 + r) \oplus (1 + r) \oplus f_{N-2}$$

Example 10-1 (Figure 10-8) has only four possible portfolios. Each plan can be seen as an independent path decomposed into stages (Figure 10a) and the optimal path is easily identified.

DECISION TREE Since we were given the initial state ($2 million) in Example 10-1, we could have combined the beginning part of the paths and branch off only as needed to find the optimal final state. Such a problem is called a *final state* problem, and a *decision tree* can be used with the *forward search* for a solution that optimizes the final state. (see Figure 10-10b).

COMPOSITION Dynamic programming may be regarded as a use of the principle of optimality to combine homogeneous states in a decision tree.

$$\max f_N(x_N) = \max [(r_N(x_N, d_N) \oplus f_{N-1}(x_{N-1})]$$

can now be written in terms of the optimal f_{N-1}° and the state x_{N-1}° from which the optimal path has been obtained:

$$f_N^\circ(x_N) = \max [r_N(x_N, d_N) \oplus f_{N-1}^\circ(x_{N-1})]$$

An asterisk is commonly used to denote the optimal value, but we have chosen to use the degree symbol $^\circ$ to avoid confusion with multiplication. More specifically, for an investment problem we can write

$$f_N^\circ = \max [(1 + r) * f_{N-1}^\circ]$$

298 Introduction to Operations Research and Management Science

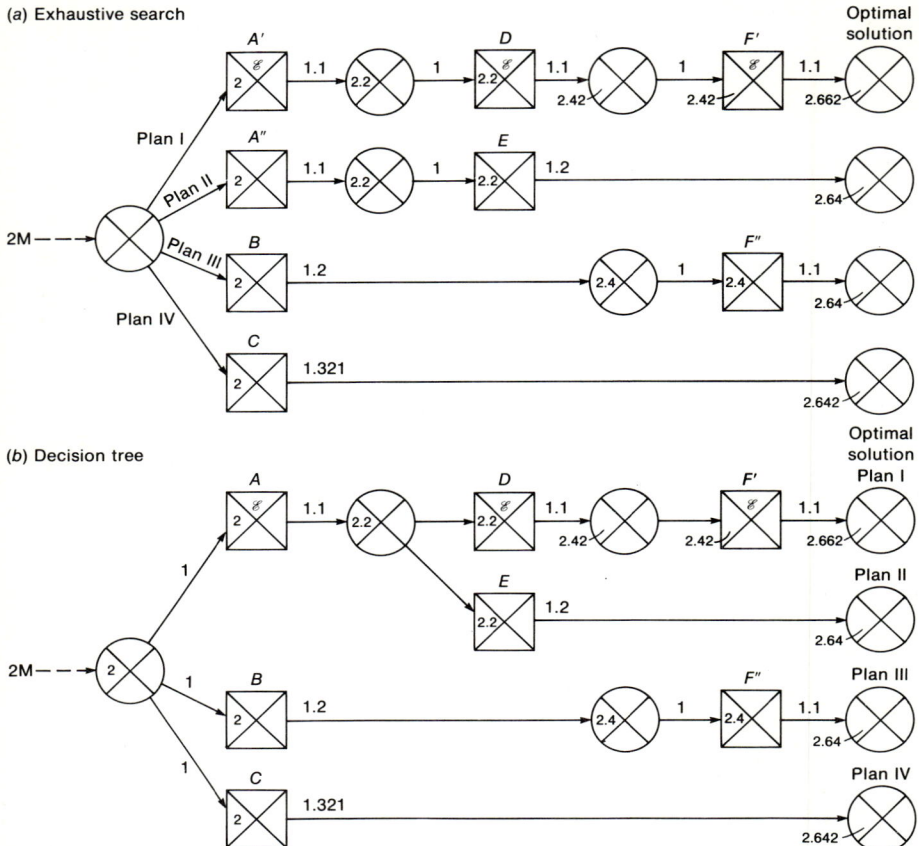

Figure 10-10 RPM networks displaying an exhaustive search process and decision tree (indicating optimal solution).

Combining the processes F' and F'' of the decision tree, we finally obtain the RPM network (Figure 10-11a) which was used in Example 10-1.

The saving brought by the optimality principle seems negligible for this simplistic example but is considerable when the problem is more involved. Unfortunately, it is not always convenient or possible to draw a detailed RPM network of the type shown in Figure 10-11a where the decision is made for each individual process on the GO(𝓔)–NO-GO (𝒪) basis. The abbreviated RPM network *b* must be used to describe complex problems. The decision variable in such a network is no longer just the rate of resource flow x_N through each node N, as in linear programming, but rather which alternative d_N to choose at each decision stage.

The network models shown in Figure 10-11a and b are suitable for both forward and backward analyses, and usually both are needed to solve complex

(a) Explicit sequential decision process (linear programming)

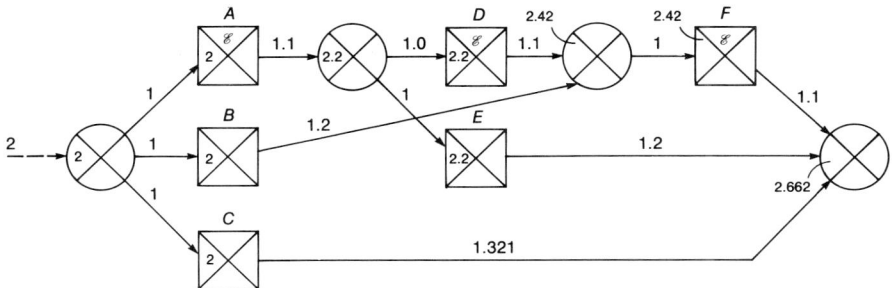

(b) Implicit sequential decision process (dynamic programming proper)

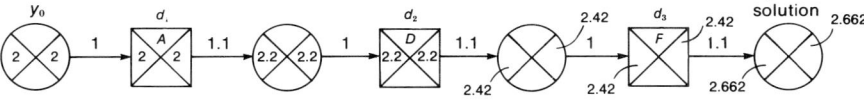

All flows in M = million

Figure 10-11 RPM networks describing sequential decision process (indicating optimal solution).

problems; one analysis verifies the feasibility, and the other checks the optimality. The labeling of the stages is arbitrary, although many researchers prefer a reverse labeling corresponding to backward analysis for an *initial state* problem formulation.[1]

10-3 Longest- and shortest-path problems

Popular dynamic programming applications to discrete models include what is known as the *longest- and shortest-path* problems. The recursive relations for these models are:

Longest-path problems $\quad f_N^\circ(x_N) = \max\ [r_N(x_N,d_N) + f_{N-1}^\circ(x_{N-1})]$

Shortest-path problems

$$f_N^\circ(x_N) = \min\ [r_N(x_N,d_N) + f_{N-1}^\circ\ (x_{N-1})]$$

The plus sign inside the brackets may be made negative depending on the labeling of stages and whether the problem is to search for the initial or the final state.

Example 10-2: *Pricing of crude oil* The petroleum industry in Wonderland is monopolized by the giant Standard Oil and Kerosene (SOAK) Company. SOAK is concerned about the pricing of its crude oil, which is presently being sold for

---

[1] See, for example, George L. Nemhauser, *Introduction to Dynamic Programming*, John Wiley & Sons, Inc., New York, 1966.

$9/bbl and has a demand of 1 million bbl/yr. The management has decided to raise the price to either $10 or $11/bbl within 5 yr. The government of Wonderland does not allow a price change of more than $1/bbl/yr (either up or down) and no more than once yearly. The company's economist has made the following forecast for the sales volume as a function of the price. What policy should be chosen to maximize the gross annual income of the firm?

	Yearly sales, millions of barrels				
Price, $/barrel	Year 1 (now)	Year 2	Year 3	Year 4	Year 5
8	NA*	1.1	1.2	NA	NA
9	1.0	1.0	1.2	1.5	NA
10	NA	1.0	1.1	1.4	1.7
11	NA	NA	1.1	1.2	1.6
12	NA	NA	NA	0.8	NA

*Not applicable

COMPUTATION OF IMMEDIATE RETURNS Assuming that the economist is correct, we know both the volume and price of crude oil sold each year. If we construct an RPM network, we have a resource flow corresponding to the product of the two (Figure 10-12). If we were using linear programming, this would have the effect of assigning the crude oil price as the resource marginal value. But since we are going to use dynamic programming, let us insert the total resource flow in place of the marginal value. Thus, we have 9×1.0 million bbl = $9 million for year 1; 8×1.2 million bbl = $9.6 million, 9×1 million bbl = $9 million, and

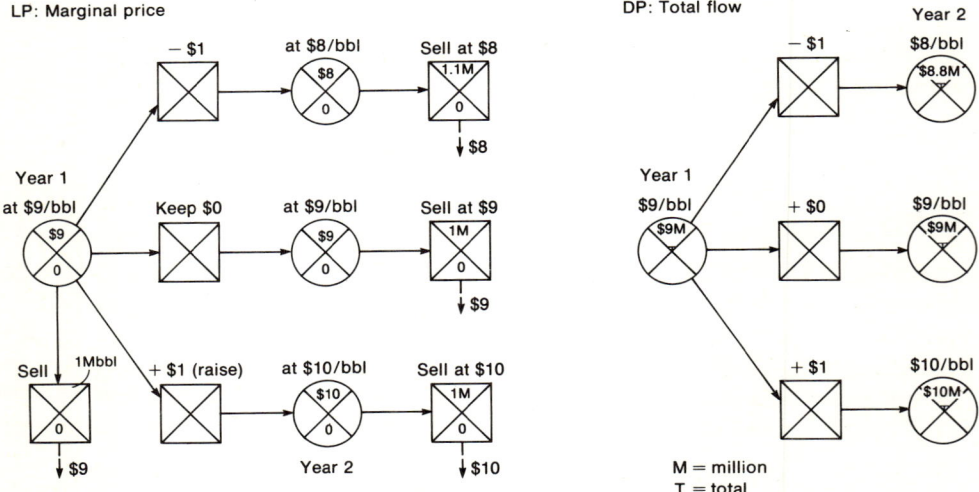

Figure 10-12 Assigning immediate returns for Example 10-2.

10×1 million bbl = $10 million for year 2; and so on. The results are shown in Figure 10-13.

This assignment of resource values in dynamic programming may be interpreted as inserting nature's policy for countering our actions. We have seen how the resource node can be interpreted as our opponent in a zero-sum two-person game (Chapter 6). The economist's forecast for the demand at different price levels is an attempt to outguess the market (nature).

FORWARD ANALYSIS The forward analysis can be performed easily on Figure 10-13 by making use of our longest-path recursive expression:

$$f_N^\circ(x_N) = \max\ [r_N(x_N, d_N) + f_{N-1}^\circ(x_{N-1})]$$

Figure 10-14 shows the graphic interpretation of both forward and backward analyses and recursive formulas. Figure 10-15 illustrates the results of the forward analysis. Once the final state has been identified ($11/bbl at year 5), we can treat the problem as an initial-state problem and proceed with the backward analysis.

BACKWARD ANALYSIS The backward analysis (Figure 10-14b) makes use of the reverse recursion expression:

$$g_{N-1}^\circ(x_{N-1}) = \min\ [g_N^\circ(x_N) - r_N(x_n, d_N)]$$

Figure 10-16 illustrates the final solution for $62.7 million over the 5-yr period. The optimal policy is as follows:

	Year 1	Year 2	Year 3	Year 4	Year 5
Price, $/bbl	9	10	11	10	11
Demand, millions of barrels	1	1	1.1	1.4	1.6
Revenue, millions of dollars	9	10	12.1	14	17.6
Cumulative, millions of dollars	9	19	31.1	45.1	62.7

ADAPTIVITY ANALYSIS The total slacks are easily computed for all processes by merely taking the difference between the left cell f_N and subtracting it from the entry in the right cell g_N. The basic path passing through nodes with zero residues identifies the solution. The total slack is $= g_N - f_N$. For the resource node, the residue is computed as the right-cell value g_N° from which we subtract both the left-cell entry f_{N-1}° and the value of the resource r_N. The total slack for the resource node is $g_N^\circ - f_{N-1}^\circ - r_N$.

These slacks can be used to determine how much regret the company would incur if it were to deviate from the optimal plan. Caution must be exercised,

302 Introduction to Operations Research and Management Science

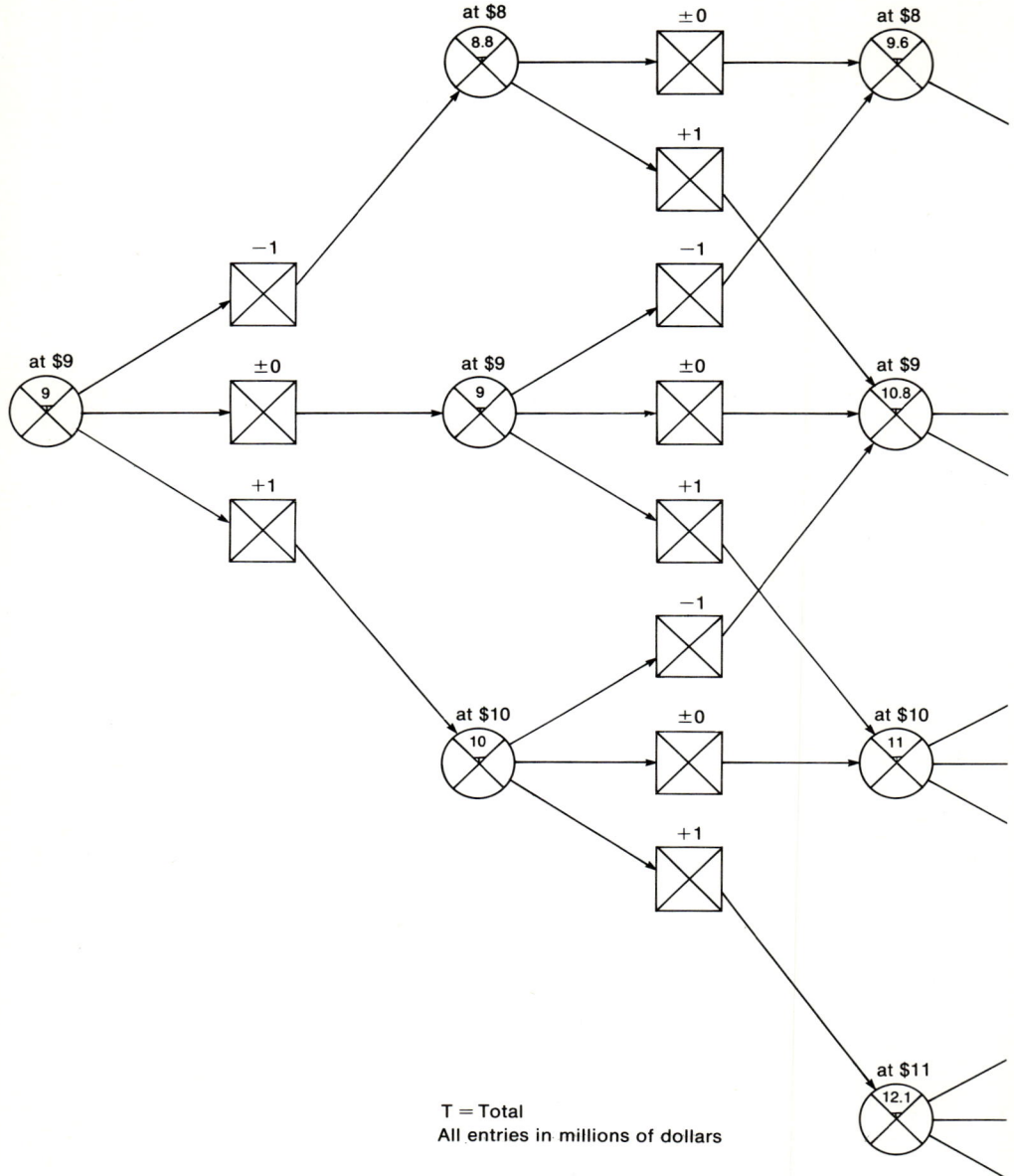

Figure 10-13 RPM network readied for DP analysis (Example 10-2).

Sequential Decision Process: Dynamic Programming 303

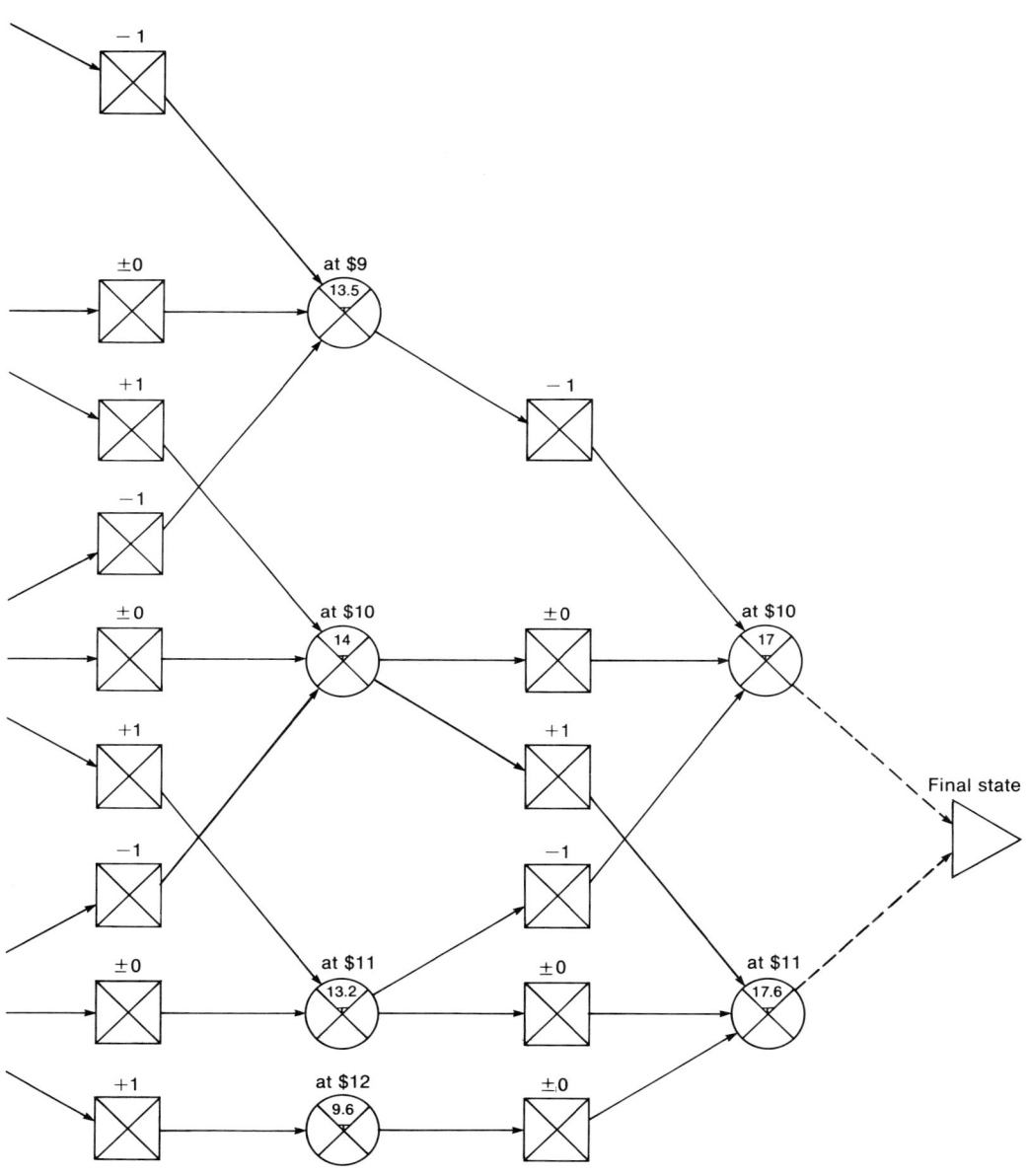

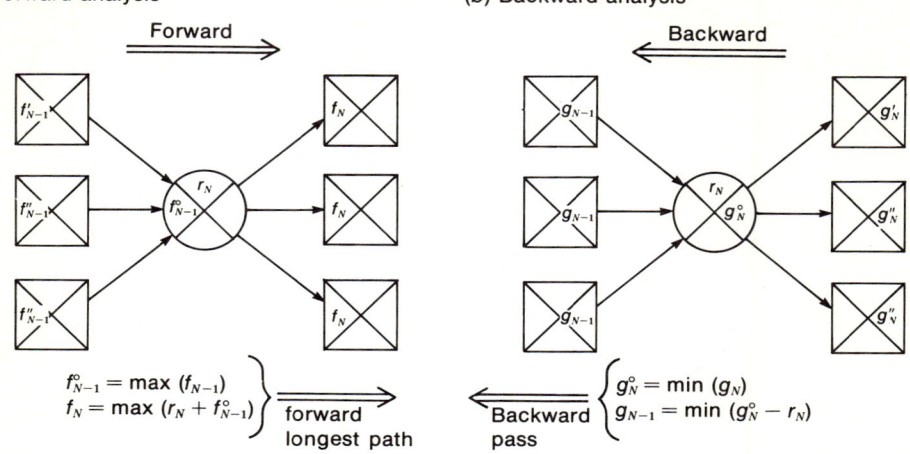

Figure 10-14 Forward and backward analyses of the longest-path problem (Example 10-2).

however, so as not to count the same penalty twice. The safest method is to count only the opportunity costs at the resource nodes since this is where the profit is being made. The regrets for the activities make it possible for management to see quickly which direction to follow and what would be the least penalty incurred by doing so. More penalties can accumulate if the mistakes are compounded and the management stays off the basic path longer than necessary.

Figure 10-16 illustrates the final DP analysis including all slack computations. For instance, the slack at $8 on year 2 was computed as $20.3 − $9 − $8.8 = $2.5 million, and the slack for +1 going from $8 in year 3 to $9 in year 4 was computed as $32.2 − $0 − $27.6 = $4.6 million. Instead of the optimal $9 → $10 → $11 → $10 → $11 path, if we took the $9 → $9 → $10 → $10 path, we would lose $2.1 + $1.3 + $0 + $0.6 = $4 million.

SECTION 10-3 TUNE-UP Stagecoach problem

Solve the shortest-path problem in Fig. 10-17 using the RPM network skeleton given in Figure 10-18, page 311.

10-4 Resource allocation

Another popular application is the allocation of a limited resource among alternatives. Again we assume that the allocation has to be discrete rather than continuous, so that linear programming cannot be used. First we shall use the RPM de-

Sequential Decision Process: Dynamic Programming   305

tailed network and solve the problem as we have previously. Then we shall introduce a tabular method that will alleviate having to draw complex RPM networks and handle larger-size problems.

Example 10-3: *Budget allocation* The Wonderland Health, Education, and Welfare (WHEW) Commission has a special research and development budget of $8 million. The commission has requested project proposals from the three major areas, health, education, and welfare, and has received proposals from all areas. The following required budgets and potential benefits have been suggested for each proposal.

1	Areas	Health			Education				Welfare			
2	Proposal ID	H0	H1	H2	E0	E1	E2	E3	W0	W1	W2	W3
3	Budgets, millions of dollars	0	5	6	0	2	3	7	0	1	4	8
4	Benefits, millions of dollars	0	8	9	0	4	6	10	0	2	7	12
5	Net payoff (4 − 3), millions of dollars	0	3	3	0	2	3	3	0	1	3	4

No more than one grant (but maybe none) is to be awarded in each area, and it is desired to maximize the sum of individual net payoffs.

RPM NETWORK SOLUTION The RPM network in Figure 10-19 is constructed in a manner similar to the longest-path problem of Example 10-2. There are three optimal solutions, but one is obviously favored. $H1$-$E2$-$W0$ and $H1$-$E1$-$W1$ produce net payoffs of $6 million, and so does $H0$-$E2$-$W2$; but the last solution does it for only $7 million, while the other two solutions require the entire $8 million.

THE METHOD OF PECKING ORDER Let us assume that the proposals in these three areas are judged by three different administrators. The fund first goes to the health division and is used to fund health projects that are obviously superior to other proposals. Then whatever is left is funneled down to the education division. Finally, the welfare division receives whatever remains. This is not to say that these administrators are crooks. Rather, let us assume that they are quite aware of each others' needs and often forego their own needs when there appear to be better proposals in other areas. Thus, we have a case where decisions are made sequentially rather than simultaneously. Figure 10-20 compares simultaneous decision-making using linear programming with sequential decision-making using dynamic programming. Let us suppose, however, that the welfare administrator is becoming tired of always receiving the allocation the night before the budget deadline. To remedy the situation, she has gathered all her proposals for the next funding and formulated a table detailing exactly what to do regardless of the amount of money that is actually available. Figure 10-21 shows the detailed decision table. The education administrator happens to see Figure 10-21 and

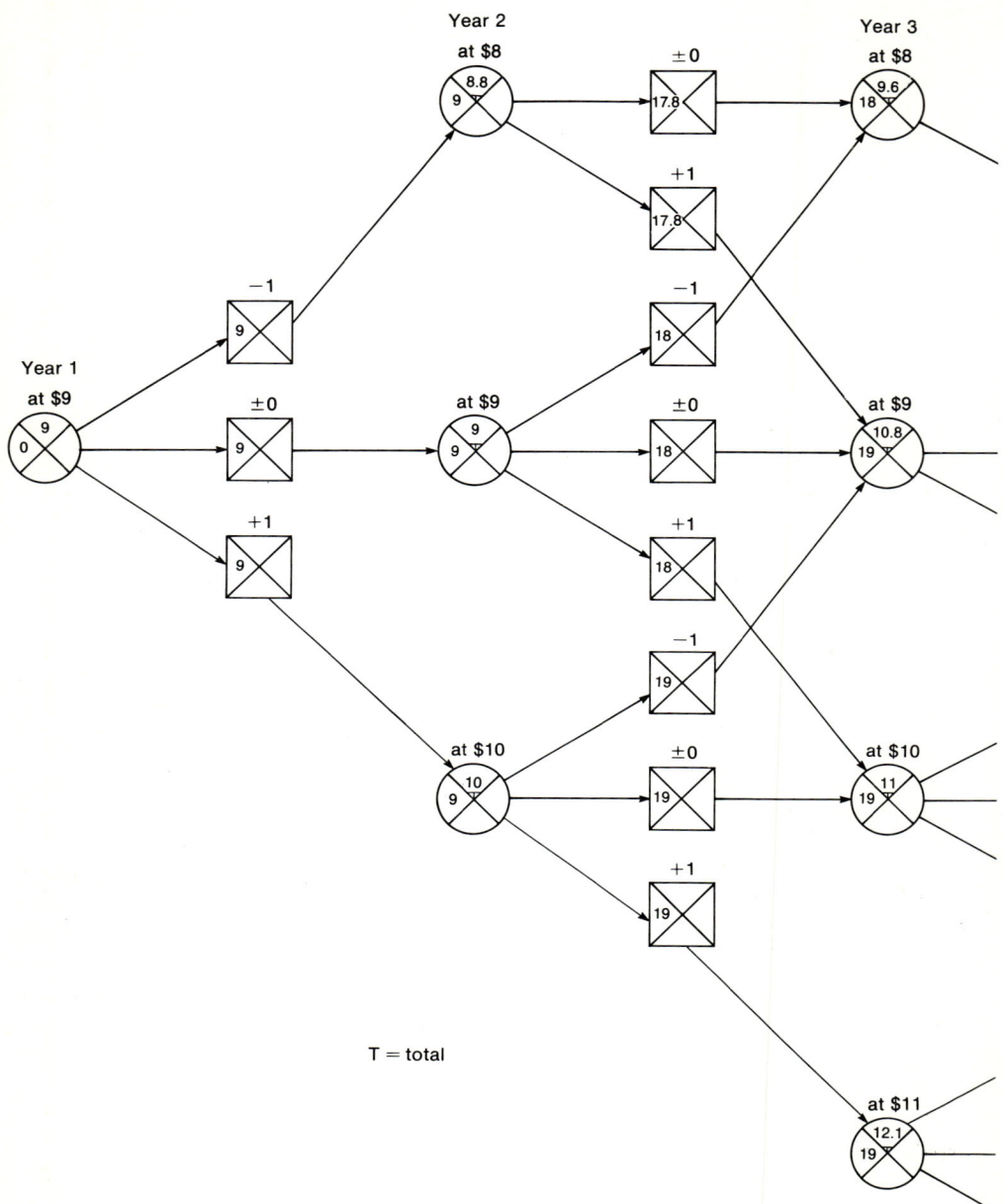

Figure 10-15 Forward analysis for SOAK Oil Company (Example 10-2).

Sequential Decision Process: Dynamic Programming

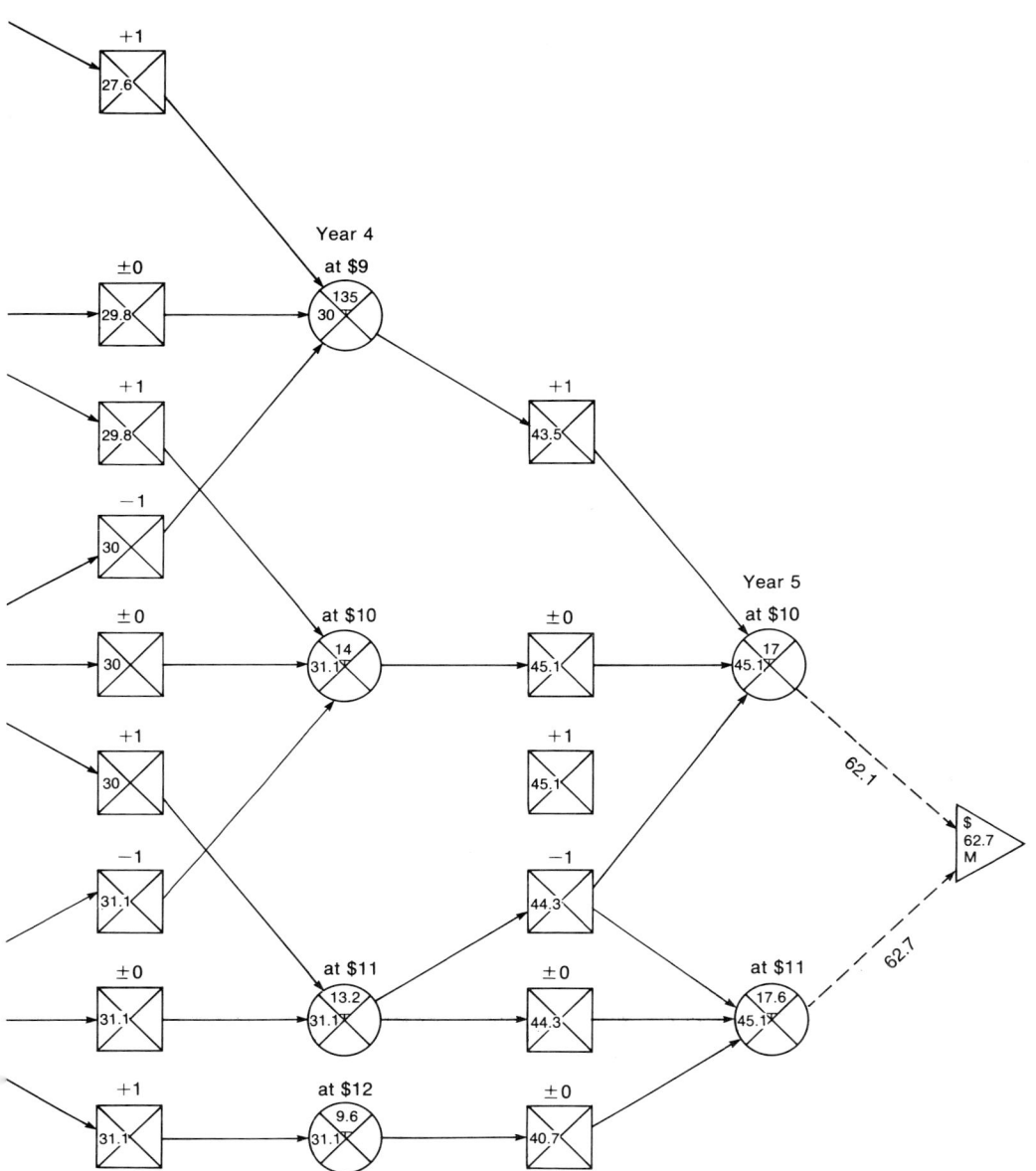

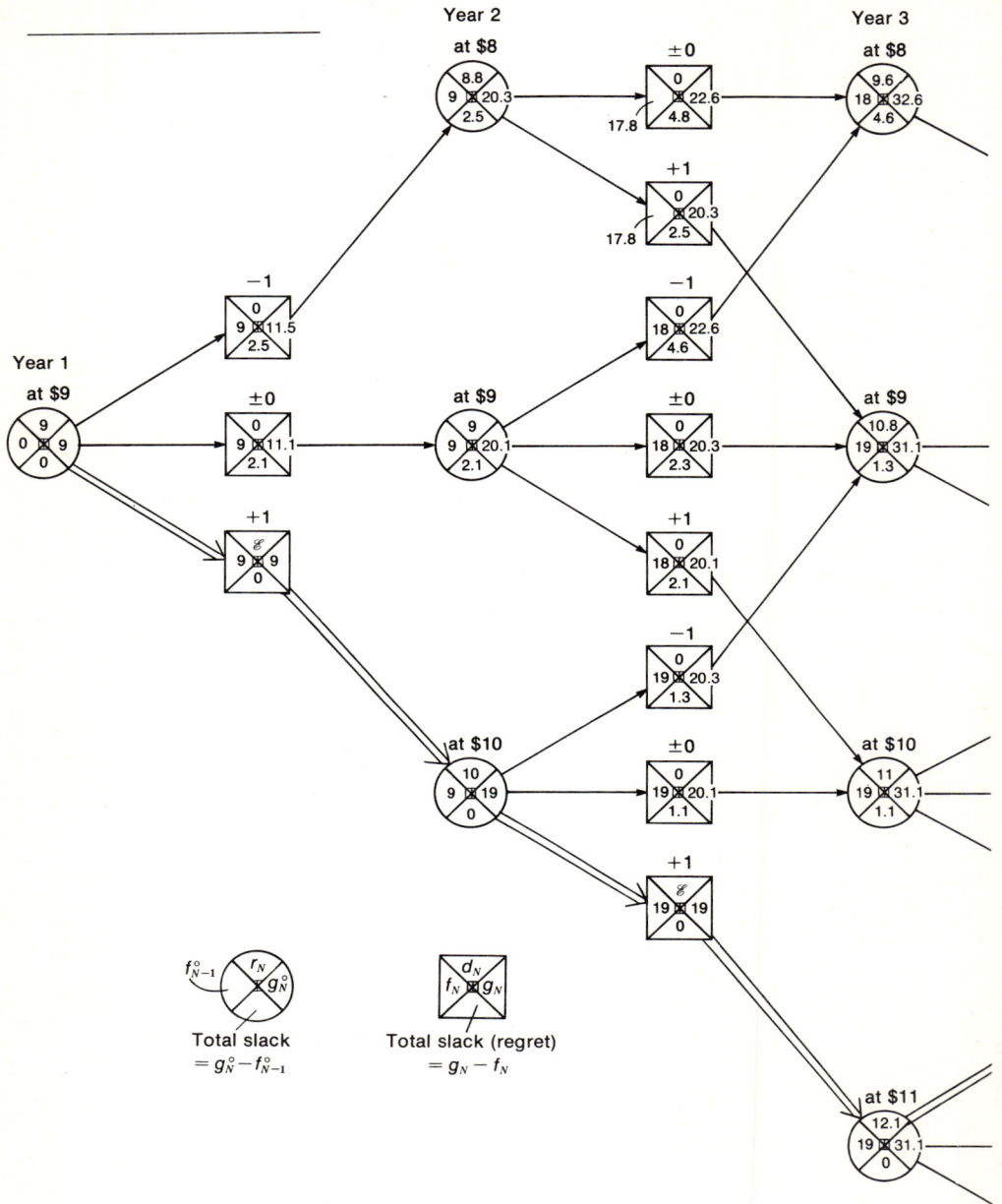

Figure 10-16 Completed DP analysis for Example 10-2.

Sequential Decision Process: Dynamic Programming 309

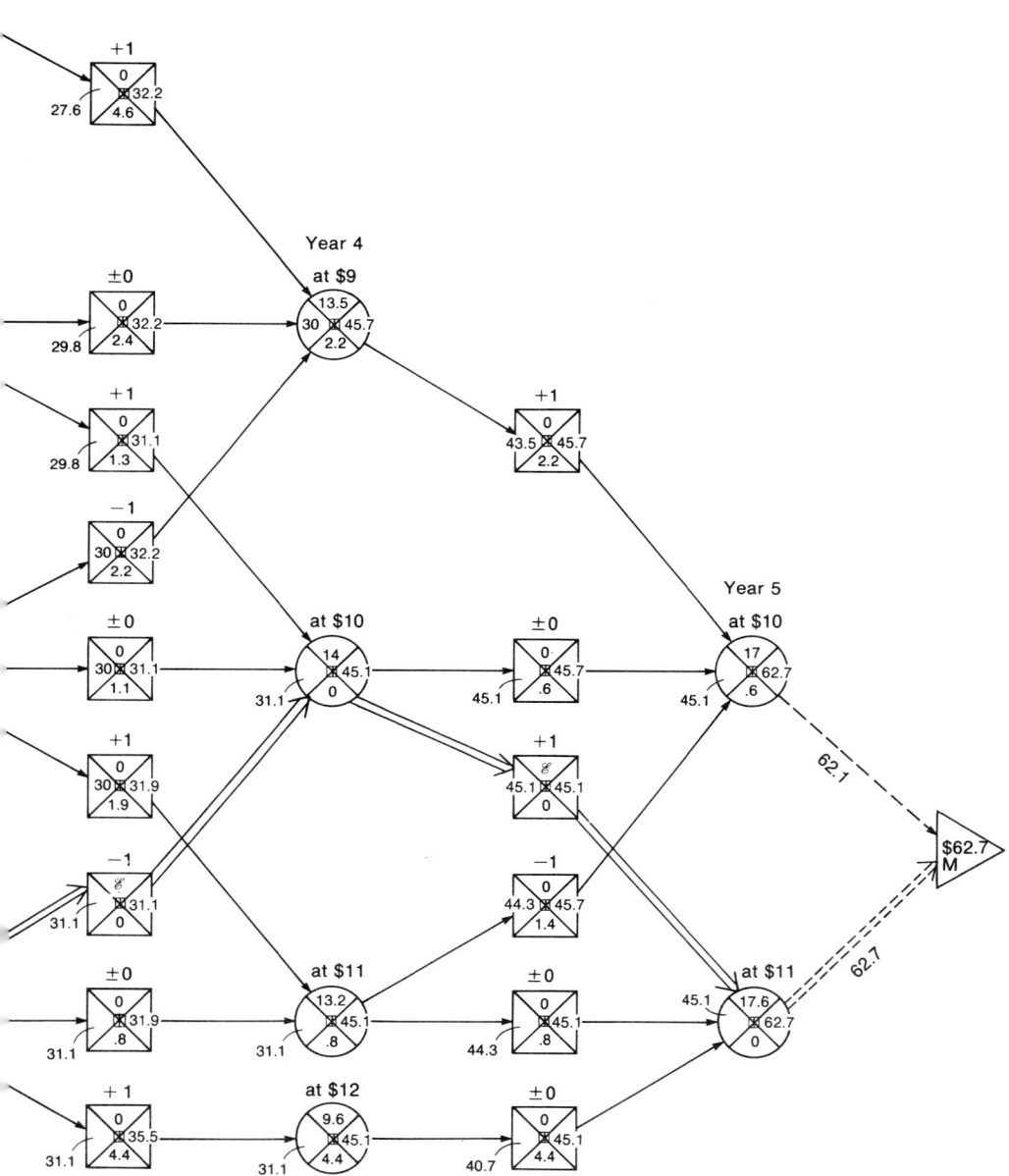

A problem which was specially constructed to illustrate the features of dynamic programming is the "Stagecoach Problem." This problem concerns a mythical salesman who had to travel west by stagecoach through unfriendly Indian country about a hundred years ago.

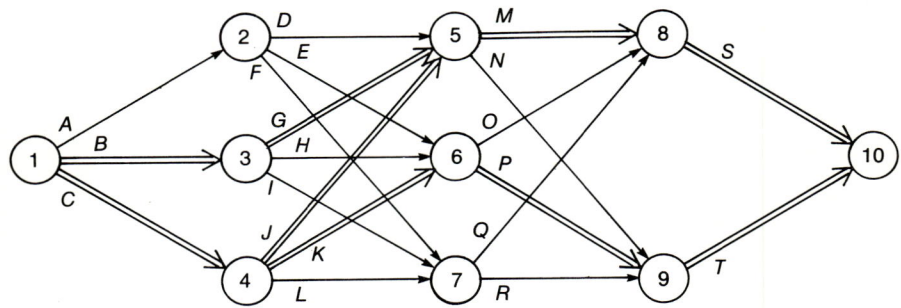

Four stages were required to travel from his point of embarkation in state 1 to his destination in state 10.

This salesman was a prudent man who was quite concerned for his safety on this trip. After some thought, a rather clever way of determining his safest route occurred to him. Life insurance policies were offered to stagecoach passengers. Since the cost of each policy was based on a careful evaluation of the safety of that run; the safest route should be the one with the cheapest life insurance policy.

The cost for the standard policy on the stagecoach run from state i to state j, which will be denoted by c_{ij}, is given below.

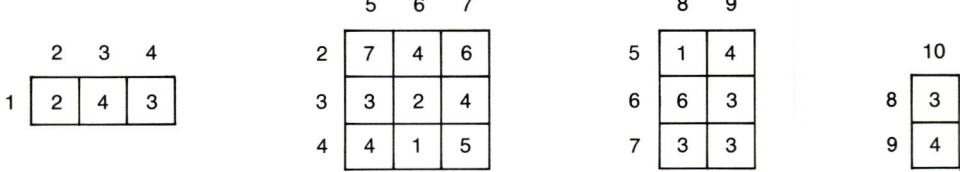

Which route minimizes the total cost of the policy?

Figure 10-17 Stage-coach problem for Section 10-3 Tune-up. The stage-coach problem was developed by Professor Harvey M. Wagner of Stanford University, and presented by Dr. Donald Guthrie to his operation's research class at Oregon State University in 1963. It now appears in several OR books including Wagner (1969).

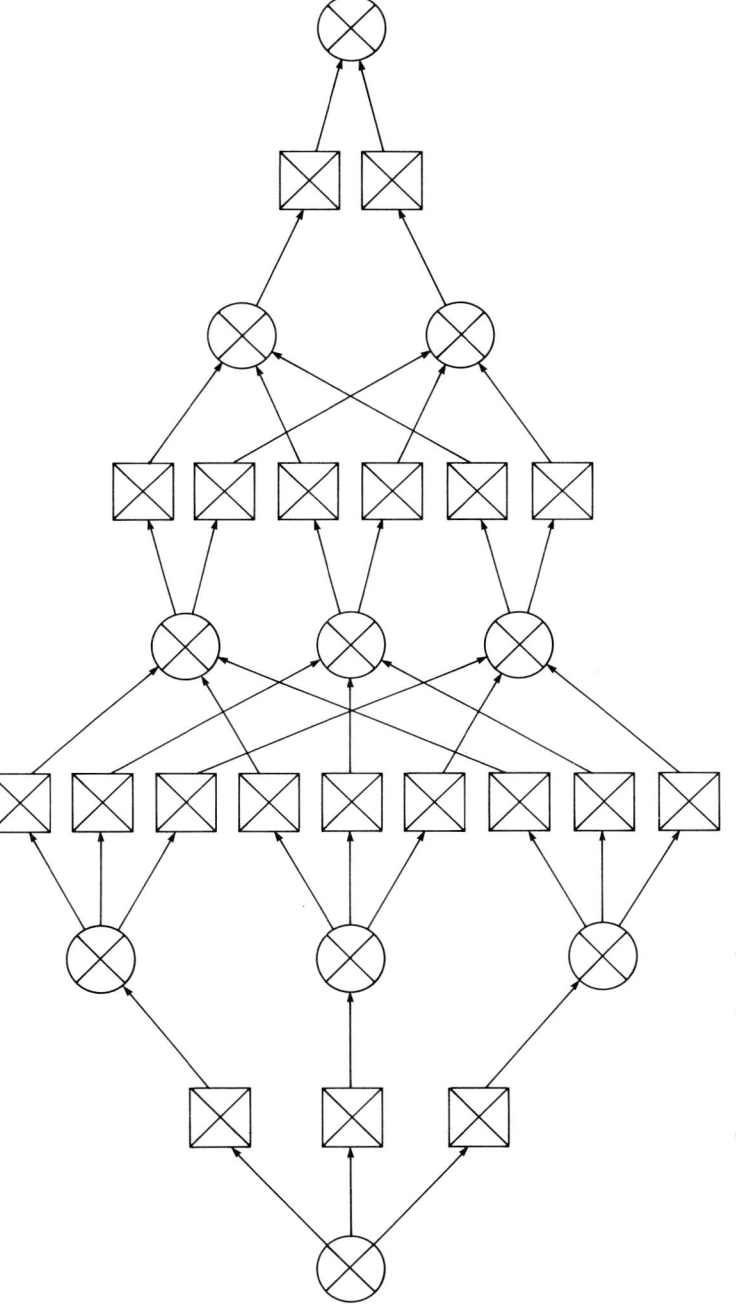

Figure 10-18 Stage-coach problem worksheet for Section 10-3 Tune-up.

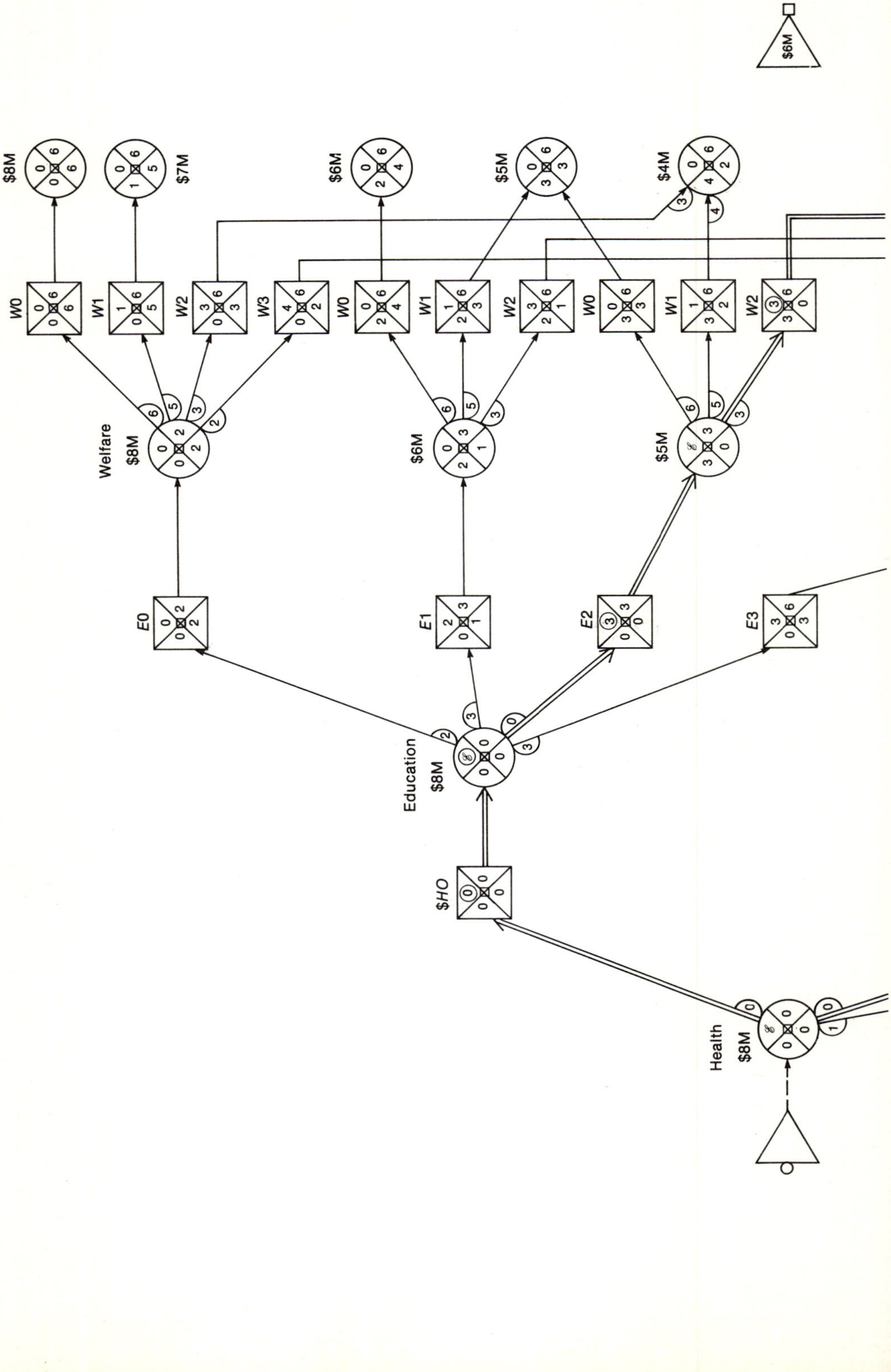

Health
$8M
$HO
Education
$8M
E0
E1
E2
E3
Welfare
$8M
$6M
$5M
W0
W1
W2
W3
W0
W1
W2
W0
W1
W2
$8M
$7M
$6M
$5M
$4M
$6M

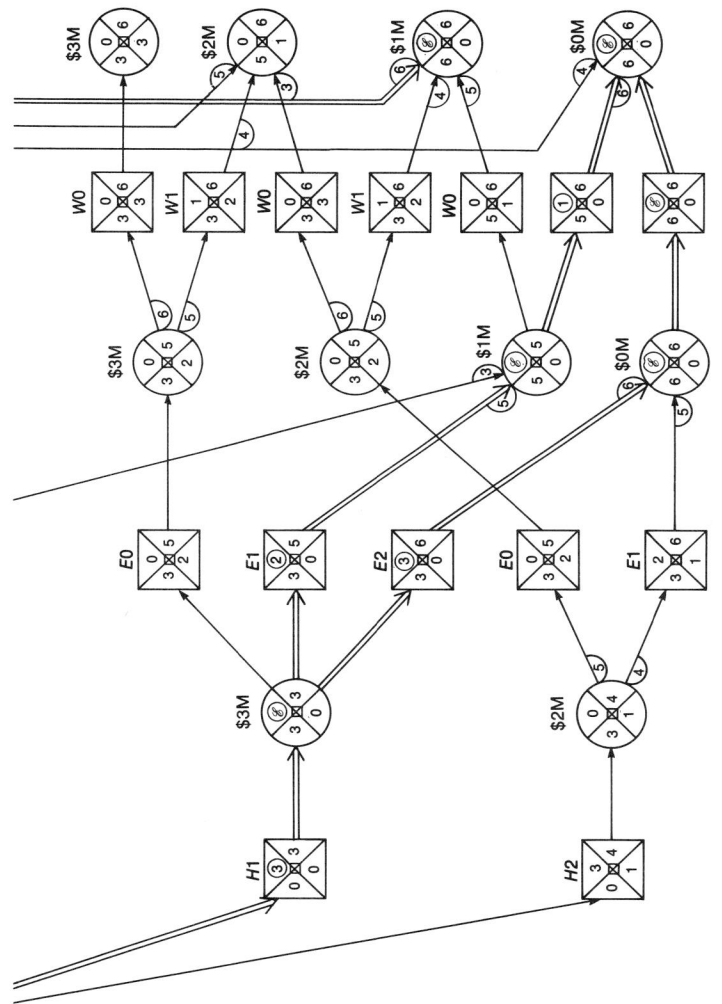

All entries in M = million

Figure 10-19 Detailed RPM network for the WHEW (Example 10-3).

(a) Linear programming approach

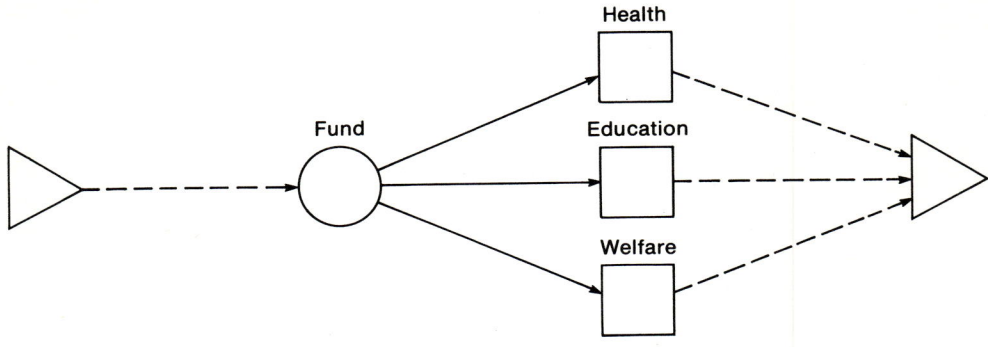

(b) Dynamic programming approach (sequential decision process)

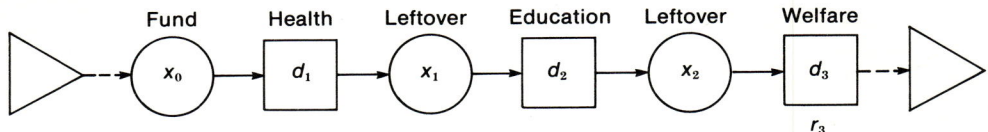

Figure 10-20 (a) Simultaneous decision-making using linear programming; (b) sequential decision-making using dynamic programming.

If W receives from stage 2	Then, from the alternatives open to W				W will choose	For the net pay-off of	With a leftover
	Budget Net	W0 0 0	W1 1M 1M	W2 4M 3M	W3 8M 4M			
0	$f_3(x_3)$	0°	—	—	—	W0	0	0
1M		0	1M°	—	—	W1	1M	0
2M		0	1M°	—	—	W1	1M	1M
3M		0	1M°	—	—	W1	1M	2M
4M		0	1M	3M°	—	W2	3M	0
5M		0	1M	3M°	—	W2	3M	1M
6M		0	1M	3M°	—	W2	3M	2M
7M		0	1M	3M°	—	W2	3M	3M
8M		0	1M	3M	4M°	W3	4M	0
x_3						d_3°	$f_3^\circ = r_3$	x_4

° indicates the value of $f_3^\circ(x_3)$.
M = millions of dollars

Figure 10-21 Decision table for welfare administrator (stage 3).

If E receives from stage 1	Then from the combination of d_2° and					E will choose	For the cumulative pay-off of	What is sent to stage 3
	Budget Net	E0 0 0	E1 2M 2M	E2 3M 3M	E3 7M 3M			
0	$f_2(x_2)$	$0 + 0°$	—	—	—	E0 + W0	0	0
1M		$0 + 1°$	—	—	—	E0 + W1	1M	1M
2M		$0 + 1$	$2 + 0°$	—	—	E1 + W0	2M	0
3M		$0 + 1$	$2 + 1°$	$3 + 0°$	—	E1 + W1 or E2	3M	1M 0
4M		$0 + 3$	$2 + 1$	$3 + 1°$	—	E2 + W1	4M	1M
5M		$0 + 3$	$2 + 1$	$3 + 1°$	—	E2 + W1	4M	2M
6M		$0 + 3$	$2 + 3°$	$3 + 1$	—	E1 + W2	5M	3M
7M		$0 + 3$	$2 + 3$	$3 + 3°$	$3 + 0$	E2 + W2	6M	4M
8M		$0 + 4$	$2 + 3$	$3 + 3°$	$3 + 1$	E2 + W2	6M	5M
x_2						$d_2^\circ + d_3^\circ$	$f_2^\circ = r_2 + f_3^\circ$ maximum	x_3

° indicates the value of $f_2^\circ(x_2)$.
M = millions of dollars

Figure 10-22 Decision table for education administrator (stage 2).

mentions to the welfare administrator that he, too, is worried about the budget deadline. He asks to borrow Figure 10-21 and tries to compile the most equitable way of splitting whatever funds are allocated between the two areas. Figure 10-22 shows the resulting decision table. Now the health administrator announces that a budget cut may be forthcoming and that the actual funding may be delayed pending the decision of the president. The three administrators decide to collaborate, and the resulting decision table is shown in Figure 10-23.

Figure 10-23 confirms our RPM network solutions, and the three administrators can now rest at ease knowing that a plan is ready whatever the funding level turns out to be. The opportunity cost shown in the RPM network is also shown in the tables inside the $f_N(x_N)$ section. All we have to do is to take the difference between the values of the alternatives and compare it with the optimal value $f_N^\circ(x_N)$.

SECTION 10-4 TUNE-UP: Zilch rent-a-buggy service

In Wonderland, there is a rent-a-buggy service by the name of Zilch with the motto "We are the last and we try the hardest!" The company has just bought six new buggies, and the management is interested in deciding where they should be assigned. There are three branch offices: one inside Micropolis, one in Eastport, and one near Port San Angelos. Each branch-office manager claims to be entitled to more buggies, and the management has called in a market research firm to conduct a study of

316   Introduction to Operations Research and Management Science

If the total allocation is	Then from the and Budget Net	combinations of d_3^o, d_2^o H0 0 0	H1 5 3	H2 6 3	H will choose	For the cumulative pay-off of	What is sent to stage 2
0	$f_1(x_1)$	$0 + 0°$	—	—	H0 + E0 + W0	0	0
1M		$0 + 1°$	—	—	H0 + E0 + W1	1M	1M
2M		$0 + 2°$	—	—	H0 + E1 + W0	2M	2M
3M		$0 + 3°$	—	—	H0 + E1 + W1 H0 + E2 + W0	3M	3M
4M		$0 + 4°$	—	—	H0 + E2 + W1	4M	4M
5M		$0 + 4°$	$3 + 0$	—	H0 + E2 + W1	4M	5M
6M		$0 + 5°$	$3 + 1$	$3 + 0$	H0 + E1 + W2	5M	6M
7M		$0 + 6°$	$3 + 2$	$3 + 1$	H0 + E2 + W2	6M	7M
8M		$0 + 6°$	$3 + 3°$	$3 + 2$	$\begin{cases} H0 + E2 + W2 \\ H1 + E1 + W1 \\ H1 + E2 + W0 \end{cases}$	6M	$\begin{cases} 8M \\ 3M \\ 3M \end{cases}$
x_1	$f_1(x_1) = r_1 + f_2(x_2)$				$d_1^o + d_2^o + d_3^o$	$f_1^o = r_1 + f_2^o$ maximum	x_2

M = millions of dollars

Figure 10-23 Decision table for health administrator (stage 3).

the approximate increase in revenue that will result from adding more buggies to these offices. The following data are proposed:

	Increase in revenue, thousands of dollars/wk		
Allotment, units	Micropolis	Eastport	Port San Angelos
0	0	0	0
1	20	12	16
2	20	15	20
3	30	20	21
4 or more	30	30	30

The Micropolis manager becomes exuberant about these statistical forecasts and tells the corporate management that the Micropolis office should receive at least four buggies since its statistics obviously *dominate* all other payoffs. Do you agree?

10-5 Planning horizon

When questioned about the origin of the name *dynamic programming*, R. E. Bellman told the authors that he simply needed a name that was noncommittal and one that would give him maximum freedom of research. As it turned out, the name was rightly chosen, much more appropriate than the possible alternative *sequential decision theory*. Although other mathematical programming models have static objective functions, dynamic programming is a scheme that keeps pushing its objective function ahead (or back) until the entire chain of decisions has been scanned. This dynamic nature makes it possible to use the ending point of a decision process as the basis for further optimization, and this basis for decision is called the *planning horizon*.

In Example 7-2 of Chapter 7 we presented an illustration of production scheduling that assumes the constant cyclic (seasonal) demand and price patterns. Aside from having to assume that the same demand and price fluctuations are repeated every year, this model has several limitations. One major limitation stems from its inability to take into an account any abrupt change in parameters. The LP model is not able to handle setup costs which are incurred only if the production run is started and not at all if the production is not to run. Discounts for ordering quantities above a minimum order and replacing obsolete equipment when the frequency of breakdowns becomes intolerable are other examples of discretely changing parameters that are hard to model by linear programming.

Dynamic programming can easily handle these conditions, although admittedly it is subject to its own "curse of dimensionality." It also provides a wealth of information in its solutions. When a problem is solved, an answer is found not only to the original question "What shall we do under a given situation?" but also to the yet unasked question "What shall we do when we cannot do what is best?" In other words, dynamic programming carries enough data with it to "plan" the future when we have more information as to what is possible.

However, carrying all the data through its planning stages could make dynamic programming as useless as a collection of archives full of old documents with no updated index. Fortunately, the principle of optimality resolves this problem by a very practical method called the *planning horizon theorem*. Applied to the situation where a decision must be made between producing (or procuring) the quantity P_{t_2} at time t_2 versus producing (or procuring) it at time t_1, the theorem can be stated officially as follows.

Planning horizon theorem: If in the forward algorithm the minimum cost decision at t_2 occurs for $P_{t_1} > 0$, $t_1 \leq t_2$, then in periods $t > t_2$ it is sufficient to consider only periods j so that $t_1 \leq j \leq t$. In particular, if $t_1 = t_2$, then it is sufficient to consider programs so that $P_{t_2} > 0$.

We may propose an alternative layman's version of this theorem that conveys its meaning, if not its mathematical rigor:

The spirit of planning horizon: If a newer brew turns out better at any time than all older brews, throw away all old batches for they will never again be as good as the newer brew.

Thus, the planning horizon theorem permits us to forget about carrying dynamic programming data that will no longer be used. The power of this theorem as well as its meaning are best explained by means of an example.

Example 10-4: *Dynamic production scheduling for N periods* Gryphon Winery Company is a manufacturer of specialty wines and spirits. Its pride and joy is Royal Red Queen, a wine made from choice cranberries and tiger lily seedpods. Because of the seasonal nature of both the demand for the product and the supply of tiger lilies, together with the high cost of the setup necessary to produce a new batch of wines, the present production scheme is not profitable. The company is eager to continue the production of this traditional specialty wine, and you have been called in to conduct a study of how the schedule may be changed to optimize total production costs. The present production policy is to produce the total annual demand at once, incurring a high storage cost throughout the year but enabling the tiger lily seedpods to be purchased when the price is the lowest. Knowing that the heavy demand for the wine is during the outdoor season, you have gathered the following forecasts for the demands and supplies, as well as the marginal processing and storage costs as derived from a linear programming study of the overall company operation.

Month	Demand, cases (24 bottles)	Raw material purchase cost, dollars/case	Process-setup cost dollars	Processing variable cost, dollars/case	Between-months storage cost, dollars/case
1	20	1	50	5	1
2	15	2	40	4	1
3	25	3	40	5	2
4	30	4	50	6	2
5	40	3	20	2	1
6	20	4	30	6	

The present policy calls for the production of 150 cases in month 1, resulting in the total cost of $1,515.

Figure 10-24 is an RPMS network illustrating Gryphon Winery's production problem. Using the traditional linear program would not produce an optimal answer because of the once-only nature of the setup costs. For example, $50 per setup would be incurred for the first month if any production takes place in that month but not otherwise. The "marginal" cost of the setup will depend on the quantity to be produced that month, and this dual value is needed to utilize any linear programming procedure. In dynamic programming we use the *total* value corresponding directly to the contribution made to the objective function at each stage, and therefore we are not limited by the discrete nature of the setup cost. In effect, a temporary objective function is created at each stage, which is made up from the immediate return generated from a decision that is newly available at this stage and from the cumulative return from all previous stages that are needed to implement the new decision.

Stage 1. Assuming that there is no leftover inventory, the first month's production is easily obtained, as shown in Figure 10-25 (row 1). There is no choice but to produce the quantity demanded (20 cases). If there were a leftover supply, all we need to do is to subtract it from the demand to adjust the production. Purchasing 20 cases of raw materials at the rate of $1 per case ($20), setting up the process ($50), and processing 20 cases

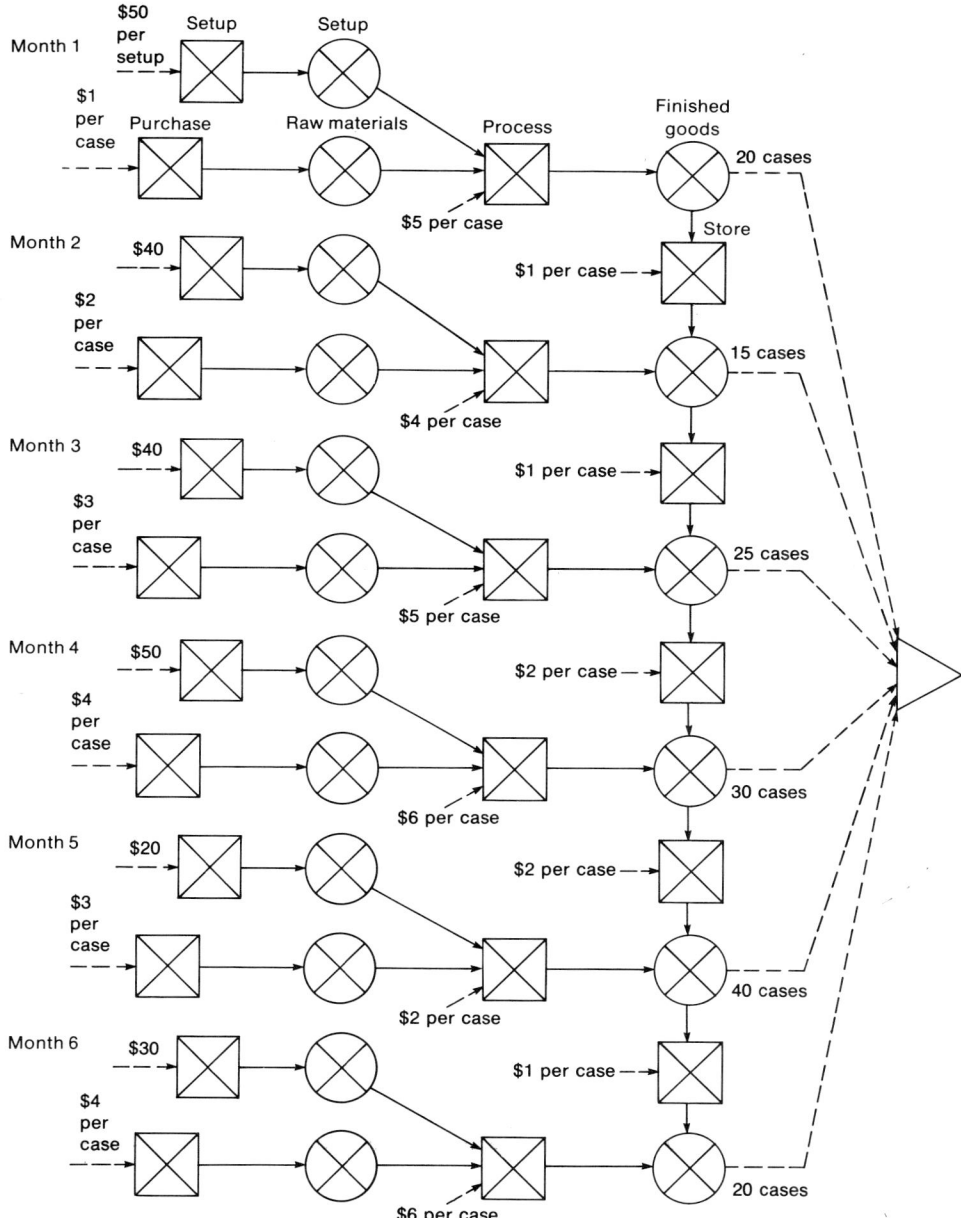

Figure 10-24 RPMS network model for the dynamic scheduling model (Example 10-4).

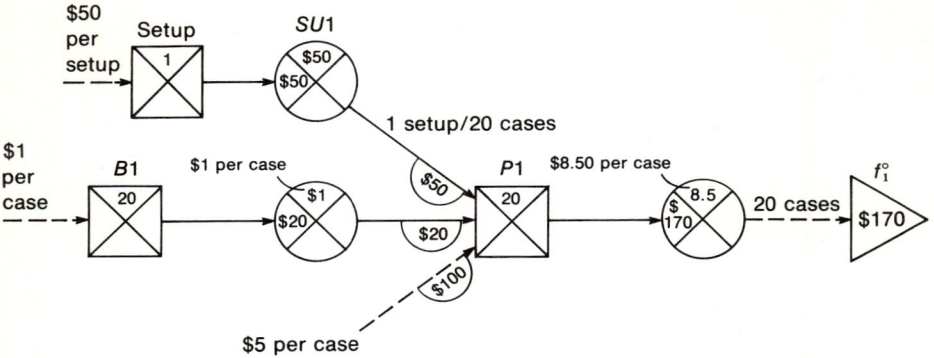

Figure 10-25 Stage 1 decision of Gryphon Winery.

at $5 per case would yield products that are worth $170 total, or $170/20 = $8.50 per case.

Since there is no other alternative available at this stage, the cumulative return f_1 resulting from the immediate return of $170 and the accumulated past return $f_0 = 0$ will constitute the optimal return of $f_1^o = 170$.

Stage 2. In the second stage, two options are available. We can produce 2 mo worth of demand at once during the first batch or 20 cases in the first month and 15 cases in the second. These two alternatives (see Figure 10-26, row 2) indicate that the optimal solution in stage 2 is to increase the first month's production to 35 cases ($f_2^o = 275$) rather than make a new batch of 15 cases for the immediate return of $130 and add this to the accumulated return of $f_1^o = 170$ for a total cost of $300. Since the optimal solution still relies on the first month's production, we cannot apply the planning horizon theorem to discard the statistics for the first month's production costs.

Stage 3. At this stage three alternatives are available to produce the additional demand of 25 cases: (1) to include it in the first month's production ($475); (2) to include it in the second month's production ($305) independently of the first month's production that takes care of the first month's demand ($170) for a total cost of $475; and (3) to produce a separate batch of 25 cases for $240 and adding this to the accumulated cost $f_2^o = 275$ for a total cost of $515.

$$f_3^o = \min\,(475, 475, 515) = \$475$$

is degenerate between the first and second option. By choosing the second month's production alternative, we can eliminate the viability of further extending the first month's production to cover future needs by making use of the planning horizon theorem.

Stage 4. Again, we have three alternatives. (Without the planning horizon, we would have had to check four alternatives and would have found that the first is not needed in finding an optimal solution.) $f_4^\circ = 745$ falls in the second month's production, and no simplification is available from the planning horizon theorem at this stage.

Stage 5. $f_5^\circ = \$965$ indicates that a new batch is in order. This means that we can now eliminate the statistics for previous productions from future considerations. All new demands will be met from the fifth or sixth month's production.

Stage 6. $f_6^\circ = \$1,085$ is the current cumulative cost, and the answer to the original problem. If Gryphon Winery obtains future demand statistics, we need to worry about adjusting the fifth and/or subsequent month's production schedule only. This means that Gryphon can go ahead and fix its production schedule for the first four months without having to correct it when future demand data become available from the forecast. $1,085 is more than a 28 percent saving over the old production cost ($1,515) and should make the Gryphon Winery happy to continue the production of Royal Red Queen.

INTERPRETATION After the solution has been obtained by dynamic programming, it may be converted into an LP-type marginal-cost analysis. Figure 10-28 shows the graphic inventory variations for all DP alternatives that have been considered (assuming constant usage rates), and Figure 10-29 illustrates the marginal-cost interpretation of the optimal solution f_6°.

SECTION 10-5 TUNE-UP: Taking advantage of quantity discounts

Looking-Glass and Mirror Manufacturing Company buys sheet glasses for processing into various types of mirrors. The need for these sheets for the next 6 mo is as follows:

Month	1	2	3	4	5	6
Demand, tons	100	150	80	200	120	80

The price is fixed at $100/ton for up to 100 tons, but discounts are available for larger quantities: 10 percent discount for 100 to 249 tons; 25 percent discount for 250 to 499 tons; and 40 percent discount for 500 tons or more. The storage holding cost of $20/ton-mo is high because of the insurance rate adjusted to vandalism and accidental breakage, and the company is torn between wanting to take advantage of the quantity discount prices and lower storage costs. You have been asked to identify the optimal ordering schedule to minimize costs and to display the results in an RPM network.

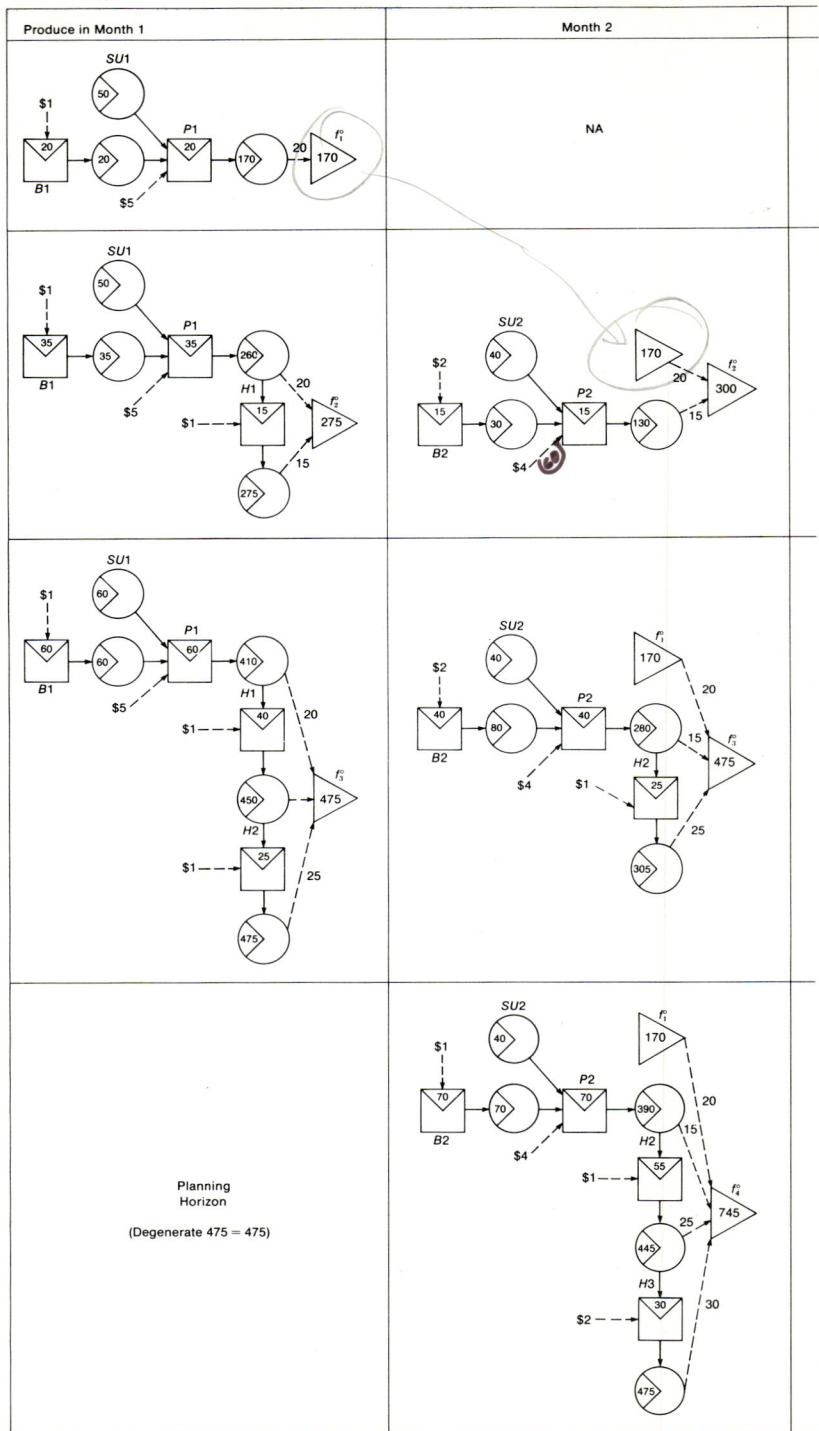

Figure 10-26 RPMS representation of the first 4-mo DP analysis for the Gryphon Winery.

	Month 3	Month 4	Demands	
	NA	NA	$\frac{20}{20}$	Month 1
	NA	NA	$\begin{array}{c}20\\15\\\hline 35\end{array}$	Months 1-2
	[diagram: $B3$ (25) → (75) → $P3$ (25) → (240) → f_3^o 515; $SU3$ (40) with $\$3$; f_2^o (275); $20+15=35$; $\$5$]	NA	$\begin{array}{c}20\\15\\25\\\hline 60\end{array}$	Months 1-3
	[diagram: $B3$ (55) → (165) → $P3$ (55) → (480) → f_3^o 815; (30) → (540); $SU3$ (40) with $\$3$; f_2^o (275); 35; $\$5$; $\$2$; 25; 30]	[diagram: $B4$ (30) → (120) → $P4$ (30) → (350) → f_4^o 825; $SU4$ (50) with $\$4$; f_3^o (475); $35+25=60$; $\$6$; 30]	$\begin{array}{c}20\\15\\25\\30\\\hline 90\end{array}$	Months 1-4

324   Introduction to Operations Research and Management Science

	Month 1	Month 2	Month 3
	$SU1 = \$50$ $B1 = \$1\,(20) = 20$ $P1 = 5\,(20) = 100$ $H0 = 0$ $f_1^\circ = r_1 = \$170$		
	$SU1 = \$50$ $B1 = 1\,(35) = 35$ $P1 = 5\,(35) = 175$ $H1 = 1\,(15) = 15$ $\overline{r_2 = 275}$ $f_0 = 0$ $\overline{f_2^\circ = \$275}$	$SU2 = \$40$ $B2 = 2\,(15) = 30$ $P2 = 4\,(15) = 60$ $H1 = 1\,(0) = 0$ $\overline{r_2 = 130}$ $f_1^\circ = 170$ $\overline{f_2 = \$300}$	
	$SU1 = \$50$ $B1 = 1\,(60) = 60$ $P1 = 5\,(60) = 300$ $H1 = 1\,(40) = 40$ $H2 = 1\,(25) = 25$ $\overline{r_3 = 475}$ $f_0 = 0$ $\overline{f_3^\circ = \$475}$	$SU2 = \$40$ $B2 = 2\,(40) = 80$ $P2 = 4\,(40) = 160$ $H1 = 1\,(0) = 0$ $H2 = 1\,(25) = 25$ $\overline{r_3 = 305}$ $f_1^\circ = 170$ $\overline{f_3^\circ = \$475}$	$SU3 = \$40$ $B3 = 3\,(25) = 75$ $P3 = 5\,(25) = 125$ $H1 = 1\,(0) = 0$ $H2 = 1\,(0) = 0$ $\overline{r_3 = 240}$ $f_2^\circ = 275$ $\overline{f_3 = \$515}$
	Planning horizon (degenerate)	$SU2 = \$40$ $B2 = 2\,(70) = 140$ $P2 = 4\,(70) = 280$ $H2 = 1\,(55) = 55$ $H3 = 2\,(30) = 60$ $\overline{r_4 = 575}$ $f_1^\circ = 170$ $\overline{f_4^\circ = \$745}$	$SU3 = \$40$ $B3 = 3\,(55) = 165$ $P3 = 5\,(55) = 275$ $H2 = 1\,(0) = 0$ $H3 = 2\,(30) = 60$ $\overline{r_4 = 540}$ $f_2^\circ = 275$ $\overline{f_4 = \$815}$
		$SU2 = \$40$ $B2 = 2 \times 110 = 220$ $P2 = 4 \times 110 = 440$ $H2 = 1 \times 95 = 95$ $H3 = 2\,(70) = 140$ $H4 = 2\,(40) = 80$ $\overline{r_5 = 1015}$ $f_1^\circ = 1170$ $\overline{f_5 = \$1185}$	$SU3 = \$40$ $B3 = 3 \times 95 = 285$ $P3 = 5 \times 95 = 475$ $H2 = 1\,(0) = 0$ $H3 = 2\,(70) = 140$ $H4 = 2\,(40) = 80$ $\overline{r_5 = 1020}$ $f_2^\circ = 275$ $\overline{f_5 = \$1295}$
		New planning horizon	

Figure 10-27   Tabular analysis for the RPMS of Figure 10-26.

Sequential Decision Process: Dynamic Programming 325

	Month 4	Month 5	Month 6	Supply / Demand	
	NOT AVAILABLE			$D1 = 20$	Month 1
				$D2 = 15$	Months 1–2
				$D3 = 25$	Months 1–3
	$\begin{array}{ll} SU4 & = \$50 \\ B4 = 4\,(30) & = 120 \\ P4 = 6\,(30) & = 180 \\ H2 = 1\,(0) & = 0 \\ H3 = 2\,(0) & = 0 \\ \hline & r_4 = 350 \\ & f_3^\circ = 475 \\ \hline & f_4 = \$825 \end{array}$			$D4 = 30$	Months 1–4
	$\begin{array}{ll} SU4 & = \$\ 50 \\ B4 = 4\,(70) & = 280 \\ P4 = 6\,(70) & = 420 \\ H2 = 1\,(0) & = 0 \\ H3 = 2\,(0) & = 0 \\ H4 = 2\,(40) & = 80 \\ \hline & r_5 = 830 \\ & f_3^\circ = 475 \\ \hline & f_5 = \$1305 \end{array}$	$\begin{array}{ll} SU5 & = \$\ 20 \\ B5 = \$3\,(40) & = 120 \\ P5 = 2\,(40) & = 80 \\ H2 = 1\,(0) & = 0 \\ H3 = 2\,(0) & = 0 \\ H4 = 2\,(0) & = 0 \\ \hline & r_5 = 220 \\ & f_4^\circ = 745 \\ \hline & f_5 = \$965 \end{array}$		$D5 = 40$	Months 1–5
		$\begin{array}{ll} SU5 & = \$\ 20 \\ B5 = \$3\,(60) & = 180 \\ P5 = 2\,(60) & = 120 \\ H5 = 1\,(20) & = 20 \\ \hline & r_6 = 340 \\ & f_4^\circ = 745 \\ \hline & f_6 = \$1085 \end{array}$	$\begin{array}{ll} SU6 & = \$\ 30 \\ B6 = \$4\,(20) & = 80 \\ P6 = 6\,(20) & = 120 \\ H5 = 1\,(0) & = 20 \\ \hline & r_6 = 230 \\ & f_5^\circ = 965 \\ \hline & f_6 = \$1195 \end{array}$	$D6 = 20$	Months 1–6

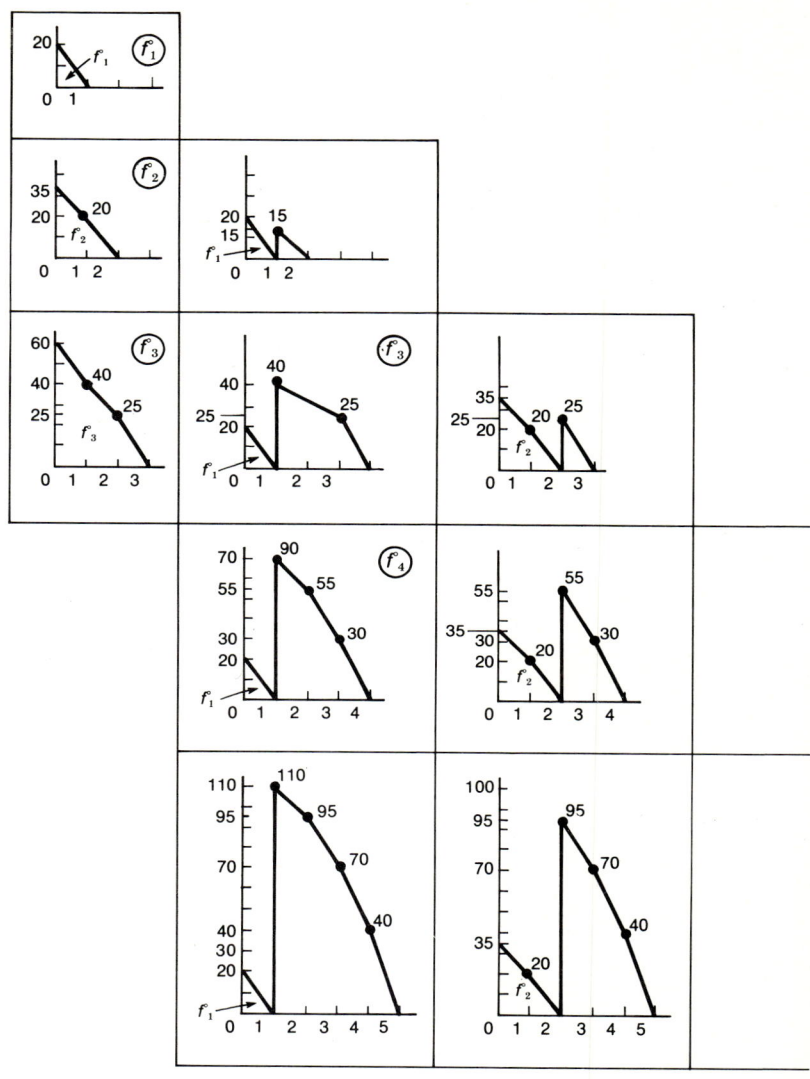

Figure 10-28 Inventory patterns for DP alternatives.

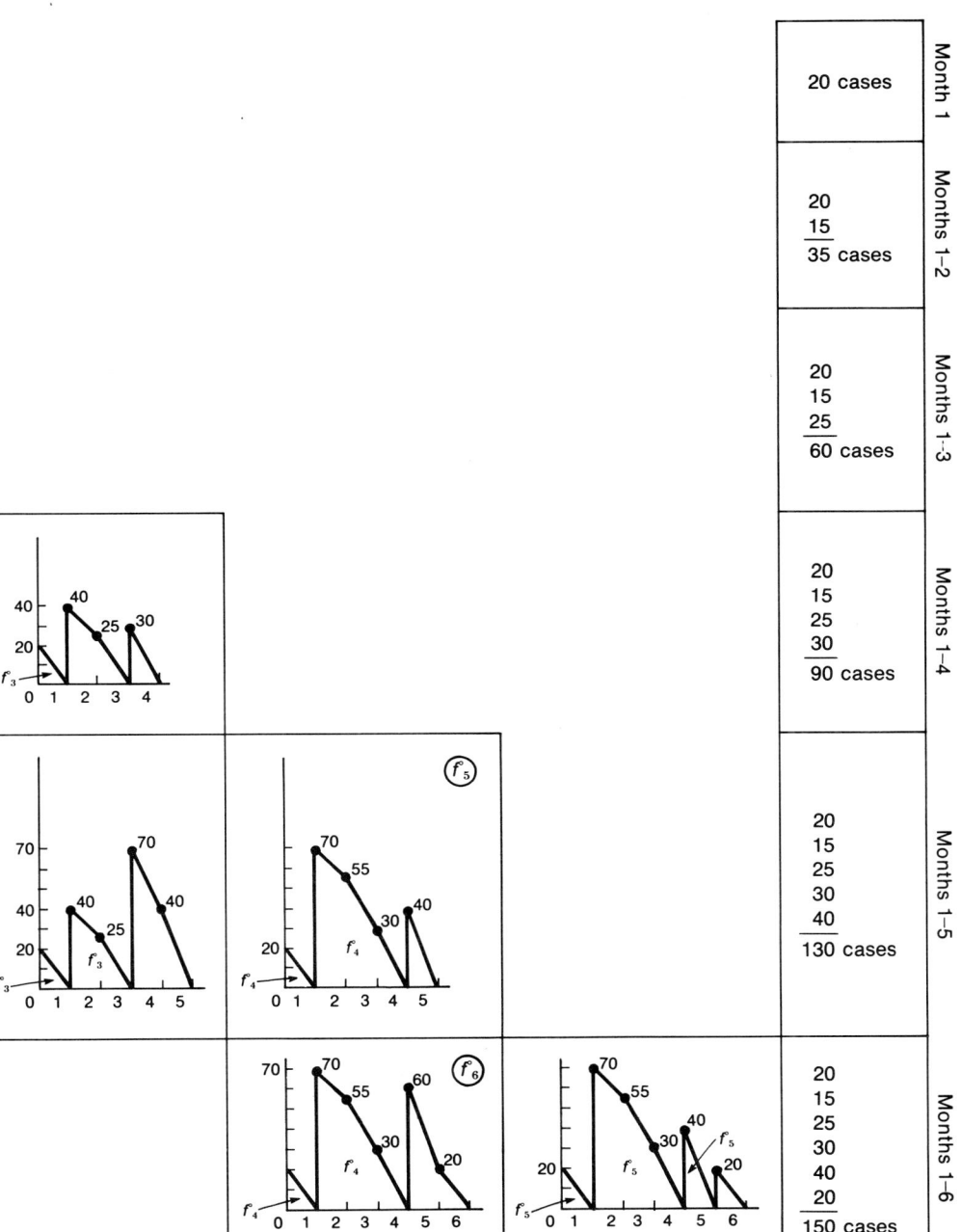

328 Introduction to Operations Research and Management Science

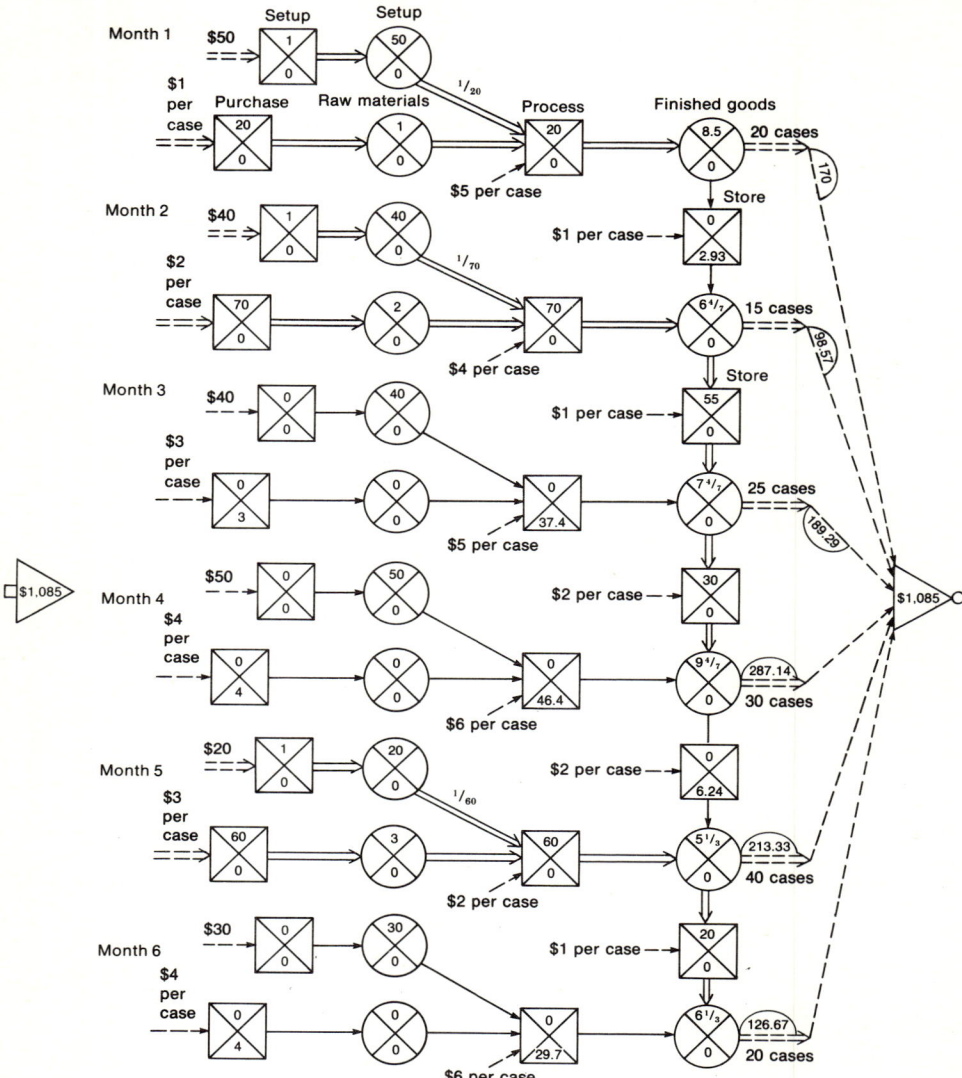

Figure 10-29 Marginal cost analysis of Gryphon Winery solution.

10-6 Combining linear and dynamic programming

Because of the curse of dimensionality, many LP problems are too cumbersome to be solved by dynamic programming, although theoretically it is always possible to do so. On the other hand, some linear programming problems would involve

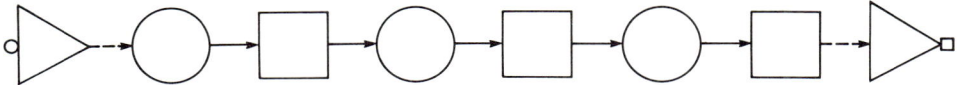

Figure 10-30 Example of a linear programming problem that is more easily solved by dynamic programming than by a formal simplex tableau analysis.

many iterations by a simplex algorithm but could be solved trivially by dynamic programming. Figure 10-30 is an example of such a problem.

Many LP problems are similar in nature to the one in Figure 10-30, though not as trivial. Even then, we may be aided by utilizing an intuitive approach similar to dynamic programming but performed more informally. Marginal-cost and residue analyses are used to test for feasibility and optimality. If the solution is nonoptimal or nonfeasible, it may be remedied by adopting a stepping-stone-type correction measure similar to the one introduced in Chapter 8.

Example 10-5: A caterer's problem A caterer is faced with the task of catering a series of OR/MS convention banquets. The convention lasts from Monday to Friday (5 days), and a banquet is held every night. The expected attendances are 200, 150, 185, 300, and 120. Experience with previous OR/MS conventions has shown that only 90 percent of the cloth napkins are salvageable after each banquet because the guests draw RPM networks and otherwise mutilate their napkins during the heated discussions at the dinner table. A total of 20 napkins are left over from last year's convention, and the caterer has three options for procuring the napkins for this year's convention:

1. Use a 24-hr dry-cleaning service at 10 cents per napkin to clean soiled napkins from one banquet for the banquet two nights later.

2. Use a 48-hr washing-and-ironing service at 5 cents per napkin to clean the napkins from one banquet for the banquet three nights later.

3. Purchase new napkins at 20 cents per napkin for each banquet.

Find the optimal solution to the caterer's problem.

The formulation of an RPM network and the identification of the optimal solution are intuitively obvious; we just do what comes naturally. Figure 10-31 displays the network and solution. The intuitive process may proceed as follows: On Monday night, buy as many napkins as needed for that night, $(200 - 20 = 180)$, recycle them the cheapest way by the washing-and-ironing service. Similarly, buy the napkins for Tuesday and Wednesday nights and wash what can be used (dry-clean them if more are needed urgently). After all the primal values have been filled in intuitively, we can check for the dual values. (If we find any negative residue or negative resource value, we would simply try out an alternative route.)

The fact that optimal or almost optimal solutions are often found in this manner

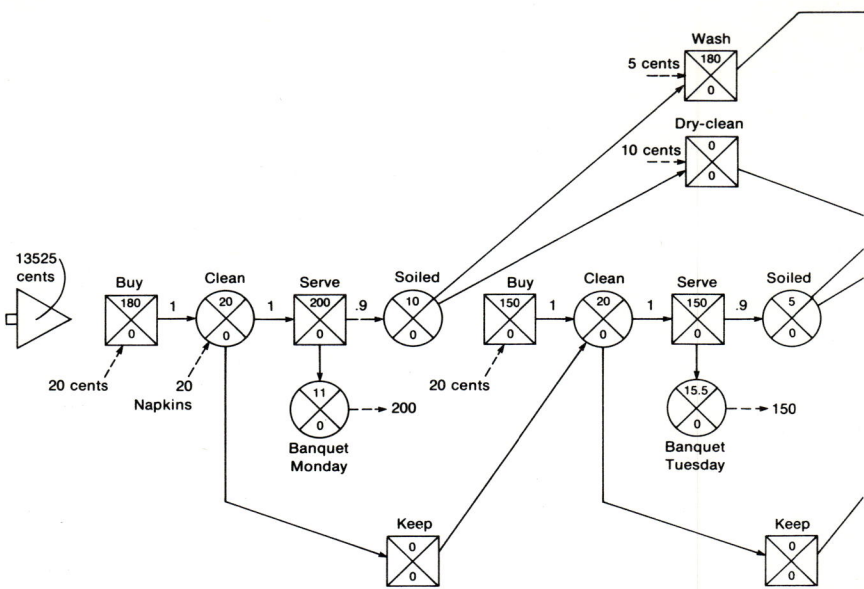

Figure 10-31 RPM network with its optimal solution for the caterer's problem (Example 10-5).

for simpler OR/MS problems shows that some management decisions can be optimized intuitively. An astute manager could arrive at the same optimal solution that would result from a rigorous OR/MS study. As we shall see in Chapter 11, the cost of an OR/MS study can outweigh any advantages that could result from its use. More important, a timely suboptimal decision may be preferred to a delayed optimal solution that is too late to be implemented.

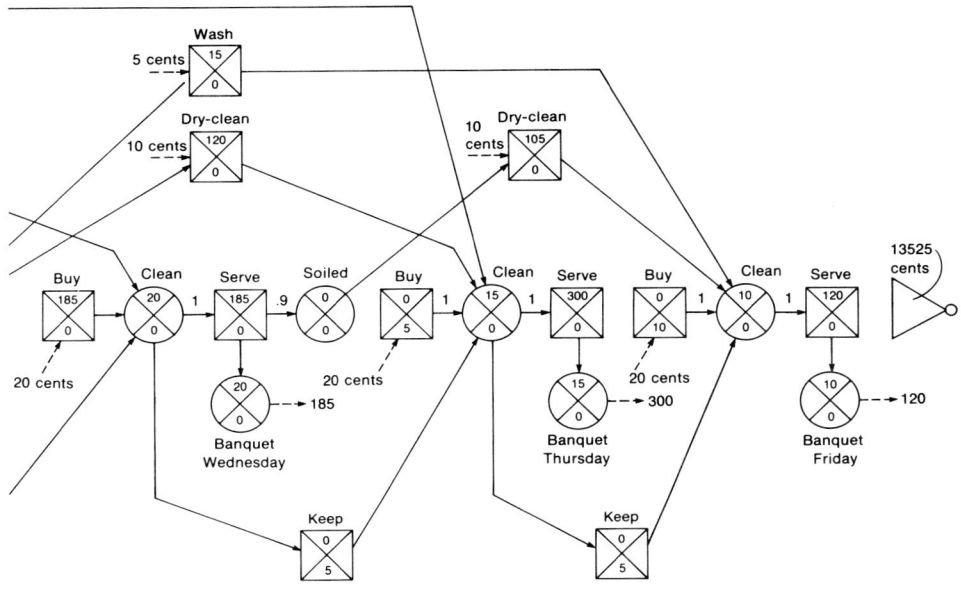

TUNE-UP SOLUTIONS

Section 10-1

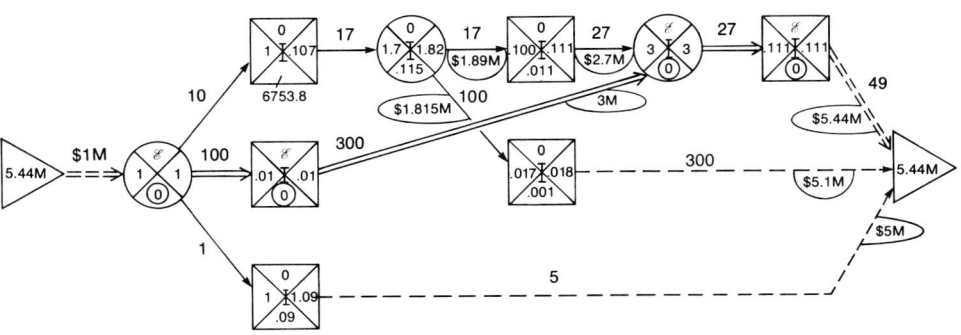

all flow values in M = 1,000,000

Section 10-3

The RPM network on page 332 reveals three optimal paths via its backward analysis: *B-G-M-S*; *C-J-M-S*; and *C-K-P-T*.

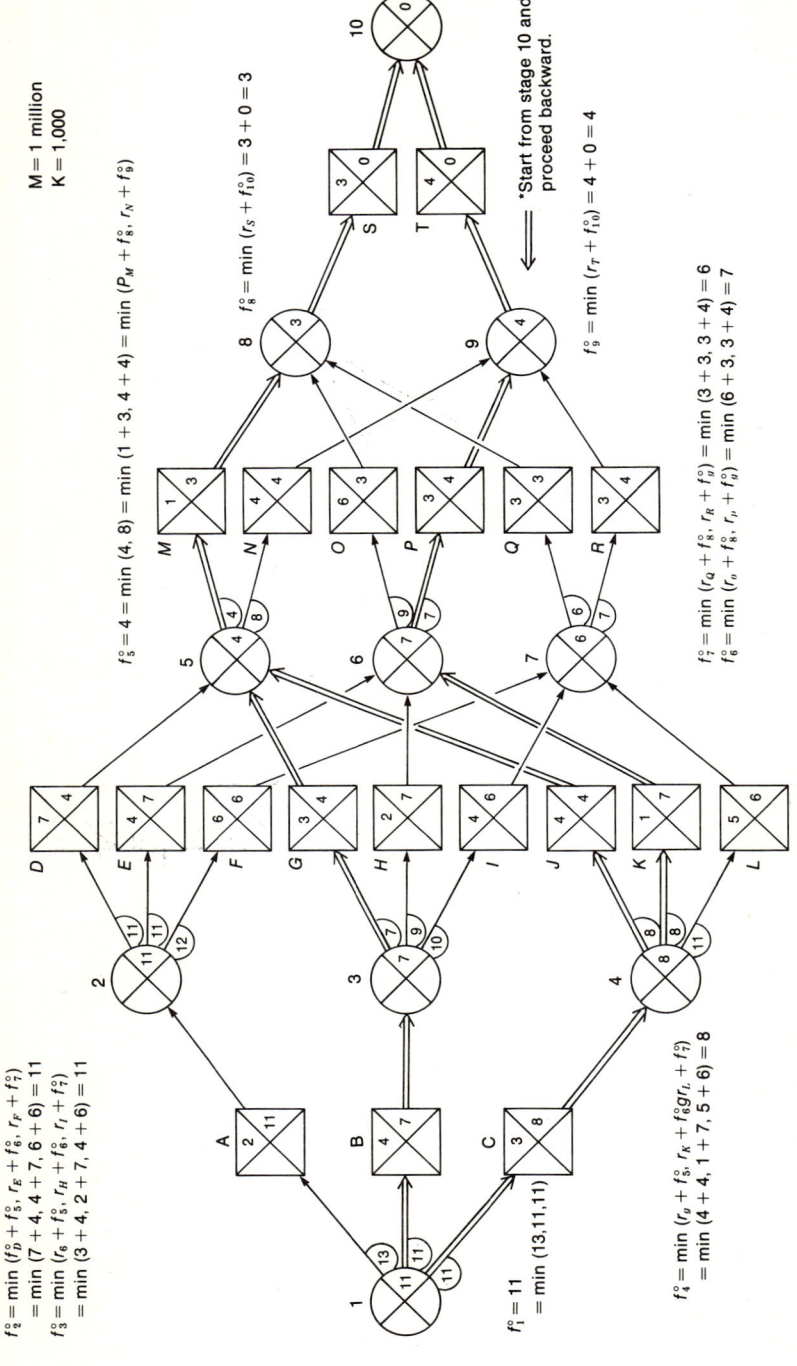

Section 10-4

Decision table for Port San Angelos (stage 3)

If Port San/Angeles receives from stage 2	Then from the alternatives open to P						For total return	Buggies left over
	d_3	P0	P1	P2	P3	P4		
	Buggies	0	1	2	3	4		
	Returns	0	16	20	21	30	Choose	
x_3	$f_3(x_3) = r_3(x_3, d_3) + f_4^\circ(x_4)$						d_3°	f_3°	x_4°
0	0 + 0°						P0	0	0
1	0 + 0	16 + 0°					P1	16	0
2	0 + 0	16 + 0	20 + 0°				P2	20	0
3	0 + 0	16 + 0	20 + 0	21 + 0°			P3	21	0
4	0 + 0	16 + 0	20 + 0	21 + 0	30 + 0°		P4	30	0
5	0 + 0	16 + 0	20 + 0	21 + 0	30 + 0°		P4	30	1
6	0 + 0	16 + 0	20 + 0	21 + 0	30 + 0°		P4	30	2

Decision table for Eastport (stage 2)

If Eastport receives from stage 1	Then from the alternatives open to Eastport						For total return	Buggies passed on to stage 3
	$d2$	E0	E1	E2	E3	E4		
	Buggies	0	1	2	3	4		
	Returns	0	12	15	20	30	Choose	
x_2	$f_2(x_2) = r_2(x_2, d_2) + f_3^\circ(x_3)$						d_2°	f_2°	x_3
0	0 + 0°						E0 + P0	0	0
1	0 + 16°	12 + 0					E0 + P1	16	1
2	0 + 20	12 + 16°	15 + 0				E1 + P1	28	1
3	0 + 21	12 + 20°	15 + 16	20 + 0			E1 + P2	32	2
4	0 + 30	12 + 21	15 + 20	20 + 16°	30 + 0		E3 + P1	36	1
5	0 + 30	12 + 30	15 + 21	20 + 20	30 + 16°		E4 + P1	46	1
6	0 + 30	12 + 30	15 + 30	20 + 21	30 + 20°		E4 + P2	50	2

Decision table for Micropolis (stage 1)

If Micropolis receives from headquarters	Then from the alternatives open to Micropolis						For total return	Buggies passed on to stage 2
	$d1$	M0	M1	M2	M3	M4		
	Buggies	0	1	2	3	4		
	Returns	0	20	20	30	30	Choose	
x_1	$f_1(x_1) = r_1(x_1, d_1) + f_2^\circ(x_2)$						d_1°	f_1°	x_2
6	0 + 30	20 + 46°	20 + 36	30 + 32	30 + 28		M1 + E4 + P1	66	5

The optimum solution is to allocate 1 buggy to Micropolis, 4 to Eastport, and 1 to Port San Angelos for a total increase in revenues of $66,000/wk. If Micropolis were to receive 4 buggies, the maximum revenue increase that could be expected would be $58,000/wk.

Section 10-5

P1: $100 \times 100 = \$10000$
$f_1^o = r_1 = 10000$

P1: $75 \times 250 = \$18750$
H1: $20 \times 150 = 3000$
$f_2^o = r_2 = 21750$

P1: $75 \times 330 = \$24750$
H1: $20 \times 30 = 4600$
H2: $20 \times 80 = 1600$
$f_3 = r_3 = \$30950$

P2: $90 \times 150 = \$13500$
$r_2 = 13500$
$f_1^o = 10000$
$f_2 = 23500$

P2: $90 \times 230 = \$20700$
H2: $20 \times 80 = 1600$
$r_3 = 22300$
$f_1^o = 10000$
$f_3 = \$32300$

P3: $100 \times 80 = \$8000$
$r_3 = 8000$
$f_2^o = 21750$
$f_3^o = 29750$

P3: $75 \times 280 = \$21000$
H3: $20 \times 200 = 4000$
$r_4 = 25000$
$f_2^o = 21750$
$f_4 = \$46750$

P3: $75 \times 400 = 30000$
H3: $20 \times 320 = 6400$
H4: $20 \times 120 = 2400$
$r_5 = 38800$
$f_2^o = 21750$
$f_5 = 60550$

P4: $90 \times 200 = \$18000$
$r_4 = 18000$
$f_3^o = 29750$
$f_4 = 47750$

P4: $75 \times 320 = 24000$
H4: $20 \times 120 = 2400$
$r_5 = 26400$
$f_3^o = 29750$
$f_5 = 56150$

P4: $75 \times 400 = 30000$
H4: $20 \times 200 = 4000$
H5: $20 \times 80 = 1600$
$r_6 = 35600$
$f_3^o = 29750$
$f_6 = 65350$

P5: $90 \times 120 = 10800$
$r_5 = 10800$
$f_4^o = 46750$
$f_5 = 57550$

P5: $90 \times 200 = 18000$
H5: $20 \times 80 = 1600$
$r_6 = 19600$
$f_4^o = 46750$
$f_6 = 66350$

P6: $100 \times 80 = \$8000$
$r_6 = 8000$
$f_5^o = 56150$
$f_6 = 64150$

EXERCISES

10-1 The state of Appallakia in Wonderland has been hit with the worst epidemic in its history, and you have been asked to dispatch medical units to five key towns in the area. You have 10 medical teams available, and you need to allocate them in such a way as to maximize the overall benefit. It is estimated that the number of epidemic patients will decrease as the number of medical units sent to each area increases. The following table was compiled to show the expected number of epidemic patients at the end of 1 wk if the given level of medical assistance is provided:

No. of Medical Teams	No. of Patients			
	Town A	Town B	Town C	Town D
0	1,000	2,000	2,500	4,000
1	500	1,600	2,000	3,000
2	10	800	1,500	2,000
3	5	300	1,000	500
4 or more	3	100	100	10

What will you do?

10-2 A cannery operates for 4 mo during summers only and requires 10 workers. It costs the company $2,000 to train any number of new employees up to 100 by means of videotaped instructions, and $1,000 in salary and fringe benefits to retain a worker for 1 mo regardless of productivity. One worker quits or is laid off at the end of each month and must be replaced either by hiring and training new employees or by extra idle workers on payroll. Assuming that there is no trained worker at the beginning of the summer but that the videotaped instructions can train new employees in no time at all, find the optimal schedule for hiring personnel during the 4-mo period. An employee who quits receives a full month's salary.

10-3 A college student is traveling through Wonderland using the same itineraries as in Section 10-3 Tune-up. While traveling, the student takes orders for sets of encyclopedias, "The Wonder Books," to earn a living during the summer, and so it is necessary to choose the itinerary that will maximize the expected revenue from the orders that are received. Assuming that the payoff table is the same as the one in Section 10-3 Tune-up, find the most optimal itinerary for the college student.

IMPLEMENTING THE IMPLEMENTATION: Project Planning and Management

Chapter 11

11-1 Value of OR/MS studies

An OR/MS study is usually a rewarding experience for an organization but seldom an inexpensive one. It is not uncommon to see a preliminary study save a company unnecessary expenses many times the cost of the OR/MS project. Planning effective utilization of limited resources is not only an economically advantageous move but a social obligation that all firms must consider seriously.

A simple routine inventory or production-system analysis may cost several thousands of dollars and require weeks or months to complete. An extensive project, such as the design of a regional airport, may cost several million dollars and require several years of investigation. Most projects require that two or three full-time OR/MS analysts (in addition to the multidisciplinary assistance provided by the management) spend a year or more on the study.

There are consulting firms (the so-called think tanks) that specialize in OR/MS projects, but most large corporations prefer to have their own OR/MS researchers. These in-house researchers work in departments bearing such names as operations research, corporate planning, economic analysis, management science, industrial engineering, systems, and activity analysis. The projects undertaken by such departments are statistical analysis (29 percent), simulations (25 percent), linear programming (19 percent), inventory theory (6 percent), critical path scheduling (6 percent), dynamic programming (4 percent), nonlinear programming (3 percent), queuing (1 percent), etc.[1] Athough 86 percent of all OR/MS project solutions are at least partially implemented, only 48.1 percent are implemented in full.

The evidence supports other surveys' findings [...] that the simplest techniques are the ones most frequently used. A major factor here is the ability to present and explain simple techniques (such as simulation) in a rather short time to the nontechnical managers.[2]

The value of an OR/MS study is judged by the effectiveness of the solutions that are implemented from the study. To derive a solution that is both timely and appreciated, the OR/MS project must be planned and managed with foresight. To implement a solution effectively, it is necessary to use a plan that is easy to follow and a schedule that is realistic and controllable by the management. In fact, the OR/MS team must set up a temporary management information system (MIS) to plan, schedule, and manage the implementation. Projects are then viewed as temporary profit centers which subcontract most if not all of the actual work that is required.

11-2 History of project management

The word *project* means "to throw or cast forward, or extend beyond something else" (Webster). An OR/MS project is partly exploratory and partly developmental. Finding a solution to a new problem requires extensive investigation and creative effort. Even the solution often turns out to be innovative and requiring the reeducation of operating personnel. Because of this creative aspect, an OR/MS project is plagued by the same uncertainty that is found in most research and development projects. You cannot force an OR/MS researcher to uncover an ideal solution to an unsolved problem overnight, no more than you can ask an artist to turn out inspired masterpieces on a mass-production basis.

Yet time is an essential resource and the only real constraint that we cannot arbitrarily change, trade, or buy. A feasible solution that is suboptimal but available

---

[1] Efrain Turban, "A Sample Survey of Operations Research Activities at the Corporate Level," *Operations Research*, vol. 20, no. 3, pp. 708-721, May-June 1972. Also, Lars Lonsteadt, "Factors Related to the Implementation of Operations Research Solutions," *Interface*, vol. 5, no. 2, pt. 1, pp. 23-30, Feb. 1975.

[2] Op. cit., p. 717.

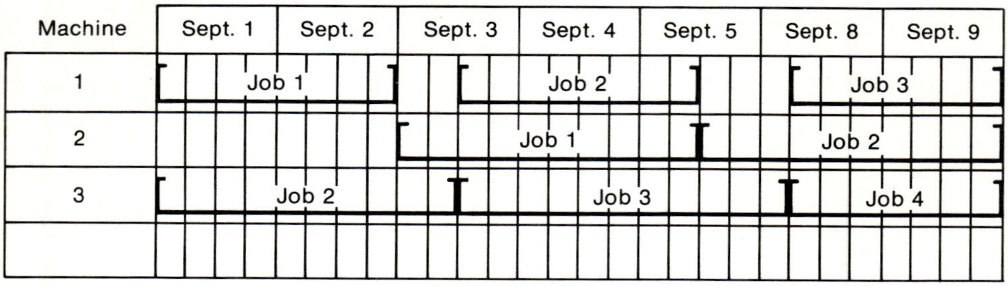

Machine	Sept. 1	Sept. 2	Sept. 3	Sept. 4	Sept. 5	Sept. 8	Sept. 9
1	Job 1			Job 2		Job 3	
2				Job 1		Job 2	
3		Job 2			Job 3		Job 4

Figure 11-1 Gantt chart.

on time is always preferred over optimal solutions that are too late to be implemented. Hindsights are abundant, but foresights are appreciated. It is imperative that we have some idea of when we can obtain a solution for a project if we plan to use it in a real-life situation.

GANTT CHART Henry L. Gantt developed the *Gantt milestone chart* for use in production scheduling during World War I (ca. 1910). It is a time-scaled bar chart showing the utilization of each major resource, with milestones indicating the end of one activity and the beginning of the next (Figure 11-1). The chart was very useful in scheduling routine activities where interrelationships were implicitly obvious. (Everyone knows that a foundation must be laid before the frame for a house can be built, and that the frame must be set up before a roof can be built.) However, when applied to more complicated projects, such as those in OR/MS, the chart was found wanting in explicit communication of precedence relationships among activities utilizing different resources.[1]

CRITICAL-PATH METHOD Today's project-scheduling techniques originated in 1956 in the Integrated Engineering Control (IEC) Group at E. I. duPont de Nemours & Company, which started to use a network model to schedule its own engineering design and construction activities. The original scheme represented activities on nodes, with the direction of arrows indicating the time flow for the precedence relation. Figure 11-2 illustrates the concept of *activity on node*. Several such chains could usually be found in a project, and the one consuming the most time (the longest path) was called the *main chain*. The scheme worked so well that it was applied to projects that were too big for manual computations.

Since DuPont used UNIVAC computers, it naturally turned to the Remington Rand Corporation for implementation of this scheduling tool on the computer. J. W. Mauchly and J. E. Kelley revamped the activity-on-node concept in favor of

---

[1]As technology progressed, several attempts were made to create a management tool for project scheduling. O'Brien (1969, p. 34), for example, reports on a *target commitment scheduling* by Professor Boyan at MIT ("Lecture Notes for Course 15:71," 1946) which has many of the features of modern project-scheduling tools.

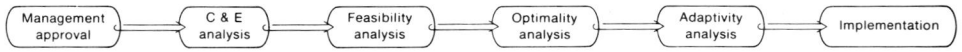

Figure 11-2 "Chain" of activities represented by activities on node.

a network where arrows represent activities; the arrows are joined at nodes called *events* and identify the activities which were then referred to by their beginning and ending node numbers.

By February 1957, the program was sufficiently implemented so that a test case could be run, and the construction of a $10 million chemical plant in Louisville, Kentucky, was selected by Kelley of UNIVAC and Morgan Walker of IEC for this trial run. The resulting network contained over 800 activities and was created and monitored by a team of six engineers whose introduction to the critical-path method (CPM) consisted of a 40-hr crash course. The success of this application was followed by another $2 million project (1958) and by a project to schedule the shutdown and overhaul of the neoprene processing plant at Louisville. The first application of CPM at Louisville reduced the maintenance time from 125 to 93 hr (26 percent), and the second CPM application reduced it to 78 hr (almost 38 percent reduction), to gain almost 1 million lb of production annually.

The original intention of the DuPont IEC group was to construct algorithms for time-cost tradeoffs that would maximize the effective use of resources. As it turned out, today CPM is used almost exclusively to compute time schedules based on single time estimates for all its activities.

PROGRAM EVALUATION AND REVIEW TECHNIQUE At about the same time CPM was being developed, the U. S. Navy's Special Project Office (SP) was put in charge of the Fleet Ballistic Missile (FBM) project. This so-called Polaris project was to involve 250 prime contractors and 9,000 subcontractors, all of them working together on a project that had no precedence in the history of the Navy. SP became cognizant of the potential difficulties of coordinating all activities and staying abreast of inevitable scheduling hardships. It felt that no existing scheduling tool could cope with the complexity of this project and was eyeing the progress of CPM applications. On January 27, 1958, SP organized a study group consisting of representatives from Booz, Allen, and Hamilton (a consulting firm), Lockheed Missile System Division, and SP to investigate further the possibility of adopting an approach similar to CPM. The method they developed has been named *program evaluation and review technique,* or simply PERT. As it turned out, PERT is very similar to CPM and is also considered to be an extension of the Gantt chart:

> *Prior to that time a form of Gantt charting involving thousands of individual milestones was used as the primary method of planning and control. The task of assessing program status by continually updating and reviewing each milestone was laborious and taxed the limits of human comprehension. PERT*

provided a means of knitting these milestones into objective oriented plans enabling top management to readily determine the time phased relationship between tasks and the interactions between performing organizations.[1]

The main difference between PERT and CPM is that PERT makes its activity-duration estimates using three criteria: optimistic a, most likely m, and pessimistic b. Thus, the estimated time has an expected duration t_e that is computed simply as a weighted average:

$$t_e = \frac{a + 4m + b}{6}$$

with a statistical variance

$$V = \left[\frac{b - a}{6}\right]^2$$

This statistical information can be used to predict the probability of completing the critical path by a given date. By assuming that the project duration obeys a *normal distribution*, we may add individual variances along a critical path and then take the square root to estimate the standard deviation of the normal distribution, with the length of the critical path (the longest chain of t_e's) used as its mean. It then suffices to make use of a standard normal distribution table to estimate the probability of a project duration falling within a certain range and meeting a deadline. (We shall discuss more PERT applications later in this chapter.) Today, PERT and CPM are considered synonymous and are often referred to as CPM/PERT or CPS (*critical-path scheduling*).

CRITICAL-PATH SCHEDULING A modern CPS analysis is a full-fledged OR/MS study incorporating (1) planning (feasibility analysis), (2) scheduling (optimality analysis), and (3) control (adaptivity analysis and implementation). Although CPS may still be known as CPM, PERT, or by some other name,[2] the name no longer implies just a technique, but rather "a way of thinking" (Riggs and Heath, 1966, p. 16). For example, the PERT Coordinating Group at the Department of Defense claims that:

PERT is a set of principles, methods, and techniques for effective planning of objective-oriented work thereby establishing a sound basis for effective scheduling, costing, controlling and replanning in the management of programs.

---

[1]PERT Coordinating Group, U. S. Dept. of Defense, "PERT GUIDE," 1963, p. 45.

[2]For example, cost planning and appraisal (CPA), least cost estimating and scheduling (LESS), network management technique (NMT), program evaluation procedure (PEP), and planning network (PLANNET), and project evaluation and cost scheduling (PECOS).

1. *Planning:* The planning phase includes the establishment of the study objective (system identification), a product-oriented work-breakdown structure (C & E analysis), and the creation of an arrow network or a precedence diagram depicting the chronological ordering of all activities and events (network modeling). An arrow network is an *event-on-node* representation, while a precedence diagram is essentially the same as the original *activity-on-node* representation. As we shall soon see, an RPM network is easily converted into either form.

2. *Scheduling:* The end product of the planning phase, a network model depicting only the activities that must be carried out (i.e., a network representing only basic paths), is then used to compute the elapsed-time estimates and identification of critical paths in the network. The computational algorithm is the same as in the longest-path dynamic programming model studied in Chapter 10.

3. *Control:* The schedule obtained from the second phase must then be adapted to the situations facing the management. What is needed is "a schedule which attempts to balance the objectives, the network flow plan, and resources availability."[1] More precisely, this involves resource management, time-cost tradeoffs, and probabilistic estimation of when the project will be completed. In PERT terminology, these are known as PERT/TECH, PERT/COST, and PERT/TIME, or simply PERT. The control phase must of course include a continuous updating of the schedule, taking into consideration all the previously mentioned factors. This requires an "analysis of the interrelated networks, schedules and slack values as a basis for continuous evaluation of program status, forecast of overruns, and the identification of problem areas in time for management to take corrective action."[2]

11-3 Planning Phase

A CPS study starts after an initial OR/MS study has been completed. The OR/MS study focuses attention on *what to do*, selecting basic variables out of all possible alternatives; then it is time for the CPS study to investigate *how to do it*. A CPS network model is therefore a representation of basic paths from the original OR/MS study's RPM network. The traditional emphasis in CPS has been to identify activities and events marking the beginnings and ends of these activities. Neither the arrow network nor the precedence diagram has provisions for expressing resources explicitly.

The planning phase is often regarded only as a preliminary step that is necessary to get to the scheduling phase. But communication is often the biggest

---

[1] PERT Coordinating Group, U. S. Dept. of Defense, "PERT GUIDE," 1963, p. 3.
[2] Ibid., p. 3.

stumbling block in a project implementation, and in the planning phase all personnel involved in the project are compelled to meet and to exchange information. The merits of this phase could very well outweigh any benefits that would accure from more sophisticated CPS analyses conducted later. Explicitly, the advantages include:

1. Limiting the possibility of overlooking jobs that belong in a project

2. Showing interrelationships of all jobs in the project

3. Giving a clearer picture of relationships that control the order of performance of various jobs that can be given in a typical Gantt chart

WORK-BREAKDOWN STRUCTURE The PERT Coordinating Group of the U. S. Department of Defense claims that a product-oriented work-breakdown structure reflecting the organization of objectives is essential to any PERT installation. This structure resembles an organizational chart, but it is *product-oriented*, meaning that each level describes a set of resources (products are units of accomplishments) included within the resource classification of the level above. The structure is developed downward from the definition of the program objective (the system) through successive levels down to the details required for effective planning, scheduling, and management. It is, in fact, a C & E analysis using a block diagram (see Figure 11-3).

PRECEDENCE DIAGRAM An increasingly used network model in CPS is the activity-on-node, or precedence, diagram. Computer programs are available for printing such a diagram on a line printer, and its block-diagram appearance is easily accepted by novices in OR/MS. The conversion from an RPM network to a precedence diagram is simply a matter of copying basic process nodes and connecting them by arrows wherever there is a basic resource node. The RPM network cannot include feedback loops and must obey chronological ordering; in short, we need a P-network model (see Chapter 4, Section 4-3). Figure 11-4 shows a simple example of the conversion of an RPM network into a precedence diagram.

ARROW NETWORK The other (and still the most popular) type of network model used for CPS study is an arrow network. Instead of representing each activity by a block, an arrow is used to tie the beginning event (I node) to the ending event (J node). While an arrow in a precedence diagram is used exclusively to indicate the precedence relationship, an arrow in an arrow network must do the double duty of indicating an activity in addition to its precedence relation.

The arrow-network convention has advantages of appearing very simple and adapting conveniently to computer programming. Each activity is identified in the program by the beginning- and ending-node pair I-J. When an activity's ending node J is the same as another activity's beginning node I, we know that the latter

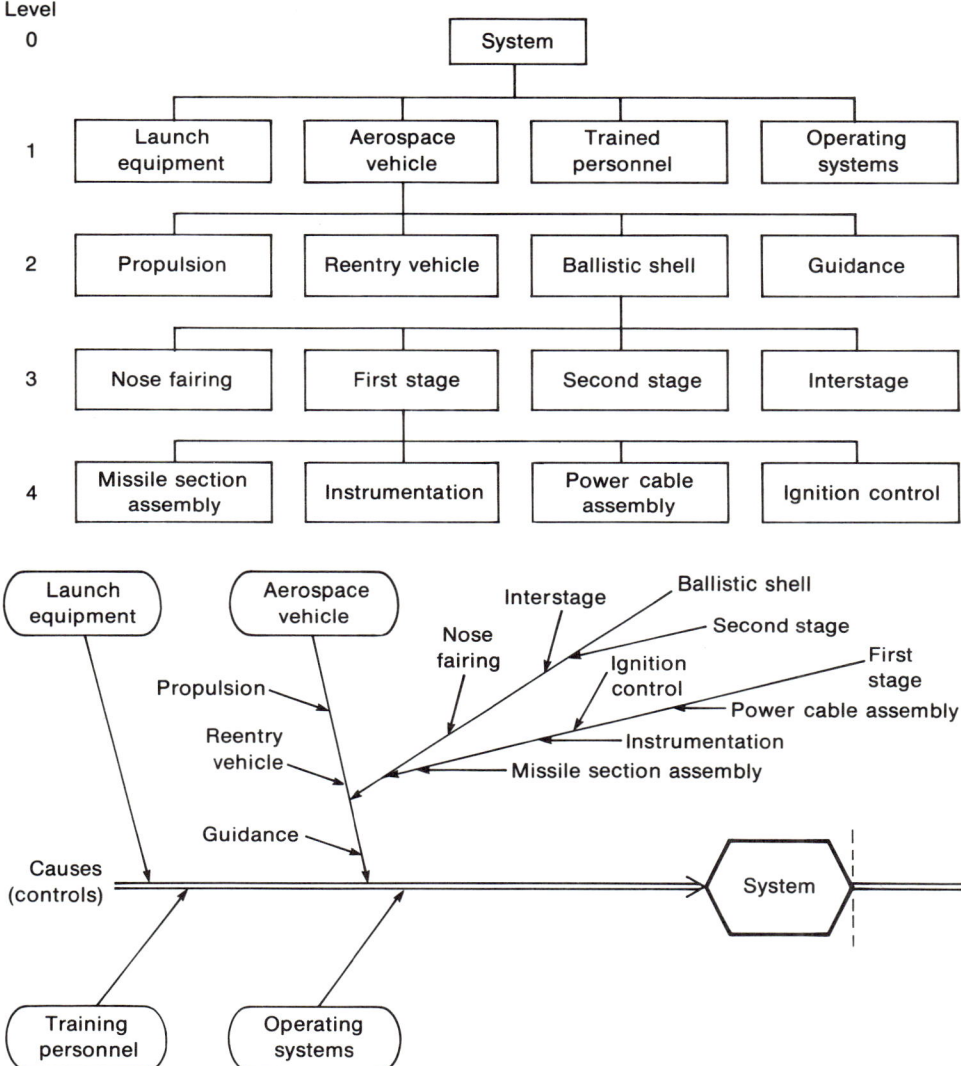

Figure 11-3 CPS work-breakdown analysis versus RPMS C & E diagram. (Adopted from DOD, 1963, p. 4.)

must follow the former. But since a node represents at once the ending of all preceding activities and the beginning of all following activities, it is not possible to express directly the relationship where only certain preceding activities are prerequisites to specific following activities. Also, if there are two activities sharing the same logical beginning and the same logical ending, the *I-J* numbering will not be adequate to differentiate between the two activities.

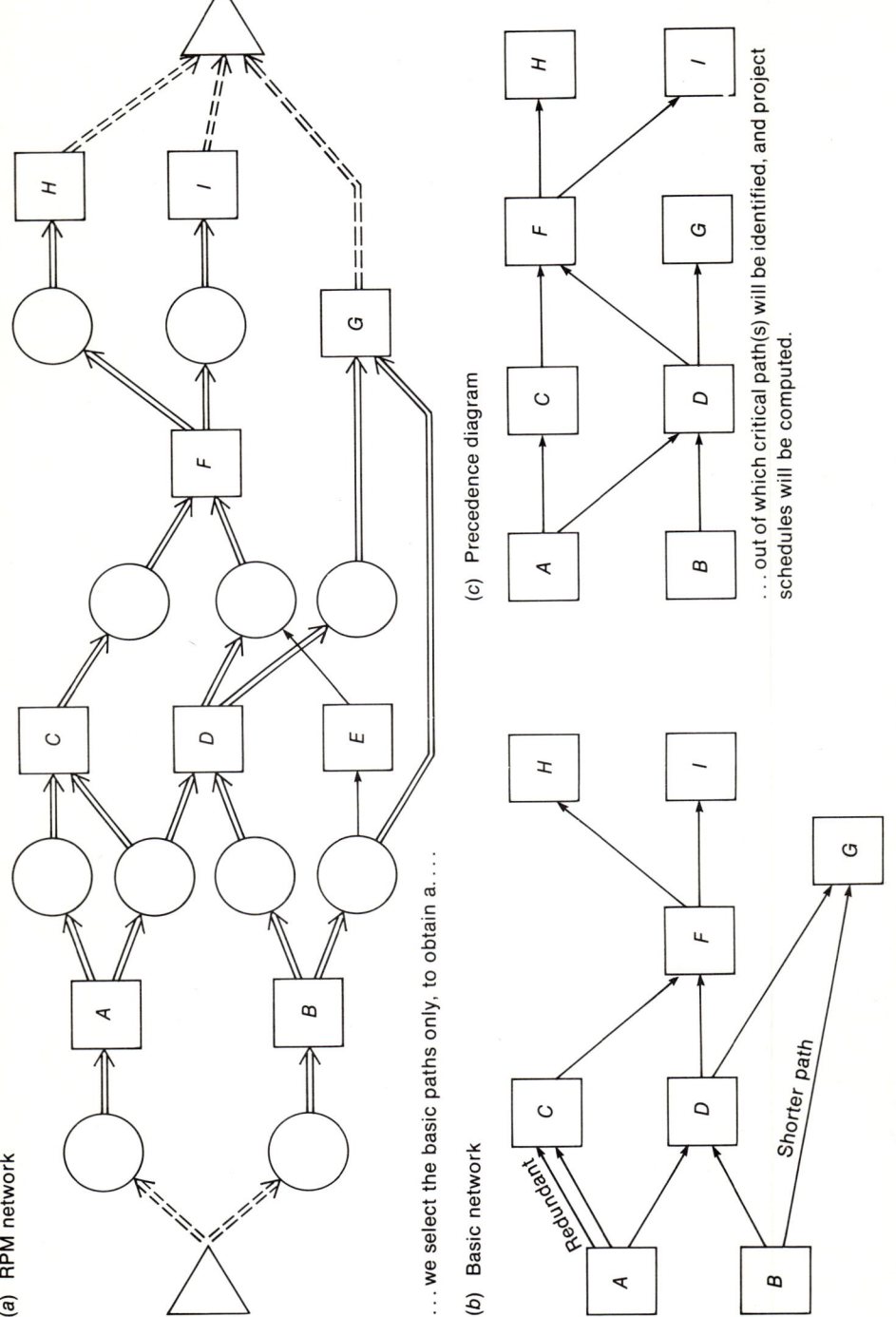

Figure 11-4 Converting an RPM network into a Precedence Diagram.

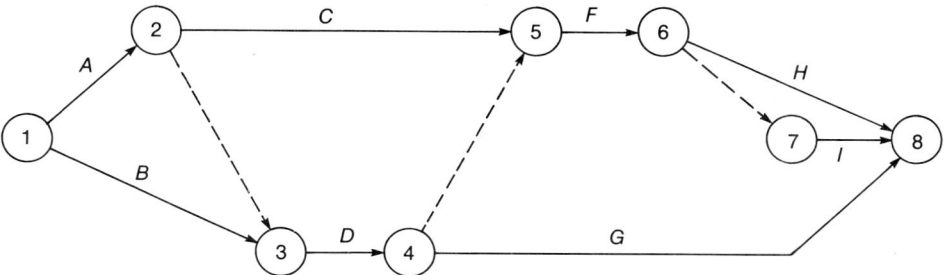

Figure 11-5 Arrow-network representation of Figure 11-4 showing dummy arrows.

To alleviate these difficulties, *dummy* arrows have been created. These are dotted (or dashed) arrows that represent technological relations but no activity, or, in other words, artificial activities with zero time duration. Figure 11-5 is an arrow-network representation of Figure 11-4. [Note that it is customary to have one project-start (1) and one project-end (8) node.] Three dummy arrows are shown in the figure: 2-3, 4-5, and 6-7. The first two are logical dummies used to indicate that A precedes both C and D but B precedes only D and not C, and that D and C are both prerequisites to F but G only needs D to be completed. If these logical dummies were eliminated, the network would then imply that both A and B must be completed before either C or D, and that both C and D must be completed before either F or G. The dummy 6-7 is called an *artificial dummy* and is used solely to give a different *I-J*-node designation (7-8) to I than H has (6-8). Without this dummy arrow, both H and I would be identified as 6-8. This need for an artificial dummy is eliminated in many modern computer programs that identify activities separately even if they share the same node numbering.

IDENTIFICATION OF LOGICAL DUMMIES The identification of when and where a logical dummy should be placed is often a difficult problem for a novice. It is similar to the problem facing a computer-logic designer who wants to come up with a most efficient and yet logically correct circuit to perform a specified function. In an RPMS network, a process node implies an AND relation among inputs and outputs while a resource node implies an OR relation; in a CPS network, *all* works must be performed sooner or later, only how soon they can be performed depends upon the technological relations shown by the arrows.

A simple logical scheme has been devised to facilitate the conversion from the basic paths of an RPM network to an arrow network, and this procedure will also work in converting from a precedence diagram to an arrow network. The procedure is as follows:

1. Construct a matrix having as rows the set of all activities preceding some activity or activities in the second set, and as columns the set of all activities following one or more activities from the first set. For a full matrix, the entire set of activities can be listed both as rows and columns (Figure 11-6a).

2. Enter a slash (/) in the cell corresponding to where a relation exists from an activity in the row to an activity in the column. All resource nodes between the same two activities will be represented by a single slash in the cell corresponding to this pair.
3. Consider each row at a time. If a row contains only one slash, there is no need for a dummy for this connection; if a row contains more than one slash, some of them may turn out to need dummies.
4. To see which of the slashes in step *3* needs a dummy, compare the columns corresponding to these dummies. If all columns are identical and each column contains the same set of slashes contained in the others, there is no dummy. If a column contains a slash that is not in one or more of the other columns of the set, then the original slash in *3* for the column containing this excess slash is a dummy. Mark this as Ø.
5. Repeat steps *3* and *4* for all rows containing more than one slash.

The procedure is completely symmetrical; and all rows and columns can be interchanged and the algorithm will still hold. Thus, a check can be made by turning the matrix around 90° and running through the algorithm again to see if all the Ø's have been identified correctly. Figure 11-6 illustrates how the logical dummies for Figure 11-5 can be identified from the RPM network. Note that the activity *E* was omitted altogether from the matrix as it was not a basic variable. Similarly, the redundant short path *B* to *G* was eliminated in favor of the longer path *B-D-G*, a process that will be discussed (page 348).

After having entered all pertinent slashes from the RPM network in the matrix, we can proceed with the algorithm. Obviously it is not necessary to include all ac-

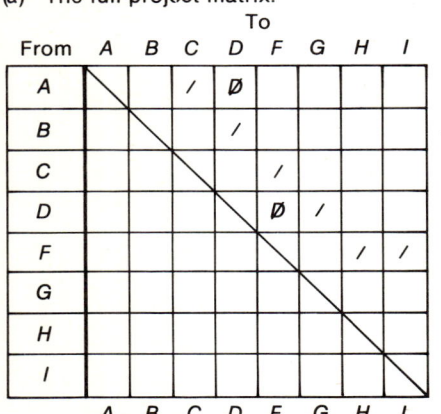

Figure 11-6 Identification of logical dummies for Figure 11-5.

tivities in one matrix, and Figure 11-6b shows two partial matrices that can be used in place of Figure 11-6a. The diagonal line in Figure 11-6a shows the identity elements (activity A to A, B to B, and so on).

Following the algorithm step 3, we identify rows A, D, and F as containing more than one slash. At row A, columns C and D are compared according to step 4. Column C contains only one slash (cell A-C), which is of course contained in column D (cell A-D). Column D, on the other hand, contains a slash in row B (cell B-D) that is not in column C (cell B-C contains no such slash); thus, the original cell A-D must be marked as ∅. Row D contains two slashes also (D-F and D-G), and we compare column F with G and find that C-F is contained in F but not in G (C-G has no slash); thus, D-G is marked as ∅. Column G contains no slash that is not in column F. Row F does contain two slashes, but columns H and I are identical and so there is no need for a dummy.

To double-check our findings, we interchange the roles of rows and columns. Columns D and F are the only ones containing more than one slash. At column D, we must compare rows A and B, and we find row A containing one slash that is not in row B, meaning that the cell A-D needs a dummy. At column F, we check rows C and D and again find that D-F needs a dummy.

IDENTIFYING PATHS IN THE PRECEDENCE MATRIX The full project matrix (Figure 11-6a) contains all the information that is on the arrow network (Figure 11-5), and all paths in Figure 11-5 can be seen in Figure 11-6a. Using the diagonal as the base, a staircase pattern can be formulated for each path. Because the matrix is really a picture of the arrow network, it is called a *CPS tableau*.[1] This identification of paths is facilitated by adding two more elements to the matrix of Figure 11-6: PS, meaning *project start*, and PE, meaning *project end*. A slash is entered in the PS row whenever there is an exogenous resource starting a project activity, and a slash is entered in the PE column when an activity has an observable endogenous output that terminates the project. Thus, any column that has no slash in Figure 11-6 will have a slash in the PS row indicating that these are starting activities (that is, a slash is entered in PS-A and PS-B cells); likewise, any row that has no slash will have a slash in column PE (rows G, H, and I). Then the staircase patterns can be discerned for PS-A-C-F-H-PE, PS-A-D-F-I-PE, PS-B-D-G-PE, PS-B-D-F-H-PE, and so on, for all eight possible paths. Figure 11-7 illustrates the arrow-network construction procedure:

1. Construct the tableau including PS and PE and all slashes.
2. Identify all logical dummies.
3. Ignoring all dummies, identify all slashes belonging to the same cluster by the same node number. By a *cluster* we mean all slashes in the same row or col-

---

[1] James L. Riggs and Michael S. Inoue, "Critical Path Scheduling: Tableau Method," *Proc.*, 17th *Annual AIIE Conference*, 1966, pp. 273-282.

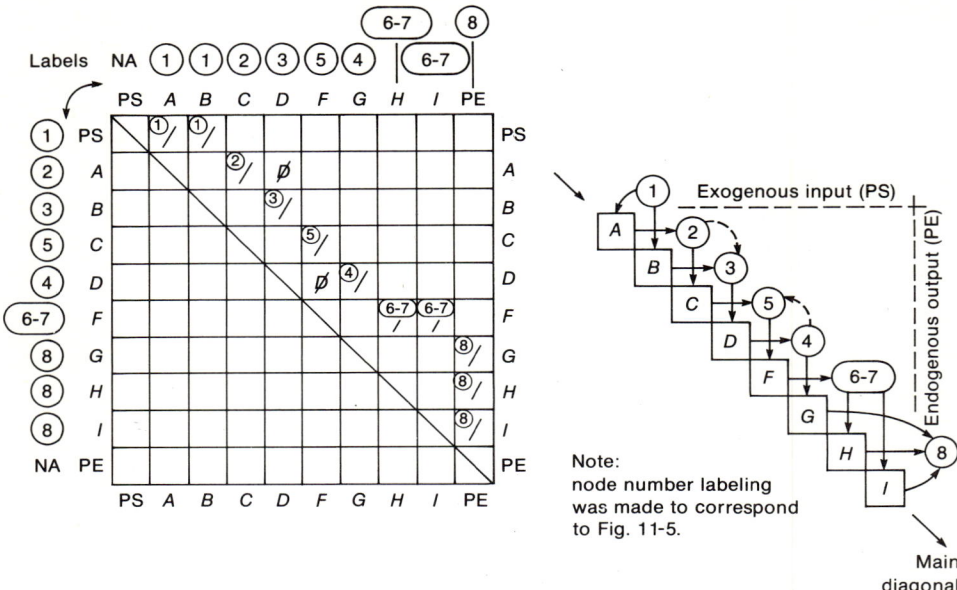

Figure 11-7 Conversion of RPMS to arrow network via tableau.

umn, so that there is no more than one label for each row or column slashes. For example, in Figure 11-7 the row PS and all slashes in the row are labeled one, and then all columns containing those slashes are also labeled one. We alternate between rows and columns until all slashes in the same cluster have been identified, and then move on to the next cluster: two for row *A*.

4. Any row or column that is left unlabeled is suspect for redundancy. Check first to see if there is a longer path; and if there is, remove the slash by marking it as $\not{R}$.

5. Repeat step *3* for any $\not{R}$ by reinstating the $\not{\emptyset}$'s. If a row or a column remains unlabeled after all redundancies have been removed, label it according to clusters of $\not{\emptyset}$'s.

6. Create nodes for labels and connect them with slashes; then implement $\not{\emptyset}$'s. (For older computer programs, it is necessary to relabel nodes in a technological order so that any arrow will always have $I < J$ and insert artificial dummies.)

IDENTIFICATION OF REDUNDANT SLASHES IN THE TABLEAU   In Figure 11-6, care has been taken to remove the redundant slash in cell *B-G*. The procedure just described will automatically identify any such shortcuts. Figure 11-8 (*a* and *b*) shows how row *B* and column *G* remain unlabeled when the

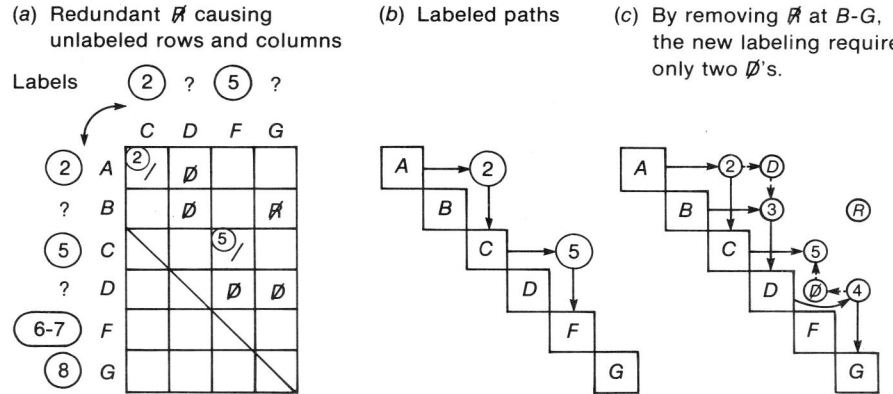

Figure 11-8 Partial tableau showing the redundant / at B-G.

redundant slash is left in the tableau. By removing R̸ the new labeling produces Figure 11-8c.

To identify which slash is to be removed, probably the simplest approach is to trace the path through the original RPM network (if one is available), or mentally trace all the ∅ paths in the tableau (Figure 11-8c). The path B-D-G is easily seen to be a longer path than B-G.

SECTION 11-3 TUNE-UP

Figure 11-9 shows several CPS tableau segments with slashes already inserted. In Figure 11-9a to c, PS and PE must be filled out, and these may or may not contain redundant connections. The tableau segments in Figure 11-9d portray segments of arrow networks. Use ∅ to mark the logical dummies and R̸ to mark the redundant connections.

11-4 Scheduling phase

The completion of a network model, be it an RPM, precedence, or arrow network, enables us to begin the scheduling phase. The traditional CPM approach requires that a time estimate (DUR) be collected for each activity, either directly or through the three-value estimation method of PERT, and be applied to the network to obtain scheduling data for activities. The longest-path dynamic programming application to RPMS, with additional data on resource availability, can furnish scheduling data for resources as well. The benefits resulting from this scheduling phase include:[1]

---

[1]James L. Riggs and Charles O. Heath, *Guide to Cost Reduction Through Critical Path Scheduling*, Prentice-Hall, Inc., Englewood Cliffs, N.J., 1966, p. 20.

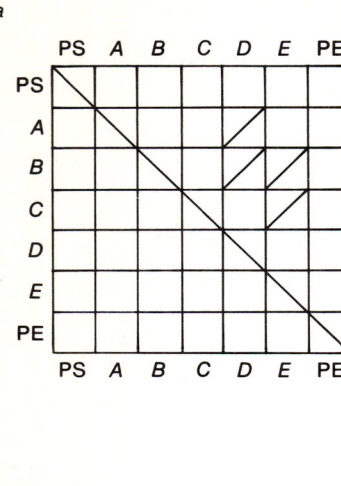
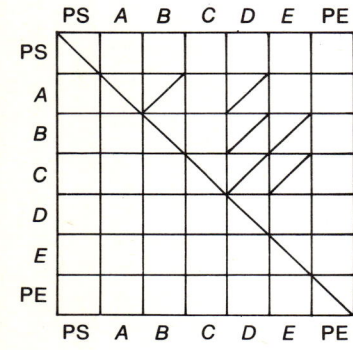
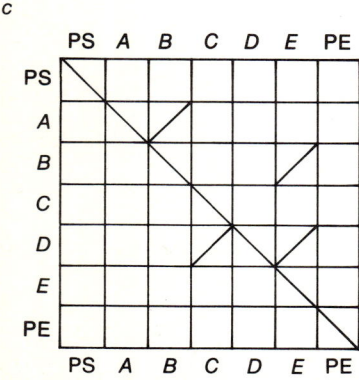

Figure 11-9 CPS tableau segments for Section 11-3 Tune-up.

1. Providing a time schedule containing much more information than the classical Gantt chart
2. Identifying those jobs that are critical in order to complete the project by the completion time
3. Predicting trouble areas; revealing nature, timing, and magnitude of future problems
4. Permitting an accurate forecast of resource requirements according to type, amount, and date
5. Providing a method of resource allocation to meet limiting conditions and minimize overall costs

ACTIVITY-SCHEDULING TERMINOLOGY A CPS analysis yields an earliest and a latest schedule for each activity to be performed and the flexibility of changing the activity schedule between the two; PS, PE, and all DURs are given. The earliest schedule shows when an activity can be undertaken if all other activities follow their earliest schedules. ES and EF indicate the *earliest start* and *earliest finish* dates, respectively, where $EF = ES + DUR$ for each activity. The latest schedule shows how late the undertaking of an activity can be delayed and still have the entire project completed by the target date PE if all other activities also follow their latest schedules. LS and LF indicate the *latest start* and *latest finish* dates, respectively, for each activity, where $LS = LF - DUR$.

The *total float* (TF) is the slack available in scheduling each activity: $TF = LS - ES = LF - EF$. TF is the leeway that would be made available, for example, if all preceding activities followed their earliest schedules and all subsequent activities followed their latest schedules. An activity is critical if $TF = 0$. There are three subclassifications of total float:

1. *Free float* (FF): The portion of TF that can be used by an activity without affecting the earliest schedules of the following activities. It corresponds to the slack available to schedule an activity if all other activities follow their earliest schedules.
2. *Safety float* (SF): The portion of TF that can be used by an activity without affecting the latest schedules of all preceding activities. It corresponds to the slack available to schedule an activity if all other activities follow their latest schedules.
3. *Independent float* (IF): The portion of TF that can be used by an activity without affecting either the earliest or the latest schedule of any other activity in the project.

RESOURCE-SCHEDULING TERMINOLOGY In addition to the CPS scheduling information, an RPM network can provide scheduling information for each individual resource item.

1. *Resource start* (RS): The date when the said resource can be made available for scheduling. It may be given exogenously or computed as the latest of the EFs of all preceding activities providing this resource. If an exogenous date is given in addition to the computed RS date, the latest (the largest numerical value) of the two must be chosen.

2. *Resource end* (RE): The date when the said resource must be made available for scheduling. It may either be a milestone or a target date that must be met for producing that resource or the earliest of the following LSs so that other activities can be completed on time for PE. The earliest of these two dates will prevail.

3. *Resource committed* (RC): The duration between the preceding activities and the ensuing activities that must be reserved for reasons other than shown by the arrow connections. For example, a resource may be used elsewhere in the project or may be scheduled for a rest period between activities. (A commercial airline crew, for instance, is required to take a minimum layover time between transoceanic flights. A machine may be due for maintenance between processes, and there may be training time required to condition personnel before starting up a new activity.)

4. *Resource residue* (RR): The slack available to schedule a resource while keeping in mind all its commitments: $RR = RF - RS - RC$. A critical resource has $RR = 0$.

If all $RC = 0$, the RPMS scheduling will yield the same activity schedules as a traditional CPS analysis.

RPMS P-NETWORK SYMBOLOGY Since $EF = ES + DUR$ and $LS = LF - DUR$ are easily computed, these values are not explicitly shown in an RPM network. The symbology shown in Figure 11-10 is consistent with our discussion of the longest path DP problem in Chapter 10.

Example 11-1: *Wonderland air mail service* Let us assume that Figure 11-5 (repeated as Figure 11-11) illustrates a network of airmail service from the west coast to the east coast of the Wonderland, with nodes 1, 2, 3, . . . , 8 representing the eight major airports throughout the country (Port San Angelos, Northwest Point, Micropolis, Eastport, Key South, etc.) The post office of Wonderland (POW) is initiating the Wonder air mail service (WAM) to promote the use of airmail over first-class mail which is also transported by air. POW promises that any airmail deposited in the mailbox of any of these airports before midnight (hour 0) will reach city 8 by the start of the business day, 10 A.M. The flight

Abbreviation	Description	RPMS computation	CPS computation
DUR	Activity duration in minutes, hours, days, etc.	Given or DUR = $(a + 4m + b)/6$	Given (CPM) or DUR = $(a + 4m + b)/6$ (PERT)
ES	Earliest start date for an activity	ES = max (RS + RC) of all preceding resources	ES = max (PS or EF of all preceding activities.).
EF	Earliest finish date for an activity	EF = ES + DUR	EF = ES + DUR
LF	Latest finish date for an activity	LF = min (RF − RC) of all following resources	LF = min (PE or LS of all following activities.)
LS	Latest start date for an activity	LS = LF − DUR	LS = LF − DUR
TF	Total float (residue) available to an activity	TF = LS − ES = LF − EF	TF = LS − ES = LF − EF
PS	Project start date which is usually set to 0	Exogenously given, or min RS of all resources	Given
PE	Project end date which is usually computed as the critical path duration	PE = max (given date or EF of all resources	PE = max (EF)
RS	Resource start date when the resource is either exogenously or endogenously made available	RS = max (given date or EF of all preceding activities)	Not available
RF	Resource finish date when the resource must be produced for either external or internal accounting	RF = min (given milestone due-date or LS of all following activities)	Not available
RC	Resource commitment that is externally defined	RC = required duration for resource commitment as exogenously specified	Not available
RR	Resource residue	RR = RF − RC − RS	Not available

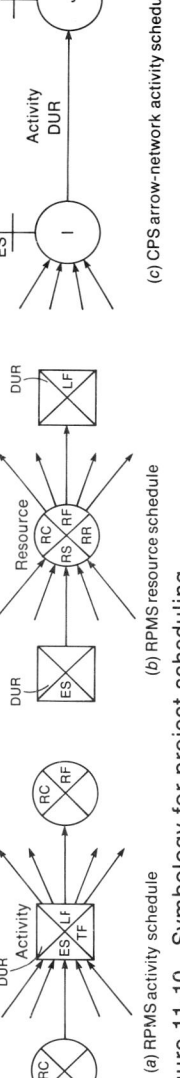

(a) RPMS activity schedule

(b) RPMS resource schedule

(c) CPS arrow-network activity schedule

Figure 11-10 Symbology for project scheduling.

times between cities (airports) are tabulated as follows:

Flight ID, activity	From, I	To, J	Estimated DUR, hr	Comments (Restrictions)
A	1	2	4	Connects to flight C directly. Connects to D via helicopter service
B	1	3	2	Connects to flight D directly
Dummy	2	3	0	Airport to airport helicopter service
C	2	5	1	Connects to flight F directly
D	3	4	2	Picks up mail from A and B and will connect directly to G and via an interairport rapid transit to F
Dummy	4	5	0	Interairport rapid transit system
F	5	6	2	Must connect to flights H and I
G	4	8	4	Transports mail from D and city 4 to 8
H	6	8	2	Continuation of F with limited mail
Dummy	6	7	0	Overflow mail from flight H loaded on I
	7	8	1	SST commuter service to city 8

Using this information (known in CPS as an activity and restriction list), it is desired to find the earliest and latest flight schedules that are possible.

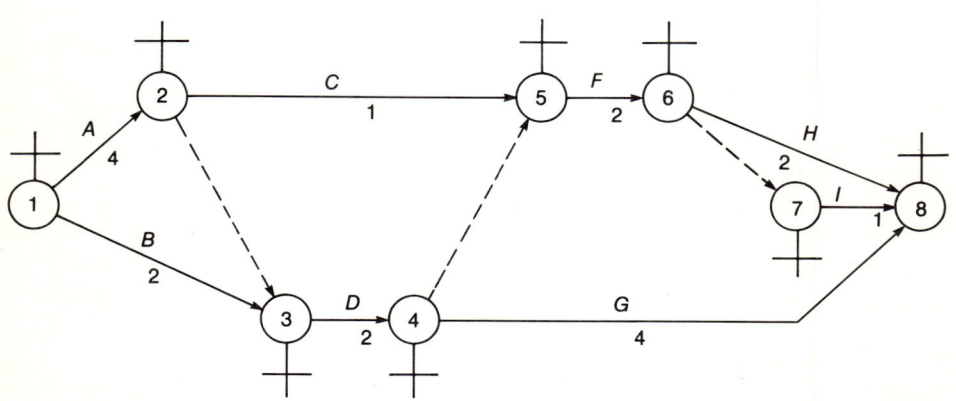

Figure 11-11 WAM airmail service (Figure 11-5 with DUR; Example 11-1).

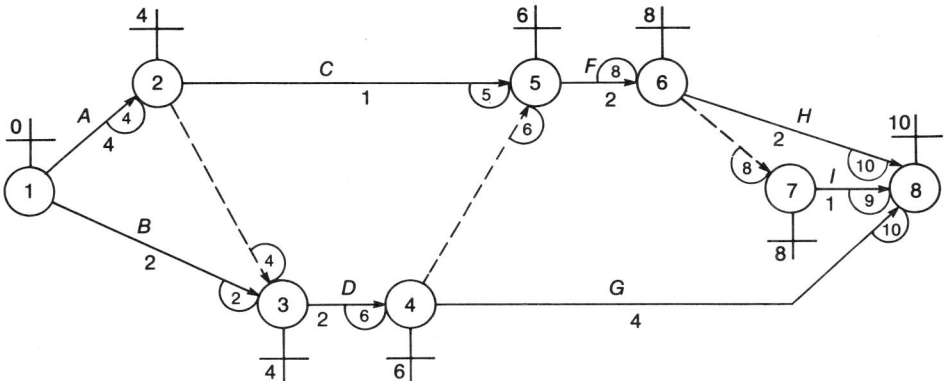

Figure 11-12 Earliest schedule for WAM.

EARLIEST SCHEDULE Each flight out of a city must wait for the city closing time (midnight = 0) and the arriving connecting flights from cities further west. The earliest departure time ES is the latest of those figures; the earliest arrival EF at the destination is easily computed as the ES plus the time required in transit DUR. Both flights A and B have the same ES = 0, which is the closing time PS at city 1. Flight A arrives city 2 at 4 A.M. (EF = 0 + 4 = 4), at which time C can depart with its ES = 4 and expect to arrive at city 5 by 5 A.M. (EF = 4 + 1 = 5). Flight B must wait for flight B's arrival (0 + 2 = 2) and the helicopter bringing mail from airport 2 (4 + 0 = 4); its ES is max (0, 2, 4) = 4, where 0 is the closing time at city 3. D arrives at city 4 by 4 + 4 = 8 = EF. This analysis is shown in the arrow network in Figure 11-12, with bags containing EF values at the arrowheads and ES to the left of the $+$ marker.

LATEST SCHEDULE Knowing that all mail must be in city 8 by 10 A.M., we can compute backward when each flight must arrive at its destination J. Then we can also find out when it must leave its city of origin I, and this may permit POW to set city I's closing time as late as possible. Flights H, I, and G must all be in city 8 by 10 A.M., which means that they must leave cities 6, 7, and 4 by $10 - 2 = 8$, $10 - 1 = 9$, and $10 - 4 = 6$ A.M., respectively. These departure times are known as LS, and their arrivals as LF. Note that all LFs at node 8 are the same, just as all ESs at each node are identical. Using the right side of the marker $+$ at each node for LF and hanging the LS in the bags at the root (tail end) of the arrow, we can indicate the latest schedule in the same arrow network (Figure 11-13). In passing, we note that there are different conventions for marking ES and LF on nodes. One popular method is to use a square for ES and a circle for LF. For example, node 7 could have been marked ⑧⑨, but this method makes it harder to identify the node to which these times are associated. We prefer to use 8|9/⑦ for clarity.

CRITICAL PATHS In Figure 11-13, we have used double arrows to indicate those flights where the earliest and the latest schedules are the same. Those activ-

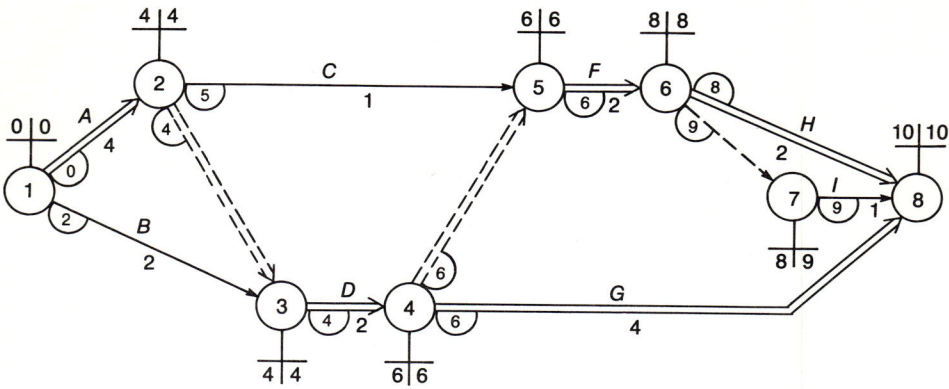

Figure 11-13 Completely scheduled arrow network for WAM.

ities where ES = LS and EF = LF are called *critical activities*. There are two *critical paths* through the network—*A-D-F-H* (1-2-3-4-5-6-8) and *A-D-G* (1-2-3-4-8). Any delay in any of the critical activities would mean that the mail will not get to city 8 by 10 A.M. Notice that the due date (10 A.M.) happens to coincide with the EF of *H* and *G*. If the due date were any earlier, the schedule would not be possible; if it were any later, there would be no critical path but only what we might call *more critical* paths, or paths with the least float.

BOUNDARY TIMETABLE Although it is possible to have the computer display an arrow network graphically, it is expensive and time-consuming. The usual reporting is performed by printing a *boundary timetable*. The exact form varies from one program to another, but they are all similar to Figure 11-14 shown below. If a graphic display is needed, a bar chart is printed on a line printer; this is faster, easier, and less expensive than using a plotter to plot an arrow network.

I	J	Description	Duration	Early start	Late start	Early finish	Late finish	Total float	Free float
001*	002	Flight A	4.0	0.0	0.0	4.0	4.0	0.0	0.0
001	003	Flight B	2.0	0.0	2.0	2.0	4.0	2.0	2.0
002	005	Flight C	1.0	4.0	5.0	5.0	6.0	1.0	1.0
003*	004	Flight D	2.0	4.0	4.0	6.0	6.0	0.0	0.0
005*	006	Flight F	2.0	6.0	6.0	8.0	8.0	0.0	0.0
004*	008	Flight G	4.0	6.0	6.0	10.0	10.0	0.0	0.0
006*	008	Flight H	2.0	8.0	8.0	10.0	10.0	0.0	0.0
007	008	Flight I	1.0	8.0	9.0	9.0	10.0	1.0	1.0

*Denotes critical activities

Figure 11-14 Boundary timetable for Example 11-1.

Implementing the Implementation: Project Planning and Management   357

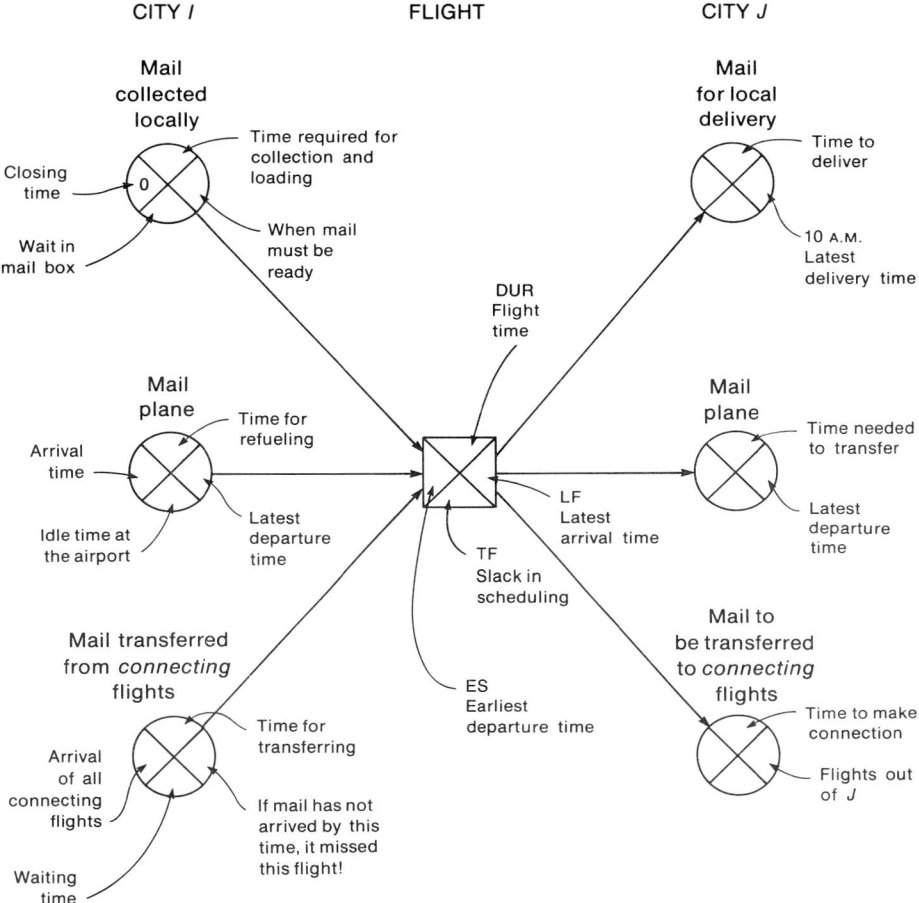

Figure 11-15 C & E diagram for a mail flight activity (Example 11-1).

RPM NETWORK SOLUTION The precedence relationship that is shown in an arrow network stems from an activity needing a resource that is produced or released by another activity. An RPM network shows this technological relationship explicitly. Because it carries more information, it is also more cumbersome in appearance. In the arrow network of Figure 11-13 solid arrows represent flights between cities. A simple C & E diagram (Figure 11-15) can be built for a typical flight, say, flight D, as an activity requiring as input resources a mail plane in transit at city I's airport, mail collected at city I, and mail transferred onto this plane from another flight. As the output of this activity, we may show the mail plane at city J, with mail to be transferred to other connecting flights and for local delivery.

358

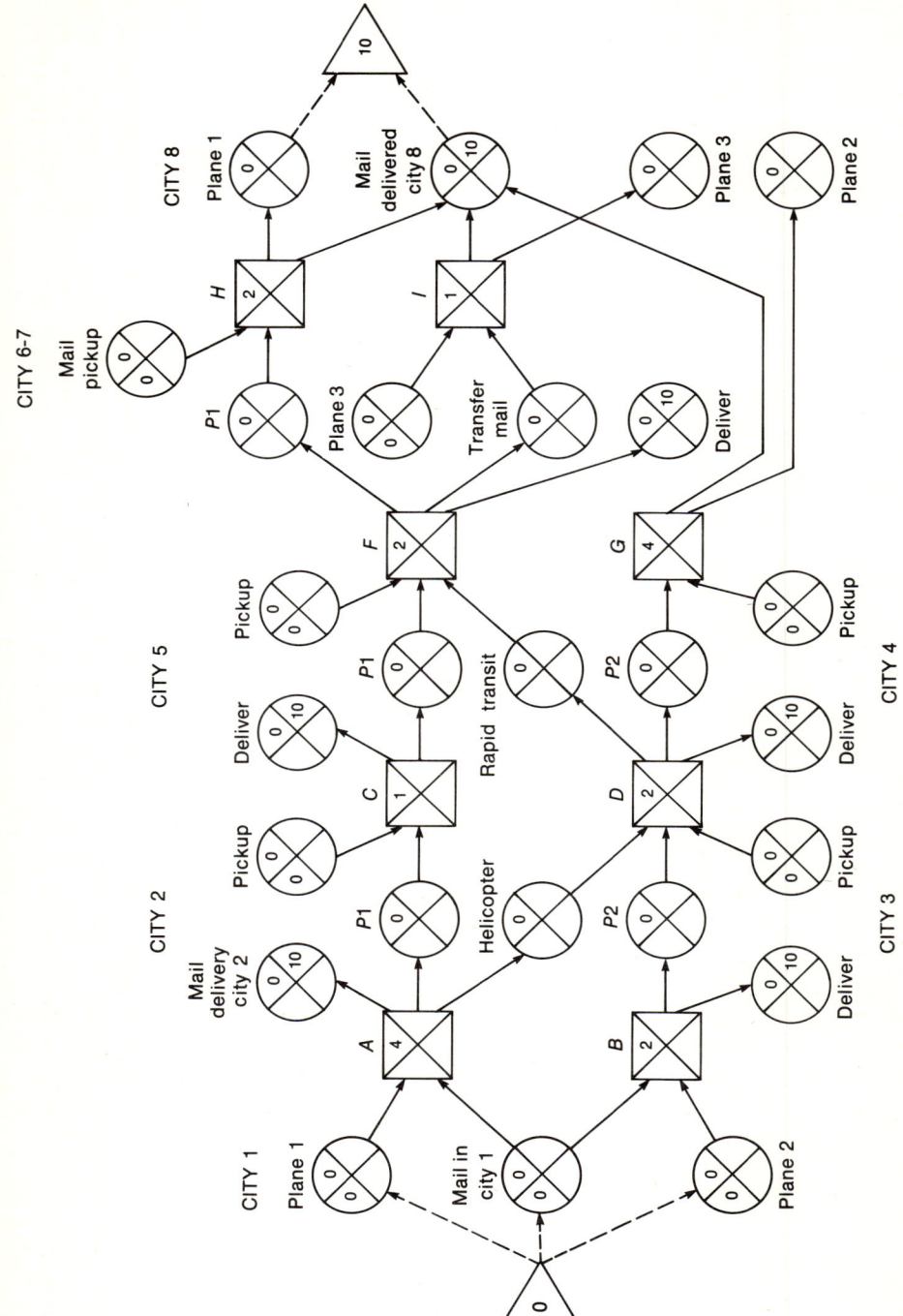

Figure 11-16 RPM network model for WAM service.

Cascading C & E diagrams such as the one in Figure 11-15 will produce an RPM network (Figure 11-16). The forward application of dynamic programming will compute the earliest schedule, and the backward application will produce the latest schedule. The residues are the slacks available for each resource and activity. In order to make this RPM analysis compatible with the CPS analysis, we must make an artificial assumption that all resource commitments take 0 time: 0 time to refuel the airplane, 0 time to transfer mail, 0 time to collect mail; and so on. Figure 11-16 also includes known PS = 0 (midnight) for all exogenous resources, such as mail to be picked up in all cities and availability of airplanes. PE = 10 (10 A.M.) is also included as RF for endogenous resources.

The computation of the earliest schedule is easy. We add the left entry (ES or RS) to the top value (DUR or RC) and hang the value at all outgoing arrows (Figure 11-17). Then for the new left entry (ES or RS) we take the longest path, which means the largest of all hanging values. For example, at D we are waiting for the helicopter transfer (4), the plane from flight B (2), and the local mail pickup at midnight (0), and take the latest arrival, max (4, 2, 0) = 4, to be the ES for the activity D. The plane departing at 4 A.M. would then arrive at the destination (city 4) at ES + DUR = 4 + 2 = 6 A.M. = EF, and this value is hung on three output resources: rapid transit, P2, and delivery at city 4. Since these are unique inputs to these resources, RS for all three resources are set to 6. RS + RC = 6 + 0, and we now have 6 hanging at F and G.

Proceeding in this manner, we can convert Figure 11-16 into Figure 11-17. (Again, the inclusion of the hanging bags is not necessary but is used to explain the process.) The critical paths follow along arrows where the hanging values are selected to enter the left-hand side of the connecting node. For example, starting backward from city 8, we find that either H or G will give us the 10 in mail delivery at city 8. Using H, we can backtrack to $P1$ and F; 6 in F is chosen from the rapid transit, which leads us back to D and then through the helicopter to A. Thus, A-D-F-H is identified as a possible critical path. Had we taken G instead of H, we would have traced the other critical path A-D-G. [Note that the direction of the earliest schedule is forward (left to right) and coincides with the point of the triangle cells we have been filling. At the end of the earliest schedule computation, all top and left cells of nodes must be filled out.]

The computation of the latest schedule proceeds in exactly the opposite manner. We move from right to left and subtract the top value from the right cell to obtain the hanging value. The smallest hanging value is inserted in the right-hand cell of the node. Figure 11-18 shows the result of this computation. The residue is computed by taking the left-hand value and subtracting from it the top and right-hand values. The nodes with 0 residue mark the critical paths.

SECTION 11-4 TUNE-UP: Wilderness cabin project

One of the projects selected for funding by the Wonderland Health, Education, and Welfare Commission (see Example 10-3) is called Wilderness Recreation for Youth (WRY), a proposal to make Wonderland's wilderness areas more accessible to young

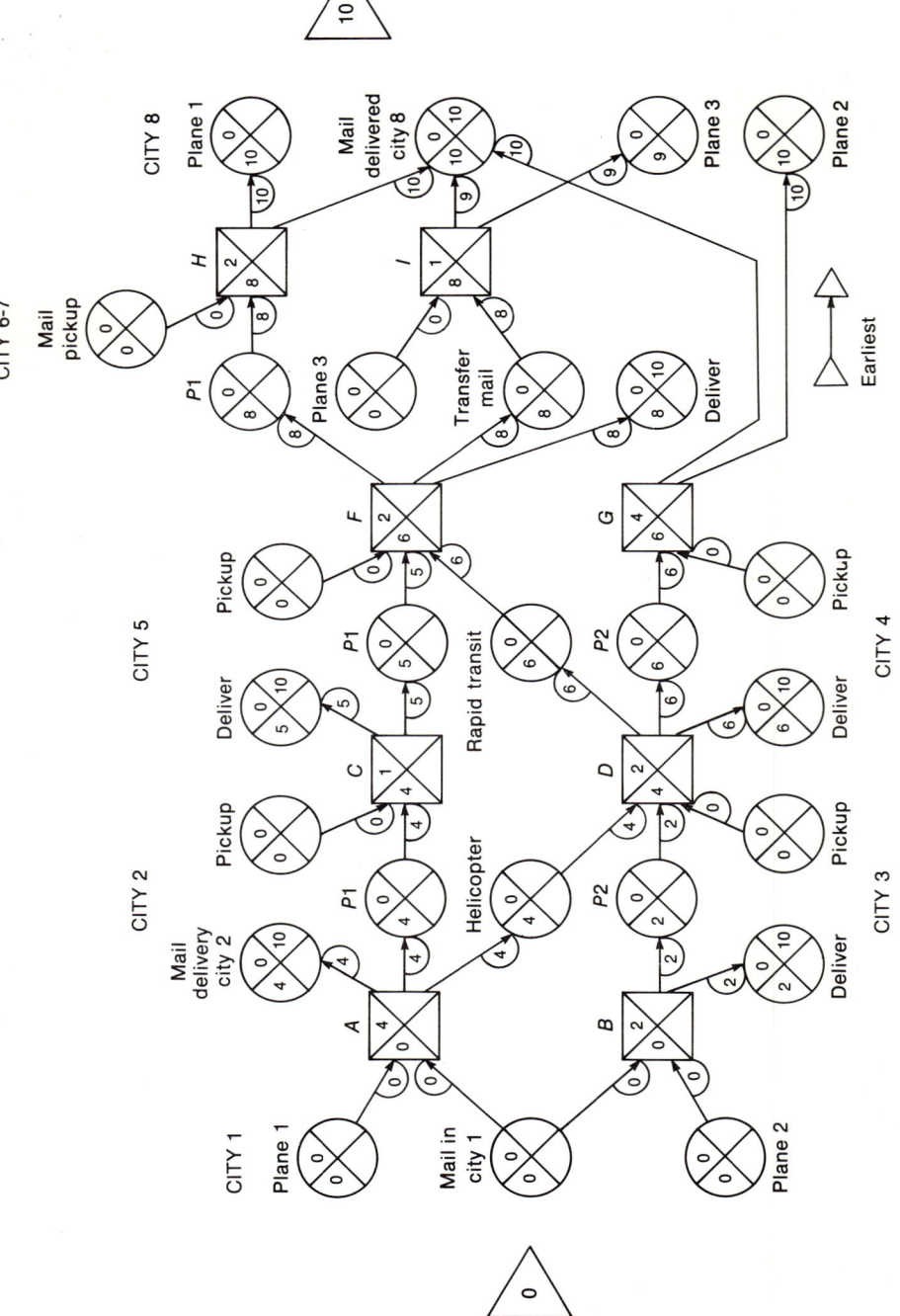

Figure 11-17 RPM network model of Figure 11-16 with the earliest schedule included.

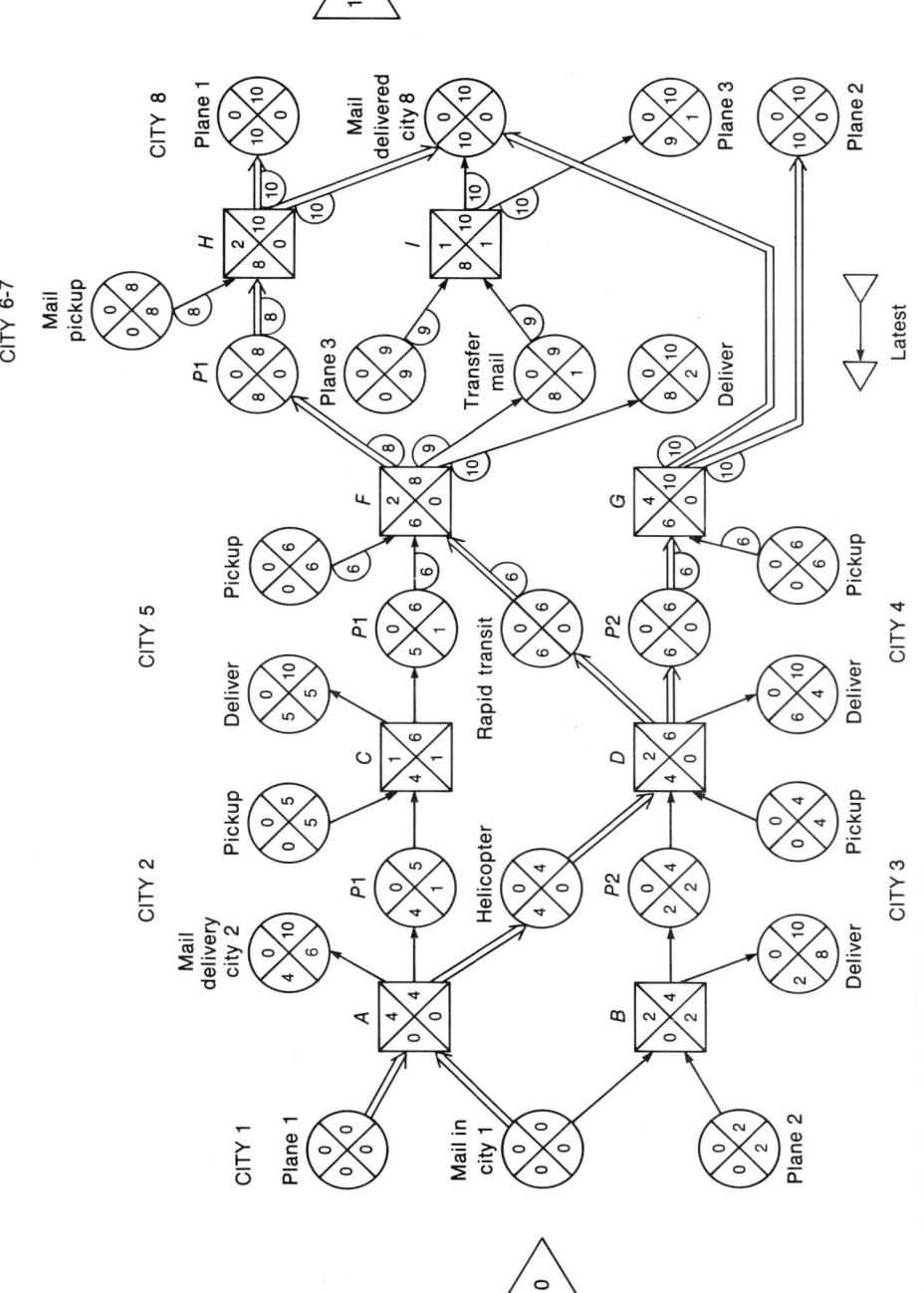

Figure 11-18 Completed WAM schedule.

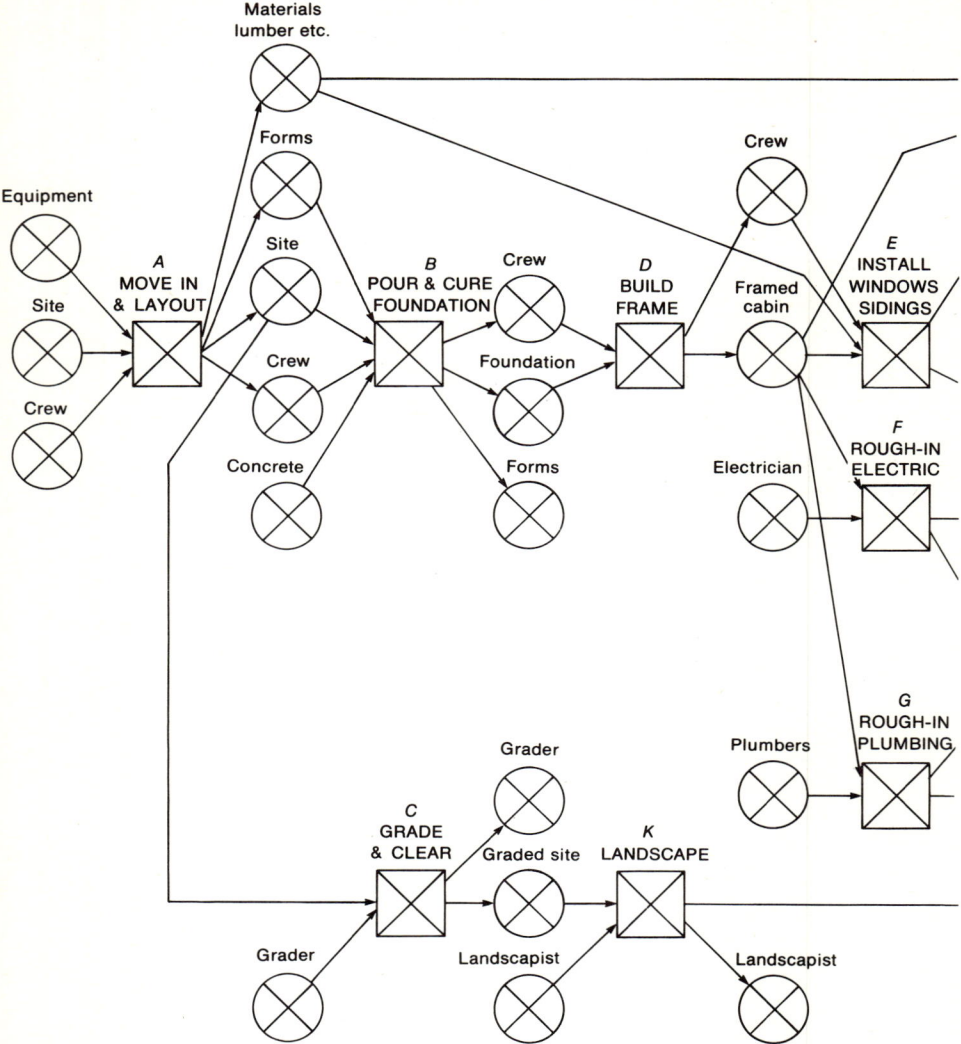

Figure 11-19   RPM P-network model for Section 11-4 Tune-up.

people while preserving the natural environment. It asks that dormitory-style cabins be built in selected locations near wilderness areas and that they be made available to young adults at a nominal charge. The feasibility study for this project was funded, and an OR/MS study was made as to the location, style, layout, and budget for the construction of the cabins. It was decided that a two-story A-frame cabin of 1,000 ft^2 livable space be built at each location, using mainly student crews hired during summer months. The cabins are to be completed in *turn-key* condition (meaning that they are ready to be occupied) and turned over to nonprofit organizations for management.

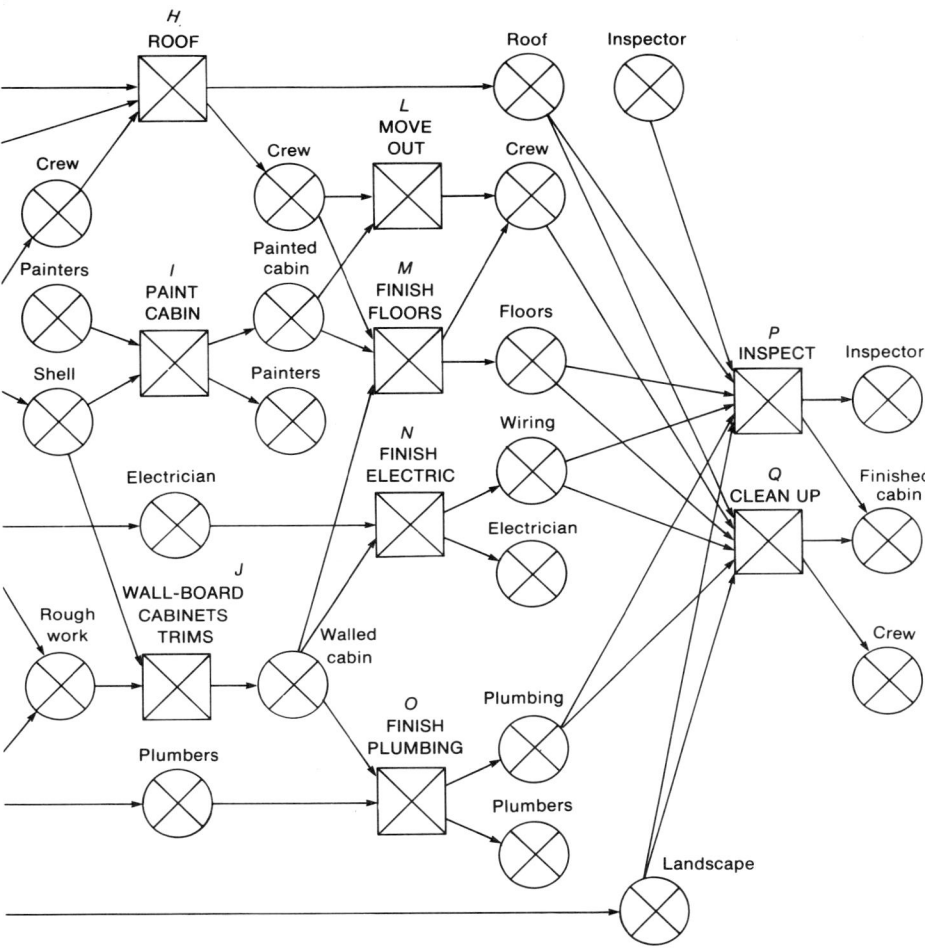

The funds are made available for the actual construction of these cabins, and it is necessary to set up a schedule to estimate the amount of time it will take to complete each cabin. The basic paths are lifted from the original RPM network and supplemented by activities that were not included in that network, but are considered essential to the actual construction project: for example, move in, clean up, and grade.

Figure 11-19 shows an RPM P network for this project. Construct an arrow network from the P network and check for accuracy against the activity and restriction list for CPS in Figure 11-20. Then, making use of estimated activity durations, compute the earliest, latest, and total float schedules for all activities. Mark critical paths on the

Activity list	Estimated duration (days)	Restriction list
(a) Move-in and layout	2	Must come before any other activity
(b) Pour and cure foundation	7	Cannot be done before (a)
(c) Grade and clear site and driveway	1	Cannot begin before (a)
(d) Build frame	6	Must follow (b)
(e) Install sidings and windows	1	Must have frame (d)
(f) Rough-in electric	2	Must have frame (d)
(g) Rough-in plumbing	2	Must have frame (d)
(h) Roofing	5	Must have sidings (e)
(i) Paint cabin	5	Must have sidings (e)
(j) Install wallboards, cabinets, and trims	2	Must have rough-ins (f and g) and sidings (e)
(k) Landscape including trails	2	Must be graded (c)
(l) Move-out	1	Cabin must be painted (i) Roof must be on (h)
(m) Finish floors	2	Walls (j) and paint (i) must be finished
(n) Finish electric	1	Walls must be up (j)
(o) Finish plumbing	1	Walls need be up (j)
(p) Inspect	1	(k), (m), (n), (o)
(q) Cleanup	1	(k), (l), (m), (n), (o)

Figure 11-20 Activity and restriction list for Section 11-4 Tune-up.

arrow network by using double arrows. Artificial dummies need not be shown, but all logical dummies must be identified correctly.

11-5 Resource management

For a project to be feasible, all required resources must be available at the time they are needed by the particular activity. In most practical situations the man-

Implementing the Implementation: Project Planning and Management   365

agement is in charge of more than one project at a time, and the resources, although potentially available, may not be ready in time in the right quantities. Sharing an expensive piece of equipment is a common practice. Computer time is often allotted to competing accounting, engineering, administrative, and clerical uses. Even management time must be allocated. When a manager is busy, it is essential to rate activites in an order of priority and delegate responsibility where possible. Of the activities that only the manager can handle, the pressing ones should be done first leaving the least important ones until last.

To illustrate how the allocation of resources may be made, let us assume in our Example 11-1 that it takes 30 min to refuel an airplane at each stop, 30 min to pick up or deliver mail at the airport post offices, 1 hr for the helicopter connection, 30 min for transferring from flight F to flight I, and 1 hr of rapid transit time between cities 3 and 5. It has also been decided to maintain the mail pickup at midnight and delivery at 10 A.M. if possible, or as soon after as feasible if the 10 A.M. delivery cannot be met. All three planes are available for refueling by midnight at cities 1 and 7, and one plane must be refueled and ready to fly from city 8 by 2:30 P.M., 3:30 P.M., and 4:30 P.M. Figure 11-21 shows the revised RPM network including all these restrictions. The revised time schedule is shown in Figure 11-22. The landing restriction at city 3 means that flight B should not be started earlier than 5 A.M., and this marks the beginning of critical paths throughout the network. The 10 A.M. delivery can be met at all cities except city 6-7 at 2 P.M. and city 8 at 3:30 P.M. To compute the latest time schedule, we must first decide on the allocation of airplanes at city 8 using the earliest time schedule. Both planes 2 and 3 are available in city 8 by 2:30 P.M. after their refueling, and plane 3 by 3:30 P.M. Since there are two planes leaving city 6-7, we have decided to pick up the local mail on flight I instead of flight H and to assign plane 2 to the earliest 2:30 P.M. departure on the next leg. In this manner, any delay in flight schedule should not affect the departure of I, and flight H, without the burden of additional mail, should be able to continue to city 8 at its convenience. Plane 2 will then have 1 hr of slack for its 3:30 P.M. flight, and plane 1 will have 1 hr of float for its 4:30 P.M. flight.

The latest schedule tells us that flights A, C, and G are no longer critical and that mail pickup (closing time for outgoing mail) can be delayed in many cities: 2 A.M. in city 1; 7 A.M. in city 3; 8 A.M. in city 2; 10 A.M. in city 5; and 10:30 A.M. in city 4. This information may, in turn, be used to schedule work hours for postal workers so that an extra work force will be available during critical moments such as the mail transfer between planes.

Because it is easier to relate resources from one project to another, RPM networks are suitable for multiproject scheduling where a resource from one project may be borrowed temporarily to perform work in another.

SECTION 11-5 TUNE-UP: RPMS scheduling of cabin project

In the wilderness cabin project of Section 11-4 Tune-up, let us assume the following conditions (turn to page 368):

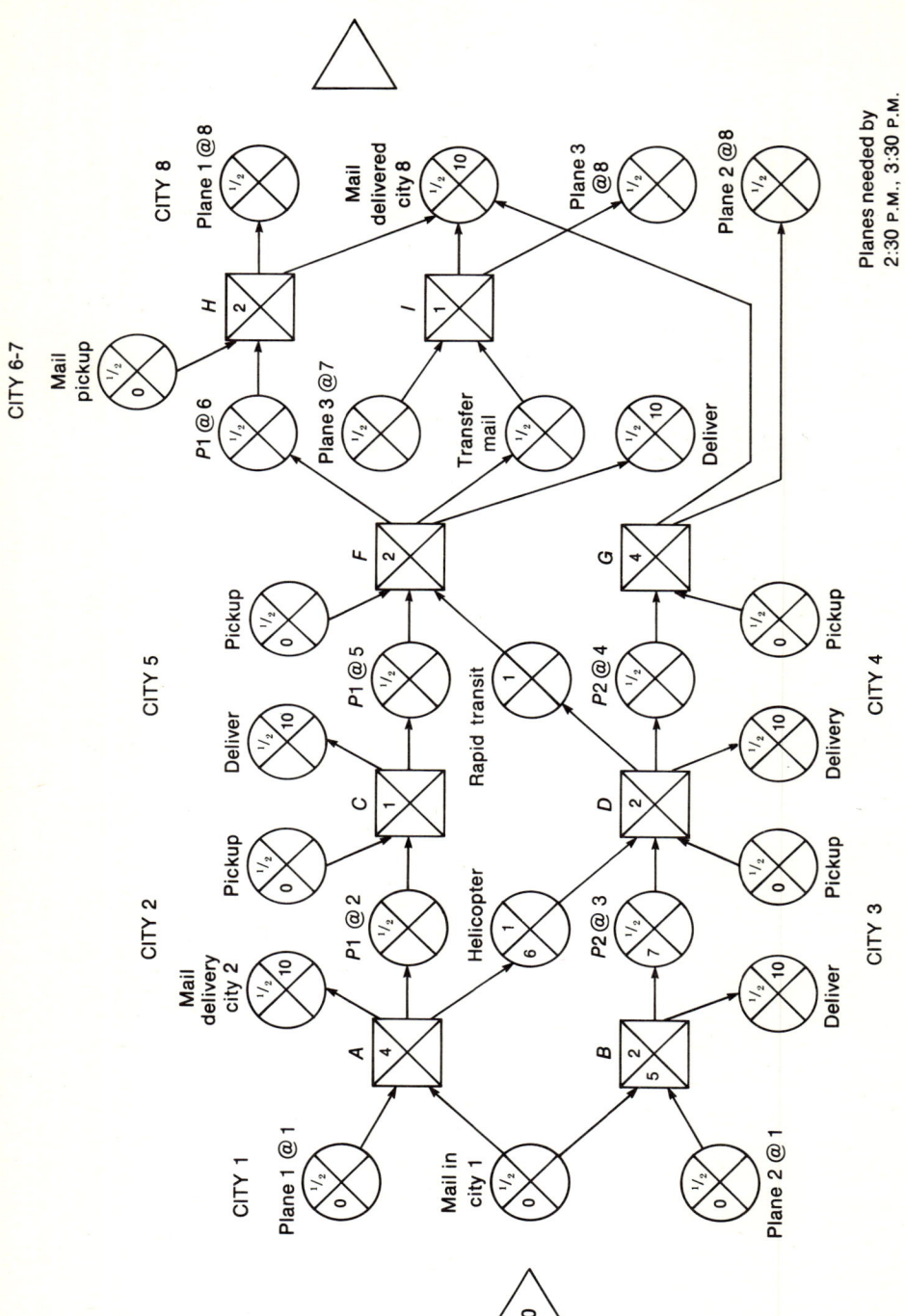

Figure 11-21 WAM with resource restrictions.

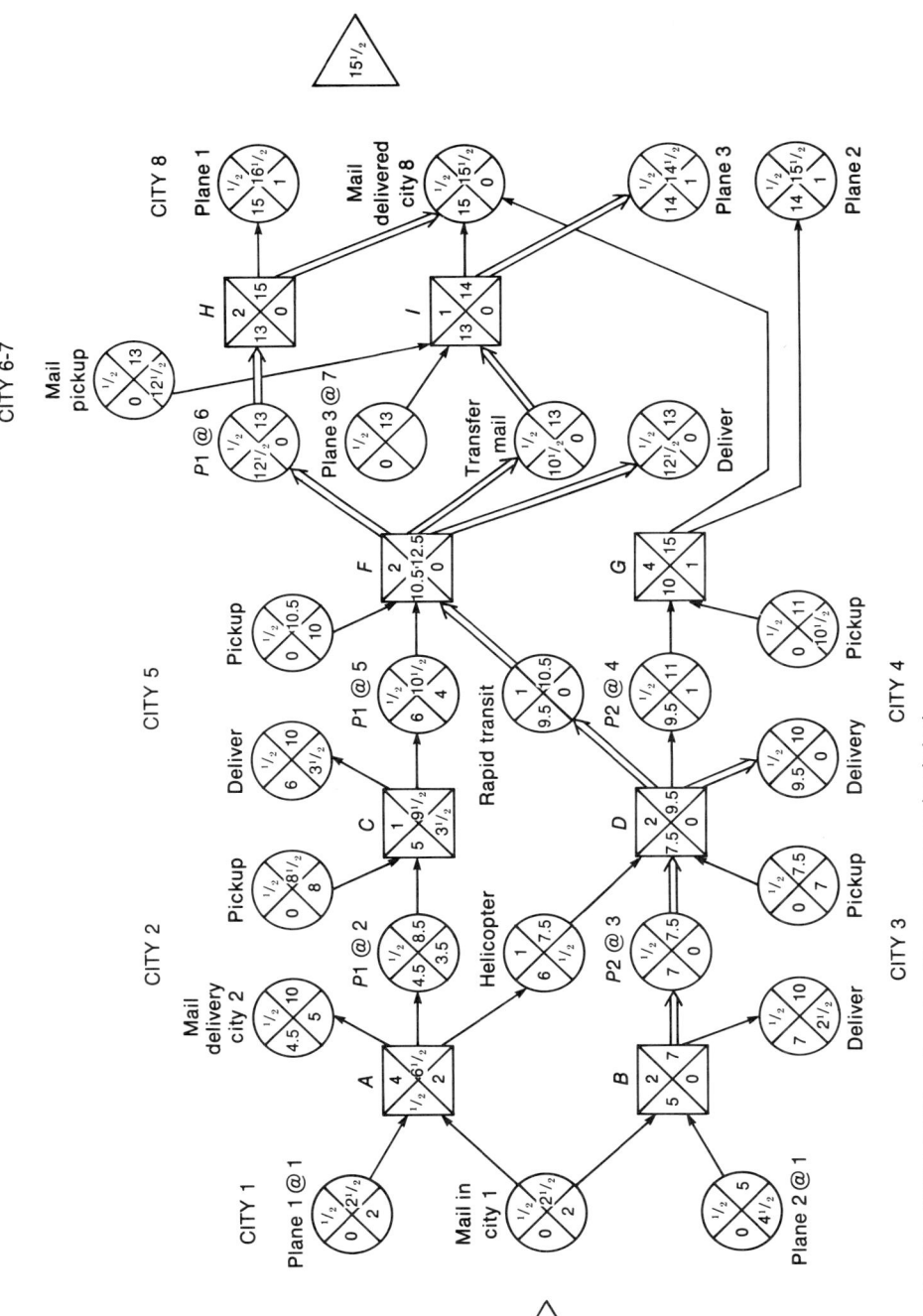

Figure 11-22 WAM RPM network with resource scheduled.

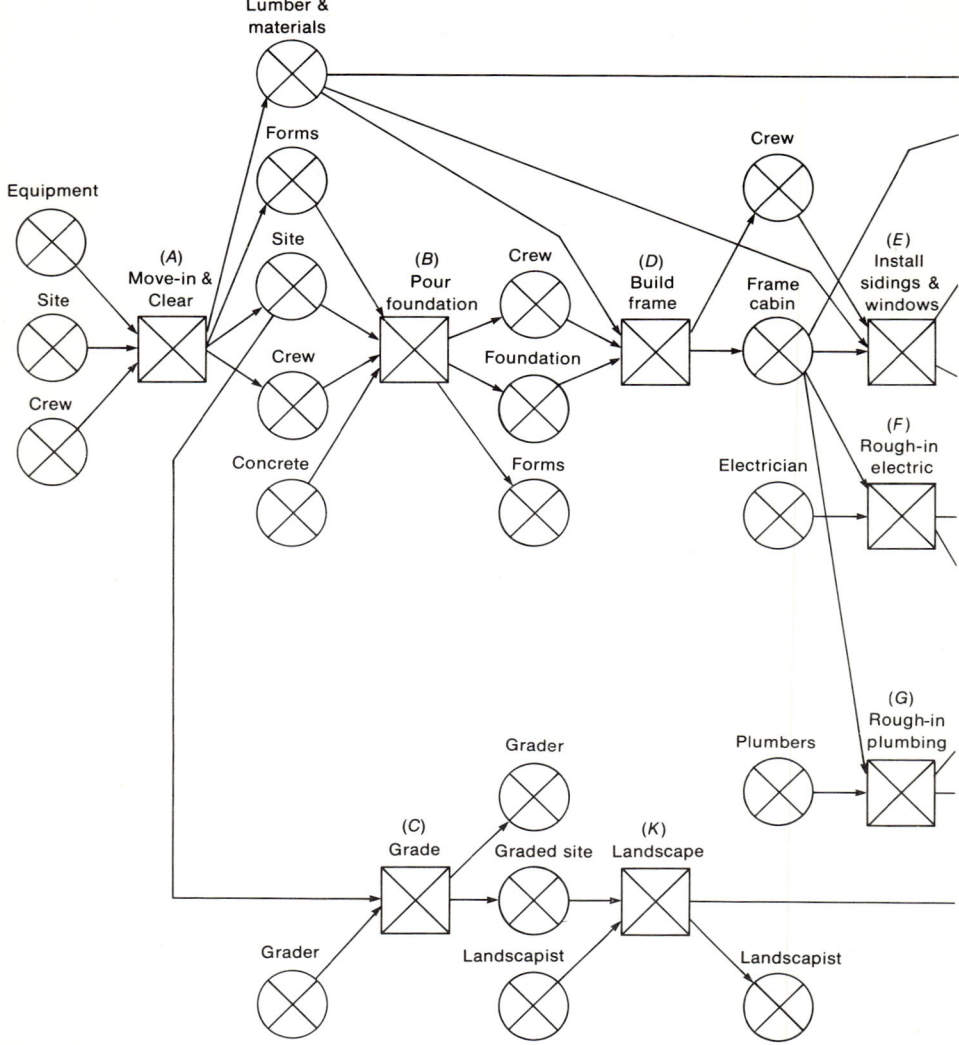

Figure 11-23 RPM network for CPS computations including resource restrictions.

1. The students for industrial training (SIT) decided to bargain for better working conditions in this project. They are asking that a 2-day hardship break be made available between activities involving the use of student crews.
2. The grader will not be available until the tenth day of the project.
3. The landscaper is needed on another project by the twentieth day of this project.

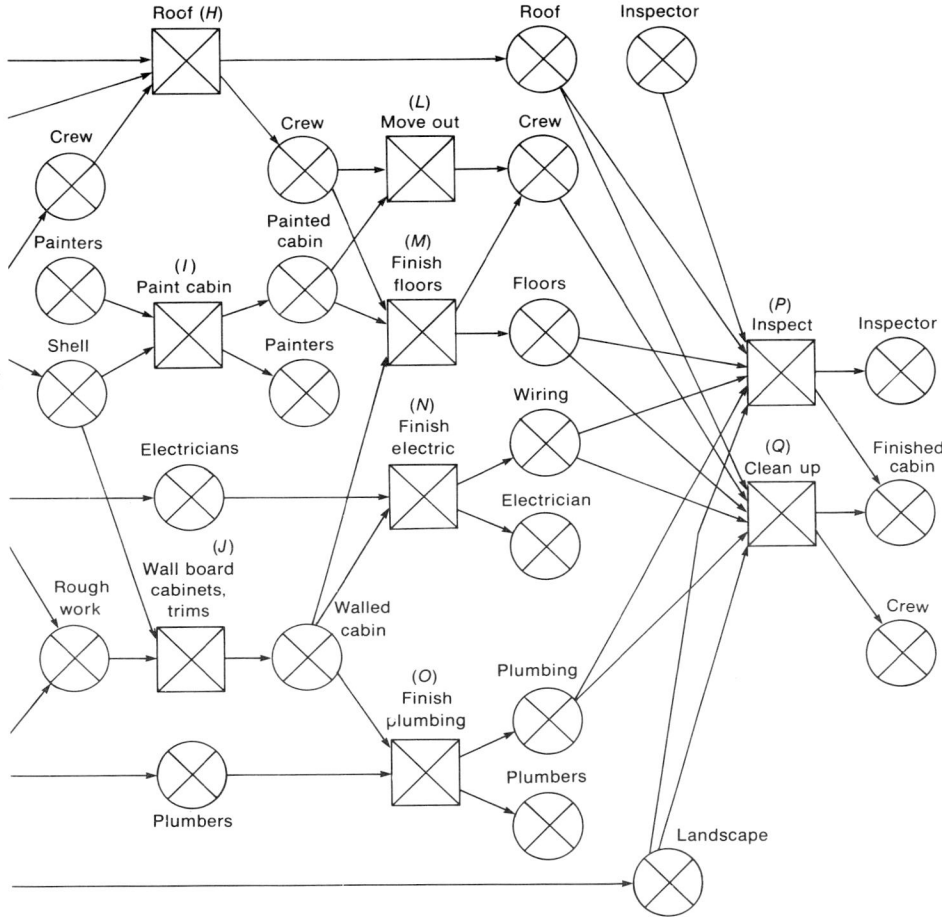

4. Two days must be included to dry the painted cabin before undertaking any other activity on the cabin.

5. It is being proposed that the plumbers do the painting instead of painters.

Include the estimated time (DUR) for each activity and the above conditions in the RPM network of Figure 11-23. Compute the earliest, latest, and total float schedules.

11-6 LP interpretation of scheduling problems

In RPMS so far we have become accustomed to minimizing our expenditures and maximizing our total return. Ever since our application of RPMS concepts to game theory models in Chapter 6, we have learned to ask nature to be our partner in optimization: If we maximized our outputs, we asked nature to minimize the inputs, and vice versa. In scheduling, we have used *time* as our essential resource, and we have acted as though we had control over this resource. It is possible to set up a scheduling model that tries to minimize the *time budget* for going from the source to the sink, which would lead us to a shortest-path problem in contrast with the CPS longest-path problem.

SHORTEST-PATH PROBLEM Consider the WAM problem of Figure 11-11 (Example 11-1), which is reproduced as part of Figure 11-24. Let us assume that our concern is merely to find a passage from city 1 to city 8 that would minimize the total flight time for air freight of a perishable commodity. The RPM network interpretation of this model is straightforward (Figure 11-24*b*), and so are the primal and dual LP representations. Figure 11-24*c* illustrates the shortest-path solution. Note that the resource-node values indicate event times while the residues in activities correspond to the slack available. The shortest path is *B-D-K-F-I* as indicated by activities which carry the primal value of 1.

LONGEST-PATH PROBLEM Converting from the shortest-path problem, where the inputs (activity durations) are minimized, to the longest-path problem, where the inputs must be maximized, is a simple matter of exchanging the minimizing source node with the maximizing sink node. An optimal solution (critical path) can indeed be found in this manner. Unfortunately, the event times (resource-node values) computed using this approach will indicate a *countdown* of the time budget; that is, the first node will have the highest event time, gradually decreasing to zero at the last node. This is a natural accounting practice for capital budgeting and for stating lead time in line-of-balance applications, but it is contrary to our practice for evaluating time schedules.

We do not usually count down to the completion of a project (except, perhaps, for the last few hours before blasting off a spacecraft) but rather count up from day 1. In critical path scheduling the progress of a project is traditionally measured by the days spent rather than days remaining.

To reconcile this difference, we must make sure that an activity *I-J* has event time t_I to be smaller than t_J by at least the duration DUR of the activity. Thus $t_J > t_I + \text{DUR}$, and the arrow direction must point toward the earlier (smaller) event time, contrary to the arrow-network convention. In fact, in CPS it is common practice to write the precedence restriction as $A < B$ and indicate this by the chain of activities $_o\overset{A}{\rightarrow}_o\overset{B}{\rightarrow}_o$. Figure 11-25 illustrates these concepts by comparing the arrow network solution with the RPM solution. Note that the values of the resource nodes are earliest start (ES) times while the residues of activities are the total floats (TF), and critical paths join nodes with zero residues.

It is significant to note the role played by nature. In the game problem, nature assigned probabilities to resource nodes; here, it assigns the event times as we decide on which activities to include in our critical paths.

SECTION 11-6 TUNE-UP

Using the following list of activity durations and restrictions, construct an arrow network and solve both the shortest and longest-path problems using RPMS.

Activities	Durations	Constraints
A	2	A < C, D
B	3	B < E
C	4	C < E
D	9	
E	6	

11-7 Time-cost tradeoff

At the beginning of this chapter we noted that the original CPS programming included cost optimization as an integral part of its scheduling procedure. Early computer programs (such as LESS/COST and PECOS) were all excellent programs created explicitly for optimizing CPS projects. All these programs were parametric in nature, meaning that an optimal schedule was produced for each discrete project-time duration; the total cost for the project was then computed for each project duration, and the lowest cost schedule was chosen. With our knowledge of the LP interpretation of the longest-path problem it is possible to set up a linear model that will provide us directly with the optimal total-project cost schedule.

COST ANALYSIS As mentioned previously, a project is often considered to be a cost center responsible for its own budget and resource allocation. The expenses are then divided into two groups: direct cost, associated with activities, and indirect cost, associated with the management of the overall project. For the sake of optimization, it is convenient to distinguish among three types of costs: fixed cost, which is invariant and must be encumbered if the project is to be carried out at all; direct cost, which varies inversely proportional to the duration of each activity; and indirect cost, which varies proportionately to the total project duration. The approximate relationships between direct and indirect costs are shown in Figure 11-26. It should be noted that these costs may or may not vary linearly—some have quantum jumps, and others have irregular curves—but a fair analysis of time-cost tradeoff is possible by assuming piecewise linear approximation.

The main idea behind the optimization in time-cost tradeoff is to shorten activities to save indirect costs until direct costs start to cost more than the saving. In Figure 11-26, going from time 8 to 7, the indirect cost has decreased $30 and the direct cost has increased $28; going from time 7 to 6, on the other hand, the

THE SHORTEST-PATH (NOT CPS) PROBLEM

(a) Arrow network (artificial dummy omitted)

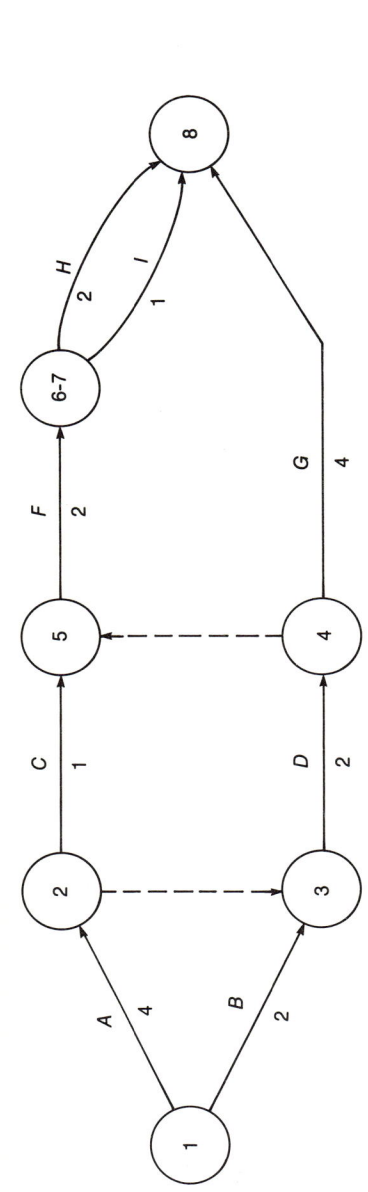

(b) RPM network

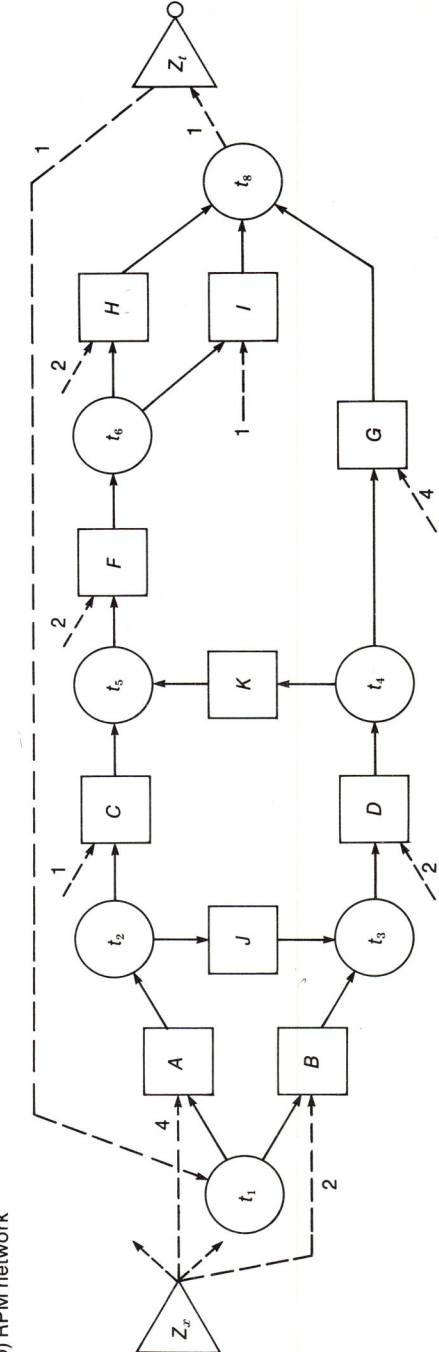

373

PRIMAL MODEL

min $Z_x = 4A + 2B + 1C + 2D + 2F + 4G + 2H + 1I$

subject to $1 \geq A + B$ at t_1
$A \geq C + J$ at t_2
$B + J \geq D$ at t_3
$D \geq K + G$ at t_4
$C + K \geq F$ at t_5
$F \geq H + I$ at t_6
$H + I + G \geq 1$ at t_8

All values nonnegative

DUAL MODEL

max $Z_t = t_8 - t_1$

subject to $t_1 + 4 \geq t_2$ at A subject to $t_1 + 2 \geq t_3$ at B
$t_2 + 1 \geq t_5$ at C $t_3 + 2 \geq t_4$ at D
$t_5 + 2 \geq t_6$ at E $t_4 + 4 \geq t_8$ at G
$t_6 + 2 \geq t_8$ at H $t_6 + 1 \geq t_8$ at I
$t_2 \geq t_3$ at J $t_4 \geq t_5$ at K

All values nonnegative

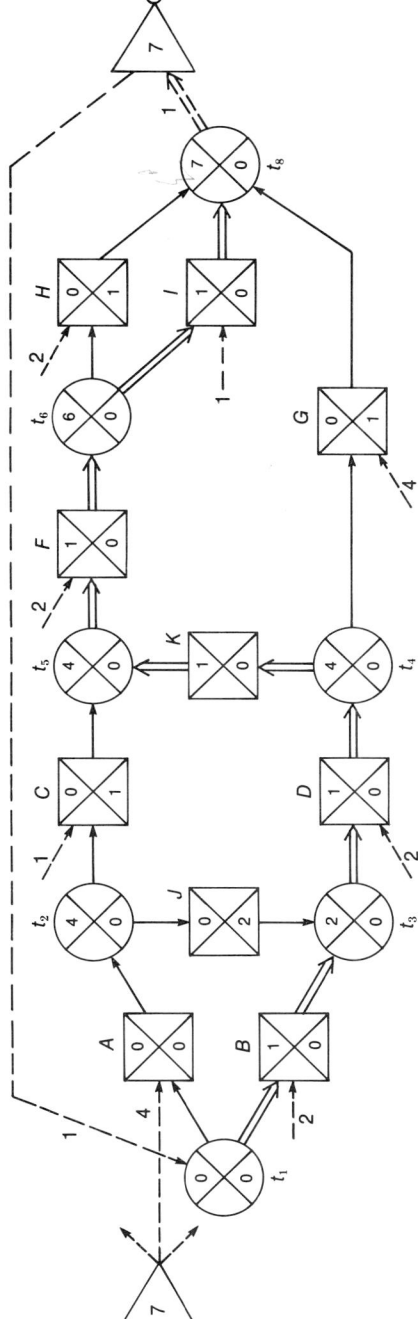

(c) RPM solution showing event time t_j and time residue (float)

Figure 11-24   Shortest route WAM.

374

THE LONGEST-PATH (CPS) PROBLEM

(a) Arrow network showing the critical paths

(b) RPM network accommodating our project schedule convention

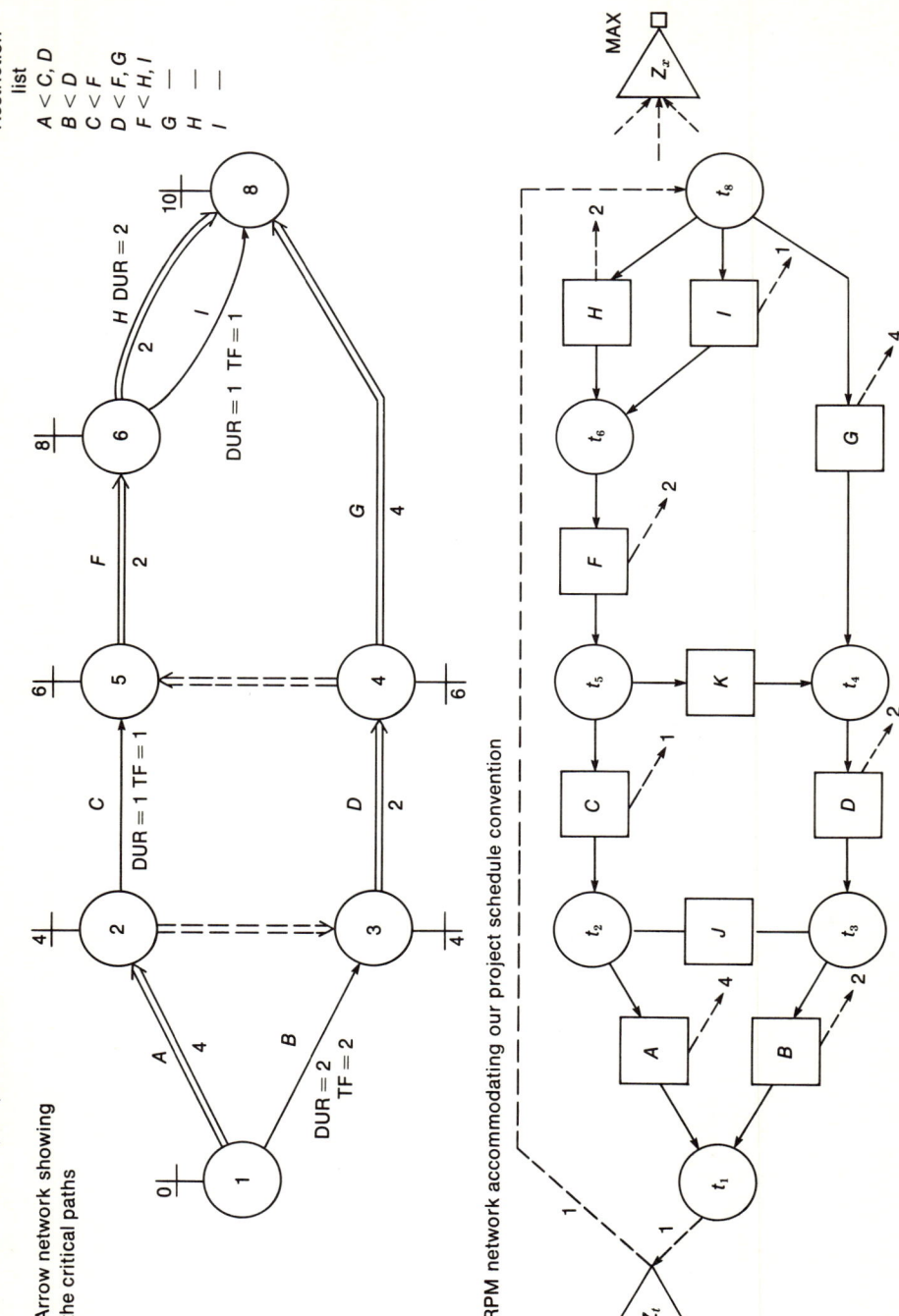

PRIMAL MODEL

max $Z_P = 4A + 2B + 1C + 2D + 2F + 4G + 2H + 1I$

subject to $A + B \geq 1$ at t_1
$C + J \geq A$ at t_2
$D \geq B + J$ at t_3
$G + K \geq D$ at t_4
$F \geq C + K$ at t_5
$H + I \geq F$ at t_6
$1 \geq G + H + I$ at t_8

All values nonnegative

DUAL MODEL

min $Z_t = t_8 - t_1$

subject to $t_2 \geq t_1 + 4$ at A subject to $t_3 \geq t_1 + 2$ at B
$t_5 \geq t_2 + 1$ at C $t_4 \geq t_3 + 2$ at D
$t_6 \geq t_5 + 2$ at F $t_8 \geq t_4 + 4$ at G
$t_8 \geq t_6 + 2$ at H $t_8 \geq t_6 + 1$ at I
$t_3 \geq t_2$ at J $t_5 \geq t_6$ at K

All values nonnegative

(c) RPM network representing a solution (note that the degeneracy could have allowed G to assume 1 and K, F, and H to assume 0 for the same solution)

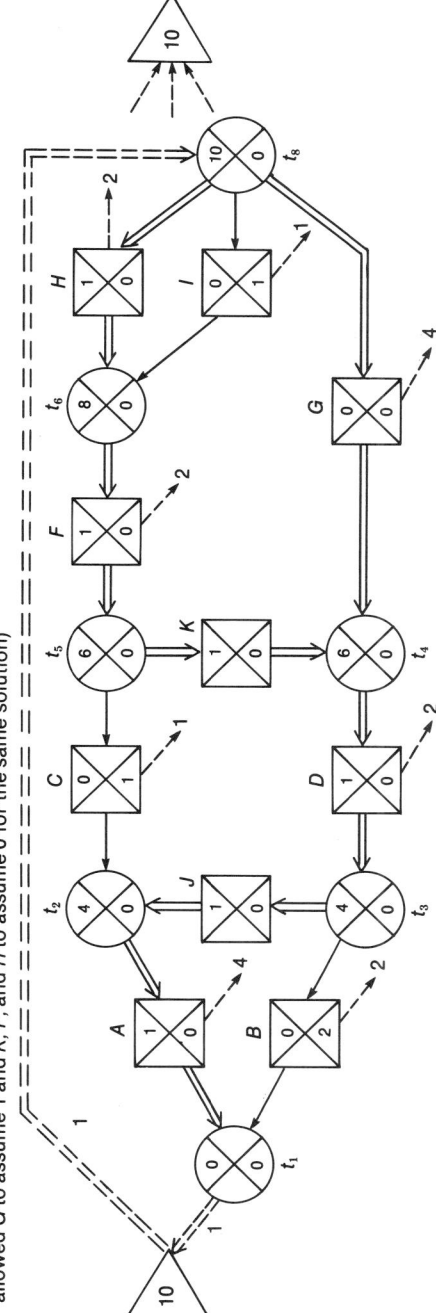

Figure 11-25 Longest-path WAM.

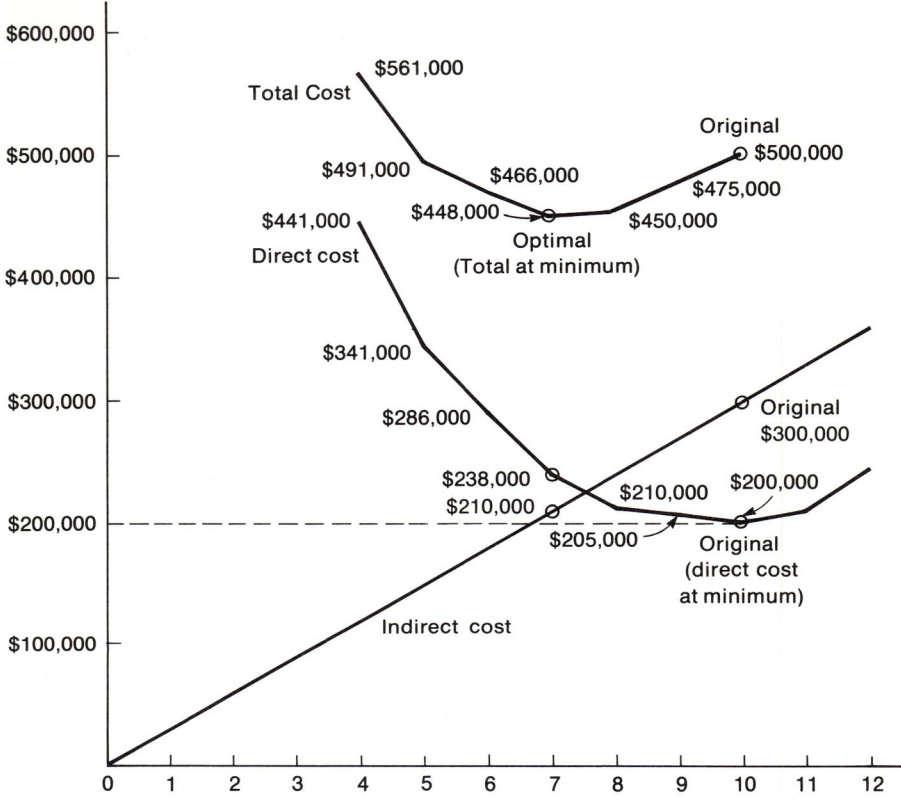

Figure 11-26 Cost curves for varying project duration.

direct cost has increased to $48 versus a $30 saving in indirect cost. The optimum project duration is therefore 7.

If we are free to set the project duration, then we need to achieve a balance between direct and indirect costs. The shorter the project, the more expensive our crashed activities become. Extra crews are hired, workers are paid overtime, additional equipment is rented, and other expensive measures may be adopted. If a project is too long, the administrative overhead increases, workers are kept on payroll for a longer time, warehouse and equipment leases may need to be renewed, and insurance and taxes may increase accordingly. In a time of rapid inflation, the problem may become even more critical. Any profit margin may quickly be eaten up by rising costs.

Even when we are not free to set the project duration, savings can frequently be made by shortening some activities and lengthening others. For a simple project, this may be done by a trial-and-error procedure (Riggs and Heath, 1966, p. 112) or by setting up a dual network comprising possible cuts (J. L. Riggs and M. S.

Implementing the Implementation: Project Planning and Management   377

Inoue, "CPS Tableau Method, "*Proc. AIIE Conference*, 1966, pp. 273–282). When linearity may be assumed, we can also make use of linear programming.

APPLICATION   The RPM network in Figure 11-25 showed a flow of 1 from node t_8 through a critical path to t_1. This use of 1 is similar to the $\mathscr{E}$ that was used in Chapter 10 to indicate the execution of those activities containing this as their primal value. Instead of using this fictitious quantity, we can "buy" the project duration by paying the indirect cost at t_8; then, we will try to recoup this expense by accumulating a direct-cost saving at each activity. Thus, no project duration will be bought that cannot be paid back by an equivalent saving. These concepts are presented in Figure 11-27.

Example 11-2: Time-cost tradeoff for WAM Returning to the Wonderland airmail (WAM) service of Example 11-1, let us now consider the possibility of optimizing the time-cost tradeoff. The service now requires 10 hr from city 1 to city 8, and it is estimated that the indirect cost is being accumulated at the rate of $30,000/hr,

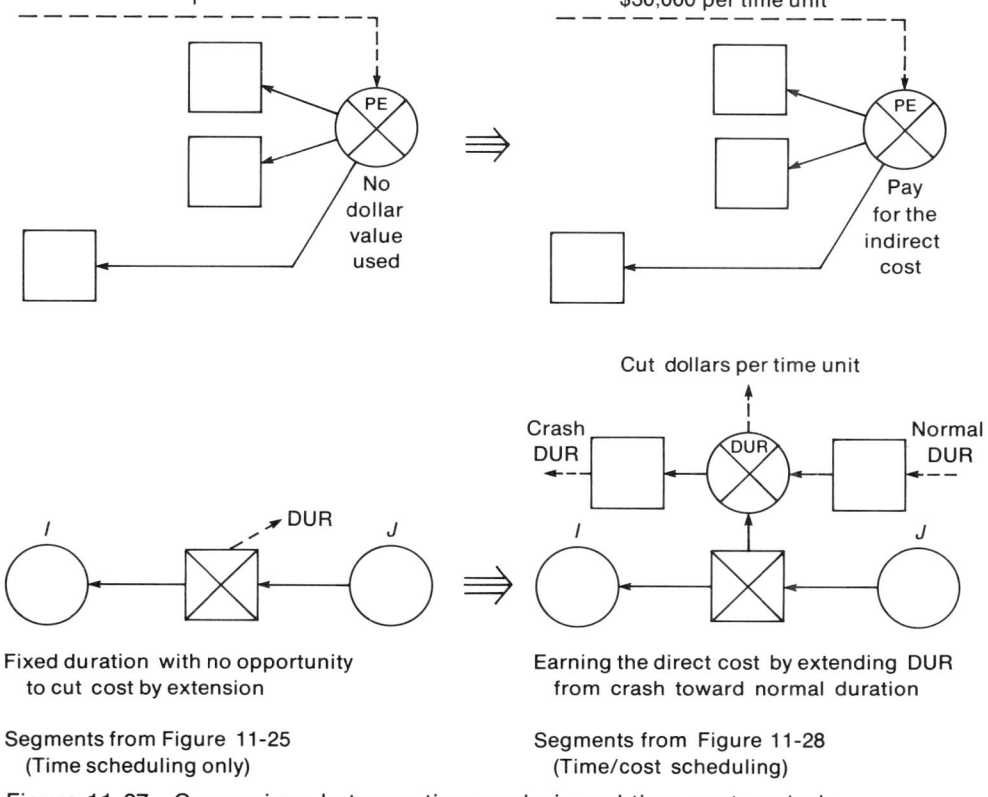

Figure 11-27   Comparison between time analysis and time-cost analysis.

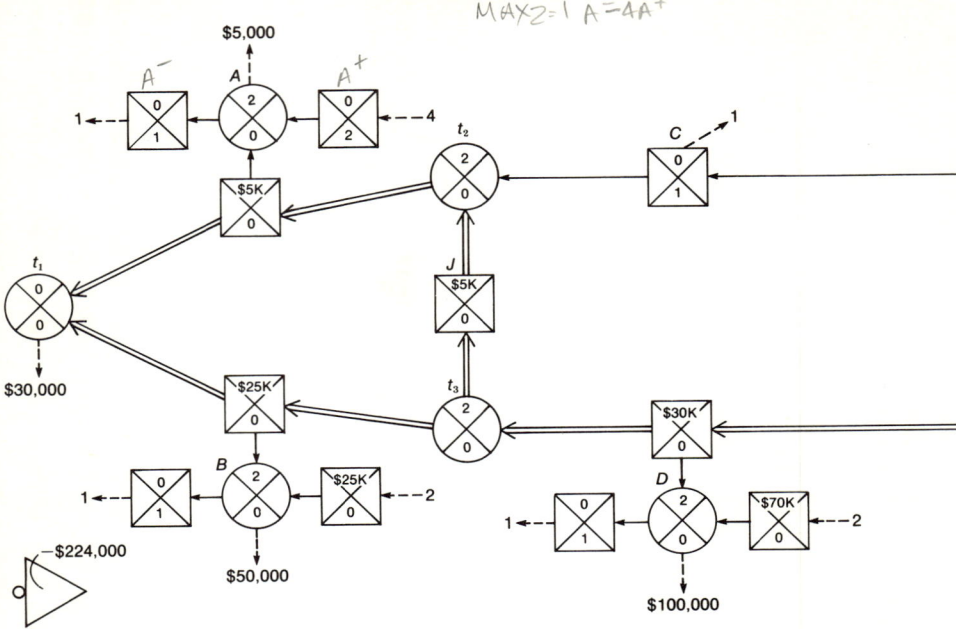

Figure 11-28 RPM LP-network and solution to Example 11-2.

or $300,000/10$ hr. This cost could represent, for example, the socioeconomic effect of mail delay, which must be considered in relation to the cost of speeding up the mail delivery. For different legs of the mail flight service, we have corresponding increases in direct costs, which may include the cost of acquiring a faster type of aircraft that consumes more fuel or the cost of delivering mail at wrong addresses for lack of time to sort mail more carefully. Let us assume that the results can be tabulated as follows.

			Normal (original)		Crashed		Cost slope	
							Thousands of dollars,	
			Time,	Direct cost, thousands of	Time,	Direct cost, thousands of	$S_{ij} = \dfrac{(C_c - C_n)}{(D_n - D_c)}$	
i	j	Activity	D_n	dollars, C_n	D_c	dollars, C_c		$S_{ij}D_c$
1	2	A	4	20	1	35	5/hr	5
1	3	B	2	20	1	70	50/hr	50
2	5	C	1	20	1	20		
3	4	D	2	20	1	120	100/hr	100
5	6	F	2	20	1	30	10/hr	10
4	8	G	4	20	2	56	18/hr	36
6	8	H	2	20	1	50	30/hr	30
6	8	I	1	20	1	20		
2	3	J	0	20	0	20		
4	5	K	0	20	0	20		
Total				200		441		231

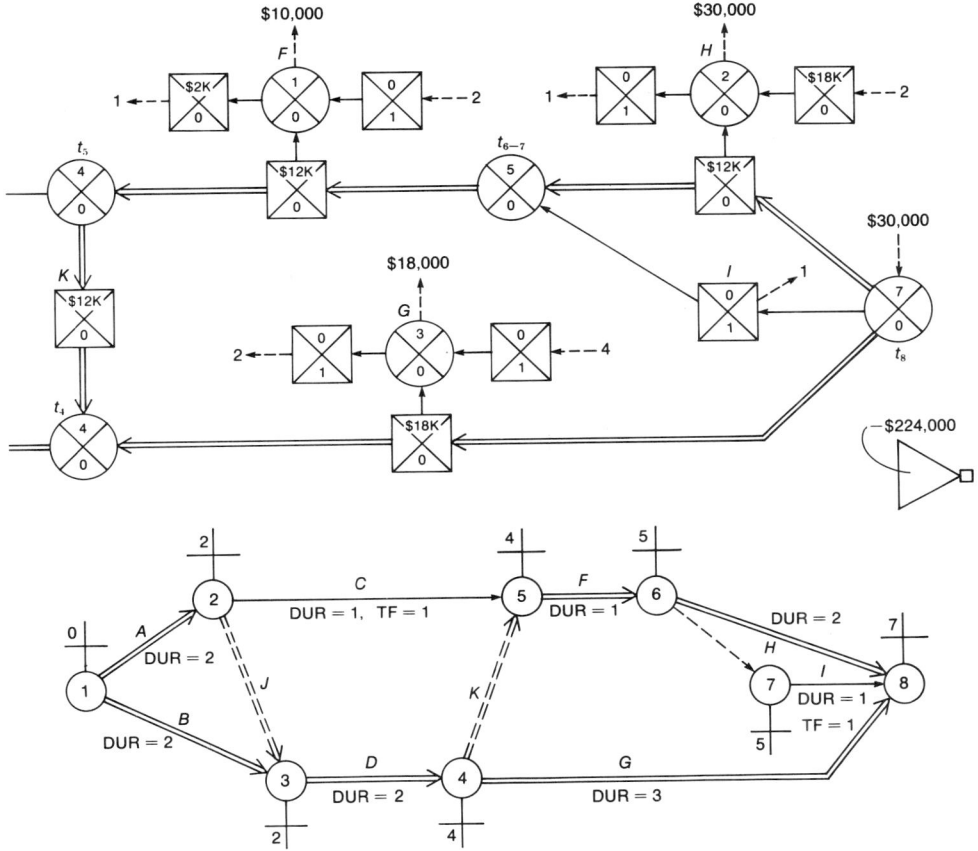

From our discussion of Figure 11-27, we can set up an LP/RPM network (Figure 11-28). The event nodes indicate the new schedule, completing the entire project in 7 instead of 10 hr. The objective-function value of $-\$224{,}000$ can be translated into the actual project cost by considering it as the saving from the all crashed schedule where the cost slope would start at time 0 for each activity. Thus, the total project cost at the optimum schedule is

$\Sigma C_c + \Sigma S_{ij} D_c +$ (RPM objective function value) $= \$441{,}000 + \$231{,}000 - \$224{,}000 = \$448{,}000$.

The actual cost curves for this example are illustrated in Figure 11-26. To obtain any specific duration other than the optimal $t_8 = 7$, we can force t_8 to assume that value by freezing it with a dummy activity node. In a simple problem like this one, we can identify an optimal schedule for each project duration from a time-scaled arrow network (known as a *time chart*). Figure 11-29 illustrates the time chart for the original problem and for the optimal solution. The costs indicated on charts are the additional expenses incurred when the activity is shortened by that

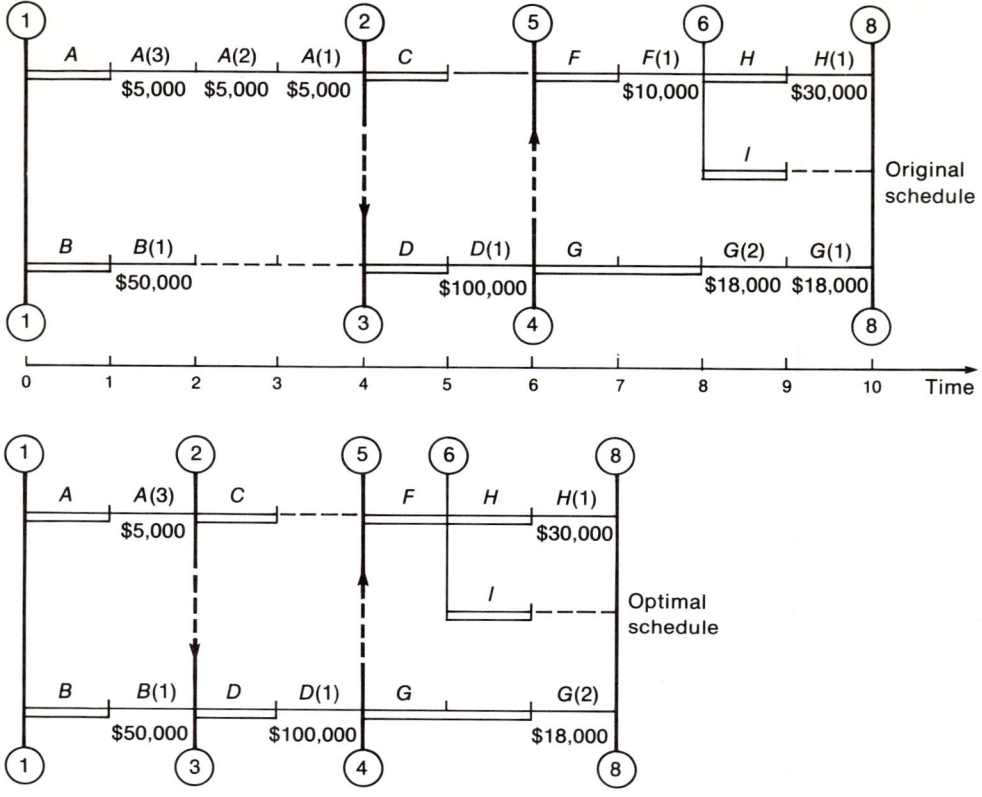

Figure 11-29 Time charts for the WAM time-cost tradeoffs (Example 11-2).

time length (1 hr). The minimum cut from the top to the bottom of the chart identifies the optimal increase in direct cost for reducing the project by 1 day. Thus the first cut from the 10-hr schedule was made through $A(1)$ and the float from B, the second in the same way with $A(2)$, the third through $F(1)$ and $G(1)$, and so on. The results are the same as when using the LP algorithm.

11-8 PERT probability analysis

An important contribution of PERT is its ability to make an estimate as to when a project will be completed, or more exactly, the probability of completing a project by a target date. The procedure is simple once the three time estimates are obtained for each activity. The estimated duration is computed by using the formula already introduced in Section 11-2:

$$t_e = \frac{a + 4m + b}{6}$$

After the critical path(s) has been determined, we use the formula

$$V = \left(\frac{b-a}{6}\right)^2$$

to compute the variance along the critical path and take the square root of the sum to obtain the standard deviation. When there is more than one critical path, the one with the largest total variance is chosen. The standardized deviation of the estimated project completion t_p from the target time t_t is computed as

$$Z = \frac{t_t - t_p}{\sqrt{\Sigma V}}$$

and the normal distribution table is used to find the probability of meeting the target date.

Example 11-3: *WAM PERT* In Example 11-1 let us assume that the three times estimates were obtained for each flight. It is desired to compute the probability of the mail being delivered by 9 A.M., 10 A.M., and noon and to estimate what arrival time at city 8 will have at least 80 percent probability.

Activity	Time estimates			Estimated Duration, $t_e = \dfrac{a+4m+b}{6}$	Variance, $V = \dfrac{(b-a)^2}{36}$
	Optimistic, a	Most likely, m	Pessimistic, b		
A	3	4	8	4.5	0.6944
B	1	2	3	2	0.1111
C	1	1	1	1	0.0
D	2	2	6	2.667	0.4444
F	1	2	2	1.833	0.0278
G	2	4	10	4.667	1.7778
H	2	2	2	2	0.0
I	1	1	6	1.833	0.6944

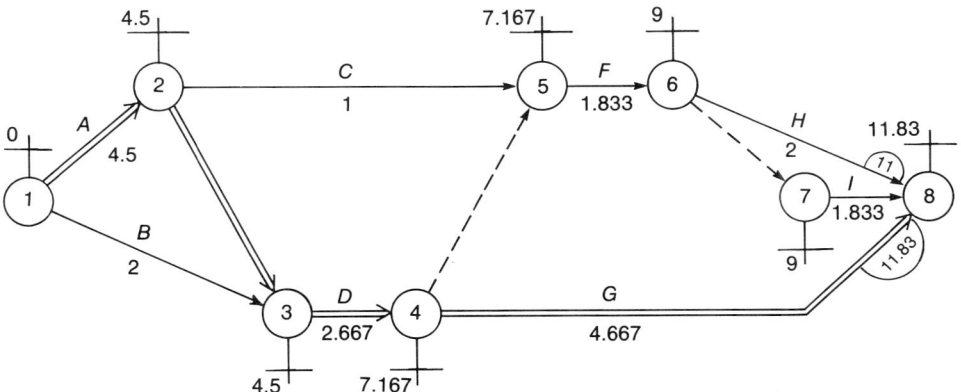

The variance along the critical path sums to

$$0.6944 + 0.4444 + 1.7778 = 2.91664 = (1.708)^2$$

The probability of arriving before 9 A.M. corresponds to

$$Z = \frac{9 - 11.83}{1.708} = -1.657$$

or 5 percent from the table. The probability of arriving before 10 A.M. corresponds to

$$Z = \frac{10 - 11.83}{1.708} = -1.07$$

or 15 percent from the table. And the probability of arriving by noon is

$$Z = \frac{12 - 11.83}{1.708} = 0.0995$$

or 54 percent from the table. To obtain the arrival time with 80 percent probability at city 8, we need $Z = 0.85$. Then

$$0.85 \times 1.708 + 11.83 = 13.3$$

and 1:20 P.M. is the earliest arrival time with the 80 percent confidence level.

TUNE-UP SOLUTIONS

1

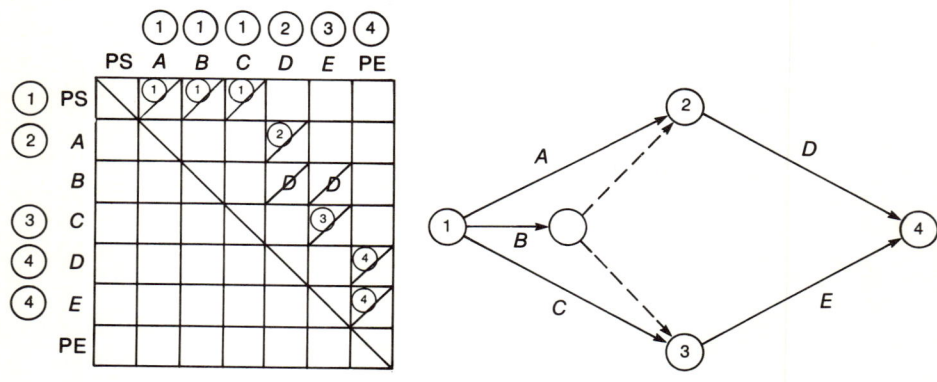

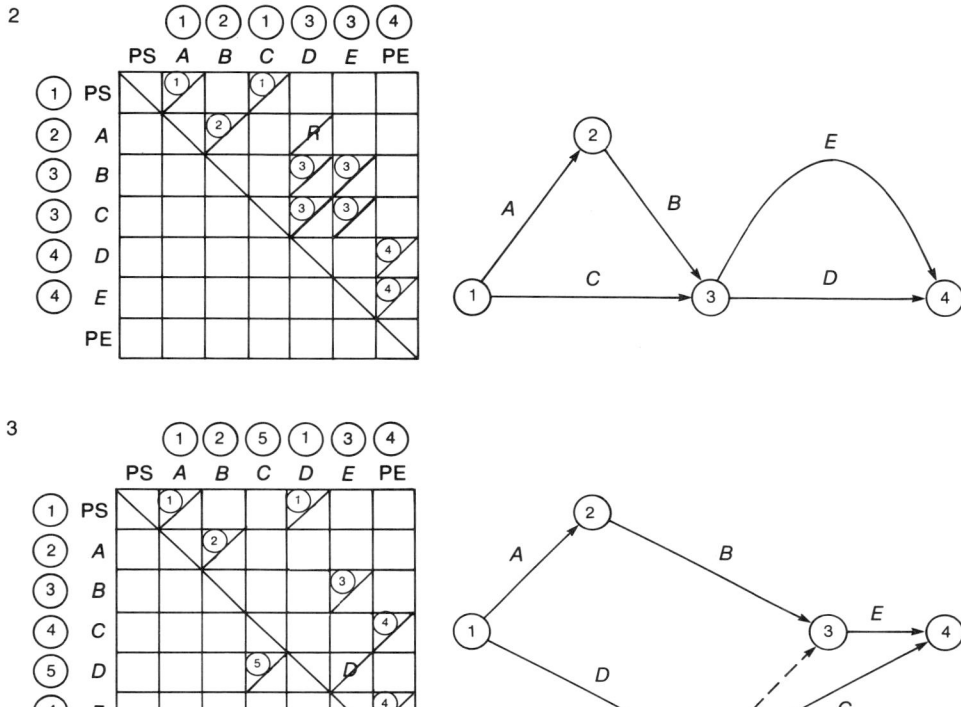

Section 11-3

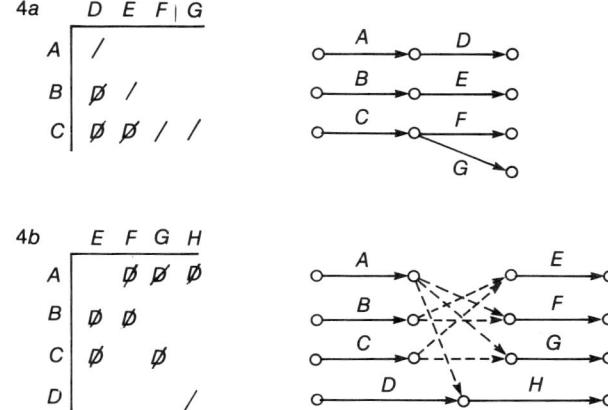

4c

	D	E	F	G	H
A	/	/	Ø		
B			Ø	/	/
C	/	/	Ø		

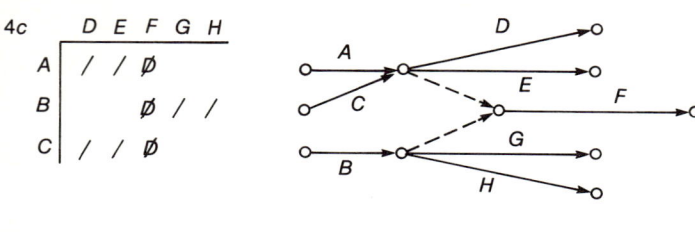

4d

	F	G	H	I	J	K
A	/		/	/	/	
B	/		/	/	/	
C		/				/
D	/		/	/	/	
E		/				/

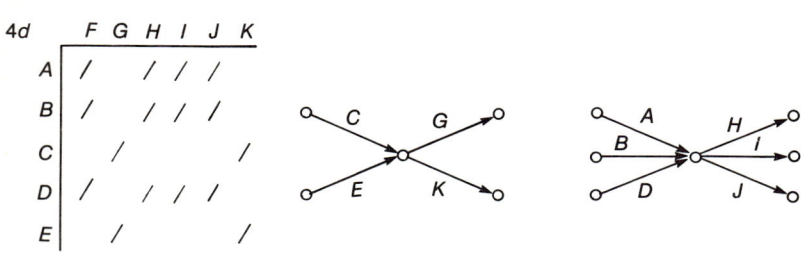

Section 11-4

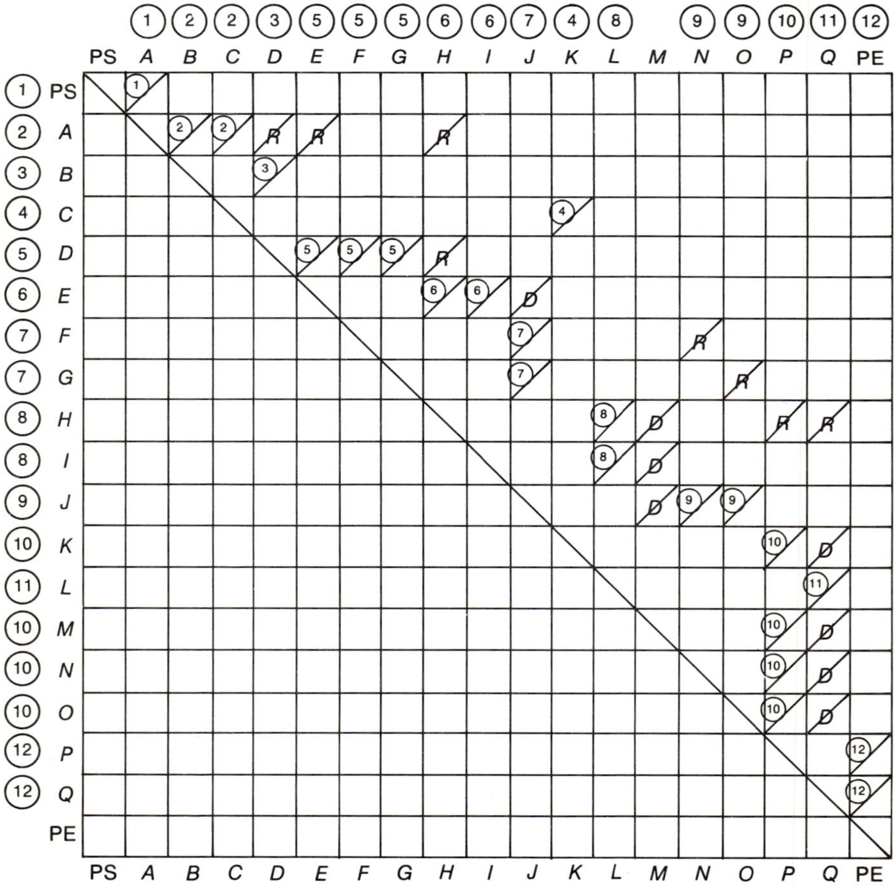

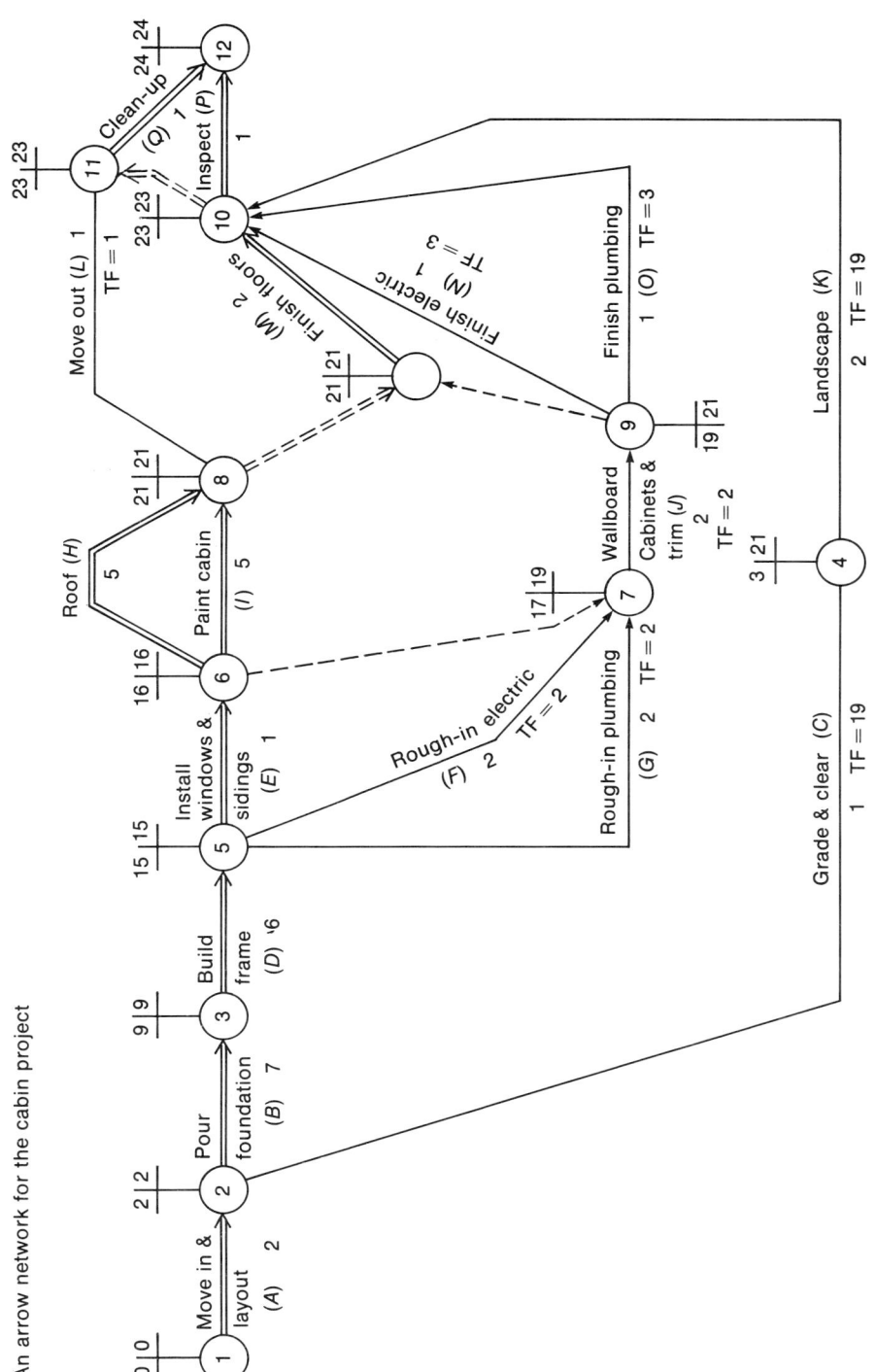

An arrow network for the cabin project

Section 11-5

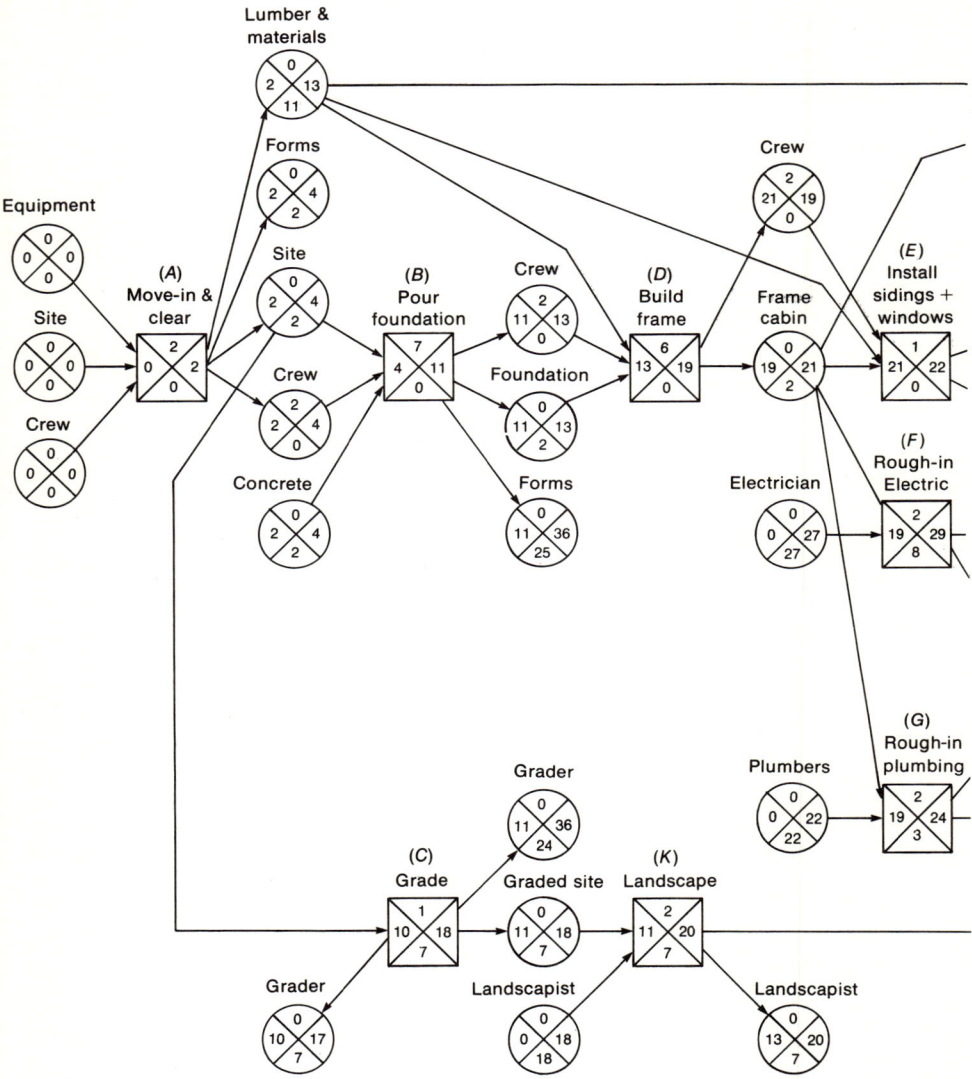

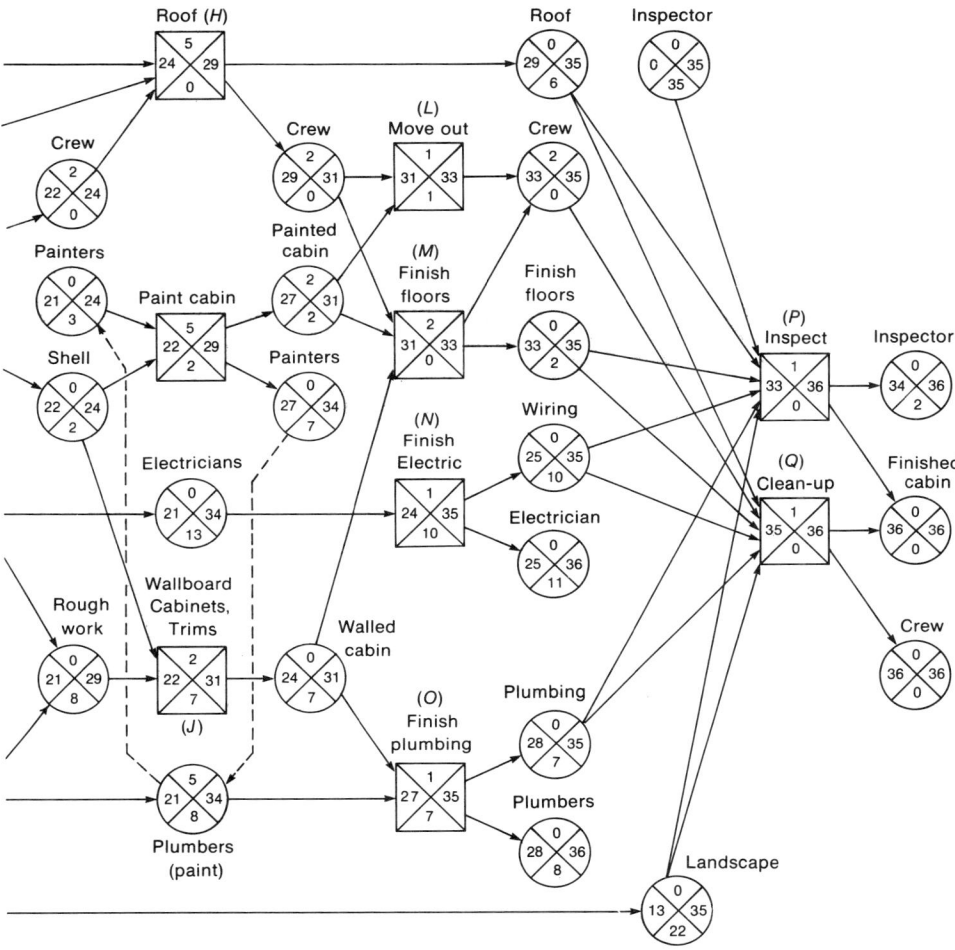

Section 11-6

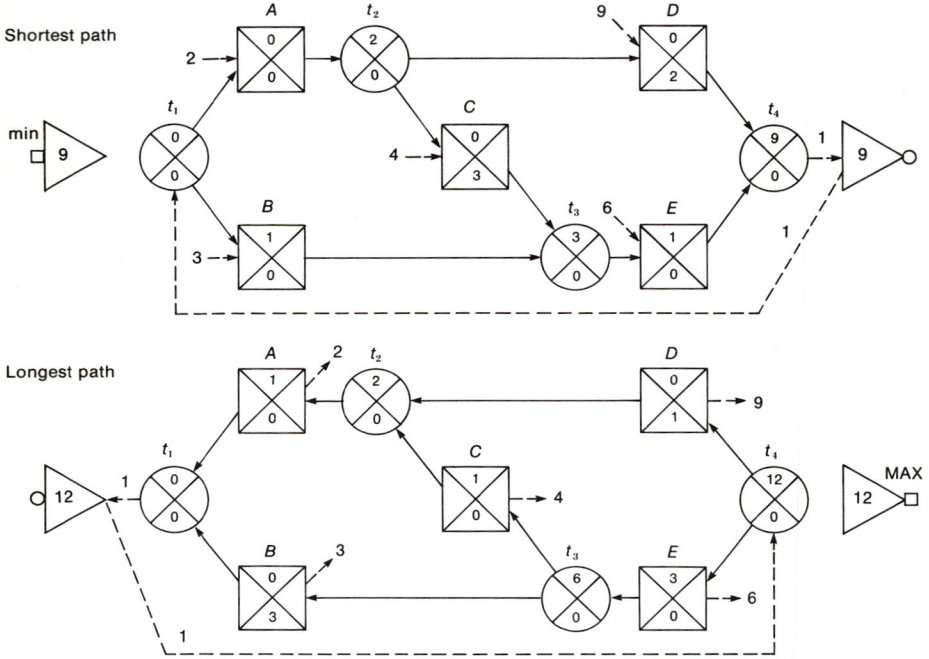

EXERCISES

11-1 Construct arrow network segments for the following precedence relations.

(a)

	D	E	F	G
A	/	/		
B		/	/	
C			/	/

(b)

	E	G	H	I	J
A	/	/		/	
B			/		/
C	/	/		/	
D	/	/		/	
E				/	/

(c)

	E	F	G	H
A	/		/	
B		/	/	
C		/		/
D	/			/

(d)

	E	F	G	H
A	/	/	/	/
B		/	/	/
C			/	/
D				/

11-2 The following RPM *P*-network has been prepared to show the process of preparing and mailing an advertisement brochure (all time data are in days).

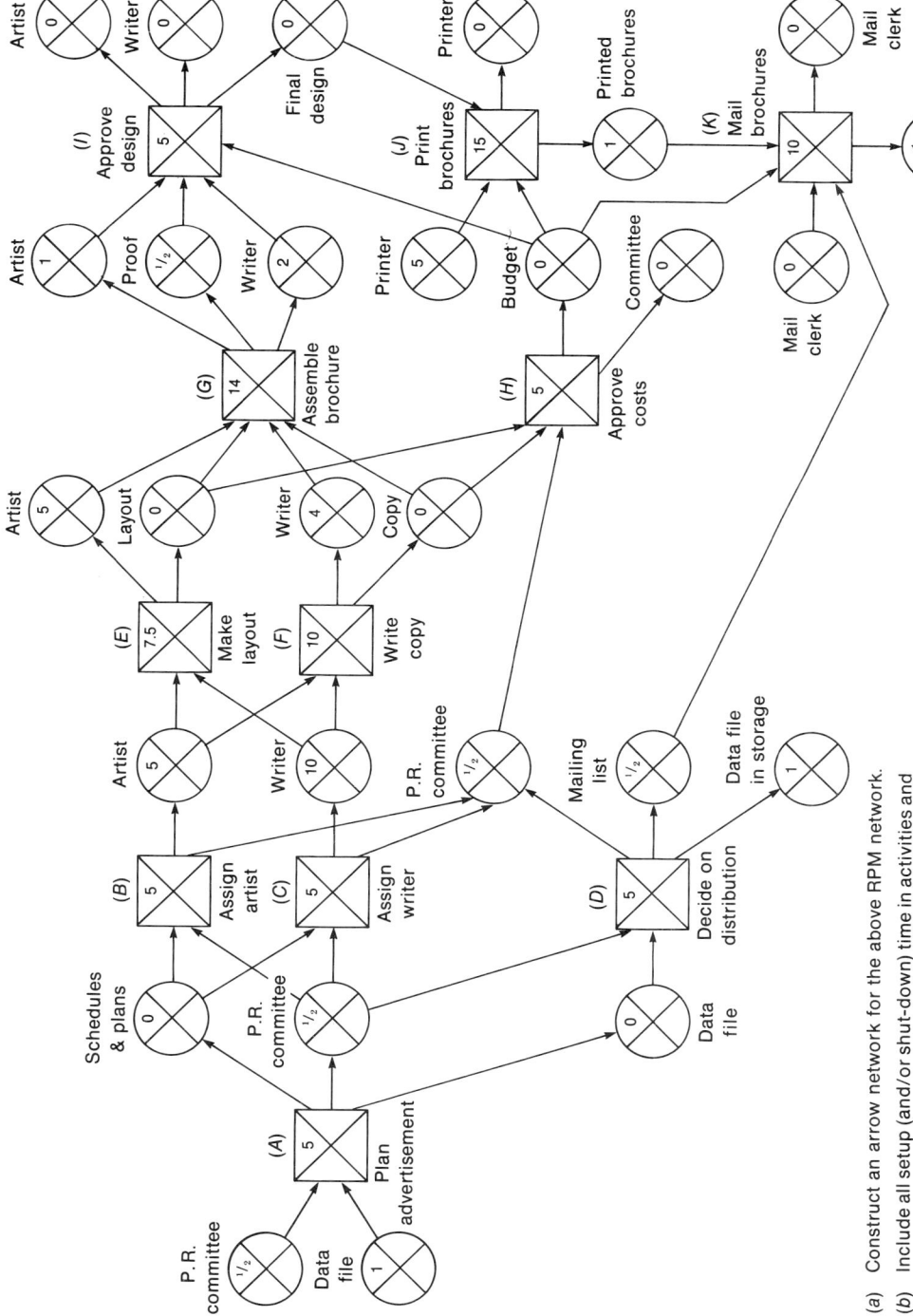

(a) Construct an arrow network for the above RPM network.
(b) Include all setup (and/or shut-down) time in activities and compute the earliest and latest schedules on your arrow network.
(c) Identify all critical activities.

11-3 In Exercise 11-2, compute all activity and resource times for the RPM *P*-network and answer the following questions, assuming the project is completed in $83^{1}/_{2}$ days.

  a. When will the data file be put back in storage?
  b. When should the printer be informed of this job?
  c. When can your clients expect to receive your brochures?
  d. What will be the total duration of your committee assignment on this task?
  e. If the committee could work only one task at a time, what effect would this have on the total project completion?
  f. If the artist must work on another job for 5 consecutive days while this project is in progress (say, between activities *B* and *I*) what schedule change should be allowed to least affect the project completion?

11-4 In Exercise 11-2, the committee is composed of four people and the normal processing costs are $100/hr (the setup and shutdown costs are constant). Processing can be speeded up proportionately by increasing the work force: what is done in 5 days by a committee of 4 will take 2.5 days by a committee of 8, et cetera. The minimum crash time for any activity is $^1/_2$ day, or 4 hr. Discuss how you would model such a situation on LP.

11-5 Using the data in the RPM network and CPS arrow network on page 391 portraying its solution,

  a. Compute the objective function value of the RPM network.
  b. State the dual LP model.
  c. Interpret the original problem.
  d. Knowing that the crash direct cost for each activity is $1,000 per activity, compute the actual total project cost for the optimal solution shown in the networks.

11-6 The two projects on pages 392, 393 are to be undertaken using the same electrician and painters. Find an integrated schedule that will minimize the total time required to complete both projects.

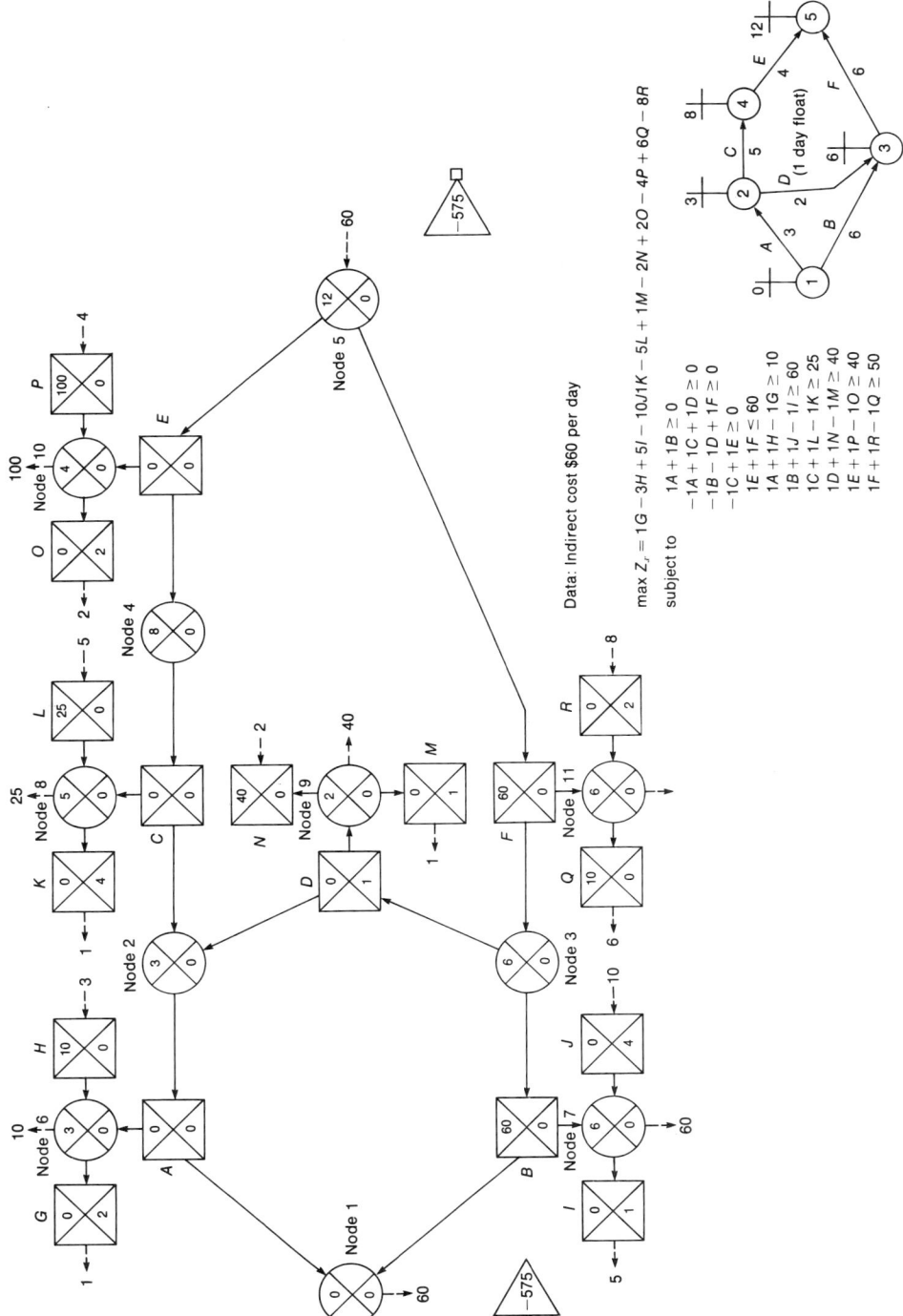

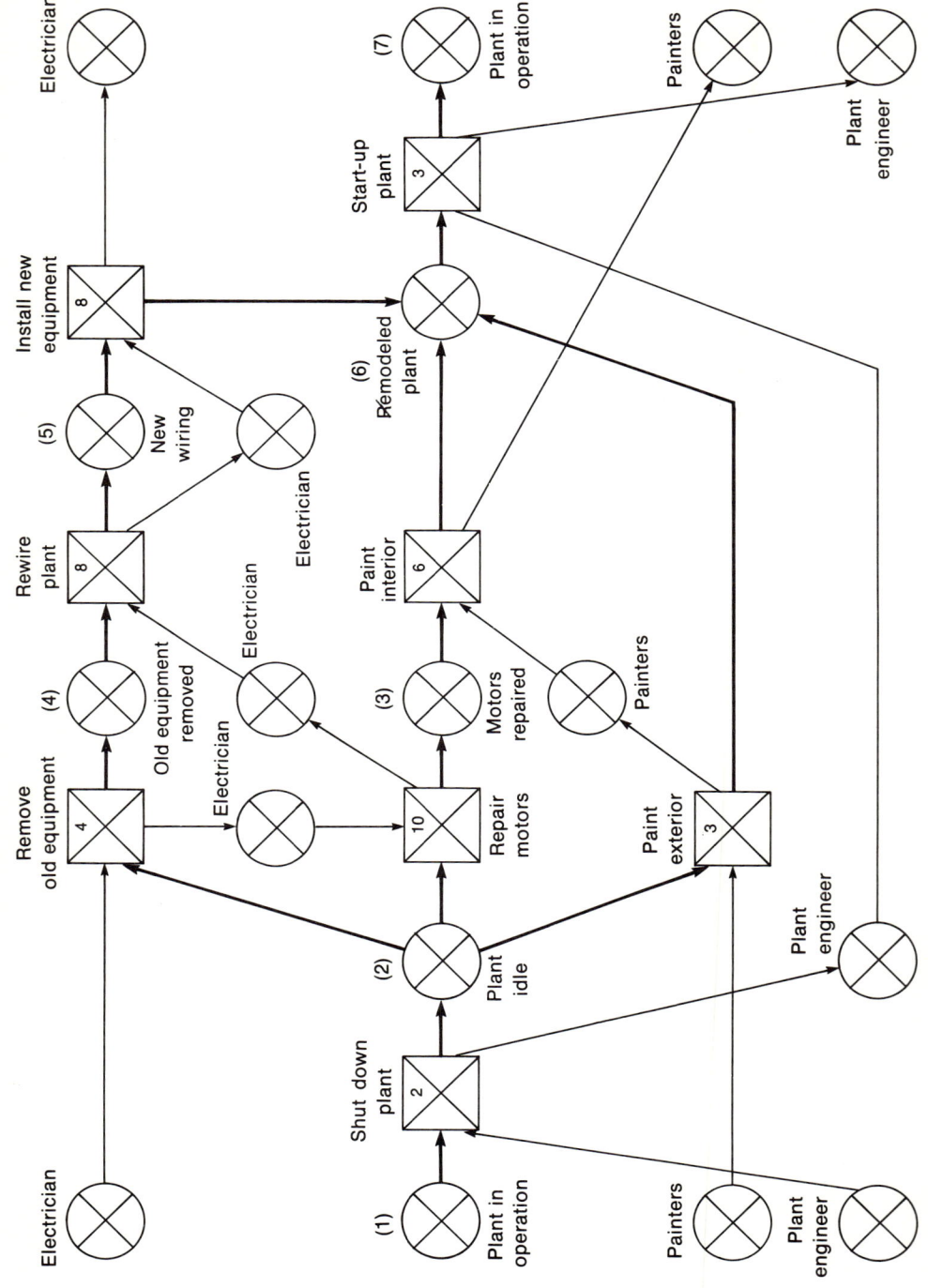

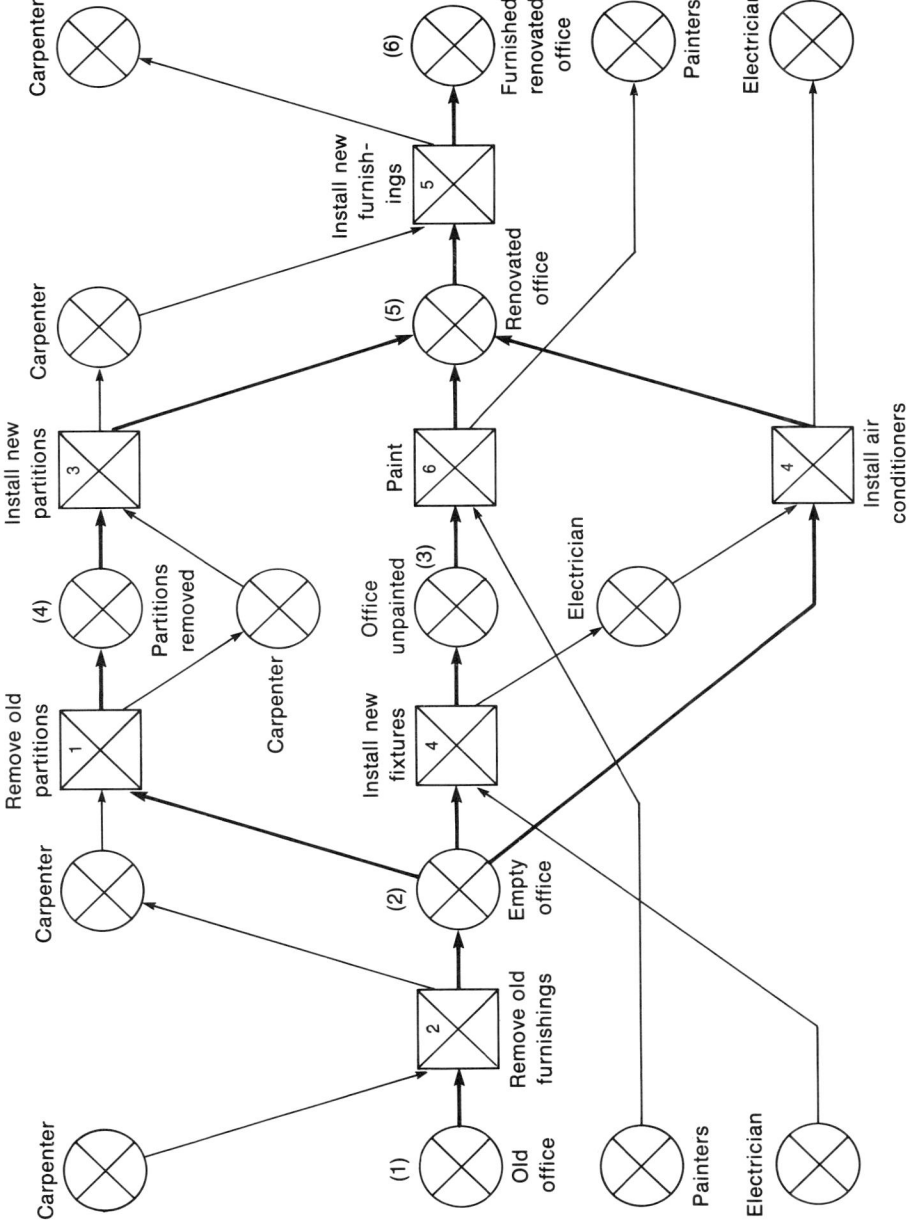

SYSTEMS EVALUATION: Queuing Models and Simulation

Chapter 12

12-1 Diagnostic tools for systems

The job of an OR/MS researcher is not finished when a system has become successfully implemented. The fact that the system was obviously feasible and adequate (if not optimal) at the time of implementation does not discharge the OR/MS practitioner's responsibility to watch over its performance during its lifetime. A civil engineer who designed a bridge would be held responsible for its collapse even if the collapse occurs after many years of satisfactory service.

Not only is it the responsibility of the system designer to incorporate a margin of safety and an automatic auditing and correction mechanism into a system, but it is the responsibility of the entire OR/MS team to catch any error or obsolescence in a system that has been entrusted to one of its members. The medical profession will stand behind a physician who needs advice on a difficult case; the legal profession does not hesitate to disbar a member who is no longer qualified; and an engineer cannot become registered in any state (or most countries) before having acquired the minimum years of professional experience. In each case, a professional is expected to consult with peers when a problem extends beyond his experience and training. Thus, an OR/MS analyst who suspects that a system is no longer operating satisfactorily should alert the appropriate persons and offer assistance.

Just as a fever is an indication of an individual's failing health, an excessive delay in a system is an indication of its failing effectiveness. When a system is not tuned up properly, it expends resources unnecessarily, and any such "illness" eventually wastes time. A chronic shortage of cash, mis- or uninformed personnel, frequent breakdowns of machinery, and low employee morale are examples of organizational illnesses that usually cause delays. Work stoppages and slowdowns are methods traditionally used by workers to call the attention of the management to the fact that all is not well. Delays, whether avoidable or unavoidable, waste the most precious resource available: time.

An equivalent of a physician measuring the temperature of a patient is an OR/MS researcher comparing the amount of actual delays against what is expected from the system as originally designed. The benchmarks can be established in one of two ways: theoretically or by simulation. From the model of the system, its delay characteristics (such as the average queue length, occupancy rate, and time a customer must spend in the system) can be computed analytically, or the model can be subjected to a set of exogenous conditions simulating the actual environment and system operation. Queuing theory and Monte Carlo simulation are valuable tools in setting these benchmarks.

12-2 Basic queuing theory

Queuing theory originated in the telephone traffic theory, which was developed by the Danish scientist A. K. Erlang (1878-1929) who was concerned about the rapid increase in telephone traffic. Erlang published several fundamental papers during the first quarter of this century, and today he is remembered by a statistical distribution that bears his name, the Erlang distribution. The telephone traffic theory states:

> "*The basic purpose of Telephone Traffic Theory is to find the conditions under which adequate service is given to subscriber demand whilst economic use is made of the facility providing this service.*"[1]

There are several features that distinguish queuing theory and Monte Carlo simulation techniques from other OR/MS techniques we have studied. First, they deal primarily with stochastic models. [Although probabilistic concepts were touched upon in our discussions of Pareto analysis (Chapter 3), game theory (Chapter 7), and PERT (Chapter 11), our emphasis has been on deterministic models.] Second, in spite of the original intent of telephone traffic

---

[1] Petr Beckman, *Introduction to Elementary Queuing Theory and Telephone Traffic*, Golen Press, Boulder, Colo., 1968, p. 10.

theory, neither queuing theory nor the Monte Carlo simulation is an optimization tool per se. Yet, as we shall see later in this chapter, it is possible to make use of the RPM representation to include cost considerations in queuing models. This approach is similar to the procedure (outlined in Chapter 11) of mating a CPS arrow network with RPMS. Instead of an arrow network, however, we shall make use of another network modeling tool that is more adapted to representing state transitions in queuing models: the signal flow graphs.

SIGNAL FLOW GRAPH A signal flow graph (SFG) has an appearance that is almost identical to that of an arrow network. The only distinguishing graphic feature is that the arrow symbol is placed in the middle rather than at an end of the edge joining the two event nodes. The development of the SFG is usually credited to Samuel J. Mason, who published an article on feedback theory in 1953 using SFG notations; but the true origin seems obscure and is thought to have occurred considerably earlier.[1] Arnold Tustin applied the SFG representation to modeling economic structures in "The Mechanism of Economic Systems," also published in 1953.[2]

The basic idea of SFG is simple. It represents variables by circle nodes that resemble event nodes on CPM arrow networks. Functions represented by arrows relate the independent variable at the tail of the arrow to the dependent variable at the head of the arrow. Thus, a simple expression $y = f(x)$ can be expressed by the independent variable node x, the dependent variable node y, and the arrow portraying the transformation $f(\ )$. SFG may be cascaded to show intermediate variables and transformation of dependent variables; therefore,

$$z = g(y) = g[f(x)]$$

can be shown as two arrows in series: $f(\ )$ and $g(\ )$ (Figure 12-1). The most common transformation is a simple multiplication by a constant. In such a case, SFG simply has the scalar value (say, a) in place of the transformation [say, $f(\ )$]. A common addition can be illustrated by parallel arrows, and Figure 12-2b shows how to represent $y = ax_1 + bx_2$.

MARKOV CHAIN The particular application of SFG we are interested in is the representation of *state transition* of a queuing model. For example, a system may be either *idle* (state 0) or *operating* (state 1), and there may be a finite probability that at any time interval the system may move from one state to another. Figure 12-3 shows an example of a state-transition SFG where the transitions are expressed in terms of an average number of jobs arriving every hour, λ, and an average number of jobs that the system can handle every hour, μ. The actual transition will occur from one state to another if the system is in that state and the transition opportunity arises. Thus, the transition rate of the system going

---

[1] For example, C. E. Shannon, "The Theory and Design of Linear Differential Equation Machines," *CSRD Report 411*, Jan., 1942.

[2] Arnold Tustin, *The Mechanisms of Economic Systems*, William Heinemann, 1957.

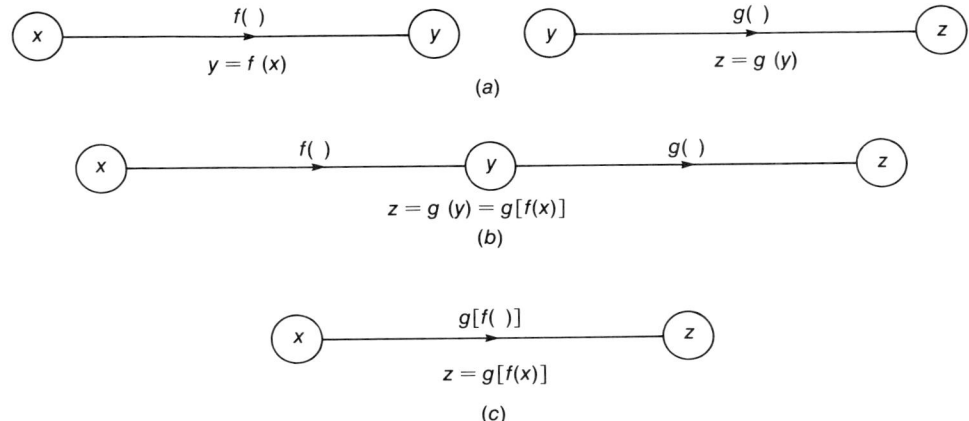

Figure 12-1 Simple SFG cascading.

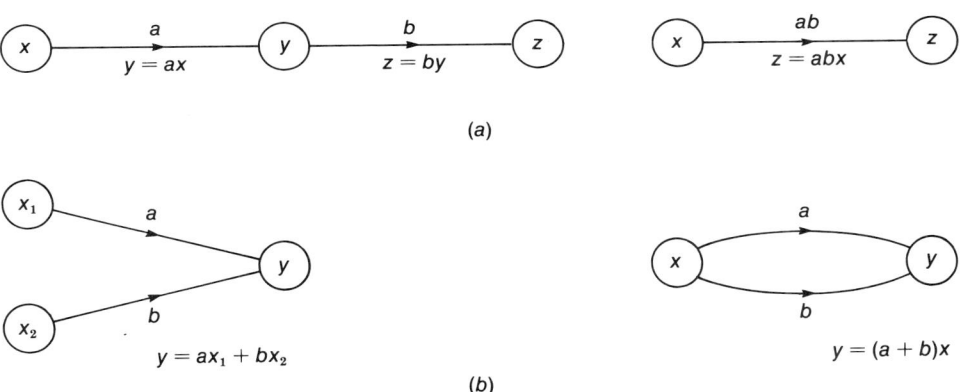

Figure 12-2 Scalar SFG.

Figure 12-3 Simple state-transition SFG expressing a Markov process.

from state 0 (idle) to state 1 (operating) is the probability of being in state 0, P_0, multiplied by the job-arrival rate λ. Similarly, we can express the rate of transition from 1 (operating) to 0 (idle) as the product of the probability of being in state 1 and the service rate μ. The frequency of the system going from idle to busy is obviously the same as that of going from busy to idle, and the two transition rates must equal each other: $\lambda p_0 = \mu p_1$.

The SFG model in Figure 12-3 has the property that the transition from one state to another is dependent only on the probability of being at the particular state at the time of transition and not on the previous history of the system. This "memoryless" feature of not having to remember where the system has been in order to compute the probability of where it will go next is called the *Markovian property* in honor of the Russian mathematician and professor at St. Petersburg, Andrei A. Markov (1856–1922). The SFG model portraying this Markovian property is called a *Markov chain*, or, more strictly, a *first-order Markov chain* (*order* refers to the number of states remembered; *first-order* indicates the dependency on the present state only). Although it is not necessary to make use of SFG or the Markov chain to discuss queuing theory, they provide us a visual map to follow throughout our discussion which is also compatible with our RPMS (Section 12-5).

SECTION 12-2 TUNE-UP

Express the following Markov chains in SFG. (Equations are written inputs = outputs.)

1. $2p_1 = 4p_2$; $4p_2 = 3p_3$; $3p_3 = 2p_1$
2. $5p_2 = 4p_1$; $1p_1 = 2p_3$; $3p_1 + 2p_3 = 4p_4$; $4p_4 = 5p_2$
3. $4p_2 = p_0$; $p_0 + 5p_3 = 2p_1$; $2p_1 = 7p_2$; $3p_2 = 5p_3$
4. $p_0 + 3p_1 = 5p_0$; $4p_0 + 1p_2 + 2p_1 = 7p_1$; $2p_1 + 5p_2 = 6p_2$

12-3 Finite-queue single-server models

A *single-server model* is a queuing system in which one customer is treated at a time. Customers may or may not be allowed to line up on a queue to wait for the service, and the queue length may or may not be limited to a finite length. (The term *customer* is used to mean a job that needs processing.) The common assumption is that a customer arrives randomly and that we know only the average rate of arrival λ. For example, if $\lambda = 3$/hr, every minute there is a $3/60 = 5$ percent probability that a customer will arrive and a 95 percent probability that no customer will arrive. The odds may be simulated by any "fair" method such as drawing straws or tossing coins. Such an arrival mechanism is called a *Poisson process* [after Simeon Denis Poisson (1781-1840), a professor at the Ecole Polytechnique of Paris, France, and a renowned statistician] and follows a *Poisson distribution*.

The service mechanism is also assumed to be random. For example, $\mu = 6/\text{hr}$ would mean that an average of $60/6 = 10$ min service time is spent per customer. This is also a Poisson process but is usually referred to as a negative-exponential service time, and described by the same cumulative curve as the one we encountered in the Pareto analysis (Chapter 3). As in the case of the Pareto analysis, this is a safe distribution to assume when we have no detailed knowledge about the operating mechanism except that it behaves in an unbiased random manner.

An SFG portraying such a Markovian process will have the number of states correspond to the number of customers allowed in the system (either being serviced or waiting in a queue) with states connected by either an arrival rate λ or a service rate μ. Such a model is commonly called a *birth-and-death (B & D) process*.

B & D PROCESS WITH NO QUEUE ALLOWED Figure 12-3 portrays the simplest possible birth-and-death process where no queue is allowed to form. The system must be either idle with probability p_0 or busy with probability $1 - p_0 = p_1$. Since $\lambda p_0 = \mu p_1$, we can write

$$p_1 = \frac{\lambda}{\mu} p_0 \quad \text{and} \quad 1 = p_0 + p_1 = \left(1 + \frac{\lambda}{\mu}\right) p_0$$

The ratio $\lambda/\mu = p_1/p_0$ indicates the utilization rate of the system and is commonly expressed by $\rho = \lambda/\mu$, also known as the *service factor*, or *coefficient of utilization*. It follows that

$$p_0 = \frac{1}{1+\rho} \quad \text{and} \quad p_1 = \rho p_0 = \frac{\rho}{1+\rho}$$

Example 12-1: Wonderland price control The finance minister of Wonderland likes to impose price control on commodities whenever it appears that their prices are rising too sharply. On the average, there are two such crises per year, and the average duration of a price control is about 3 mo. What is the utilization rate of the price control?

The two states can be identified as *free trading* (0) and *price control* (1) and the arrival rate of the crisis is 2/yr. The service rate is 12 mo/3 mo $= 4 = \mu$. Thus, the utilization rate and state probabilities are

$$\rho = \frac{\lambda}{\mu} = \frac{2}{4} = 50 \text{ percent}$$

$$p_0 = \frac{1}{1+\rho} = \frac{2}{3} \approx 67 \text{ percent}$$

and

$$p_1 = \rho p_0 = \frac{1}{3} \approx 33 \text{ percent}$$

Common sense might have given us a false result—that the price control is effective about one-half of the time. $p_0 \neq p_1 < 0.5$ because crises are averted while

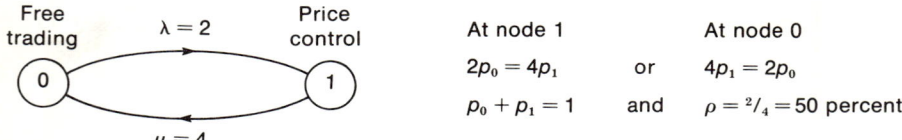

Figure 12-4 Wonderland "mixonomics."

prices are controlled. This "mixonomic" (mixing free trade with price control) phenomenon is portrayed graphically in Figure 12-4.

B & D PROCESS WITH A FINITE QUEUE Let us now consider the situation where a customer, finding the system occupied, decides to wait in line, but there is a limit as to how many customers can be in the system at the same time. Let us assume that a system allows two customers to wait in line in addition to the customer being serviced. The system states include 0 (idle), 1 (customer being served), 2 (one customer in line), and 3 (two customers waiting). The first-order Markov assumption can be interpreted to mean that only one customer can either arrive or depart at any one time. Two customers arriving simultaneously or one customer arriving while another is departing can be interpreted as a succession of two events taking place one after another. In other words, we do not indicate an arrow going, for example, from 0 to 2 bypassing state 1. Figure 12-5 illustrates the situation.

It is also conceivable that the arrival rate for the customers depends on the number of customers already in the system. If there is only a limited demand for a service, the market will be decreased by the number of customers now waiting in line; and even if the market is not decreased, a customer seeing a long line may decide to seek a competing service elsewhere. We denote the arrival rates by subscripting them with the state node at the tail of the arrow. By the same token, the service rate may also depend on the number of customers in the system. A barber may give an extra long haircut service to a single customer when no customers are waiting, but may give rush haircuts to a long line of lunch-time customers. A typist seeing a mountain of papers to be typed may become discouraged and slow down the work pace rather than speed it up. We shall denote these service rates also by the state of the system before the departure takes place.

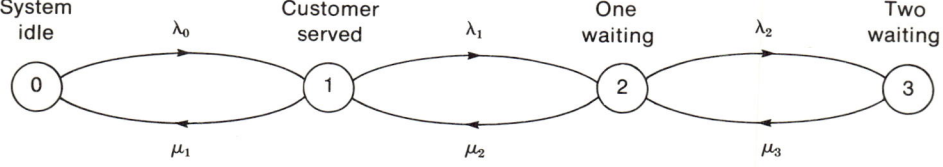

Figure 12-5 Finite-queue Markov-chain birth-and-death process.

The birth-and-death balancing equations (births = deaths, or inputs = outputs) can be written around each state node:

Node	Inputs	=	Outputs
0	$\mu_1 p_1$	=	$\lambda_0 p_0$
1	$\lambda_0 p_0 + \mu_2 p_2$	=	$(\mu_1 + \lambda_1) p_1$
2	$\lambda_1 p_1 + \mu_3 p_3$	=	$(\mu_2 + \lambda_2) p_2$
3	$\lambda_2 p_2$	=	$\mu_3 p_3$
	Births	=	Deaths

These balancing equations can be used to express all state probabilities in terms of p_0:

$$p_1 = \frac{\lambda_0}{\mu_1} p_0$$

$$p_2 = \left(\frac{\mu_1 + \lambda_1}{\mu_2}\right) p_1 - \frac{\lambda_0}{\mu_2} p_0 = \frac{\lambda_0 \lambda_1}{\mu_1 \mu_2} p_0$$

$$p_3 = \frac{\lambda_2}{\mu_3} p_2 = \frac{\lambda_0 \lambda_1 \lambda_2}{\mu_1 \mu_2 \mu_3} p_0$$

Since the system must be in one of the four states, we can also write

$$1 = p_0 + p_1 + p_2 + p_3 = \left(\frac{1 + \lambda_0}{\mu_1} + \frac{\lambda_0 \lambda_1}{\mu_1 \mu_2} + \frac{\lambda_0 \lambda_1 \lambda_2}{\mu_1 \mu_2 \mu_3}\right) p_0$$

Defining $\rho_i = \lambda_{i-1}/\mu_i$, we can write

$$p_0 = \frac{1}{1 + \rho_1 + \rho_1 \rho_2 + \rho_1 \rho_2 \rho_3}$$

$$p_1 = \frac{\rho_1}{1 + \rho_1 + \rho_1 \rho_2 + \rho_1 \rho_2 \rho_3}$$

$$p_2 = \frac{\rho_1 \rho_2}{1 + \rho_1 + \rho_1 \rho_2 + \rho_1 \rho_2 \rho_3}$$

$$p_3 = \frac{\rho_1 \rho_2 \rho_3}{1 + \rho_1 + \rho_1 \rho_2 + \rho_1 \rho_2 \rho_3}$$

If all arrival rates are the same and all service rates are also the same, these expressions can be simplified considerably by using $\rho = \lambda/\mu$:

$$p_n = \frac{\rho^n}{\sum_{i=0}^{3} \rho^i}$$

where $n = 0, 1, 2,$ or 3

and

$$p_n = \rho p_{n-1} = \rho^n p_0$$

The average number of customers in the system L_s is then computed:

$$L_s = 0p_0 + 1p_1 + 2p_2 + 3p_3 = \sum_{n=0}^{3} np_n = \text{expected value of } n = E(n)$$

The average length of queue L_q is also computed:

$$\begin{aligned} L_q &= 1p_2 + 2p_3 \\ &= L_s - 1\,(p_1 + p_2 + p_3) \\ &= L_s - 1 + p_0 \\ &= \sum_{n=0}^{3} np_n - 1 + p_0 \end{aligned}$$

To compute how long an average customer must wait in line before being serviced, we must consider what happens to the customer when he arrives at the system:

0. The system is idle (0) when the customer arrives and the service is immediate.

1. The customer finds one customer being serviced (1) and needs to wait $1/\mu$ time before being served.

2. The customer finds two customers in the system (2), and needs to wait $1/\mu$ time before getting into the state (1), or a total time of $2/\mu$.

3. The customer finds the system full (more than two customers already are waiting in line) and goes away. This is called *balking*.

Since these incidences occur with the frequencies of p_0, p_1, p_2, and p_3, respectively, we can compute the expected waiting time:

$$W_q = \frac{1}{\mu}(1p_1 + 2p_2) = \frac{1}{\lambda}(1\rho p_1 + 2\rho p_2) = \frac{1}{\lambda}(1p_2 + 2p_3) = \frac{L_q}{\lambda}$$

Thus the total time in the system is computed as the waiting time plus the service time:

$$W_s = W_q + \frac{1}{\mu} = \frac{1}{\mu}(1p_0 + 2p_1 + 3p_2) = \frac{1}{\lambda}(1\rho p_0 + 2\rho p_1 + 3\rho p_2) =$$

$$\frac{1}{\lambda}(1p_1 + 2p_2 + 3p_3) = \frac{L_s}{\lambda}$$

How good are these estimates in actually predicting a system's performance? The common statistical device to measure how close the average expected value is to the observed data is the variance (var), defined as the expected square of the deviation of the observed value X from its expected value $E(X)$:

$$\text{var } X = E\{[X - E(X)]^2\}$$

But the expected value of X^n is defined as

$$\bar{X}^n = E(X^n)$$

$$= \sum_{p(x)>0} x^n p(x)$$

So that we can say

$$\bar{X} = E(X)$$

$$= \sum_{p(x)>0} x p(x)$$

and

$$\text{var } X = E(X - \bar{X})^2$$

$$= E(X^2 - 2\bar{X}X + \bar{X}^2)$$

$$= E(X^2) - 2\bar{X}E(X) + E(\bar{X}^2)$$

$$= E(X^2) - 2\bar{X}^2 + \bar{X}^2$$

$$= E(X^2) - \bar{X}^2$$

$$= E(X^2) - [E(X)]^2$$

In this manner, we can compute, not only the expected value, but also the variance of such queue statistics as L_s, L_q, W_s, and W_q.

Example 12-2: *The circuit court of Eastport* The small community of Eastport and its surrounding area are served by a circuit court. An average of two cases is brought in every week, and the court is able to handle one case a day on the average (five cases per week). Since a delay of over 1 wk is considered intolerable by Wonderland's effective judicial system, any overload (over five cases in the system) is handled by another court. Find the pertinent queuing statistics.

Since there is no additional information, we may assume that the arrival is Poisson-distributed with a mean of $\lambda = 2$, and independent of the court's caseload. The service may also be assumed to be exponentially distributed with a mean service time of $1/\mu = 1/5$ (or $\mu = 5$), again independent of the number of pending cases. The SFG for the finite queue model can be built as shown in Figure 12-6.

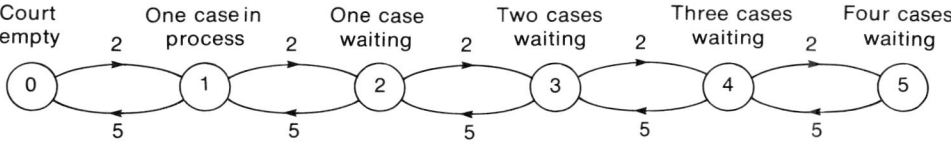

Figure 12-6 Circuit court of Eastport (Example 12-2).

Node	Birth inputs	=	Death outputs	
0	$5p_1$	=	$2p_0$	$p_1 = 0.4p_0$
1	$2p_0 + 5p_2$	=	$7p_1$	$p_2 = 1.4p - 0.4p_0 = 0.16p_0$
2	$2p_1 + 5p_3$	=	$7p_2$	$p_3 = 1.4p - 0.4p_1 = 0.064p_0$
3	$2p_2 + 5p_4$	=	$7p_3$	$p_4 = 1.4p_3 - 0.4p_2 = 0.0256p_0$
4	$2p_3 + 5p_5$	=	$7p_4$	$p_5 = 1.4p_4 - 0.4p_3 = 0.01024p_0$
5	$2p_4$	=	$5p_5$	$p_5 = 0.4p_4 = 0.01024p_0$

$$1 = \sum_{n=0}^{5} p_n = p_0 + p_1 + p_2 + p_3 + p_4 + p_5 = (1.0 + 0.4 + 0.16 + 0.064 + 0.0256 + 0.01024)\, p_0$$
$$= 1.65984\, p_0$$

$p_0 = 1/1.65984 = 0.6024677 \approx 0.602$ $\qquad\qquad = 60.2\%$

$p_1 = 24.1\%$ $\qquad$ $1p_1 = 0.241$ $\qquad$ $1p_1 = 0.241$
$p_2 = 9.6\%$ $\qquad$ $2p_2 = 0.192$ $\qquad$ $4p_2 = 0.384$
$p_3 = 3.9\%$ $\qquad$ $3p_3 = 0.117$ $\qquad$ $9p_3 = 0.351$
$p_4 = 1.6\%$ $\qquad$ $4p_4 = 0.064$ $\qquad$ $16p_4 = 0.256$
$p_5 = 0.6\%$ $\qquad$ $5p_5 = 0.030$ $\qquad$ $25p_5 = 0.150$

$\sum_{n=0}^{5} p_n = 1.0 = 100\%$ $\qquad$ $E(n) = \sum_{n=0}^{5} np_n = 0.644$ $\qquad$ $\sum_{n=0}^{5} n^2 p_n = 1.382 = E(n^2)$

$L_s = E(n) = 0.644$ cases pending or in the court on the average

$L_q = E(n) - 1 + p_0 = 0.246$ cases in queue

The average waiting time in the queue is computed as either

$$W_q = \frac{1}{\mu} E(n) \simeq 0.12 \text{ wk} = 0.6 \text{ day}$$

or

$$W_q = \frac{L_q}{\lambda} \simeq 0.12 \text{ wk} = 0.6 \text{ day}$$

The average total time in court is

$$W_s = W_q + \frac{1}{\mu} \simeq 1.6 \text{ day}$$

or

$$W_s = \frac{L_s}{\lambda} \simeq 1.6 \text{ day}$$

The variance for L_s is

$$\text{var } n = E(n^2) - [E(n)]^2 = 1.382 - (0.644)^2 \simeq 0.967$$

The standard deviation is estimated as

$$\sigma = (0.967)^{0.5} \simeq 0.983$$

Thus, a rough estimate of three standard deviations is $E(n) \pm 3\sigma = 0.6 \pm 3$.

From our knowledge of statistics (Figure 3-3, page 45), we conclude that it is very unlikely to find more than four cases in the court at any one time, and that the overflow out of this court (more than five cases) is practically nil.

12-4 Infinite-queue single-server models

When the queue is allowed to grow to any length, the SFG representation becomes cumbersome if not impossible. Queuing theory models assume that the utilization factor is less than unity to prevent the queue length from growing indefinitely. All the computations we have indicated so far assume the balance is reached between births and deaths (or arrivals and departures from any node) and that the system is at its *steady-state* condition.

The formula we have derived for queue statistics can be simplified in the case of infinite queue length:

$$p_0 = \lim_{n \to \infty} \frac{1}{\sum_{n=0}^{\infty} \rho^n} = 1 - \rho$$

since $1 + \rho + \rho^2 + \rho^3 + \rho^4 + \ldots$ converges to $1/(1-\rho)$ for $\rho < 1$. $p_n = \rho^n p_0$ can be written $p_n = \rho^n(1 - \rho)$. Similarly, knowing that the series $\Sigma_{n=0}^{\infty} n\rho^n$ converges to $\rho/(1-\rho)^2$ for $\rho < 1$ helps us rewrite the other expressions in more compact formats. Readers who are skeptical about these convergences should carry out simple long divisions as shown below:

$$(1 - \rho) \overline{\big) 1 }^{\displaystyle 1 + \rho + \rho^2 + \rho^3 + \rho^4 + \cdots}$$

$$\begin{array}{r} \underline{1 - \rho} \\ \rho \\ \underline{\rho - \rho^2} \\ \rho^2 \\ \underline{\rho^2 - \rho^3} \\ \rho^3 \\ \underline{\rho^3 - \rho^4} \\ \rho^4 \cdots \end{array}$$

$$(1 - \rho)^2 = (1 - 2\rho + \rho^2) \overline{\big) \rho }^{\displaystyle \rho + 2\rho^2 + 3\rho^3 + 4\rho^4 \cdots}$$

$$\begin{array}{r} \underline{\rho - 2\rho^2 + \rho^3} \\ 2\rho^2 - \rho^3 \\ \underline{2\rho^2 - 4\rho^3 + 2\rho^4} \\ 3\rho^3 - 2\rho^4 \\ \underline{3\rho^3 - 6\rho^4 + 3\rho^5} \\ 4\rho^4 - 3\rho^5 \\ \underline{4\rho^4 - 8\rho^5 + 4\rho^6} \\ 5\rho^5 - 4\rho^6 \end{array}$$

Similarly, we have:

$$L_s = \sum_{n=0}^{\infty} n p_n = \sum_{n=0}^{\infty} n \rho^n (1-\rho) = (1-\rho) \sum_{n=0}^{\infty} n \rho^n = (1-\rho) \frac{\rho}{(1-\rho)^2}$$

$$= \frac{\rho}{1-\rho} \quad \text{or} \quad \frac{\lambda}{\mu - \lambda}$$

$$L_q = \frac{\lambda^2}{\mu(\mu - \lambda)}$$

$$W_s = \frac{1}{(\mu - \lambda)} = \frac{L_s}{\lambda}$$

$$W_q = \frac{\lambda}{\mu(\mu - \lambda)} = \frac{L_q}{\lambda}$$

In the case of Example 12-2: $\lambda = 2$, $\mu = 5$, $\rho = 2/5 = 0.4$, and we have:

$p_0 = 1 - \rho$

$\quad = 0.6 \quad$ instead of 0.602 for the finite queue

$p_1 = \rho(1 - \rho)$

$\quad = 0.24 \quad$ instead of 0.241 for the finite queue

$p_2 = \rho^2(1 - \rho)$

$\quad = 0.096$

$p_3 = 0.0384$

$L_s = \frac{\lambda}{\mu - \lambda}$

$\quad = 2/3$

$\quad = 0.667$

$L_q = \frac{4}{5(5-2)}$

$\quad = 4/15$

$\quad = 0.267$

$W_s = 1/3$

$\quad = 0.333$

$W_q = 2/15$

$\quad = 0.133$

If you were the circuit court judge (in Example 12-2), you would probably be interested in knowing how your workload would stack up. You already know that you spend an average of $1/\mu = 1/5$ wk = 1 day per case presented to the court. Similarly, you can assume that there will be an average of $1/\lambda = 1/2$ wk = 2.5 days between arrivals of cases. Thus, you would be busy 1 day out of every 2.5 days, or $1/2.5 = 40$ per cent of the time; and that is, of course, the utilization factor ρ.

If you are busy 40 percent of the time, then obviously you must be idle 60 percent of the time ($p_0 = 1 - \rho$), and you might then wonder what is the probability of skipping off on a week-long fishing trip without anybody missing you during your absence. To sneak out of the court without anyone suspecting, you must choose a time when the court is not in session and no case is pending p_0. Then to have your week-long vacation, the system must stay in the state 0 for 5 days. Figure 12-7 reproduces the portion of SFG of Figure 12-6 that interests us. It shows the probability of exit from state 0 in terms of days instead of weeks: The arrival rate λ of 2 cases per wk can be expressed as the daily probability

$$\lambda t = 2 \times 1/5 \text{ wk} = 0.4 \text{ cases per day}$$

If the probability of exiting from the state 0 is λt, then the probability of staying in the state must be $1 - \lambda t$ for each t (day). To have a 5-day vacation you have to be this lucky for 4 more days:

$$P(\text{lucky 5 days}) = p(\text{lucky to be in } 0) \, p(\text{lucky 2d day}) \ldots p(\text{lucky 5th day})$$

$$= p_0(1 - \lambda t)^4$$

$$= 0.6(1 - 0.4)^4 = 0.6^5 = 0.0777$$

Thus there is a 7.77 percent probability of being lucky for 5 days. The lucky 7 percent combination appears to be almost too lucky, and you may wish to verify the computation. We used $t = 1/5$ to check the daily probability of transition, but to be more accurate you may wish to repeat the computation using hours instead of days.

$$P(\text{lucky } 5 \times 8 \text{ hr}) = p_0(1 - 2/40)^{39} = 0.6 \times 0.1353$$

$$= 0.081166 = 8.1\%$$

The 8.1 percent probability is even better than the previous computation, and you start to wonder if you can improve your odds further by carrying out your computation on the basis of minutes, seconds, nanoseconds, etc.

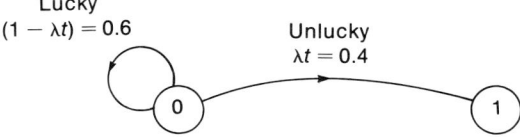

Figure 12-7 Segment of SFG explicitly displaying a simple method for generating a Poisson process.

This example is not unlike the situation where a person finds out that a bank that compounds the interest rate on a savings account on a monthly basis gives a higher dividend than another bank that uses the same interest rate but compounds it quarterly. A person might then try to locate a bank that would compound the savings daily—or even by the hour! But there is a limit to this utopian pursuit, and, as you may have guessed, it is our old friend the negative exponential function. More formally, we can write:

$$\lim_{n \to \infty} \left(1 - \frac{\lambda t}{n}\right)^n = e^{-\lambda t}$$

Thus, using $\lambda = 2$ and $t = 1$ week, we can compute:

$$P(t \geq 1 \text{ wk}) = e^{-2} = 0.1353$$

Thus, the probability of having a week-long fishing trip and not getting caught is

$$P = p_0 e^{-2} = 8.12\%$$

Interpreted another way, you may say that on the average there will be 4 wk out of the 50-wk year in which there is a 5-day or more gap between court sessions.

Extending our court example even further, you may want to know the probability that there will be exactly n number of cases during any particular week. We already know what this is for zero cases:

$$P(0) = e^{-\lambda t}$$

For one case, we need to move from state 0 to state 1:

$$P(1) = \lambda t e^{-\lambda t}$$

For two cases, A and B, A may come before B or B before A, and the joint probability of arrival is $(\lambda t)^2$:

$$P(2) = \frac{(\lambda t)^2 e^{-\lambda t}}{2}$$

For three cases, there will be $3! = 6$ permutations ($ABC, ACB, BAC, BCA, CBA,$ and CAB) each with the probability of $(\lambda t)^3$:

$$P(3) = \frac{(\lambda t)^3 e^{-\lambda t}}{3!}$$

For the general case of n, the expression that provides these probability values is known as the *Poisson distribution*:

$$P(n) = \frac{(\lambda t)^n}{n!} e^{-\lambda t}$$

To make sure that we do indeed obtain our original relationship, we can check the ratio of probabilities between $n - 1$ and n:

$$P(n - 1) = \frac{(\lambda t)^{n-1}}{(n - 1)!} e^{-\lambda t}$$

Thus $P(n)/P(n-1)$ can be found:

$$\frac{P(n)}{P(n-1)} = \frac{(\lambda t)}{n}$$

and this is as it should be for our negative exponential distribution.

These reasonings for the Poisson and negative exponential description of arrivals can be applied analogously to the service mechanism. Indeed, Figure 12-6 is a symmetrical SFG, and the roles of λ and μ can be reversed merely by turning the network around. Nonetheless, our common practice of referring to arrivals as events and to services as time-consuming activities dictates our usage of the expression *Poisson-arrival and negative-exponential-service queue models*.

SECTION 12-4 TUNE-UP

The Fast and Slimy State Park has a campground that receives an average of 20 campers per hr during the peak hours of summer days. The visitors check in at the gate, pay a nominal camping fee of $1/night, and proceed to a campground that is fully equipped with running water, hot showers, and barbecue grills. Arriving at the gate of this campground, you find a queue of 10 campers in front of you (1 being checked in and 9 more in the queue) and only one state park ranger on duty. You are thinking of perhaps going to another campground where the line is shorter or leaving for a short time to eat, but you are concerned that you may not find a place to camp if you leave this line.

Assuming no further knowledge, estimate how long you will have to wait to get into the campground. What is the average time spent by the officer registering each visitor? If you leave the queue to eat and then return, how many campers will have registered while you were gone?

12-5 RPMS representation of queuing models

An RPM network can be used to represent any system of linear equations and inequalities. The SFG network models in this chapter have been used to generate birth-and-death balances for the steady-state conditions, and these can always be represented by RPM networks. The advantage of utilizing an RPM network over an SFG in describing a Markov chain is that it is capable of representing two types of flows on the same network. The resources flow through the network and are identified by the primal values; the evaluation of resources is conducted by the dual model, and the values of resources constitute the dual set of flows. We are free to define any quantity as the primal commodity and choose any easily quantified measure to evaluate its value. The roles of the primal and dual values are completely interchangeable, as are the two players using the same zero-sum payoff table in the game theory model of Chapter 5.

The queuing theory was developed primarily as an analytical rather than an optimization tool. It is concerned with the primal flows which enable us to compile all the queue statistics we may wish to obtain from a system, but not how the system can be improved. To optimize a system, as well as to analyze it, we need to provide an objective function that assigns decision criteria to the alternatives.

Different problems have different solution procedures that are best suited for a given set of circumstances. The versatility of RPMS modeling is revealed by a simple example that illustrates the advantage of utilizing the dual interpretations of RPMS.

Example 12-3: FIASCO Joe Blow is an astute and hard-working individual who has decided to augment his income by moonlighting as a tax consultant. He has studied tax regulations through a correspondence course, received his state registration, and opened up a one-man consulting office: Financial Investigation and Advising Services Company (FIASCO).

To beat the competition, Joe has decided to conduct all his business by telephone. He advertises grandly in local newspapers that he will let clients call and explain their tax problems over the phone. He will perform the necessary computations on a pocket-size electronic calculator, and give answers immediately. This service turns out to be fairly popular among people who are too shy to confront tax consultants face to face. Joe charges his clients by the minute and has even come up with a catchy slogan for his service: "A dollar a minute will save you hundreds!"

An average service takes 10 min and Joe estimates that he will receive three calls on an average evening hour if his phone is free to receive incoming calls. By taking on this moonlighting job, Joe had to forego his overtime work at the plant where he works during the day, and he estimates this loss to be worth $12/hr. At the present, Joe has only one telephone line. Describe this as a queuing model.

NO-QUEUE SINGLE-SERVER RPM MODEL This simplest case is represented by the same SFG model as in Figure 12-3. Since there are only two possible states, the state occupancy rates are computed easily as P_0 (idle) $= 2/3$ and P_1 (consulting) $= 1/3$. Also,

$$\rho = \frac{\lambda}{\mu} = (3 \text{ customers per hr})/(6 \text{ customers per hr}) = 0.5$$

The relationships $\lambda p_0 = \mu p_1$ and $p_0 + p_1 = 1$ are easily modeled in RPMS (Figure 12-8). Figure 12-9a shows the numerical values for this no-queue single-server model of FIASCO, and Figure 12-9b illustrates symbolically how the dual values were computed, starting from an arbitrary value of $Z_q = Z$.

By balancing the flows around the node p_0 to find q_1, and then around p_1, we can write $Z + \mu(Z + C_0/\lambda) = C_1$ which gives

$$Z = \frac{\lambda C_1 - C_0}{\lambda + \mu}\mu$$

This expression is independent of the state probabilities. Thus, the formula can be used to design the system parameters such as C_0, C_1, λ, and μ without having to

The SFG

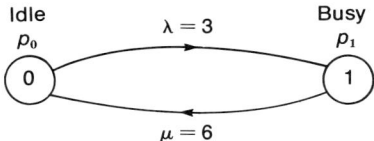

representing:

	Births	=	Deaths
At node 0	$6p_1$	=	$3p_0$
At node 1	$3p_0$	=	$6p_1$

can be represented by an RPM network

To this, we must add the implicit requirement that the system must be either in 0 or 1 state: $p_0 + p_1 = 1$. This creates the node q_0.

The cost structure can be superimposed to indicate the cost of being idle, $C_0 = \$12/\text{hr}$, and the profit from consulting, $C_1 = \$60 - 12 = \$48/\text{hr}$.

Now the RPM network reads as:
PRIMAL: MAX $Z_p = 48p_1 - 12p_0$
subject to $1 = p_0 + p_1$ at q_0
$\qquad\qquad 3p_0 = 6p_1$ at q_1
$p_0, p_1 \geq 0$

DUAL: min $Z_q = q_0$
subject to $q_0 + 12 = 3q_1$ at p_0
$\qquad\qquad 6q_1 + q_0 = 48$ at p_1
$q_0, q_1 \geq 0$

Since all logical constraints are strict equalities, all values are easily solved:
$p_0 = 2/3$; $p_1 = 1/3$; $Z_p = \$8/\text{hr}$ (i.e., \$8 over the \$12/hr previous income)

Then, $Z_q = \$8$, and $q_0 = \$8$. At p_0, we have $12 + 8 = 3q_1$; $q_1 = 20/3$.
A check can be made at p_1: $6(20/3) + 8 = 48$. Q.E.D.

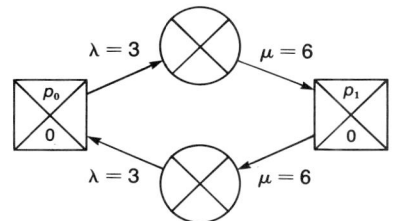

which can be condensed as

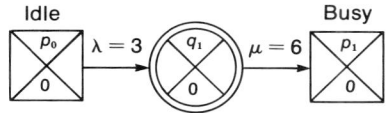

$$Z \neq \mu\left(Z + C_0/\lambda\right) - C_1$$

$$Z = \frac{\lambda C_1 - C_0}{\lambda + \mu} \mu$$

Figure 12-8 Graphic derivation of the RPM network for a no-queue single-server model.

(a) Primal and dual numerical values

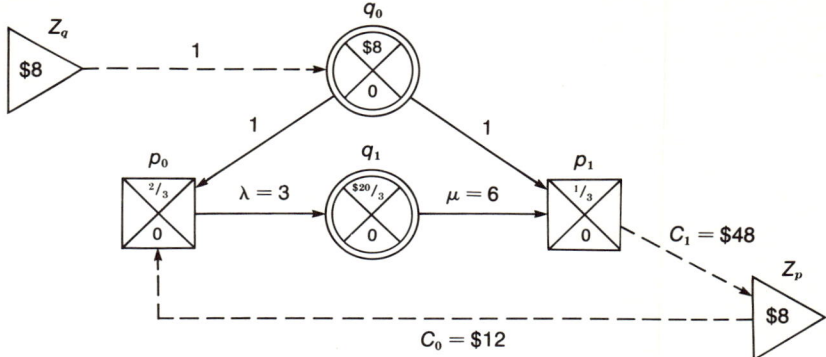

(b) Dual value computation

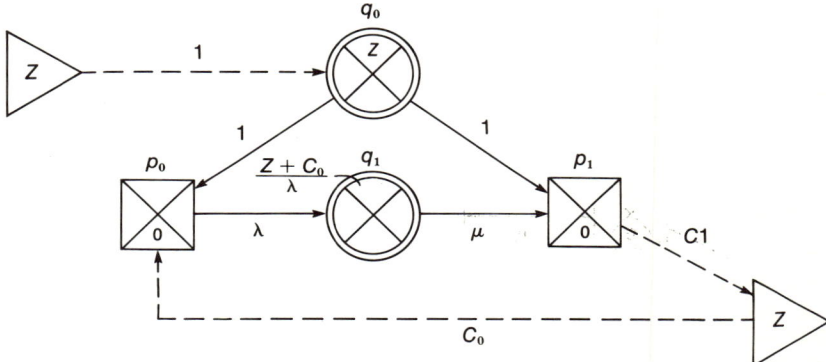

Figure 12-9 Primal and dual values for a no-queue single-server RPM model.

know probability values. To illustrate this advantage, the following questions are answered on Figure 12-10:

1. How much should Joe charge his customers to make $10/hr net profit over his $12/hr benchmark?

2. If he had to keep $C_1 = \$48$, what can Joe do to raise his profit to $10/hr?

3. How low can the demand for his service fall before Joe should think about returning to his old job?

INFINITE-QUEUE SINGLE-SERVICE RPM MODEL Suppose that Joe's FIASCO has done so well that he has now decided to use a telephone answering service to take messages while he is busy with a client. A client who calls while Joe is on the telephone leaves a telephone number with the answering service and

(a) How much should Joe charge his customers to make $10/hr net?

$6 \times {}^{22}/_3 + 10 = C_1$ at p_1

$C_1 = \$54$

$C_1 + C_0 = 54 + 12 = \$66/hr$

$ = \$1.10/min$

Answer:
Charge $1.10/min instead of $1/min.

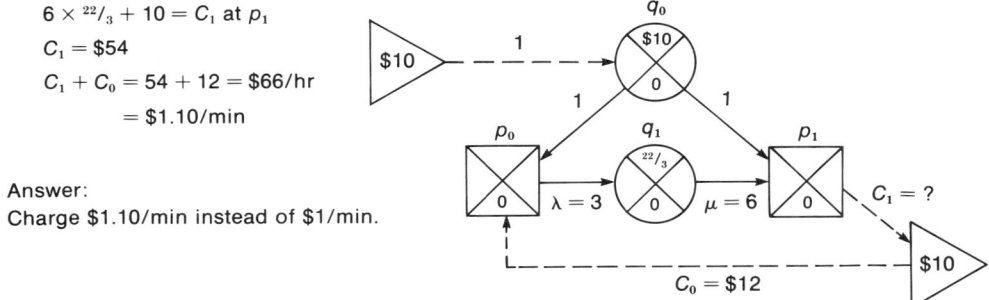

(b) How could Joe make $10/hr net without raising his fee?

$\mu \times {}^{22}/_3 + 10 = \$48$ at p_1

$\mu = \dfrac{48 - 10}{{}^{22}/_3} = \dfrac{114}{22} = 5.182/hr$

$1/\mu = 11.58$ minute per customer

Answer:
Spend 12 minutes per customer instead of 10 minutes.

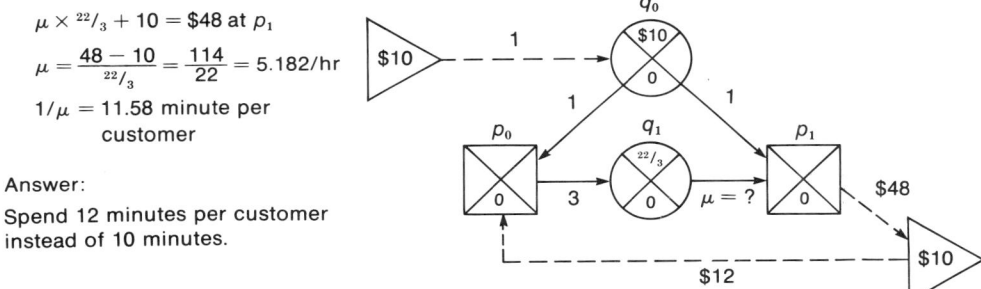

(c) What is the break-even arrival rate for FIASCO?

$6[12/\lambda] + 0 = 48$ at p_1

$\lambda = \dfrac{72}{48} = 1.5$ customer per hour

Answer:
Go back to overtime work if the demand falls to 50 percent of the present (1.5 customers per hour instead of 3 customers per hour).

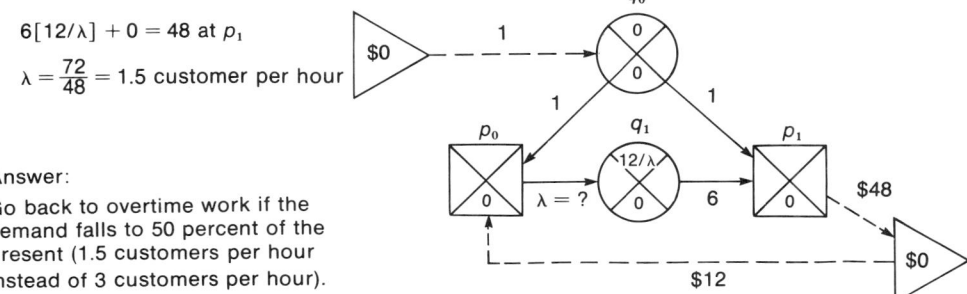

Figure 12-10 Examples of dual value computations for FIASCO.

Joe calls the answering service to obtain the number when he is free. The answering service has many lines, and any number of customers may be put on the waiting list. Also, it takes practically no time at all for Joe to obtain the next client's number from the answering service. The answering service increases the cost of Joe's operation from $12/hr to $22/hr. Will this operation be profitable?

414 Introduction to Operations Research and Management Science

This telephone answering service provides a waiting line (queue) of indefinite length for Joe. If we were to draw an SFG for the clients, we would have to make the queue long enough to accurately predict Joe's business. From Joe's point of view, however, there are still only two states: he is either (1) busy with the probability of p_0, or (2) not busy with the probability of p_1. The problem would be reduced to a two-state model if we could find the equivalent parameters.

Figure 12-11a shows the SFG for an infinite queue, Figure 12-11b its two-state equivalent model, and Figure 12-11d the RPM network for the reduced problem. It is reasonable to assume that the arrival rate would remain the same for Figure 12-11a, but the "apparent" service rate v would be different from the original μ.

(a) SFG representation of an infinite-queue single-server model

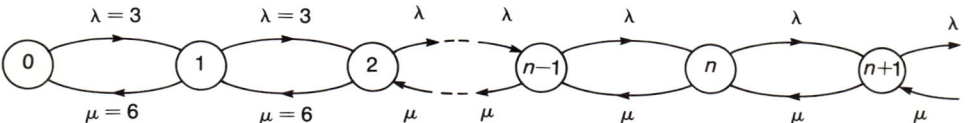

(c) RPM for (a).

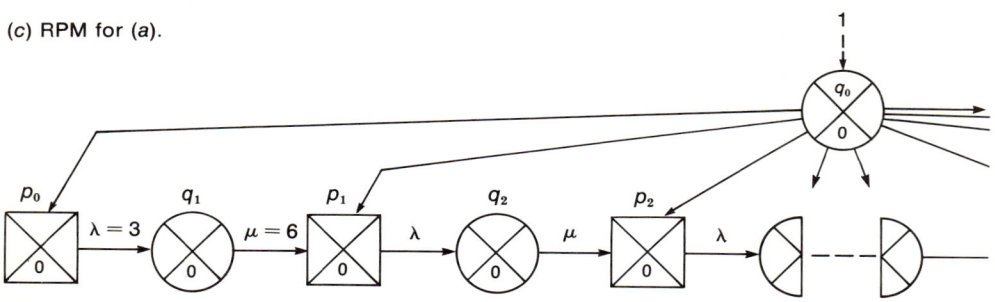

(d) RPM network for (b)

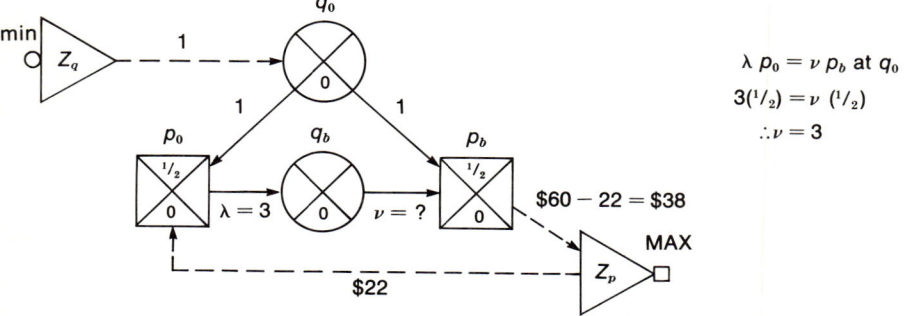

$\lambda p_0 = v p_b$ at q_0
$3(1/2) = v (1/2)$
$\therefore v = 3$

Figure 12-11 Infinite-queue model for FIASCO.

Systems Evaluation: Queuing Models and Simulation   415

From our previous calculations we know that $p_0 = 1 - \rho$, where $\rho = \lambda/\mu$ is the utilization rate (or load factor). Thus,

$$p_b = 1 - p_0 = \rho = 0.5$$

and this bit of information on the RPM network enables us to find $v = \mu - \lambda = 3$. The remaining computations are straightforward, and in Figure 12-11e we find that the profit is the same as before: $8/hr net.

Thus, it does not seem profitable for Joe to use the answering service unless he expects more clients to call. The maximum profit he can expect is for $P_b = 1$, or $Z = \$38$/hr, which is lower than the $48/hr profit without using the answering service. Of course it would be dangerous for Joe to base all his decisions on this

(b) An equivalent two-state model

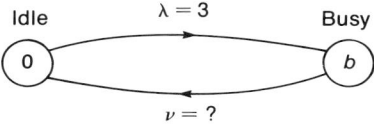

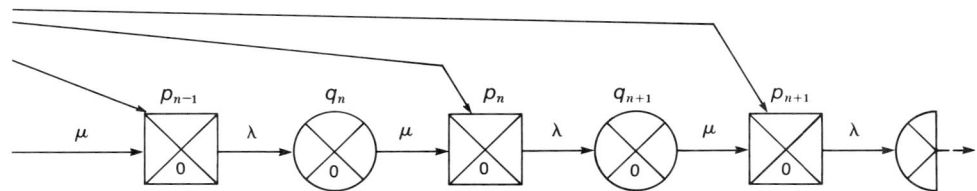

(e) Cost computation on (d)

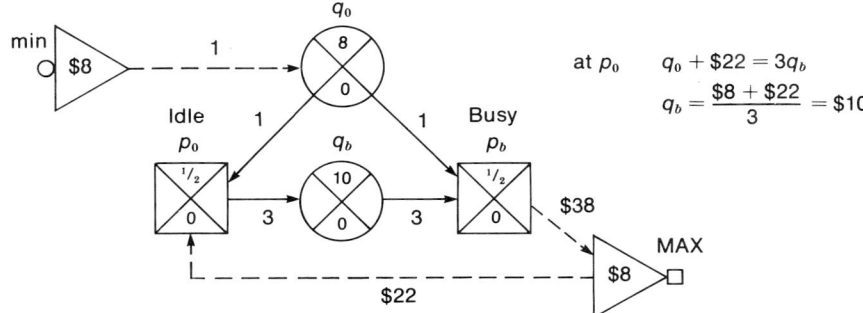

simplistic queuing analysis. There are many intangible factors that need consideration for such a seasonal business as tax-return preparation. The subject of intangible and irreducible factors will be discussed further in Chapter 13.

SECTION 12-5 TUNE-UP

As a freelance OR/MS consultant, you are successful on bidding an average of 2 projects per yr. A project lasts about 3 mo, and you charge $10,000/mo in addition to expenses. You estimate your expenses to be $15,000/yr when you have no project to charge your expenditures to.

1. Your present policy is to bid on new projects only after you are finished working on a current project. Estimate the state probabilities and your annual income.
2. You estimate that one-half of your customers (1 customer per yr) may be willing to wait for you to complete your current project before starting theirs if a suitable incentive such as a discount is offered. If you were to maintain your present level of income and wish to sign a contract on just one more project in addition to a current project, what discount would you be able to offer to entice customers to wait for your services?

12-6 Multiserver systems

Our discussion of queuing systems can be extended to cases of multiservers. Let us illustrate with a few simple examples.

PARALLEL QUEUES When we have n servers with the identical service rate μ operating independently with customers forming n separate queues, each server can be analyzed separately. It suffices to divide the arrival rate λ by n and use λ/n as the arrival rate for each station.

SINGLE-QUEUE PARALLEL SERVERS Some banks and post offices have adopted a single-queue parallel-server system. All customers wait in one line, and the customer at the head of the line goes to the first server that becomes free, which is the equivalent of speeding up the service rate μ by the number n of identical parallel channels (servers) $n\mu$.

The fact that this system is more efficient than that of parallel queues is easily seen by comparing W_q for each case. For the single-server case in Section 12-4, we have

$$W_q = \frac{\lambda}{\mu(\mu - \lambda)}$$

Let us assume $\lambda = 10$, and $\mu = 4$, and $n = 5$. Then, in the case of parallel queues, we have

$$W_q = \frac{\lambda/n}{\mu[\mu - (\lambda/n)]} = \frac{10/5}{4[4 - (10/5)]} = 0.25$$

and in the case of single-queue parallel servers, we have

$$W_q = \frac{\lambda}{n\mu(n\mu - \lambda)} = \frac{10}{5 \times 4 (5 \times 4 - 10)} = 0.05$$

(one-nth the waiting time of the parallel queues.)

SERIAL SYSTEM In a supermarket, it is a common practice for a checkout-counter clerk to be assisted by a bagger. Often, the bagger is another clerk who could open up another counter where she will be the sole clerk, doing both the checking and the bagging.

Let us consider a simplistic no-queue serial system to illustrate the application of SFG to such a problem. Let each state be identified by a pair of numbers (I, J) where I identifies the state of the checker (0 = idle, 1 = checking, b = blocked by the bagger who has not finished bagging the previous customer's groceries) and J identifies the state of the bagger (0 = idle, 1 = bagging). Then, using λ for the arrival rate of the customers, μ_1 for the service rate of the checker, and μ_2 for the service rate of the bagger, we may construct the SFG as shown in Figure 12-12. The original formulation of this model to the best of our knowledge is due to Sheldon M. Ross (1972), a professor at the University of California, Berkeley.

Using the birth-and-death balance equations as in Section 12-3, all queue statistics can be computed. It is easily seen that this system is even less efficient than the parallel-queue system.

COMPOSITE SYSTEMS Series and parallel constructions can be combined to describe complex mechanisms. A typical application is to illustrate the reliability of a system such as the one shown in Figure 12-13. There are two major parallel-path groupings: the subsystem I, consisting of A, B, and C, and the subsystem II, which is D. We can assume that the system is partly functioning if either subsystem is operating. The simultaneous failures of ABD, ACD, BCD, or AD would cause the system to be completely inoperative. Expressing the state of the system

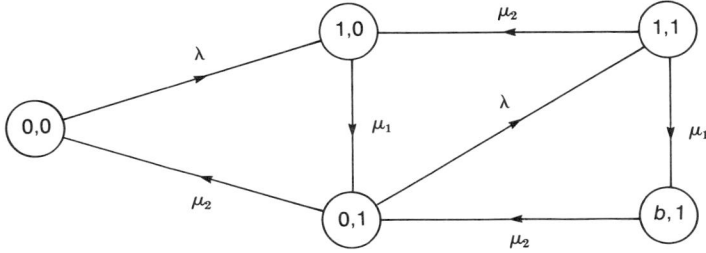

Figure 12-12 SFG for the checker-bagger serial system.

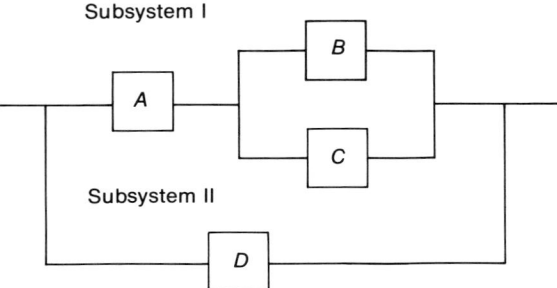

Figure 12-13   Block diagram of the reliability example.

by the four-digit label $ABCD$, with 0 indicating operative and 1 inoperative, the SFG can be built to show possible failure patterns.

Figure 12-14 illustrates the SFG network. The arrival rates are for the occurrence of failures, and once the path is disrupted it is assumed that no further failure can occur in that path; hence there is no 1111 state. Such a diagram is useful in planning strategies for maintenance and repair. A standard operating procedure

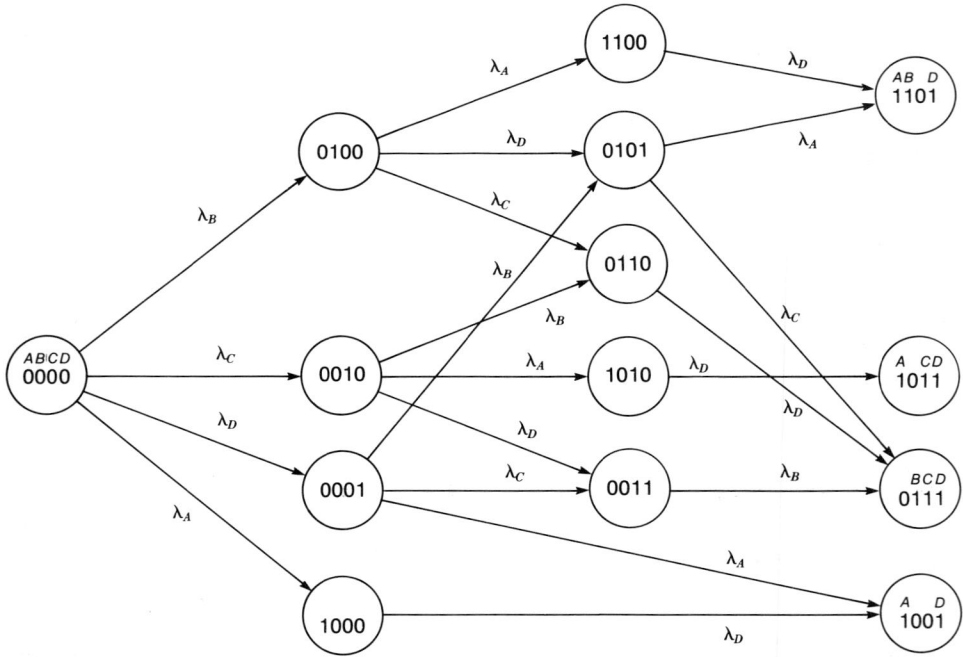

Figure 12-14   A project input-output matrix that traces the relationship of project activities and resources.

can be written for each case to minimize the potential down time for the entire system.

12-7 Monte Carlo simulation

One sure way to find out if a system will work under a given set of circumstances is to try it out, but unfortunately, the systems designed by OR/MS researchers are often too impractical, too costly, or too complex to be tried out. As the aerodynamic characteristics of supersonic transports can be tested using wind-tunnel models, the queuing characteristics of an OR/MS system may be evaluated using computer-simulation models.

It is often tempting to bypass a theoretical analysis and immediately begin to construct a simulation model for evaluating a system's performance. Computer simulation is often regarded as being the "method of last resort" to be used "when all else fails" or, at best, as a systematic approach to improve on intuitive "seat-of-the-pants" analysis (Wagner, 1969, pp. 889–890). It is also said that "simulation yields only an empirical form of knowledge, fraught with the danger that the stochastic model is not truly representative" (Flagle et al., 1960, p. 446).

In spite of all the criticisms that have been made about computer simulation, it has proved to be one of the most useful tools in OR/MS. When IBM first decided to construct its series 360 computers it built a special simulation language for the purpose of evaluating the new computers' performance. The models built with this language were so successful that IBM decided to market the software program then known as Gordon's Simulator.[1] Since that time, several versions of general purpose simulation system (GPSS) have appeared, and today, GPSS is considered to be the most popular simulation language in the world.

There are many stochastic simulation languages besides GPSS. SIMULA is a popular language in Europe; SIMSCRIPT is a FORTRAN-based language; GASP requires users to write their own FORTRAN programs using the supplied subroutines; and GERT is an ideal language for simulating Markov chains. All these stochastic simulation languages have one feature in common that distinguishes them from nonstochastic simulation languages such as DYNAMO (see Chapter 13), ECAP, and CSMP. This feature is called *Monte Carlo simulation*. In short, it is akin to tossing a coin or a pair of dice or spinning a wheel (thus the origin of the name Monte Carlo) to determine the state transition of the system being modeled. In the case of a Markov chain, it suffices to indicate all transitions as probabilities that can be generated by a mechanism known as a *pseudo-random-number generator*.

---

[1] Informally named after its inventor, Geoffrey Gordon of the Advanced Systems Development Division of International Business Machines Corporation, and progressively renamed from *General Purpose Systems Simulator* to *General Purpose Simulation System*.

The most common pseudo-random-number generator is called the *Multiplicative Congruential Method*. One example may be written as

RANDOM $(N + 1) = 11 \times$ RANDOM (N) [modulo 128]

where 128 and 11 are numbers chosen more or less arbitrarily and [modulo 128] means that we should divide the number in front of it by 128 and record the residue. The first number used is called a seed, and this, too, can be chosen arbitrarily. Let RANDOM (1) be 1,234; then $11 \times$ RANDOM $(1) = 13,574$. The largest multiple of 128 that is smaller than 13,574 is $106 \times 128 = 13,568$. $13,574 - 13,568 = 6$, and this is the next random number: RANDOM $(2) = 006$.

RANDOM $(3) = 11 \times 006$ [modulo 128] $= 66$ [modulo 128] $= 66$ (since 66 is smaller than 128)

RANDOM $(4) = 11 \times 066$ [modulo 128] $= 726$ [modulo 128] $= 726 - (5 \times 128) = 726 - 640 = 086$

RANDOM $(5) = 11 \times 086$ [modulo 128] $= 946$ [modulo 128] $= 946 - (7 \times 128) = 956 - 896 = 050$

The result of this arithmetic exercise will be a series of unordered (i.e., random-looking) uniformly distributed numbers between 000 to 127. If we then divide these numbers by 128, we will obtain a close facsimile of random numbers between 0.000 to 0.999 (actually 0.99218...). Our series 006, 0666, 086, 050, ..., translates to 0.046875, 0.515625, 0.671875, 0.390625, and so on.

Well, what good is all this? Let us return to the example of the circuit court judge who wants to go fishing for a week (Section 12-4). His SFG in Figure 12-7 is duplicated in Figure 12-15. To simulate this process, we assign random numbers 0.000 to 0.599 to the 60 percent lucky loop and 0.600 to 0.999 to the unlucky jump to node 1. To find out whether the simulated day is lucky or not, we pick up a random number and see if it is smaller than 0.599 or larger than 0.600. If the number is smaller, it simulates the lucky day; if the number is larger, it simulates the unlucky day. If the numbers are generated randomly, there will always be 60 percent chance of remaining lucky and 40 percent chance of exiting to the unlucky node 1.

In our case, the first number generated is 0.046875, which is obviously less

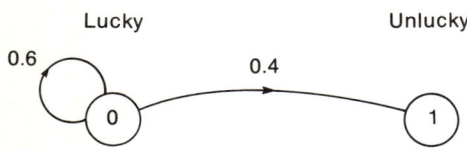

Figure 12-15 Monte Carlo simulation of a Markov-chain Poisson process.

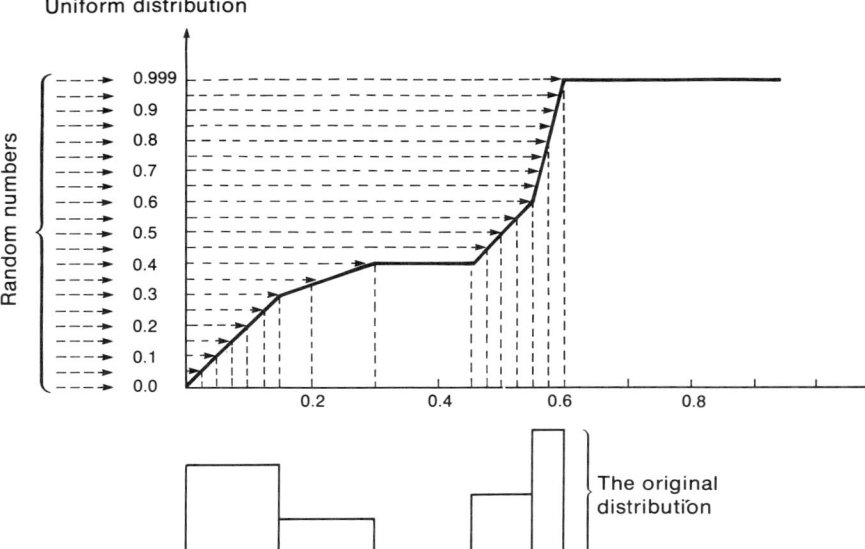

Figure 12-16 Random-process generation.

than 0.599; thus the simulated day is a lucky day. The second is 0.515625, and again we are lucky. The third number is 0.671875, which is larger than 0.600 and simulates an unlucky day for the judge, who must now get back to work. If we keep repeating this experiment, we would find that the judge will have a string of 5 lucky days only about 8 percent of the time. This, in essence, is the Monte Carlo approach.

The *uniform distribution* is a useful tool in generating any statistical distribution. All that is required is to make up a table corresponding to the ogive of the distribution (as we have done several times in Chapter 3) and project the uniform distribution (the generated random numbers) on the coordinate. The corresponding ogive readings, if accumulated, will duplicate the original distribution. Figure 12-16 portrays this process.

The name *pseudo-random-number generator* comes from the fact that the generator will eventually recycle. In our example, we know that eventually the number 006 (or another such number that has already been generated) will appear and from there on the same series of numbers will appear. It is then possible to change the seed and start over with a new set of numbers.

It is worthwhile to remind ourselves that *to simulate* is no more than "to feign the appearance of, without the result really being the thing simulated" (Riggs, 1970). In other words, the results of a simulation are never better than the data used to build the model itself.

TUNE-UP SOLUTIONS

Section 12-2

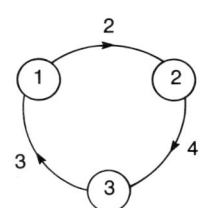

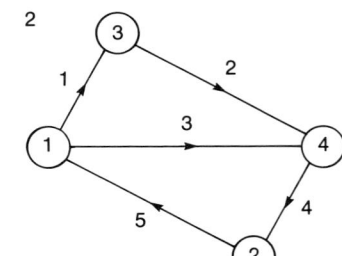

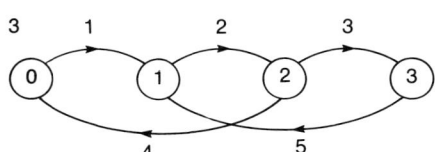

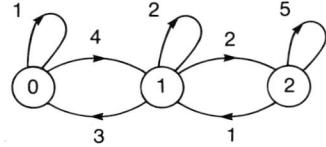

Section 12-4

μ = 22 campers per hr   since

$L_s = 10 = \dfrac{\lambda}{\mu - \lambda}$

$\quad = \dfrac{20}{\mu - 20}$

$W_s = \dfrac{1}{(22 - 20)}$

$\quad = 0.5$ hr

$\quad = 30$ min

$\dfrac{1}{\mu} = \dfrac{60 \text{ min}}{22}$

$\quad = 2.73$ min per camper

2 hr × 20 = 40 campers

Section 12-5

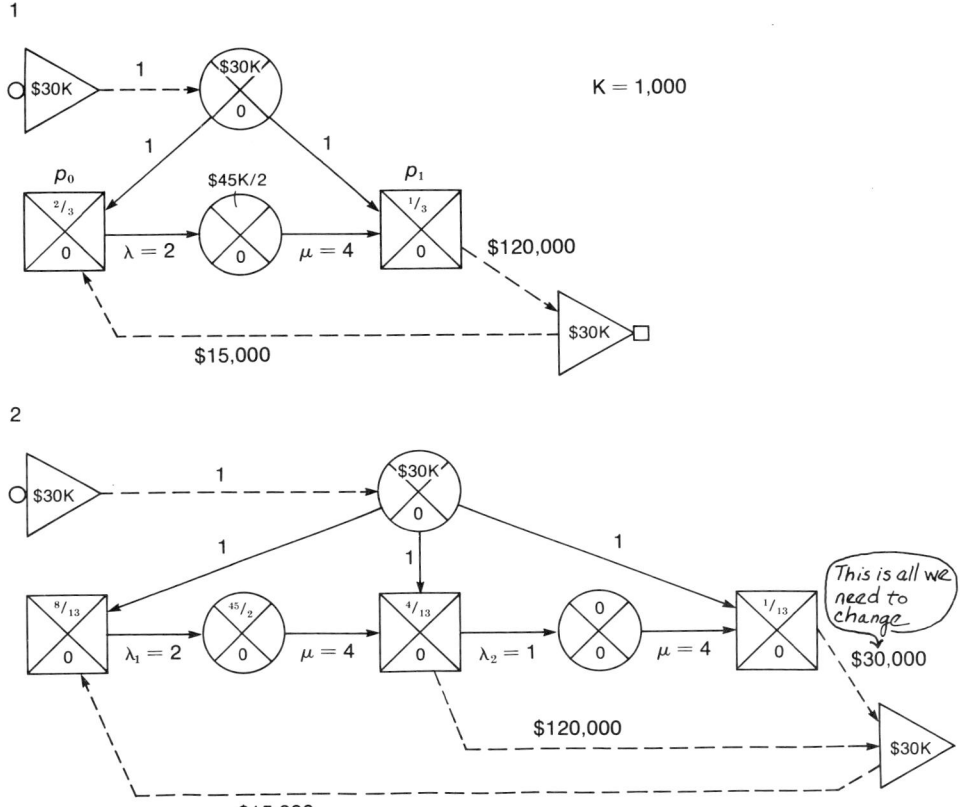

EXERCISES

12-1 Given a multiplicative congruential random-number generator

RANDOM $(N + 1) = 5 \times$ RANDOM (N) [modulo 64]

compute the values of RANDOM (1) through RANDOM (4) if RANDOM (0) = 11.

12-2 The interarrival mean time for a single-server system is 10 min, and the mean service time is 5 min. Assuming a Poisson arrival and a negative-exponential service mechanism, compute the utilization rate for this infinite-queue model. What is the probability of finding two or more customers in the system?

12-3 In Exercise 12-2, what is the average queue length and what is the average time the customer can expect to wait before being serviced?

12-4 A computer system is in one of three possible states at any time: 0, down and being repaired; 1, up and operating but idle; 2, serving a customer. The SFG for the corresponding Markov chain is:

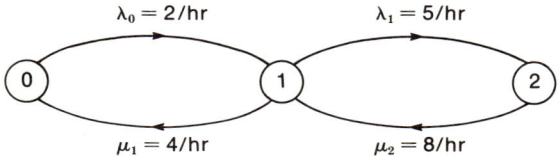

Assuming that it costs $10/min to be in state 0, and $5/min to be in state 1, how much should the company charge per minute for the use of the computer in order to net $90/min? Determine this without computing state probabilities.

12-5 In Exercise 12-4, compute the state probabilities p_0, p_1, and p_2. Use the results to check the answer to the original exercise.

RPMS: A Tool for General Systems Analysis

Chapter 13

13-1 Think ahead—think behind

In previous chapters we observed many types of problems and the tools designed to evaluate them. These tools have become well known and accepted because they serve a useful function in helping us cope with similar problems that are frequently encountered. Many other tools have been developed but are less familiar because they treat only specific types of problems that are rarely encountered.

In this chapter we shall explore some difficulties that beset any OR/MS practitioner, which are characteristic of all attempts to analyze systems seriously. Experience can be helpful in handling these problems through knowing what can be ignored with relative safety, and yet no one has all the answers. The tools and approaches that will be described are usually more powerful than one would imagine.

SHAKY NUMBERS OR/MS tools rely on number manipulations to provide a solution and to indicate a preferred course of action. Occasionally it is very difficult to secure the numerical values needed to apply our tools. It normally takes a lot of digging to expose necessary data, and sometimes the cost of securing data is beyond the value that can be derived from the numbers once they are exposed. Assuming we know enough about hidden numbers, the decision to search rests on a breakeven analysis between the value of an answer and the cost of obtaining it. This can be a tough question, but it is not as consuming as a situation where numbers are uncertain or do not exist, and yet the situation demands analysis.

Numbers do not exist naturally for characteristics aptly called *intangibles*, or *irreducibles*. What is the value of peace of mind, a beautiful view, freedom from bad odors, or good will? Such values are increasingly needed to evaluate reforms deemed important to our society. Clever attempts to develop numbers for intangible factors utilize rating scales, utility functions, and relative costs. C. West Churchman, R. D. Luce, Howard Raiffa, John Von Neumann, and others have suggested ways to assign numbers to characteristics, but the numbers so developed cannot be employed without recognizing their limitations; that is, characteristics are rated on an interval scale (temperature measurements are examples of interval-scale ratings), and the resulting numbers cannot be used as freely as ratio-scale numbers (dollars, weight, distance).

CHURCHMAN-ACKOFF EVALUATION OF OUTCOMES An example of an interval-scale ordering of utility is the so-called *Churchman-Ackoff procedure* developed in 1954.[1] It is based on the following assumptions:

1. To every outcome O_j there corresponds a real nonnegative number Y_j to be interpreted as a measure of the true relative importance of O_j.

2. If O_j is more important than O_k, then $Y_j > Y_k$; and if O_j and O_k are equally important, $Y_j = Y_k$.

3. If O_j and O_k have utilities Y_j and Y_k, respectively, the utility of the combined outcome $O_j + O_k$ is $Y_j + Y_k$.

The O_j and O_k are assumed to be independent and therefore not mutually exclusive; the method also assumes the linear additivity of utilities. Although these assumptions may be questionable, they have been useful in creating an interval scale for a set of ordered utilities. The construction procedure is roughly described as follows:

1. Have the decision maker rank the n outcomes in order of preference. Let O_1 represent the most preferred and O_n the least preferred.

2. Assign 1 to the utility of O_n and have the decision maker assign numbers to the remaining outcomes that reflect their relative values. (Conceal these numbers during the next step.)

---

[1] Discussed in Russel L. Ackoff and Maurice W. Sasieni, *Fundamentals of Operations Research*, John Wiley & Sons, New York, 1968, p. 51.

3. Present the decision maker with a program of choice comparing the most favored outcome O_1 with a decreasing combination of other outcomes $O_2 + O_3 + \cdots + O_n$, $O_2 + \cdots + O_{n-1}$, $\cdots$, until it is shown that the single outcome is equal to or greater than the combination offered. Repeat this for O_2 versus $O_3 + \cdots O_n$, $O_3 + \cdots O_{n-1}$, and so on for all other O's until all limits are found.

4. Check these limits against the numbers originally assigned in step 2. If the numbers are not consistent, change them as little as possible to make them fit the constraints created in step 3.

An alert reader will easily see that this procedure can be handled as a linear programming problem, using the figures from step 2 as an objective function and the data from step 3 as a set of constraints.

More important, the ordinal preference of the type discussed by this Churchman-Ackoff method can be incorporated into an existing RPM network to reflect management's policy. For example, if the production of a resource Y_1 is preferred over that of resources Y_2 and Y_3 (one unit of each), then we can incorporate this as a primal node, say, X_m, using Y_1 as an input and Y_2 and Y_3 as the output. This dummy primal node X_m will force Y_1 to have a dual value that is consistently higher than (or equal to) the sum of Y_2 and Y_3. Figure 13-1 illustrates the example.

BENEFIT-TO-COST ANALYSIS A different approach for rating intangibles is used in some benefit/cost analyses that evaluate government projects. An intangible such as the social value of having a place to picnic or hike is derived from calculating the current cost to enjoy such benefits at existing facilities (travel, admission, etc.). Then these derived values are included as benefits expected from similar facilities provided by a new project. For example, a fisherman's day on a lake can be given a value of about $5, a camper's night is worth approximately $2, and a picnic outing is valued at $1 per person. The purpose of developing such

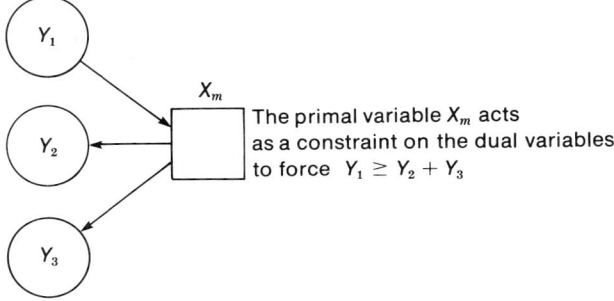

Figure 13-1 Inclusion of an ordinal utility constraint in an RPM network.

numbers is to be able to put a value on societal improvements that will benefit both current and future generations.

The most reliable numbers that we can work with are those taken from today's events. Numbers from the past may be very accurate, but they probably do not reflect current values; for example, the use of base-year statistics, such as current prices stated in 1968 dollars, helps give comparative meaning to monetary values collected over a period of time. The numbers given to actions expected to take place in the future always involve some amount of guesswork because there is no way to make forecasts with complete accuracy.

MULTIPLE FUTURES Even today's data used for today's decisions must be handled with caution. Most numbers are based on the average or most expected value of an outcome. For instance, when we include a delivery time in a model as being one week although we know the delivery might arrive a day earlier or several days later, we do so because the 1-wk estimate seems a good, average time that is neither overly optimistic nor overly pessimistic. This is the *deterministic* approach.

Another approach is to use a *stochastic model*, that is, one that includes a probability distribution of events. For our example of delivery times, a stochastic model would involve estimates of the probability for each delivery period (e.g., the probability of a delivery arriving on the fifth, sixth, and seventh days, etc.) and the anticipated cost resulting from each delivery interval (e.g., later deliveries rapidly increase costs owing to inconvenience or actions required to find substitute resources). Deterministic models also can be used to evaluate the effects of uncertain futures through a *sensitivity analysis* (Section 5-3). Putting different numbers into a deterministic model of a problem will logically alter the solution. The sensitivity of a factor in the problem is measured by determining how much that factor can vary before the solution is no longer acceptable or the outcome suggests an alternative course of action. This concept has been demonstrated repeatedly in our discussions of dual values. Shadow prices reveal how much the numbers given in the problem statement can vary before a different solution emerges.

A similar method of testing sensitivity involves setting an *aspiration level* for a given factor. In a manufacturing system the standards of performance for different jobs are aspiration levels. Used-car sales personnel and buyers base their bargaining positions on personal aspiration levels for a given car. In a deterministic model an aspiration level can be set for a factor where only shaky estimates are possible; this aspiration level is then considered to be a firm figure in the analysis. By rerunning the analysis with different aspiration levels, a decision maker may evaluate options without knowing the actual distribution of unknown values. For example, if the delivery time for supplies is uncertain and even the range is obscure, a selected delivery duration can be put into a model to observe its effect on total costs. When a calculated cost is acceptable, the only remaining question is whether the aspiration level that produced the acceptable cost was reasonable.

It is much easier to judge whether a factor will be above or below a certain level than to estimate the likelihood of every possible value for that factor.

Example 13-1: *The first resort* Snowmore Mountain is a popular skiing area near a large metropolitan population. A group of skiing enthusiasts with OR/MS training developed plans to build a modern resort and secured capital pledges of $500,000 to finance their plans. As part of the fund raising, they contracted with a quick-food chain to operate a restaurant that will occupy most of the ground floor of their envisioned two-level lodge. Now the group must decide the room layout for guests.

The season at Snowmore lasts about 100 days, and during this period other resorts on the mountain average 90 percent occupancy. The group aspires to make a 15 percent return on their investment, or $0.15 \times \$500,000 = \$75,000$, per season. Of this amount $15,000 will be returned from the restaurant lease, and therefore, $60,000 must be earned from rentals. Thus the aspiration level is set at $600/day. There is considerable uncertainty about the occupancy rate as a function of the prices a new facility can charge. The daily rates for similar facilities with established reputations are $40 for a suite and $7 for a dorm space. These rates should yield net returns of $21 and $4, for suites and dorm space, respectively, after deducting fixed charges and assuming 80 percent occupancy. An RPM network based on the known cost figures, physical conditions, and revenue aspiration level is shown in Figure 13-2.

The allocation plan for an 80 percent occupancy rate meets the aspiration level of $600/day by allotting the entire space to individual suites. All the figures that are involved in the solution have a historical foundation except the 80 percent capacity factor. If 80 percent is considered conservative, additional cost data could be generated for a more optimistic 90 percent capacity factor. Assuming the variable cost drops faster for a dorm space than for a suite as greater utilization increases total revenue, the net returns expected at a 90 percent occupancy are

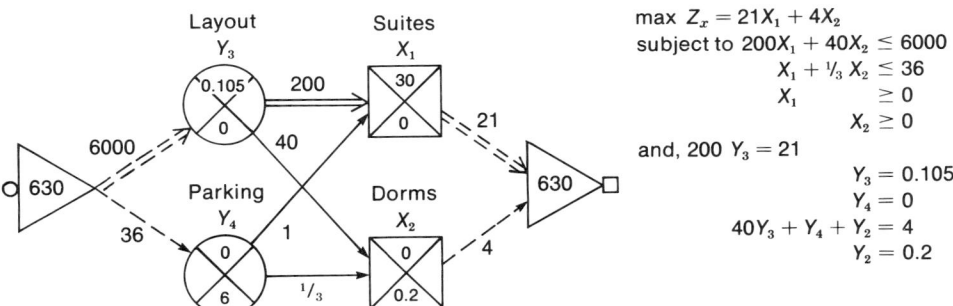

Figure 13-2 Optimal space allocation at 80 percent resort occupancy (Example 13-1).

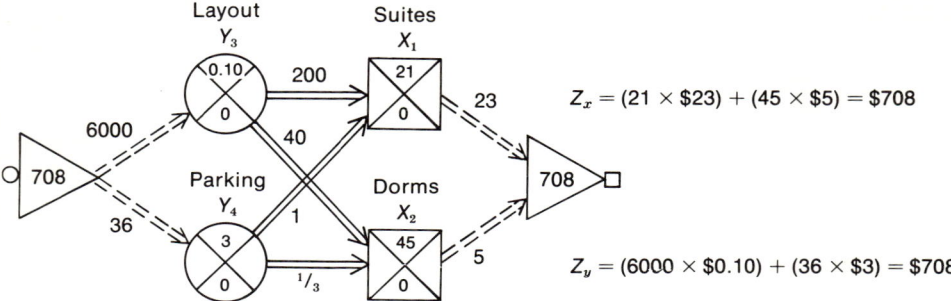

Figure 13-3 Optimal space allocation at 90 percent resort occupancy (Example 13-1).

$23 for a suite and $5 for a dorm space. The optimal solution for this mix is shown in Figure 13-3.

Greater returns are a normal consequence of raising the utilization of a facility, and they are evident in the increase of $708 − $630 = $78 shown by the new optimal mix. Now the resort planners can evaluate the effects of uncertainty. Both the 80 percent and 90 percent occupancy rates meet the cutoff objective of $600. The change in layout between the two rates is probably more significant than the increase in total return, which was naturally expected at the more optimistic utilization estimate. The likelihood of attaining 90 percent occupancy is surely influenced by the type of guests provided for at the lodge. Having space for guests seeking either rooms or dorm space may increase the probability of reaching 90 percent, or it may decrease it. There might already be adequate dorm space at Snowmore and therefore providing more would be a losing proposition. Such considerations must enter into the decision. It is not enough to consider only the probability of an uncertain factor such as a utilization rate; the ramifications of each aspiration level must also be explored.

SECTION 13-1 TUNE-UP
1. Would any mix reach the $600/day aspiration level for the Snowmore resort described in Example 13-1 if the net returns at 75 percent occupancy for suites and dorm space were $19 and $3.75, respectively?
2. What purpose was served by identifying an aspiration level of $600/day?

13-2 Think big–think small

Several definitions of a system were offered in Chapter 4. Both common sense and the definitions suggest that a system can be very large—even too large to comprehend. One of the tasks of OR/MS analysts is to identify boundaries for a system that capture the critical factors of a problem yet are restrictive enough to allow a reasonable solution search. In other words, all the key inputs and outputs should receive attention without cluttering the analysis with irrelevant factors. But the nagging doubts that accompany a decision on what is or is not relevant can age an analyst.

It would have been easy to model physical systems in the Dark Ages when it was believed there were only four elements—earth, water, air, and fire—and that all substances were supposedly composed of these elements. It was thought that earth and water were pulled down by gravity while air and fire tended to rise because they possessed levity; however, air was likely to have earth particles mixed with it so that it never rose very far. Even gravity was not regarded as we know it today; it was assumed that something in an object made it aspire to rush to the earth instead of being pulled downward by the earth. Given these beliefs, most observable physical phenomena could be explained quite simply and with surprising reasonableness.

Less than 100 years ago operations of most commercial organizations could be represented by an austere model. Owing largely to limited communication, businesses were smaller, less complex, and less affected by outside influences such as government agencies and policies; consequently, fewer factors were required to represent the functions of an organization realistically. Today we live in a very complex environment. Information flows abundantly and rapidly. Government and commerce are inextricably bound together. Multinational interests are linked with domestic concerns for conservation of raw materials, improvement in conditions of employment, utilization of energy, and environmental programs. Some very sophisticated models have been developed to improve our understanding of these interrelationships and to investigate future conditions.

MAJOR MODELS Several organizations have constructed models of the United States economy. These *econometric* models utilize a multitude of inputs that characterize the economic health of the nation; and, by altering magnitudes or relationships among the inputs, the effects of different economic actions can be theoretically experienced before they are actually implemented. Economic models provide guidance in answering such questions as "Will increased foreign trade raise the domestic inflation rate?" or "Will an energy shortage reduce gains in the gross national product, and, if so, how much?" The models developed to date do not always foretell what actually will happen, but they provide insights into the workings of a system and promise greater accuracy as complex interrelationships become more evident. They are necessarily *dynamic models* because relationships must be frequently adjusted to reflect new forces at work in the economy.

World models are obviously more ambitious than national models and are beset with the same limitations, only magnified. Jay W. Forrester, a professor at M. I. T. who was a leading figure in the development of the digital computer, has spurred computer simulation through his pioneering efforts in *systems dynamics*. The titles of his books reveal the progressive scope of his modeling: "*Industrial Dynamics*" (1961), "*Urban Dynamics*" (1969), and "*World Dynamics*" (1971).

The most recent book describes a model for simulating the major ecological forces at work in the world today.

The future projected by Forrester is sobering. Although his model necessarily simplifies many interactions, it incorporates an array of data ranging from expert opinions to hard facts about the world's known resources, population growth rates, incidence of pollution connected with power plants, etc. These variables interact to affect a measure of performance called *quality of life*, a composite condition that reflects the material standard of living, crowding, pollution, and food supply. A representative scenario begins with an understanding that human population cannot grow without additional food supplies. Since most of the world's best land is already under cultivation, more farm output can be realized only through increased use of tractors, fertilizers, pesticides, and other industrial products. But extra industrial output makes a heavier drain on our already scarce natural resources and inevitably creates more pollution. Then greater pollution ultimately interferes with both the growth of food and population, which closes the vicious circle.

Forrester cites numerous computer runs that have traced many possible futures. One run has postulated that current conditions will progress until growth is halted and reversed by pressures arising from the scarcity of natural resources. Another run has assumed undiscovered natural wealth becomes available, say, from deposits under oceans, and has extrapolated trends to show how accelerated industrialization could result in runaway pollution that would overwhelm the biosphere. A modification of this run allowed advances in technology to control pollution, but these advances caused the population to soar until the land could not provide sustenance. A graph of one scenario is shown in Figure 13-4.

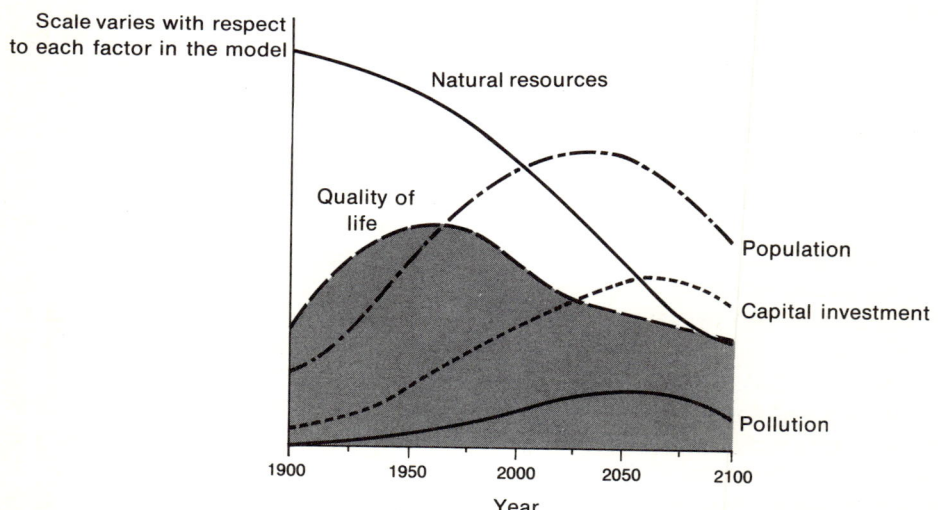

Figure 13-4 Simulated future conditions showing growth halted by a shortage of natural resources. [Adapted from Forrester (1971).]

MORE MODEST SYSTEMS Most OR/MS practitioners will never analyze a major system, but they can expect to encounter more modest system problems. Analyses of simpler systems usually rely on approximations, restrict the number of interacting variables, and assume a static rather than dynamic environment. Although some reality is lost by the simplifying techniques, they are defensible from the standpoint that decisions are needed quickly and the resulting analysis is probably more comprehensive and recordable than conventional intuitive techniques. For example, a transportation model assumes rigid transfer costs for a specific point in time, largely ignores environmental influences, and is immune to political pressures, but it produces an optimal solution for the given circumstances that challenges comparable results by intuition.

Systems associated with the world of commerce typically attempt to organize the resources of men, capital assets, and procedures to produce the highest payoff. In these systems, two tasks are combined: determining the structure of the model and ascertaining the best decision or course of action. The former usually suggests a closed, relational system; and the latter implies an open, optimization system. An RPMS representation offers a format for both tasks.

A descriptive diagram of a manufacturing system is shown in Figure 13-5. According to RPM conventions, circles indicate the resources and boxes show the activity or process. Taken as a whole, the closed system can represent the functions of a company as it sells its products to consumers, uses the results of sales to plan production, converts the plans to manufacturing schedules and orders, produces products, and sells to consumers. This framework emphasizes the internal functions of the company. The external environment is merely implied, but exogenous factors can be included by extending the scope of the system to explicitly show competitors, legal considerations, market conditions, political influences, etc.

The lower-right section of Figure 13-5 is the purchasing subsystem. By isolating the purchasing function from the rest of the closed system we can examine its effectiveness as an open system. In effect, the total system is considered as the environment for the purchasing subsystem; equivalently, the isolated purchasing subsystem can be considered as the environment for the rest of the system to see how it is affected by the purchasing function. From either view the purchasing function becomes an open system which is amenable to OR/MS optimizing procedures. The isolation is accomplished by putting *gates* on all the flow links between purchasing and the rest of the system.

The isolated purchasing subsystem is shown in Figures 13-6 and 13-7. Figure 13-6 indicates the placement of the gates, shown as double triangles; these gates represent minimizing or maximizing objectives for purchasing. The flows and nodes are labeled in Figure 13-7, which is drawn as a conventional RPMS diagram. Inputs and outputs of the open system are obtained by integrating the flow with its associated resource or process. Thus the input to the material list resource node Y_1 is $b_1 = a_{11}X_1$. The physical meaning of b_1 is the portion a_{11} of time made available to prepare material lists by the manning level X_1 at the production-control department.

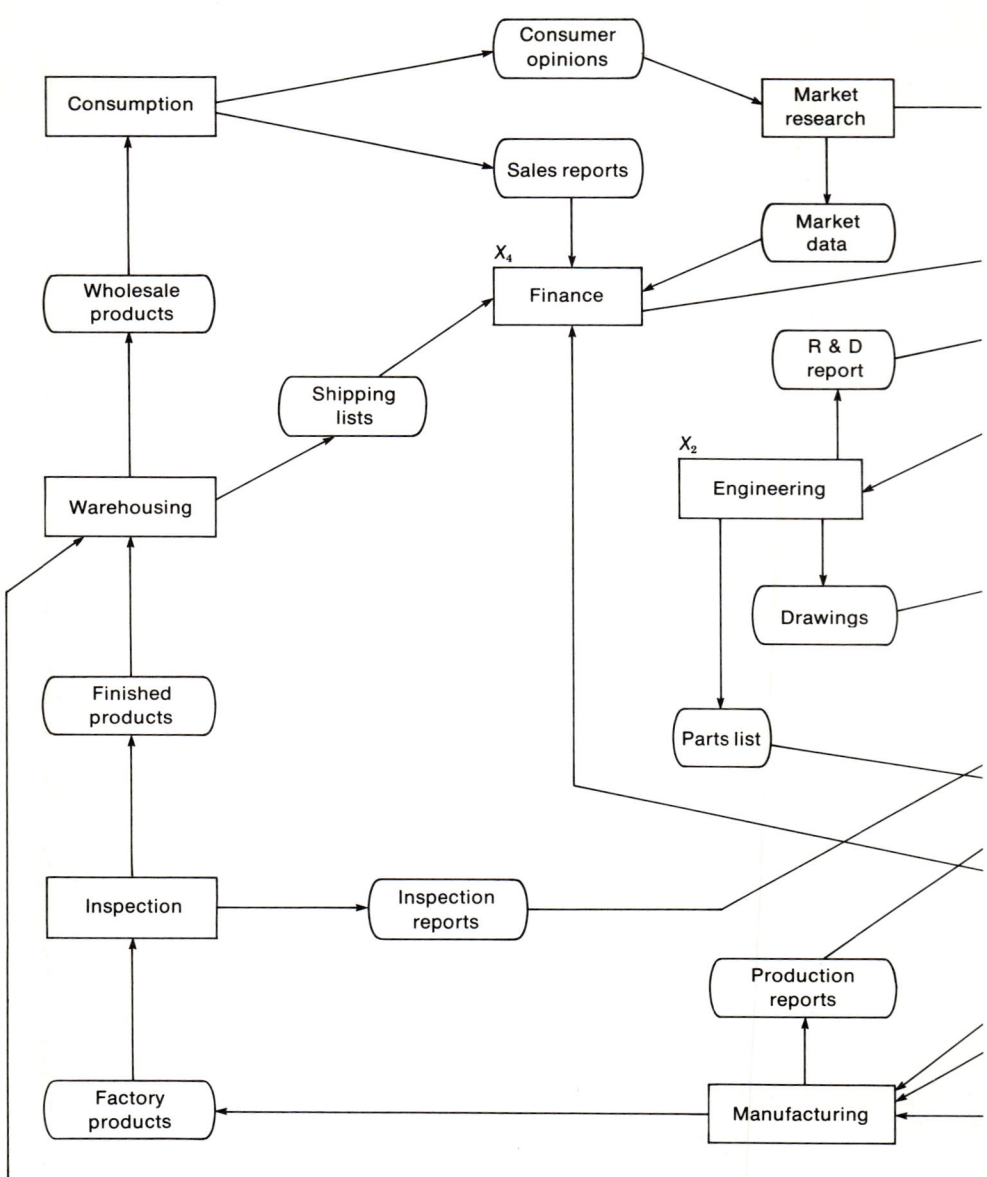

Figure 13-5 Closed-system model of a manufacturing organization.

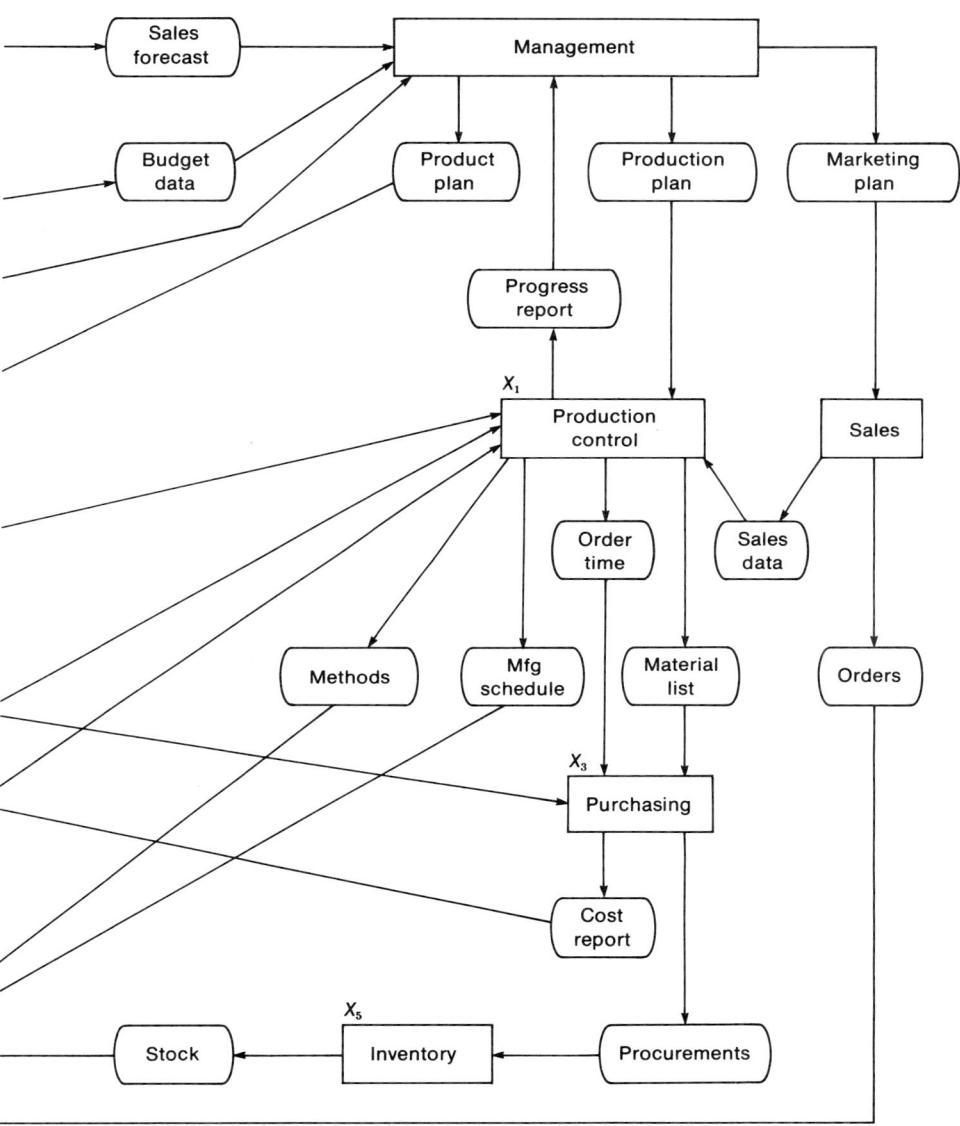

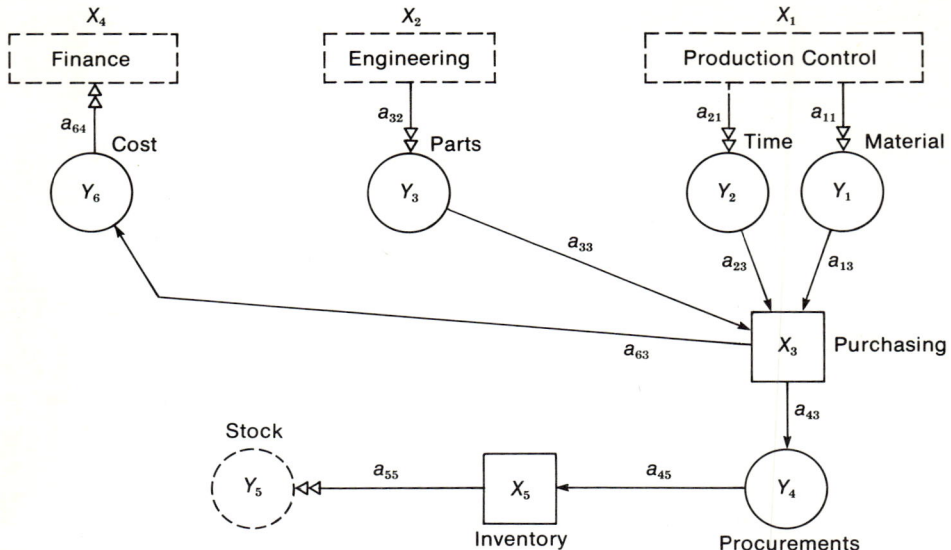

Figure 13-6 Purchasing function isolated by gates from the rest of the system.

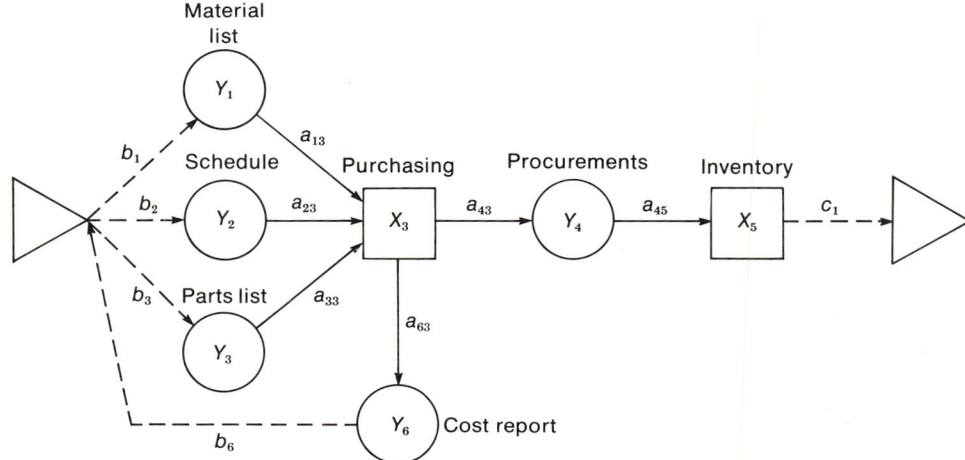

Figure 13-7 Purchasing function diagrammed as an open system with exogenous transmittals. The environment is represented by triangles and comprises the rest of the closed system shown in Figure 13-5.

Similarly: develop a schedule in the department (X_3) to procure goods (Y_4) and

$b_1 = a_{11}X_1$ total labor available (person-hr) for preparing material lists

$b_2 = a_{21}X_1 =$ total time available for purchasing

$b_3 = a_{32}X_2 =$ portion a_{32} of engineering efforts X_2 diverted to preparing parts lists

$b_6 = a_{64}X_4 =$ cost reports required by the finance department to maintain its activity level X_4

$Y_1 =$ per unit contribution to company profit made by the material list

$Y_2 =$ unit value of time spent by procurement

$Y_3 =$ unit contribution of the parts list to the overall company profit

$Y_4 =$ unit value of the purchased parts (what it will do to the profit if one unit is short)

$Y_6 =$ per unit contribution of cost reports to the company profit

$X_3 =$ activity level at the purchasing department (person-hr/wk)

$X_5 =$ activity level at the inventory (units of goods received for storage per week)

$a_{13} =$ amount of material-list efforts required to maintain one activity level X_3

$a_{23} =$ time required to effect one unit of purchasing activity X_3

$a_{33} =$ parts lists needed to maintain one unit of purchasing activity X_3

$a_{43} =$ units of purchased procurements produced by one unit of X_3

$a_{45} =$ amount of procurements handled by a unit level of inventory activity X_5

$a_{63} =$ cost reports produced per person-hour of purchasing department effort

$c_1 = a_{55}Y_5$

  $=$ contribution of a level of X_5 to stocks, evaluated in dollars

From the given relationships a familiar model is easily developed. The primal LP model is

max $Z_x = c_1 X_5$ maximize the dollar value of stocks received from inventory

subject to

$b_1 - a_{13}X_3 \geq 0$ material-list-efforts availability

$b_2 - a_{23}X_3 \geq 0$ time constraint

$b_3 - a_{33}X_3 \geq 0$ parts-list-efforts availability

$a_{63}X_3 - b_6 \geq 0$ to satisfy the finance department's activity needs

$a_{43}X_3 - a_{45}X_5 \geq 0$ to provide enough procurements to the inventory department

The inequations for the primal resulted from balancing flows around Y_1, Y_2, Y_3, Y_4, and Y_6. The dual LP model for the same system is developed by balancing flows around the process nodes X_3 and X_5 (all variables are nonnegative):

$$\min Z_y = b_1 Y_1 + b_2 Y_2 + b_3 Y_3 - b_6 Y_6 \quad \text{minimize the cost of operation}$$

subject to

$$a_{13}Y_1 + a_{23}Y_2 + a_{33}Y_3 - a_{43}Y_4 - a_{63}Y_6 \geq 0 \quad \text{cost accounting at } X_3$$

$$a_{45}Y_4 - c_1 \geq 0 \quad \text{cost accounting at } X_5$$

After the symbols are replaced with numerical data, the models can be solved using the procedures described in previous chapters.

SYSTEM SHAPES AND SLICES   An object may take different shapes and meanings when viewed by different people or by the same people at different times. An optical illusion can baffle the senses as it seems to change shape before your eyes, and a modern painting imparts different messages to its viewers. Also, the same system diagram can be interpreted in diverse ways, reflecting the individual interests of observers.

A purchasing agent looking at the closed system in Figure 13-5 would focus on the *purchasing* node and is likely to feel that the diagram did injustice to his specialty. The agent could recite a long list of factors that affect his actions. Many of the factors are exogenous to the system as diagrammed because they are part of the larger system environment in which the organization exists. If a satisfactory analysis is impossible without explicitly considering outside factors, the system can be expanded to encompass them. For example, the purchasing agent might insist that the supplier from which materials and parts are purchased must be included; also, the agent might say that the general market which includes competing purchasing agents should be added. As shown in Figure 13-8, such factors can be incorporated into the open system, and after the inclusion, the analysis can proceed as before. In doing so, it is important to recognize the relationship of the newly defined environment to the newly included factors.

By changing the location of the gates that isolate the open system, a different slice is exposed for examination. A segment containing only the *procurements* resource and the *inventory* process is shown in Figure 13-9. This segment can be called the *inventory system*, and it represents a function that has received a lot of attention from management scientists. If time scheduling is of primary interest to an observer of the inventory system, the system can be reassembled in the form of a critical-path network; then it would take the shape shown in Figure 13-10, and the analysis would focus on the schedule for a particular order of goods. A flowchart for record keeping in the inventory system would be important to ad-

RPMS: A Tool for General Systems Analysis   439

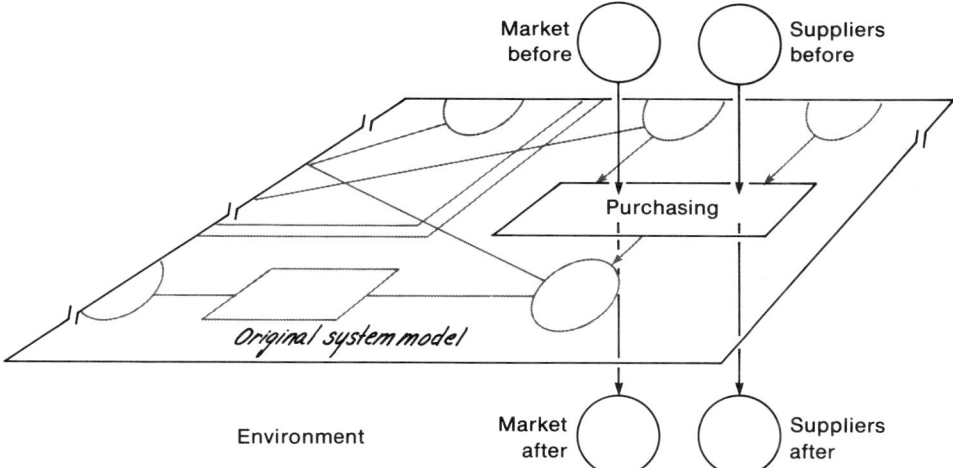

Figure 13-8 Variables added to enrich the system model of Figure 13-5. Both the "before" and "after" conditions for added environmental factors are shown to present a more complete cause-and-effect relationship.

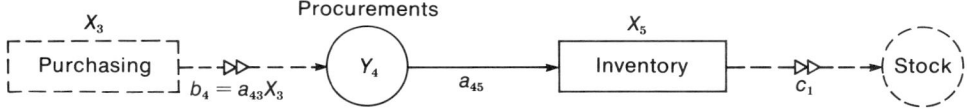

Figure 13-9 Inventory RPMS model.

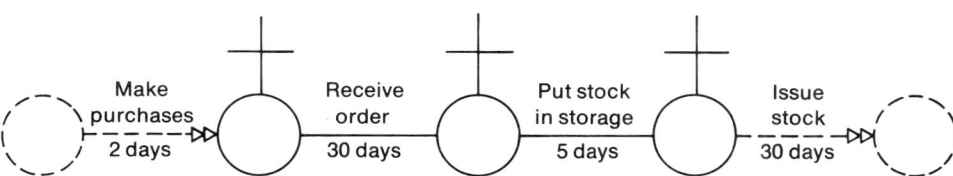

Figure 13-10 Inventory critical-path network.

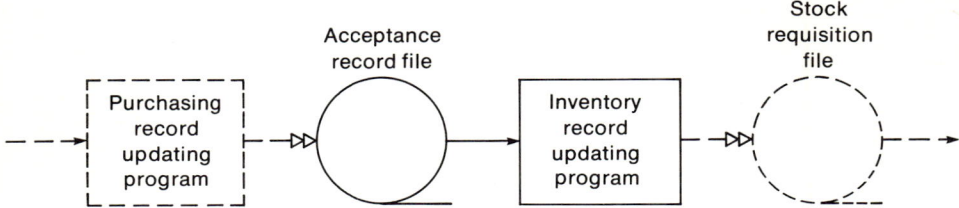

Figure 13-11   Inventory-records flowchart for computer data processing.

ministrators in order to know the state of purchase orders, invoice payments, inventory files, and stock requisitions. The data processing tasks associated with the inventory system can be shown using traditional electronic data processing (EDP) flowchart symbols (Figure 13-11).

PARAMETRIC INTERACTIONS   Most of the RPMS examples studied in this book have assumed the parameters to be constants. In Chapter 12, however, we have introduced the idea that a parameter can be the decision variable whose value is to satisfy the system's requirements. Thus, we were able, for example, to choose the service rate for a queuing model that optimized the average operation of the system. Taking the idea a step further, we can envision a system where parameters are linear (or even nonlinear) functions of variables determined elsewhere in the system. It is also conceivable that decision variables themselves are dependent on each other and the objective functions are not simple linear sums of weighted variables. The recent trend toward the use of benefit/cost ratios instead of the LP-type *benefit-minus-cost* objective functions to measure the effectiveness of a program is an example.

Although RPMS models can still be built to represent such systems, it is no longer certain that an optimal solution can be found for such models. LP methods are of limited use in such a case, and Dynamic Programming (Chapter 10) and Branch and Bound (Chapter 8) methods are often too cumbersome and impractical. But this is not to say that attempts to model such systems should be abandoned. Indeed, there are many OR/MS models that include such features while remaining simple and practical in solving industrial and societal problems. One such example is the celebrated *Wilson's formula* for inventory control.

Example 13-2: Inventory control for WAM packing cartons   The Wonderland airmail service (WAM) uses recyclable packing cartons. It is estimated that the annual demand D for such cartons is 200,000 and that there is an adequate circulation of such cartons among WAM customers, thanks to the abundant supply created during a more affluent era. When WAM is in need of cartons, it launches a campaign to collect reusable cartons from its customers. Each such campaign incurs trucking and labor costs of $c_1 = \$60$ regardless of the number of cartons collected (annual ordering cost $= c_1 N = 60 N$, where N is the number of such campaigns per year). Each carton must be repaired and sanitized at the cost of $c_0 = \$0.80$ before being allowed back into the service (annual cost of goods $= c_0 D = \$160,000$). The storage of the cartons is expensive because of bulk and fire insurance, running $c_2 = \$0.10$ per carton (annual holding cost $= c_2 \times$ average number of cartons in storage). In order to minimize the cost of the operation, it has been proposed not to collect cartons from customers until the warehouse is empty, and to ask the post office industrial engineer to determine the optimal frequency N and the *economic ordering quantity* Q of the carton-collection operation.

Figure 13-12 is an RPM network for the WAM problem. The usage of the cartons is assumed to be uniform throughout the year. If WAM collects Q number of cartons N times per year, there will be NQ cartons to satisfy the demand D (flow balance around the demand node: $NQ = D$). If WAM waits for the stock to become depleted before replenishing it with Q cartons, the average number of cartons in the warehouse will be $Q/2$. Per carton cost of holding drops to $c_2/2 = \$0.05$. Since $NQ = D = 200,000$, the decision made on N would automatically determine the value of $Q = D/N$. Furthermore, the RPM network in Figure 13-12 uses Q and N as parameters of transmittance.

The total cost

$$Z_q = c_0 NQ + c_1 N + c_2 Q/2$$

must equal

$$Z_p = DP = D\left[\frac{C_2}{2N} + \frac{C_1}{Q} + C_0\right]$$

and a simple substitution of $D = NQ$ proves this to be true. The annual cost of goods $c_0 NQ = c_0 D = \$160,000$ is a constant that is independent of the value of Q or N by itself. The minimum for Z_q or Z_p will occur when the annual ordering cost $c_1 N = Dc_1/Q$ is equal to the annual holding cost $c_2 Q/2 = Dc_2/(2N)$ since one is inversely proportional to the other with respect to the variable Q or N. $Dc_1/Q = c_2 Q/2$ yields $Q = \sqrt{2Dc_1/c_2}$, and $c_1 N = Dc_2/(2N)$ yields $N =$

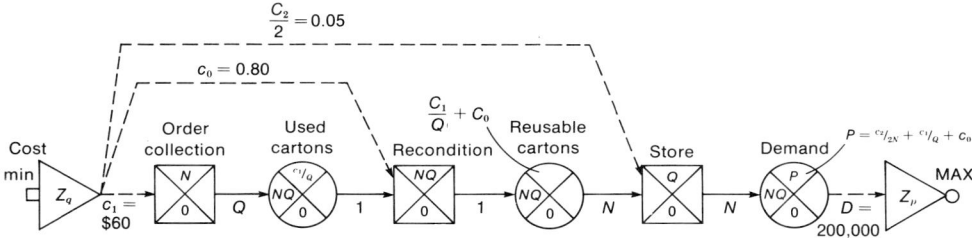

Figure 13-12 Inventory system for recyclable WAM packing cartons.

$\sqrt{Dc_2/(2c_1)}$ for the optimal values of Q and N. $QN = \sqrt{2Dc_1/c_2}\sqrt{Dc_2/2c_1} = D$ as it should be. In the case of WAM,

$$EOQ = Q = \sqrt{240{,}000{,}000}$$
$$= 15{,}492 \quad \text{cartons/order}$$
$$N = 12.9 \quad \text{or roughly 13 times per yr}$$

The optimal total annual cost is

$$Z_q = Z_p = c_0 D + c_1 N + \frac{c_2 Q}{2} = c_0 D + \sqrt{\frac{Dc_1c_2}{2}} + \sqrt{\frac{Dc_1c_2}{2}}$$
$$= Dc_0 + \sqrt{2Dc_1c_2} = \$161{,}500$$

The formula for $EOQ = \sqrt{2Dc_1/c_2}$ is commonly known as *Wilson's formula*.

SECTION 13-2 TUNE-UP

1. In "World Dynamics" Forrester recommends global cooperation and careful long-range planning to avoid collapse of our civilization: "The short run is more visible and more compelling. It speaks loudly for immediate attention. But a series of actions all aimed at short-run improvement can eventually burden a system with long-run depressants so severe that even heroic short-run measures no longer suffice".[1] As shortages are becoming more apparent each year, some short-range actions are being initiated (e.g., search for new energy sources and greater exploration for raw materials). Suggest some longer-range policies to avert the projected disasters and diagram the basic resource/process relationships involved.

2. Every year the federal budget includes billions of dollars for research, and a significant portion of the total research money is awarded to projects conducted by universities. Federal funds are used to support research studies, educate scientists, and provide extension services. These activities produce new technologies, which promote industrial or public benefits, and scientists prepared to carry on future research. In turn, the benefits and scientific personnel contribute to the national economy that provides the federal funds to initiate the cycle. The nature of this closed system is diagrammed in Figure 13-13.[2]

    The continued health of a program depends on its ability to satisfy expectations. For example, a research program should continue to receive support as long as it is making sufficient progress in meeting societal needs. One way to examine the effectiveness of the components of a program is to isolate them from the rest of the system's components and evaluate the resulting structure as an open system. Some interesting observations can be made even without specific numerical data to define relationships among the components. Using the symbols given in Figure

---

[1] Jay W. Forrester, *World Dynamics*, Wright Allen, Cambridge, Mass., 1971.
[2] M.S. Inoue and J.L. Riggs, "Resource Planning and Management (RPM) Network," *Proc. International Symposium on System Engineering and Analysis*, vol. II, 1972, pp. 187–192.

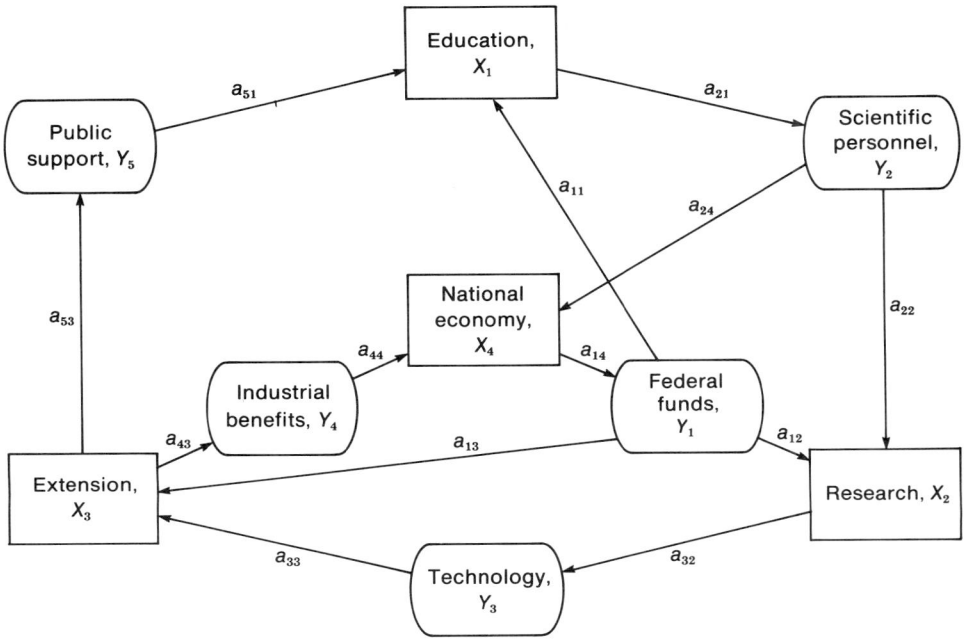

Figure 13-13 RPMS representation of a closed system that encompasses basic and applied research, education, and training of scientists and technologists, and extension and advisory services to the public.

13-13, examine the effectiveness of federal funding derived from the national economy X_4 and Y_1 by placing gates at a_{11}, a_{12}, a_{24}, a_{44}, and a_{13}. The remaining nodes X_1, X_2, X_3, Y_2, Y_3, Y_4, and Y_5 are the environment affected by the federal budget and can be assembled as an open system.

Draw an RPMS diagram of the open system and briefly describe the inputs and outputs. For instance, the input to education can be labeled c_1 and results from integrating a_{11} over Y_1 ($c_1 = a_{11} Y_1$); it is interpreted as the amount of federal funding allocated to education. Similarly, b_2, the output from Y_2, is the number of scientists to be trained to meet national needs ($b_2 = a_{24} X_4$). After the network has been constructed, write the corresponding primal and dual LP models and briefly interpret the meaning of each statement in the models.

13-3 Think again

After all the specialized techniques of OR/MS are sorted out, the unifying theme is the *OR/MS way of thinking*. It is easy to lose this theme in the fascination engendered by clever number manipulations and thought-provoking diagrams. But the tools of the trade are of little use unless they are accompanied by discipline and logic in practicing them. It is appropriate to conclude this introduction to OR/MS with some keys to thinking that should help open the door to OR/MS applications.

RESOURCEFULNESS Abundant examples and sample applications have been cited in this text, but rarely can they be copied exactly to solve actual problems. They should be viewed as prototypes because they exhibit general formats for analyzing different classes of problems. One of the prominent features of an RPM network is the assistance it provides in identifying the basic structure of a problem. Too often a solution method is chosen before the structure of a problem is confirmed. An OR/MS analyst who tries to apply a favorite solution procedure, such as the transportation method, to every problem is like a golfer who uses only one club or a doctor who prescribes the same pills for every ailment.

Sometimes none of the OR/MS tools are just right for evaluating a certain situation. Then an analyst can display resourcefulness by adapting familiar methods to suit the unusual situation. Such modifications might be the translation of data into different units or the examination of facts from a different angle. For example, the increasing attention devoted to energy conservation has led to proposals that units of output be measured, not just by man-hours, but by materials consumed per unit and by the energy needed per unit. Such factors included in productivity studies could easily produce a more realistic appraisal and alter the attractiveness of previously proposed designs.

Another example of resourcefulness is to apply conventional tools in unconventional ways. In Chapter 11 we observed the use of a precedence matrix in developing critical-path networks. This use of the input/output (I/O) matrix can be extended to other situations. In Figure 13-14, the rows and columns represent research projects being conducted by an organization. Project directors are asked to indicate where the results of their projects can be expected to contribute to other projects. The expected contributions are noted by O's in the I/O matrix. As shown, resources from project A should benefit projects C, D, and I; then, by imposing a staircase pattern on the matrix (similar to Figure 11-6), a path of related work in the total research structure is identified. This path traces mutually supporting activities (boxes) and the resources (circles) that provide the support. From this pattern an RPM network can easily be developed.

PATIENCE To the uninitiated the most obvious characteristic of OR/MS is its extensive use of numbers or symbols to represent numbers. Few people are naturally prepared to accept this extreme dedication to quantification. After all, it took mankind thousands of years to develop a number system, and only in the last few decades have numbers been associated with management. Now system planners and operators are being asked to use complex numerical formulations to guide their decision-making, and in many cases their reluctance is understandable. C. Grayson Jackson, Dean of the School of Business Administration of Southern Methodist University, nicely capsulizes the problem of implementation:

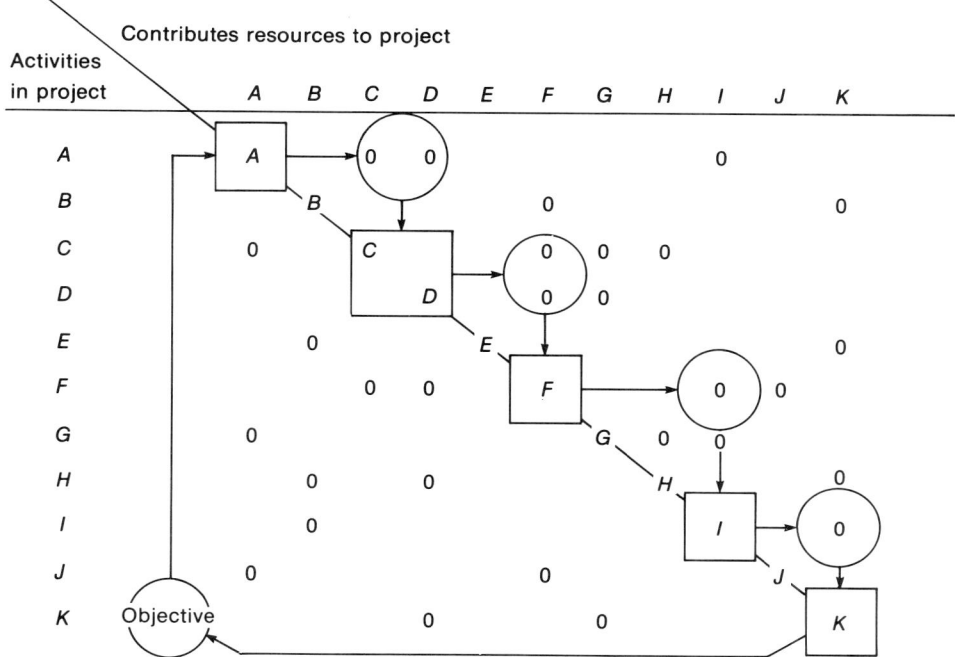

Figure 13-14 A project input-output matrix that traces the relationship of project activities and resources.

" 'What we need to do is humanize the scientist and simonize the humanist.' This dictum is a popularization of C. P. Snow's view of science and the humanities as two distinct cultures, and it is all too true when applied to management. Management and management scientists are operating as two separate cultures, each with its own goals, languages, and methods. Effective cooperation—and even communication—between the two is just about minimal. And this is a shame."[1]

Both OR/MS advocates and management personnel must learn from each other, but OR/MS analysts should make the greater effort because their expertise is meaningless until put into use. The effort requires patience. The following are among the obstacles to be overcome:

1. Lack of time: Many OR/MS modeling techniques take considerable time to develop, and decisions may be needed before the models are ready.

[1] C. Grayson Jackson, "Management Science and Business Practice," *Harvard Business Review*, July–August, 1973, p. 41.

2. Lack of data: Needed figures usually exist, but they may be buried in files or otherwise inaccessible owing to distance, rules, form, tradition, or lack of retrieval facilities.

3. Lack of sympathy: Frequently, operating personnel are not familiar with the language of OR/MS, and they may not appreciate the technical issues involved.

4. Lack of precision: Because models are frequently based on simplifying assumptions, they may not possess the realism necessary to give the precise directions managers expect to have for making important decisions.

These and other obstacles cannot be overcome immediately or completely, but they can be alleviated by making continuous, patient efforts to explain what OR/MS is and can do, getting operating personnel involved in the OR/MS side of a study, organizing data for future use, designing OR/MS studies to produce usable results quickly while establishing the framework for more complete analyses, following up studies to correct accepted models for changing conditions, and directing OR/MS tools at real problems, with real figures, to provide real service.

MATURITY As we become increasingly competent in OR/MS, our horizons should continually expand. At first we focus on small problems with limited constraints and objectives, but as our competence increases, we are capable of recognizing more subtle aspects of problems and the ways in which one problem relates to others. Very few things are truly independent. In a complex system it is safe to say that any action will have more effects than just the intended effect. A mature (complete) general systems analysis considers exposed and concealed data, bold and tenuous relationships, and obvious and obscure effects.

SENSIBILITY Bertrand Russell once quipped: "Mathematics may be defined as the subject in which we never know what we are talking about, nor whether what we are saying is true."[1] Russell's definition may seem too severe when we think of arithmetic, but it is worth noting from two OR/MS perspectives: Some relationships defy exact formulation, and mathematical solutions are only one phase of the total solution to a problem. Most real-world situations involve subjective values. Even if these subjective values can be represented accurately in mathematical expressions, people still must be convinced of their authenticity. Then the results suggested by the mathematical exercises must be converted into physical actions, and the conversion process often raises questions that were not fully quantified, such as acceptability by a union, biases of executives, or preferences of buyers. The mathematics of management are powerful but fragile.

RPMS was designed to encourage thinking that invites resourcefulness, patience, maturity, and sensibility. Its pictorial, systematic, and versatile features should assist initial understanding, improved diagnoses, and practical prescriptions. But it is still the craftsman, not his kit of tools, that determines quality.

---

[1]Bertrand Russell, "Mathematics and the Metaphysicians." *Mysticism and Logic*, 1917.

TUNE-UP SOLUTIONS

Section 13-1

1. No. The best that can be done is 30 suites at $19/suite-day to yield $570.

2. The aspiration level eliminated the consideration of the probabilities associated with all occupancy levels below 80 percent. Thus, effort is concentrated on a refined analysis of the effects of occupancy rates above 80 percent.

Section 13-2

1. Four possible long-range strategies to alleviate deleterious future conditions are diagrammed here. Several additional factors could be added to each diagram to increase the richness of the model. Even the basic diagrams suggest the difficulties that can be expected in controlling the process functions.

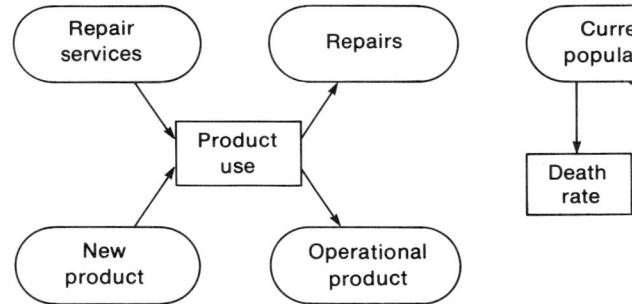

Design and build to maximize product life and minimize repair difficulties

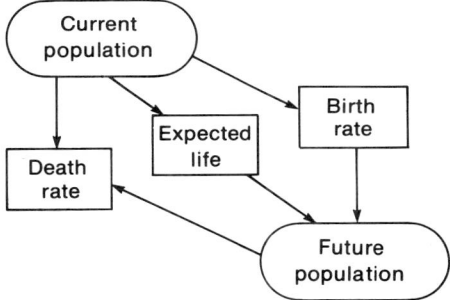

Encourage steady or declining population

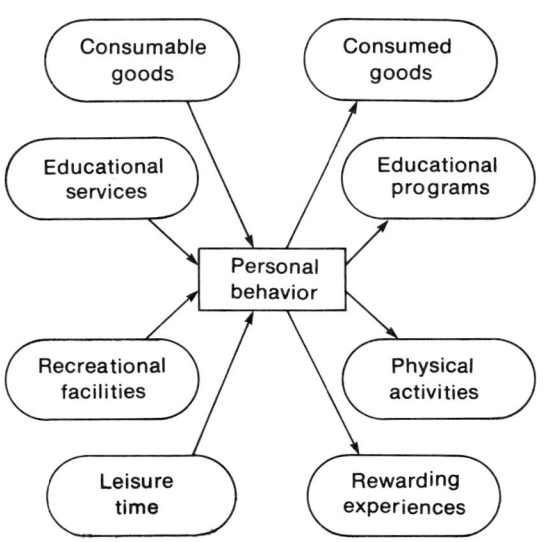

Encourage people to maximize the use of services such as education and recreation (athletics, arts, etc.) to minimize consumption of material goods.

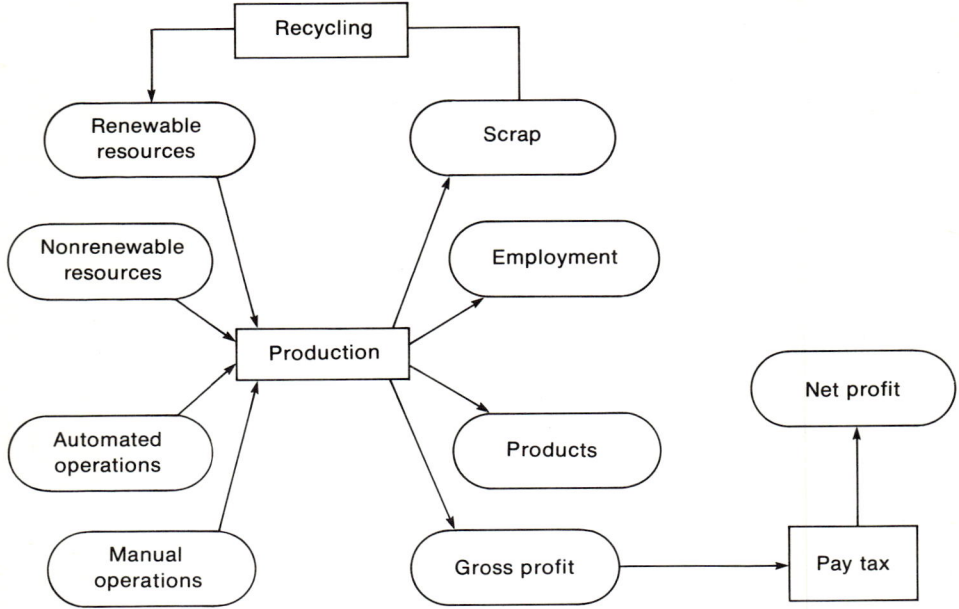

Encourage the use of renewable resources and manual operations by regulating tax rates. Maximize recycling wherever possible.

2. The open-system RPMS diagram of the resources and processes in Figure 13-13, after isolating the national economy and federal funds, is shown in Figure 13-15. The optimization goals suggested by the diagram are to minimize the federal budget while maximizing societal benefits. These strategic goals are contradictory of course, but compromising tactics can be developed by analyzing the relationships that link the components of the system. Several interactions are revealed in the primal and dual models.

The primal model is:

$\min Z_x \quad = c_1 X_1 + c_2 X_2 + c_3 X_3 \qquad$ total federal budget

subject to

$a_{21} X_1 - a_{22} X_2 \geq b_2 \qquad$ national demand for scientists

$a_{32} X_2 - a_{33} X_3 \geq 0 \qquad$ demand for new technology

$a_{43} X_3 \geq b_4 \qquad$ demand for industrial benefits

$a_{53} X_3 - a_{51} X_1 \geq 0 \qquad$ need for public support

with all X's nonnegative.
The dual model is:

$\max Z_y \quad = b_2 Y_2 + b_4 Y_4 \qquad$ total societal benefit

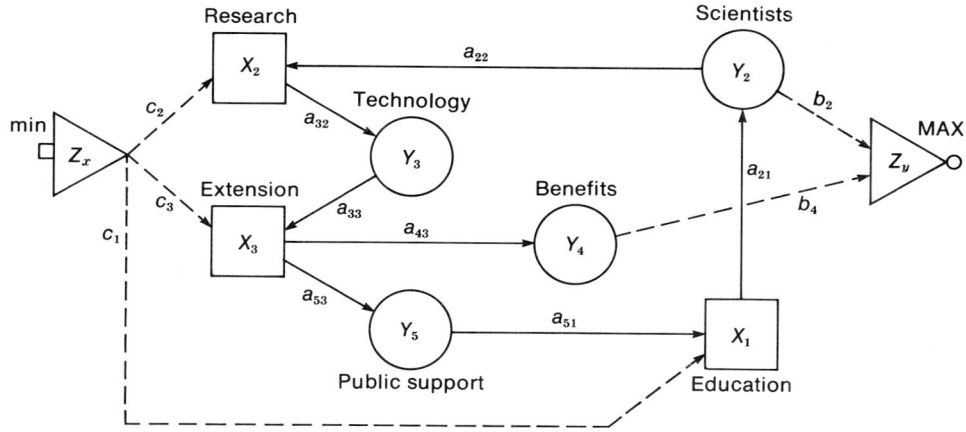

Figure 13-15 Prima model. (M.S. Inoue and J.L. Riggs, "Resource Planning and Management (RPM) Network," *Proceedings of the International Symposium on Systems Engineering and Analysis*, vol. II, p. 191, 1972.)

subject to

$a_{51}Y_5 + c_1 \geq a_{21}Y_2$ to keep education solvent

$a_{33}Y_3 + c_3 \geq a_{43}Y_4 + a_{53}Y_5$ to provide enough money and technology for extension

$a_{22}Y_2 + c_2 \geq a_{32}Y_3$ to keep research going

where all Y's are nonnegative.

EXERCISES

13-1 Evaluate another segment of the system shown in Figure 13-13 to study the effects of not including extension X_3. Place gates at a_{32}, a_{13}, a_{14}, a_{24}, and a_{53}.
  (a) Draw an RPM network of the isolated subsystem.
  (b) What activities are to be maximized, and which resources are to be minimized?
  (c) Explain how the subsystem functions.

13-2 A closed system is diagrammed in Figure 13-16.

X_1 = political process
X_2 = administration
X_3 = economic activity
X_4 = demographic component
X_5 = land use
X_6 = government services

Y_{10} = pollution generated
Y_{11} = social stratification
Y_{12} = housing demand
Y_{13} = recreational demand
Y_{14} = demand for services
Y_{15} = zoning

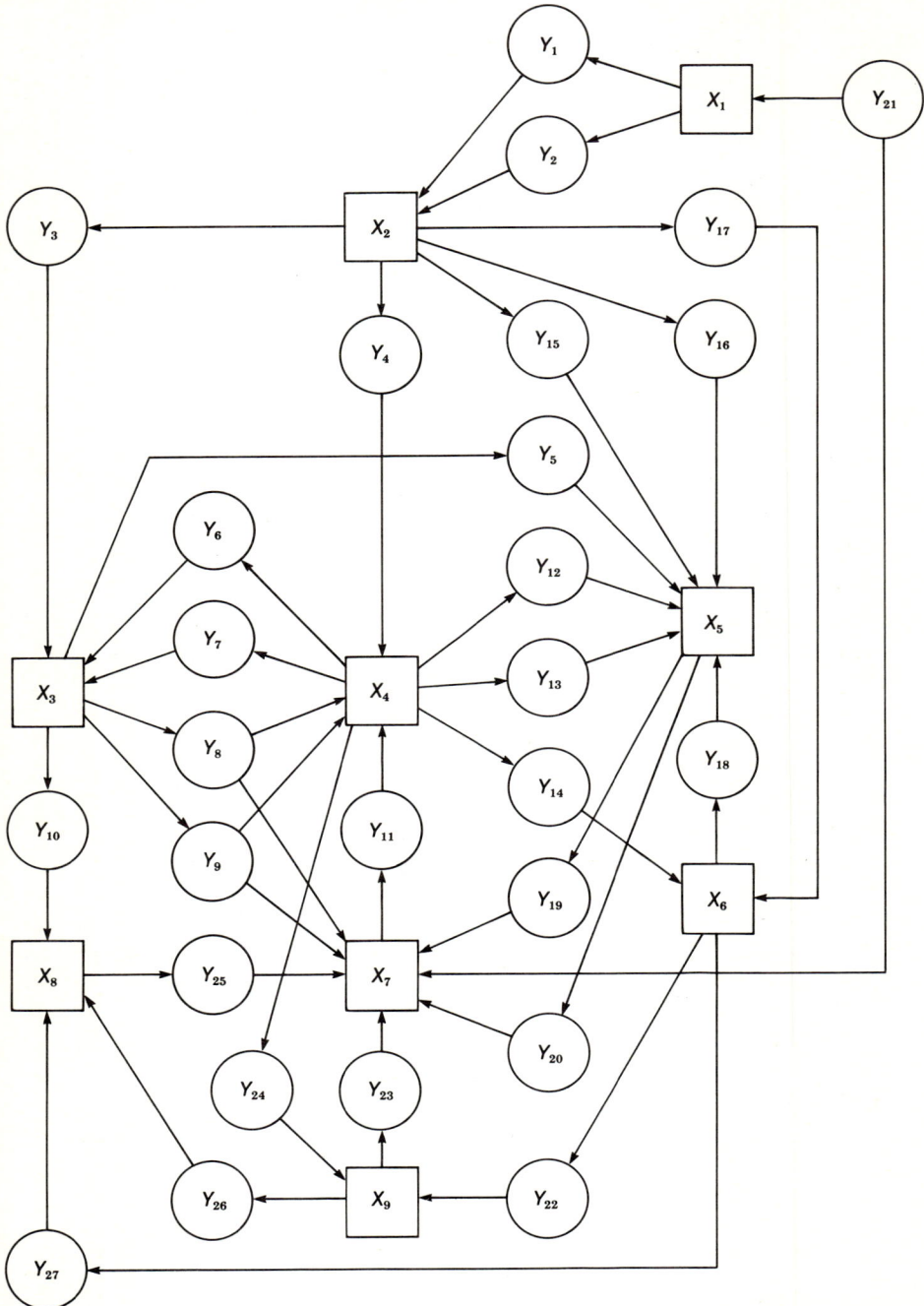

Figure 13-16 General system model for regional regulation of the quality of life.

X_7 = quality of life
X_8 = pollution impact
X_9 = transportation
Y_1 = policy
Y_2 = budget
Y_3 = standards
Y_4 = incentives
Y_5 = demand for industrial land
Y_6 = demand for goods
Y_7 = labor available
Y_8 = employment
Y_9 = income

Y_{16} = taxes
Y_{17} = budget
Y_{18} = land requirements
Y_{19} = quality of housing
Y_{20} = quality of recreation
Y_{21} = living conditions
Y_{22} = facilities
Y_{23} = crowding
Y_{24} = demand for travel
Y_{25} = pollution levels
Y_{26} = pollution generated
Y_{27} = abatement facilities

(a) What segment of the total system should be isolated to study the treatment of energy problems? Discuss how the flows suggest actions that could lead to energy conservation and the harmful effects that could result from faulty energy allocations.
(b) What exogenous factors influence Y_1?
(c) If Y_8 were expanded to reveal the activities involved in pollution control, what measurement areas would likely be present?

13-3 For an engineering project, the following simplified C & E diagram (Figure 13-17) has been created.
(a) Knowing that the management authorization must precede basic research data and external data, basic research data must precede R & D prototype data and blueprints and specs, external data must precede blueprints and specs, and blueprints and specs as well as R & D prototype data must precede the purchase order, construct an I/O matrix to show the relationships.
(b) Construct an RPM network for the engineering project and identify all the nodes.

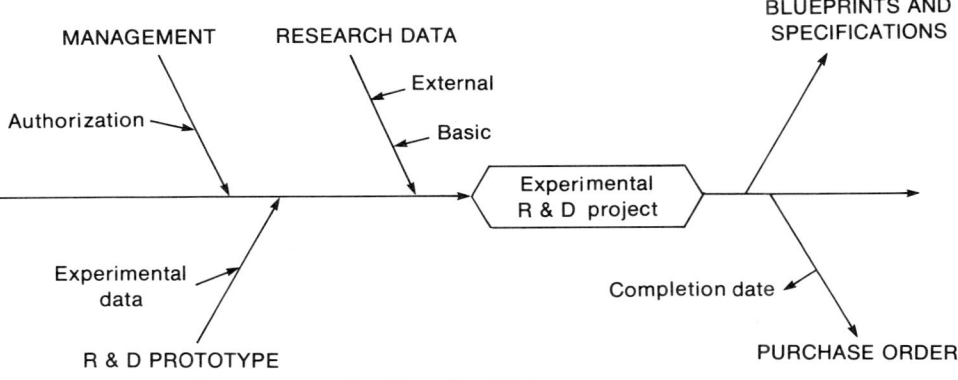

Figure 13-17 C & E diagram for Exercise 13-3.

CONVERSATIONAL COMPUTER PROGRAMS FOR LINEAR PROGRAMMING:

Appendix A

There are basically two types of linear programming software that are widely in use today: conversational programs modeled after the Basic program developed at Dartmouth College for General Electric time-sharing computer systems, and batch-oriented programs similar to the MPS used on IBM machines. The former is an excellent pedagogic tool, while the latter is more practical as an industrial tool.

In this appendix and in Appendix B, we shall introduce four programs: the GE Basic program and a typical adaptation, and the IBM/MPS program and its adaptation to a non-IBM machine. It is likely that a computer installation will have its own version of one or both types of linear programming programs, and anyone with access to a computer will have little difficulty in adjusting to the particular system being used. For those who are seriously interested in utilizing RPMS to solve LP problems, there is no better alternative than to sit at a terminal or a keypunch and actually prepare, run, and interpret examples with your own "canned" (i.e., preprogrammed software) LP package. For those of us who prefer to do without a computer, a careful study of computer run examples incorporated in the text and in these appendixes should provide an appreciation of how actual computer runs are made.

At present, there is no commercially available RPM computer program. Thus we must convert our networks into traditional LP languages and interpret their outputs accordingly. In a sense this is a blessing, for this teaches us classic OR terminology and an appreciation of works of our predecessors.

A-1 Time-sharing terminals

There are numerous different types of communication terminals that can be used with a time-sharing computer system. Some are portable and equipped with an acoustical coupler so that any telephone may be used to communicate with a computer. However, the most popular types are still the Teletype model 33 (automatic send and receive, ASR-33), which seems to have the appeal of the rugged model-T Ford, and, to a lesser extent, its companion ASR-35. Figure A-1 illustrates the keyboard of these two models. With the exception that only uppercase letters (capitals) can be used, the two keyboards are similar to the keyboard of a typewriter. The special key to note is the RETURN at the right of the second row. This RETURN key must be depressed at the end of each message to have it transmitted to the computer. We indicate the use of this key by a (r) in our printout copy of the terminal input. The underlined messages are typed in by the user, while the nonunderlined portion is received from the computer.

A-2 LINPRO***

Although no longer in the computer manufacturing business, the General Electric Company should be credited for being the first successful commercial time-sharing operator. GE supported a research grant with Dartmouth College, where the Basic (*beginner's all-purpose symbolic instruction code*) language was developed for the time-sharing system installed in 1964. The GE-265 system consisted of a GE-235 computer and a Datanet-30 communications controller (essentially another minicomputer) and was so successful that it soon became the prototype for an extensive commercial time-sharing service. Although more advanced systems (GE's Mark II and III, Control Data Corporation's Cybernet, and many others) are available today, GE-265 is still an inexpensive and versatile system that is widely used and imitated.

LINPRO*** was one of the earlier programs written in Basic. It uses the two-phase method and automatically supplies residues [called *slack variables* for less-than-or-equal-to (.LE.) constant constraints and *surplus variables* for greater-than-or-equal-to (.GE.) constant constraints] and artificial variables needed for our simplex algorithm. The program *maximizes*, so that a minimization problem must be stated using a negative form: e.g., min $10x_1 + 20x_2$ is changed to

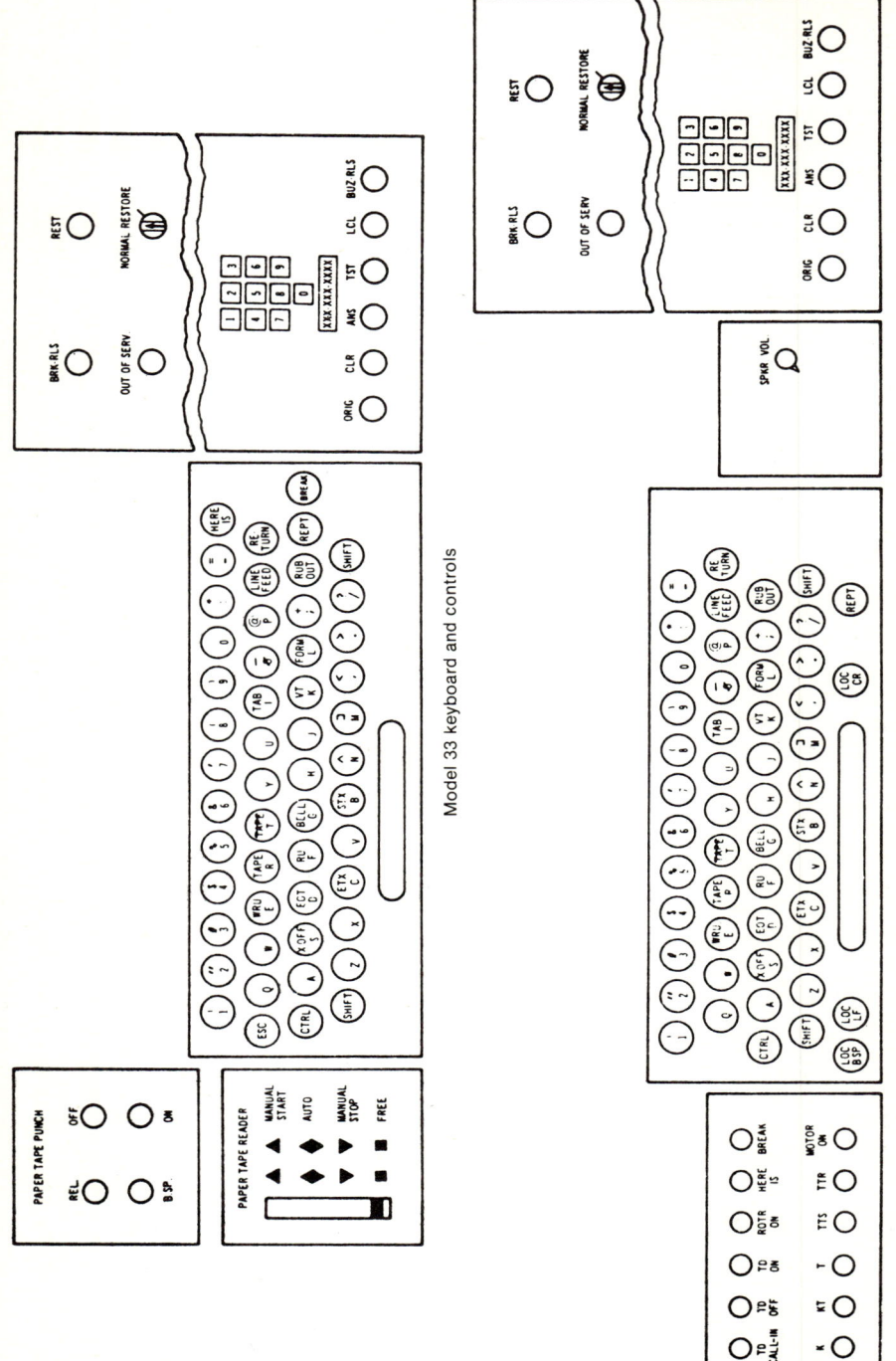

Figure A-1 Teletype terminals commonly used for time-sharing.

max $- 10x_1 - 20x_2$. The general procedure is described in Figure A-2. An example is illustrated in Figure A-6 using a variant of LINPRO***.

Step 1. Convert the RPM network to the standard LP model with a maximizing linear objective function subject to a set of linear constraints. Make all constants (exogenous or endogenous flows) positive and put all other terms on the left side of the inequality ($\leq$ or $\geq$) or equality ($=$) signs. For example, the motors and alternators problem of Chapter 5 (Section 5-3 Tune-up) may be stated as

$$\max Z_x = 4x_1 + x_2$$

subject to

$$6x_1 + 6x_2 \leq 360$$
$$1x_1 \leq 50$$
$$x_2 \leq 40$$
$$x_2 \geq 20$$
$$x_1 = 30$$

Step 2. Rearrange all constraints in the following order, supplying the necessary 0s and 1s. All .LE. ($\leq$) constraints of $ax_1 + bx_2 \leq c$ type, of which we have three, must come first:

$$6x + 6x_2 \leq 360$$
$$1x_1 + 0x_2 \leq 50$$
$$0x_1 + 1x_2 \leq 40$$

All .EQ. ($=$) constraint of $ax_1 + bx_2 = c$ type, of which we have one, must follow:

$$1x_1 + 0x_2 = 30$$

All .GE. ($\geq$) constraints of $ax_1 + bx_2 \geq c$ type, of which we have one, must be placed last:

$$0x_1 + 1x_2 \geq 20$$

Step 3. Go to a terminal, call up the computer by depressing the ORIG button and dialing the computer center's telephone number. If you do go through an operator, indicate that you are about to transmit data and request a high-grade line.

Step 4. Log on by answering appropriate questions and providing identification and account numbers. Some systems require terminals to have coded *answer-back* messages that are acknowledged by the computer center. Depressing the key marked HERE IS will print out the answer-back mes-

456

Category **MATHEMATICAL**
Name **LINPRO * * ***
Number **M 17 06 1**
Language **BASIC**
Character **4000**

PURPOSE

To maximize an objective function using the two-phase method. It automatically supplies slack, surplus, and artificial variables as required for the solution.

INSTRUCTIONS

NOTE:

More detailed instructions may be obtained by listing programs LPINST * * * and LPINS2 * * *.

Before using this program arrange all constraints (i.e. linear restrictions on the problem variables) as follows:

1. The "less than or equal" inequalities.
2. The strict equalities.
3. The "greater than or equal" inequalities.

To use this program enter the data starting at line 10,000, in this order:

FIRST: COEFFICIENTS OF EACH OF THE PROBLEM VARIABLES (INCLUDING ZEROES FOR VARIABLES NOT APPEARING) IN EACH RESTRICTION, STARTING WITH THE FIRST RESTRICTION AND PROCEEDING IN ORDER UNTIL ALL COEFFICIENTS OF ALL RESTRICTIONS HAVE BEEN ENTERED IN DATA STATEMENTS,

THEN: THE ELEMENTS OF THE "B" VECTOR (THE CONSTANTS COMPRISING THE RIGHT SIDE OF ALL RESTRICTIONS) IN THE SAME ORDER AS THE RESTRICTIONS,

LAST: THE COEFFICIENTS OF THE (LINEAR) OBJECTIVE FUNCTION, IN THE SAME ORDER AS USED IN THE RESTRICTIONS, INCLUDING ZEROES IF NEEDED.

THEN TYPE "RUN."

Additional instructions may be found in the listing.

SAMPLE PROBLEM

Maximize the function $30 \times X1 + 45 \times X2$ while satisfying the following constraints:

```
          X1                  <  =  6000
  2.5  x  X1  +  2.0  x  X2   <  =  4000
         X1                   <  =  2400
                     X2       >  =  1000
  3.0  x  X1                  -     1000
  2.5  x  X1  +  2.0  x  X2   >  =  0
                     X2       >  =  10000
```

The data would be entered starting at line number 10000, in the following order:

First: Coefficients of each of the problem variables in each constraint.
Ex : 10000 Data 1, 0, 0, 1, 2.5, 2, 1, 0, 0, 1, 3, -1, 2.5, 2
Then: The values on the right side of the constraints.
Ex : 10001 Data 6000, 4000, 24000, 1000, 1000, 0, 10000
Last: The coefficients of the objective function.
Ex : 10002 Data 30, 45

As the program runs, the values "7,2" would be supplied for "M, N." M being the number of constraints and N being the number of variables. When "I, J and K" are called for "3, 0, 4" would be supplied. "I" being the number of < = restrictions, 0 being the number of = restrictions and 4 being the number of > = restrictions.

NOTE:

The problem solution is X1 = 6000, X2 = 4000

This problem was run 3 times to illustrate all output options. ← *Only one run is shown on Fig. A-2.*

SAMPLE SOLUTION

This sample solution is a copy of the printout that will appear at your teletypewriter.

NOTE:

All user supplied information is underlined.

COMPUTER TIME-SHARING SERVICE

Figure A-2 General Electric's time-sharing service's LINPRO***

458   Introduction to Operations Research and Management Science

sage. A typical exchange of messages is shown below. The user types in the underlined portion and follows it with the return key (r).

```
HELLO OR/MS                              The answer-back (optional)
ON AT    18:02   PX FRI 02/10/77         Computer center acknowledges.
USER NUMBER--Z12345 (r)                  User identifies the validity code.
SYSTEM--BASIC (r)                        LINPRO is written in BASIC and is
NEW OR OLD--OLD (r)                        stored as an old program under the
OLD PROGRAM NAME--LINPRO*** (r)            call name LINPRO***

READY                                    The computer sought out the
                                         program.
```

Step 5. Construct the data file for the LINPRO*** program. Figure A-3 is the BASIC program, which has line numbers 10000 to 19999 reserved for data to be used by the program. It is recommended to use line numbers in increments larger than 1 so that extra data may be inserted later if necessary. Data must be introduced in the following order: internal transmittances, exogenous flows, and endogenous flows.

```
10000 DATA 6,6,1,0,0,1,1,0,0,1 (r)       The transmittances;
10010 DATA 360,50,40,30,20 (r)           the exogenous flows; and
10020 DATA 4,1 (r)                       the endogenous flows
                                         (the [MAX] obj. fn. coefficients) } LAST.
```

Step 6. We now ask the computer to translate the Basic language into machine instructions by using a dictionary (Basic interpreter) and to execute the algorithm by following those instructions. This is done by the RUN command.

```
RUN (r)                                  Instruct the computer to compile
                                         and execute the LINPRO using
LINPRO    18:09    PX FRI 02/10/77       data above included as a part of
                                         the BASIC program.
TYPE '2' FOR OUTPUT OF TABLEAUS AND BASIS
AT EACH ITERATION, '1' FOR THE BASIS ONLY,   Options available to
OR '0' FOR JUST THE SOLUTION. WHICH?  0 (r)  users.
```

Step 7. The RUN time instructions must be answered as requested by the program. The output option (0, 1, or 2), the number of resource (M) and process (N) nodes, and the types of constraints (LE, EQ, GE) are asked.

```
WHAT ARE M AND N OF THE DATA MATRIX?   5,2 (r)   5 resources (M) and 2
                                                 processes (N).
HOW MANY 'LESS THANS','EQUALS','GREATER THANS'?  3,1,1 (r)
```

```
100 GOTO 20000
101 LET O=1
102 DIM A(18,30)
103 PRINT "TYPE '2' FOR OUTPUT OF TABLEAUS AND BASIS"
104 PRINT "AT EACH ITERATION, '1' FOR THE BASIS ONLY,"
105 PRINT "OR '0' FOR JUST THE SOLUTION. WHICH."
108 INPUT P5
108 PRINT
110 PRINT "WHAT ARE M AND N OF THE DATA MATRIX";
116 INPUT M,N
120 PRINT
124 PRINT "HOW MANY 'LESS THANS', 'EQUALS', 'GREATER THANS'";
128 INPUT L, E, G
132 IF L+E+G = M THEN 144
136 PRINT "INPUT DATA NOT CONSISTENT."
140 STOP
144 LET B=M+N+G+1
148 LET W=M
152 IF B*(W+1)>540 THEN 164
156 PRINT "PROBLEM TOO LARGE"
160 STOP
164 IF B>30 THEN 172
168 IF W+1< 18 THEN 180
172 PRINT "CHANGE DIM STATEMENT (NO. 102) FOR A "W+1"BY"B"MATRIX"
176 STOP
180 LET M=M-1
184 LET H=1
188 FOR I=0 TO W+1
192 FOR J=1 TO B
196 LET A(I,J)=0
200 NEXT J
204 NEXT I
208 FOR I=0 TO M
212 FOR J=1 TO N
216 READ A(I,J)
220 NEXT J
224 NEXT I
228 FOR I=0 TO M
232 READ A(I,B)
236 NEXT I
240 FOR J=1 TO N
244 READ A(W,J)
248 LET A(W,J)=-A(W,J)
252 NEXT J
256 FOR K=1 TO M+1
260 LET A(K-1,N+G+K)=1
264 LET A(K-1,N+K)=K+N-G
268 NEXT K
272 IF B>0 THEN 280
276 IF G=0 THEN 340
280 FOR K=L+E+1 TO M+1
284 LET A(K-1,N+K+L-E)=-1
288 NEXT K
292 LET W=W+1
296 LET Q=0
300 FOR J=1 TO N+G
304 LET S=0
308 FOR I=M-G-E+1 TO M
312 LET S=S+A(I,J)
316 NEXT I
320 LET A(W,J)= -S
324 IF A(W,J)>Q THEN 336
328 LET Q=A(W,J)
332 LET C=J
336 NEXT J
340 PRINT
344 PRINT "           YOUR VARIABLES"J"THROUGH"N
348 IF G=0 THEN 356
352 PRINT "  SURPLUS VARIABLES"N+1"THROUGH"N+G
356 IF L=0 THEN 364
360 PRINT "    SLACK VARIABLES"N+G+1"THROUGH"N+G+L
364 IF G+B=0 THEN 372
368 PRINT "ARTIFICIAL VARIABLES"N+G+L+1"THROUGH"B-1
372 IF P5=0 THEN 380
376 GOSUB 636
380 OF Q=0 THEN 540
384 OF P5=0 THEN 564
388 LET H=H+1
392 LET Q=1E76
396 LET R= -1
400 FOR I=0 TO M
404 IF A(I,C)<=0 THEN 420
408 IF A(I,B)/A(I,C) > Q THEN 420
412 LET Q=A(I,B)/A(I,C)
416 LET R=I
420 NEXT I
424 IF R>= -.5 THEN 440
428 PRINT "AOLUTION UNBOUNDED"
432 GOSUB 636
436 STOP
440 LET P=A(R,C)
444 LET A(R,0)=C
448 FOR J=1 TO B
452 LET A(R,J)=A(R,J)/P
456 NEXT J
460 FOR I=0 TO M
464 IF I=R THEN 492
468 FOR J=1 TO B
472 IF J=C THEN 488
476 LET A(I,J)=A(I,J)-A(R,J)*A(I,C)
480 IF ABS(A(I,J))>1E-8 THEN 488
484 LET A(I,J)=0
488 NEXT J
492 NEXT I
496 FOR I=0 TO M
500 LET A(I,C)=0
504 NEXT I
508 LET A(R,C)=1
512 LET Q=0
516 FOR J=1 TO N+G
520 IF A(W,J)>Q THEN 532
524 LET Q=A(W,J)
528 LET C=J
532 NEXT J
536 GOTO 380
540 LET W=W-1
544 LET K=K+1
548 GOTO 512
552 PRINT
556 PRINT
560 PRINT "ANSWERS:"
564 PRINT
568 IF Q=0 THEN 576
572 PRINT "BASIS BEFORE ITERATION"H
576 PRINT "VARIABLE", "VALUE"
580 FOR I=0 TO M
584 IF A(I,0)=0 THEN 592
588 PRINT A(I,0), A(I,B)
592 NEXT I
596 IF Q <> 0 THEN 388
600 PRINT
604 PRINT "DUAL VARIABLES:"
608 PRINT "COLUMN", "VALUE"
612 FOR J=N+1 TO B-G-1
616 FOR I=0 TO M
620 PRINT J,A(W,J),
624 NEXT J
628 GOSUB 636
632 GOTO 70000
636 PRINT
638 IF P5=1 THEN 676
640 PRINT
644 PRINT "TABLEAU AFTER "H-1" ITERATIONS"
648 FOR I=0 TO M
652 FOR J=1 TO B
656 PRINT A(I,J),
660 NEXT J
664 PRINT
668 PRINT
672 NEXT I
676 RETURN
10000 DATA 4E44  { to be replaced by the
20000 READ G9        user's data file }
30000 IF G9=4E44 THEN 60000
40000 RESTORE
50000 GOTO 101
60000 PRINT "LIST THE FILE 'LPINST***'"
70000 END
```

Figure A-3   BASIC program listing of GE's LINPRO***

Using these data and instructions, the computer program generates appropriate residue and artificial variables. The residue variables are called *slack* variables when they correspond to .LE.-type constraints and *surplus* variables when they correspond to .GE.-type constraints. Note that although data must be inputted in the order of .LE., .EQ., and then .GE. constraints, the variables are numbered in the order of decision variables first, surplus (.GE.) variables next, slack (.LE.) variables third, and artificial variables last. Thus, in our example, we have:

$$6x_1 + 6x_2 + x_4 = 360$$
$$1x_1 + x_5 = 50$$
$$1x_2 + x_6 = 40$$
$$1x_1 + x_7 = 30$$
$$1x_2 - x_3 + x_8 = 20$$

$$\min \quad x_7 + x_8 \quad \text{(during phase 1)}$$
$$\max \ 4x_1 + 1x_2 \quad \text{(during phase 2)}$$

This assignment is printed out by the computer.

```
         YOUR VARIABLES  1  THROUGH 2
     SURPLUS VARIABLES  3  THROUGH 3
       SLACK VARIABLES  4  THROUGH 6
  ARTIFICIAL VARIABLES  7  THROUGH 8
```

The RPM network interpretation of these variables is shown in Figure A-4.

The solution is produced by LINPRO*** in the form of a list using the same labels: Variables in solution (primal values) are given first, followed by dual values.

```
ANSWERS:

VARIABLE        VALUE
  5              20.
  3              10.
  6              10.
  1              30.
  2              30.

DUAL VARIABLES:
COLUMN          VALUE
  4              .166667
  7              3.
```

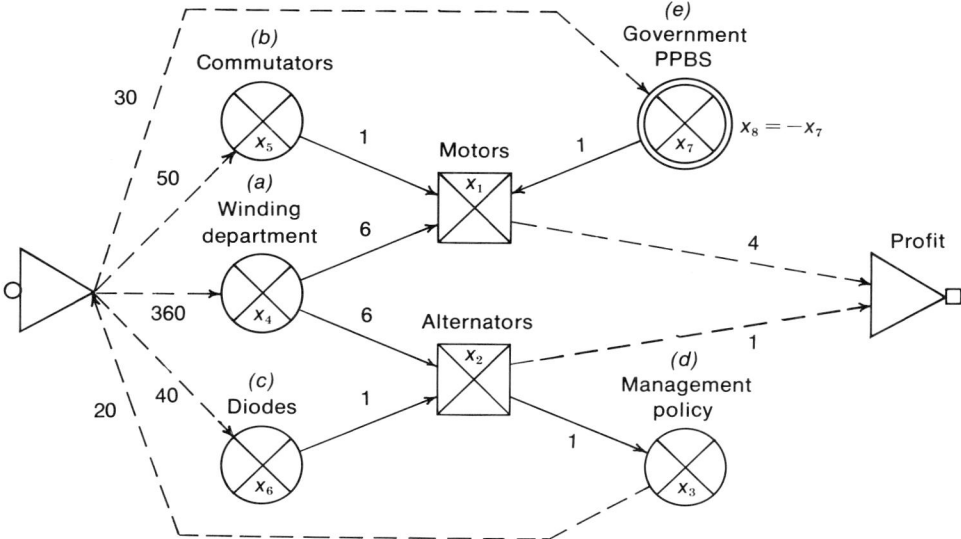

Figure A-4 RPM network for the GE LINPRO*** variable assignment.

These values can then be copied onto the RPM network, and the basic paths identified. In this particular example, it is clear that the government's regulation is the costliest constraint. Each unit of additional motor allocation would contribute $3 to the company's profit. Also, the winding department's work force could be increased profitably if each hour could be bought at less than 16.7 cents. Figure A-5 illustrates the resulting network.

Step 8. The program can be rerun simply by changing the data file and retyping RUN. When we no longer desire the service of the time-sharing system, we type BYE. When the return key is then depressed, the terminal will type out the farewell messages, log off, and terminate the telephone connection.

```
BYE ⓡ
*** OFF AT 18:14   PX FRI 02/10/77.
```

SECTION A-2 TUNE-UP

Figure A-2 illustrates a complete LINPRO*** example. Construct an RPM network, interpret the numerical solution in the network, and identify the basic paths.

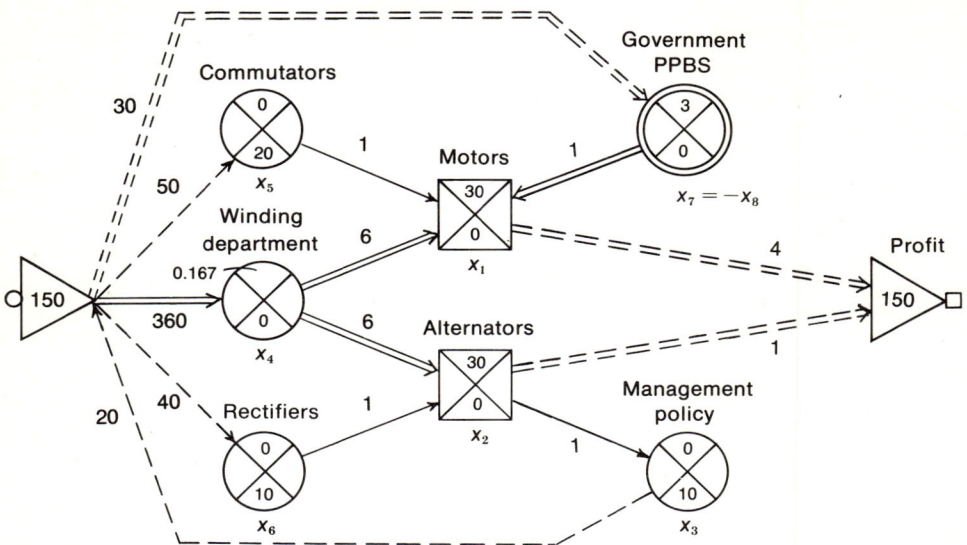

Figure A-5 RPM interpretation of LINPRO*** output.

A-3 Customized conversational linear programs

Originally, General Electric Company maintained a generous software policy of making all time-sharing library programs available for listing by its users. All one had to do was to say LIST and a complete copy of the program was obtained. Figure A-3 is such an example.[1] This open-door policy contributed greatly to the quick popularization of time-sharing services. In 1967 more than twenty different types of time-share services were operating. GE had its processing centers in Chicago, Cleveland, Dallas, Detroit, Los Angeles, Lynchburg (Virginia), New York, Wichita Falls (Texas), Phoenix, San Francisco, Schenectady (New York), and Washington, D. C. Each such center served between 30 to 80 terminals of the teletype 33 and 35 types. Other characteristics of this Mark I System included a 6-μs memory cycle, 16,000-word storage for the CPU and 18-million-character disk storage (DS-20) and 110 interrupts per second allocating 3 to 12 seconds of processing time to each user.

LINPRO*** is one of the earliest time-sharing efforts in OR/MS software development, and, as mentioned earlier, it has been copied widely. The program in Figure A-6 is an example of how a private system may adopt LINPRO***

---

[1]Figure A-3 lists the LINPRO*** source program with the permission of the General Electric Company. This program may not run directly on another computer as it makes use of special features of GE BASIC. For example, a dimensioned variable in GE BASIC is permitted to have the value of 0 for its subscript. LPINST*** is a separate descriptive file containing an explanation of how to create the data file and run the program.

for its own educational use. The printouts from the terminal are self-explanatory, especially after the detailed description of GE's LINPRO***. The present program, also called LINPRO (or, more exactly, *LINPRO), has several improved features and was developed at Oregon State University. It has done away with the data file by asking all data entries to be made at the execution. It has an option to print out tableaux at all iterations ahd has several debugging features that are convenient to novices. The value of objective function is now printed at each iteration (this was *not* the case with the original LINPRO***) and slack and surplus variables (S's) are distinguished from artificial variables A's and real primal variables $A, B, C, \ldots$.

Two examples are included: the same motor alternator example as in GE's LINPRO*** in Figure A-6 and the woodwork shop example from Chapter 5 (Example 5-1) in Figure A-7. The second example has deliberate errors (−9 instead of +9; L80 instead of 180) and a rerun with a new set of values for the objective function to illustrate the versatility of this program.

SECTION A-3 TUNE-UP

Illustrate all four iterations of the motor-alternator tableaux with RPM networks. Identify each case by stating whether the solution is feasible, infeasible, optimal, or nonoptimal.

```
≠HI (r)
  NOV  5, 1978    9:34 AM            (r) means depress (return) key
MAX  S          30.00                 _____ are user's entries.
MAXTIME         360
SFBLKS            0
SFBLKLIM         10
MFBLKLIM         25
NO. USERS        26
JOB NO.     730,222
TERMINAL       047

≠LINPRO (r)
THIS LINEAR PROGRAMMING MODEL WILL HANDLE UP TO 25 VARIABLES
AND 20 CONSTRAINT EQUATIONS. PLEASE TERMINATE ALL RESPONSES
WITH A CARRIAGE RETURN. THANK YOU.

DO YOU WANT A TABLEAU FOR EACH ITERATION (TYPE 1)
OR ONLY THE FINAL TABLEAU AND SOLUTION (TYPE 2)?        1 (r)

HOW MANY VARIABLES ARE IN YOUR OBJECTIVE FUNCTION?  2 (r)
PLEASE TYPE IN THE COEFFICIENTS.
4 1 (r)                    [MAX] $Z_x = 4X_1 + 1X_2$
THANK YOU.

YOUR OBJECTIVE FUNCTION IS:
  +     4.00A  +       1.00B        $A = X_1$   $B = X_2$
CORRECT?     YES (r)

HOW MANY OF YOUR CONSTRAINT EQUATIONS USE LESS THANS AS OPERATORS?
3 (r)
PLEASE TYPE IN THE COEFFICIENTS AND THE CONSTRAINT CONSTANT FOR
EACH.
1 0 50  (r)           $X_1 \leq 50$
6 6 360 (r)           $6X_1 + 6X_2 \leq 360$
0 1 40  (r)           $X_2 \leq 40$

HOW MANY USE EQUAL SIGNS AS OPERATORS?    1 (r)
PLEASE TYPE IN THE COEFFICIENTS AND THE CONSTRAINT CONSTANT FOR
EACH.
1 0 30 (r)            $X_1 = 30$

HOW MANY USE GREATER THANS AS OPERATORS?    1 (r)
PLEASE TYPE IN THE COEFFICIENTS AND THE CONSTRAINT CONSTANT FOR
EACH.
0 1 20 (r)            $X_2 \geq 20$
THANK YOU.

YOUR CONSTRAINT EQUATIONS ARE:
 1)
  +      1.00A  +         0B    <     50.00
 2)
  +      6.00A  +       6.00B   <    360.00
 3)
  +        0A   +       1.00B   <     40.00
 4)
  +      1.00A  +         0B    =     30.00
 5)
  +        0A   +       1.00B   >     20.00
CORRECT?     YES (r)

YOUR VARIABLES        A     THROUGH     B
SLACK VARIABLES       S1    THROUGH     S4
ARTIFICIAL VARIABLES        A1    THROUGH    A2
```

Figure A-6a *LINPRO example of woodwork shop problem (a).

TABLEAU NUMBER 1

	A	B	S1	S2	S3	S4
OBJ FNCTN	4.00	1.00	0	0	0	0
S2	1.00	0	0	1.00	0	0
S3	6.00	6.00	0	0	1.00	0
S4	0	1.00	0	0	0	1.00
A1	1.00	0	0	0	0	0
A2	0	1.00	-1.00	0	0	0
SIMPLEX CR	4.00	1.00	-0	-0	-0	-0

	A1	A2	CONSTANTS
OBJ FNCTN	0	0	
S2	0	0	50.00
S3	0	0	360.00
S4	0	0	40.00
A1	1.00	0	30.00
A2	0	1.00	20.00
SIMPLEX CR	-0	-0	-0

VALUE OF OBJECTIVE FUNCTION =   0

TABLEAU NUMBER 2

	A	B	S1	S2	S3	S4
OBJ FNCTN	4.00	1.00	0	0	0	0
S2	1.00	0	0	1.00	0	0
S3	6.00	0	6.00	0	1.00	0
S4	0	0	1.00	0	0	1.00
A1	1.00	0	0	0	0	0
B	0	1.00	-1.00	0	0	0
SIMPLEX CR	4.00	-0	1.00	-0	-0	-0

	A1	A2	CONSTANTS
OBJ FNCTN	0	0	
S2	0	0	50.00
S3	0	-6.00	240.00
S4	0	-1.00	20.00
A1	1.00	0	30.00
B	0	1.00	20.00
SIMPLEX CR	-0	-1.00	-20.00

VALUE OF OBJECTIVE FUNCTION =   20.0000

TABLEAU NUMBER 3

	A	B	S1	S2	S3	S4
OBJ FNCTN	4.00	1.00	0	0	0	0
S2	0	0	0	1.00	0	0
S3	0	0	6.00	0	1.00	0
S4	0	0	1.00	0	0	1.00
A	1.00	0	0	0	0	0
B	0	1.00	-1.00	0	0	0
SIMPLEX CR	-0	-0	1.00	-0	-0	-0

	A1	A2	CONSTANTS
OBJ FNCTN	0	0	
S2	-1.00	0	20.00
S3	-6.00	-6.00	60.00
S4	0	-1.00	20.00
A	1.00	0	30.00
B	0	1.00	20.00
SIMPLEX CR	-4.00	-1.00	-140.00

VALUE OF OBJECTIVE FUNCTION =   140.0000

Figure A-6b *LINPRO example of woodwork shop problem (b).

TABLEAU NUMBER 4

	A	B	S1	S2	S3
OBJ FNCTN	4.00	1.00	0	0	0
S2	0	0	0	1.00	0
S1	0	0	1.00	0	.17
S4	0	0	0	0	-0.17
A	1.00	0	0	0	0
B	0	1.00	0	0	.17
SIMPLEX CR	-0	-0	-0	-0	-0.17

	A1	A2	CONSTANTS
OBJ FNCTN	0	0	
S2	-1.00	0	20.00
S1	-1.00	-1.00	10.00
S4	1.00	0	10.00
A	1.00	0	30.00
B	-1.00	0	30.00
SIMPLEX CR	-3.00	-0	-150.00

VALUE OF OBJECTIVE FUNCTION =   150.0000

ANSWERS:

VARIABLES IN SOLUTION	UNITS
S2	20.0000
S1	10.0000
S4	10.0000
A	30.0000
B	30.0000

VARIABLES NOT IN SOLUTION	SIMPLEX CRITERIA
S3	.1667
A1	3.0000

DO YOU WANT TO CHANGE ONE OR MORE PARAMETERS AND RERUN? NO ⓡ

*HI ⓡ
NOV 5, 1978   9:48 AM
MAX $ 30.00
MAXTIME   360
SFBLKS   0
SFBLKLIM   10
MFBLKLIM   25
NO. USERS   38
JOB NO.   730222
TERMINAL   047

*LOGOFF ⓡ
COST $1.26
CPU TIME SEC.   8.9
WC TIME MIN.   15.7

Figure A-6c *LINPRO example of woodwork shop problem (c).

NOVEMBER 5, 1978   9:52:35 AM TERMINAL 047

*LINPRO (r)
THIS LINEAR PROGRAMMING MODEL WILL HANDLE UP TO 25 VARIABLES
AND 20 CONSTRAINT EQUATIONS. PLEASE TERMINATE ALL RESPONSES
WITH A CARRIAGE RETURN. THANK YOU.

DO YOU WANT A TABLEAU FOR EACH ITERATION (TYPE 1)
OR ONLY THE FINAL TABLEAU AND SOLUTION (TYPE 2)?   <u>2</u> (r)

HOW MANY VARIABLES ARE IN YOUR OBJECTIVE FUNCTION?   <u>2</u> (r)
PLEASE TYPE IN THE COEFFICIENTS.
<u>-9 9</u> (r)   *Note -9 was <u>NOT</u> intended*
THANK YOU.

YOUR OBJECTIVE FUNCTION IS:
-     9.00A   +   9.00B
CORRECT?   <u>NO</u> (r)
PLEASE TYPE IN THE COEFFICIENTS.
<u>9 9</u> (r) $Z_x = +3X_1 + 9X_2$
THANK YOU.

YOUR OBJECTIVE FUNCTION IS:
+ .   9.00A   +   9.00B
CORRECT?   <u>YES</u> (r)

HOW MANY OF YOUR CONSTRAINT EQUATIONS USE LESS THANS AS OPERATORS?
<u>2</u> (r)
PLEASE TYPE IN THE COEFFICIENTS AND THE CONSTRAINT CONSTANT FOR
EACH.
<u>30 20 L80</u> (r)   *Note L80 is <u>not</u> 180*
<u>6 12 60</u> (r)

HOW MANY USE EQUAL SIGNS AS OPERATORS?   <u>0</u> (r)

HOW MANY USE GREATER THANS AS OPERATORS?   <u>0</u> (r)
THANK YOU.

YOUR CONSTRAINT EQUATIONS ARE:
1)
+   30.00A   +   20.00B   <   80.00   ← *L was ignored in L80.*
2)
+   6.00A   +   12.00B   <   60.00
CORRECT?   <u>NO</u> (r)

PLEASE ENTER THE EQUATION NUMBER AND WHETHER IT IS A
COEFICIENT (1) OR A CONSTANT (2)?   <u>1 2</u> (r)
WHAT IS THE NEW VALUE?   <u>180</u> (r)   *L80 corrected to 180*
DO YOU WANT TO MAKE ANY ADDITIONAL CHANGES?   <u>NO</u> (r)
DO YOU WANT TO LIST THE EQUATIONS AGAIN?   <u>YES</u> (r)

YOUR CONSTRAINT EQUATIONS ARE:
1)
+   30.00A   +   20.00B   <   180.00
2)
+   6.00A   +   12.00B   <   60.00
CORRECT?   <u>YES</u> (r)

YOUR VARIABLES   A   THROUGH   B
SLACK VARIABLES   S1 THROUGH   S2

Figure A-7a   *LINPRO example of motor-alternator problem (a).

TABLEAU NUMBER 3

	A	B	S1	S2	CONSTANTS
OBJ FNCTN	9.00	9.00	0	0	
A	1.00	0	.05	-0.08	4.00
B	0	1.00	-0.03	.13	3.00
SIMPLEX CR	-0	-0	-0.22	-0.38	-63.00

VALUE OF OBJECTIVE FUNCTION =   63.0000

ANSWERS:

VARIABLES IN SOLUTION	UNITS
A	4.0000
B	3.0000

VARIABLES NOT IN SOLUTION	SIMPLEX CRITERIA
S1	.2250
S2	.3750

DO YOU WANT TO CHANGE ONE OR MORE PARAMETERS AND RERUN? <u>YES</u> (r)
DO YOU WANT TO CHANGE THE OBJECTIVE FUNCTION?   <u>YES</u> (r)
PLEASE TYPE IN THE COEFFICIENTS.
<u>15 10</u> (r)
THANK YOU.

YOUR OBJECTIVE FUNCTION IS: *This is problem 5-3.*
   +   15.00A   +   10.00B
CORRECT?   <u>YES</u> (r)

DO YOU WANT TO CHANGE ANY OF THE CONSTRAINT EQUATIONS?   <u>NO</u> (r)
DO YOU WANT TO LIST THE EQUATIONS AGAIN?   <u>YES</u> (r)

YOUR CONSTRAINT EQUATIONS ARE:
 1)
 +   30.00A   +   20.00B   <   180.00
 2)
 +   6.00A   +   12.00B   <   60.00
CORRECT?   <u>YES</u> (r)

YOUR VARIABLES   A   THROUGH   B
SLACK VARIABLES   S1   THROUGH   S2

Figure A-7b *LINPRO example of motor-alternator problem (b).

TABLEAU NUMBER 2

	A	B	S1	S2	CONSTANTS
OBJ FNCTN	15.00	10.00	0	0	
A	1.00	.67	.03	0	6.00
S2	0	8.00	-0.20	1.00	24.00
SIMPLEX CR	-0	-0	-0.50	-0	-90.00

VALUE OF OBJECTIVE FUNCTION =   90.0000

ANSWERS:

VARIABLES IN SOLUTION	UNITS
A	6.0000
S2	24.0000

VARIABLES NOT IN SOLUTION	SIMPLEX CRITERIA
B	0
S1	.5000

DO YOU WANT TO CHANGE ONE OR MORE PARAMETERS AND RERUN? NO (r)

LOGOFF (r)
COST $0.69
CPU TIME SEC.   4.8
WC TIME MIN.   8.8

Figure A-7c *LINPRO example of motor-alternator problem (c).

TUNE-UP SOLUTION
Section A-2

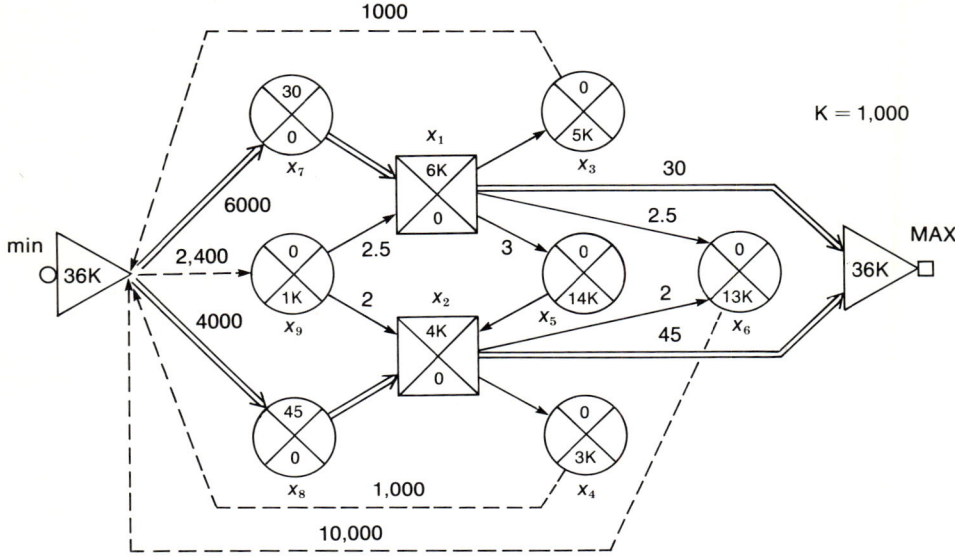

Note that all unit transmittances have been implied. The objective-function value can be computed *exogenously* as $6{,}000 \times 30 + 4{,}000 \times 45 = 36{,}000 = Z_y$; *endogenously* as $30 \times 6{,}000 + 45 \times 4{,}000 = 36{,}000 = Z_x$; or *internally* as $y_7 \times a_{71} \times x_1 + y_8 \times a_{82} \times x_2 = 30 \times 1 \times 6{,}000 + 45 \times 1 \times 4{,}000 = 36{,}000$. Values that are off the basic paths are null.

Section A-3

Tableau number 1 (not feasible at s_1 and A_1; not optimal at A and B)

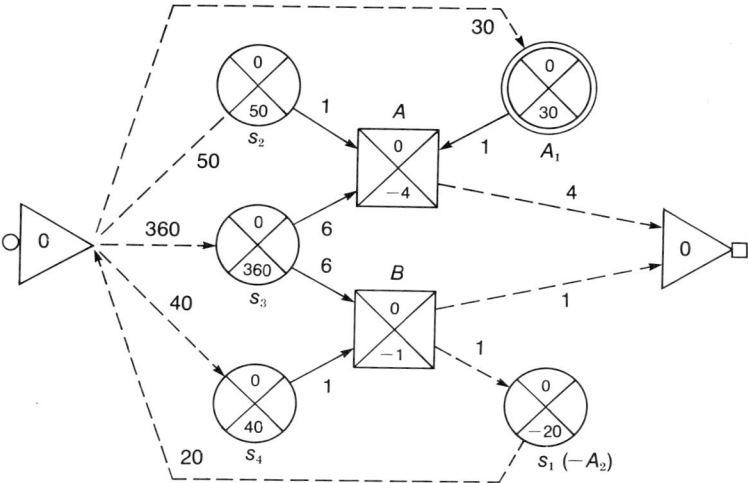

Tableau number 2 (not feasible at A_1; not optimal at A and s_1)

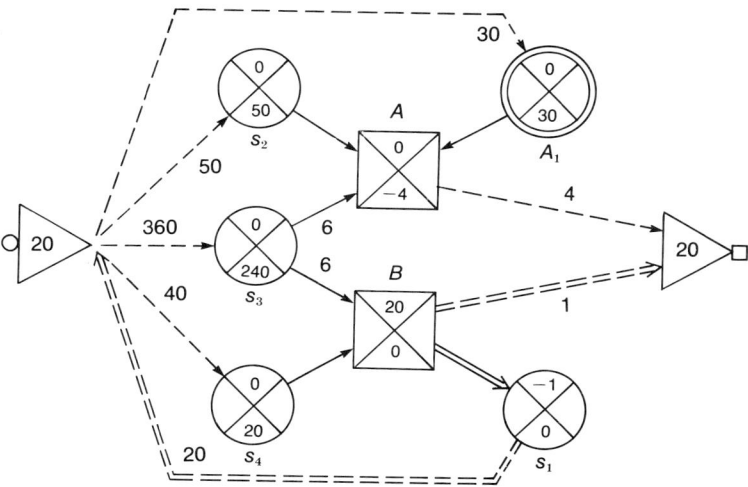

Tableau number 3 (feasible but not optimal at s_1)

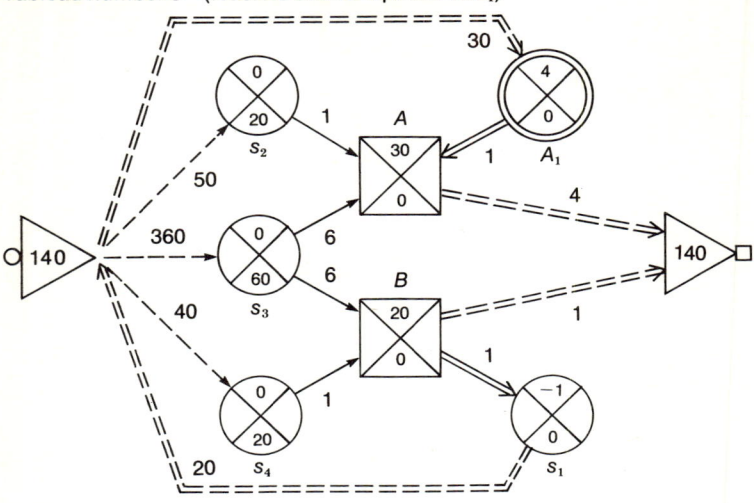

Tableau number 4 (feasible and optimal)

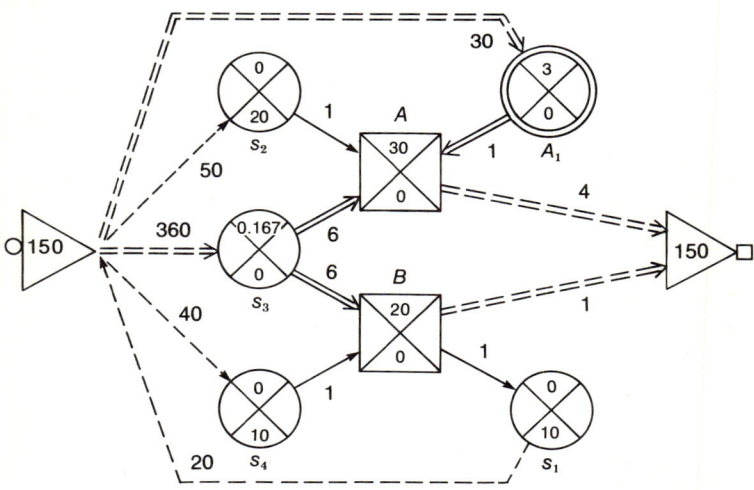

MATHEMATICAL PROGRAMMING SYSTEM: The Product-Form Approach

Appendix B

B-1 Revised simplex production form

In Chapter 9 we studied simplex procedures, which were touted as being the most popular procedures for solving linear programming problems. There is no introductory operations research or management science book that does not discuss the simplex method in minute details. Yet, we must now confess that most industrial problems are *not* solved by the textbook simplex algorithm, the big-M method, or the two-phase procedure.

The procedure used by computers to solve large-scale problems is based on the *revised* simplex procedure that is commonly referred to as the *product-form* approach. In looking at a regular simplex tableau, we note that there is a very large number of empty cells, a fact that makes its RPM network representation more practical. The product-form approach saves space by storing only the portion of the matrix that is essential and discarding the useless zeroes and ones that can be recreated from other available information. It is used in conjunction with a data preparation routine bearing such a name as MATGEN or *matrix generator*.

Users of a particular make of computers often band together in a group, which helps the members and the manufacturer to determine what hardware, software, and services are needed to promote more effective use of the computers. SHARE is such a users group for International Business Machines. A large number of OR users also belong to the SIGMAP (special interest group for mathematical programming) of ACM (Association for Computing Machinery). SIGMAP was, and still is, the popular forum for exchanging information about LP algorithms, and SHARE members designed a standard format for handling data in simplex computations.

IBM and other computer manufacturers took the SHARE standards and developed various LP computer programs that have great similarities as far as computer users are concerned. Some revered names include LPS, MPS, LP/600, ILONA, and OPHELIE. A few such packages are capable of handling nonlinear programming problems (e.g., integer and quadratic problems) and of decomposing larger problems into smaller problems with solutions that are easier to find. The decomposition algorithms were originally developed by Dantzig and Beale (see Chapter 9 for Beale's contribution to cycling) and permits us to use local solutions to smaller problems to identify the global optimum for the larger problem.

A feature of particular interest to OR/MS practitioners is the mixed-integer programming (MIP) option of specifying some discontinuous (or integer) conditions to otherwise continuous variables. Examples of such conditions are: discounting costs for larger purchases; incurring a one-time construction cost if a facility is to be used at all but none if this option is not chosen; and choosing at least one out of several alternatives in a given set of variables (e.g., if one variable from a set is chosen, use a variable from another set). Not all computer programs can accept such specifications, and those that do may be expensive to run. The branch-and-bound and dynamic programming methods discussed in Chapters 8 and 10, respectively, could be effectively interfaced with regular LP programs to handle such situations.

It is not our intention to elaborate on these more advanced mathematical programming concepts in this appendix; nor shall we identify all the idiosyncrasies of a particular computer program or installation. Many excellent books are available (see the Annotated Bibliography) and reference to the latest computer manual and consultation with the data processing staff are recommended to the OR/MS analyst before embarking on the use of an unfamiliar computer system. On the other hand, there are some useful features of the MPS-type programs (typified by the IBM's MPS/360, MPSX, and LPS/1130) that are quite different from the LINPRO-type programs discussed in Appendix A.

B-2 MPS

IBM's mathematical programming system (MPS) includes a program that is widely used by OR/MS practitioners to solve LP problems. Unlike the LINPRO program, which accepts resource constraints one row (one resource node) at a time, MPS requires that flows (branch coefficients) into or out of each process node be specified one branch at a time. A constraint in LP can be written as:

$$F_i(X) = \sum_{i \neq j} a_{ij} x_j \left\{ \begin{array}{c} \geq \\ = \\ < \end{array} \right\} b_i$$

In an MPS-type program, each column j of the simplex tableau is entered one coefficient a_{ij} at a time, preceded by the name of the activity (column j) and the name of the resource (row i).

The actual sign to be used by the coefficient depends upon the specification of the type of resource node. MPS treats each constraint i as an equation including the primal residue x_i:

$$F_i(X) + x_i = \sum_{\text{all } j} a_{ij} x_j = b_i \qquad \text{where } a_{ii} = 1$$

Four types of constraints can be specified under the ROWS section of MPS: N, E, L, and G, depending on the range that the residue x_i is allowed to vary (Figure B-1), and an objective function is treated as a free variable N.

The matter of choosing the correct sign for the a_{ij} coefficient can be greatly simplified by using only L-type constraints ($<$) and one objective function which must be specified as an N constraint. Unlike LINPRO, which is made to *maximize* its objective function, an MPS program without a specific instruction to the contrary will *minimize* its objective function. Figure 6-5 (p. 120) illustrates how easy it is to encode such a minimization problem with only L-type constraints. Looking at an RPM network, the analyst needs to remember only that

CODE	Constraint type	Relationship to exogenous flow b_i (RHS)	Permitted range for residue x_i	Equation assumed
N	Free constraint or objective function	$F_i(X) - b_i$	$-\infty \leq x_i \leq +\infty$	$F_i(X) + x_i = b_i$
E	Exact equality (=)	$F_i(X) = b_i$	$x_i = 0$	$F_i(X) = b_i$
L	Less than (<) or equal to a constant	$F_i(X) \leq b_i$	$x_i \geq 0$	$F_i(X) + x_i = b_i$
G	Greater than (>) or equal to a constant	$F_i(X) \geq b_i$	$x_i \leq 0$	$F_i(X) = b_i + |x_i|$

Figure B-1 MPS input data.

inflow is positive and outflow is negative, and this will apply to all activity nodes (the boxes). For a maximization problem, the same rule holds *except* for the dotted arrows to the primal (maximizing) objective function where the signs must be reversed. Figure B-2 illustrates a maximizing problem of the familiar woodworking shop example from Example 5-1 (Figure 5-10, p. 93). Note that all entries in the COLUMNS section are positive, even though the $9 arrows flow out of BOOKCASE and DESKS. Figure B-5 (p. 484) at the end of this appendix summarizes the sign convention.

MPS INPUT DATA FILE The prerequisite to running the MPS is the creation of a data file containing at least the three main sections, ROWS, COLUMNS, and RHS. These are sandwiched between NAME and ENDATA.

NAME: A one- to eight-character alphanumeric name must be given to LP model in columns 15 to 22 of the first card containing the word NAME in the first four columns of the punched card. This name identifies the input data file to be called in by the MPS compiler and optimized during the execution.

ROWS: The primal objective function N and all resources (L if possible) must be given unique alphanumeric names of one to eight letters. No space is permitted within the name, and you may not use $ as the first letter. The punched card containing the word ROWS in its first four columns must be followed by data cards with the type code (N, L, E, G) in column 2 or 3 and resource names in columns 5 to 12.

COLUMNS: Following the card containing the word COLUMNS in columns 1 to 7, as many data cards as are necessary should be included to specify all nonzero arrow coefficients a_{ij}'s and c_j's. Many computer programs, such as the LPS used on smaller computers, require that only one coefficient be specified per card. The MPS/360 allows two entries but will also accept cards containing only one coefficient. The column name must appear starting in column 5 (NAME 1) and follows the same rule as row names. A process (column) name must *not* be the same label used by a resource or another process. The first resource name (NAME 2) appears in columns 15 to 22, followed by the coefficient (preceded by a minus sign if negative) in columns 25 to 36. Another arrow on the same activity may be specified as the second constraint in NAME 3 (columns 40 to 47) with its coefficient in VALUE 3 (columns 50 to 61).

RHS: The dual objective function (the terminal node for the resources) must also be given a one- to eight-character alphanumeric name. Following the card containing the word RHS in the first three columns, there must be as many cards as necessary describing the values of the endogenous and exogenous flows (dotted-arrow values). NAME 1 (columns 5 to 12) must contain the terminal-node name; NAME 2 (columns 15 to 22) and NAME 3 (columns 40 to 47) must contain the resource nodes to which the flow values (VALUE 2 in columns 25 to 36 and VALUE 3 in columns 50 to 61) are connected. If all resources are stated as

IBM MATHEMATICAL PROGRAMMING INPUT FORM

Printed in U.S.A.
X20-1761-0 U/M025

ID (73–80)

JOB ________ ANALYST ________ DATE _/_/_ PAGE ____ OF ____

	Indicator (2–3)	Name 1 (5–12)	Name 2 (15–22)	Value 2 (25–36)	Name 3 (40–47)	Value 3 (50–61)	62–72
1	NAME		WOODWORK				
2	ROWS						
3	N	PROFIT					
4	L	LUMBER					
5	L	SPACE					
6	COLUMNS						
7		BOOKCASE	PROFIT	9.	LUMBER	30.	
8		BOOKCASE	SPACE	6.			
9		DESKS	PROFIT	9.	LUMBER	20.	
10		DESKS	SPACE	12.			
11	RHS						
12		RESOURCE	LUMBER	180.	SPACE	60.	
13	ENDATA						
14							
15							
16							
17							
18							
19							
20							

N, Objective function, FX, fixed; FR, free; E, is equal to; L, is less than or equal to; G, is greater than or equal to; MI, minimum infinity; PI, positive infinity

Figure B-2 MPS input data example.

L-type (<), flows into the resource node will be positive and flows into the terminal will be negative. (Again, the second name and value are optional.)

ENDATA: A card containing the word ENDATA in the first six columns must be the last card for the data file. Another data file may directly follow an ENDATA card if it has a different name.

OPTIONAL SECTIONS RANGES for constraints and BOUNDS for activities are two optional sections that assist ROWS by delimiting the freedom of variables.

BOUNDS Following a card containing the word BOUNDS in the first six columns (and before the ENDATA card), several boundary statements may be entered. The codes in columns 2 and 3 may be one of the following:

UP (upper bound)	$x_j \leq$ VALUE 2	(value in columns 25 to 36)
LO (lower bound)	$x_j \geq$ VALUE 2	
FX (fixed)	$x_j =$ VALUE 2	
FR (free)	$-\infty \leq x_j \leq +\infty$	(x_j may be negative and corresponds to a double box in RPMS)
MI (nonpositive)	$x_j \leq 0$	(lower limit is MInus infinity)
PL (nonnegative)	$0 \leq x_j$	(upper limit is PLus infinity)

Columns 5 to 12 must contain a name for the bounding constraint; VALUE 2 must be specified for UP, LO, and FX but has no meaning for others.

RANGES: After a card containing the word RANGES in the first six columns, data cards for specifying the opposite limits for constraining resources may be added. For example, an L-type resource may be given a lower limit and a G-type resource may be given an upper limit. NAME 1 (column 5 to 12) is the new boundary (another resource name); NAME 2 (column 15 to 22) is the old resource name; and VALUE 2 (column 25 to 36) is the range of the interval. If the old resource had a lower limit of b_1 and the range were r_1, the new constraint would be an upper limit of $b_1 + r_1$; but if the old resource had an upper limit instead, the new constraint would be a lower limit of $b_1 - r_1$.

SCALING: ROWS and COLUMNS, but neither BOUNDS nor RANGES, may be scaled by including the word SCALE in NAME 2 and the divider in VALUE 2. This will cause the value in VALUE 3 to be effectively divided by VALUE 2.

The optional features are really unnecessary in most cases and tend to make the interpretation of output and comparison with the RPM network more confusing. They do, however, eliminate some repetitive tasks and break the monotony of having to keypunch the same set of data repeatedly. There are many other such gimmicks available. For example, punching a D in the first column of a ROWS card, a new constraint NAME 1 of the type (columns 2 to 3) code L, E, or G may be formed as a weighted sum of an already specified constraint NAME 2 multiplied by its weight VALUE 2 and added to another already specified constraint NAME 3 multiplied by its weight VALUE 3; that is, NAME 1 = (NAME 2) (VALUE 2) + (NAME 3) (VALUE 3).

MODIFY, DELETE, BEFORE (add new data before), and AFTER (add new data after) are commands that permit the user to revise an old data file. A REVISE data file need only contain those changes in their appropriate sections.

MPS CONTROL PROGRAM Once the data file has been created, control cards must be prepared. Columns 1 to 8 contain the label (optional), and the program will ignore the entire card if the first column contains an asterisk. Columns 10 to 71 contain the program, and any nonblank character in column 72 will indicate that the statement could not fit in one card and is to be continued onto the next.

First the *job-control cards* (// cards used by the particular computer installation and including the account number, user code, JOBLIB, and SYSIN) must be prepared in consultation with your EDP personnel. The control program includes a PROGRAM card, a TITLE card, and an INITIALZ section. The latter serves to MOVE the data file into XDATA, the objective function into XOBJ, and the dual objective function into XRHS. It must then CONVERT the input data file into a PROBFILE; SETUP the problem as a MAXimization or MINimization problem, and select applicable constraints if there are more than one set; ask (optional) for the BCDOUT printout of the PROBFILE; ask (optional) for a PICTURE of the simplex tableau; conduct a PRIMAL or DUAL optimization; print the SOLUTION; conduct an adaptivity analysis for a limited RANGE; EXIT; and terminate (PEND). Figure B-3 illustrates the woodwork example of Chapter 5.

MPS OUTPUT It is impossible in this short appendix to describe all outputs that can be produced from even a simple MPS program. Fortunately most reports are not difficult to interpret once some vocabulary has been acquired. The *section*-1: *rows report* is a standard output with the following heading and meaning:

NUMBER	A sequential line number, 1, 2, 3, ... (index i of y_i)
..ROW..	The name of a resource or the objective function
AT	Followed by BS for a basic solution variable, LL for a resource at its low limit, UL for a resource at its upper limit, EQ for a resource that is an equality, and FR for an unbounded constraint

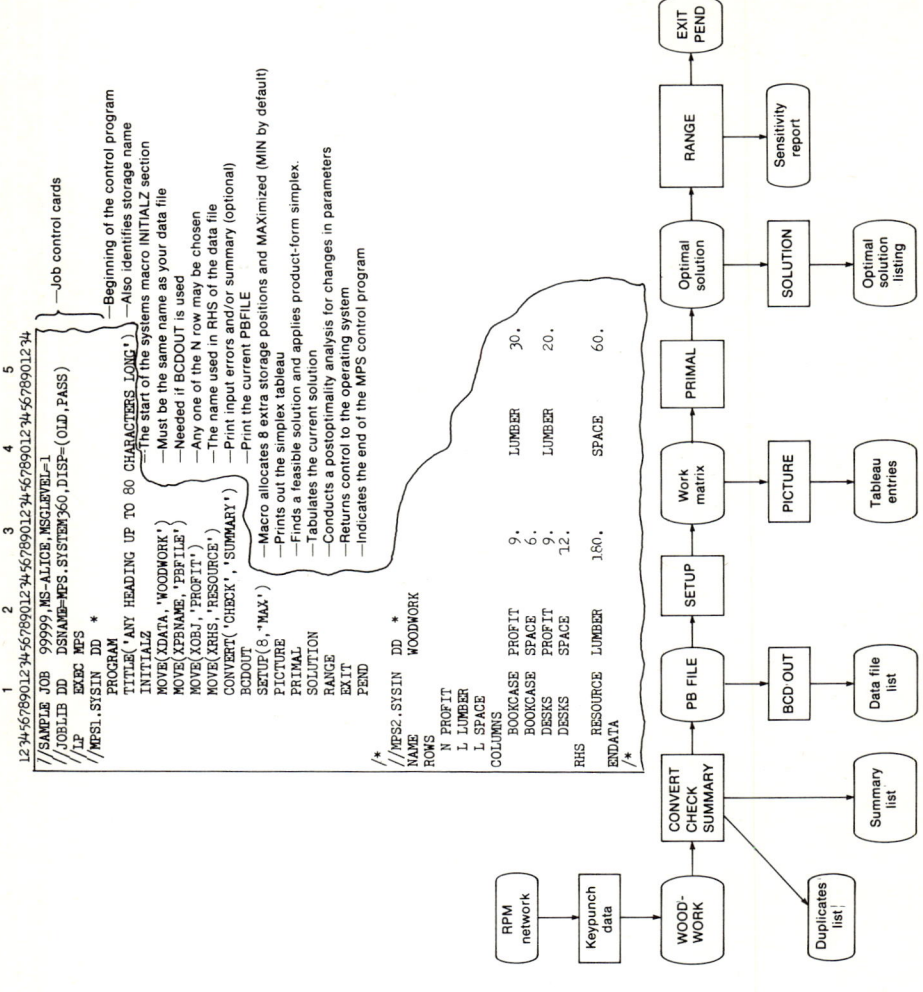

Figure B-3 *REX of the desk-bookstore problem from terminal.

...ACTIVITY...	Amount of resource flowing through the node
SLACK ACTIVITY	The residue x_i to be entered at the bottom of the resource node (x_i = total inflow = total outflow)
..LOWER LIMIT.	The outgoing dotted arrow from the resource node
..UPPER LIMIT.	The incoming dotted arrow to the resource node
.DUAL ACTIVITY	The shadow price of the resource (y_i on top of the node)

Similarly, the *section*-2: *columns report* includes a heading with

NUMBER	The continuation of the line number (index j of x_j)
.COLUMN..	The name of an activity
AT	BS for an activity in the basic paths, LL for a nonbasic variable at its lower limit, UL for a nonbasic variable at its upper limit, EQ for a nonbasic artificial or fixed variable, and FR for a nonbasic free variable
..INPUT COST..	The dotted arrow to the primal objective function
..LOWER LIMIT.	The lowest feasible value allowed to the activity
..UPPER LIMIT.	The highest feasible value allowed to the activity
.DUAL ACTIVITY	The opportunity cost y_j to bring a nonbasic activity x_j into the base

The identification section, which precedes these two reports, identifies the SOLUTION as INFEASIBLE, NONOPTIMAL, or OPTIMAL, and gives the TIME in minutes and the ITERATION NUMBER at the time of output. The FUNCTIONAL value of the objective function and of special rows and columns (if desired, ACTIVITY, and definition are also printed.

The BCDOUT report prints out the input data file, and the CHECK report includes the computed ROW ERROR between the actual value of RHS and the solution value of RHS for each resource constraint exceeding the CRitical tolerance (for example, 10^{-30}). The most challenging output is the RANGE report that includes five sections: (0) identification section for the RANGE with TIME, ITERATION NUMBER and a selected listing of rows and activities, and sensitivity analyses for (1) nonbasic resources (ROWS AT LIMIT LEVEL), (2) nonbasic activities (COLUMNS AT LIMIT LEVEL), (3) basic resources (ROWS AT INTERMEDIATE LEVEL), and (4) basic activities (COLUMNS AT INTERMEDIATE LEVEL). Each resource in (1) or (3) is given LOWER and UPPER LIMIT, LOWER and UPPER ACTIVITY, lower and upper UNIT COST, LOWER and UPPER COST, and lower and upper LIMITING PROCESS with their status (AT). The UNIT COST is the change in the objective-function value as the resource flow is shifted by a unit value toward its lower or upper limit. The LIMITING PROCESS indicates the resource or activity which must either be brought into or taken out of the base when the LOWER or UPPER ACTIVITY level is reached. The ACTIVITY LEVEL, of course, is not allowed to go beyond the LOWER or UPPER LIMIT. Each activity in (2) or (4) is given a similar treatment showing the deviation up toward the UPPER LIMIT or down toward the LOWER LIMIT. As long as the variation is maintained within the LOWER and UPPER ACTIVITY, the corresponding UNIT COST is a valid opportunity cost.

B-3 *REX

Most computer installations have their own version of a linear program, and it is impossible to describe them all. As an example of a customized LP package with added flexibilities of operating from a time-sharing terminal, input and output from the *REX system is shown in Figure B-4. *REX is a product-form, composite, bounded variable, multipricing, simplex linear programming package developed by H. Lynn Scheurman at Oregon State University. The woodwork example is shown in Figure B-4. The underlined data are entered by the operator while the computer prints out all the nonunderlined statements.

Most users will find that an MPS or *REX data file can be constructed more easily from an RPM network than from a simplex tableau or another mathematical representation. Figure B-5 has helped many users to overcome their initial problem of translating RPM arrows into data file parameters with the proper signs.

```
██████████        Log-on
NOVEMBER 5, 1973  10:02:08 AM TERMINAL 047

#EDIT
                    error correction (\) single character,
                              upper case L.
]INPUT
00001:ROWS
00002:$PROFIT <LUMBER <SPACE
00003:COLUMNS
00004:BOOKCASE PROFIT 9 LUMBER 30 SPACE 6
00005:$DESKS PROFIT 9 LUMBER 20 SPACE 12
00006:RHS
00007:RESOURCE LUMBER 180 SPACE 60\
00008:MISTAKE TO BE DELETED
00009:
]ERASE 8 ← delete the last line and continue input.
]APPEND
00008:ANOTHER MISTAKE
00009: (CR)
]LIST ← To see what we got so far.
00001:ROWS
00002:$PROFIT <LUMBER <SPACE
00003:COLUMNS
00004:BOOKCASE PROFIT 9 LUMBER 30 SPACE 6
00005:DESKS PROFIT 9 LUMBER 20 SPACE 12
00006:RHS
00007:RESOURCE LUMBER 180 SPACE 60
00008:ANOTHER MISTAKE
                      Replace a line
]REPLACE 8 ← error correction — reset to the
00021:MISTAKE<EOF       beginning of the line
]LIST
00001:ROWS
00002:$PROFIT <LUMBER <SPACE
00003:COLUMNS
00004:BOOKCASE PROFIT 9 LUMBER 30 SPACE 6
00005:DESKS PROFIT 9 LUMBER 20 SPACE 12
00006:RHS
00007:RESOURCE LUMBER 180 SPACE 60
00011:EOF
]RESEQ ← renumber (00) sequentially
]LIST
00001:ROWS
00002:$PROFIT <LUMBER <SPACE
00003:COLUMNS
00004:BOOKCASE PROFIT 9 LUMBER 30 SPACE 6
00005:DESKS PROFIT 9 LUMBER 20 SPACE 12
00006:RHS
00007:RESOURCE LUMBER 180 SPACE 60
00008:EOF
                     OPTIONAL
]OUT,*WOODWORK ← create a public (*) file
                      could have been replaced by:
                          ]OUT,1
                          ]REWIND,1
]EQUIP,1=WOODWORK
]EQUIP,2=FILE   }  Make
]EQUIP,3=FILE   } files available for future use.
```

```
]REWIND,1 }
]REWIND,2 }  were not needed here, but it is a good practice to rewind all files
]REWIND,3 }        none/Acclass/
]EQUIP,4=LP ← Eqip Line Printer (LP) as Logical Unit Number (LUN) 4.
]LABEL,4/*****SAVE FOR M.S.INOUE******APPENDIX B****BOOKCASES/
                                    Label LP printout for identification
*FRTY,*REX ← Callout FORTRAN compiler and the *REX program.
<<< REX V1.4  -- 053     -- 11/07/73 >>>         Optional title
TITLE, APPENDIX B ****** BOOKCASES OR DESKS?*************
                 TITLE APPENDIX B ****** BOOKCASES OR DESKS?
[00:00:10]        Data input  Listing on file (LUN1)
INPUT,1=1,L=2,S=2}         Summary on file (LUN2)
[00:00:10]
                 INPUT,1=1,L=2,S=2
NO INPUT ERRORS ← Wait for this before typing in CTL
CTL,L=2,C=2 ← Control with List and comment on LUN2.
                 CTL,L=2,C=2
[00:00:12]
MAXIMIZE ← You may MAXIMIZE or MINIMIZE
OUTPUT,L=2,S=3 ← Output Listing (L) and Summary (S) on LUNS 2 and 3.
END       You need this to get the Execution.

END OF FORTRAN EXECUTION

COPY,1=3/R,0=4 ← Copy the summary file from LUN 3/Rewind onto teletype.
     TITLE  APPENDIX B ****** BOOKCASES OR DESKS?************
     OBJ  = PROFIT
     RHS  = RESOURCE
     MAXIMUM =         63.000000
     ROWS
     PROFIT      Z     63.000000        -63.000000    MINF    PINF
     LUMBER      U    180.000000          0           MINF   180.000000
     SPACE       U     60.000000          0           MINF    60.000000
     COLUMNS
     BOOKCASE    B      4.000000          9.000000      0        0
     TABLES      B      3.000000          9.000000      0        0
     EOF

COPY,1=2/R,0=4 ← Copy LUN 2 onto Line Printer (LP=LUN4)
LABEL,4/*****NEXT COMES FILE 3****** ← Label LP for LUN3 printout.
COPY,1=3/R,0=4 ← Copy LUN 3 onto Line Printer (LUN4)
LOGOFF
```

Figure B-4 Line-printer output.

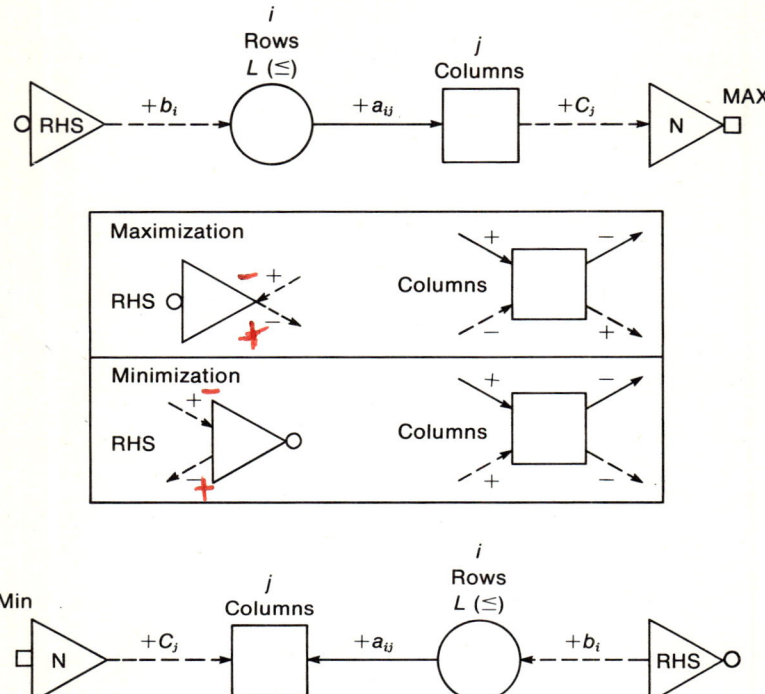

Figure B-5 Sign convention for MPS and *REX interpretation of RPM networks.

ANNOTATED BIBLIOGRAPHY

Many worthwhile books have been omitted from the following selected list of references to limit its size, and apologies are extended to their authors. Each reference is accompanied by a brief annotation to aid the reader in selecting the book with a proper *content* rather than a proper title. As with many tools, a book can be improved with intelligent usage. Comments, constructive criticisms, and suggestions for additions and deletions to improve the text as well as this bibliography will be greatly appreciated by the authors.

Ackoff, R. L., and M. W. Sasieni (1968): "Fundamentals of Operations Research," John Wiley & Sons, Inc., New York. A concise but comprehensive coverage of OR techniques including branch-and-bound applications.

Agrawal, R. C., and E. O. Heady (1972): "Operations Research Methods for Agricultural Decisions," Iowa State University Press, Ames, Iowa. An OR/MS introduction primarily intended for agricultural economists but requires no knowledge of agriculture to appreciate it. It has two good chapters on game theory, many numerical examples, but no exercise problems.

Ashby, W. R. (1966): "Design for a Brain," Science Paperbacks and Chapman & Hall, Ltd., London. Along with "Introduction to Cybernetics" by the same author and publisher (1964), this book provides easy reading on some challenging systems concepts.

Au, T., and T. E. Stelson (1969): "Introduction to Systems Engineering, Deterministic Models," Addison-Wesley Publishing Company, Inc., Reading, Mass. An OR text written for engineering students, it provides a transition from the familiar methods of calculus to LP models.

———, R. M. Shane, and L. A. Hoel (1972): "Fundamentals of Systems Engineering, Probabilistic Models," Addison-Wesley Publishing Company, Inc., Reading, Mass. A sequel to the preceding reference, this book can also be read independently as a text in statistical theory.

Baumol, W. J. (1965): "Economic Theory and Operations Analysis," 2d ed., Prentice-Hall, Inc., Englewood Cliffs, N. J. An excellent introduction to the economic significance of shadow prices and dual variables.

Beer, S. (1968): "Management Science: The Business Use of Operations Research," Doubleday & Company, Inc., Garden City, N. Y. An enjoyable picture book that introduces OR/MS concepts in a nontechnical manner.

Bellman, R. E. (1957): "Dynamic Programming," Princeton University Press, Princeton, N. J. The most authoritative book on dynamic programming.

Berge, C. (1962): "The Theory of Graphs and Its Applications," Methuen & Co., Ltd., London, translated by A. Doig. A classic in its field, this book provides the mathematical interpretations needed to utilize graph theories. Its appendix treats the general theory of games.

Bierman, H., Jr., C. P. Bonini, and W. H. Hausman (1973): "Quantitative Analysis for Business Decisions," Richard D. Irwin, Inc., Homewood, Ill. An up-to-date introduction to OR/MS with good examples.

Calson, J. G., and M. J. Misshauk (1972): "Introduction to Gaming: Management Decision Simulations," John Wiley & Sons, Inc., New York. A good coverage of the role and potential of simulation for solving difficult problems.

Carroll, L. (1960): "Alice in Wonderland and Other Favorites," Washington Square Press, a division of Simon & Schuster, Inc., New York. In case you are wondering where our inspiration has come from!

Charnes, A., and W. W. Cooper (1961): "Management Models and Industrial Applications of Linear Programming," John Wiley & Sons, Inc., New York. A major early contribution to linear programming and operations research with abundant examples.

Chestnut, H. (1965): "Systems Engineering Tools," John Wiley & Sons, Inc., New York. A comprehensive coverage of hardware- and software-oriented tools, including a few pages on linear and dynamic programming.

Churchman, C. W. (1968): "The Systems Approach," Delacorte Press, Dell Publishing Co., Inc., New York. A nonmathematical introduction to modern systems concepts.

———, R. L. Ackoff, and E. L. Arnoff (1957): "Introduction to Operations Research," John Wiley & Sons, Inc., New York. A classic OR/MS text which was way ahead of its time and is always refreshing to read.

Copper, R. B. (1972): "Introduction to Queueing Theory," The Macmillan Company, New York. A solid introudction to basic mathematical theory of waiting lines.

Cox, D. R., and W. L. Smith (1961): "Queues," John Wiley & Sons, Inc., New York. A classic in queuing theory.

Dantzig, G. B. (1963): "Linear Programming and Extensions," Princeton University Press, Princeton, N. J. The most authoritative work on linear programming. The introductory chapters giving the history and presenting paradigms using input/output relationships among primal variables are enjoyable to read even by laymen.

de Neufville, R., and D. H. Marks (eds.) (1974): "Systems Planning and Design," Prentice-Hall, Inc., Englewood Cliffs, N. J. A collection of actual systems analysis case studies divided into introduction, systems modeling, optimization, and evaluation.

Elmaghraby, S. E. (1966): "The Design of Production Systems," Reinhold Publishing Corp., New York. An advanced book on production analysis and design with several fine algorithms and unique contributions.

Fabrycky, W. J., P. M. Glare, and P. E. Torgerson (1972): "Industrial Operations

Research." Prentice-Hall, Inc., Englewood Cliffs, N. J. An award-winning text that first develops a basic foundation for statistical and economic analysis before discussing OR/MS applications which include quality control and inventory management.

Finer, S. E. (1966): "Vilfredo Pareto: Sociological Writings," Frederick A. Praeger, Inc., New York, translated by D. Mirfin. A detailed discussion of the sociological contributions of Pareto.

Flagle, C. D., W. H. Huggins, and R. H. Roy (eds.) (1960): "Operations Research and Systems Engineering," The Johns Hopkins Press, Baltimore. A masterpiece that clearly illustrates basic concepts behind every major tool used in OR/MS and systems engineering; enjoyable but serious reading intended for laymen.

Ford, L. R., and D. R. Fulkerson (1962): "Flows in Networks," Princeton University Press, Princeton, N. J. The most widely quoted work on optimization using networks.

Forrester, J. W. (1961): "Industrial Dynamics," John Wiley & Sons, Inc., New York. Systems dynamics applied to industrial systems.

——— (1968): "Principles of Systems," Wright-Allen Press, Cambridge, Mass. Preliminary edition containing 10 chapters on basic concepts behind systems dynamics.

——— (1969): "Urban Dynamics," The M. I. T. Press, Cambridge, Mass. Application of systems dynamics to urban problems.

——— (1971): "World Dynamics," Wright-Allen Press, Cambridge, Mass. A controversial book predicting the future of our world using systems dynamics models.

Gass, S. I. (1969): "Linear Programming," 3d ed., McGraw-Hill Book Company, New York. A widely quoted work on linear programming, this book also includes a section on nonlinear programming.

Gaver, D. P., and G. L. Thompson (1973): "Programming and Probability Models in Operations Research," Brooks/Cole Publishing Co., Monterey, Calif. A large text that begins with transportation models and continues with detailed discussions of probability models; numerous problems and answers are included.

Gordon, W. J. J. (1961): "Synectics," Collier-Macmillan Canada, Ltd., Toronto, Canada. A paperback on training group creative capacity.

Gue, R. L., and M. E. Thomas (1968): "Mathematical Methods in Operations Research," The Macmillan Company, New York. Mathematical foundations for a wide range of OR/MS techniques, including continuous and discrete maximum principles of Pontryagen.

Hadley, G. (1962): "Linear Programming," Addison-Wesley Publishing Company, Inc., Reading, Mass. Another classic in linear programming that is widely adopted as an operations research text.

——— (1964): "Nonlinear and Dynamic Programming," Addison-Wesley Publishing Company, Inc., Reading, Mass. A sequel to Hadley's "Linear Algebra" (1961) and "Linear Programming."

Hall, A. D. (1962): "A Methodology for Systems Engineering," D. Van Nostrand Company, Inc., Princeton, N. J., 1962. A comprehensive non-OR/MS coverage of systems engineering, including a fascinating chapter on psychological aspects of synthesis.

Hall, W. A., and J. A. Dracup (1970): "Water Resources Systems Engineering," McGraw-Hill Book Company, New York. Of special interest to civil engineers, this book also includes a chapter largely devoted to linear programming.

Hare, Van Court, Jr. (1967): "Systems Analysis: A Diagnostic Approach," Harcourt, Brace & World, Inc., New York. An informational analysis of systems endorsed by W. R. Ashby and M. K. Starr.

Hillier, F. S., and G. J. Lieberman (1967): "Introduction to Operations Research,"

Holden-Day, Inc., San Francisco. The first publication of OR lecture notes at Stanford University; a well-written, comprehensive introduction to OR/MS (2d ed. in 1974).

Howard, R. A. (1960): "Dynamic Programming and Markov Processes." The M. I. T. Press, Cambridge, Mass. A fascinating introduction to dynamic programming and optimization using Markov chains based on his Ph. D. dissertation.

Huggins, W. H., and D. R. Entwisle (1968): "Introductory Systems and Design," Blaisdell Publishing Company, a division of Ginn and Company, Waltham, Mass. A voluminous but enjoyable book on hardware applications of signal-flow graphs, especially suited for self-learning.

Jacobs, O. L. R. (1967): "An Introduction to Dynamic Programming," Barnes and Noble, Inc., New York. A sound coverage of basic dynamic programming principles and applications.

Johnston, J. B., G. B. Price, and F. S. Van Vleck (1966): "Linear Equations and Matrices," Addison-Wesley Publishing Company, Inc., Reading, Mass. An enjoyable and worthwhile text for any reader seriously wanting to review linear algebra or to learn its business and economics applications.

Klir, G. J. (1969): "An Approach to General Systems Theory," D. Van Nostrand Company, Reinhold Publishing Corporation, New York. Theory of systems using the *universe and coupling (UC)* and *state-transition (ST)* structures.

Kuester, J. L. and J. W. Mize (1973): "Optimization Techniques with FORTRAN," McGraw-Hill Book Company, New York. An outstanding collection of FORTRAN programs for linear, dynamic, and nonlinear programming.

Kuhn, H. W., and A. W. Tucker (1963): "Linear Inequalities and Related Systems," Princeton University Press, Princeton, N. J. A technical exposition of key mathematical relationships that are widely employed in operations research.

Lee, S. M. (1972): "Goal Programming for Decision Analysis," Auerback Publishers, Inc., Philadelphia, Pa. An introductory presentation of goal programming which includes a dozen case studies with numerical data, actual models used, and a FORTRAN program specifically designed for goal programming.

Levin, R. I., and C. A. Kirkpatrick (1971): "Quantitative Approaches to Management," 2d ed., McGraw-Hill Book Company, New York. A delightful text on fundamental OR/MS concepts.

Maisel, H., and G. Gnugnoli (1972): "Simulation of Discrete Stochastic Systems," Science Research Associates, Inc., Chicago. Computer simulation of queuing models and introduction to GPSS, a computer simulatiion language.

Maki, D. P., and M. Thompson (1973): "Mathematical Models and Applications," Prentice-Hall, Inc., Englewood Cliffs, N. J. Provides a solid mathematical foundation for those interested in models used in the social, life, and management sciences.

Martin, M. J. C., and R. A. Denison (eds.) (1971): "Case Exercises in Operations Research," Interscience Publishers, a division of John Wiley & Sons, Inc., New York. A collection of real-life open-ended cases, presented with an excellent instructor's manual.

McMillan, C., and R. F. Gonzalez (1973): "Systems Analysis, A Computer Approach to Decision Models," 3d ed., Richard D. Irwin, Inc., Homewood, Ill. An excellent text for those wanting to build OR/MS models using Fortran, Basic, or GPSS.

Meadows, D. H., et al. (1972): "The Limits to Growth," Universe Books, New York. A short, thought-provoking treatise about what world conditions may be like in the next century based on simulation models.

Miller, D. W., and M. K. Starr (1969): "Executive Decisions and Operations Research," 2d ed., Prentice-Hall, Inc., Englewood Cliffs, N. J., A management-oriented introduction to OR/MS.

Moder, J. J., and C. R. Phillips (1971): "Project Management with CPM and PERT," 2d ed., Reinhold Publishing Corporation, New York. A wide-ranging book that effectively presents both the practical and theoretical aspects of network analysis.

Muth, J. F., and G. L. Thompson (1963): "Industrial Scheduling," Prentice-Hall, Inc., Englewood Cliffs, N. J. An excellent exposé of the mathematics behind scheduling techniques.

Nadler, G., (1963): "Work Design," Richard D. Irwin, Inc., Homewood, Ill. Ideal systems concepts are detailed in the first section.

Naylor, T. H., J. L. Blaintfy, D. S. Burdick, and K. Chu (1966): "Computer Simulation Techniques," John Wiley & Sons, Inc., New York. One of the early and popular texts in computer simulation.

Nemhauser, G. L. (1966): "Introduction to Dynamic Programming," John Wiley & Sons, Inc., New York. A clear and concise introduction to dynamic programming.

O'Brien, J. J. (1969): "Scheduling Handbook," McGraw-Hill Book Company, New York.
A very readable, comprehensive coverage of scheduling techniques, including precedence diagrams.

Odum, H. T. (1971): "Environment, Power, and Society," Interscience Publishers, a division of John Wiley & Sons, New York. A fascinating paperback using energy-flow network diagrams to illustrate problems in ecology, economics, politics, and even religion.

Orchard-Hays, W. (1968): "Advanced Linear Programming Computing Techniques," McGraw-Hill Book Company, New York. A fine collection of techniques that make the most of linear programming.

Plane, D. R., and G. A. Kochenberger (1972): "Operations Research for Managerial Decisions," Richard D. Irwin, Inc., Homewood, Ill. A broad introduction to OR/MS including decision theory, zero-one integer programming using backtracking, and Fortran programs for LP, zero-one, and Lagrange multiplier methods.

Raiffa, R. D. (1958): "Games and Decisions," John Wiley & Sons, Inc., New York. Renowned presentation of basic and advanced techniques for decision-making.

Riggs, J. L. (1968): "Economic Decision Models for Engineers and Managers," McGraw-Hill Book Company, New York. An entertaining way to acquire a working knowledge of engineering economy.

——— (1970): "Production Systems: Planning, Analysis, and Control," John Wiley & Sons, Inc., New York. A comprehensive coverage of all major quantitative methods used in production management.

——— and C. O. Heath (1966): "A Guide to Cost Reduction Through Critical Path Scheduling," Prentice-Hall, Inc., Englewood Cliffs, N. J. Provides a mastery of CPM and PERT through numerous examples, exercises, and solutions.

——— and A. J. Kalbaugh (1974): "The Art of Management," McGraw-Hill Book Company, New York. An introduction to the quantitative aspects of management that stresses the value of graphic representations.

Ross, S. M. (1970): "Applied Probability Models with Optimization Applications," Holden-Day, Inc., Publishers, San Francisco. A rigorous mathematical treatment of probabilistic models in OR/MS.

───── (1972): "Introduction to Probability Models," Academic Press, Inc., New York. An excellent introduction to probability models, especially those expressed as Markov chains.

Saaty, T. L. (1961): "Elements of Queueing Theory with Applications," McGraw-Hill Book Company, New York. A well-known text that presents a thorough and understandable introduction to queuing.

Samuelson, P. A. (1973): "Economics," 9th ed., McGraw-Hill Book Company, New York. Classic in economics, it has many inspirational thoughts that are useful in OR/MS and are incorporated in this book. In addition, it offers a world-famous presentation of economic principles and relationships.

───── (1965): "Foundations of Economic Analysis," Atheneum Publishers, New York. For those who are seriously interested in economics.

Sasieni, M., A. Yaspan, and L. Friedman (1959): "Operations Research, Methods and Problems," John Wiley & Sons, Inc., New York. Another classic in OR/MS that is still refreshing to read.

Schmidt, J. W., and R. E. Taylor (1970): "Simulation and Analysis of Industrial Systems," Richard D. Irwin, Inc., Homewood, Ill. A Fortran-based introduction to Monte Carlo simulations of industrial models.

Shamblin, J. E., and G. T. Stevens, Jr. (1974): "Operations Research: A Fundamental Approach," McGraw-Hill Book Company, New York. An excellent introduction to OR/MS via basic statistics and matrix studies.

Simmonard, M. (1966): "Linear Programming," Prentice-Hall, Inc., Englewood Cliffs, N. J., translated by W. S. Jewell. An English translation of an authoritative French work.

Simmons, D. M. (1972): "Linear Programming for Operations Research," Holden-Day, Inc., San Francisco. A theoretical introduction to linear programming.

Smythe, W. R., and L. A. Johnson (1966): "Introduction to Linear Programming, with Applications," Prentice-Hall, Inc., Englewood Cliffs, N. J. LP theory, exercises with answers, and 18 pages on applications.

Starr, M. K. (1971): "Management: A Modern Approach," Harcourt Brace Jovanovich, New York. Inspiring reading on management philosophy and techniques.

Taha, H. A. (1971): "Operations Research: An Introduction," The Macmillan Company, New York. An excellent introduction to all OR/MS subjects with numerous numerical examples, especially in the beginning sections on linear programmers.

Tustin, A. (1953): "The Mechanism of Economics Systems," William Heinemann Ltd., London. The classic work on the application of signal-flow-graph techniques to modeling economics systems.

Vadjda, S. (1961): "Mathematical Programming," Addison-Wesley Publishing Company, Inc., Reading, Mass. A rigorous introduction to linear programming and related topics.

───── (1962): "Readings in Mathematical Programming," John Wiley & Sons, Inc., New York. Excellent reference on LP paradigms; concise but includes numerous numerical examples.

van Gigch, J. P. (1974): "Applied General Systems Theory." Harper & Row, New York. A successful integration of OR/MS tools with systems theory at an introductory level.

Von Neuman, J., and O. Morgenstern (1947): "Theory of Games and Economic Behavior," Princeton University Press, Princeton, N. J. The classic work tying the economic theory to linear programming.

Wagner, H. M. (1969): "Principles of Operations Research," Prentice-Hall, Inc., Englewood Cliffs, N. J. An award-winning OR/MS text, voluminous and comprehensive but more valuable than the abridged version, "Principles of Management Science" (2d ed. in 1975).

White, D. J. (1969): "Dynamic Programming," Holden-Day, Inc., San Francisco. A rigorous introduction to dynamic programming, including different DP formulations for identical models.

White, H. J., and S. Tauber (1969): "Systems Analysis," W. B. Saunders Company, Philadelphia. Hardware-oriented introduction to systems engineering.

Whitehouse, G. E. (1973): "Systems Analysis and Design Using Network Techniques," Prentice-Hall, Inc., Englewood Cliffs, N. J. A strong reference book for GERT which also discusses CPM, PERT, flowgraphs (SFG), and maximal flow models.

Wiener, N. (1954): "The Human Use of Human Beings: Cybernetics and Society," revised 2d ed., Doubleday & Company, Inc., Garden City, New York. Entertaining thoughts are mixed in with serious considerations of cybernetic models.

―――― (1961): "Cybernetics," 2d ed., The M.I.T. Press, Cambridge, Mass.

Wiest, J. D., and F. Levy (1969): "A Management Guide to PERT/CPM," Prentice-Hall, Inc., Englewood Cliffs, N. J. A small paperback that packs in a large amount of practical information about network analysis techniques.

Wilde, D. J., and C. S. Beightler (1967): "Foundations of Optimization," Prentice-Hall, Inc., Englewood Cliffs, N. J. A masterpiece on the theoretical foundation of OR/MS techniques.

Williams, J. D. (1954): "The Compleat Strategyst," McGraw-Hill Book Company, New York. The most enjoyable way to become infatuated with game theory, written for laymen.

INDEX

ABC rule, 44, 46
Ackoff, Russel L., 426
Activity start and finish times (in CPS), 351, 353
Adaptivity analysis, 13, 85, 95, 96, 301
Additivity assumption, 184
AIDS (American Institute for Decision Science), 2
AIIE (American Institute of Industrial Engineers), 2
Algorithm, meaning of, 50
AND (logical intersection), 76, 153
Aquinas, Saint Thomas, 61
Arbitrage problem, 177–179
Aristotle, 30, 31, 71
Arrival rate (λ), 396–398
Arrow network, 342–345
Artificial variables, 250
Aspiration level, 428
Assignment method, 213–216
Auditing, 14

Back-tracking, 232
Backward analysis, 292–294, 301
Balking, 402
Basic, computer language, 453, 459
Basic feasible solution (BFS), 90, 91
Basic nodes, 72, 101, 129
Basic path, 72, 101, 124, 293
Basic variables, 72, 101, 129
Beal, E. M. L., 275, 494
Beckman, Peter, 395
Bellman, Richard, 99, 289, 316
BFS, 90, 91
Bibliography, annotated, 485–491
Big M method, 250, 268
Birth-and-death (B & D) process, 399–403
Black box diagram, 20

Blackett's circus, 4
Blending problems, 161–165
Boundary time table, 356
Bounded flows, 155, 156
Brainstorming, 32
Branch and bound method, 231–235
Breakeven chart, 41
Budget allocation model, 305

C & E diagram (*see* Cause-and-effect diagram)
Cabinet-maker problem, 86
Camp-Meidel extension, 43–45
Canonical form, 248
Capacitated flows, 154–156
Cartesian coordinate system (see E^n FSS)
Caterer's problem, 329
Causality, 30, 31, 67, 71
Cause-and-effect (C & E) diagram, 19–37, 119
  applications, 32–34, 41, 75, 87, 343
  construction, 20–25
  history, 30–32
  variations, 26–29
Central limit theorem, 43
Charnes, A., 161
Chinese restaurant problem, 106
Churchman, C. West, 426
Churchman-Ackoff procedure, 426
Coefficient of utilization (ρ), 399
Complementary slackness theorem, 139, 152, 206, 294
Composite queuing systems, 417, 418
Computer, 113, 251, 419
  languages, 419, 462, 463
  models, 64
  programs, 113, 452–484

Index 493

Conservation of resources postulate, 71
Constraints:
   .LE., .GE., and .EQ., 114, 184, 266
   nonnegativity, 71, 92, 93, 137, 139
   real and fictitious, 6–8
   satisficing, 92
   technological, 158–160
Continuity assumption, 181
Contraction, RPM, 129–131
Controllable inputs, 20, 24, 85, 87
Conversational computer programs, 452–472
Convex hull, 294
Cooper, W. W., 161
Corner-point (extreme-point) theorem, 86
Cost analysis, scheduling, 371, 376
Cost curves, 376
CPS (see Critical-path scheduling)
Creativity, 8, 32
Critical activities, 356
Critical-path method (CPM), 338, 339
   (See also Critical-path scheduling)
Critical-path scheduling (CPS), 340, 341
   PERT probability analysis, 380, 381
   planning phase, 341–349
   resource management, 364–370
   scheduling phase, 349–365
   tableau, 347
   time-cost tradeoff, 371, 376–380
Critical paths, 355, 356
Curse of dimensionality, 99, 113, 244, 317
Cut-set network, 186, 188
Cybernetics, 246, 248
Cycle, LP, 255
Cyclic scheduling, 165–168
Cycling, simplex method, 275, 277–279

Dantzig, George B., 113, 114, 117, 200, 248, 474
Darwin, Charles R., 73
Data:
   collection, 63
   handling, 38, 44, 425–427
Decision tree:
   branch and bound, 232
   dynamic programming, 297, 298
Decision under uncertainty, 10, 11
Decomposition principle, 297
Degeneracy, 96–98, 226, 227, 269, 275
Delphic oracles, 3
Descartes, René, 86
Diet problem, 117, 161
Dimensional scaling, 253, 255
Discrete programming, 181
Documentation, 33
Dominance, 125
Double circle, 115, 153
DP (see Dynamic programming)
Dual values, 221, 247–249
Duality principle, 10, 99–101, 246–248, 275

Dummy arrows (in CPS):
   artificial, 345
   logical, 345, 346
Dummy node (in LP-RPM), 167
Dynamic programming (DP), 288–330
   backward analysis, 292–294
   characteristics, 296–299
   forward analysis, 290–292
   relationship to LP, 294, 328, 329

Economy, 246–248
Eliminating, LP equations, 255, 264
E^n FSS (n-dimensional Euclidean feasible solution space), 85, 86, 89, 90, 244
Endogenous flows, 89, 251
Entropy, 246
Epsilon (ϵ), transportation method, 227
Equality constraints, 89
Erlang, A. K., 395
Euclid, 85
Euclidean space (see E^n FSS)
Evaluation factor, 24, 33
Events in CPS, 339
Execute ($\mathscr{E}$), DP, 293, 298
Exogenous flows, 71, 251
Expected duration (t_e), 340, 380
Experimentation, 13, 33
Extreme point theorem, 86, 98, 152, 244

Factors of production, 60
Feasibility analysis, 84, 88–92, 184, 185, 208, 264
Feasible solution, 25, 104
Feasible solution space (FSS), 6, 85
   construction, 86–88, 243
   unbounded, 269
Feedback, 167, 246
Fictitious constraints, 5–7
Final state problem (DP), 290
Finite queue models, 398–405, 410–412
Float:
   free, (FF), 351
   independent (IF), 351
   safety (SF), 351
   total (TF), 351
Flood's technique, 213–216
Flow diagram, 132
Flowcharts, 132, 440
Forrester, Jay W., 431, 442
Forward analysis, 290–292, 301
Free variable, 115, 155, 157
Frozen variable, 115, 155, 157
FSS (see Feasible solution space)
Fulkerson, D. R., 13

Game theory, 9–12, 140–145
Gantt, Henry L., 338
Gantt chart, 338, 339, 342
General systems theory, 64, 65

Geometry, 85
GIGO, 63
Goal programming, 92, 184
Golden rules of RPMS, 151–153
Gordon, Geoffrey, 419
GPSS (general purpose simulation system), 68
Graphical analysis, LP, 84–111, 243, 244
Guesstimates, 46
Guthrie, Donald, 310

Hall, Arthur D., 70
Hasegawa, T., 181
Heath, C. O., 340, 349, 376
Heisenburg's principle, 31
Hitchcock, Frank L., 113, 199, 248
Hungarian method, 213–216
Hyperplanes, 244

Ideal system, 24
IFORS (International Federation of Operational Research Societies), 2
Imputed costs, 61, 102
  (See also Shadow price)
Industrial engineering, 2, 60
Infinite queue models, 405–409, 412–416
Information, 246
Initial state formulation, 290, 299
Initial tableau, 260
Inoue, M. S., 19, 36, 66, 347, 376, 442, 449
Input/output matrix, 444, 445
Intangibles, 426
Inventory control, 44, 440–442
Inventory process, 438–442
Investment analysis, 68, 69, 160, 161, 289–294
Irreducibles, 426
Ishikawa diagram (see C & E diagram)
Isoquants, 94
Iteration, LP, 255

Jackson, C. Grayson, 444, 445

Kelly, J. E., 338
Kirchhoff's law, 73
Koopmans, Tjelling C., 113, 199
Kuhn-Tucker conditions, 152

Labeling, 186
Lee, Sang M., 184
Leftovers, 136–139
  (See also Residues)
Length of queue (L_q), 402
Linear programming (LP), 76, 113
  computer programs, 452–472
  game theory interpretation, 140–145
  models, 114, 125, 129
  paradigms, 175–181
  relationship to dynamic programming, 295, 328, 329
  relationship to scheduling, 370
  RPM golden rules, 152
  simplex algorithms, 243–277

Linear programming (LP):
  simplification, 125–136
  standard form, 114
  transportation method, 199–204
Linearity assumption, 181, 184
LINPRO, 120–123, 453–470
Logical AND (in RPM), 76, 153
Logical dummy (in CPS), 345
Logical relationships in RPMS, 76
Logical variables (in LP), 248
Longest path:
  CPS, 338, 370, 374, 375
  DP, 299
Lonsteadt, Lars, 337
LP (see Linear programming)
Luce, R. D., 426

Main chain, 338
Management by exception, 46
Management science, 2
Manufacturing organization, 434, 435
Marginal cost analysis, 295, 318, 321
Markov, Andrei A., 398
Markov chain, 68, 396–398, 400, 419
Mason, Samuel J., 396
Mathematical programming system (see MPS program)
Mauchly, J. W., 338
Max-flow min-cut theorem, 184–186
Maximax principle, 10
Maximization (transportation method), 229, 230
Mellon, B., 161
Milestone chart, 338
Milestone date, 24, 339, 340
Mine, H., 181
Minimax principle, 10
Mixed integer programming, 474
Mixonomic problem, 400
Model:
  construction, 12–14, 61, 63, 64, 431–433
  dual, 11, 99–101, 246–251
  primal, 10, 101, 251, 437
Models:
  descriptive, 63, 433
  mathematical, 64, 167, 296, 395, 431
  normative, 63, 151
  simplification, 129, 253–255, 264
MODI (modified distribution) method, 217–223
Money, 246, 247
Monotonicity, 244
Monte Carlo simulation, 419–421
MPS program, 120–123, 154, 475–482

Naddor, Eliezer, 232
Nadler, G., 24
Negative exponential distribution, 43–45, 399, 409
Nemhauser, George L., 299
Network:
  arrow, 342–245
  dual (cut-set), 186, 188

Index **495**

Network:
  programming, 198, 199
  RPM, basic pattern, 153–157
Network algorithm, 49–54
Nodes:
  arrow network, 342, 343, 345
  basic, 129
  dummy, 167
  OR and AND, 119, 121, 153
  primal and dual, 101, 247, 248
  side cells, 291
Nonfeasible solutions, 185
Nonnegativity, 92, 93, 104
Normal distribution, 43, 340
Normalizing, 255, 264
Northwest-corner rule, 209–211

Objective function, 73, 91, 97, 99, 100, 184, 253
Observable output, 20, 84, 87
Odum, Howard T., 71
Ogive (cumulative distribution), 40
Oil pricing model, 299
Omit symbol (σ), 293, 298
Operations research, 2, 4
Optimal solution, 104
Optimality, principle of, 289
Optimality analysis, 13, 84, 91–95, 215, 260
Optimality check, 214, 260
Optimization postulate, 72, 73
OR (logical union), 76, 153
OR/MS (operations research and management science):
  applications, 443–446
  approaches, 3, 38, 51, 430–433
  experimentation, 84
  practices, 63, 64, 247, 394, 395, 425, 426
  studies, 44, 63, 336, 337, 419
ORSA (Operations Research Society of America), 2
Out-of-kilter conditions, 105

Parallel flows, 129
Parallel queues or servers, 416, 417
Parametric programming, 277
Paretian optimality, 39, 40, 184
Pareto, Vilfredo, 39
Pareto diagram, 40, 44, 164–166
Pareto distribution, 39, 41–43, 399
Pascal, theory of bets, 9–11, 142, 145
Pereyra, W. T., 36
PERT, 339–341, 380–382
Pivot column (pc), 260
Pivot point (pp), 264, 265
Pivot row (pr), 264, 265
Pivoting, LP, 255, 264
Planning, schedules, 341–349
Planning horizon theorem, 317
Poisson, Siméon Denis, 398
Poisson distribution, 398, 407–409
Poisson generator, 420

Postoptimality analysis, 96
  (*See also* Adaptivity analysis)
Postulates, RPMS, 71–73, 152
Precedence diagram, 342
Precedence matrix, 347–349
Precedence network, 65, 68, 342, 349
Primal model, 10, 101, 246, 251
Principle of optimality, 289
Problem identification, 21, 75
Process flowchart, 132
Process nodes, 66, 71, 157
Processes, scaling, 253, 255
Product form, revised simplex, 473, 474
Product mix problem, 131
Professionals, 35
Program Evaluation and Review Technique (*see* PERT)
Programmability assumption, 184
Programming, 112, 140
  computer, 113, 452–484
  definition of, 112, 113
  discrete, 181
  integer, 181
  mathematical, 113, 167
  mixed integer, 474
  parametric, 277, 371
  zero-one, 181
Programs, computer, 419, 474
  LINPRO, 120–123, 482–484
  MPS, 475–482
  REX, 120–123, 482–484
Project, definition of, 337
Project management, 337, 338
Project scheduling, 349, 351
  symbology, 352, 353
  terminology, 351, 352
Proportionality assumption, 184
Pseudo-random-number generator, 419–421
Purchasing function, 436
Purpose of a system, 73–74

Quality of life, 432
Quantity discount problem, 321, 328
Queuing:
  finite-queue single-server models, 398–405, 410–416
  inifinite-queue single-server models, 405–409, 412–416
  multi-server systems, 416–419
  RPMS representation, 409–416
  theory of, 395–398

Raiffa, Howard, 426
Range report, 94
Ratios:
  between processes, 157
  between resources, 160
Regret:
  branch and bound, 234

Index

Regret:
  dynamic programming, 301, 304
  VAM, 211, 214, 218
Residues, 71, 89, 90, 211, 248, 352, 353
Resource:
  allocation, 304, 315
  flows, 290, 291
  management, 364, 365
  nodes, 66
  ratios between, 160
  scaling, 253
  scheduling, 351, 352
  sharing, 153
  value of, 60
Resource committed (RC), 352
Resource residue (RR), 352
REX program, 119–123, 155, 482–484
Riggs, J. L., 19, 66, 340, 347, 349, 376, 421, 442, 449
Rim conditions, 200, 202, 264
Ross, Sheldon M., 417
Rowe, W. D., 70
RPM network, 66, 344
  construction, 75–77, 119, 153–157
  critical path scheduling, 344, 357–361, 377
  dynamic programming, 292–294, 305
  interpretation, 105, 115, 116, 246–248, 290
  queuing, 409–416
  simplex tableau, 280
  transportation, 201, 204
RPMS (resource planning and management system), 61, 65
  definition of, 70
  dynamic programming, 290
  game theory representation, 142–145
  linear programming, 151–153
  postulates, 71–73, 152
  queuing models, 409, 410
  scheduling, 352, 353, 357–361
Russell, Bertrand, 446

Saddle point, 144
Sales scheduling problem, 169–175
Samuelson, Paul, 247
Sasieni, Maurice W., 426
Satisfice, 13, 72
Scaling, dimensional, 253, 255
Schedule, CPS: earliest, 355
  latest, 355
Scheduling:
  cyclic, 165–168
  phases, CPS, 349–365
  production, DP, 318–321
  resource, 351–353
  staff, 125–129
Scientific approach, 9
SCOOP (Scientific Computation of Optimum Programs), 113
Self-optimizing, 246
Sensitivity analysis, 96, 103, 428

Sequential decision process, 305, 314
Serial system queues, 417
Service factor (ρ), 399
Service rate (μ), 396, 398
Sewage treatment problem, 179–181
SGSR (Society for General Systems Research), 2, 65
Shadow price, 102, 218, 219, 260, 428
Shannon, C. E., 396
Shortest network, 47–54
Shortest path (in DP), 299, 370, 372
Signal flow graph (SFG), 396–398, 407, 418
Simplex:
  algorithm, 117, 243, 255–277
  figure, 86, 244
  manual computations, 266
  method, 202, 243–280
  revised product form, 473, 474
  tableau, 244, 248–251
    within RPM, 280
Simulation, 419–421
Single-server queuing model, 398
Sink node, 66, 76, 89
Slack variables, 248
Societal constraint, 8
Software, computer, 452, 453
Solution space, 5, 6
Source node, 66, 76
Spencer, Herbert, 73
Staff-scheduling model, 125, 169
Stagecoach problem, 304, 310
State probabilities, queues, 417
State transition, Markov process, 396, 397
Statistical model, 65, 419, 428
  (See also Ogive; Simulation; Stochastic model)
Steady-state system, 73, 405
Stepping stone method, 215–217
Stigler, G. J., 117
Stochastic model, 65, 428
Structural (real) variables, 248
Surplus variables, 249, 250
System, 9, 65, 430
  closed, 433–435
  definition of, 70, 79, 82
  enrichment, 439
  open, 433, 436
Systems study, 12–14, 62, 78, 431–433
  (See also Model construction)

Tableau:
  CPS, 347–349
  simplex, 248–251
  transportation, 200
TAPE, 8, 20
Tchebychev's inequality, 43, 45
Technological constraints, 65, 66, 158–160
Time budget, 370
Time chart, 379, 380
Time-cost tradeoff, 271–380
Time-sharing terminals, 453, 454

TIMS (The Institute of Management Science), 2
Total float, CPS, 351
Total slack, DP, 294, 301
Traffic problem, 181
Transformation of resources, 154
Transportation method:
 demand and supply, 200, 227–231
 extensions, 226–231
 MODI mithod, 217–223
 Northwest-corner rule, 209–211
 problem, 199
 stepping stone method, 215–217
 tableau, 200, 201, 230
 VAM, 211–213
Transshipment problem, 157, 158, 199, 225, 226
Travelling-salesman problem, 232, 235
Triangular model, 113
Trim loss problem, 175–177
Tucker diagram, 114, 115, 141, 248
Turban, Efrain, 337
Tustin, Arnold, 396
TV cable model, 47–54
Two phase method, 250, 268

Unbalanced assignment problem, 230
Unbalanced supply and demand, transportation method, 227–231
Unbounded model, 167, 185, 269
Uniform distribution, 421
Utilization rate, queues, 399, 415

Vajda, S., 117

VAM (Vogel's approximation method), 200, 211–213
Variable:
 artificial, 250
 basic, 129
 free, 115, 155
 frozen, 115, 155, 157
 logical, 248
 slack, 248, 453
 structural, 248
 surplus, 249, 453
Variance:
 expected duration, 340, 381
 queue statistics, 402, 403
Vogel, W. R., 205
von Bertalanffy, Ludwig, 64, 65
von Neumann, John, 114, 426

Wagner, Harvey M., 289, 419
Waiting line (see Queuing)
Waiting time, 402
Walras, Leon, 39
Weiner, Norbert, 246
Wilson's formula, 440, 442
Work-breakdown analysis, 342, 343

Yovits, M. C., 56

Zero-one programming, 181
Zero-sum two-person game, 140–142
Zipf's law, 72, 152